REVEALING OUR SOCIAL WORLD

A Brief Introduction to Sociology

First Edition

Mark Plume

Reynolds Community College

Bassim Hamadeh, CEO and Publisher
Kassie Graves, Director of Acquisitions
Jamie Giganti, Senior Managing Editor
Miguel Macias, Senior Graphic Designer
Lara Braff, Specialist Acquisitions Editor
Michelle Piehl, Project Editor
Alexa Lucido, Licensing Coordinator
Chelsey Schmid, Associate Editor

Printed in the United States of America

ISBN: 978-1-63487-414-4 (pbk) / 978-1-63487-415-1 (br)

DEDICATION

To Nickie

CONTENTS

ACKNOWLEDGMENTS

If it takes a village to write a book, then I have an entire community to thank for encouraging and helping me with this one. I want to begin by thanking the team at Cognella Academic Publishing, who took a chance on an unproven author. A special thanks to my editor, Michelle Piehl, without whose patience, guidance, and firm hand I would still be dodging deadlines. I am particularly indebted to those who took the time to review chapters of this book: Richard Hoeser, Wayne Knight, Michael Cline, and Minturn Wright. I am extremely grateful to my colleagues at Reynolds Community College, who graciously suffered my irritability, curtness, and absentmindedness during the writing of this book. Thank you Linda Pinney, Doug Gava, George Kugler, Nancy Morrison, and Glenda Potts.

This book would never have seen the light of day if it weren't for the efforts of RJ. We first met when he was my TA at Virginia Commonwealth University, where he completed his MS in sociology. He is bright, self-directed, and meticulous. He acted as my research assistant on this book, digging up graphs, charts, and obscure scholarly works as well as the most current research in a number of subfields. He reviewed each chapter with honesty and a critical eye, all the while tolerating my writing style. The amount of work he did to complete this book is immeasurable, and I will forever be in his debt.

Finally, I have to thank the one person who endured the most during the writing of this book, Nickie Enos, my wife. She endured countless lonely weekends and holidays as I toiled on this book. She picked up my slack in all household and family duties and tolerated a sometimes testy husband. Moreover, she did this with a smile while offering words of encouragement, sometimes leaving me "cheer" notes on the kitchen counter. During this whole process Ellie, our miniature schnauzer, remained blissfully oblivious to my work, lucky her.

1

THE BASICS: Stuff You Have to Know

CHAPTER 1

The Sociological Perspective

CHAPTER 2

Doing Sociology: Investigating Human Behavior in Everyday Life

CHAPTER 3

Culture Is Everything, Everything Is Culture

CHAPTER 1

THE SOCIOLOGICAL PERSPECTIVE

"It can be said that the first wisdom of sociology is this—things are not what they seem."

— Peter Berger

Do You Know How Things Really Work?

Do you use a computer? Silly question—of course you do. As of 2013, the latest census data available, around 84% of Americans owned a computer, and nearly 75% had home access to the Internet (File and Ryan, 2014). I would wager that both those numbers are higher today. You would probably agree that most people in the U.S. have and use computers daily, just like you. Do you know how your computer works? If you are like most people, you probably don't. Just as people use their computers every day, they engage society every day. People travel the highways, go to work, raise families, shop for new computers, pay their taxes, and seek out happiness. However, they have no idea what governmental agencies really do with their taxes, they don't know why why women tend to make less than men or why some groups seem to be more privileged than others, and they are unaware of the social forces and historical circumstances that have brought them to where they are in their lives. The vast majority of people in the world are "end users" of society—they know how to navigate it, but they don't know how it works.

Fig. 1.1 Computers have become a part of our daily lives. We use them, but most of us have no real idea how they work.

Sociology, by its very nature, is a critical discipline; sociologists ultimately seek to *reveal* the workings of a society even if it means criticizing widely held beliefs and behaviors or provoking change in social institutions or the established social order. For example, most Americans believe in our system of meritocracy, the idea that you will get ahead if you work hard, and that we can experience social mobility through hard work (which many times includes education). Mobility is the idea that our hard work translates into rising up the ladder of social class/success. A number of examples of extreme mobility are frequently mentioned, usually in grade school or during political elections, about how anyone can become president. These stories usually include Abraham Lincoln, Bill Clinton, and Barack Obama. These support the myth of social mobility. In fact, your chances of becoming president of the U.S. is about 1 in 10 million; you are more likely to be hit by lightning *twice*, those odds being about 1 in 9 million (Carter, 2012; Parsons, 2011). The *reality* of social mobility is that the vast majority of Americans will die in the same social class in which they were raised. The reality is there is little social mobility in the U.S. How do we know this reality? Through research done by social scientists (Chetty et al., 2014; Isaacs, 2008; Corak, 2006; Causa and Johansson, 2011; Krugman, 2012; Krueger, 2015). Sociologists want to pull back the curtain of illusion to show how society is really constructed and how it really operates—not the way people believe it works or how they wish it worked.

Many students take an introductory sociology class because they have to or they think that sociology is about working with or helping people. While I would like to believe that sociology helps every student who studies it, and that sociology as a discipline benefits humankind, the real work of sociology is to systematically investigate the complex relationships between individuals, groups, and social structures to better understand the connections between social forces, human behaviors, and social order. Figure 1.2 illustrates the connection of social forces to behaviors, and how those behaviors contribute to social order.

Take for instance your decision to go to college. Social forces that are beyond the control of individuals influence many human behaviors. Asking a simple question like "Why are you in college?" reveals the many forces and circumstances that influenced your decision. You might think

Fig. 1.2 The relationship between social forces, our behaviors, and social order.

that you can't get a good job without a college education (*economic forces*) or maybe you decided to go because you received enough financial (*governmental forces*) to afford college. Maybe you felt there was a social expectation to go to college or all your friends were going (*social conformity and expectation*). Perhaps, the college you are attending is accessible to someone like you in this point in history (*historical forces*). Whatever the reasons, there were economic, social, historical and cultural forces at work influencing your decision. Ultimately, attending college by millions of students helps regulate social order by producing an educated citizenry, which participates in the work force, pays taxes, votes, and will in large part, transmit similar values and beliefs to another generation.

A Note on Social Order

There will be a great deal of discussion about social order in this chapter and in nearly every chapter of this book. There are about 323 million people in the U.S., which means there are 323 million individual identities and social agendas. How is it possible for so many people with so many different personalities and points of view to all, for the most part, get along and live out their daily lives with such social regularity? A great deal of understanding sociology is exploring how many parts of social life contribute to this regularity, what sociologists call social order. One obvious way to see social order is in contrast to social disorder or chaos. If you're like me, you probably wake up each morning and carry on without worrying if the electricity will work, if the roads will be safe, and if the economy and government have collapsed. This regularity of daily life is achieved in part because we accept our social order and help to maintain it by obeying laws, paying taxes, working and participating in social life. In more general terms social order can be thought of as the way social life is organized and how that organization patterns the way we relate and behave. Basically, social order means that we believe and behave in ways that maintain and reproduce our way of life. As we will see later in the chapter, there are competing views on how social order is established and maintained.

Dispelling Commonly Held Ideas and Beliefs: Better Living through Sociology

Sociology is Not …

Sociology is not common sense, it is not common knowledge, and it is not conventional wisdom. Sociology attempts to understand the obvious, and many times in doing that, reveals reality. Let's start with common sense. Common sense is what appears to be obvious behavioral reactions to certain social circumstances. For example, *common sense* to me means that you do not stop in a busy doorway to have a conversation with a friend, thus bottlenecking the doorway. Unfortunately, many people have yet to get the memo on this. Sociology does not teach common sense, but some sociologists may choose to investigate behaviors like this. Can common sense even be taught?

How about common knowledge? Sociology is a scientific discipline, and, through research, it seeks to uncover the real workings of a society, not how people want to believe it works. What do you think about violent crime? Is it pervasive and on the rise? When asked, most Americans say violent crime is a problem and is on the rise. In fact, in 2015, 70% of those surveyed believed that crime had increased in the past year (McCarthy, "More Americans Say Crime Is Rising," 2015). Perhaps because crime stories are so prominent on the evening news and digital media, people view crime as an immediate and rising problem. However, violent crimes rates in the U. S. have been on the decline since 1993 (Zimring, 2006). In fact, the murder rate in the U.S. is half of what it was in 1993 (FBI, "Crime in the United States," 2013). Again, the belief that violent crime is on the rise is another example of *inaccurate* common knowledge. While the vast majority of Americans *think* violent crime is all around them and on the rise, the *reality* is that it is on the decline.

Sometimes, research may reinforce common knowledge. The General Social Survey (an annual survey of thousands of Americans) has shown in each year that it has been administered that the vast majority of Americans believe in a God (Hout, Fischer, and Chaves, 2013). Most people think that most people believe in a God. This is reinforced common knowledge.

Finally, we come to conventional wisdom. The uber-famous economist John Kenneth Galbraith, who is said to have coined the term *conventional wisdom,* wrote that social behaviors "are complex, and to comprehend their character is mentally tiring. Therefore, we adhere, as though to a raft, to those ideas which represent our understanding. We associate truth with convenience" (Galbraith, 1958).

What he means is that we have assumptions about how the world works that most of us buy into, even if they're not necessarily true. Diet and exercise are multibillion-dollar industries in the United States. Due to media influence and little real education about diet and exercise, millions of Americans believe they can do particular exercises that will reduce specific body parts, for example. This belief in "spot reducing" is misguided and downright wrong. Men will do one hundred sit-ups and crunches, determined to reduce their keg to a six-pack, and women all over the country will do who knows what to reduce the size of their butts, hips, and thighs. In fact, there are products advertised that you simply wear around the house while you relax or watch TV that electrically stimulate your abdominal muscles, thus relieving you of the tedium of exercise or dieting. The truth is you lose weight all over your body first, and then you can strengthen areas of your body through training. It seems more convenient to believe in the misplaced wisdom of spot reducing.

Sociology in a way, is the "anti-conventional wisdom". Sociology does not seek to understand the world in a simple way, rather to unravel and expose social complexities. Many times, convenience and comfort are the *opposite* of what social research and sociological thinking reveal. For example, most of us would agree that if we were at a party and we had too many martinis, we should not drive, especially if our apartment or dorm was nearby and we could opt to simply walk home. Conventional wisdom would lead us to believe that we have done a good deed and we are much safer by walking anyhow. However, Levitt and Dubner (2009) have shown that a drunk walker is eight times more likely to be killed than someone who chooses to drive drunk. Even if you consider others who may be involved (passengers, occupants of other vehicles), who may be killed by a drunk driver, a drunk walker is still five times more likely to be killed than a drunk driver is. Neither drunk driving nor drunk walking are good ideas. Therefore, the best thing to do is call a cab or a sober friend to come pick you up or just stay where you are if you can. That way you avoid drunk driving and drunk walking altogether.

THERE'S AN APP FOR THAT

Worried about whether you are sober enough to drive or walk home? Never fear, there are over twenty apps to gauge your blood alcohol content (BAC). Apps such as *Can I Drive Yet?, iDrinkSmarter*, and *Last Call* are used to let users know if they are at, below or above the legal BAC level (Everything Code Inc., 2012; Baczone, LLC, 2014; Wang, 2008). You simply plug the mouthpiece (the part you blow into) into your mobile device, exhale into it and the app calculates and displays your BAC. Once you know your BAC you can decide if you are good to drive ... or walk home, call Uber, or perhaps stay put.

Now, using fifty words or less, define rape. Just close your eyes and try to come up with a definition. According to your definition, can a woman rape a man? Another powerful example of conventional wisdom is the notion that women cannot rape men. Research from the Centers for Disease Control (CDC, 2011) finds that 1 in 21 men reported being forced to have sex with a woman. I know what you are thinking because it's conventional wisdom: men have to be erect to penetrate a woman, and therefore he wanted it. Well, like all erectile tissue (in women and men), the penis' erectile response is involuntary. Therefore, men who are raped by women become erect by mechanical stimulation, not arousal. You wouldn't, for example, see someone with erect nipples in frigid weather and think they were aroused, you would assume they were just cold. Additionally, rape is not defined solely as penetration of the vagina. The federal definition of rape was changed in January 2012, a definition that had not been altered since 1927, to be more inclusive and gender-neutral.

> *"The penetration, no matter how slight, of the vagina or anus with any body part or object, or oral penetration by a sex organ of another person, without the consent of the victim" (FBI, "Attorney General Eric Holder," 2012).*

Notice that other than the word vagina, the definition is sex-neutral. Both men and women can be considered victim or perpetrator. Did you also notice the number of sex acts that can now be considered rape? Conventional wisdom ignores the inconvenient reality that men can be raped by women. This conventional wisdom perpetuates the myth that only men can rape, and that rape is simply men penetrating women's vaginas. When most people think of rape, they automatically assume the victim is a female. Please note that the overwhelming majority of rape and sexual assaults in the U.S. are perpetrated against women. The purpose of this discussion is only to show that in sociology, we acknowledge the complexities of social interactions, and we hope to uncover the reality of those interactions no matter how much it may displace our commonly or conventionally held ideas of the social world.

Seeing Your World as a Sociologist: Thinking Sociologically

After I finished graduate school, I moved from Los Angeles to Boston for a few years. When I first started driving there, I realized Bostonians drive differently than Los Angelinos. In Los Angeles, drivers recognize that if they are turning left, they must yield to oncoming traffic. However, Bostonians interpret the green light as a starting gate for the left-hand turn. That is, drivers turning left yank their wheel to the left and gas it through the turn, dangerously close to the oncoming traffic and endangering everyone involved. I noticed this behavior repeatedly. Why do Bostonians drive like that but you don't see that behavior in other parts of the country?

Well, I thought about this for months and came up with a variety of explanations. Many of them involved stupidity or a bad upbringing. However, I was not thinking sociologically. When I did, the answer was obvious: their behaviors were a result of the structure of their roads. The roads in the city of Boston are rather narrow, and dedicated left-hand turn lanes are few and far between. The structure of the roads was, in a sense, forcing drivers to take risky left-hand turns. Without dedicated left-hand turn lanes, local drivers feel that they must rush the left turn in order to get through the intersection. In addition, the narrow roads cause traffic to pile up rapidly, and in order to get through an intersection, many just rush the left turn. Of course, after a time, this behavior becomes normalized through habitual practice. The behavior has become part of the driving culture in Boston (we'll discuss this in Chapter 3). You are expected to rush the left-hand turn or you may suffer the consequences.

To this day in Boston, if you are turning left and yielding to oncoming traffic, you may get a honk from the drivers behind you for not rushing the turn. In contrast, the wide boulevards with left-hand turn lanes at nearly every intersection in Los Angeles shape a different driving behavior, one that does not include the rushed and dangerous left-hand turn. There is no need for this behavior because the structure of the roads allows for left-hand turns to be completed through a designated left-hand turn lane with a separate green arrow.

Private and Public

Much like understanding the effect of the roads on drivers' behavior in Boston, sociology attempts to understand the influence social structure has on our social behaviors and interactions. Most people like to believe that their actions are solely a result of their decisions, what I call a "private" view. But the reality is that our lives are much more "public" than we think. When you drive a car here in the U.S., do you drive on the right-hand side of the road? (I hope you said yes!) Why? Because it's the law. Therefore, the government has an influence on your life in the way you drive. You stop at red lights and go on green lights—again the laws influence your behavior—and you don't want a ticket (we'll discuss that effect in Chapter 6). So, your driving behavior is not "private": you don't decide which part of the road to drive on, and you don't go on red and stop on green. Rather, your driving behaviors are "public," or influenced by a host of reasons. You want to obey the laws, you want to avoid punishment, you want to be a safe driver, and you want to be a good person.

The Sociological Perspective

We could very simply define *sociology* as *the study of society*, but it is so much more than that—it is a way of seeing the world. The sociological perspective is exactly that: a perspective, a way to see the world. The Sociological Perspective attempts to see the way social forces, patterns, and circumstances come to affect individual and group life. The sociological perspective is also new to nearly all of my students. While you have been taking math, history, and English classes since first grade or before, you have most likely never taken a sociology course. So, don't be hard on yourself or freak out if you don't understand the material right away. The good news is that while you have not taken sociology before, you have the capacity to understand the sociological perspective due to all your life experiences. In fact, I would wager that you have actually thought about the world using the sociological perspective and not even realized it! Has a homeless person ever asked you for some spare change? Have you ever wondered why that person is on the streets and thought that in this economy maybe she lost her job, couldn't pay her rent, and couldn't get another job? If you have ever thought in those terms, then you were thinking sociologically.

Most individuals are consumed with the "private" nature of their lives, the decisions they make and their interactions with others they believe are purely a result of their own will. While we all have agency or the ability to make choices, sometimes social circumstances force our hand. For example, what if Maria, a single mom, lost her job cleaning houses in Los Angeles but manages to find another job in Pasadena. Sadly, she can't afford to move, and she doesn't have a car (she never learned to drive). The bus from El Segundo runs too late in the morning for her to get to the new job on time, so she can't take the job. On top of all that, her two daughters are going to need child care while she looks for work, but she can't afford to pay for that. Are all those circumstances her fault—her bad decisions? No. Economic forces, the effects of ethnicity, gender, and social class, as well as structural effects such as the bus system (government) influence her life. These "public" effects influence all of our lives. Without much education and being poor, Maria is like many people in the U.S.: they want to work, but social forces and circumstances keep them from it.

The Sociological Imagination: Seeing Our Lives as Public

> *"Neither the life of an individual nor the history of a society can be understood without understanding both."*
>
> — *C. Wright Mills*

In 1959, a sociologist named C. Wright Mills wrote *The Sociological Imagination*, which seeks to understand the relationship between two complex and opposite concepts—the individual and society. The central idea in his book was that we all have the capacity to employ the sociological perspective using our **sociological imagination**—seeing and understanding how our own lives are shaped not only by our decisions, but also by larger social and historical forces.

How do we do this? He argued that we need to see the intersection between our own biographies (lives) and the larger social and historical landscapes in which we are enmeshed. Let's think about it this way: as human beings raised by other humans in a human society, we cannot escape the influences of others and the historical and social forces that society exerts on us. By virtue of being raised among others and being a part of a society, we have the ability to step back and see the social, cultural, and historical influences on us.

Most of my students, whether they are at a community college or a four-year university, are in school to get a college degree so they can get a good job, make more money, buy a house, and go in debt! This is their typical response when I ask my students why they are in college (except the debt thing—I added that, but it's true). There is a sense among a great number of my students that a college education is a requirement of the American Dream, that somehow, obtaining that dream demands a college degree. Many of them seem to be aware that in this historical period, a college degree is necessary as a sort of passport needed to enter the middle class.

Let's employ our Sociological Imaginations to explore why you are in college. Think about who you are—male or female, young or older, working class or middle class, white or black, Latino or Asian. Think about your background and all the experiences you have had in your life, even the neighborhood you grew up in, which have led up to this point in your life.

Now imagine it is 1955 in the U.S. Would you be in college? If you are a black man or woman, chances are great that you would not be in college, and the same goes for most Latinos and Asians. Even most whites (male and female) would be excluded from college. College was typically an upper middle class, white, male experience prior to the end of World War II. Let's think about all the social influences that affect your ability/decision to go to college. We can start with the historical period in which we live and all the changes that have happened since 1955. Are you attending a community college? The open enrollment community college is a relatively new institution. There are also economic changes that demand a more educated and sophisticated work force. For example, you may be in college because you can't get a promotion at your job without a college certificate or degree.

How about financial aid? Most of my undergraduate students receive financial aid, and for many, it is the only way to afford college. In fact, during the 2013-14 academic year, college undergraduates in the U.S. were awarded a record $184.5 billion in financial aid (College Board, 2014). Figure 1.3 (page 12) breaks down how that amount was awarded across various aid categories. Additionally, there have been significant changes in laws and social policies that prohibit colleges from discriminating against potential students. These programs, including financial aid, all emerged in the last half of the twentieth century, making the college experience a much more common event for a greater number of Americans (Gladieux, 1995). In 2012, the latest data available, there were 20.6 million students enrolled at some type of degree-granting institution (National Center for Education Statistics, 2013). This is a lot of people in college. Why so many? Can you think of other social and cultural reasons there are so many Americans in college?

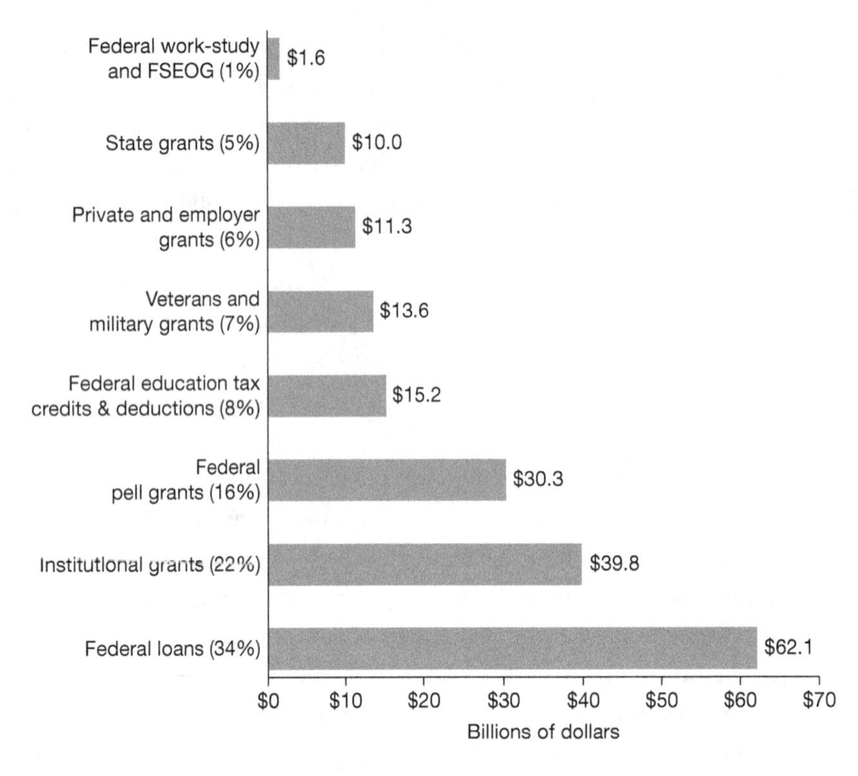

Fig. 1.3 Total Undergraduate Student Aid by Source and Type (In Billions), 2014–2015
Trends in Student Aid website (trends.collegeboard.org), Table 1A

Now, take a mental step back and look at the current social landscape in regards to who goes to college. You live in a time in which there is unprecedented access to a range of community colleges, state and private colleges, and universities. The elite liberal arts and Ivy League schools are no longer the only game in town. A record number of financial aid dollars are awarded each year, making college more affordable to a greater number of students from a wider range of class, ethnic, and social backgrounds. Figure 1.3 above shows that undergraduate college students in the U.S. received 183.9 billion dollars in aid during the 2014-2015 academic year, a record amount. New social policies have opened up accessibility to colleges around the country. Also, there seems to be a social attitude or expectation that most people will attend college, which permeates nearly all strata of society.

Men of my father's generation and social class could realize a good living with just a high school diploma. However, in today's economic and social atmosphere, most people view a college education as the pathway to greater earnings. The real difference in earnings, over one's working life (ages twenty-five to sixty-four), between someone with a high school diploma and someone with a four-year college degree is nearly $1 million (Day and Newburger, 2002). The intersection between who you are and these historical circumstances has a tremendous effect on whether you go to college, what college you attend, what type of employment you will find after college, and

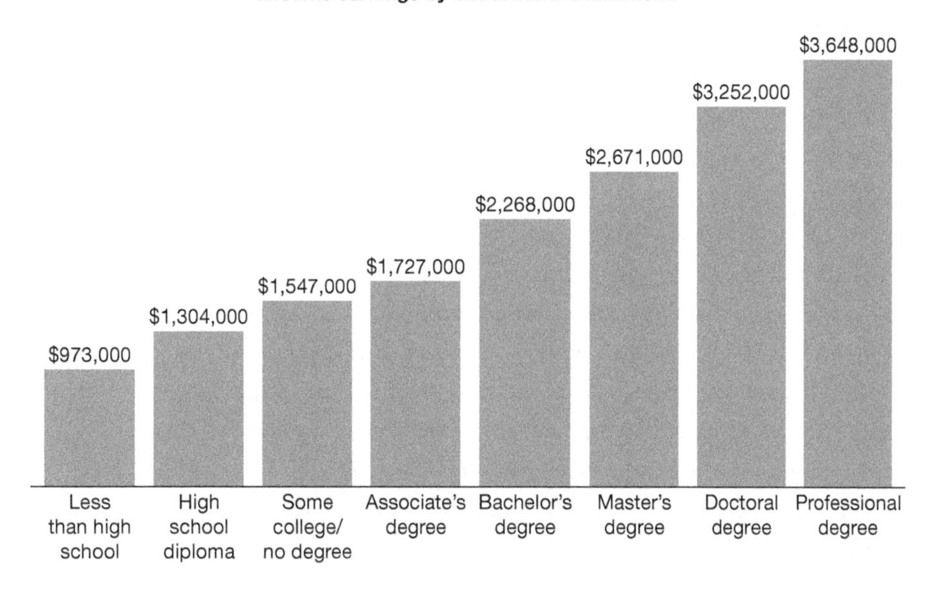

Fig. 1.4 Lifetime Earnings by Education Level

your lifelong earnings potential. Figure 1.4 shows differences in lifetime earnings by educational attainment. Is your college degree worth it?

Can you see how "public" your decision to go to college is? It was not just your decision to apply to college (private)—it is all those historical, social, and economic forces that influenced you (public) and led you to your college. Taking that step back and seeing that *intersection* between who you are and the myriad influences created by our times is using your *Sociological Imagination*.

READ MORE

- *The Sociological Imagination* by C. Wright Mills. In this book, Mills attempts to reconcile the agency of individuals with the influence that historical and social forces exert on individuals. He sees individuals as both products of their social environments and influencing their social environments.
- *Invitation to Sociology* by Peter Berger. A concise and insightful view of what sociology is. This is a quick read and the turn of every page will leave you thinking "This is so obvious, why didn't I think about this before?" This book will leave you seeing the world in a whole new, exciting and critical way.

Micro- and Macrosociology

Actually, in the section above, we were discussing both micro- and macrosociology. When C. Wright Mills asks us to examine our own lives (micro) in the context of the larger society (macro), he is urging us to see the connection between the micro (small) level and macro (large) level.

Microsociology focuses on interactions between individuals and within small groups. Microsociology might examine any number of social interactions like anonymous homosexual sex in public bathrooms, conversations between men and women, teacher-student interactions, crack dealers and their customers, or how people greet each other. In our daily lives, we may buy a cup of coffee, have an argument with a boyfriend, attend a boring sociology class, or send a text to a parent—these all occur at the micro or "small" level.

Say you wanted to study the different ways people greet each other on the street. You could go out and observe a bunch of people in public. You might notice two young men walking down the boardwalk on Venice Beach, California, and as they pass each other, one says "Sup?" and the other replies "Sup?" Now suppose you are in Rangoon, Burma (Myanmar), and you observe two people walking down Dalhousie Street. As the two pass each other, one asks "Where you going?" and the other replies "Over there." ("Over there" is their generic answer, like when here in the U.S. someone asks you "How are you?" and you respond "Fine.") While these are very different ways to greet each other, they are both appropriate to the respective social setting. These styles say something about how people interact and what is appropriate in each culture. Therefore, *microsociology* is concerned with interpersonal interactions that may be emblematic of larger social structures or how behaviors illustrate cultural patterns.

Some behaviors are influenced and limited by "large" social structures. You must be a certain age to get a driver's license, you cannot (legally) drink alcohol until you are twenty-one, and you need to get financial aid to stay in college. These behaviors are influenced by "large" (macro) social structures such as the law (government) and the economy.

Macrosociology is concerned with examining and understanding large social structures such as a society's class structure, social institutions, or society's belief systems. A macrosociologist may study a range of issues such as religion, workplace inequality, or poverty. One common measure of poverty, for example, is the Gini coefficient. The Gini coefficient of inequality measures the distribution of income or wealth within and across countries of the world. Gini coefficients range from 0 (perfect income equality) to 1 (perfect income inequality). So, if a country had perfect equality of income (everyone had the same income), the Gini coefficient would equal 0, and perfect inequality of income would have a value of 1 (if one person had all the income of a country). The Gini coefficient in the U.S. has been increasing over time, indicating that the income inequality is growing larger, which means the gap between the wealthy and the poor is widening. Macrosociologists use the Gini coefficient to compare the income inequality between

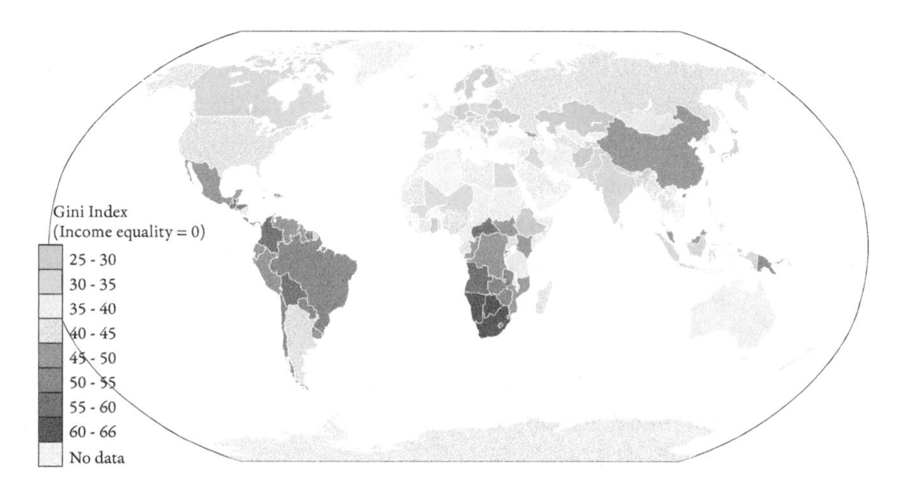

Fig. 1.5 All values are in hundredths (i.e., 25=.25).

countries, attempting to understand how economic, political, and social systems interact to create differences in income inequality, and determine how those systems create and maintain poverty and inequality. The map above (figure 1.5) shows the income inequality - Gini coefficient - distribution by country. As you look around the map, can you think of reasons you see the levels of inequality in a given country? What kind of company does the U. S. keep in terms of income inequality?

You can think of the difference between micro- and macrosociology as bottom-up versus top-down. Microsociology assumes that interpersonal interactions ultimately shape larger social structures (bottom-up)—that is, the way we act toward each other shapes social reality (society). Macrosociology posits that society's large social structures pattern individual interactions (top-down).

The Development of Sociology: A Brief Description Whom Do We Have to Thank for Sociology?

It would be impossible to present a complete history of sociology here in this text. What I can do is illustrate some historical high points that are regarded as connected to the modern discipline of sociology. I will present the dots; you make the connections.

Probably before modern man emerged from Africa nearly 70,000 years ago, humans were living in collectives and therefore subject to the social forces and pressures of living together. As long as we have been living together, people no doubt have been wondering about the dynamics of the group, clan, or tribe. So, as a species, we have had the potential to think sociologically since we first huddled together in some dark cave in the Great Rift Valley.

Fast-forward to around 400 BCE, where we find Plato discussing which type of social organization is best for people. In his dialogue, *The Republic,* Plato essentially discusses which form of government would best meet the needs of its constituents, concluding that "philosopher kings" would be the superior rulers. They would rule as kings rule over men and still be truth-loving, just philosophers, thus creating a society where people can find justice and happiness (Plato, 1941). It is interesting to note that there are elements of Plato that appear much later in the theoretical works of some social philosophers and sociologists such as August Comte, Emile Durkheim and Karl Marx.

Fast-forward to around 350 BCE, where we find Plato's student, Aristotle, discussing the individual and society. He basically sees humans as social creatures and urges governments to be rational and considerate of individuals in their deliberations. This quote from Aristotle sums up his idea about the individual and society.

> *"Man is by nature a social animal; an individual who is unsocial naturally and not accidentally is either beneath our notice or more than human. Society is something that precedes the individual. Anyone who either cannot lead the common life or is so self-sufficient as not to need to, and therefore does not partake of society, is either a beast or a god." (Aristotle, 1920).*

Fast-forward to the late 1300s CE, where we find Ibn Khaldun. This Muslim thinker wrote extensively on politics, economics, urban life, and social change. His social and political analyses were so insightful they were used by later historians to track the rise and fall of the Ottoman Empire. He even connected the idea of social cohesion with the success or disruption of social life, illustrating that members of a society need to work together cooperatively at some level to produce social order. Sometimes referred to as the father of Eastern Sociology, Ibn Khaldun, is widely believed to be one of the founders of modern sociology, but he rarely appears in introductory or sociological theory textbooks (Gates,1967; Dhaouadi, 1990). Why do you think this Muslim thinker is largely ignored in sociology?

Fig. 1.6 Ibn Khaldun. Some think he used sociological analysis well before sociology emerged in the West.

Fast-forward to the Age of Enlightenment. The Enlightenment, or the Age of Reason, was a time of tremendous political, economic, and social upheaval throughout Europe. This period, thought to begin in the late seventeenth century, was marked by a move away from tradition, faith, and superstition and toward a scientific understanding of the world. Enlightenment thinkers believed that through reason, logic, and observation all things could be understood or discovered. Many new discoveries had been made in this era: Newton's laws of thermodynamics, the law of gravity, and the movement to a heliocentric view of the solar system. This new and profound understanding of the physical world led many social philosophers to believe that these systematic rules of investigation could be applied to the social world to improve conditions for whole nations and move toward more democratic societies.

The work of Enlightenment thinkers such as Benjamin Franklin, Thomas Jefferson and others led to the creation of the American Declaration of Independence, the Constitution and its Bill of Rights. In fact, the American Revolution was a direct result of these writings and the political ideals of this period. Ultimately, the literature, discoveries and movements of the Enlightenment set much of the world on a path to understanding the social world through scientific inquiry rather than mysticism or religion. This period also saw an end to colonial rule in some countries, and the movement toward more equalitarian governments in others. The material in this section shows that some of history's greatest thinkers have contributed, perhaps in distant ways, to the development of sociology.

The Major Players

Auguste Comte

Out of this fever of inquiry called the Enlightenment and the turmoil of the French Revolution emerged a man widely considered to be the father of sociology, Auguste Comte (1798–1857). It is commonly reported that Comte coined the term sociology. Apparently, if you name something, you become the father or mother of it. However, another thinker may have beat him to the punch; the term *sociologie* was believed to have been coined by Emmanuel-Joseph Sieyes in an unpublished manuscript around 1780 (Guilhaumou, 2006).

Fig. 1.7 Auguste Comte. Considered to be the father of sociology.

The values, beliefs and ideas of the Enlightenment were tremendously influential on Comte's thinking and views on society. Much like his counterparts in the physical sciences who had discovered laws of the physical world (gravity, etc.), he believed he could discover "laws of society." He believed this could be achieved through the practice of positivism. **Positivism** was Comte's belief that the true workings of social life can be revealed through observation. He believed that only through a deep scientific understanding of how society operates was it possible to construct a better society.

Comte wanted to build the discipline of sociology into what he called the "Queen Science." He believed there was, in a sense, a hierarchy of scientific disciplines, and sociology was at the top of the heap, all other disciplines subsumed by sociology. Again, Comte wanted sociology to be the dominant science used to investigate society and to provide ways in which society could be more just and egalitarian.

In order to show the connections between the various part of society and that human societies changed and grew over time he drew *organismic* analogies—making comparisons between living organisms and society—in an attempt to link sociological analysis to the more respected, empirical discipline of biology. Parts of society were seen as analogous to "elements, tissues and organs" of living organisms (Durkheim, 1978). Social development and change were viewed as the growth or evolution of living organisms.

Comte's sociology included two important elements he called social statics and social dynamics. *Social statics* refers to the parts of society and their relationship to each other. Sociologists, Comte argued, had to identify the parts of society and understand how they functioned together. For example, public schools are necessary for creating literate citizens, who, in turn, obey social rules like getting jobs, then take part in the work force and pay taxes, which ultimately contributes to social order.

Social dynamics, on the other hand, was Comte's idea that society, like a living organism, develops and grows over time. His study of social dynamics, or social change, attempted to understand how human societies have progressed from primitive forms to highly developed civilizations. This social evolution is expressed in his work on the law of the three stages.

In one of his most important works, *The Course in Positive Philosophy* (1842), Comte states that human society was guided by the "Law of the Three Stages" as societies evolved. He argued that human explanation for events in the world has progressed from the **theological stage**, guided by the belief in supernatural beings, magic, and superstitions, through the **metaphysical stage**, wherein some larger universal force or power guides events in the world, to the **scientific or positivist stage**, where events in the world are understood through empirical observation so clear connections between social forces and social behavior can be shown to exist.

In the scientific stage, the highest form of knowledge is gained through the practice of positivism. For Comte, this was the one true way to understand events in the world that was free from superstition, magic, intuition, or cosmic forces. Positivism freed us, Comte believed, from knowledge derived from belief to knowledge based on observation. Thus, the beginnings of the modern scientific method as it relates to sociology are found in Comte's positivism.

Ultimately, Comte wanted sociology to be a science that could explain the complex interconnectedness of social structures and social change. He believed that using a positivist approach sociology could determine the past development of human society as well as predict its future course. He recognized that human societies were complex endeavors that could only be understood through observation, which should be done by highly trained scientists called sociologists.

Harriet Martineau

Harriet Martineau (1802–1876) was an English author who wrote on a number of topics such as women's suffrage and the abolition of slavery. Sometimes referred to as the first female sociologist or the "founding mother of sociology," she was aware that all major elements of society, such as government, the economy, and religion, must be investigated to gain a full understanding of any social phenomenon, specifically gender, race and class inequality (Pichanick, 1980: Webb, 1960). Like Comte she was a positivist and believed that through observation one could determine the complex interplay between individuals and social structures and the progressive evolution of human society.

Fig. 1.8 Harriet Martineau

She was a bit obsessed with human happiness. She believed that all humans have the inalienable right to happiness, and this belief drove all of her theoretical and empirical work. Much of her work focused on how gender, race and social class influenced individuals' ability to find happiness within a given society. Interestingly, she used a cross-cultural comparative method to examine different societies in order to determine how they had progressed in their treatment of women and minorities. She examined how the organization and the practices of various societies either allowed or denied women and minorities the same freedoms that others enjoyed. Those that were more progressive were more inclusive and women and minorities were able to find happiness compared to less progressive societies (Hill and Hoecker-Drysdale, 2003; Hoecker-Drysdale, 1992).

She even traveled to the United States in 1835 spending two years observing what she referred to as the *American experiment*—our nascent American democracy. In her book *Society in America* (1837), she criticizes America and Americans mostly for denying women full participation in society and maintaining the institution of slavery. She pointed out the hypocrisy of a nation founded on democratic ideals, such as all people are created equal, to promote freedom but deny women and slaves their most basic rights.

Her translation of Comte's *Cours de Philosophie Positive (The Course in Positive Philosophy),* as the *Positive Philosophy of Auguste Comte* (1855) in English, made Comte's ideas more accessible and was arguably her most significant contribution to the modern discipline of sociology. This translation had a profound influence on English-speaking sociologists and the sociology movement in America (Wheatley, 1957). She also wrote *How to Observe Morals and Manners* (1838), which is essentially a primer on how to conduct participant observation research, which we will discuss further in Chapter 2.

For her the purpose of sociology was to understand and describe social manners—patterns of interaction and the structured practices that make up social institutions—and social morals—a society's collective ideas of how to behave, what we commonly refer to as values and behaviors. Furthermore, she believed this understanding of manners and morals should be used to change society for the better. Ultimately, for her sociology should focus on the mechanisms and structures that contribute to social inequality and change them. In turn, this would lead to what she considered the overarching value of sociology, achieving the greatest happiness for the greatest number of people.

Herbert Spencer

If you are the guy who writes the first textbook in sociology, help define what sociology should study and contribute to the foundations of structural-functionalism, *one* of the *three* major theoretical perspectives in sociology, you are going to end up in every introductory textbook on sociology for a long time to come. Herbert Spencer (1820–1902), a British polymath (someone who is an expert in many subject areas), made several contributions to the development of sociology, but here I will discuss two, of which I will dismiss one.

In his book *The Study of Sociology* (1873), Spencer describes some of the fundamental assumptions of what would become the *Structural-Functionalist* (functionalism) perspective. The functionalist approach views society as a complex system of interconnected parts that work together cooperatively to promote solidarity and stability (we will discuss this later in the chapter). Spencer builds on Comte's earlier organismic analogies of social systems by comparing society to the human body. In Spencer's analogy, he recognized "morphology" (structure) and "physiology" (process); this should sound familiar ... a lot like Comte's *social statics* and *social dynamics*. Spencer argued that all societies are composed of social structures (family, polity, religion, etc.), and all societies change and evolve over time. He viewed sociology as a discipline that seeks to understand these universal properties of societies—that all societies have structure and change over time.

Like the human body is made up of many *structures*, such as the nervous system, cardiovascular system, skeletal-muscular system, etc., society is made up of social structures like religion, government, education, and culture, among others. These structures of the human body need to function together properly for you to be a healthy person; similarly, social structures need to *function* together in order to maintain social order (a healthy society). He also introduced the idea that society tends to move toward equilibrium, or balance. He argued that even when social conditions change social structures (social institutions like the government, economy, religion, etc.) rally to bring the system back into balance, back to normal, restoring the status quo (Spencer, 1898). We will see later in the chapter that this is a key component of functionalism and one of its chief criticisms.

After reading Darwin's (1859) *On the Origin of Species,* Spencer believed Darwin's ideas could be applied to humans and human society. This led to Spencer's more controversial idea, that of *social Darwinism*—the belief that like living creatures, society evolves over time from simple to more complex forms through adaptation to the physical environment, and that the social arrangements found in society are natural and inevitable. Spencer even proposed that Darwin's phrase "natural selection" be replaced with his now-infamous phrase "survival of the fittest," which refers to the concept that individuals who are best adapted (fittest) for particular social conditions will prevail (survive), while those who are unfit are eliminated. (Interestingly, Darwin did swap the phrase "survival of the fittest" for "natural selection" in later printings of *On the Origin of Species.*)

You should know that Spencer (1851) did not believe that society should provide any welfare systems, sanitation, vaccinations, public schools, or any form of what he called "poor laws." This seems like a rather mean-spirited position to take, and while it might appear that way, he really thought the concept of survival of the fittest could be applied to human society, therefore eliminating the need for social programs that would only encourage survival of the weak. In his version of social Darwinism, Spencer views human social order as a result of the survival of the fittest—the strongest members of society would flourish, while the weak and unfit would die off—with no need for social programs that would only preserve the weak and pollute society. Spencer wrote, "A nation which fosters its good-for-nothings will end by becoming a good-for-nothing nation." Wow! You can probably see how this goes sideways fast.

Let's put his thinking in historical context. Think about *when* he was writing about these things, his social position, and the global domination of the British Empire on which the sun never sets, and you can get a glimpse into his thought process. As Spencer surveyed human society from his vantage point as a privileged, white, British man—who deserves to be at the top of the heap because he represents the most fit humans—there seems little room in the world for variation or compassion because the arrangement of the social world is a result of natural evolution. His social Darwinism, then, becomes a rationalization for the domination of men over women, the rich over the poor, and the subjugation of people of color by whites. Fortunately, over time, social Darwinism has become a hollow concept, ultimately devolving into racism, sexism, and nationalism (not to mention Nazism, eugenics, and human euthanasia). Unfortunately, around the world today, social Darwinism (in its various incarnations) acts as a mechanism to oppress millions of people. However, for more *evolved* people and societies everywhere, it has been relegated to the trash heap of history.

While his attempt to use social Darwinism as a lens for understanding the organization of societies was ultimately flawed, he made many contributions to sociology. Spencer argues that sociology must take a holistic approach to understanding human social experiences, and consequently there are multiple causes for all social conditions. He emphasized that societies move toward equilibrium or a stable state, and in the final analysis society is held together by common values, traditions and beliefs (Perrin, 1976).

Karl Marx

The intellectual influence of the Enlightenment combined with the massive industrialization and urbanization of nineteenth-century Europe, as well as all the problems, challenges, and changes that accompanied them, created a sort of perfect storm for the development and growth of sociology. Perhaps no other social thinker of the time was more affected by these changes than Karl Marx (1818–1883). He despised capitalism, loved humankind, articulated a solution for destroying capitalism, and designed a utopian state for the working masses.

Fig. 1.9 Karl Marx

Capitalism: Setting the Stage

As with all the thinkers we examine, you need to keep in mind *when* Marx was writing. Marx witnessed great economic and social upheaval in mid-nineteenth-century Europe. Industrialization was sweeping across Europe along with urbanization, and there was an exodus of millions of people from agrarian country life to noisy, congested, smelly urban environments. The world was changing in a profound way. For thousands of years, most people in the world were farmers; both economic production and consumption were done in the context of the home, which was typical of traditional societies. But Marx was observing a radical change in human society. It was becoming heavily industrialized, and people were leaving the farms and moving to the cities in record numbers—the world was modernizing. Marx struggled to understand this transition from traditional to modern society.

The greatest social and economic change, for Marx, was the rise of capitalism—an economic system in which the means of production (capital) is controlled by private owners for profit. The form of capitalism Marx observed was what I call *raw* capitalism. This type of capitalism was harsh; there were no child labor laws, no safety requirements, no standardized hiring methods, and no wage regulations. Marx recognized that all those farmers coming to the cities to find jobs had nothing to offer but the "sweat of their brow"—their labor. For Marx, capitalism was designed to exploit the worker and profit the elite class (Marx, 1867). For example, if you worked in a chair factory and you built a chair, for which the factory owner paid you ten dollars, he then sells that chair for one hundred dollars, profiting ninety dollars from *your* labor, *not* his. In part, this is why Marx disliked the capitalist system so much: it exploited workers.

Alienation, or Why Marx Hated Capitalism

Karl Marx was a hippie who was born one hundred years too soon. By this, I mean he was deeply concerned with the plight of the working masses—he wanted people to be happy and free, much like the hippies of the 1960s. Marx saw capitalism as an economic system that prevented workers from achieving happiness and freedom. Specifically, Marx argued that the capitalist economic system was unique in creating conditions that led to the alienation of workers.

According to Marx, the most human thing we can do is labor—not for someone else, but to labor for ourselves. He argued that in pre-capitalist conditions, someone like a baker would own his own shop, determine his own hours and working conditions, create his own baked goodies, and decide how they would be distributed. He would have personal relationships with those he worked and dealt with on a daily basis. This free expression of ourselves through labor is what Marx referred to as our "species-being." Marx contends that workers will ultimately lose control over their lives by losing control over their labor (Marx, 1975).

In contrast, under capitalist conditions, workers are nothing more than replaceable cogs in a large, impersonal production apparatus. They work prescribed hours under dire conditions, are closely supervised, and their work is often monotonous. The consequence of these conditions, according to Marx, was workers' loss of control over the process of production, over the products they make, and over their own human nature. This process of **alienation**—the estrangement or separation of workers from their labor and, ultimately, from their human nature—was the engine that drove Marx's hatred for capitalism.

Marx describes alienation in his Economic and Philosophic Manuscripts of 1844 this way:

> *"... estrangement appears not only in the fact that the means of my life belong to another and that my desire is the inaccessible possession of another, but also in the fact that all things are other than themselves, that my activity is other than itself, and that finally—and this goes for capitalists too—an inhuman power rules over everything" (Marx, 1844).*

Marx distinguishes four types of alienation:

- *Alienation from our human nature.* Capitalist conditions create forced labor, which is not done freely by oneself, tears the individual away from his true free self, the "species-being," which Marx understood to be free and productive activity. Capitalism alienates the worker from labor, which is the essence of human nature, *separating* the worker from his human nature.
- *Alienation from the product of labor.* In the past, a person who was laboring for himself produced things that he needed or could sell or barter to get what he needed. A baker produced baked goods to consume or sell. Under capitalism, what the worker makes is not what they need or want. Workers build houses they will never live in, assemble cars

they will never buy and sew clothes they can't afford. Workers are *alienated* from what they produce.

- *Alienation from the labor process.* That is, because you work for someone else on his time, his pace, and for pay, your labor is essentially forced labor. The conditions of capitalism coerce the worker to labor for others, *alienating* the labor.
- *Alienation from our fellow human beings.* The structure of capitalism alienates workers from their capitalist oppressors, they are simply exploiting their labor and workers only connect to others through the buying and selling of commodities they produce. While our lives may be touched by many people every day, other workers who made the food we eat, the clothes we wear or the phone we use, we only know them through the objects we buy and consume. Therefore, people are *alienated* from one another because we don't know each other as individuals, but as extensions of capitalism (Fisher, 1996; Marx 1975; Ollman, 1971; Meszaros, 1986).

Class Conflict

Marx maintained that the history of mankind is the history of class struggle—the idea that throughout the history of human society, there has been one class that dominates others—and capitalism was no exception. He viewed capitalism as a system that created a division between the **owners of the means of production (bourgeoisie)**—the elite class who owned the factories, machinery, money, etc.—and those who labored for them, the **workers (Proletariats)**. This class difference between the owners of the means of production (haves) and the workers (have nots) is the source of social and economic conflict, according to Marx.

Communism, or How to Kill Your Boss in the Name of the Revolution

Most people only know of Karl Marx because of his association with communism. Actually, Marx never wrote a book or a single essay about communism per se; however, descriptions of it are scattered throughout his writings. Marx's conception of communism was *not* what has been perceived as communist states here on planet earth. In fact, Marx's conception of communism is diametrically opposed to any country ever claiming to be communist. For Marx, communism was a utopian society free of the class differences and struggles that had plagued all previous human societies.

Marx believed that conflict between the *haves* and *have nots* would intensify as the capitalist class continued to exploit the proletariats in their pursuit of greater and greater profits. Ultimately, Marx argued, the workers would grow tired of their treatment, unite, and engage in a bloody revolution that would sweep aside the capitalist class. What emerges from the revolution is a "dictatorship of the revolution" or socialism, a temporary state that ultimately transforms into a classless society—communism. In *The Communist Manifesto*, Marx and Engels (1848) encourages workers to unite and rise up in bloody revolution, basically calling on the working class to kill their bosses. The book got him kicked out of Belgium and France! Essentially, Marx constructs a sociological argument in which the conflict between the capitalists and workers becomes so intolerable that workers are mobilized to revolution, bringing about social change and moving society toward a more egalitarian form, thus laying the foundation for the *conflict perspective*. Marx's work has significantly contributed to the theoretical perspective known as the conflict approach. The general assumption in this approach is that social life is shaped by the struggle (conflict) between individual and groups to acquire valuable social resources and social equality. Many consider Marx to be the father of the conflict perspective.

Ultimately, Marx believed his greatest argument for communism was humankind's desire to live in a classless society where all freedoms are enjoyed by all. Basically, Marx believed that workers of the world would become sick and tired of their mistreatment, rise up, kill their bosses, and take control of society, thus transforming it into a utopian world, because it made the most sense. Wouldn't you want to live in a society in which everyone is equal, everyone enjoys all the same rights and freedoms, and there is abundance?

As we have seen in the work of Comte and Spencer and we will later see in Durkheim and Weber, their work represents a struggle with radical social change, and Marx was no different. These social thinkers were witnessing a profound social transformation from our traditional agrarian world to a modern, industrialized, and urbanized one in which the fate of humankind was unknown. These were stressful and scary times! What do you do when you are stressed to the point of fear? If you are like me and most people, you probably seek out some form of comfort: mac and cheese, ice cream, alcohol, curling up into the fetal position, or watching romantic comedies. This is what Marx's communism represents—his comfort. His communism represents one possible outcome for human society, a utopian outcome that is comforting.

Marx's legacy in sociology is the generalized conflict approach, which argues that the *conflict* between groups competing for access to and possession of valuable social resources bring about social change and contributes to social order (we will discuss this more later in the chapter). His work showed the profound effect economic forces have on individuals and groups within society as well as the way ideology is used to reproduce dominance by elite classes. Broadly, in sociology his work has influenced modern stratification theory, social class theory, feminist, race and even queer theory.

READ MORE

- *The Manifesto of the Communist Party* (commonly referred to as *The Communist Manifesto*) by Karl Marx and Friedrich Engels. Essentially a blueprint for the overthrow and dismantling of capitalist systems, this book discusses why communism is superior to other social forms and calls for workers of the world to unite because they have nothing to lose but their chains of oppression

Emile Durkheim

Fig. 1.10 Emile Durkheim

While Marx focused on economic inequality in the context of society's transition to modernity, Emile Durkheim (1858–1917) struggled with the effects that transformation would have on social order. Durkheim was instrumental in advancing sociology as an academic discipline. He was the first professor of sociology in France and promoted **empirical sociology**—knowledge of the social world gained through observation/data collection—through his study of suicide.

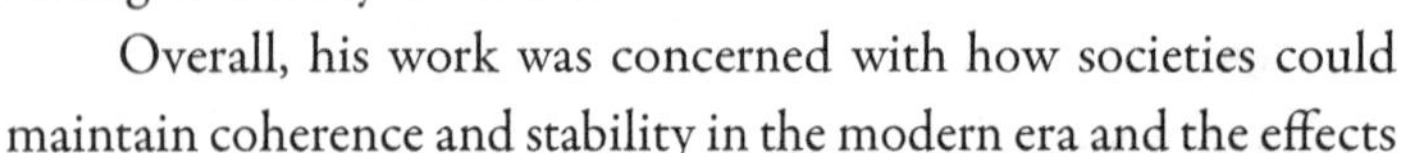

Overall, his work was concerned with how societies could maintain coherence and stability in the modern era and the effects the loss of social cohesion could have on individuals. Additionally, he showed that human behaviors are influenced by social-structural forces, or what he called "social facts." **Social facts** are social rules, customs, and social institutions that are external to and coercive of the individual. Traffic laws, for example, are external to you, and they strongly influence you (coerce) your driving behavior; you drive on the right-hand side of the road, do the speed limit, and stop for school buses. Durkheim argued that social facts transcended individuals. That is, people are born and die but social facts like values, the economy, government, and religion persist, and they act to constrain people's behavior, thereby preserving social order (Durkheim, 1895). Essentially, the behaviors of individuals are constrained through social influences such as laws, religious instruction and conformity to bring about social cohesion and help maintain social order.

Specifically, Durkheim attempted to show through empirical means (observation/data collection) the effect of social forces on suicide. When most people hear about suicide, their thoughts go immediately to depression and mental illness as the cause. But what brings people to a state of such depression that they are willing to take their own life? Durkheim argued that the causes of suicide were to be found in social factors, not in traits of the individual. That is, there were social forces that may make individuals feel less connected to others and their community, driving them to suicide.

He compared suicide rates of Catholic and Protestant communities and found Protestants had higher rates of suicide than Catholics. He discovered that members of Catholic communities expressed higher levels of **social integration**—a sense of connectedness with others and community—than did their Protestant counterparts. Members of Catholic communities, Durkheim argued, experienced more social control (regulation of behavior to gain conformity), instilling a greater sense of sameness, which was lacking in Protestant communities, resulting in lower rates of suicide among Catholics. Durkheim described those in Protestant communities as experiencing higher levels of **anomie**, meaning normlessness, or a sense that there is a lack of social control or guidance. This state of anomie and all its associated problems, Durkheim feared, could be the fate of societies as they confronted the modern era (Durkheim, 1897).

Durkheim's work on suicide showed that an act that is commonly conceived of as personal, is also influenced by social forces. Moreover, this work was an early example of empirical investigation, which helped establish sociology as a scientific endeavor. Much of his work focused on the forces that hold society together, which was instrumental in the further development of *structural functionalism*, one of the major theoretical perspectives in sociology.

Max Weber

(We retain the German pronunciation, VAY-bear)
Weber's contributions to sociological thought, like the other major contributors, are considerable and beyond the scope of this chapter. However, I will briefly outline what I believe to be his major contributions to sociology. Like many social thinkers of his time, Max Weber (1864–1920) struggled with understanding the effects of society's transition from traditional form to the modern era.

Fig. 1.11 Max Weber

As he witnesses society modernize, Weber noticed that old patterns of running organizations were being replaced by more efficient, rational, administrative models called bureaucracies. Bureaucracy literally means rule by desks or offices, but it is best thought of as a rational/logical way for an organization to arrange itself to achieve its goals efficiently. The college you are attending is a bureaucracy; the Department of Motor Vehicles and hospitals are also good examples of bureaucracies (although one could question how efficiently they do things). While Weber had problems with bureaucracies, he ultimately saw them as the best way for societies to organize themselves to deal with the increasing complexity of social systems. Realizing bureaucracies were here to stay, he outlined the characteristics of the ideal type bureaucracy, which refers to traits that a perfect bureaucracy should possess but may not be found in any real-life bureaucratic organization (I will discuss this in detail in Chapter 5). Because bureaucracy was such an efficient way of organization, Weber saw the increased bureaucratization of most spheres of social life as an "inescapable fate" for modern societies (Weber, 1925).

Perhaps Weber's best-known work is his 1905 book, *The Protestant Ethic and the Spirit of Capitalism*. In this work, Weber highlights the connection between Calvinists' religious beliefs and the rise of capitalism as the preeminent economic system. In many societies, the pursuit of profit was interpreted as a transgression, but many denominations of Protestantism viewed economic profits as a sign of salvation, specifically in Calvinism. It was this moral justification that led to the expansion of profit seeking and the rise of the capitalist system, argued Weber. You can see how a belief system that saw economic profits as a "sign" that one was saved would lead people to seek profit through capitalist endeavors to assure their place in heaven.

Unlike Comte and Durkheim's insistence on a positivist approach to sociology—that knowledge about the social world can only be derived from what we can observe and measure—Weber described sociology as a science that should concern itself with "interpretive understanding of social action" (Weber 1925, 1978). What he meant was that sociology had to go beyond mere observation of behaviors and seek to understand the *motivation* for people's actions. Weber termed this interpretive understanding *verstehen*, which is the German verb "to understand." Weber meant it to be interpreted in a deeper way: that we should have some subjective way of understanding individuals' motivations and behaviors from their perspective. Think about his meaning of verstehen like the old saying "walk a mile in someone else's shoes." Once you have walked in someone else's shoes, you gain a greater insight into why she acts the way she does and how she sees the world.

TABLE 1.1 Comparison of Marx, Durkheim, and Weber

	Theorist		
	Marx	**Durkheim**	**Weber**
View of the individual	Shaped almost entirely by individuals' relationship to the economy in the capitalist system. You are part of the elite class or the working class. However, Marx believed that the self-realization of the individual was the highest goal of socialism (discovering that under capitalism, you were an alienated and exploited worker, but now, under socialism, you are a free individual). The liberation of the individual, free from any type of exploitation, was the ultimate goal of dismantling state rule of any type.	Believed that humans were unlimited in their desires, and without proper social constraint (social control), they would run amuck. Social structure is necessary to control the individual and create conformity and compliance to social rules to achieve social cohesion.	Of the three thinkers, Weber imbued individuals with the greatest amount of agency. In fact, he argued that sociology should not be concerned so much with observing behavior as much as understanding the motivation or *reason* people engage in various behaviors.

Theorist

	Marx	Durkheim	Weber
View of Society	Society is controlled by the wealthy, by ideological as well as economic means, to maintain their dominance. Until the proletariat/workers develop a true class consciousness (realize the truth about their own exploitation), they will continue to be exploited by the elites.	Society exists beyond the individual. Cultural norms, values, beliefs, and institutions act to constrain individual actions in order to gain social conformity. This social control is necessary to maintain social stability and social order.	As society transitioned from a traditional to a modern form, rational social organization expanded into nearly all spheres of social life. This modern rationality—in the form of *bureaucracy* - becomes a dominating social force that is expressed through increasingly rigid rules, which ultimately constricts individuality.
View of social change	A bloody workers' revolution. Ultimately, the conflict between the owners of the means of production and the workers—continued alienation and exploitation of the working class—will result in a revolution, ending in a workers socialist state.	Durkheim's notion of social change can be seen in his explanation of the transition from traditional to modern society in which the division of labor becomes more specialized and the relationships between individuals become more complex. Also, his idea of "collective effervescence" describes great times in history in which collectives rise to heightened levels of exaltation, which can lead to great changes in society such as the American revolution or the civil rights movement.	Sees the continued rationalization and bureaucratization of society bringing about a sort of social staleness that needs a jump-start to bring about change. He argued that charismatic leaders can bring about substantial social change. They have new ideas, which challenge the established social order in time of crisis, which brings about social change. Mahatma Gandhi and Martin Luther King, Jr. are good examples.

W.E.B. Du Bois

(Pronounced due-BOYZ)

Many of Du Bois' predecessors struggled with issues of society's transition to the modern era, analyzing the effects of modernization on social structures, but W.E.B. Du Bois (1868–1963) represents the transition to modern sociology. That is, while Marx, Weber, and Durkheim had one foot in the past and one in the present, Du Bois' focus on understanding the social and economic consequences of membership in minority groups and seeking racial equality was planted firmly in the modern era. His work focused on the sociological plight of black Americans and sought to increase knowledge of social injustice through grassroots activism.

Fig. 1.12 W.E.B. Du Bois

He was the first African American to earn a Ph.D. from Harvard University and was one of the founders of the National Association for the Advancement of Colored People (NAACP), which raises awareness of the tremendous inequalities that black Americans face and seeks to redress them. The mission statement of the NAACP clearly indicates what the organization aims to achieve:

> *"The mission of the National Association for the Advancement of Colored People is to ensure the political, educational, social, and economic equality of rights of all persons and to eliminate race-based discrimination" (NAACP, 2015).*

Even though Marx had earlier examined social inequality, his analysis focused on class and economic conflict. Du Bois sought to shine a sociological light on the inequality of race, highlighting white power, racial prejudice, and discrimination. He was a strident advocate for racial justice in the first half of the twentieth century, writing prolifically about the history and sociology of black Americans. His work *The Philadelphia Negro* (1899), a case study of a black community in Philadelphia, highlighted not only the low social status of blacks, but also the physical and social separation of blacks from whites, which he would later refer to as the "color line" in America.

In his 1903 book *The Souls of Black Folk,* Du Bois presents a number of essays describing the economic and sociological forces that had shaped the black experience in America. He lived at a time in the United States when politicians, academics, and the clergy were publically declaring blacks an inferior race with no social worth. In order to change this view of blacks, Du Bois advocated social activism and the use of his scholarly work. He believed that a scientific, sociological analysis of the lives of blacks in the United States would alter public opinion and, in turn, change racist laws and policies. He was right, in part, though he did not live to see the passing of the Civil Rights Act of 1964.

Much of his professional life was devoted to seeking racial equality in the United States; his role in the founding of the NAACP highlights his commitment to improving the social position of blacks and his belief that organizing could produce black power and effect change from within the black community. However, Du Bois clearly recognized that blacks alone could not change their social conditions; rather, it was the responsibility of whites, who had the *power* to bring about social, legal, and economic equality for black Americans. His legacy of sociological inquiry into social injustice is represented not only in current theories on race, but also on feminist and queer theories that seek social justice for other historically oppressed social groups.

READ MORE

- *The Souls of Black Folk* by W.E.B. Du Bois (1903). The book is composed of several essays, the theme being equality for black people in the United States. The essays illustrate various dimensions of inequality between whites and blacks, and they make compelling arguments for removing barriers to the black vote and making educational opportunities available for black Americans. The content of the essays will resonate with readers because many of these issues persist in society.

Major Theoretical Perspectives in Sociology

Theories are necessary to make sense of the social world and of the observations/data that sociologists collect. Theories in sociology help us make sense of what we see around us in the social world; they answer the question *why*. How does society hang together? How do some social groups dominate others? Why do women on average earn less than men? Why did crime rates fall dramatically in the 1990s? Sociological theories offer *explanations* for why we think and act the way we do.

However, sociological theories explain social phenomena at different levels and from different perspectives. While some theories focus on society as a whole to get the "big picture," some are concerned only with the interactions between individuals, and yet others look at particular groups within society, like the differences between young and old. Some theories concentrate on social inequality, some are particularly interested in how society remains cohesive and stable over time, and still others look at how our shared understanding of symbols help us navigate social life.

Sociologists have developed thousands of theories to explain social life, but in order to make sense of this vast number of theories they are generally organized into three major theoretical perspectives, approaches, or schools of thought: Structural-Functionalism (functionalism), Conflict, and the Interactionist approaches. Each *perspective* or point of view is just one way to look at how society is organized and how it functions. In general, each represents an attempt to explain how society is arranged, how it functions, and ultimately, how it all hangs together—social order. You may be tempted to ask which theory is "right." Don't think about these theories in terms of "right" or "wrong," rather think about them as *different* perspectives on the same phenomena. Think about it this way: Imagine three people seated at different places around a baseball park, all of them watch a player slide into home plate. Each has a different perspective on the play and will *explain* it from his vantage point. It's not about safe or out (the umpire determined that) but how they *see* the play.

Structural Functionalist Perspective

Rooted in the work of Comte, Spencer, and Durkheim, structural functionalism, or functionalism, is a macrosociological theoretical perspective that attempts to explain the organization and functioning of society in terms of the interconnectedness of various social elements such as norms, traditions, customs, institutions, etc. This approach emphasizes that society is a complex system whose various component parts work through cooperation to maintain social cohesion and stability. Functionalists further believe that society is bound together by social consensus; members of society agree upon and strive together to maintain a social order. That is, a state of social equilibrium or balance is achieved because members of society share a common system of values, beliefs and behaviors, which allows society to operate smoothly. Functionalism's emphasis on value consensus is a major ingredient in nearly all its interpretations of social order.

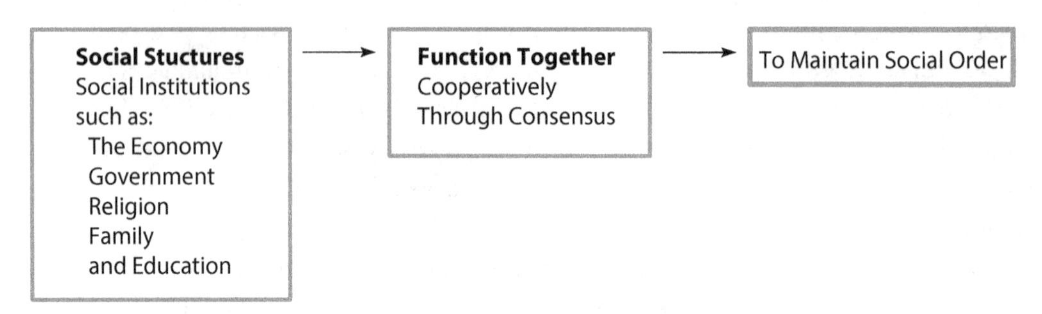

Fig. 1.13 Diagram of Structural Functionalism

Functionalism became widely popular in the United States between the 1940s and 1960s. Robert Merton (1949) became a central figure in the expansion of functionalism by including three key concepts:

Manifest function: the explicit purpose of any given social structure, the intended consequences that people expect from a social institution. These are the functions we expect institutions to fulfill. FoPr example, we expect our education system to teach our children basic academic subjects in order to create literate citizens.

Latent function: the unintended or unforeseen consequences of organizational structure and interactions among its members. One could argue, for example, that schools are essentially training grounds for work later in life. Students are expected to arrive on time, take recess (coffee break), work cooperatively under instruction, break for lunch, return to afternoon work, then "punch out" when the school day (shift) ends.

Dysfunction: tension, strain, or contradictions within social elements. Remember earlier in the chapter, Spencer presented functionalism as an analogy between society and the human body? Social dysfunctions can be viewed as analogous to illnesses in the human body, where various structures have to rally to bring balance (health) back to the individual, such as white blood cells rushing to a wound to fight infection. For example, the great recession of 2007-2008 produced serious economic damage to society such as increased unemployment, partial market crashes, downward social mobility, and general economic fear. Other social structures adjusted to address the economic damage and bring society into balance (health): the government provided a multibillion-dollar Wall Street bailout, more financial aid was made available for those who had lost their jobs, and many junior and community colleges increased certificate and workforce programs, helping the unemployed to "retool" themselves for the job market.

Conflict Perspective

Originating in the works of Karl Marx, **conflict theory**, in contrast to the functionalist approach, argues that social order is not maintained through value consensus, but rather preserved involuntarily by the dominance of more powerful groups (read: they have more of the goodies) over less powerful groups. That is, all societies are unequal in the distribution of valuable resources (goodies), land, money, cattle, education, power, etc.; consequently, society is arranged into classes—groups of people that have similar access to and possession of those valuable resources. Modern conflict theorists assert that conflict is not just based on class struggles but occurs on a much wider level and among other groups, such as the young and old, men and women, people of color and whites, and heterosexual and LGBTQ communities. The "conflict" between these groups is the engine for social change that moves society in the direction of equalitarianism, or at least *less* inequality.

Looking at Figure 1.14, you can see that the first assumption of the conflict perspective is that all societies are unequal; therefore, valuable social resources will be distributed unequally. It is this inequality of access to and possession of valuable social resources that produces the conditions of conflict between various groups in society. This conflict is natural because all societies are unequal therefore the conditions for conflict exist in all societies. Social conflict is also necessary because it pushes along social change, which ultimately contributes to social order. The conflict approach argues that dominant social groups manipulate social institutions, and use coercion and sometimes force to maintain their power over subordinate groups. When subordinate groups resist or rebel against the dominant groups' control social change results.

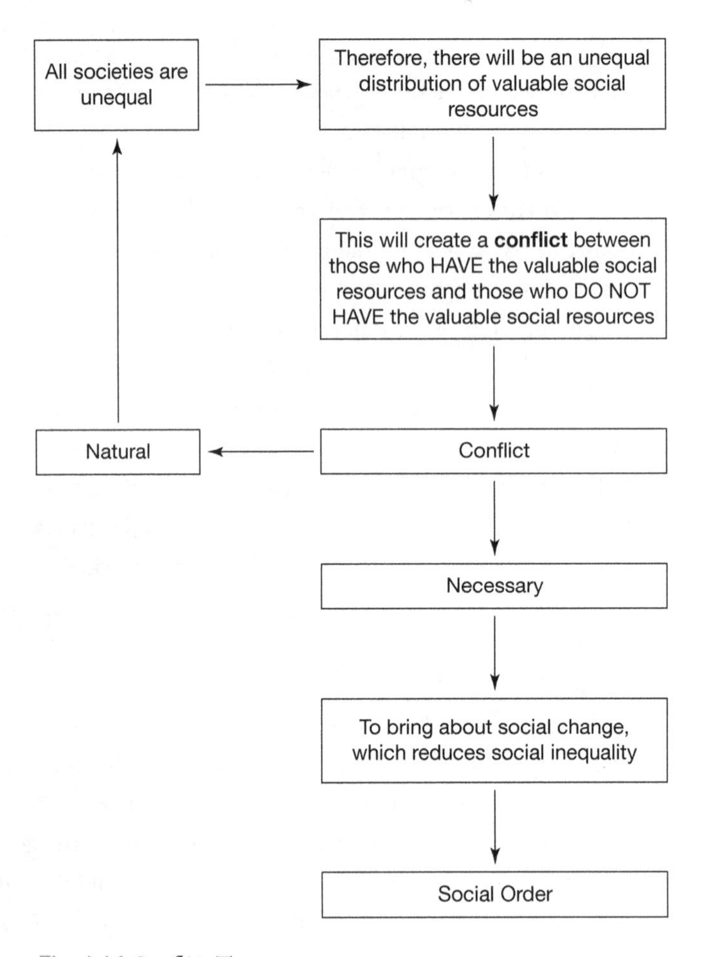

Fig. 1.14 Conflict Theory

The conflict perspective, like all three of the perspectives, acts as a type of umbrella approach under which many other theories have flourished, such as feminist theory, which examines the inequality between men and women, and race theory, which looks at the inequality between blacks and whites. Other emergent voices, such as that of queer theory and critical race theory, can trace their theoretical roots to a Marxist origin (Holmes, 2010).

Interactionist Perspective

Whereas the other two approaches take a large-scale, macrosociological approach to explaining social phenomena, interactionism focuses on everyday interactions between individuals (micro-sociological) and the meaning they attached to those interactions. Functionalists and conflict theorists analyze how social structures pattern our behaviors. Economic and other social forces make us get up and go to work, obey traffic laws, and raise families in similar ways, instilling in children conventional social values. This represents what I call a *top-down approach*—large social structures like the economy and government pattern our daily behaviors and interactions.

In contrast, interactionism represents a *bottom-up approach* - in which society is the product of everyday interactions. That is, interactionists maintain that a society's social structure—social reality—is brought into being only by human interaction. Through interaction, members of society negotiate a social reality, then act on that reality, which, in turn, helps maintain social order. This perspective is more difficult for most people to get their minds around, so I will briefly outline three interactionist approaches with examples in the hope that I can make interactionism a bit clearer.

Fig. 1.15 Diagram of interactionist process of social interaction leading to social order.

Symbolic Interactionism sounds intimidating but simply means that we *interact* with each other using sets of *symbols*. Associated with the work of Harold Blumer, George Herbert Mead, and Charles Horton Cooley, symbolic interactionism is the most prominent theory in the interactionist array. As we meet and interact with people, we use a host of symbols, but language is the largest set of symbols that we use in our day-to-day interactions. Through the use of language and other symbols (body language, gender, race, clothing, etc.), we negotiate a social reality that is made up of expected behaviors, which contributes to social order. Think about it this way: we have relationships with lots of people, but those relationships are not all the same—some friends knock on your front door and wait for you to come and open it, other friends walk right through the front door, go to the fridge, grab a beer, sit down, and wait for you. Through interacting with your friends using symbols (mostly language), symbolic interactionists would argue, you construct social realities with each friend, which guide your behaviors and make your relationships run smoothly because each of you knows how to behave in the context of that friendship. Try to apply this perspective to your romantic relationships. You probably developed different relationships with different partners; even though you are the same person, you have a different set of expectations from each partner based on how you negotiated your relationship through the use of symbols.

Ethnomethodology is another ominous-sounding theory, but when we break it down, it's pretty straightforward. Let's start at the end: "-ology" means the study of. Jumping to the front, "ethno" refers to race, people, or culture, and "method" means ways of behaving. Put it all together, and we get the *study of a people's ways*. **Ethnomethodology** focuses on the analysis of micro-processes of everyday life to determine the "methods" (ways) used by people to achieve a sense of social order—what we call society. While some see this approach as a bunch of nonsense, others have a cult-like devotion to it.

Harold Garfinkel (1967), the father of ethnomethodology, was fascinated with informal social norms, those unspoken, unwritten rules of social engagement like shaking hands when you are introduced to someone or being quiet and facing forward in an elevator. He understood that social rules like these helped maintain social order. He argued that one could understand the normal social order of everyday life by disrupting it.

A common strategy in ethnomethodology is the violation, or "breaching," of informal social rules. Garfinkel had his students go out into the community and violate a number of informal social rules, such as acting like a guest at their own home or saying "What do you mean by that?" when asked "How are you today?" He also had students turn and face a crowd in an elevator and engage them in conversation. Garfinkel found that people became confused and angry when students violated these "taken for granted" behaviors.

Ethnomethodologists believe that consensus is needed for human interaction, and consensus is built in part by shared, "taken for granted" social rules of conduct. They assume that people in society share these social rules, and when they are violated, one can get a glimpse of why the rules exist and gain a better understanding of society. For example, violating "rules" of elevator behavior may reveal those rules exist to preserve personal space. Ultimately, ethnomethodology hopes to uncover social rules and behaviors (ways) that help maintain social order.

Dramaturgy is not a laundry detergent even though it sounds like one ... Dramaturgy, it gets your whites, whiter! It is an interactionist approach that analyzes social interaction in terms of theatrical performance, hence the *drama* in dramaturgy. In his book *The Presentation of the Self in Everyday Life*, Erving Goffman (1959) laid out his notion of dramaturgy. This perspective studies social interactions, emphasizing the ways in which individuals work to create, maintain, dismantle, and present a shared understanding of reality. Unlike the other sociological perspectives we have discussed, which focus on explaining human behavior; dramaturgy focuses on understanding the effect of social context, social statuses, and roles on behavior.

Central to this approach is the interpretation of daily behaviors in theatrical terms such as *stage* (social context—work, school, home, etc.), *role* (your character—student), and *script* (your behaviors—study, attend class, etc.). Life is a never-ending theatrical performance in which we find ourselves on numerous stages taking on multiple roles and using untold numbers of scripts. We move between the stages of home as parent, to office as supervisor, to social events as party-goer, playing out our parts. In each setting, we are constantly trying to show others that we are good at our roles: good mother, competent worker, and reliable friend.

Goffman makes a distinction between "front-stage" and "back-stage" behaviors. Front-stage behaviors are public—at work interacting with others or giving a toast at a wedding. Back-stage behaviors are out of the public eye, such as at home in your pajamas, curlers in your hair, and eating Ben and Jerry's right from the container.

Dramaturgy argues that all behaviors are social performances that attempt to manage a desired impression of the self to others. This "impression management" is how we all act out our particular roles, using scripts to produce a desired result. For example, what type of *impression* would you like to *manage* in a job interview? You would most likely want to give the impression that you are the person for the job, and you would do that by showing up on time, wearing a suit, being polite, speaking clearly, and making eye contact with the interviewer. Given the "stage" of a job interview, you would act very differently from how you would act at the party you throw after you get the job.

TABLE 1.2 Theoretical Perspectives

Theoretical Perspective	Level of Analysis	General Approach	Example
Structural-Functionalism	Macrosociological	Social structures (social institutions such as government, the family, religion, education, and the economy) function together cooperatively to promote social stability and maintain *social order*.	The *federal government* provides financial aid for *families* of *college students* so they can get a college education and become taxpayers and productive participants in the *economy* and maintain the social order or our way of life.
Conflict	Macrosociological	Groups within society compete for access to and possession of valuable social resources. Those with the greatest economic power promulgate consensus through domination, ensuring *social order*. However, when the existing order is challenged by subordinate groups and they rebel, this can bring about social change.	Centuries of unequal treatment of African-Americans was challenged by members of black communities throughout the south of the United States in the late 1950's and early 1960's, culminating in the passing of the Civil Rights Act of 1964. This social change brought about more equality between the races.

(*Continued*)

Theoretical Perspective	Level of Analysis	General Approach	Example
Interactionist (Symbolic Interactionism)	Microsociological	Through interpersonal interactions, using a number of symbols, social reality is negotiated, which helps individuals interpret and understand social roles, which, in turn, guide *social order*.	Through symbols that include photos and text, images of women are sexualized in popular magazines, creating social expectations about how women should look and act. This can lead to girls to want to look like models and engage in eating behaviors to achieve model-type bodies, which are unrealistic.

The Bottom Line

Sociology is a scientific discipline that seeks to understand human social behavior, especially the origins, development, and organization of human society. Topics of study in sociology range from crime to the paranormal, from the individual to the state, from the divisions of race, gender, and social class to the shared beliefs of a common culture, and from social stability to radical change in whole societies. What links these diverse topics is sociology's unique perspective on how human action and consciousness both shape and are shaped by surrounding cultural and social structures.

We have seen that sociology is not common knowledge or common sense but rather the opposite. The sociological perspective seeks to reveal the social world as it is, not as we believe it to be, or how we would like it to be. We have also discussed that we all have the capacity to see the world through the lens of sociology by employing our sociological imagination, which allows us to see the connections between our own lives and the larger social and historical forces at work in the world.

Sociology developed, in part, out of the Enlightenment period in which traditional lines of authority were being challenged with new ideas of reason, scientific investigation, and individualism. This transition compounded with industrialization and urbanization led to great social upheaval in Western societies. The rise of sociology was in part a response to these dramatic changes. The early thinkers in sociology such as Comte, Marx, Weber, and Durkheim were fascinated with this change in social organization as they witnessed the transition from traditional to modern society.

We see the work of Spencer, Marx, Weber, and Durkheim coalesce into modern-day sociological perspectives. The work of Comte, Spencer, and Durkheim had the most influence on contemporary structural functionalism. While the roots of conflict theory lie in the work of Marx, it has been greatly expanded into neo-Marxism (which is the foundation of critical theory), race, feminist, and queer theories.

Over the course of about two hundred years, sociology has gone from an obscure element of social philosophy to a prominent scientific discipline whose analyses inform law, social, educational, and economic policies. Sociology is an integral part of the liberal arts education, and at least an introduction to the discipline is required as part of the general education of thousands of college students. While Comte's hope for sociology to become the "Queen Science" has not been fully realized, sociology's importance has been recognized by a range of organizations and institutions. In fact, as of 2015, the Medical College Admissions Test (MCAT) includes a section on sociology, recognizing the importance of the sociological perspective in the practice of medicine (Association of American Medical Colleges, 2015; Kain, 2012).

TRY THIS

These eight assumptions are essential to the sociological perspective. They are necessary to understand how sociologists view the social world (Buechler, 2008). Try and think of examples for each one of the eight assumptions listed in the table below. Each one of the assumptions below was discussed in this chapter.

TABLE 1.3 The Fundamental Sociological Assumptions

Assumptions	Meaning	Question	Example (s)
Society is a social construction (see the discussion on Durkheim on page 26)	Society is a human creation. Society has a dual nature: while it is created by the actions of individuals, it becomes an objective reality that persists over time and influences the actions of the individual.	What is a social construction? How could you show using cross-cultural comparisons that society is a social construction? Give at least two examples from your own life circumstances of how you are affected by society as a social construction.	

(*Continued*)

Assumptions	Meaning	Question	Example (s)
Society is an emergent reality (see the discussion on dysfunctions on page 33)	The reality of society is that it emerges from the interaction of individuals but is more than just the sum of the individuals. A social reality emerges that is greater than the sum of the parts.	Using the recent economic downturn as an example, show how the idea that society is an emergent reality can create new social realities.	
Society is a historical product (see the discussion about the sociological imagination on page 10)	In order to understand current social arrangements, we need to look at historical social organizations. This allows us to engage in comparative analysis and understand social change.	We have discussed the idea of change and the effect of historical period on biography extensively. Give two examples of how society has changed in your lifetime. Also, imagine you were born in 1915 in America. How could that historical reality have impacted your life? Give at least three examples of how that historical period in America could have impacted your life.	
Society consists of social structures (see the discussion about structural functionalism on page 32)	Society is made of social structures that constrain the individual but are also shaped by actors' actions.	We have discussed social structure in terms of social institutions. Give at least two examples of how institutions can constrain behavior and why they do.	
Society consists of reflexive actors (see the discussion on symbolic interaction on page 35)	We are aware of ourselves and others. We monitor and adjust our actions and beliefs based on the perceived social context and other elements of social interactions.	Give an example of how in a specific social situation you are aware of yourself and others and how that can influence how you act.	

Assumptions	Meaning	Question	Example (s)
Society is an interaction of agency and structure (see the discussion on the interactionist perspective on page 34)	Our interactions are shaped by social structures like the economy and social structures are shaped by our interactions.	Give one example from your life of how you interact with a particular institution.	
Society has multiple levels (see the discussion about micro- and macro-sociology on page 14)	Microsociological analysis focuses on the reality created through day-to-day interactions between individuals, and macrosociological analysis seeks to find the "big picture" by investigating large social structures, institutions, and large-scale patterns.	Give one example of micro-sociological analysis and one example of macrosociological analysis.	
Society involves unintended consequences (See the discussion about manifest and latent functions on page 32)	Sometimes, our actions have unintended consequences and affect ourselves or another person in a way we did not intend. Anytime a collective of humans is engaged in an endeavor, there is the *manifest* function of that endeavor and *latent* or unintended consequences of the interactions.	Give an example from your own life of how your actions had an unintended consequence and affected you or another person in a way you did not intend.	

Figure Credits

Fig. 1.1: Copyright © Depositphotos/AlexBrylov.

Fig. 1.3: Source: http://trends.collegeboard.org/student-aid/figures-tables/total-undergraduate-student-aid-source-type-2013-14.

Fig. 1.4: Source: http://educationcrossroads.utk.edu/GraphicsPage.asp.

Fig. 1.5: Copyright © M Tracy Hunter (CC BY-SA 3.0) at https://commons.wikimedia.org/wiki/File:2014_Gini_Index_World_Map,_income_inequality_distribution_by_country_per_World_Bank.svg.

Fig. 1.6: Copyright © Waqas Ahmed (CC BY-SA 3.0) at https://commons.wikimedia.org/wiki/File:Ibn_Khaldun.jpg.

Fig. 1.7: "Auguste Comte," https://commons.wikimedia.org/wiki/File:Auguste_Comte.jpg. Copyright in the Public Domain.

Fig. 1.8: "Harriet Martineau," https://commons.wikimedia.org/wiki/File:Harriet_martineau_portrait.jpg. Copyright in the Public Domain.

Fig. 1.9: John Jabez Edwin Mayall, "Karl Marx," https://commons.wikimedia.org/wiki/File:Karl_Marx.jpg. Copyright in the Public Domain.

Fig. 1.10: "Emile Durkheim ," https://commons.wikimedia.org/wiki/File:Emile_Durkheim.jpg. Copyright in the Public Domain.

Fig. 1.11: "Max Weber," https://commons.wikimedia.org/wiki/File:Max_Weber_1894.jpg. Copyright in the Public Domain.

Fig. 1.12: "W.E.B. Du Bois," https://commons.wikimedia.org/wiki/File:Du_Bois,_W._E._B..jpg. Copyright in the Public Domain.

CHAPTER 2

DOING SOCIOLOGY: INVESTIGATING HUMAN BEHAVIOR IN EVERYDAY LIFE

Casual Investigation vs. Systematic Investigation

Imagine you are on vacation in Paris, France. You are having a wonderful time eating crêpes, drinking wine, falling in love, and seeing the sights. One day, you find yourself lost in the city. No matter how long you stare at your map of Paris, you just cannot find the Eiffel Tower (all you really have to do is look up). So you approach a woman on the street and ask her politely if she could point you to the Eiffel Tower. She shrugs, grunts, and pushes you aside as she moves on. What may you conclude from this observation? That Parisians are rude. They do not like Americans. They hate to give directions. That they smell. Well, you walk around some more and finally look up ... ah, there it is, the Eiffel Tower. Later that evening, you return to your hotel and there in the lobby is the rude Parisian woman you asked for directions earlier in the day. Come to find out (from the nosy desk clerk) the woman is a German tourist on holiday, and she did not know where the Eiffel Tower was, either.

Fig. 2.1 The skyline of Paris

This is what I refer to as *casual investigation* of the social world. We all engage in casual investigation. You cannot live among others and not wonder about their behaviors. I bet just today you saw someone do something and wondered why she did it, or why she did it the way she did, or even think how you would never have done that. I bet you definitely wondered about someone else's behavior if you drove today! To this day, I wonder why women do the things they do. Moreover, I am sure women wonder the same thing about men. Not only do we make observations and then wonder about others' behaviors, but we usually attempt to *explain* those behaviors. These explanations are what I call a *mini-theory* that attempts to explain the behaviors we have just observed. However, these observations and mini-theories are flawed because we have conducted casual investigation. We have not conducted our investigation in any systematic or scientific way that allows us to eliminate the errors found in casual investigation.

In the example above, we draw incorrect conclusions from a faulty observation. You assumed that the woman you asked for directions was a Parisian and she knew her way around Paris. That was a faulty observation. Then you drew an incorrect conclusion about the French being rude and not liking Americans (this is also a faulty *mini-theory* ... or is it?).

Recently, the Paris Chamber of Commerce and the Regional Tourism Committee concluded a massive campaign aimed at teaching salespeople, waitstaff, and sightseeing guides to be less rude to tourists. The program culminated with the distribution of 30,000 manuals on how to create a better welcome to Paris (Gallo, 2013). To learn more, go to www.doyouspeaktouriste.fr.

In sociology, we conduct social research on human behavior, and from that research, we draw conclusions that become published scientific findings. Many times, those findings are used to inform laws and social policies, influence therapeutic practices, or develop social theory. Therefore, as responsible sociologists/scientists, we cannot afford to make poor observations and draw faulty conclusions because our conclusions inform laws, policies, and practices that have the potential to affect peoples' lives. If our work as sociologists may affect the lives of many people, we must take care to use a method of systematic investigation that avoids the pitfalls of casual observation.

What Is Social Research?

"Research is formalized curiosity. It is poking and prying with a purpose."
— Zora Neale Hurston

Social research is the systematic investigation of the social world. Social research helps us understand the world beyond our immediate experience and provides us with an understanding of how the social world operates. Topics in social research might include poverty, race/ethnicity, social and gender inequality, social networks, interpersonal attraction, and the influence of peer pressure. Research on topics like these and others have the potential to provide vital information to government agencies, policymakers, non-governmental organizations and other interested groups.

Many times, research is driven by personal interests. Some say that many social researchers are propelled into research by their own biographies, experiences in their own lives that create their research interests—sometimes referred to as "me-search." I know that for me this is true. My PhD dissertation was an examination of the well-being of adult children of alcoholics. I grew up in an alcoholic home, and I was fascinated by the topic, especially how children can emerge from such damaging home lives and still be well-adjusted, productive adults.

While research on a topic may be influenced by personal interest, the collection, analysis and interpretation of data must remain objective. A researcher has to let the data fall where it may and not influence the data to fall in the direction he *wishes* it to fall. Subjective biases and value judgments should never cloud the research process.

The Value of Social Research

"Research is to see what everybody else has seen, and to think what nobody else has thought."
— Albert Szent-Gyorgyi

In our daily lives, we are confronted with the findings from social research: everything from the architecture of the buildings at your college, to how billboards for tobacco products are placed in certain neighborhoods, to the way products are arranged on supermarket shelves. For me, social research is important for several reasons:

1. **It can be counterintuitive and dispel myths:** Let's take a common belief about the death of a spouse. There is a widespread belief that it is more difficult for a husband or

wife to deal with the sudden death of his or her spouse than a long, anticipated death. Carr et al. (2001) showed that especially for older men who lost a wife suddenly, it was easier to handle psychologically than a lingering illness. These are valuable findings for therapists and bereavement specialists who counsel widowers.

2. **It can explain why people behave the way they do:** It is one thing to describe *what* behaviors teenagers engage in, such as alcohol or substance use, but perhaps more important is understanding *why* they do these things. Research conducted by Alexander Jensen and Shawn Whiteman (2014) has shown a strong relationship between parental favoritism and teenage alcohol and substance use. While most parents admit to having a favorite child, they try to hide those feelings and treat all children alike, but when non-favorites feel that they are treated unfairly, problems arise. This research showed a correlation between feeling on the outs and substance abuse (alcohol, drugs, and cigarettes). *Why* teenagers engage in substance abuse can, in part, be connected to their feelings of not being their parents' favorite child.
3. **It creates new knowledge about the social world:** Who do you think is more likely to be successful in high school: boys or girls? How about college? Research from Zimbardo and Coulombe (2015) shows that there may be a "demise of guys" in terms of their once-social and academic eminence. From elementary school to graduate school, men in the U.S. currently lag behind women. Males are 30% more likely to drop out of high school than girls and are 10% less likely than females to obtain a bachelor's degree or higher. Moreover, males make up 67% of students enrolled in special education and remedial classes nationwide. Coupled with these academic failings, boys and men in the U.S. are reporting greater worries about intimacy and relationships. This, and other research like it, shows that society is being confronted with a new social landscape in which boys and men are underperforming academically and struggling with intimacy.
4. **It can potentially influence social policies and create laws:** Scenic Vermont saw a 770% rise in heroin use between 2000 and 2014 (DiSalvo, 2014). In January 2014, the governor of Vermont, Peter Shumlin, devoted his entire state of the state address to heroin addiction. Seeking to remedy the growing crisis, the state has adopted several programs that will hopefully service recovering addicts and reduce access and use. One of the programs it has initiated is a Syringe Exchange Program (SEP) in an attempt to make intravenous drug use safer and reduce the spread of blood-borne diseases. The decision to adopt such a program was based mainly on social research on needle exchange programs conducted over the past twenty-five years (U.S. Department of Health and Human Services, 1998; Vlahov and Junge, 1998; Marmor et al., 2000: Wodak and Cooney, 2004; CDC, 2008). This rich body of social research helped convince policymakers in Vermont that an SEP would be effective dealing with at least one element of their heroin epidemic.

THE TRANSYLVANIA EFFECT

A connection between phases of the moon and other phenomena such as suicide, violent behavior, mood swings, and natural disasters is referred to as the "Transylvania Effect." Hundreds of studies have been conducted and lots of ink has been spilled attempting to find a connection, but no correlations have been found. The "Transylvania Effect" is a good example of information that seems to be common knowledge but is just downright wrong!

Knowledge and Social Research

As a society, how do we know what we know? That is, where does our knowledge come from? Much of our knowledge is, in a sense, transmitted through *tradition*—the handing down of customs and beliefs from one generation to another. Displaying the flag on Memorial Day, having the bride's family pay for the wedding, and wearing black to a funeral are all typical American traditions. Why do we do these things? Because it's the way it has always been done; it's tradition.

Another type of knowledge is *authority*—the power to influence thought, opinion, or behavior by socially accepted sources such as your parents, the police, government officials, religious/community leaders, and experts (authorities) like your professors. Information from these sources is viewed as legitimate because it comes from some authority figure like your professor, who is an authority, or your mom, or from your family physician. Information from these people has to be right ... right?

Not necessarily. The problem with using knowledge based on tradition or authority, or even our own intuition, is that many times, it is misleading or just plain wrong. Ever heard that more babies are born during a full moon? I have actually heard nurses say this is true. I have also heard that it was just an urban myth. So which is it: more babies born during the full moon or not? Well, an astronomer and physicist named Dan Caton (2002) conducted the largest study ever that examined this supposed phenomenon. He looked at twenty years of data from the National Center for Health Statistics (Natality Statistics Branch), which added up to about seventy million U.S. births, and he found zero correlation between full moons and increased deliveries!

TRY THIS

Ask a number of people like friends, family, coworkers, and people on the street if they think that there is an increase in births during a full moon. Keep track of how many think it's true and why, and track those who say no and why. What type of knowledge are the believers basing their opinions on? What type of knowledge are the non-believers basing their opinions on? I bet you will find that most people believe this to be true, and you will see different sets of reasoning (knowledge) used across the two groups.

The Scientific Method

Think back to the last time you were in a heated discussion with someone and each of you was trying to *prove* your point. Invariably, one of you will ask the other to provide "proof" or evidence that supports (proves) your point. If you offer up your feelings, intuition, say your mom told you or everyone knows that, your opponent will most likely (and deservedly) laugh at you. Typically, in our Western rational culture, we expect people to offer scientific evidence to support their arguments.

In your discussion with your friend, you may cite the results of social research. You hear it on the news every day, you read about it, and your professors probably tell you about it each time you meet. You have probably used it to prove a point or win an argument. But how is it conducted? What are the methods or techniques researchers use to investigate the social world? In addition, what is the process they employ to achieve valid and reliable (we'll discuss these things later) findings?

As we have discussed, knowledge derived from non-scientific methods can be inaccurate or wrong and is not generalizable—used to describe groups larger than those observed. Moreover, people are dubious of "proof" that does not come from scientific inquiry. Using the scientific method—the set of systematic techniques of investigation and analysis used to organize and design research—sociologists conduct research that generates findings, which can be applied to larger populations, and draw conclusions that help explain social behavior. The father of sociology, Auguste Comte, envisioned sociology as science of society equivalent to the natural sciences of physics and chemistry. This vision has influenced generations of sociologists who use the scientific method in an attempt to "legitimate" sociology as a scientific discipline.

Nuts and Bolts: Some Important Research Terms

Before we move on, I want to introduce some important terms that will help make each step in the research process a bit more clear and consistent. All research starts with considering some set of **concepts**, which are abstract ideas, notions, or mental images that correspond to elements of our social lives. "Social class," "marital satisfaction," "poverty," and "gender" are all good examples of concepts. One of the problems with concepts is they are abstract, difficult to define and measure, mostly because they cannot be directly observed. Can you directly observe social class or marital satisfaction? You can observe indicators of social class, such as someone driving a Bentley, living in Beverly Hills, and shopping on Rodeo Drive. Witnessing a husband and wife argue throughout their entire flight from Los Angeles to Tahiti might indicate they are not satisfied in their marriage ... or they just like to fight on planes. So, how do we as researchers measure what we cannot directly observe?

Our objective is to take a fuzzy concept like social class and turn it into a measurable variable. In order to do this, we must operationalize social class. **Operationalization** is the process of indicating exactly how a social concept will be measured. We could operationalize social class by measuring income, educational level and wealth. While we cannot directly observe social class, we *can* measure income, educational level and wealth. Therefore, when we set out on a path of research, we must operationalize each of our concepts by defining how we will measure them.

The language of research is a language of variables. In fact, this language of variables would allow me and Sheldon Cooper to discuss research even though he is a theoretical physicist and I am a sociologist. When discussing social research, it is common to talk in terms of variables in order to understand what was being studied, how a researcher views the relationship between variables, and to understand the conclusions he draws. A typical conversation between sociology geeks might sound like this: "How did you operationalize your independent variables, and what exactly was the dependent variable in your latest study?" asks Nathan. "Well, I constructed a nested dependent variable because I was using a repeated measures MANOVA design ... blah, blah," replies Nellie.

A **variable** is anything that has quality or quantity and can vary—something that *varies* or changes. Common variables in sociology include age, sex, race/ethnicity, and religion. You can see that age can change over time or between individuals, sex can be either male or female, and people can belong to many religions.

Variables come in two flavors: independent and dependent. An **independent variable** is any element whose characteristics have an influence on the dependent variable. The **dependent variable** is any element whose characteristics or variations are influenced, affected, or caused by independent variables. Sometimes, the dependent variable is referred to as the *outcome variable,* because its outcome *depends* on the values of independent variables.

Now let's put it all together. The *concept* of social class—placing people into groups based on a vague notion of similar levels of income, wealth, education, consumption patterns, and life-styles—is too vague to investigate or measure directly. For us to create the *variable* social class, we must *operationalize* it by defining it as measured by: *income*—the amount of money an individual earns each year from jobs and investments; *education*—the highest level of education a person has attained; and *home ownership*—whether an individual owns his primary residence or not. So, now you have a clear way to measure a fuzzy concept.

Causation or Correlation?

Let's look at how independent and dependent variables are related. Social research has shown a strong association between growing up in an alcoholic home environment and becoming an alcohol abuser (White, Johnson, and Buyske, 2000; Ellis, Zucker, and Fitzgerald, 1997). However, social researchers would not say that growing up in an alcoholic home *causes* alcoholism, because they cannot show that there is a cause-and-effect relationship, and there are other genetic issues involved (McGue et al., 1997). Rarely in sociology do we talk about causation, or the idea that an independent variable causes a dependent variable. What researches can say is that there is a strong likelihood or connection between growing up in an alcoholic home and becoming an alcoholic. Social researchers are likely to talk about the correlation—the measure or degree of relationship between two variables—when describing how variables are associated. So, in this case, we can say that there is a strong correlation between growing up in an alcoholic home environment and becoming an alcoholic. Researchers on this topic use language like children growing up in alcoholic homes are *more likely* to become alcoholic, or alcoholic homes *contribute to* adult children's alcoholism, but not alcoholic home life *causes* alcoholism (Jacob and Johnson, 1997).

Figure 2.2 below expresses the connection between independent variable (X) and dependent variable (Y). The arrow in the diagram can be interpreted as X causes Y, X influences Y, or X affects Y.

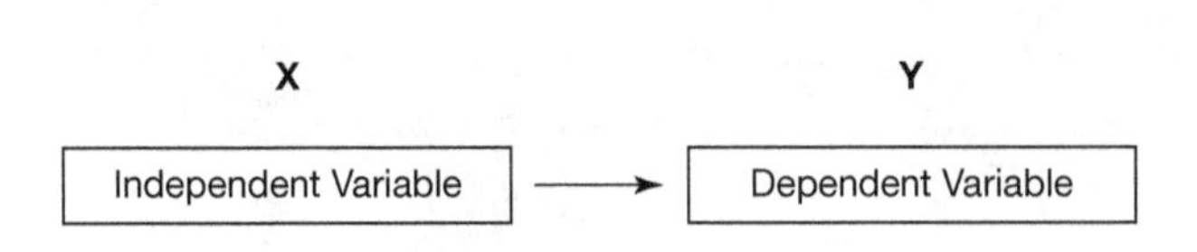

Fig. 2.2 This is the typical representation of the relationship between Independent and Dependent Variables

Not all research is conducted using the same logical reasoning. Researchers working on topics that have well-developed theories are interested in supporting those theories with empirical evidence. Many times, investigators begin research by noticing patterns that appear in the data they have collected. Commonly in research, we refer to two broad methods of reasoning as the deductive and inductive approaches.

The deductive approach works down from the most general to the most specific, from theory to hypothesis to observations. It is sometimes called the "top-down" or "theory-driven" approach. Figure 2.3 (A) shows how deductive research can start with a theory, generate a hypothesis to be tested, and then make observations that either do or do not support the hypothesis. For example, starting from a more general theory of classroom environment and children's health, researchers Melissa Milkie and Catharine Warner (2011) hypothesized that negative classroom factors, such as the lack of heat and basic supplies, would be associated with emotional and behavioral problems in first grade students. Their hypothesis was supported, indicating that particular features of a classroom environment can contribute to or heighten emotional and behavior problems among first-graders. Imagine the deductive approach as a theory in search of evidence to support it—a solid explanation of some social phenomenon that needs data to support it.

In contrast, the inductive approach begins with the specific and builds to the general. This approach moves from specific observations to broader generalizations and then theories, sometimes called "bottom-up" or "data-driven" research. Inductive approach researchers collect significant amounts of data on a topic of interest to them. Next, they step back and try to get a "bird's eye" view of the data, looking for patterns that may appear. Finally, they attempt to construct a theory that could explain these patterns. Someone investigating interpersonal attraction, for instance, may collect personal bios from online dating sites and notice a clear pattern in the language men and women use in describing themselves as potential partners. Confirming these patterns, she may then develop a theory of how people present themselves on online dating sites.

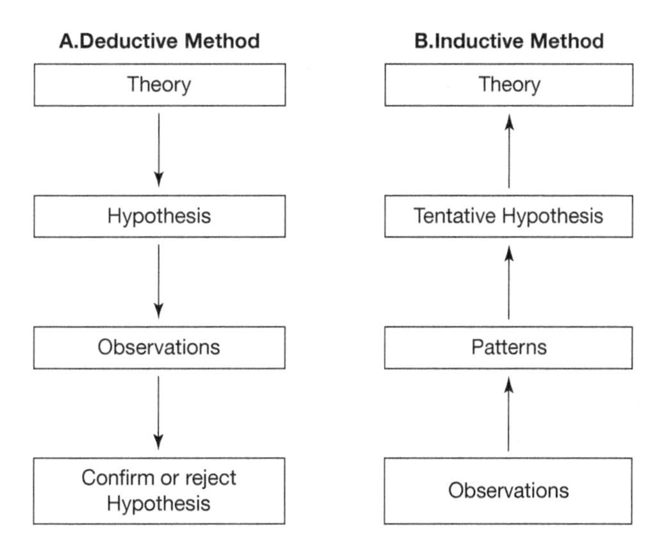

Fig. 2.3 (a) Deductive vs. (b) Inductive Research

In figure 2.3 (B) you can see how the steps in the inductive process are essentially reversed from that of deductive research. The inductive approach to research can be thought of as data in search of a theory—many observations that form clear patterns that need some way to be explained.

REPLICATION IN RESEARCH: A BAD EXAMPLE

In 1989, two researchers, B. Stanley Pons and Martin Fleischmann, claimed to have achieved nuclear fusion in a jar of water at room temperature (cold fusion). This was cutting-edge research, and the cold fusion process had the promise to provide an abundant, clean, and cheap energy source (Fleischmann and Pons, 1989). The scientific community was abuzz with excitement, and immediately, other researchers attempted to replicate Fleischmann and Pons' work (trying out their recipe).

That's when things turned ugly. NO other research team could replicate Fleischmann and Pons' work—they had a bad recipe! The inability to replicate their work signaled to the larger scientific community that Fleischmann and Pons either conducted sloppy research or lied about their findings. As a result, cold fusion research has largely been discredited and marginalized by the scientific community. Ultimately, both researchers were discredited, and they quietly left the U.S. and worked abroad.

The Process of Social Research

Social research is a systematic investigation of the social world that contains procedures and rules of conduct that guide the research process. The research process is exactly that—a process that contains a number of steps that should be followed in a particular order. Figure 2.4 below illustrates the sequence of steps in the research process that sociologists typically follow.

Think about conducting research being similar to writing a recipe. Recipes must be accurate and precise; how much of an ingredient you use is just as important as the order in which ingredients are combined as well as the oven temperature and cook time. As a researcher, you have to describe in detail how you conducted each step in the process so that your work, like a recipe, can be followed and others will get consistent results or, at the very least, be able to conduct the research the same way you did. If you give someone your recipe for chocolate chip cookies and he follows it, he should get chocolate chip cookies. You if give someone your recipe for chocolate cookies, he uses it and gets banana bread, that's a bad recipe!

In scientific research, replication—repeating research in all its important details to achieve consistent results—is necessary to assure that research findings are valid and reliable. Additionally, independent replication of research acts as a checks-and-balances system that helps detect faulty or dishonest work. On page 52 is an example that shows the importance of replication to illuminate shoddy research.

Steps in the Research Process

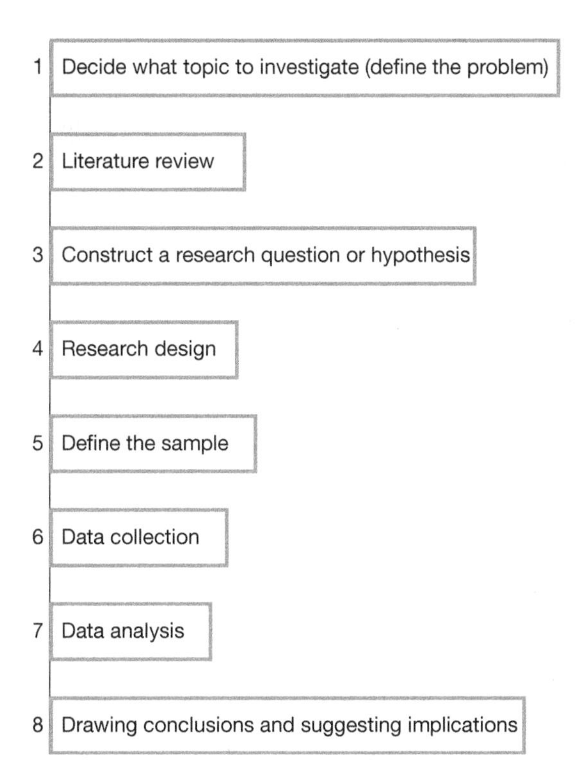

Fig. 2.4 Steps in the Research Process

STEP 1. Decide What Topic to Investigate (Define the Problem)

Topics of investigation are unlimited in social research. Research topics can range from the effect of peer pressure on childhood memories to human trafficking to alternate urban economies. You can do research on anything you find interesting or intriguing. As I mentioned above, much of the research in sociology is biography. This means that many researchers end up studying things that have some connection to their own lives. For example, W.E.B. Du Bois, the first African American to earn a doctorate from Harvard, wrote prolifically on the plight of African Americans in the U.S. Many feminist scholars base their work on their own life experiences as women, and queer scholarship reflects the experiences of researchers who identify with the LGBTQ community.

STEP 2. Review of the Literature

Once you have decided on a topic, the next step is to summarize the relevant research that has been conducted on that subject and show how your work is connected to previous and current research. The *literature review* is, for me, perhaps the most important step in the research process. This review gives you both a sense of the breadth and depth of the literature produced on your topic, and reveals past and current work as well as suggestions for future investigation. You will discover many things about your topic and the work that has been devoted to it. You may find a dearth in the research or inadequate theoretical structure, or you may find that your work could extend existing theories. You may find that your topic is not well-investigated or there has not been any work done on it in a long time. You may discover that there are conventional ways to define or measure your variables that are well-accepted within the field. However, you would never know any of this without doing a comprehensive review of the literature.

A thorough review of the relevant literature is an imposing task that will most likely require the use of digital, print, and other archival materials. While the Internet has made literature reviews faster and easier, material for some topics have yet to join the ranks of digital literature. For example, a friend of mine who recently finished his doctorate in marine archaeology told me that he spent nearly all his time reviewing original sources in Seville, Spain, hunched over stained, aging manuscripts and manifests. Many delicate original documents like this have yet to be digitized or will never be digitized. The "lit review" for my doctoral dissertation took more than a year in an era before the Internet. Fortunately, much, but not all, of the material you will need has been digitized and is available via the Internet or through academic library sources.

STEP 3. Develop a Hypothesis or a Research Question

Now that you have decided on your topic and have completed your literature review, you can move to the next step in the research process, which is developing a research question or hypothesis. Research questions are broad and typically not specific. That is, research questions do not predict the direction or strength of the relationship between independent and dependent variables. Hypotheses, on the other hand, are specific predictions of the behavior of variables. Below, I have shown a sample of both a research question and a hypothesis.

Research question: Does heavy marijuana use affect academic performance?

Hypothesis: Heavy marijuana use will negatively affect academic performance, specifically grade-point average.

I think from the example above it is easy to see the difference between the research question and hypothesis. The research question is exactly that: it is a question about the relationship between two or more variables that leaves room for discovery and interpretation. Hypotheses, on the other hand, are specific statements about the relationship of the variables and the direction of the effects of some variables on others. Hypotheses can be considered little ways to test a larger theory. That is, theories are too broad to test directly. We typically test theories by breaking up little pieces of those theories, and we call those pieces hypotheses, which are more easily tested or investigated. While hypotheses can be more manageable ways to test larger theories, they don't have to be. Regardless of how your research is guided, by a research question or a hypothesis, it has to be testable, like the examples above. Asking, "What is the meaning of life?" is not a testable research question.

Some people use research questions as broad guides as they investigate topics, which help them develop more specific hypotheses. For instance, "What are the effects of marijuana use on college students' behaviors?" would be an example of a research question that could guide the development of hypotheses like the one above. Not all research is hypothesis driven; research questions can stand alone to guide research projects.

Recent research on marijuana use and academic performance shows that heavy pot use (those who smoked fifteen times or more a month) contributed to "college students skipping more classes, spending less time studying, earning lower grades, dropping out of college, and being unemployed after college." These findings come from a very cool study that looked at twelve hundred college students over a ten-year period. The researchers found that not only did heavy pot use affect their academic performance, but it also had the potential to disrupt their working lives downstream of college (Arria et al., 2013).

STEP 4. Develop a Research Design

Now that we have a testable research question or usable hypothesis, we are now able to develop an overall design for our research. Research design is influenced by several things such as time, topic, access to respondents, cost, and many other factors. Many times, these are beyond the control of the researcher. However, many obstacles can be overcome by a creative researcher who can manage to come up with a usable design and collect the data.

For me, the most influential factor influencing research design is your topic. If you are researching something relatively innocuous, such as how people intend on voting in the next election, you can come up with a number of designs to elicit that information from individuals. For example, you could stop people on the quad of your college and ask them about their voting habits, you could call people up after dinner and ask how they will vote in the next election, or you could easily send out an Internet survey asking about people's decisions to vote in the next election. My point is that something as banal as how you will vote in the next election allows you to ask people in a variety of ways and settings that are nonthreatening and not terribly personal. Additionally, questions about voting behaviors will not make people feel threatened, or feel like they have to give a desirable answer, or feel that the information is sensitive.

But what if you are investigating something more sensitive? For example, what if you were investigating people's interest in and practice of sadomasochism/bondage and domination, or SMBD? That's right, kinky sex. It would not be productive to call people on the phone after dinner and ask if they were into Latex. A phone survey would not be appropriate for this topic for a number of reasons. For one, this is a highly sensitive topic. In addition, your odds of calling a house and getting someone on the phone who is into SMBD is remote; you could waste months or years without getting a single respondent (we'll discuss these and other issues later in the chapter). You can see how your topic will help guide your design—the set of methods you will use to elicit the information from your respondents.

Quantitative and Qualitative Designs

Generally speaking, research designs are either quantitative or qualitative in nature. However, there are many studies that incorporate both a quantitative and a qualitative research component; we call these multi-methods or mixed-methods studies. For now, let's start with highlighting the differences between qualitative and quantitative research.

Quantitative research is research in which the findings are summarized using numbers or statistics—the data has been quantified. Overwhelmingly, sociologists like to use quantitative research. This may be a function of our positivist roots; we seem to feel the need in our Western rational society to present quantitative evidence to support our arguments, and people seem to be more impressed with "hard" data.

Quantitative Research Designs—And the Survey Says?

Surveys are, by far, the most popular research design used by sociologists, mainly because they are cheap, fast, and can capture relatively large samples. I bet you have taken part in some type of survey. Have you ever been stopped at the mall while shopping by someone with a clipboard wanting to know about your shopping behaviors or your attitude toward the economy? Has someone ever called your home and asked you what type of breakfast cereal you prefer? Alternatively, have you received an email asking you to take a short survey about your cell phone service? Have you ever filled out an in-class survey about your professor's performance? If you answered yes to any of these questions, you have taken part in a survey. Even if you didn't answer yes to any of the questions above, you've been part of the ultimate survey—you have been counted in the census.

The census represents the ultimate survey and is perhaps the oldest type of survey. A **census** is an attempt to enumerate a given population using systematic methods. The ancient Egyptians supposedly took a census as long ago as 3340 BCE—that's more than 5,300 years of the government trying to track us down (Office for National Statistics, 2014). It didn't stop there: ancient civilizations such as Greece, Rome, China, and India conducted censuses so they could get their money through taxation and find out who was fit enough for military service. While most ancient censuses were invasive, looking at how much stuff you had so the government could tax you appropriately or press healthy men into military service, today's U.S. census is much more benign, seeking to count and describe American households.

Survey Types

Interview Surveys

Surveys come in a variety of forms or types. Surveys can be conducted in person, over the phone, online, or be self-administered. Let's take a look at each type in turn.

Face-to-face or in-person surveys can be effective for certain types of research but have some drawbacks. Marketing firms frequently use face-to-face surveys because samples can be obtained fast. Again, think about your topic. Most people are not going to be offended by an in-person interview about what type of gum they prefer. Another popular use of the in-person interview is the exit poll, a survey of voters as they exit polling stations. Asking what political party you just voted for is not that invasive. While it seems face-to-face surveys should be used for research on innocuous topics, Alfred Kinsey (1948, 1953) used them to ask people about their sexual orientation, experiences, and habits. In his groundbreaking and socially influential work, Kinsey and his associates conducted face-to-face interviews with more than 18,000 men and women. Among a host of other social changes, their work influenced the radical changes in our attitudes toward sexuality that emerged during the 1960s and '70s. Behold the power of research!

In-person interviews have some advantages, such as immediate responses, high response rates, and typically fewer "I don't know" responses. Additionally, the interviewer is able to clarify the meaning of questions to respondents. Face-to-face surveys typically have higher response rates than other survey types because people can't slam the door shut on an interviewer, throw away a survey they received in the mail, or ignore or delete an online survey. In-person interviews also have the advantage of giving the researcher the ability to probe a respondent's answer, asking them to clarify or expand on their responses. Face-to-face research also allows interviewers to gather other information about respondents while conducting the interview by observing their appearance, noting demeanor, speech and other traits. This is a feature you can't get in any other survey style.

Generally, face-to-face survey research is conducted either by well-funded studies that many times demand high response rates or by researchers who seek a small number of respondents and are looking for a sample of convenience or a grab sample (more about sampling later). It comes down to face-to-face surveys being really expensive and time- and labor-intensive. Interviewers have to be extremely well-trained and disciplined in order to not bias responses, and that training/practice is expensive and time-consuming. Kinsey found that he had to spend a great deal of time training his interviewers so that they didn't chuckle, chortle, or snicker at individuals' responses or, more importantly, so they would not respond with disgust or shock to participants' answers. He developed a rigorous interview schedule that had to be followed precisely. In fact, many of his interview designs and innovations are still incorporated in today's interview research.

THERE'S AN APP FOR THAT

KinseyReporter as the name suggests, is a mobile survey platform for sharing data about sexual behaviors. Participants are encouraged to submit anonymous reports of sexual or intimate activity within 24 hours of an encounter. Users have the option of reporting their own sexual behavior or that of others. Material that has been submitted so far includes sexual behaviors and events, health issues, sexual violence, public displays of affection and a range of other experiences (Indiana University, 2015).

Phone Surveys

Phone surveys are, unsurprisingly, surveys conducted over the phone. Nearly all current phone surveys employ a number of high-tech ways to create samples and capture data. Random Digit Dialing (RDD) allows researchers to randomly dial phone numbers within a given area code and an exchange region (the first three digits of phone numbers). Therefore, all possible phone numbers that have been assigned in a given geographical area can be dialed by RDD, even cell phone numbers and unlisted numbers, which can reduce bias toward and type of phone. Among the many tools phone survey researchers have at their disposal is Computer Assisted Telephone Interviewing (CATI). This system allows interviewers to randomly dial a phone number (using RDD) and follow an electronic script on the screen in front of them while they conduct interviews. Using CATI, the interviewer sticks to a script that allows him to ask all respondents the same questions in the same order.

Like all survey types, phone surveys have both advantages and disadvantages. The real advantage of phone surveys is the sheer volume of interviews one interviewer can conduct. Imagine a researcher trudging around a neighborhood in a snowstorm, banging on people's front doors and trying to conduct face-to-face interviews, versus sitting in a nice, warm room with a steaming cup of hot chocolate. Which would you rather do? And which scenario will most likely yield more completed surveys? With the assistance of RDD and CATI, a single interviewer can dial hundreds of numbers and complete dozens of surveys in a single shift.

The interviewer's appearance is not an issue with phone surveys. Keeping to the script and using a monotone voice reduces cues for socially desirable answers. Like the face-to-face interviewer, the phone researcher can probe the respondent for more complete answers. However, unlike our friend slogging from door to door all alone, the phone interviewer can get assistance from others in the phone center if he needs help with a particular question or respondent.

While phone surveys are wildly popular among some of the most powerful research organizations (Pew, NORC, ICPSR), they do present their own set of problems. Because of the proliferation of marketing phone research, legitimate research is hindered by the public's perception of the call being a telemarketing scheme. Many times, my wife's response to a sales call is to ask the caller to remove us from their call list. She recently received a call from someone claiming to be from the IRS. He stated that she owed a large sum of money in back taxes and that severe punishment, even the possibility of prison time, was imminent unless she paid up. She was immediately suspicious because the caller had a thick foreign accent, used poor grammar, and ended the call with "may God help you." Ultimately, she alerted the local police and the IRS to the potential scam. Obviously, then, phone survey researchers have to overcome resistance to participation because people think their call is just another telemarketer or multinational scam artist, especially when personal information could be involved. My wife has one foolproof way to avoid dealing with the dinnertime interlopers: she simply hangs up. Like the survey you get in the mail and use as kindling in your fireplace or simply throw in the garbage, the ability to hang up abruptly on a phone survey is a serious downfall. Finally, the proliferation of caller ID and voicemail to screen one's calls can negatively impact the access to and responses from potential research participants.

Self-Administered Surveys

Online Surveys

I have to be honest: I receive dozens of requests to participate in online surveys every month through my email, and I usually just delete them. What do you do when you are asked to participate in online surveys? Do you always take part? Are you an online survey snob, only taking the ones you deem worthy? Or do you just hit delete?

While websites like SurveyMonkey.com and Zoomerang.com allow the public to create and distribute online surveys, the massive increase in online surveys has been mainly a result of the private sector's desire to sell us more stuff by finding out more about us. Companies like Nielson (yup, the TV ratings guys), Harris Interactive (which Nielson owns), and Knowledge Networks conduct thousands of online surveys each year to gain general marketing information and targeted research they conduct for their clients. Collecting data online is here to stay. As the Internet expands globally and people around the world spend more and more time online, private sector businesses, government organizations, and academic research will become more Internet based. Big data (or mega-data) is used by tens of thousands of organizations, both private and public, to understand both the changing commercial habits of people and changing social habits and attitudes.

Online surveys provide researchers with some real advantages, such as no printing costs and no postage costs, and as with all self-administered questionnaires, the respondents have the ability to work at their own pace in the privacy of their own home. Most people feel comfortable online, and that comfort may in part help reduce people's reluctance to take online surveys. Just like those surveys you get in the mail and immediately trash, the online survey is easily deleted. Hacking episodes like the ones that affected millions of shoppers at Target and the Ashley Madison infidelity hook-up site, have given rise to issues of security on the Internet. Many people do not take online surveys because they are unconvinced that their personal information and responses are safe.

BIG DATA

What is big data? A business type named Doug Laney (2001) said that big data is comprised of the three V's: volume, velocity, and variety. **Big data**, then, are large data sets being created so fast out of such a variety of data that conventional data management and analysis methods are inadequate to interpret them. Ever been on the Internet doing a little shopping or browsing? When you switched sites, did you see ads at the top or sides of your screen pitching you items similar to those you were browsing earlier? That's big data.

The more time we spend on our various devices, the more key strokes we make, the more information is compiled about us. Big data reflects our increased use and dependency on digital devices and access to the Internet. As the number of ways to collect data about individuals and organizations grow—cell phones, closed-circuit TV, computers, tablets, the Internet, and credit cards and pets embedded with Radio Frequency Identification (RFID) chips—the more data is collected. IBM estimates that since 2012, 2.5 exabytes of data are created every day. (A measurement of digital data, one exabyte equals *one billion gigabytes*. That flash drive you keep on a lanyard around your neck that has *lots* of storage is just sixty-four gigabytes.) Think about it this way: it has been estimated that all words *ever* spoken by humans total five exabytes, which is a mere *two days* of digital data collection—that's big data! (Klinkenborg, 2003)

Mail Surveys

With the explosion of the Internet, there has been a massive decline in mail-out surveys. However, I am sure that you still get one in the mail every once in a while. I will not spend much time discussing them, but let's look at the features, advantages, and disadvantages. What can I say ... they are sent out through the mail. I don't think mail surveys have any real advantage over other self-administered surveys like online surveys. The one possible advantage is the sense of security may be higher for mail surveys—people probably feel better about mailing something containing possibly sensitive material than sending it into the ethers of cyberspace. Mail surveys, then, share the same advantages that other self-administered surveys provide: they are relatively inexpensive, longer surveys can be used, and more complex questions about more sensitive issues can be asked. The real advantages of mail surveys are anonymity and convenience. While mail surveys are much less expensive than face-to-face surveys and telephone surveys, they remain more expensive than online surveys.

THERE'S AN APP FOR THAT

Polldaddy is and app that allows you to create, store and use surveys right on your iPad. You can simply create a survey, load it onto your iPad then go out into the world and use the survey portion offline, collect your data then when you connect to the internet just sync your responses to Polldaddy.com. The site will manage the data so you can perform a range of analyses (Automattic, 2016).

Cross-Sectional and Longitudinal Surveys

Surveys are the most commonly used tools in sociological research, and cross-sectional surveys—surveys that are taken at one point in time—are the most frequently used by social researchers. In reality, most survey research uses cross-sectional designs. While they can provide us with useful information, they are limited to that *particular* sample *at the point in time* in which the survey is conducted. Cross-sectional surveys can use any data collection method, including face-to-face interviews, telephone surveys, and mail-out and web-based surveys. Cross-sectional surveys are popular because they are inexpensive, can be conducted easily, and have the potential to yield large samples. For example, when Gallup, the mega-polling/survey company, used a cross-sectional survey to ask people if they approved of gay marriage in 1996, only 27% of Americans thought gay marriages should be recognized (McCarthy, "U. S. Support for Gay Marriage", 2015). Well, that was true for Americans at that point in time—1996. However, that survey does not reflect current attitudes toward gay marriage. According to a Pew Research study (2015), 57% of

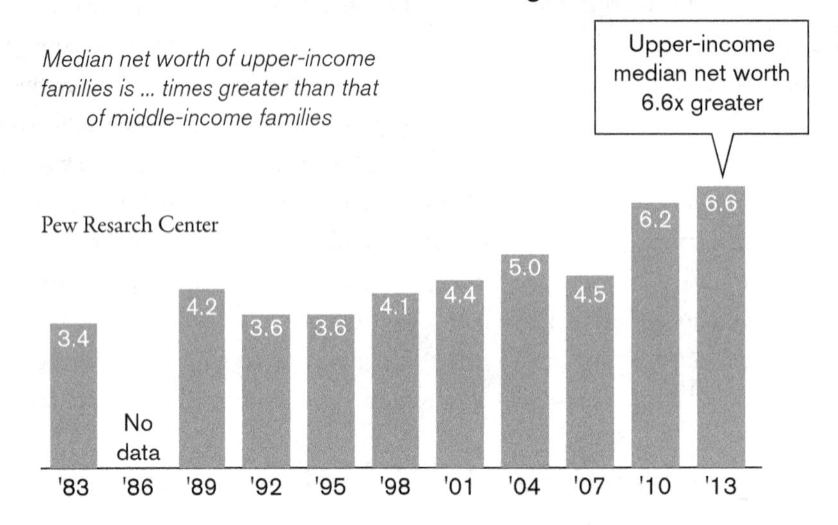

Fig. 2.5 Trend showing widening gap between the earnings of upper- and middle-income families in the U.S.

Americans now favor same-sex marriages. It is easy to see that cross-sectional surveys are convenient but they are limited to when and who is being surveyed.

In contrast, **longitudinal studies** interview/survey the same individuals throughout time, or the same variables are measured repeatedly over time. There are several versions of longitudinal survey designs. In trend analysis, multiple cross-sectional studies are compared across time. For example, the graph in figure 2.5 shows the trend in the increasing gap between upper-income families and middle-income families. The chart clearly shows the gap between upper-income families is growing. In 1983, upper-income families made 3.4 times as much as middle-income families, but those differences have swollen to the upper-income families earning 6.6 times as much as middle-income families in 2013 (Fry and Kochhar, 2014). Therefore, the *trend* indicates a widening gap between the earnings of upper- and middle-income families.

While trend analysis can reveal changes over time, it is not very good at showing how or why the changes occurred. *Panel studies* (these are really the type of studies we think of when we think about longitudinal research) offer insights into how and why changes occur over time. In panel studies, the *same people* are interviewed/surveyed at two or more points in time. While the data collected from longitudinal studies are rich, especially in terms of developmental processes, longitudinal designs have problems of their own. They are incredibly expensive, they are labor-intensive, and their logistics can become overwhelming. Issues of *attrition* contribute to many of the problems of longitudinal research. Attrition refers to the factors that influence the diminishing of the sample. People move, change their names, change their sex, become institutionalized, or no longer want to take part in the research. You could imagine the logistics, labor, and cost associated with maintaining your sample and how, over time, the sample might shrink. In addition, researchers don't live forever. At some point, the investigators must retire or hand the work off to other researchers. (See box on the USC Longitudinal Study of Generations for an example of a panel study.)

THE USC LONGITUDINAL STUDY OF GENERATIONS

At the University of Southern California (USC), Vern Bengtson (2009) initiated a study of about three hundred California families in 1971 that is still ongoing. He has studied the members of those families for over forty years, producing hundreds of journal articles, conference presentations, and a number of scholarly books. The study has yielded surprising findings about the family in America. Below is a detailed description of how the study is constructed and what variables it focuses on.

"The Longitudinal Study of Generations (LSOG), with a fully elaborated generation-sequential design, allows comparisons of sets of aging parents and children at the same stage of life but during different historical periods. These comparisons make possible the investigation of the effects of social change on inter-generational solidarity or conflict across 35 years and four generations, as well as the effects of social change on the ability of families to buffer stressful life transitions (e.g., aging, divorce and remarriage, higher female labor force participation, changes in work and the economy, and possible weakening of family norms of obligation), and the effects of social change on the transmission of values, resources, and behaviors across generations. The study also examines how intergenerational relationships influence individuals' well-being as they transition across the life course from early, to middle, to late adulthood. The LSOG contains information on family structure, household composition, affectual solidarity and conflict, values, attitudes, behaviors, role importance, marital relationships, health and fitness, mental health and well-being, caregiving, leisure activities, and life events and concerns. Demographic variables include age, sex, income, employment status, marital status, socioeconomic history, education, religion, ethnicity, and military service" (Association of Religion Data Archives, 2015).

The Experiment

Experiments are common in medical research, psychology, and other areas of inquiry but not as common in sociology. The major reason is control. **Experiments** are highly controlled research designs that typically compare two groups to assess the effect of a manipulated independent variable(s) on the dependent variable. Many of the variables in the topics we investigate in sociology cannot be rigidly controlled or it would be unethical to control them. Imagine conducting an experiment on the effects of poverty and children's development, then going to your local hospital's maternity ward and randomly assigning newborns to poor families and others to middle-class families—that's not going to happen. We cannot artificially control variables like that in sociology, but many times, others like psychologists and medical researchers can.

Most experimental research can be identified by three common characteristics:

- Participants are randomly assigned to either an experimental or control group
- The researcher *manipulates* the key independent variable(s)
- Participants in each group are treated identically with the exception of the manipulated key variable(s)

Let's say we are interested in seeing if there is a relationship between being unconnected (having no access to the Internet or other digital networks) and one's anxiety level. We could design a nice little (hypothetical) experiment. Say I have two hundred undergraduate students who have volunteered for my study; I randomly assign them to one of two groups of one hundred students:

- The *control group*—business as usual and digitally connected
- The *experimental group*—the digitally deprived and unconnected (no phones, tablets, computers, or connected devices of any kind, including TV)

We will ask those in the experimental group to go two full days without being connected in any way. We won't know if taking away the students' connectivity will affect their anxiety levels unless we know what those levels are to begin with. In the classic experiment, both groups are given a pre- and post-test to compare groups and/or measure change resulting from the experimental treatment (digital deprivation in our case). So, we will pre-test students to see what their baseline anxiety levels are to see if the digital deprivation will affect those levels.

After we pre-test everyone, I have all two hundred students stay in my laboratory dormitory where I can control access to phones and all other devices. The control group is allowed to conduct themselves as usual with respect to all their devices, while the experimental group goes two days without any connectivity.

At the end of the two days, we post-test everyone's anxiety levels, and we find no difference between the pre- and post-test anxiety levels of those in the control group. However, in the experimental group, the post-test scores reveal a huge increase in anxiety levels. We may conclude that college students who experience digital deprivation for two days, experience a rise in their anxiety levels. The design and results of this (hypothetical) experiment are shown in table 2.1 below.

How would you respond to having all your connectivity taken away for two days? A study conducted by the International Center for Media and the Public Agenda (2013) asked students at the University of Maryland to go unplugged for 24 hours. Researchers found that many students couldn't go the full 24 hours and opted out once they realized they were "addicted" to using their devices to stay connected to family, friends and the world. Others felt "depressed" and "isolated" (Moeller et al., 2011).

TABLE 2.1. Design of the Experiment to Assess the Effects of Digital Deprivation on Anxiety Levels

Group	Pre-test	Intervention	Post-test
Experimental (N=100)	Anxiety level measured before intervention	Digital deprivation	Anxiety level measured after intervention (elevated anxiety levels, change from pre-test)
Control (N=100)	Anxiety level measured before intervention	Business as usual	Anxiety level measured after intervention (no change from pre-test)

Qualitative Research Designs

> *"What people say, what people do, and what people say they do are entirely different things."*
>
> — *Margaret Mead*

Qualitative research involves gathering non-numerical information, and the research findings are summarized using a narrative. That is, a qualitative researcher will present a story that summarizes what he found rather than report numerical findings. Qualitative research is typically more interested in process and practice and less with outcomes. This means that qualitative researchers tend to focus on the process while observing their participants' perceptions, experiences, and how they make sense of their lives (Crossman, 2015). Techniques used in qualitative sociology include participant observation, ethnography, case studies, and action research.

I will discuss some qualitative research methods below and highlight each with an example. Remember how earlier in our discussion of research design, we looked at the research topic being a driving force in creating a design and choosing a data collection method. So, as you read through these examples, think about why these researchers chose their particular investigative method. Focus on their topics. Were their designs appropriate choices for their topics? Could they have used another method and been more effective? Could they have produced such rich understanding of their subjects by using quantitative methods?

Also referred to as *field research,* qualitative research typically involves the researchers going to the community or event that they wish to investigate—they go into the field. This has the distinct advantage of observing individuals in their natural setting while letting events unfold normally and naturally. Qualitative researchers seek to understand their subjects' lives on a subjective level, to understand and see the world through the eyes of those they observe. To achieve this, qualitative investigators commonly engage in a data collection technique called participant observation. **Participant observation** is the practice of researchers *taking part* in an event or lifestyle or practices of the group being *observed.* This is a common practice among anthropologists as well as sociologists.

In her book, *On the Run: Fugitive life in an American City,* Alice Goffman (2014) weaves a gripping and vivid tapestry of the lives of young black men in an impoverished neighborhood in South Philadelphia. For six years, Goffman, hangs out with and befriends several young black men. Her work highlights how the limited choices of young black men and constant harassment by the police creates a web of presumed criminality. The constant surveillance and harassment by the police helps forge a culture of distrust of not only the police but any form of authority. She witnesses an array of crimes, comes to aid of her friends while all the time detailing the events in what becomes a troubling and insightful participant observation study that reveals the realities of urban street life, police abuse and the failed war on drugs.

Qualitative research tends to access a deeper, richer understanding of the experiences of the individuals who are the subject of the research. Many times in qualitative studies, the researcher conducts interviews with people who have shared a common experience or event in order to understand their perspective. **Ethnography**—a sociological method of inquiry that explores how people live and make sense of their lives, examining the meaning they produce through everyday interactions—is practiced by qualitative researchers across a range of settings. For example, in his book *Tally's Corner,* Elliot Liebow (1967), a white anthropologist, interviewed, hung out, and drank with a group of black men in their Washington, D.C., neighborhood for over a year. He discovered that contrary to what those on the outside looking in perceived as a bunch of poor, lazy black men, he found a collection of underemployed and other-employed men whose lives moved to a rhythm different from the mainstream and who participated in alternate urban economies.

Many times, researchers cannot live among those they want to study or they want to investigate an event like a natural disaster that a community experienced. These researchers must rely on interviews as their method of inquiry. If a researcher interviews fifty people who lived through Hurricane Katrina, that researcher will get fifty different stories. Even though that investigator will listen to fifty stories, she will hear some common themes that emerge from them. Certainly, you can imagine that any group of people who share an experience or lifestyle will report in their own way some common elements of that experience.

A vivid example of this type of investigation is Helen Benedict's 2009 book *The Lonely Soldier*, in which she interviews female soldiers who served in Iraq between 2003 and 2006. Each woman's story is interesting and compelling, but they all illuminate common themes that run through each of their experiences. Each of their stories echoed the feelings of isolation, misogyny, degradation, humiliation, and the military's deep-seated hatred of women.

READ MORE

- *The Lonely Soldier* by Helen Benedict (2010). A frank telling of how women in the military are perceived and treated and how that makes them feel.
- *Tally's Corner: A Study of Negro Streetcorner Men* by Elliot Liebow (1967). An ethnographic analysis of black urban men whose lives revolve around a Washington, D.C., street corner and how they interpret their lives.
- *On the Run: Fugitive Life in an American City* by Alice Goffman (2014). A gritty and frightening look at the lives of young, urban black men in South Philadelphia and how the police use technology and terror to create a culture of fear and distrust of all authority.
- *Righteous Dopefiend* by Philippe Bourgois and Jeffery Schonberg (2009). This book is both disturbing and insightful. For more than a decade, the authors follow a group of heroin addicts through the homeless neighborhoods of San Francisco and discover how at once they care for each other and betray each other.

Action Research

A growing qualitative research technique is **action research** (sometimes called participatory action research, or PAR), a research method that involves the participation of those affected by the issue under investigation in order to educate, take action, or effect change (Reason and Bradbury, 2008). Used by frequently by Non-Governmental Organizations (NGOs) and those actively seeking community changes. Action research focuses on community-based projects that seek to effect change through the collaboration of community members, such as bringing retail food outlets to urban food deserts or educating urban residents about creating their own subsistence gardens. Many times the community members who undertake it note how many times the positive outcomes for the community are more important than the methods used to access the change (Bogdan and Biklen, 1992; Lewin, 1948).

This community-based action research has three basic phases:

- Look—observe the problem by including the input of those affected by the problem.
- Think—interpret the input/information gathered.
- Act—create a solution to the problem.

Participatory action research requires the input and participation of community members to build a solution to their perceived problem and to put that solution into action for the benefit of the community (Stringer, 1999).

STEP 5. Sampling Design and Defining the Sample

While sampling designs are influenced earlier in the research process by topic choice and research design, in this step researchers must finalize sampling designs and define their sample. That is, as a researcher, at this point you have to decide who you are going to do it to (define the sample) and how you are going to round them up (sample design).

Let's say we are studying marijuana use among college students in the U.S. Ideally, we would like to study all college students who smoke marijuana, because that is our *population*. However, we cannot do that for several reasons: it would be too time- and labor-intensive and far too costly. What we can do is capture a sample—a subset of people who represent the population. Researchers use either probability or non-probability sampling.

- Probability sampling: Any method of sampling or selection that employs random selection. For example, *simple random sampling* is a sampling method that ensures that each person (or item) in the population has an *equal chance* of being selected into the sample. If I wanted to take a simple random sample of the students in my introductory sociology class, which has two hundred students in it, I could put all students' names on slips of paper, place all the strips in a very large hat, then draw fifty names from the hat. Every name was in the hat, so every student in the class (the population) had an equal chance of being drawn. I now know that the sample I have drawn is representative of my population, because they were selected at random, and everyone had a chance to be selected. This isn't possible for large national samples, so more sophisticated methods are used, but random selection is still preserved.

- **Non-probability sampling:** This sampling method does not involve the random selection, but the judgment of the researcher. For instance, if I were doing research on how long college students could go without telling a lie, I could simply use students from my class or grab some from my college's quad as they walked by. I am using college students, who are the focus of my study, but I am not using a probabilistic method to sample them. This limits what I can say about my sample, because I don't know how representative they are of college students.
- **Snowball sampling:** This is a sampling technique used mainly by qualitative researchers. If you are doing research on Goth culture, you really can't send out a survey or interview people on the street. You wouldn't know who is into Goth to survey, and you would end up standing in the street for days, wasting your time waiting for some Goth to walk by. Qualitative researchers would reach out to either someone in the Goth scene or someone who is attached to the scene (sometimes referred to as an *informant*). This person could introduce the researcher to a couple they know who are into the Goth scene. Then, that couple introduces the researcher to two other couples, who take them to a Goth bar and introduce our happy researcher to ten people ... you see how the researcher's sample has *snowballed* from one person to over fifteen.

STEP 6. Data Collection

At this stage, the researcher is interested in getting the information, going into the field, and collecting data. The work to be done in this step is dictated primarily by your research design. If you have designed a web-based survey, you need to create your survey (or use an existing one) and get it out to those selected for your sample. Alternately, you may have to interview people face-to-face, or observe people in the park, or collect data on student GPAs from the college's registrar.

There are many ways to collect data from people; sometimes, you do not have to talk to a single person or observe anyone to draw conclusions about behavior. This style of data collection is called **unobtrusive data collection**. For example, when I was a young researcher at a major university in Massachusetts, I made an observation about the appearance of a bronze statue that indicated to me what behaviors people in that building were engaged in. In the atrium of my building (where my office was located), there was a large bronze statue of a reclining nude woman (very tactfully done). Bronze exposed to air over time oxidizes and develops a patina (a greenish coloration) that dulls the finish. However, the oils from human hands prevent the patina from being established. That is, if you touch a bronze statue regularly in the same place, those areas will remain shiny. I was able to conclude that occupants and visitors alike were passing by our reclining nude and touching her in two spots, keeping them as shiny as the day she was installed. I never had to interview a single person, I never had to make any other observation except to notice the shiny areas of her body, and I knew what people were up to! What two areas of her body do you think everyone was touching?

Secondary Data Analysis

Many times when I teach a research methods class, my students want to collect data using surveys. They immediately set out to design their own survey, which may not always be the best decision. Why reinvent the wheel? So much data has already been collected by some good researchers using reliable and valid instruments (surveys/tests/scales) that there is no need to create your own. Another frequently used form of unobtrusive data collection is **secondary data analysis**—using and analyzing data that was collected and published by someone else. These data may include information from the General Social Survey (GSS), census data, historical documents, the FBI, the Bureau of Justice Statistics, or vital records on birth, death, marriage, and divorce. There are thousands of private and governmental agencies that have the financial and manpower abilities to collect, organize, and analyze mountains of data that can become available to the public. Because of their resources, these organizations have lots of good data that you, as a researcher, can use without having to spend time, money, and other resources just to collect data that has already been compiled and stored somewhere.

Content Analysis: A Type of Secondary Analysis

A good example of secondary data analysis that is frequently used by social scientists is content analysis. In **content analysis,** researchers don't study people; they study the forms of communication that people use. They *analyze* the *contents* of various forms of human communication. For example, Deborah Tannen (1990) analyzed the content of conversations between men and women and found that they employ different conversational styles.

Most sociological content analysis investigates the content of mass media, but not exclusively. Some examines historical documents or the literary work of a particular author. Many scholars have conducted content analysis research on the works of Hemingway, Twain and Frost, looking for themes that guide their lives the authors reveal through their writings. For example, Robert Sears (1978) and his colleagues examined the theme of separation anxiety fantasies in Mark Twain's novels using content analysis. They found that descriptions of separation anxiety were present in his writings at various stages of his life, such as when his wife was pregnant (fearing the child would be a separation threat to his marital love), and when he anticipated her death.

In her study, *Women Bleed. Period: An Exploration of Feminine Hygiene Companies' Print and Commercial Advertisements*, Charlotte Shapiro (2013) scoured both print and television feminine hygiene products advertisements looking for patterns in the way advertisers portray menstruating women. She found that most ads showed women as either embarrassed or ashamed of their bodies and many times the ads reinforced either myths or taboos about menstruation.

Another example of content analysis of the media is a study conducted by the Parents Television Council (2007) that examined the violent content of children's programming. For this study, researchers watched more than 440 hours of children's programming carried on eight separate networks and concluded that violence and vulgarity was alive and well in children's television shows. The study indicated that there was an average of 7.86 violent incidents per hour embedded in children's television.

These examples give you a sense of what content analysis is: the focused examination of some form of communication (media). In each of the examples above, the investigators combed through their targeted media for instances of particular variables, separation anxiety fantasies in Twain, and violent behavior in children's TV programming. While these were scientific studies, as individuals, we perform a sort of content analysis when we find themes in the media we consume. I'm sure that everyone has noticed that the *vast majority* of the knowledgeable characters in television ads for laundry detergent are women, implying the female character does the laundry and women are raised to know how to do laundry.

STEP 7: Analyzing the Data

The detailed process of analyzing both qualitative and quantitative data is well beyond the scope of this book, so I will present a broad outline of these types of data analyses. Once the data has been collected by whatever method was used, analyzing this information is the next step in the research process. Researchers using quantitative data need to convert responses to numbers so they can analyze them using statistical software designed for social research. This process is called *coding* the data. Basically, researchers convert answers on surveys into numbers like "male"=1 and "female"=2 or "black"=1 and "white"=2. Then, the software can do various statistical calculations once responses are converted into numeric data.

Once data analysis is completed, quantitative researchers typically present their results or findings in an easily digestible format, such as a table, chart, graph, or set of diagrams. Here, not only are findings presented, but possible reasons for the findings are discussed. In addition, support or rejection of the hypothesis is included in this step if one was being tested.

In contrast, qualitative data is not converted into numbers, but some coding is involved. This involves transcribing interviews or field notes verbatim. Then, the researcher reads each transcript while making notes that sum up what is being said in the text. This is commonly referred to as *open coding*.

Qualitative researchers face an additional challenge: performing the process of thematic content analysis. This analysis involves identifying themes and categories that "emerge from the data." This involves discovering themes in the interview transcripts and presenting those findings to readers in a cogent narrative (Gläser and Laudel, 2013).

Specialized software is available for field researchers who want help in managing and analyzing their data. It is important to note that these programs do not "analyze" the data; they simply manage the data and make handling it easier. Regardless of which type of data are being analyzed, it is important that the analysis be accurate. You will never get good answers from data if you don't ask it good questions.

STEP 8: Drawing Conclusions and Suggesting Implications

Findings that emerge from data analysis are used to draw conclusions. The conclusion section of your study refocuses the purpose of the research, revealing a recap of what was found, leading into implications of the work. Limitations of the study should be included; be sure to be aware of what your research is and what it isn't. Typically, researchers use this section to suggest what future research needs to be done on the topic and recognize any implications the research has for real-world application. There are several objectives that you want to achieve in presenting your conclusions:

- Recap the main points you made in the introduction and literature review.
- Briefly review the methods and design of the study.
- Reiterate your findings.
- Discuss the broader implications for the findings.
- Describe the limitations of the research.
- Suggest the direction of future research on this topic.
- Make suggestions about the implications of the research for practice, policy, or therapy.

Reliability and Validity

Both of these are important criteria by which we assess our research results and our measurement tools. Remember at the beginning of our discussion on research, I pointed out that the results of social research have the potential to impact social policies and/or people's lives. Researchers need to use measurement tools that are valid and reliable to produce valuable results.

Think about the most reliable friend that you have. Why do you consider her/him reliable? Most likely, it is because she/he is there to bail you out of jail, take you home, or just be there when you need her/him. You can count on her/him time after time. She/he is consistent. In research, **reliability** is the *consistency* of a test, survey, observation, or other measuring device. The Rosenberg Self-Esteem Scale delivers consistent results over time. Those who take the test on multiple occasions report consistent results, and it has proven to be reliable across groups and even when used in different languages (Tinakon and Nahathai, 2012; Supple and Plunkett, 2010).

Validity refers to whether a test, survey, or other research instrument measures what it claims to measure. If I am attempting to measure self-esteem, and I construct a measure that asks, "How many push-ups you can do in one minute?" and "How fast you can run the forty?" this is not a valid measure of self-esteem. The ten-item Rosenberg Self-Esteem Scale (RSES) is a good example of a valid measure of self-esteem; it claims to measure self-esteem, and it has been shown to do just that. Essentially, people report that their scores on the RSES truly reflect the way they feel about themselves. If valid tests or surveys actually measure the concept that they say they are measuring, they are said to be strong measures.

Ethics in Social Research

While ethical research practices are important in all fields of study, they are particularly important in sociology because we rely on human participants. I don't know if you can treat hydrogen and oxygen molecules unethically, but there is always the potential for unethical treatment of human subjects.

Take, for example, research conducted by Laud Humphreys (1970) that examined anonymous homosexual sex in public restrooms. His dissertation-turned-popular book *Tearoom Trade* was derived from his yearlong participant observation study of male-male sexual liaisons in public bathrooms ("tearooms"). In order to take part in this community of anonymous gay sexual encounters, Humphreys claimed to be a "watch queen" or voyeur/lookout. While pretending to watch, he was also gathering the license plate numbers of those involved in the trysts. He then used a friend in the local police department to get information (names, addresses, etc.) about the owners of those cars. After about a year, he went door to door in disguise and interviewed about fifty of the men he had encountered in public restrooms at their homes (sometimes in the presence of their wives and children) using the ruse of administering a social health survey. His descriptions of these men were constructed in a way that made it possible for many of the men and their families to recognize themselves once his work was published as a book. This guy had some nerve! What are the major ethical issues with this study? Humphreys defended his work by citing "situational ethics"—the idea that the application of the rules of research conduct should be taken on a case-by-case basis. What do you think of that position? Should we run red traffic lights on a case-by-case basis, depending on how late for work we are? The roads would be a mess.

At one point a few years later, the sociology department at Washington University in St. Louis, where Humphreys earned his doctorate, attempted to rescind his Ph.D. The meeting organized to determine his status actually turned into a fistfight, with Humphreys being struck by a senior professor, who later lost his position over the punch. Humphreys kept his degree, but in an ironic twist, the sociology program was ultimately disbanded years later. Interestingly, the department was re-established in 2014.

As a result of *Tearoom Trade* and other ethically challenged research, all colleges and universities, as well as governmental agencies and private organizations that engage in research with human participants, have an **Institutional Review Board** (IRB)—bodies designed to approve, monitor, and review any research conducted by an organization that involves human participation. In general, social researchers are responsible for upholding three broad but basic ethical principles when conducting research.

First, *do no harm*. That is, do no physical, psychological, emotional, financial or reputational harm to research participants. Moreover, do not create situations that have the *potential* to do harm to participants.

Second, always maintain research participants' *confidentiality*. Maintaining confidentiality, say through guaranteeing anonymity, allows participants to feel that their information is protected and they are more likely to be forthcoming.

Lastly, always get participants' *informed consent* to take part in the study. That is, participants must always know what the research is about, who will have access to the results, and what possible outcomes they may experience. Allowing people to make an informed decision about participation ensures that they are taking part in the research *voluntarily*. You cannot force people to take part in research. Deception can be used if it is vital to the aims of the research and it has been approved by an IRB. Participants in studies that include deception must be *debriefed*—informed after their participation of the deception.

Conducting ethical research in sociology is taken seriously, so much so that the American Sociological Association (ASA) has strict ethical guidelines for professional sociologists. If you want to see what ethical standards sociologists are held to, visit asanet.org, the official website of the ASA. There, you can view the ASA's *Code of Ethics*—a detailed guide of ethical behaviors for sociologists. These guidelines considerably expand on the three basic principles discussed above.

The Bottom Line

Social research is a valuable tool for investigating the social world. It helps dispel myths and helps us see the inner workings of the social world we inhabit. Moreover, it has informed social policies, laws, clinical practices, and the larger public discourse on race relations, gun control, gender identity, and marriage and divorce. However, to avoid the pitfalls of casual investigation and be socially valuable, investigators must adhere to the scientific method when conducting research so that they produce reproducible and useful results.

RESEARCHERS BEHAVING BADLY

In May 2015, a graduate student at the University of California at Los Angeles (UCLA) was exposed as a fraud. Michael LaCour, an apparent rising star in the field of political science, published a paper in the prestigious scholarly journal *Science,* only to have it retracted after independent researchers challenged his methods and findings. The paper purported to have found that personalized door-to-door canvassing is effective in altering voters' political views. Using members from an LGBT organization at UCLA, LaCour and his co-author had them make in-person contact with voters who had earlier indicated on a survey that they opposed gay marriage. The article reported, based on follow-up surveys, that the door-to-door personal contact had a significant effect in shifting those voters' views toward pro-gay marriage.

Researchers at UC Berkeley and Emory University attempted to replicate LaCour's work but had no success. Apparently, researchers could not derive similar results from the study because it seems LaCour faked the data as well as the results! He never collected the data and made up results that would get his work noticed. Further investigation of LaCour's other research papers revealed that he may have fudged or faked other data and research findings. Additional investigations into LaCour's background indicated that he may have lied about receiving honors at his college graduation, and he was found to have lied about a number of awards and grants on his curriculum vitae (Bartlett, 2015).

How did they discover his ruse? Other researchers in his field asked him to supply them with the details of his research design, which he apparently did, but they could not locate contacts and could not get the same results even using the same datasets. Wow! This guy violated so many rules of ethical conduct he has no doubt ruined his career and made himself a pariah in his field.

Despite her sociological pedigree, Alice Goffman's (2014) newest work, *On the Run: Fugitive Life in an American City*, is not above ethical scrutiny. This gritty portrayal of the lives of a number of poor, urban black youths caught up in the criminal justice system is the culmination of her six years of participant observer research. While her book has been lauded by many social scientists, it has also drawn attention from those who question its ethical soundness. It has been suggested that she may have engaged in felony criminal behavior in the course of her research, specifically conspiracy to commit murder. Further scrutiny of her work by other noted ethnographers has led to accusations that much of her work may simply be fiction and not the detailed and ethical reporting of a conscientious researcher. Many researchers have called for some accounting, but Goffman said she burned all her field notes, which created considerable controversy about basic ethical behavior in field research (Stoller, 2015). What ethical issues are involved here? Should field researchers commit crimes in the line of duty as a researcher? Should original data like field notes be destroyed? Should she be criminally investigated and held accountable? NOTE: Alice Goffman has never been charged with any crime. And while her work still has its critics, it has gained more acceptance.

While research is traditionally divided into qualitative and quantitative designs, it can be conducted in a number of creative and interesting ways, including combining both qualitative and quantitative methods. The decision to use qualitative or quantitative designs is driven in great part by the research topic as well as available resources. Whatever the design decision, social researchers are all in search of revealing, unseen, unknown, or unacknowledged social realities.

The language of research is the language of variables. We have seen that variables are the basic elements of all research and that independent and dependent variables are associated with each other in specific ways. We also discussed the need for all variables to be defined and measured in precise ways in order to create reliable and valid research that yields results that can be generalized.

Most importantly, perhaps, regardless of what topic someone is investigating, her primary concern must be the well-being of research participants. Unethical research conducted in the past has highlighted the need to protect participants if social research is to be viewed as legitimate science, receive funding, engender future participation, and ultimately thrive. Unfortunately, as we have discussed, unethical research practices continue to this day despite the best efforts of Institutional Review Boards.

Figure Credits

Fig. 2.1: Copyright © ThePromenader (CC BY-SA 3.0) at https://commons.wikimedia.org/wiki/File:Eiffel_st-jacques_horz_jms.jpg.

Fig 2.5: Source: http://www.pewresearch.org/fact-tank/2014/12/17/wealth-gap-upper-middle-income/.

CHAPTER 3

CULTURE IS EVERYTHING, EVERYTHING IS CULTURE

"Culture is as natural as life. We shortchange ourselves if we view culture as artifice to be opposed to nature. On the other hand, we must separate cultural information from genetic information. The two are in no sense opposed; indeed, the confusion arises because they are so totally commingled in our experience. In the course of growing up, we learn culture as ways to exercise our genetic capacities."

— *Paul Bohannan, 1995*

The Trobriand Islanders

In traditional Trobriand Island culture, Trobrianders do not see a connection between sexual intercourse and pregnancy. As a consequence, their culture is highly sexualized. Children as young as six years old are encouraged to engage in various sexual activities, and intercourse is encouraged

Fig. 3.1 Branislaw Malinowski with Trobriand Islanders

in those as young as eleven. Young people frequently engage in what they call "sex picnics." These picnics include food and then lots of sexual activity, including intercourse. For the Trobriand Islanders, sex includes mild violence, many times heavy scratching and drawing of blood. They particularly enjoy biting the eyelashes of their partners during orgasm. Yet, when they see Westerners kissing on the lips, they are disgusted. They enjoy these robust sexual lifestyles mainly because in their culture, they do not believe that pregnancy is the consequence of sexual intercourse. Magic plays a very important part in the Trobriand island culture, and they believe that magic and spirits are responsible for impregnating women. When they are ready, the spirits, or *baloma*, which dwell on the island of Tuma, will inhabit women, impregnating them. Then, women's magic plays an important part by placing the magic pregnancy jacket on the woman and placing her in a center of a circle of women, therefore ensuring a successful pregnancy (Malinowski, 1929).

Yams are also a central feature of the Trobriand island culture; they eat yams multiple times a day prepared in a variety of ways throughout their lives. Yams are so important to the Trobriand Islanders that their yam storage huts are sturdier and more highly adorned than their own homes. An interesting fact about yams is that they contain diosgenin, which was used to make the first birth control pills in the 1960s. So, imagine young Trobriand girls eating yams all day long over their entire lifetimes; the result would be no consistent relationship between intercourse and pregnancy because of the contraceptive effect of the yams! Are the practices of the Trobriand people good or bad, right or wrong? The ways of the Trobriand Islanders are no more or less correct or valuable than the practices of other cultures; they simply represent another way of being.

What Is Culture?
Culture is everything. Everything is culture.*

"Culture emerges from life, like life emerges from matter" (Bohannan, 1995). So where there is human life, there is culture. Culture is the total way of life of a people—their learned and shared values, beliefs, customs, and habits, the things they make and use, and the common viewpoints that bind them together. While we don't see culture directly, it shapes the way we act, what we believe, and how we see the world. Remember, we don't see the world the way it is; we see the world the way we are, and culture shapes who we are. Culture is of great interest to sociologists because it affects all aspects of our lives.

Culture influences what we eat, what we wear, the way we think, the way we see the world, and how we judge right from wrong, the sacred from the profane, and beauty from ugliness. Is going to the opera culture? Is watching NASCAR culture? Is eating birthday cake on your birthday culture? Is believing in God culture? Are the contents of your dreams culture? How about getting married, is that culture? Yes, to all.

> **Every idea, feeling, action, and thing in the world and that humans create is culture. Even elements of the natural world become coopted by human culture. Nothing escapes inclusion in human culture.*

Culture is everything. Everything is culture. Now think of something that is not culture. Yep, you read it correctly. Well, if you thought of something like the moon, you would be right—kind of. Culture, as we will learn later, is created by humankind, and the moon is not made by humans. But once humans label some natural feature like the moon, it has been *coopted* by language into culture. That is, once we have a linguistic handle on something, we can manipulate it through language and apply our own particular beliefs, values, and impression on it. Let's take the moon, for example.

Fig. 3.2 What do you see when you look at the moon?

Once we label the moon with language, we have brought it into our culture; the next step is to fold it into our world view—our collective perspective from which we see and interpret the world. Think about three things you could say about the moon. Those things would probably include the moon influences tides, it is about a quarter million miles away from earth, it's composed of rock, it orbits the earth, we only see its light side, and we have been there (if you believe that). We have been taught in our Western, rational, scientific culture all about the various objective characteristics of the moon. Our *cultural* ideas about the moon are a reflection of our rational, scientific world view. While some people in the United States still believe that phases of the moon influence things like increased birth rates, aggressive behaviors, and psychiatric illnesses (lunacy ... get it, lunar), there is NO scientific research that supports these ideas (remember our discussion on the "Transylvania Effect" from Chapter 2?).

What if we asked an Inuit person from Greenland to tell us three things about the moon? That person would most likely tell us that Anningan (the moon) chases his sister, Malina (the sun), across the sky. Anningan is so consumed by the chase that he forgets to eat and over the course of a few weeks, he becomes thinner, representing the phases of the moon. Not to worry—he disappears for three days to eat (new moon), then reappears full (gibbous moon), ready to begin the chase again. In order to keep her distance from her mischievous brother, Malina rises and sets at different times than him (Freed, 2012).

Try using that Inuit story to explain the moon to your neighbor. He will probably look at you funny and wonder what you are smoking. Our culture tends to reject animism—the idea that all animals, plants, and inanimate objects have a spiritual essence—and seeks a logical-scientific explanation. But the Inuit people, and the people of hundreds of cultures around the world, believe that objects like the moon are imbued with spirits, which help them explain how the world works. The *cultural* beliefs and practices of the Inuit are a reflection of their animistic world view.

Before we go any further, I want to make clear the distinction between the terms culture and society. *Culture*, as we have discussed, is the underlying shared characteristics (language, beliefs, values, world view, etc.) of a group of people; society refers to the people of that group and their patterned interactions with each other—people conducting their daily interactions with each other in their homeland. Let's broaden that out. Culture is not bound by any geography, but a society typically is. You can find pieces of American culture all over the world. For instance, elements of American culture like McDonald's restaurants can be found in over one hundred countries, Coca-Cola can be found all over the world, and Levi's jeans are found in just about every corner of the world. But American society can only be found in the United States. I can find sushi restaurants, which represent Japanese culture, all over my hometown, but I would have to travel to Japan to experience Japanese society.

Language and Culture

> *"If culture was a house, then language was a key to the front door, to all the rooms inside."*
>
> *— Khaled Housseini*

Language—a shared collection of symbols that allow people to communicate with each other—is the largest system of symbols that we use on a regular basis to communicate.

I believe that we can assign the relationship below to our understanding of culture.

Language (communication) = Culture

What do I mean by this? Let's go back in time, let's say fifty thousand years ago. At that time, according to the recent African origin of modern humans theory, also known as the *out of Africa theory*, modern humans had come out of Africa and inhabited much of the world, but not the Americas (Meredith, 2011). Most likely, we traveled in small bands of twenty to thirty individuals. How could this happen without language, some recognized form of communication shared by the members of the collective? It couldn't. We could have never made tools, organized hunts, or worked cooperatively without language, however primitive. When languages die, cultures die with them. Language is the vehicle upon which culture emerges, is transmitted, and flourishes.

LOSS OF LANGUAGES MEANS LOSS OF CULTURES

It has been estimated that in the past fifty years, twenty-eight of the world's language families have gone extinct. Today, there are 3,176 languages that are endangered; this represents about 46% of all living languages. This means that nearly half of all languages spoken today, as well as the richness of their cultures, could go silent (Weicha, 2013).

Ethnocentrism and Cultural Relativism

> *"People from different cultures have different definitions for beauty, isn't that sad to judge others with our standards. ... rather than appreciate them?"*
>
> *— Mizuki Namura*

Before we go any further in our discussion of culture, there are two important practices we need to discuss. These are important for several reasons, but perhaps the most important, as you will see, is how one practice leads to the subjugation and death of culture, while the other leads to a richer understanding of other cultures.

"No culture can live, if it attempts to be exclusive."

–Mahatma Gandhi

Ethnocentrism is the habit of judging other cultural practices from the perspective of one's own culture and deeming them as primitive, inadequate, or inferior. Ethnocentrism is learned in all cultures because it serves some useful functions. It promotes solidarity of the group, or that "we" feeling. It unites us though our cultural practices, and promotes the idea that our way of life is worth preserving and reproducing. In a crystal-clear example of ethnocentrism, President Obama, in a 2013 speech to the United Nations, declared, "I believe that America is exceptional." With this statement, he was obviously implying that the American way of life/world view and all Americans are superior to others and other ways of life.

However, these beliefs of superiority may hinder cooperation with other cultures. If one's ways are superior to the ways of others, there seems little incentive for promoting or practicing inferior ways. This could lead to attitudes of contempt, ridicule, and downright hostility. The very real global extension of ethnocentrism is **cultural imperialism**—imposing one's cultural values, beliefs, and practices on the members of another culture. The results of this practice fill the pages of history with the records of war and religious, economic, and racial colonialism. For centuries, it was common for the ships of colonial powers to roll up on the shores of a Caribbean paradise, the invaders telling the local people to cover themselves, to speak their language, and to worship their god and their king. As local customs and languages were extinguished, so were the local cultures. These ethnocentric practices resulted in the death of hundreds of cultures around the world, depriving humankind of the variety and richness of ways of thinking, being, and seeing the world. In some ways, this practice continues today with the destruction of the world's rainforests and the ways of life of those who dwell in them. This destruction is in large part driven by the appetites of some far-off developed nation willing to exploit others to satisfy its needs.

In contrast, the perspective of **cultural relativism** views each culture as possessing its own distinct but equally valid sets of beliefs, values, and practices, which can only be understood from the viewpoint of that culture itself. Practicing cultural relativism allows researchers to understand the beliefs, values, and behaviors of other peoples from their viewpoint and not judge them by the cultural standards of the researcher. This gives us an understanding of *why* other cultures believe what they believe and *why* they engage in their particular behaviors. You cannot come to understand or appreciate other cultures if you are comparing or judging them by your standards; you will never see the world the way others do and never know why people of other cultures do what they do and believe what they believe.

Even though this perspective was developed by anthropologists, its principles act as a sort of guide to the ethical conduct of researchers of other disciplines, such as sociology. One of the basic tenets of cultural relativism is the relative worth of a culture and its component parts. That is, one culture is not superior to others (American culture is not superior to the culture of the Tiv people of Nigeria or the Tuva people of Siberia); these cultures merely represent different ways of being. Another important element of cultural relativism is the relative importance of the contents of cultures such as language, customs, rituals, and aesthetics.

Right and wrong and good and bad are only defined within the context of each culture. Remember in the opening story, the Trobriand Islanders view sexual acts between young children as part of the Trobriand childhood experience and as acceptable for their way of life. In contrast, in the United States, most people would be appalled by sexual behavior among six- and seven-year-old children; we see that behavior as deviant in our culture. So, who's right? Both. Acceptable and unacceptable behaviors are defined in the context of culture and are relative; there are no absolutes. Pedophilia is criminally wrong in our culture; does that make it *absolutely* wrong? If so, we should not find any culture in the world practicing pedophilia. However, as a rite of passage to manhood, young Sambia boys must perform fellatio and ingest the semen of the single men of their village; many engage in homosexual relationships with the older men. This is considered wrong among Americans but is an integral part of constructing manhood among the Sambia people.

READ MORE

- *The Sexual Lives of Savages* by Bronislaw Malinowski (1929). Malinowski relays detailed descriptions of the sexual practices and beliefs of the Trobrianders.
- *The Sambia: Ritual, Sexuality and Change in Papua New Guinea* by Gilbert Herdt (1987). The author explores the lengthy (twelve years) rite of passage to manhood among the Sambia people of Papua New Guinea in striking detail.

The Characteristics of Culture

Culture is created by humans. We are the only species that possesses and uses culture to the degree that we can adapt to worlds other than earth and to the point that we can modify our own essence—our DNA. Some argue that other species possess culture; I do not view rudimentary tool making, communication, social organization, and social learning sufficient to rise to the level of culture. No other species possesses the complex interplay of concept, creation, and self-reflexivity found in human cultures. Moreover, if we understand culture to be, in part, a tool for adaptation to the physical environment, there is no single species, except for humans, that inhabits the entire

Fig. 3.3 Inuit Children

globe. However, this is my position; you may believe differently.

Culture is an adaptive mechanism. Culture is an adaptive tool used by humans; its complexity allows us to thrive anywhere on earth. Even though we essentially remain a warm-climate animal, adaptive strategies such as the use of fire, hunting technologies, shelter, clothing, and cooperative work has allowed us, as a species, to occupy all climate regions on earth. The cumulative effect of these adaptive strategies, discoveries, inventions, and cooperation is culture. Our ability to develop culture comes in part from our physical features: our large brains, binocular vision, upright posture, and free hands with an opposable thumb and a prehensile grip. This unique combination of human physical features allowed our ancestors to start the culture train rolling by fashioning crude stone tools about two million years ago.

Culture is partly a response to the challenges of adapting to various physical environments and partly creative responses to satisfying our biological imperatives. That is, humans must eat, drink, eliminate waste, sleep, and reproduce. Even a cursory look at the cultures of the world shows us that people in different cultures satisfy human imperatives/drives in myriad ways.

Take, for instance, the Inuit of Greenland. Elements of their culture such as food, clothing, and language are reflections of their adaptation to a harsh Arctic environment. Like many people around the world, the Inuit eat foods found in their local environment. However, the climate of the Arctic is not suited for agriculture, so they eat a diet high in animal protein such as whale, seal, fish, polar bear, and caribou. The high fat and protein content of their diet helps them stay warm, along with heavy clothing made from the skins of the animals they kill to eat. This makes sense—they are capitalizing on the game found in their environment. This is also true of their language—it reflects their understanding of their physical environment. You have probably heard that the Inuit have hundreds of words for snow and ice. Actually, the number of root words for snow in the Inuit language is roughly equivalent to those in English. However, the Inuit language is structured so the number of distinct words for snow that can be derived from root words is not just a few hundred, but infinite. Additionally, researchers have identified at least ninety-three terms for distinctly different forms of ice (Krupnik et al., 2010; Pullum, 1991).

In contrast, the Polynesian culture is an island culture located over a vast area of the Pacific Ocean, encompassing more than a thousand islands. Their environment is distinctly different from that of the Inuit; they enjoy coconuts, rice, sugar cane, yams, taro, fish, and many other seagoing creatures. Additionally, their clothing reflects the relatively mild year-round climate;

traditionally, both men and women would wear simple loin clothes (tapa) or nothing at all. Nowadays, men wear shorts, t-shirts, and flip-flops, and variations on the sarong are worn by both sexes. Their language reflects their connection to the ocean. Naturally, the Hawaiian (which is part of Polynesia) language has about twice as many words to describe ocean waves as English. This makes sense, as most of Polynesia is made of coral islands, and wave motion is important in navigating the coral reefs that encircle the islands—and for surfing!

As all cultures do, they develop over time in response to the physical environment, exploiting the local natural resources in order to feed, clothe, and shelter members of the collective. Language is also a response to the natural environment, developing specifically to identify in detail the features prominent in the environment: snow for the Inuit and waves for Hawaiians. However, the specificity of language is not just because the Inuit are bored and sit around making up snow vocabulary and Polynesians like to name waves. It's about survival: identifying features in the physical environment in precise ways can protect members of the group. Our seal hunter, Yoskolo, knows that he can't go out on the ice floes if Yutu tells him conditions are *qautsaulittuq*—ice that breaks after its strength has been tested by a harpoon—because he may risk falling into the frigid water. And our Hawaiian friend, Keanu, knows it is dangerous to paddle his sup when the waves are *hanupanupa*—surging waves (Krupnik et al., 2010; Pukui and Elbert, 1986).

Culture is not genetic, and people are not born with it; culture is learned. You could drop off a human infant with any family in any culture of the world, and that child would grow up to understand and accept it as her own. We are all born with our own genetic profile that says "human being," but only through learning our culture can we understand and be understood by others. Additionally, we are all born with certain biological drives like hunger and thirst, but as infants, we do not possess the instinctual patterns to satisfy them—we must learn. We are, however, genetically predisposed to learn language, which is the mechanism we use to learn, create, and share culture.

Culture is shared and transmitted. In order for each new generation of individuals to survive, the individuals have to be taught how to navigate their particular culture. Sociologists refer to this process as **socialization**—the lifelong process by which children and adults learn from others—and it is necessary to ensure the development and adjustment of all humans so they can form identities and function properly in society (Chapter 4 is devoted to the topic of socialization). For humans, it takes some time before one can successfully navigate society. We do not have the biological capacity to fend for ourselves; human infants are fragile creatures. Humans are unlike giraffes, for example, who can stand up and run with the herd within an hour of being born. Moreover, by eighteen months, both male and female giraffe calves leave their moms to form their own giraffe street gangs (sort of). Humans need nurturing, education, financial support, and considerable social experience before we are able to run with our herd. This may take anywhere from eighteen to forty years.

Culture is dynamic. It changes from place to place and over time. We have already discussed a number of cultures and how different they look from our own. We know that we will encounter differences in foods, clothing, language, and ways of behaving if we travel from place to place, but all cultures also change over time due to several factors:

- **Discovery**—the process of learning about something that was not known before. When humans discovered and controlled fire, it profoundly influenced the development of human culture. Before fire, our ancestors huddled together in caves, cold and quivering, fearing the sounds of the night, waiting for the great fiery orb in the sky to reappear. Fire extended the time early humans could devote to daily activities, and it protected them from many predators. Once they started gathering around the fire for its warmth and light, they most likely started telling stories of the hunt, which led to more celebratory behaviors like singing and dancing. In fact, Polly Wiessner (2014), an anthropologist who studied hunting-gathering societies in the Kalahari of Africa, which resemble early human groups, found that most daytime conversations were devoted to issues of hunting and gathering or gossip, while conversations around the fire at night were dominated by storytelling and magic. Also, we started cooking our food, which led to increased cranial capacity, and cooked meat proteins afforded us more nutritional value (James, 1989; Weiner et al., 1998). Other notable discoveries that have profoundly impacted human culture include gravity, penicillin, and stem cells.
- **Invention**—the creation of something completely new. Imagine culture as a still mountain lake and you take a stone and throw it into the middle of the lake. What happens? Once the stone breaks the lake's surface, it creates ripples, which move out into wider and wider rings. Invention is the stone that gets thrown into culture, creating a ripple effect of changes within culture. The invention of the plow, for example, precipitated the agricultural revolution. This transformed human society, making large, widespread crop production possible, resulting in greater food surpluses, which created huge human population growth and freed people to engage in a variety of other types of work. Air conditioning changed where we live, what our houses look like, and what we do on a hot summer evening, for example. Air conditioning also managed to influence housing architecture: no need for a porch or "sleeping porch" to cool off on, just turn up the air conditioning. It has also influenced human interaction by drawing families into their isolated, air-conditioned homes and off the front porch where they used to wave at and chat with neighbors. Paper, guns, steam engines, automobiles, the computer, and the Internet are all significant inventions in human history. Can you list ways these inventions changed our language and the way we interact with each other?

READ MORE

- *Losing our Cool: Uncomfortable Truths about our Air-Conditioned World (and Finding New Ways to get through the Summer)* by Stan Cox (2010). He explores the impact the invention of air conditioning has had on our political, social, and economic lives in the U.S. He also looks at the environmental impact of worldwide air-conditioning use.

- Innovation—refers to taking an existing object, idea, or system and modifying or improving it. Apps are good examples of innovation. They claim to enhance your dining, shopping, viewing, or listening experience by improving on previous methods of delivering goods or services. Spotify lets you stream music, gets to know what music you like, and suggests additional or alternate titles you may enjoy, which is a lot easier than going to a music store and searching through titles or dealing with physical media like CDs, cassette tapes, or eight-track tapes. YourMechanic, an app that allows you to schedule auto repairs at your home or office, didn't invent the engine, the oil change, or mechanics, but it did improve on auto-repair service by putting an auto mechanic at your fingertips—the mechanic comes to you. Uber is another good example of an app that enhances the taxi experience by not requiring in-vehicle payment; there's no need to carry cash or credit cards, and the drivers are regular citizens like you and me. My wife and I use Uber frequently, and it is much more convenient (and cheaper) than taxis. Apps make things like grocery shopping, doctor's visits, learning statistics, or finding a local restaurant with the best beer selection really simple; they are an improvement over a previous way to do these things, or at least more convenient. Other types of innovations throughout history include domestication of livestock, containerized shipping, and jet aircraft. Why are these examples of innovation and not invention or discovery?
- Diffusion—the movement of parts of one culture into another. Food is a good example of diffusion of culture; as people move around the world, they take familiar elements of their home culture with them, such as food. My wife and I regularly cook Mexican, Italian, Japanese, and Thai food. We also go out for Vietnamese, Greek, Lebanese, French, and Basque food. All this exotic food from around the world is accessible in central Virginia. What kind of food can you find in your neck of the woods? Other parts of culture become diffused like yoga, which came to the U.S. via Eastern religious and meditational practices. Do you wear *pajamas*, use *shampoo*, or know a *thug*? All these words come from the Hindi language. These and many other words were coopted by

the British when they occupied modern-day India and Pakistan, then they just spread through the English-speaking world. A few years ago, my wife and I were scuba diving in Roatan, Honduras, and on the drive from the airport to our hotel, we passed by a Bojangles fast food restaurant! Roatan is not a highly developed island, and it is located forty miles off the coast of mainland Honduras. We were surprised to see Bojangles there, to say the least. Probably the most common symbol of American culture around the world is Coca-Cola, with McDonald's a close second. You can find a McDonald's restaurant in 119 countries (there are 196 countries in the world), and you can buy a Coke in all countries of the world except for Cuba and North Korea, and I bet you can scratch Cuba off that list soon.

- **External Pressure** from outside forces can be applied directly to societies to produce cultural change. This pressure can be exercised through patterns of domination like colonization or conquest. The Islamic State of Iraq and the Levant (ISIL) has invaded parts of Syria and Iraq, leaving in its wake of destruction and barbarism a population that either converted to its interpretation of the Qu'ran and sharia (Islamic law) or were killed. The people of those regions have had to abandon their mainstream interpretation of their religion and adopt a radicalized, fundamental interpretation of Islam, altering the locals' way of life. External pressure can be applied in less militant ways. Widely viewed as a human rights violation against girls and women, female genital mutilation (FGM), sadly, is still practiced in about twenty-eight countries. The practice is a deeply held cultural custom that transcends religion but is in some areas encouraged by religious leaders. Many organizations have used a range of tactics to eliminate FGM. Pressure from the United Nations and a host of other organizations has led to the reduction in the number of cases of FGM and the criminalization of FGM in eighteen African countries. This has been achieved through education and outreach programs, lobbying governments, and sharing some African nations' abysmal human rights records with the world in an attempt to pressure them to change their laws (Center for Reproductive Rights, 2008; World Health Organization, 2008).

As we have discussed, there are a number of ways culture can change, from new inventions to adopting parts of other cultures to being forced to change from outside pressures. With all the change taking place in society, it takes time for all elements of culture to catch up with those changes. Just like when you acquire some new technology, for example, you need to learn how it works, the various ways you can use it, and, ultimately, how it changes the way you live your life. The same holds true for culture. Rules that guide social behavior take time to adjust and catch up with social changes.

Cultural lag is a term used to describe how cultural values, beliefs, and norms take time to catch up with technological advances, and this lag can create social problems and conflict. With new inventions and innovations come social change. Societies have to develop acceptable ways of behaving relative to the use of new technologies. Is it acceptable to talk on your phone or text while you are checking out at a grocery store? It seems to be a gray area of social behavior, unless you're in line behind that cell phone user—then it's pretty clear-cut. I've noticed that some stores have posted signs asking customers to refrain from cell phone use during checkout, which indicates that social rules have yet to catch up with cell phone use—we still don't quite know how to act. Similarly, rules about mobile phone use in movie theaters *lagged* behind the *technology*. I lived in L.A. when cell phone use took off, and I noticed then that people were free to gab on their phones in theaters. Over a period of time, theater owners asked moviegoers to refrain from phone use during movies, but it was completely voluntary on the part of the customers. Now, nearly all theaters prohibit mobile device use during movies, using clever and amusing short videos to make the rules crystal clear. If you have ever been in a movie theater when someone was talking or texting on his phone, you can understand the conflict this can create. You can see from these examples how rules of social behavior had to catch up to the use of new mobile phone technology.

Laws that regulate Internet usage lagged behind that technology. Widespread availability and access to the Internet dates to about 1990. Many of the first laws were aimed at preventing harassment. The Communications Decency Act of 1995 basically extended to computers a law that prohibited obscene and harassing phone calls. Laws protecting children online didn't appear until 1998. Napster, an Internet site that allowed users to swap/download music for free, burst onto the cyber scene in 1999. The music industry soon realized that Napster was costing them billions of dollars, and they went to court. Napster was essentially shut down in 2001 as a free file-swapping site, as Internet practices and copyright laws were reconciled. Napster was in violation of copyright laws and had to pay out millions of dollars (Cannon, 1996; History, 2015; Kravets, 2007). It takes some time for people to realize how new technologies can affect their lives, both positively and negatively. That time between the introduction of new technology and its regulation, formal or informal, is cultural lag.

Culture is symbolic. You may notice that there is considerable variation in the way people behave and interact, but there exist many common characteristics. Some of these common characteristics are **symbols**, which are anything that represents something else. Symbols are really important in culture because they allow us to interpret things and events, then act appropriately. The only way this works is if everyone shares the meaning behind the symbols. Symbols can be material: I wear a wedding band, for example, which symbolizes my marital status.

Symbols can also be non-material like a sound, a facial expression, or a gesture. Here in the U.S., for example, we commonly use the hand gesture for OK (thumb and index finger joined in a circle) to mean everything is, well, OK. However, if you were traveling in Brazil and you wanted to let your bartender know your caipirinha (the national drink of Brazil) is super tasty, and you throw up the OK sign, you have just told him to f**k off—oops. If you raise your hand, palm out, in the direction of another person here in the U. S., you are saying "talk to the hand" or "hold it right there, buddy." Don't use this gesture if you find yourself in Greece. The hand raised and held palm outward from the body means you're throwing shit on your Greek friend—your now-angry Greek friend. It's all about the shared meaning and keeping your hands by your sides when traveling.

These examples of hand gestures illustrate a phenomenon called culture shock, the feeling of disorientation, surprise, and even fear one can experience when encountering a new culture. Not knowing the rules of a culture, such as what gestures are appropriate, can disorient visitors to unfamiliar cultures. When I traveled through Egypt, I encountered men who I thought were in heated arguments, waving their arms about while using a very firm and loud tone. I finally realized this style of interaction was common when haggling or conducting certain transactions. I was confused and a bit fearful until I learned it was a common social interaction. Sometimes the social customs of cultures may surprise travelers. Many Americans are surprised when they find that many beaches around the Mediterranean Sea are topless, clothing optional or fully nude. Many travelers from Islamic countries are shocked when they see young women wearing what they perceive as revealing clothing here in the U.S. Most Westerners traveling to Vietnam will be surprised, and maybe sickened, when they learn that cats and dogs are common items on restaurant menus. While lounging poolside at my resort in Belize a few years ago, I saw a *fully clothed* Mennonite couple step into the pool. They proceeded to walk into the pool to about shoulder depth, stop, and stand there and talk for about fifteen minutes. Everyone around the pool was trying to look without appearing to look. You have to admit that in our culture, and many others, you wear a swimsuit in a pool. Even though they were a honeymooning couple, modesty in public is an important element of their culture.

Components of Culture: Material and Non-Material Culture

Culture can broadly be broken into two component parts: material culture and non-material culture.

Material Culture is all the things that we make and use as humans—all our stuff. These are the physical artifacts of our existence. Material culture includes clothing, iPads, food, makeup, sneakers, skyscrapers, and the International Space Station.

Most people in the world do not eat with spoons, knives, and forks; despite this, people manage to feed themselves. Most people in the world do not sleep on what we consider to be a bed, and our social rules about reproduction are considerably different than those of other cultures. For example, the Yanomamo sleep in hammocks, not in beds on or near the ground. Sleeping in an elevated hammock eliminates the risk of having some slithering, crawling creature finding its way into one of your orifices as you sleep. It also allows air to circulate around you, keeping you cool, which makes adaptive sense if you live in the thick jungles and humid rainforests of South America like they do. So, these material artifacts represent human adaptive strategies.

Fig. 3.4 (a) and (b) Automobiles and smart phones are part of our Material Culture.

While it seems on the surface that this is just stuff, you should know that stuff has meaning. That is, material objects have a symbolic nature—an object can represent or stand for something else (Oxford English Dictionary, 2015). Think about all the stuff you have; all that stuff may symbolize our materialistic culture. Think about what your car symbolizes. Do you drive a hybrid, a big SUV, a highline car, or maybe a POS (piece of shit)? Your hybrid may symbolize your concern for the environment, and that big SUV may be emblematic of the need for lots of room for your outdoor gear, the Bentley Continental GT may symbolize your social status, and that POS may say "Hey, I'm broke." There is meaning in material possessions.

We know this for several reasons, but it is best illustrated using archaeology. Rarely do archaeologists find instruction manuals for ancient cultures or things that say "Hey, this is who we were, what we believed in and valued, and how we behaved." What they do find is stuff, artifacts that humans left behind in the remote past. And what they do with those artifacts is reconstruct ancient cultures. The only way they come to know about ancient people's ways of life, their culture, is from the meaning that their possessions held for them.

For example, the Moche people (100 CE–800 CE), who inhabited the northern coastal area of modern-day Peru, left behind a surprising array of ceramics that depict a wide range of subject matter encompassing many aspects of life. Moche ceramics portray people, animals, gods at war, hunting scenes, caring for the sick, and burying the dead (Weismantel, 2004). These scenes have painted a vivid picture of many parts of Moche life and a fuller understanding of Moche culture for anthropologists. However, over five hundred pots found depict sex acts that include fellatio, masturbating male skeletons, and anal sex. The majority of sex pottery discovered represented heterosexual anal sex, usually showing an infant breastfeeding while the couple has sex. What do these artifacts say about the Moche way of life? While it is controversial, Weismantel has hypothesized that the Moche may have believed that many sex acts were responsible for pregnancy. Therefore, for them, they are simply depicting mainstream sexual habits.

Non-material Culture includes the knowledge, beliefs, values, and norms that help shape society and promote solidarity and stability. Let's start with a look at social **norms**—standards of behavior for a group or society. Norms are the rules and regulations that members of a group or society have agreed upon and are expected to adhere to or suffer some consequence. Norms also elicit conformity so that our social interactions become patterned, social life has regularity to it, and social order is maintained.

Because norms are guidelines for social interaction, they are manifested in a range of *expected behaviors*. When you pass someone on campus and greet them with "How are you doing?" you *expect* a response like "Fine," "OK," or "Good." We *expect* people in the United States to drive on the right-hand side of the road, when you are introduced to someone you are *expected* to shake their hand, and you are *expected* to use the restroom to relieve yourself, not the streets. Norms are a part of every culture, and they range in importance from very serious, such as paying your taxes, to not very important, such as wearing clean clothes.

Formal Norms are social rules that are so important that they have been written down and there is usually a serious consequence for their violation. Laws are formal norms; so are the official rules of Major League Baseball (MLB), your student handbook, and the "no turn on red" sign at your local intersection. So, formal norms are the most clearly stated and strictly enforced type of norms.

There are a great number of laws; in fact, in 2011, all U.S. states and territories created 40,000 new ones (National Conference of State Legislatures, 2013). However, the number of unwritten, mainly unspoken social rules or **informal norms**—rules that govern everyday behaviors that are widely understood and conformed to and carry no serious consequence for violation—seem infinite. These informal norms or *folkways* greatly influence our day-to-day interactions with others. From the minute we get up in the morning until we go to bed at night, our daily routines are guided by a host of informal social rules. Everything from swearing at your roommates for drinking all your beer, to how close you stand to a stranger on the bus, to where you stand in the elevator, to how you behave in the classroom is guided by informal norms.

In my sociology classes, we discuss elevator behavior as a good example of a set of informal norms. How did you learn about acceptable elevator behavior? Did your parents sit you down one day and say "It's time we had a talk about elevator behavior"? Probably not, I hope not, that would be really weird! We do learn some things that way, such as when you were told to "Look both ways before crossing the street" or "Don't talk with food in your mouth." We also learn informal norms by imitation and observation, especially observing the consequences of their violation, as part of the process of our socialization into society.

Mores are a subset of both formal and informal norms that are believed to have great moral significance, and typically, their violation produces serious consequences. As we have discussed, every day our behaviors are guided by a slew of formal and informal norms. However, not all norms have a significant moral element to them. If you speed in your car

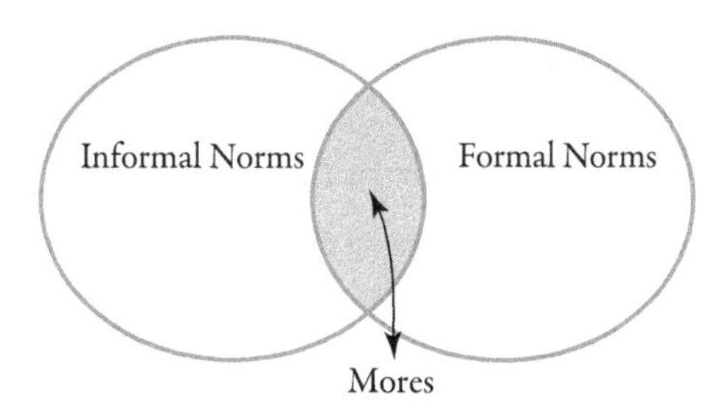

Fig. 3.5 This diagram illustrates that Mores represent the subset of all norms, both Informal and Formal that have a strong moral component.

to get to school on time, do you think you are immoral? No. If you accidently trespass on your neighbor's property, does that make you an immoral person? No. So of all the formal and informal norms that guide our lives, only a subset of them have a strong element of morality—mores. Figure 3.5 shows how mores represent only those norms that have moral significance among all possible formal and informal norms.

For example, murder and rape are highly immoral and illegal; we have formal norms or laws that prohibit these acts. Informal rules about cheating on your partner exist, and while it may not be illegal, it is still immoral, and it makes you a creep. These examples illustrate that both formal and informal norms that possess moral significance can be considered mores.

Taboos are acts that are so strongly prohibited in a culture that they elicit feelings of disgust, repugnance, and revulsion. Taboos in the United States include such acts as *incest* (sexual activity with close relatives), *necrophilia* (sexual attraction to or sex acts with a dead person), *pedophilia* (sexual attraction to or sexual contact with pre-pubescent children), *bestiality* (sexual acts with non-human animals), and *cannibalism* (eating the flesh or internal organs of other humans). Notice a common thread? All of these acts are not really productive for any collective of humans or the species in general. Sex with young children, sex with dead people, and sex with barnyard animals are all reproductive dead ends. Incest leads to physical and developmental birth defects, and eating each other just reduces the population and seems quite disgusting. These acts rise to the level of revulsion in the United States, but each of these acts is or has been practiced by some culture somewhere in world.

A Brief Discussion About Norms

Norms are a part of every culture and therefore change from place to place. For example, a friend of mine was working in the Philippines a few years ago and got to be pretty friendly with his Filipino coworker, Fred. One night after work, he was invited to Fred's house for drinks. My friend is a hearty beer drinker and gladly accepted. Fred poured my friend a beer, he finished it, and Fred immediately poured another beer. This went on for several hours, and my friend began to plot his escape, but every time he finished his beer, the glass was immediately filled. My friend, being American, did not want to be rude to his host by not finishing his beer, but he was now quite drunk. What my friend did not know is that while he was trying to be polite by finishing each beer, he was actually indicating, by finishing each beer, that Fred was a terrible host who could not supply enough beer to his guest. In Filipino culture, in order not to insult your host, you leave a small amount of beer in the glass or a tiny morsel of food on the plate, indicating that your host has been so generous you could not finish the abundance he provided. In contrast, Americans think it rude not finish all that is offered. Norms like these are subtle and many times lost on those who were not raised in the culture or who have not been fully immersed in it.

Norms also change over time within a culture. I was certain that I would grow up to have one arm longer than the other. Why, you ask? When I was a child, my mother would quite frequently yank my arm vigorously when I would not come along voluntarily or was acting the fool. When I was young, it was not uncommon for me or my friends to be spanked, struck, or hit with a belt as punishment, sometimes in public. How would an arm yank or a slap on the bottom of a child in public play out these days? A parent using physical punishment in public today could be subjected to the disapproval of other parents or even be reported to Child Protective Services. Norms about the physical punishment of children, especially in public places, has changed considerably just in the last few decades. Research indicates that it is not widely accepted to use corporal punishment on children in public or private unless there are unusual circumstances. FYI, in Sweden, it is against the law to use corporal punishment on children, and in Canada, you cannot use physical punishment on children younger than two or older than twelve. In fact, both the European Union and the United Nations have asked all nations of the world to prohibit corporal punishment by parents (Straus, 2010; Gershoff, 2010). So, if you travel with kids. ...

Norms can either encourage or restrict/prohibit behaviors. Because norms have these qualities, we make a distinction between prescriptive and proscriptive norms. **Prescriptive norms** refer to socially encouraged behaviors such as applauding after a really good Fourth of July fireworks show or wearing somber-colored clothing to a funeral. In contrast, **proscriptive norms** are behaviors that one should not or must not engage in, such as murder, placing your hands in fire, or playing air guitar during my lectures. Our social lives, then, are guided by a number of both types of norms. Can you name several prescriptive and proscriptive norms that have influenced your behavior today? Regardless of what type of norm you obey, they all encourage conformity, which promotes social stability and social order.

Norms are bound by social context. Expected social behavior may vary depending on the social setting and who is involved. Say you are at the park on a picnic with your love interest, the sun is shining, and people are out and about. You both notice a small child, about two years old, stripping off her clothes down to her diaper, laughing, and running carefree through the grass. How would you react? If you are like most people, it would probably bring a smile to your face, and you might even let out a slight giggle. Then, you turn in horror to see a forty-five-year-old man strip off his clothes down to his tighty-whities, twirling his pants about his head, laughing, and running carefree through the grass ... until he is arrested. You see, a little kid can run nearly naked through the park and she is adorable, but a grown man does the same thing and he's in jail for indecent exposure. The application of norms depends on a number of factors, such as who is involved in the behavior and where the act is taking place. Even our adorable two-year-old could not get away with her strip-down dance if she were to do it in a museum, library, or the DMV. You can get away with a lot of socially unacceptable behaviors in the privacy of your own home that you couldn't get away with on the streets of your hometown.

TRY THIS

Norm violation. Try violating some informal norm like not shaking someone's hand when you first meet them, interrupt someone's conversation or offer to trade your jacket for a cup of coffee instead of using money at your local coffee shop. There are hundreds of informal norms that guide our behaviors every day, pick one, violate it and note how people react. Then let them off the hook by telling them you were just engaging in a bit of social research. Discuss with them why they reacted the way they did. Try to get beyond that you had broken a social rule, and explore why they think the rule exists and how does it help make social interactions run smoothly.

When I was younger, I had a real issue with authority—I didn't really like obeying rules. Now I'm like the overwhelming majority of people: I have a career, a home, a family, and follow the rules ... for the most part. The big question is, why do the vast majority of people follow the rules? Like with any set of rules for behavior, there are rewards and punishments established to encourage conformity to social norms; sociologists refer to these as **sanctions. Positive sanctions** are rewards for conforming to norms like a work promotion, good grades, or a smile for holding a door open for someone. Positive sanctions are used to promote desirable behaviors like working hard, doing well on exams, and positive responses from others. These rewards are distributed so that people will continue to engage in acceptable and productive social behaviors. On the other hand, **negative sanctions** are punishments for the violation of social norms. Examples include a speeding ticket, jail time, and dirty looks from other customers when you have fifty items in the 15 or fewer items express checkout lane. Negative sanctions are applied in order to extinguish unacceptable, unproductive, or dangerous behaviors.

Fig. 3.6 Police Officers, an Umpire, and a Teacher in a Classroom are all authorized to apply formal sanctions.

Who can impose sanctions? Well, anybody really. You can't pull someone over because he failed to use his turn signal (if you lived in Virginia you wish you could), but you can shush someone for being loud in a movie theater. Sociologists make a distinction between these types of sanctions and who can apply them.

Formal sanctions are rewards or penalties that are applied by an authorized agent. For example, police are authorized to enforce laws and can write traffic tickets, issue warnings, or arrest suspects. The dean of students at your college is authorized to expel students who violate the honor code or honor students who beautify the college campus. Formal sanctions are used to promote compliance with laws or official institutional policies.

When you shake your head in displeasure, wag your finger at someone, or laugh at someone's silly behavior, you are applying informal sanctions—approval or disapproval that does not come from an authorized agent but from everyday interactions with others. These can range from mild, such as giving someone a dirty look for talking on his cell phone in an elevator, to severe, such as ending a friendship because your friend drinks too much. We all have the capacity to administer informal sanctions, and we all have. Have you ever flipped someone off after that person cut you off in traffic? If so, you applied an informal sanction.

TABLE 3.1 Some Weird (to us) Food Rules from Around the World

Country/ Region	Food Rule	Why?
Jamaica and Nigeria	Do not feed young children eggs.	They will grow up to be thieves.
China	Do not leave your chopsticks standing up in the remaining rice in your bowl.	In private homes, that practice is restricted to offerings to the ghosts of family ancestors. Doing this in a restaurant would cast a terrible curse on the owner.
Japan	If you want to share a tasty morsel with your meal-mate, do not pass the food from chopstick to chopstick. Rather, place the morsel on a separate plate and pass it to your partner.	Passing food from chopstick to chopstick references the Japanese practice of sifting through the cremated remains of loved ones looking for bones.
Alaska	It is illegal to give beer to a moose.	Have you ever seen a drunk moose?
France	As of 2011, ketchup is banned in all schools in France.	It threatens all things French. Ketchup is also viewed as an American encroachment on French culture.
The Middle East	Be sure to shake your cup after you have enjoyed your coffee with your new Bedouin friends.	If you don't, they will keep refilling it.
Nunavut (Canada) Inuit People	Be sure to fart after you finish your narwhal—the unicorn of the sea.	It shows appreciation for the meal, your host, and the cook.
Portugal	If they are not on the table, do NOT ask for salt and pepper.	To do this is to insult the cook's ability to season the food.
Thailand	Do NOT place the fork in your mouth. The fork is used to push food onto the spoon, which is then placed in the mouth.	You will appear both crude and rude.

Sources: Audiger, 2016; El Gedida, 2007; Graff and Ramadhana, 2011; Gray-Kanatiiosh, 2002; "Japanese Table Manners", 2015; Meyer-Rochow, 2009; Reid, 2012 Willsher, 2011.

THERE'S AN APP FOR THAT

The Etiquette App (Android and Apple) helps you with dining, dating, business and cultural etiquette. This could help in a variety of social situations in which you are unsure of the proper behavior. Don't know which fork to use first, unsure about how to greet your new Chinese boss, wondering how many times to kiss a French woman on the cheek or what the proper tip for the pizza delivery person is ... just use The Etiquette App and never be embarrassed again (Solaz Dazen srl, 2016).

Fig. 3.7 Eating food with Chopsticks is more widely practiced than eating with silverware.

Norms are not random. Rules for social conduct are generated by social values. That is, norms are based on the shared values of a society. All cultures possess values—culturally defined standards that guide people's interpretation about what is good or bad, right or wrong, desirable or undesirable, and just or unjust. If you want to know what a society values, take a look at its social rules. Let me start with a concrete example and move to a more abstract one. What do desert cultures value? Water. Desert cultures around the world have elaborate social rules surrounding consuming, finding, and distributing their limited water supply. The Bushmen of the Kalahari Desert have a complicated system of exchange called *hxaro,* which is guided by a complex set of social rules that determine who, how, when, and where people can, for example, drink water (Wiessner, 1977).

Fig. 3.8 San People—The Bushmen of the Kalahari.

According to University of Michigan researcher Wayne Baker (2014), one of the ten core American values is "*getting ahead*—individual achievement, status, and success." This idea of getting ahead or being successful is a fairly abstract concept, and one that people may define differently. Even so, most Americans would include possessions like a home, car, and clothing as indicators of status and success. Think about all the rules we have that protect people's stuff. You can't damage, trespass, take, or use other people's stuff. There are thousands of laws that prohibit robbery, theft, vandalism, and trespassing. These laws were established to protect the things that people work so hard for as they strive to get ahead. These laws also reflect our value of private property.

> *"Don't believe anything. Regard things on a scale of probabilities. The things that seem most absurd, put under 'Low Probability,' and the things that seem most plausible, you put under 'High Probability.' Never believe anything. Once you believe anything, you stop thinking about it."*
>
> *— Robert A. Wilson*

In daily conversations, people commonly use the terms values and beliefs interchangeably, not really making a clear distinction. We sociologists, on the other hand, like to point out the distinction between the two terms. While values are culturally defined standards about what is *good* and *desirable*, which serve as broad guidelines, **beliefs** are commonly held ideas about what is *true* or *real*. As Americans, we *value* success and we *believe* that we can be successful if we get an education and work hard. We also value freedom; therefore, we believe that people should be free to live where they want, work at what they want, be free to say what they want, and worship as they like. We also value independence, which leads to the belief that people should achieve things on their own, not rely on others, and achievement or success is an individual's responsibility. In contrast, Japanese culture values dependence; one must consider others before themselves, dependence on others is a natural part of the human condition, and contributing to the collective is emphasized.

You can see that values and beliefs are intertwined but different. One important difference between values and beliefs, and a unique characteristic of beliefs, is that people tend to maintain beliefs even when there is little or no evidence to support them or even if there is considerable evidence that contradicts them. For instance, in light of centuries of empirical evidence, including photographs, videos, and eyewitness reports (astronauts, cosmonauts, and other space men), that the earth is spherical in shape, as of 2015, there is still a Flat Earth Society, which believes the earth is a flat disc (I am not kidding: check out theflatearthsociety.org). Billions of people around the world believe in ghosts, spirits, angels, gods, and extraterrestrial beings without any support for their existence and considerable evidence suggesting they don't exist.

While beliefs can sustain people, sometimes they become the engine that drives immoral, unethical, or barbaric acts. In June 2014, for example, the Islamic State of Iraq and the Levant

(ISIL) published a manifesto, which, among other things, indicated that anyone who does not *believe* in its severe interpretation of Islam must convert or die. The extremist beliefs of ISIL's members have led them to burn, shoot, rape, torture, and behead anyone who does not believe what they believe. The group has gone as far as to produce and publish, on the Internet, videos of the gruesome beheadings of innocent people.

The Connection between Beliefs and Behaviors

The Fore (FOR-ray) people of Papua New Guinea greatly value the affection and respect of family members above nearly all other traits. According to their customs, there is only one powerful way to demonstrate one's love and loyalty to a dead relative: you must eat them. The Fore people are ritual cannibals: they eat the flesh and internal organs of deceased loved ones as a ritual celebration. They *believe* that this practice is the highest tribute of affection and respect you can bestow on your dead relative. Additionally, consuming your dead relatives keeps them near you always (Whitfield et al., 2008).

Unfortunately, one particular *behavior*, eating your dead loved ones' brains, has serious health consequences. Many times, the brains of the deceased contain a prion that causes a disease known as kuru. Kuru, or the "laughing sickness," is a spongiform encephalopathy, which is an incurable, degenerative brain disorder. It creates thousands of tiny holes in your brain so that it resembles a sponge. It is a degenerative disorder that passes through three stages. The first stage includes difficulty walking, talking, and seeing, muscle tremors, shivering, and slurred speech. In the second stage, a patient would experience the following symptoms: inability to walk without support, muscle jerks, outbursts of laughter (the "laughing sickness"), depression, and mental slowing. In the third and final stage, one would be unable to walk or sit up on his own, be incontinent, be unable to speak, and suffer a general cognitive disintegration. All this in a three- to six-month period after consuming the tainted brains.

Despite being informed of the danger associated with eating the brains of the deceased, they continued the *behavior* because the cultural *belief* in honoring the dead was so powerful. Knowing full well that they would die, and so would anyone who consumed brains of the dead, such as their children and spouses, they continued the custom. Fortunately, the ritual has effectively been extinguished. Do you believe in something so strongly you would risk the lives of your children, your parents, or other loved ones?

IS THERE LIFE AFTER LIFE?

Do you believe in past lives or reincarnation? Is there any scientific evidence to indicate that past lives are real? Well, at the University of Virginia (UVA), Dr. Jim Tucker (2013) runs the Division of Perceptual Studies (DOPS), where he and others investigate a number of paranormal events. The DOPS investigators examine paranormal activities such as near-death experiences, out-of-body experiences, and communication with the dead. However, they have a special focus on children who claim to remember past lives. DOPS researchers travel the world recording the past-life experiences of young children. They have amassed over 2,500 cases of past-life experiences and have concluded that they are real! What do you think? Check out their program at:

http://www.medicine.virginia.edu/clinical/departments/psychiatry/sections/cspp/dops/we_are-page

Dominant Culture, Subcultures and Countercultures

It is safe to say that a culture like ours is not monolithic—not solid, unbroken, and uniform. Our society is composed of a number of similar and dissimilar groups—everyone is not the same in the way they think or act. However, in the United States, like in other cultures, there is a dominant culture. The **dominant culture** refers to the mainstream culture in a society whose values, beliefs, and practices are shared and accepted by the majority of its members. That is, most people buy into our way of life without much oppositions. While there are groups who protest racial inequality, economic conditions, and gender inequality, they are exercising freedom of speech, and they don't really threaten social order. Production and maintenance of the dominant culture is usually, though not always, achieved by the majority population through control of social institutions such as schools, media, law, the political process, and the economy. In the United States, we might identify economically and politically powerful white males as those who control the dominant culture.

CONGRESS IS WHITE, RICH, AND MALE

Let's look, for example, at the racial, gender, and economic composition of Congress, which includes both the House of Representatives and the Senate. As of 2015, the U.S. Senate is 94% white and the House of Representatives is 80% white. When we add gender into the mix, we find that four out of five U.S. legislators are white men. The richest member of Congress, as of 2014, is worth more than $350 million, and the median net worth of all members of Congress was almost a half a million dollars (Dennis and Hunter, 2014; Bump, 2015).

Some would argue that as a group, the U.S. Congress has even more power than the president does, and it is overwhelmingly white, male, and wealthy. It has the power to change and make laws, including tax laws that overwhelmingly favor the rich, it holds the purse strings of education, and it can investigate anyone or any group it wants. This is not paranoia or a conspiracy theory; it is the reality that through laws, education, and finances, society can be shaped in such a way that reinforces the beliefs, values, and behaviors of the dominant group. Those who oppose the dominant culture in any serious way can be portrayed as deviant, criminal, or paranoid.

Just as there is considerable diversity of cultures across societies, there can be variation within a single society. Within nearly all cultures, there are groups of people who differ in some practice, custom, or habit from the general mainstream culture. The United States is a complex society composed of many groups; some have developed cultural patterns that are different from the dominant culture. Think about it this way: within the larger American culture, many smaller cultures, or subcultures, exist.

Subcultures are groups in society whose beliefs, behaviors and interests differ from the larger cultural patterns of society. While members of subcultures share a specific identity within that group, they are still part of and participate in the larger culture. There are countless subcultures in the United States that center around a number of social identities. Subcultures include different types of groups that can be formed by religion, age, class, region, sexual preference/identity, disability, race/ethnicity, occupation, or even interest. You can see by this list that whether we realize it or not, most of us have membership in a number of subcultures.

Ethnic and racial subcultures form around the language, food, and customs of their ancestors. Others form around shared experiences. Combat veterans are united by their unique journeys that only those who have known combat can share. Some subcultures are united by common traits, characteristics, or preferences. The corseting community, for example, embraces an aesthetic preference for tightly laced corsets and the physical sensation the members derive from wearing corsets. (There is a shop in Jacksonville, Florida, devoted to corsets and corset fashion appropriately named Subculture). Groups like Alcoholics Anonymous, Online Gamers Anonymous, and Clutterers Anonymous emerge to support those suffering from various addictions. Even though members of subcultures coalesce around their particular lifestyle, they still identify with and participate in the larger society.

Goths, hipsters, furries, and hip-hop are all examples of subcultures. Many times, like in these examples, groups have a particular style of dress, listen to certain music, and have a central focus, trait, or interest, which adds up to what members consider a lifestyle. The Goth lifestyle, the hipster lifestyle, and the vampire lifestyle represent alternate ways of living within the larger culture. Goths wear black, and hipster males have a "uniform": boots, jeans with the cuffs rolled up, plaid shirt, and oh, don't forget the facial hair. Furries like to dress as their favorite furry animal, and rap music is central to the hip-hop culture. While members of subcultures share beliefs or practices that differ from mainstream culture, they still participate in the larger general culture. I see Goths in my classes along with hipsters, athletes, and hackers, earning degrees so they can get jobs, buy homes, and have families like most in American culture.

I have many friends who ride Harleys. They wear a lot of black, take care and pride in their bikes, ride frequently, and share road stories. Many of these "weekend warriors" take on the persona of the "Harley Rider" on the weekends but are back in the classroom or office come Monday morning, participating in the big culture. Moreover, they identify with Harley bike owners no matter where they may ride—Alaska or Arizona, Croatia or Japan, membership in many subcultures is not bound by geography. When I travel to scuba dive, I meet divers from around the world, and we immediately bond over our common interest.

This is by no means a comprehensive list of subcultures. There are also many **deviant subcultures** that are less tolerated or aren't as acceptable as others. These are unusual subcultures that most people can't relate to and may mock or deride. Vampire culture, for example, is a growing subculture in which people may believe that they are vampires. Some have night jobs so they can sleep during the day and avoid daylight, they may sleep in coffins, and they may have their teeth ground down into fangs or have custom prosthetic fangs made. They dress in exotic vampire attire, and some even consume the blood of others, usually close friends who consent to the practice. But not all vampires consume blood; some get their sustenance from the psychic energy of crowds or the power in nature, such as waves or lightning. Yet others are highly spiritual, and some believe they have an immortal soul. Take a look at table 3.3 if you want to keep your vampire types straight. Finally, there are groups in society who remain marginalized because criminal activity is their central unifying activity. *Criminal deviant subcultures* include groups such as the mafia, street gangs, or drug users.

TABLE 3.2 Several Examples of Subcultures by Type

Subculture Type	Examples
Religion	Amish, Hasidim, and Fundamentalist Church of Jesus Christ of Latter-Day Saints (FLDS)
Age	Boomers, Gen Xers, Millennials
Class	Lower Class, Middle Class, Upper Class
Region	Southerner, New Englander
Sexual Preference/ Identity	LGBPTTQQIIAA+ (Lesbian, Gay, Bisexual, Pansexual, Transgender, Transsexual, Queer, Questioning, Intersex, Intergender, Asexual, Ally)
Disability	Deaf and Disabled Punk Rockers
Race/Ethnicity	African American, Latino, and German American
Occupation	Operating Room Nurses, College Professors, and Piano Tuners
Interest	Scuba Divers, Cheerleaders, and Hackers

TABLE 3.3 Know your Vampires

Vampire Type	What They're Into
Sanguinarians	Consume their own blood or that of others
Psychic (Pranic)	Thrive on the psychic or aural energy of individuals or groups
Living	Highly spiritual vampires who do not drink blood or draw on the energies of others. Organized into clans (Temple of the Vampire, Ordo Strigoi Vii and The Order of the Black Dragon)
Transcendental	Believe that they can obtain immortality by transferring their soul into the body of a younger vampire.

Source: Vampireunderworld.com

In contrast, countercultures—groups that engage in lifestyles that include beliefs and practices that are in direct opposition to the prevailing norms of mainstream culture—do not always identify with and participate in the larger society. Typically, countercultures reject some of the values, beliefs, or norms of the larger society, and unlike subcultures that operate relatively smoothly within the larger society, countercultures actively defy mainstream society by developing their own social organization, many times in isolated communities.

Some examples include the counterculture movements of the yippies (members of the Youth International Party, a political party for young progressives) and hippies of the 1960s, which opposed the war in Vietnam, the federal government, and capitalist economic systems in general. They protested the social, political, economic, and sexual inequalities of the time and essentially called for a reordering of society. Radical groups like Earth First! are in opposition to environmental policies and practices they believe don't do enough to conserve or protect natural resources. This counterculture organization advocates "monkey wrenching," or "ecotage," the practice of environmental sabotage. Followers of Earth First! are suspected of "spiking" old growth trees, putting large, hidden spikes in trees so that when loggers cut into them they are injured or killed (Roselle and Mahan, 2009; Earth First!, 2015). These acts of ecotage were meant to protest the unsustainable practice of logging old growth forests and the subsequent damage to the ecosphere and bring about radical social change.

Fig. 3.9 Hippies of the 1960's and 1970's and Black Panthers both represented counterculture groups

Some counterculture movements have lofty aims and are opposed to the larger society because they believe that they can affect real, positive social change. The hippies wanted to transform the United States into a fair and free society, and Earth First! wants human societies to stop destroying the earth so future generations can enjoy a healthy planet. However, some countercultures are more militant and antisocial. The Black Panther Party (BPP) of the 1960s and '70s was a militant counterculture movement originally formed to monitor police brutality. Then the movement grew, ultimately advocating violent revolution as the only path to black liberation. The party called on all African Americans to arm themselves in preparation for the revolution that would topple the white establishment (Bloom and Martin, 2013).

Another race-based counterculture, the White Supremacy Movement, seeks to expel or enslave all people of color and anyone who practices any religion other than protestant Christianity. Groups like the Ku Klux Klan, Aryan Brotherhood, and the Aryan Nations have popularized this movement. These groups differ slightly on tactics, but they all espouse the same message of eliminating or subjugating all non-white, non-Christians in the United States.

READ MORE

- *Vampire Culture* by Maria Mellins (2013). This thorough investigation of a world, which at first seems dark and sinister, reveals it is comprised of people from all walks of life and ages from bus drivers to teachers. They are drawn by the allure of the vampire lifestyle, fascination with the undead or social identity. A colorful account of a subculture that is largely unknown.

Theoretical Perspectives on Culture

Recall that the functionalist perspective assumes that society is a complex system of interrelated parts that work together cooperatively. Functionalists are highly concerned with social order. There are more than 323 million Americans; if people are pursuing their own self-interests, how does society hang together? The reality is people do cooperate and there is a degree of social integration, because most people are invested in their families, communities, and society. Functionalists believe that cooperation is a result, in part, of compliance and conformity to social rules. Generally, the roadways of my city and of yours run fairly smoothly because drivers cooperate with each other. People want to get to their jobs or home to their families, so they obey traffic laws, avoiding accidents and all the hassle those bring. Everyone's behavior on the road is constrained by the same rules, which leads to cooperation and creating a sort of social order of the roadways; the same is true for the larger society.

Remember from chapter 1 that the conflict perspective argues social order is maintained by the elite classes through coercion and power. Conflict theorists don't view social order as emerging from cooperation; rather, they believe the powerful classes use ideologies to maintain their positions of dominance. The dominant classes manipulate social institutions and other elements of culture, ideas, values, and beliefs to ensure their economic supremacy. The elements of culture like values, beliefs, and norms are designed to reinforce the economic relations in society. Culture is essentially constructed by the elite classes as a mechanism of social control.

The interactionist approach, as we have discussed before, emphasizes the interactions of individuals in everyday life and how they shape social life. This stands in contrast to both the functionalist and conflict approaches, which focus on how large scale social structures pattern our daily lives. The interactionist approach sees humans as continually adjusting their behavior in response to the actions of others, interpretation of the situation, and meaning found in symbols. Thus, people are seen as active, creative participants who construct their social world, not simply conform to it. For interactionists, culture is constructed through human interaction and negotiation.

For instance, imagine you find yourself at a house party, music is playing, people are dancing, and there are kegs of beer. It's Friday night, and you don't have any sociology homework, so you decide to have a few beers. You have a few beers, meet and talk with some interesting people, and dance a bit. After a few hours and many beers, you are feeling pretty buzzed, your speech is slightly slurred, your balance is a little uneven, and you're drunk. Then the music stops, the lights come on, and everyone goes silent. You are then informed that all the beer served at the party was non-alcoholic! Huh? You are now stone-cold sober. From all the symbols and given the social environment, you interpreted the situation as a party, and when you are at a party and drink beer all night long, you get drunk.

TABLE 3.4 Theoretical Perspectives and Elements of Culture

	Theoretical Perspective		
Element of Culture	**Structural Functionalism**	**Conflict Approach**	**Interactionist Approach**
Norms	Social rules are necessary for conformity and compliance, which promote solidarity and stability, maintaining social order.	Norms reinforce the economic power of the dominant group. Conformity and compliance to social rules maintain the dominant group's consent to rule.	During daily interactions, people interpret the actions of others and the social context in order to know what social rules apply.

(*Continued*)

Theoretical Perspective

Element of Culture	Structural Functionalism	Conflict Approach	Interactionist Approach
Values and Beliefs	Common values and beliefs are central to maintaining consensus, leading to stable social order. Generally, Americans share the belief that hard work will get you ahead. So, the overwhelming majority of people get jobs, work hard, pay taxes and buy stuff, helping maintain our way of life.	The powerful classes use ideologies—systems of ideas, values, and beliefs that guide the way people think and act—to maintain their positions of dominance. Members of society who do not buy into the dominant ideology are marginalized and portrayed as radical or deviant. Those who practice non-standard religions, for example, are seen as weird and pushed to the margins of society.	During daily interactions, individuals use symbols to reflect and reinforce social values and beliefs. Some political candidates use American flag lapel pins as symbols to reflect their patriotism, which people will notice during interactions.

The Bottom Line

Culture is everything, everything is culture. This is my phrase, which emphasizes that human culture is ubiquitous. Culture is what has allowed us as a species to adapt, survive, and flourish. However, the birth and development of culture was impossible without language. The development of complex languages allowed humans to organize, work cooperatively, and survive. Language is so intimately intertwined with culture that it links users in common modes of thought and perception. It also makes us uniquely human because language can relate present to past and future.

Culture has been an effective adaptive mechanism for humans, the only single species that can inhabit all geographical regions of the planet. Culture is learned, shared, and transmitted across generations, and it is dynamic. Culture changes as new discoveries and inventions are introduced and when improvements or innovations are made to existing technology. Social change comes in several forms. Language is always altered when new technologies emerge in society, because we need to label those new things the associated beliefs and behaviors. Sometimes change in behaviors lag behind the technologies, and rules about how to use the technologies have to catch up. Culture is symbolic: signs and symbols can be used as a sort of shorthand because members of the culture share their meaning.

However, languages can be extinguished through the ethnocentric practice of cultural imperialism. Human history is filled with examples of the conquest and destruction of cultures, but this has been tempered in the past century as many researchers and governments have taken a more relativistic approach to understanding other cultures. Not only has this practice preserved many cultures, it has raised awareness of cultures that are endangered by identifiable external forces.

Culture is composed of two distinct components: material culture and non-material culture. Material culture is all those things we make and use. Food, cell phones, computers, underwear, and cigars are all representatives of material culture. But these are not just things; these things have meaning. Meaning attached to material objects allows us to interpret the value, status, or worth of those objects. Non-material culture is composed of values, beliefs, and norms. Values are important shared standards of right and wrong, good and bad, desirable and undesirable, and just and unjust. These cultural standards drive beliefs about what is true and real, potentially binding us together. In turn, we act according to our beliefs. Our behaviors are constrained and regulated through the application of social norms. These rules of social conduct can encourage social cooperation and promote social stability and social order.

Within the larger culture, there exist many little cultures. And despite their distinctive values and practices, subcultures are still subsumed under the larger cultural system. Subcultures in the United States include such groups as the Hmong, Eastern Orthodox, competitive cheerleaders, and vampires. Most of us are members of a number of subcultural groups at any given time and over the course of our lives. Countercultures, on the other hand, do not operate smoothly within the mainstream culture. These groups seek to destroy or dismantle the larger culture and social structure. Many of these groups are at odds with government policies or practices, oppose cultural practices and lifestyles, or feel that members of their group are being systematically mistreated.

Finally, in this chapter, we examined the way that the three major sociological perspectives viewed culture. Functionalists argue adherence to values and beliefs promotes solidarity and consensus, contributing to stable social order. Again, conformity and compliance with social norms promotes stable social order, with all people doing what they are supposed to be doing. In contrast, the conflict approach maintains that the elements of culture are created by the elite classes to maintain their position of dominance. The elements of culture, including social institutions, are simply tools of the dominant class used to secure consent to their rule. Unlike either functionalism or conflict theories, the interactionist approach sees culture as constructed by the interaction of individuals in everyday life. For interactionists, social order is derived from interactions among individuals rather than being imposed by larger social structures. This focus shifts their interpretation away from stable values and beliefs and toward more malleable, continually readjusting social processes.

Figure Credits

Fig. 3.1: "Branislaw Malinowski with Trobriand Islanders," https://commons.wikimedia.org/wiki/File:Bronis%C5%82aw_Malinowski_among_Trobriand_tribe.jpg. Copyright in the Public Domain.

Fig. 3.2: Copyright © Saperaud~commonswiki (CC BY-SA 3.0) at https://commons.wikimedia.org/wiki/File:Moon_merged_small.jpg.

Fig. 3.3: Captain George E. Mack, "Inuit Children," https://commons.wikimedia.org/wiki/File:Enfants_Inuits_1925.jpg. Copyright in the Public Domain.

Fig. 3.4a: Copyright © Philipp Rath (CC BY-SA 3.0) at https://commons.wikimedia.org/wiki/File:Bmw_525d.jpg.

Fig. 3.4b: Copyright © Janitors (CC by 2.0) at https://commons.wikimedia.org/wiki/File:Size_comparison_of_iPhone_5C_5S_4S.jpg.

Fig. 3.6a: Copyright © Elliot Moore (CC BY-SA 2.0) at https://commons.wikimedia.org/wiki/File:G20_police_lines.jpg.

Fig. 3.6b: Copyright © Paul L Dineen (CC by 2.0) at https://commons.wikimedia.org/wiki/File:Safe_(4779502220).png.

Fig. 3.6c: Cruise Reviewer, "Jpg_port_pollenca," https://commons.wikimedia.org/wiki/File:Jpg_port_pollenca.jpg. Copyright in the Public Domain.

Fig. 3.7: Copyright © Opponent (CC by 2.0) at https://commons.wikimedia.org/wiki/File:Okonomiyaki_by_chou_i_ci_at_Sumiyoshi_Taisha,_Osaka.jpg.

Fig. 3.8: Copyright © Mopane Game Safaris (CC BY-SA 4.0) at https://commons.wikimedia.org/wiki/File:Bosquimanos-Grassland_Bushmen_Lodge,_Botswana_09.jpg.

Fig. 3.9a: Copyright © Mombas (CC by 2.5) at https://commons.wikimedia.org/wiki/File:1981_People_Pix.jpg.

Fig. 3.9b: http://www.loc.gov/pictures/item/2005677025/. Copyright © 1967 by New York World-Telegram.

PEOPLE JUST WANT TO FIT IN: Navigating Our Social Landscapes

2

CHAPTER 4

SOCIALIZATION: FITTING INTO SOCIETY AND BECOMING SOCIAL BEINGS

He said, she said

If you are a woman, think about what phone calls are like with your female friends and family members. When you call a female friend and ask her to go out on a Friday night, what do you talk about? Do you just tell her where to meet you and at what time, or are you more likely to include topics like clothes, your jobs, boyfriends/husbands, finances, and your feelings? If you are a typical American female, you probably talk about a bunch of things on that phone call unrelated to its original purpose.

If you're male, think about your last phone call to a male friend or relative. If you are like most men in the U.S., your phone calls are shorter than those of your female counterparts. If you called a male friend to go out with you on Friday night, what would the conversation be like? You most likely agreed on a time and place to meet and that would be about it ... you might ask him for some money for beer. Would you discuss fashion or relationships on that call? Why do men and women communicate differently?

In her book *You Just Don't Understand,* Deborah Tannen (1990) showed that men and women communicate using different conversational styles. Women communicate using what she calls *rapport talk*—a communication style that encourages interpersonal relations and intimacy—while men engage in what she terms *report talk*—a style that reports information with little, if any, emotional content. What accounts for these differences? Are women innately more talkative than men, or do women learn to engage in more emotionally constructive ways? Do men possess a low-word-count gene, or do men learn through interaction with others just to get the facts? (Actually, recent research shows that men talk more on average per day than women do.)

Exploring the complexities of how we come to act in the ways we do, how we come to understand who we are, and our place in society is the focus of this chapter. We will examine the influences of genetic and environmental factors on our development, as well as the social mechanisms that are constructed to help us fit in. We will also discuss how we conform to social expectations and form socially appropriate identities, ultimately becoming social beings.

Socialization

"We don't see the world the way it is, we see the world the way we are."

— The Talmud

How do we become the people that we are? How do we know how to behave appropriately in everyday life? Well, mostly through the process sociologists call socialization. **Socialization** is a lifelong, ongoing process that allows us to learn our culture, develop a sense of self, and, ultimately, help us fit into our society.

Through the process of socialization, we come to develop an appropriate social identity and learn how to navigate our social world. Socialization is really a process of learning—learning social rules, values, beliefs, learning how to operate within those rules, learning language, and learning the behaviors associated with the various social positions that we occupy. Additionally, the process of socialization allows society to pass on culture to the next generation. It is also important to know that while we are learning how to navigate our social world and becoming individuals, we are internalizing much of what we are being taught. The internalization of social rules, values, and beliefs is essential in developing functioning members of society, which is the central goal of the process of socialization.

Let's think about socialization as having two main purposes. The first is to learn our culture, and the second is to develop a sense of self or an identity, which is distinct from others. These two purposes can be viewed as producing an important and desired social effect: creating productive members of society who fit in. This is achieved through the two types of socialization: primary socialization and adult socialization.

Primary Socialization

Through **primary socialization**, we acquire the basic skills needed to navigate our social world. There are four elements to primary socialization.

1. Learning the social rules
2. Learning how to act within those rules
3. Learning language
4. Developing an appropriate social identity

As a general rule, we could think of primary socialization as being complete by the time we are done with high school (at least here in the U.S.). Typically, by the time you are finished with high school, you are able to communicate effectively using language, you know the social rules, you know how to act within those rules (whether you choose to is up to you), and you have developed a sense of self. While later life experiences may modify our sense of self as we take on new statuses and roles, this primary socialization has a profound effect on who we are. Therefore, primary socialization gives us the tools we need to be competent members of society. However, it does not provide us with all we need to navigate all the social landscapes that we will traverse throughout our lives.

A Note on Primary Socialization

Not all sociologists would agree with my perspective on primary socialization. Many sociologists view primary socialization as the processes of teaching, learning, and exploring done in the context of the family only, the first or *primary* group that a child is exposed to. Meeting physical needs such as feeding, sheltering, and clothing children is sometimes incorporated into this view of primary socialization. While most sociologists relegate primary socialization exclusively to the family and childhood, my view extends the process through adolescence so the four basic skills can be acquired.

Statuses

While in popular culture people may use status to refer to prestige or one's social rank, sociologists have a different definition and use for status. Statuses are social positions that people occupy. We all occupy a number of statuses at any given time. You may be a college student, a wife, a sister, and a NASCAR driver. These are all social positions that individuals occupy, and they represent the two general types of statuses that we recognize in sociology. Ascribed statuses are those that we are born into or acquire involuntarily later in life that we typically cannot change. Those statuses that we are born into, such as our sex, ethnicity, or birth order, we have no control over. Additionally, later in life, we may involuntarily assume a status that we also have no control over, such as a cancer patient or becoming a widow or widower. (Unless, of course, one had some control over that?)

Achieved statuses are exactly that: statuses that we achieve through our own hard work or effort. Examples include college student, professor, wife, Republican, or felon. Each of these statuses represents the result of hard work or decisions that individuals have made. Remember that while one cannot change from African American to European American, we can change some of the statuses we are born into, such as social class or religion. There are some statuses that can be achieved or ascribed. For example, Prince William of England was born royal (ascribed), but his wife, Kate Middleton, married into royalty to become a Duchess (achieved).

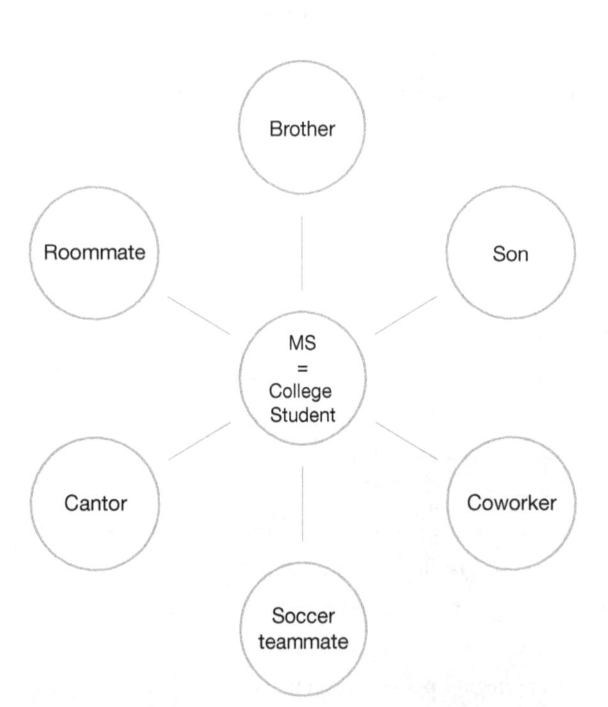

Fig. 4.1 A status set where the master status is college student. We all occupy many statuses at any given time in our lives. Our master statuses changes as we progress through life, you won't always be a college student

The master status refers to the status that tends to occupy most of your time and energy and takes precedence over your other statuses. In a sense, the master status orders how you manage all your other statuses. For many of you reading this book, college student may be your master status, or maybe being a parent is your master status right now in your life. It is important to note that your master status can and will change over your life course. You were not always a parent, which means some other status was your master status before you became a parent. And definitely remember that you will not *always* be a college student (let's hope not).

The sum total of all the statuses that we occupy at any given time in our lives is what we refer to as a status set. The status set can be illustrated using a sociogram like the one shown below in figure 4.1. Notice that the hub of the sociogram represents the master status, and the spokes radiate out to each of the other statuses that one occupies.

Roles

While we all leave high school with the basic skills needed to navigate our social world, we continue to acquire new social statuses across our life course. You did not know how to be a college student until you got to college, you did not know how to be a wife until you were married, and you did not know how to be a cashier until you got that job. As we acquire new statuses, we need to learn how to perform the roles associated with those statuses.

Roles are the expected behaviors associated with a particular social status. For example, as a college student, you are expected to attend class, pay fees, take exams, and turn your phone off in class (just a friendly reminder). As a professor, I am expected to arrive to class on time, be prepared to lecture, and give exams, among other roles. Therefore, for each status that you occupy, there are a set of expected behaviors that you must *learn*. This complex process of acquiring statuses

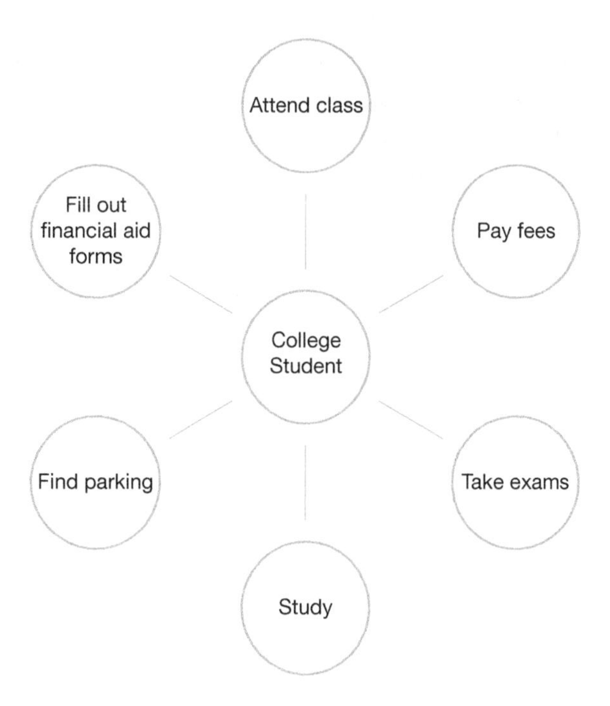

Fig. 4.2 A Role set for the status of college student. Roles are the expected behaviors associated with a given status.

and mastering roles is a large part of socialization. Additionally, the combination of statuses we occupy and how we perform the roles associated with them represents our social identity—our sense of who we are as individuals. (We will discuss this later in the chapter.)

A role set is the total number of roles (expected behaviors) associated with any status. The hub of the sociogram in figure 4.2 below contains the status (student), and the spokes radiate out to each of the roles associated with that status.

Adult Socialization

Remember, the process of socialization is a lifelong, ongoing process of learning. Adult socialization, then, is the process of transitioning into the myriad statuses that we acquire over our life course and learning the many roles that are associated with those statuses. In a sense, then, we are constantly learning as we grow older and move through our lives. Death is merely nature's way of telling us we are done being socialized.

Let's take a look at a fairly stereotypical American life course to see how we transition into new statuses and then learn how to perform (take on the roles) for these statuses.

Once you graduate from high school, you go to college and become a college student. As I stated above, you do not know how to be a college student until you become one. As you learn to be a college student, you will learn how to navigate your college's bureaucracy and learn how to behave within your college's particular culture. Once you finish college, you may take your first job, and there, you must learn how to perform your job within the larger culture of the organization. Perhaps you may learn that there are unofficial ways to get ahead at your job, but you will not know this until you are socialized into your new job and learn the general culture of the organization.

Now that you have a steady job, you may find a partner and get engaged. Do you know how to be engaged? No. Then you pop the question and you are off to get married. Now you have to learn to be married ... do you know how to be married? Trust me, you don't; neither do I, just ask my wife. But I'm learning. Ahh, wedded bliss, and along come the children. Does anyone know how to be a parent before she/he has children? No. Nevertheless, parents learn. Now, like any good American, you get divorced. Being divorced is a difficult status to learn—trust me. Again, like many good Americans, you remarry (more than one-third of all families in the U.S. are blended families) (Pew Research Center, 2011). Now you will experience the socialization process of becoming a stepparent.

The children grow and you advance at work, all the while learning how to run your entire department as you are promoted. Your children have kids of their own—congratulations, you are now a grandparent. Maybe you volunteer for Habitat for Humanity, lead a book club, or go back to school. Then you retire and begin to paint and travel and entertain all manner of family get-togethers. Whatever you do, you are learning as you take on new statuses, new roles, and new parts of yourself. This is just an illustration of socialization over the life course, the ongoing, lifelong process of learning.

Agents of Socialization

Who can we blame for socialization? In other words, if socialization is a process of learning, who is doing the teaching? Those individuals, groups, and institutions that we view as responsible for socializing members of society are **agents of socialization**. There are many socializing forces in our lives, from our parents and friends to the groups we belong to and larger social institutions such as the economy, religion and our political system. However, I focus on the four most influential agents of socialization in shaping our sense of self and helping us to fit into society.

The Family

The family is arguably the most powerful agent of socialization, especially in shaping the lives of children. For most of us, our family is our primary contact with the world. We spend more time with our family members than any other single group in our first few years of life. We spend more critical developmental time with our family, but more importantly, we share more intimate time with family members. That is, as we develop, our parents and siblings see us change and grow. Parents know how you lie, they know what you fear, and face it, they have seen you naked and changed your stinky diapers—you really cannot get more intimate than that. Chances are you will not experience that intense level of intimacy until you start a family of your own.

Your parents most likely have directly instructed you to do certain things that they believe will help you navigate culture and be a functioning member of society. Parents instruct us on how to be polite, to look both ways before crossing the street, and not to stare at people. There is also less direct or more informal learning going on. By observing their parents, children learn about how married couples interact, share intimacy, and how they argue and treat finances. These all have the potential to profoundly influence the way that children will treat their partners later in life (Siegler, 2000).

Many parents report finding themselves using the same phrases or rationale that their parents used on them when dealing with their own children. At some point in your life, usually sometime in your forties, you will look in the bathroom mirror and your father/mother will be staring back at you! You will not see the reflection of your third-grade teacher, you will not see your favorite baseball player from when you were ten looking back at you in that mirror … you will see your parent, because she/he was a profound influence on who you have become. Where your family is located in the larger social landscape may also have an effect on how you view yourself and the world. What is your family's social class and educational background? What is your ethnicity? What is your family's religious affiliation? In what part of the country were you raised? All these factors contribute to our social development and adjustment, and ultimately to the person we become.

THERE'S AN APP FOR THAT

- *Good Manners* (iPad, iPhone and iPod touch) is an app designed to teach children good manners (Solaz Dazen srl, 2016). It uses real life scenarios with animated characters and soothing background music. Scenarios include how to be a good quest, table manners, the etiquette of meeting and greeting people and caring and sharing.
- For the adults, there is *Beverly Hills Manners,* an app that can help you out of any embarrassing situation. This app provides help with topics such as social graces, party, dining, and business etiquette (Qbiki Networks, 2011).

Education

Public schools in the United States were established in the nineteenth century as a means to create a literate population. Schools established earlier in the American colonial period were designed to reinforce the ideas of the church and community. Schools have not changed much in terms of their primary goal. Schools act as agents of socialization in several ways. Obviously, schools are responsible for teaching basic knowledge such as reading, writing, and arithmetic. This is school's **manifest function**, or its evident or obvious function to educate members of society.

But schools do more than just this. When I went to public elementary school back at the dawn of time, we had to pledge allegiance to the flag and pray each morning. Behaviors like these are meant to reinforce social values and beliefs. Schools are a place that we expect children to learn not only academic lessons, but life lessons: how to share, how to obey rules, and how to navigate a bureaucracy. To a limited extent, schools also act as training grounds, where students learn the rhythm of a workday (this was more useful in the early history of U.S. public education). You arrive at school at a certain time, you have recess (coffee break), you break for lunch, and you go back to classes (work) until your day is done. Not only are schools teaching students academic lessons and larger social values and beliefs, they are also preparing the vast majority of them for the pace of a workday and the workweek. These are **latent functions**—the present but unintentional or unrecognized purposes of schools. Philip Jackson

(1968) referred to these latent functions as the *hidden curriculum* or the unstated curriculum that makes education a socialization process.

You could think about latent functions or the hidden curriculum as unintended consequences. Think back to your high school years. Did you *just* learn biology, chemistry, history, and calculus? You probably learned a lot more. Maybe you learned something about alcohol, drugs, or sex ... and not in the classroom. Maybe you learned that the attractive students seemed to be more popular and get away with more. Maybe you learned that there was a stratification of power and prestige among your teachers and the administrators. These all represent the hidden curriculum—the things we learn that are not on the menu. Latent functions are always present when we create large groups or organizations. Think about any large group or organization that you have been a part of over the years. Not only did you interact with others to perform the manifest function of that group, you most likely learned a number of things that were not intended as a result of those interactions. Ultimately, schools are powerful agents of socialization. They teach us basic education, they reinforce social values and beliefs, and they teach valuable, unintended lessons about life in a larger social context.

Peers

While your parents are powerful agents of socialization, they typically become less important as you move through adolescence. Think back to when you were fourteen. For some of you, this was just a few years ago; for others, like me, it seems like a lifetime ago. Did you want to hang out with your parents when you were that age? Did you distance yourself from them? Did you have them drop you off four blocks from where you were meeting your friends? Well, if you did any of these things, you are in good company. Social research indicates that most teenagers (thirteen- to nineteen-year-olds) report that they would rather hang out with their friends than participate in family activities (De Guzman, 2007). As children seek to form their own identities and separate from their families, they are more likely to conform to *peer pressure* in order to be accepted by their peer groups. Adolescents do not hang out with others in hopes that they will be rejected; rather, they hope to be accepted by their peers—to fit in. In order to fit in with their peers, they will ultimately have to conform to the norms (social rules) of the peer group. They must learn the rules and conform to them to be accepted.

So, if you are hanging out with a group of your peers whose behaviors include drinking alcohol, you will most likely drink to be accepted by them or risk being rejected. As a result of this desire to conform to group behaviors and their rules, teenagers tend to run in packs, many times dressing and talking alike. Therefore, as adolescents work to jettison their family identities and become their own people, they ultimately look and talk like the peers they so desperately seek to be accepted by. In addition, studies have shown that adolescents are more likely to engage in deviant behaviors (e.g., drinking and smoking) if they have best friends or friend groups that are engaging in these deviant behaviors. While peers are clearly influential during adolescence in terms of immediate interests, such as which celebrities are cool or what fashions they like, some research indicates that parents maintain influence over their children's long-term goals, such as becoming a doctor or president (Kuczynski, 2003).

Mass Media, Technology, and Popular Culture

Changing technologies like telephones, television and the Internet, have been vehicles for mass media. They have allowed mass media to expand its influence over our social lives and to boost its power as an agent of socialization. For more than a hundred years ever improved technologies have served as platforms for sharing and shaping social values, beliefs, and behaviors.

We have unprecedented access to media through inexpensive and available technologies. Recent census data indicates that nearly 84% of American households have a computer, and of those households, nearly three quarters report using the computer to connect to the Internet (File and Ryan, 2014). As of May 2013, 91% of adults in the U.S. reported having a cell phone or a smartphone. In addition, to no one's surprise, adults between eighteen and thirty-four are the biggest consumers of smartphones (Smith, 2013). We spend more and more time with our technology. A 2009 study revealed that U.S. adults spend an average of 8.5 hours in front of some type of device screen every day (Stelter 2009). What does all this technology do for us? It gives us nearly constant and instant access to information. Images of changing standards of beauty, ideas of what it means to be a real man, and advertisements customized for your browsing history bombard us with changing ideals, values, and beliefs.

In 2014, a Florida man was videoed pushing his young son down a skateboard ramp. The video was posted to YouTube, and within a week, the man had lost his job, been investigated by the local police, and started receiving hate mail and vitriolic phone calls. His boss even admitted firing him because of the video. Ultimately, he and his wife decided to move from their home. Why? Today's technology allows instant access to media and exposes how public the Internet can make our private lives. Their lives were upturned because of the power of the Internet and the comments of thousands of people who did not know them yet condemned the father's action. Fortunately, the police decided that they would not bring charges against him (Kemp, 2014).

Nature and Nurture

We cannot fully develop and become socially adjusted individuals without the interaction others. While we all have our own genetic makeup, most good evidence indicates that we need more than just our genetic code to become fully developed and adjusted social beings. We need the contact and interaction with others to make us capable of engaging in appropriate social behaviors and developing a sense of identity that separates us from others. I view the argument of nature vs. nurture as a false dichotomy. The enormous amount of research that has been done on the human genome clearly indicates that genes are impacted by environmental factors. While our genes have a profound impact on our physical and intellectual development, that development is directly linked to the presence of, and interaction with, other humans (Ledger, 2009; Freese, 2008).

THE HARLOW MONKEY STUDIES

Studies of animals raised in isolation have informed our discussion of the importance of interaction and intimacy on development. Harry and Margaret Harlow conducted a series of studies on rhesus monkeys who had been raised away from their mothers and other monkeys. Monkeys who were raised in isolation were fearful, ill-adjusted, and aggressive toward other monkeys and engaged in self-mutilation—overall anti-social behavior. Moreover, they did not mate, and those isolated females who were artificially inseminated became abusive mothers (Harlow, 1958, 1962; Harlow and Harlow, 1971).

In what is undoubtedly the most famous of these experiments, monkeys were given "surrogate mothers," wood and wire mock-ups of monkey moms. Two groups were created. One group of infant monkeys got a wire mom who could dispense milk and a cloth-covered mom who did not provide milk. The second group got a wire surrogate mother with no milk and a cloth-covered replica mom who could give milk. Regardless of which mom gave milk, all monkeys spent most of their time clinging to the cloth-covered replica mother. Even though they would take the milk from the wire mom, they would not linger with her; as soon as they fed, they went back to the cloth-covered mom.

Mothers who provided more pleasant sensations for the infant monkeys were more desirable than those mothers who gave milk. This suggested that infant love was no simple response to the satisfaction of physiological needs—providing milk. Attachment was not primarily about hunger or thirst. It could not be reduced to nursing. Harlow showed that infant-mother love was emotional rather than physiological, substantiating that continuity of care—"nurture"—was a far more determining factor in healthy psychological development than "nature."

Picking up on Harlow's claims that his experiments translated to human development, the media regularly reported that his findings as were applicable to the concepts of love and attachment and development in human beings. These monkey love experiments had powerful implications for understanding the separation of mothers and infants, as well as child-rearing in general. While this research is interesting in that it highlights clearly the nature/nurture debate, it has some issues. Can we generalize animal studies to humans? Are there some ethical issues with Harlow's work? Could we conduct such research today? Certainly not with humans, and probably not with monkeys.

Let's look at the case of Genie. Genie (not her real name) was a girl who had been denied affection and contact with other family members for nearly all of her life. She was thirteen when she was discovered in a suburb of Los Angeles in 1970. She spent the vast majority of her time bound to a potty chair in a dark room. It was reported that when she was found, she had callouses in the shape of the potty-chair seat on her buttocks. Her father believed her to be "mentally retarded" and demanded that she be bound and kept in the dark. Her mother was legally blind and apparently also a victim of her husband's abuse. When Genie was found, she was taken to a children's research hospital in Los Angeles. There, it was discovered that she could not speak, had a strange, bunny-like gait, and did not know how to interact appropriately with others. It was determined that her isolation had created such a profound deficit in cognitive, behavioral, and emotional development that it was likely she could never function independently in society (McMahan, 2014).

While Genie possessed normal genetic sequencing, the isolation and lack of human contact had such a devastating effect on her development that she could never fit into our society. Therefore, while genes are necessary for us to appear human, it is the contact with others and the social environment that allow us to be fully engaged in social life and all that comes with it. So, it is not *nature vs. nurture*, but rather *nature and nurture*, which interact to make us who we are.

Gender Socialization and the Nature/Nurture Debate

From the moment children are born, adults treat infant boys different than they treat infant girls. To this day in most hospitals around the U.S., infant girls are covered with pink blankets and boys are given blue ones. Research indicates we are more likely to hold baby boys further away from our bodies than baby girls, and we are more likely to use full English sentences with baby boys—"who's my little man?"—versus nonsense syllables with infant girls—"how's the chochee wittle girl?" On average, baby boys are larger, heavier, and have larger heads, are more physical, take greater physical risks, and are more likely to visit the emergency room than their female counterparts. Baby girls, on average, are more likely to hold eye contact, be more interested in human faces, be earlier at understanding speech, and be earlier talkers than baby boys (Brizendine, 2006; Eliot, 2009). But are these differences a result of our genetic make-up, our social environments or some combination of both?

Margaret Mead's (1935) pioneering research *Sex and Temperament in Three Primitive Societies*, conducted in New Guinea, provides a cross-cultural insight into the construction of gender roles and child-rearing practices. Mead's work among the Arapesh, Mundugumor, and the Tchambuli showed that gender roles and child-rearing practices were not universal and not bound by gender. In fact, among the Arapesh, both men and women were pacifists and did not engage in aggressive or warlike behaviors. Both sexes were nurturing and spent time with the children. And, in turn, Arapesh children grew up to mirror these attributes. What many societies view as *maternal* attitudes and behaviors extended to both men and women, making gender roles indistinguishable among the Arapesh.

In contrast, the Mundugumor were a warlike people who barely tolerated children. These were not nurturing people; in fact, harsh treatment and punishment of children was commonplace. Children were encouraged to be aggressive and violent. So, early on, children realized the importance of aggression and found that physical violence was a socially accepted solution to their problems small and large. Both boys and girls, men and women exhibited these traits, so gender roles were unidentifiable. The Tchambuli (now Chambri) exhibited what Westerners would perceive as gender-role reversal. The men were passive, vain, and decorated themselves. The women were the breadwinners, engaging in all the work, such as fishing and weaving, while the men stayed near the home, practicing dancing and art.

From these observations, Mead concluded that a society's ideas of masculine and feminine are not biologically determined, but rather culturally constructed. If masculine and feminine were absolutes, then we would find all women of the world and all men of the world behaving the same way, but we don't. There is tremendous variation in gender roles around the world. Parents all over the globe try to raise their children to be well-adjusted members of their collectives, and in doing so, they instill in them the conventions of their culture, including the ideas of masculine and feminine.

However, in the decades since Mead conducted her research tremendous advances in genetic and neurological sciences have been made, which indicate there may be some real biological difference between women and men that impact their social development. For example, men on average tend to excel at tasks that demand manipulating objects in three dimensions. Women are better, on average, than men remembering where things are. As a consequence, most women navigate based on landmarks while men have a general sense of north, south, east, and west. Women can detect slight variations in color better than men can. Women also tend to worry more than men. This is linked to the fact that women produce about half as much serotonin (a neurochemical responsible for depression) and they have half as many transporters in their brains for recycling it. This turns out to be an asset, those who worry more tend to anticipate problems and develop strategies to handle them. What does this all mean? While research shows that there are neurochemical and neuroanatomical differences between males and females, it does not mean that our conceptions of gender are biologically determined (Tabatadze et al., 2015; Miller and Halpern, 2013; Abramov et al., 2012; Cashdan et al., 2012). A more informed approach acknowledges these biological differences, while understanding that others and our social environments help shape our gender identities (we will discuss this in detail in Chapter 9).

Development of the Self: How We Become Me, Myself, and I

How do we become who we are? Well, from the story of Genie above, we certainly know that it takes the contributions of others to shape who we are. Who am I? Why am I different from others? These are profound questions that have no doubt been examined since we as a species first appeared. Humans, in general, are complex, but understanding the formation of the individual is a profoundly complicated issue.

Theoretical Approaches to the Development of the Self

The Interactionist Approach

> *"All children are born pure egoists. They perceive their needs to the exclusion of all others. Only through socialization do they learn that some forms of gratification must be deferred and others denied."*
>
> — *Andrew Vachss*

Cooley and the Looking Glass Self

> *"I am not what I think I am, and I am not what you think I am. I am what I think you think I am."*
>
> — *Charles Horton Cooley*

In his *looking glass self theory*, Charles Horton Cooley (1902) argued that our sense of self grows out of our social interactions with others. Cooley believed that our sense of self is shaped not only by the direct contemplation of our own personal qualities, but also by our perceptions of how we are being perceived by others. Generally, he believed that we all act like mirrors, reflecting back images of how we think others see us and images of ourselves to one another that include evaluations of character. Specifically, this happens in three steps:

- **We imagine how we appear to others**: Have you ever worn some new clothes to school and felt good about yourself because you feel fly and you get smiles of approval from everyone you see? The people you encountered are, in a way, mirrors that reflect your sense that you look good. You imagine that others are seeing you positively because of how they are responding to your new clothes. We imagine we look good to others.

- **We imagine how others judge us**: How do your classmates see you? Do they think you are smart and inquisitive, or do they see you as a teacher's pet? How about your boss—does she judge you to be a competent employee or a lazy layabout? How about your spouse—does she/he see you as a trusting spouse? We imagine how each person in our life judges us, especially those who are significant in our lives. You imagine how they judge you as a person in terms of your character: funny, smart, loving, or devoted.
- **We revise our beliefs and behaviors based on how we believe others perceive us**: If we imagine that others see us as a smart, devoted student, we may strive hard to be successful in college. If our spouse judges us to be a trustworthy person, we may take steps to reinforce that trust by communicating frequently throughout the day, coming home when we say we will, or completing all our household chores. The key to this step is that we react to the judgments that we *believe* others hold about us, which may not be the way they really see us, and revise or continue our behaviors.

According to the looking glass self-perspective, people shape their self-concept based on their perceptions of how others view them. So while at first glance you might think that Cooley is saying that we are being influenced by the opinions of others, but what he really means is that we are being influenced by what we *imagine* the opinions of others to be. This is seen as an ongoing process as we interact with others on a daily basis. Ultimately, the view of our *self* is shaped by how we *believe* others *perceive* us, in an ongoing process of revision to both our beliefs and behaviors.

Mead: Self and Society

Like Cooley, George Herbert Mead (1934, 1964) was an interactionist and focused on the self arising from social interaction. However, Mead believed that we come to understand ourselves through taking on the roles of others –putting ourselves in the place of others—so we can come to understand how our behavior will be defined from the standpoint of others. Role taking is used throughout the developmental process as the self is constructed and refined. Unlike Cooley, Mead argued that the development of the self unfolded in our childhood as we moved through three stages.

Imitation (Preparatory) stage (About 0–3 years): In this stage, children learn by imitating the behavior of others, especially parents. Ever notice how infants will mimic your facial expressions? If you smile, they will smile; if you look surprised, their eyes widen in surprise. Sometimes, very young children will imitate actions like playing with pots and pans while their parents prepare dinner. At this point, they really don't understand the meaning of their behavior; they are simply following your lead. While there is no role taking at this stage, as children imitate others, they are learning to be social beings.

Play stage (About 3–5 years): Children in the play stage engage in pretend play and role playing, or mentally assuming the role of another person and then acting on that perceived point of view. That is, their play is constructed around taking the role of others they have observed in their environment, such as their parents. Kids in this stage play house, doctor, and cops and robbers. Unlike in the imitation stage, children don't just imitate social interactions—they are actually creating them. This role taking of **significant others**—those people in their environment who are important to them—is fundamental to developing the ability to place one's self in the positions of others and to anticipate their responses. This is important not only for the emergence of self-consciousness, but also for the general development of the self.

When I was quite young, my older sister would force me to play house with her (she was older and much larger than me then). She would pretend to be our mother and tell me to go to work like my father, and I would leave the room and go to "work" by sitting in the hallway. After a while, she would tell me to come home from work and eat dinner. At that point, I would come back into the room and pretend to eat dinner at the table she had set for us. My sister spoke like she was Mom and most likely began to appreciate how Mom saw her and me. In contrast to the imitation stage, the value of this stage is that the child starts to understand how alike or different she is from others in the world.

Game stage (About 6–9 years): The important element of this stage lies in a child's ability to take on multiple roles, not just a single role of a parent as they did in the play stage. Children figure out that those in their environment have multiple roles. That is, moms are not just moms—they may also be nurses and volunteers. As a young child, I remember thinking that my teachers were just teachers until one day, while at the public library with my mom, we bumped into my teacher and her boyfriend. It blew my mind, and I realized that she had a home life like me and my family; she had many more roles than just my teacher.

At this stage, children can function in organized groups and can determine what they have to do within a specific group. In order for a child to take part in a game, he must know the rules and simultaneously understand the roles of all the other players. For example, in baseball, if a ball is hit to the second baseman with a runner on first, the shortstop has to cover second, the catcher backs up first, the pitcher covers home, and the third baseman will back up the shortstop. They all have to know what others will be doing so they can perform their own role.

Children also realize that they don't act solely on what they personally believe; they should act in ways in which others—society in general—expect them to behave. This is what Mead referred to as the **generalized other**—a representation of society at large, which holds certain values and expectations about appropriate social behaviors. The expectations of the generalized other are the expectations of the whole of society.

Imagine you are driving along a desolate stretch of highway in west Texas. It is flat and clear, and you can see for miles in every direction. As far as the eye can see, there are no other cars on the road. In the distance, you see something, and as you get closer, you realize it is a stop sign at an intersection. As you come to the stop sign, what do you do? (Please say stop.) Even though you can see no other cars for miles around in every direction, you will probably stop, or at least take your foot off the accelerator and poise it over the brake, without really thinking about it. Everywhere we go, we take the generalized other with us; it represents all others in society and their expectations of how we should behave—like stopping at stop signs.

So, as we grow up, we realize that the world does not revolve around us, that there are others in the world who interact and fit together, and we seek to find our place among them. We come to understand that while we have our own voice and motives, there are a great number of social expectations about how to express those parts of our selves.

Fig. 4.3 Sigmund Freud completely changed the Western understanding of personality development, childhood and what motivates humans.

Mead's "I" and "Me"

The self, according to Mead, was composed of two distinctive parts, the "I" and the "me." The "I," according to Mead, was the impulsive part of the self, and the "me" was the part of the self that regulates the "I," remaining aware of social rules and social context. While the "I" is impulsive and selfish, it is also authentic and creative. The "I" is raw and unfiltered, which is not always wanted but sometimes needed. In contrast, the "me" is the part of the self that has internalized appropriate social values and behaviors, reining in the "I" so you act to fulfill your desires using socially appropriate channels. As infants and toddlers the "I" is the most apparent part of the self as we demand things and depend on others to satisfy our needs. However, Mead stressed that for most of us, through the course of socialization, the "I" becomes less powerful and moves from the foreground to the background as we internalize social values and expectations about appropriate social behavior - the "me" moves to the foreground. The socialized self, then, is represented by a dominant, appropriately behaving "me" regulating your impulsive, creative "I."

Psychological Approaches to the Development of the Self

Freud

Our man Sigmund Freud (1930) sees the development of the self differently than our other psychologists. Freud argued that our personality is shaped by the struggle between biological desires and our internalized awareness of appropriate social behavior. According to Freud, the mind is composed of three constructs that must interact properly for us to be well-adjusted members of society: *The id, the superego,* and *the ego.*

Id: The id represents our basic physical desires, wants, and needs, particularly our sexual drives. It is impulsive and wants what it wants when it wants it—immediate self-gratification. You can imagine that in an infant, this is valuable (this should sound familiar ... it is similar to Mead's notion of the "I"). Unable to fend for one's self, the infant needs to alert caregivers to its needs. So, when a baby is hungry it cries, when it is cold or wet it cries, demanding that its physical needs be met. Obviously, as we age, we learn other ways to satisfy these drives. Watching a grown man cry, stomp his feet, and jump up and down in a fit because he is hungry is not a pretty sight and completely socially inappropriate.

So, if the id represents our primitive desires, individuals who were guided solely by their id would be seeking to satisfy their needs whenever they felt like it. In the process, they would violate social norms and act inappropriately, suffering the wrath of others and possible punishment. Go to the nearest window and pull back the curtain; now imagine you are looking out onto a world ruled by the id. The world would be on fire. People would be running naked through the streets with another naked person under their arms. Everyone would have drinks in their hands and chocolate smeared all over their faces, and they would be pooping in the streets. While we all have these desires, we must develop socially appropriate ways to satisfy them. People who are uncontrollably impulsive and give into these drives end up in serious emotional trouble, incarcerated, or dead.

Superego: In contrast to the id and its drive toward seeking pleasure, the superego represents the internalization of social rules that we learn through socialization. The superego can be thought of as the conscience encouraging us to conform to social norms and values and punishing us with feelings of guilt when we don't. The superego is designed to work out socially appropriate means to satisfy our sexual, bodily, and aggressive drives (this should also sound familiar ... it is similar to Mead's idea of the "me"). An individual with an overly powerful superego would find his ability to function normally in society tremendously inhibited by a strict adherence to rules and an overwhelming sense of guilt.

Ego: Figure 4.4 below shows how the ego seeks to balance the competing demands of the id and superego. The ego essentially resolves conflicts between the id and the superego, finding a balance of need and satisfaction through appropriate means. The ego ultimately represents our *self* as we find a balance between meeting our needs and following the rules. People with strong egos regularly resist impulsive urges to satisfy basic drives, and those with weak egos give into their temptations frequently, finding themselves in trouble. Putting all three together might go something like this: your normally strong ego gives into your id's desire for a bacon

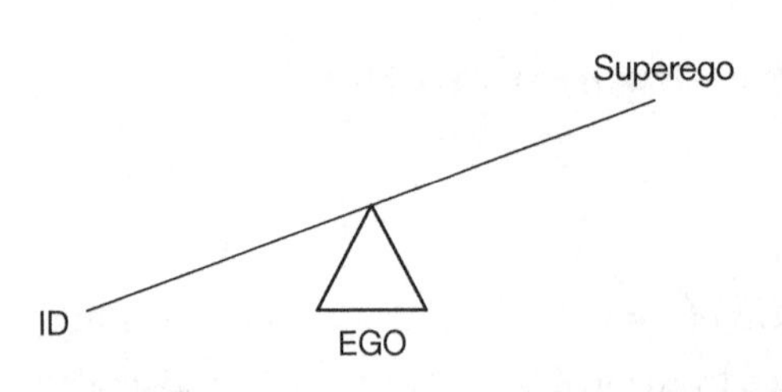

Fig. 4.4 Freud's relationship between the Id, Ego and Superego. Shown here as an individual's attempt to balance her id (impulses) with her superego (internalized social rules).

double cheeseburger, and after you have inhaled that bad boy, your superego will make you feel guilty about it.

The Much-Overlooked Lev Vygotsky: The Forgotsky Vygotsky

Fig. 4.5 Lev Vygotsky

Lev Vygotsky should be included more often in any discussion of socialization, especially in the context of the sociological approach. Why? Well, even though he presents a theory of cognitive development, it focuses on the role of culture in a child's development. Vygotsky recognized that learning always occurs and cannot be separated from a social context. So, fundamental to his theory is the idea that development results from the interaction between children and their social environment. Interactions involve those present in a child's social world such as parents, siblings, teachers, classmates, and peers. While his theory is incomplete and fairly complex, three main themes emerge:

1. **Social interaction precedes cognitive development**: Vygotsky (1978) argued that social learning precedes development. According to Vygotsky, everything in a child's development happens twice: first between people (social interaction/teaching), then inside the child's mind. For example, you learned to ride your bike because your parents, or maybe a sibling, showed you how.
2. **The more knowledgeable other (MKO) helps move development along**: MKOs are others in a child's environment who have greater understanding or higher ability levels. The MKO could be a parent, teacher, more advanced peer, or even computers. Think about how your parents, teachers, or computer programs have helped you learn a variety of things. Your parents, who are more knowledgeable about bike riding, helped you learn to ride a bike.
3. **The zone of proximal development (ZPD) is the optimal zone for learning**: Vygotsky maintained that children follow an adult's example and gradually develop the ability to perform certain tasks without help or assistance. So, the ZPD represents the distance between what a child can do with help and what she can do without guidance. The first few times you rode your bike, your parents would hold you up and run alongside until you no longer needed their support and you rode on your own.

So why am I discussing yet another developmental psychologist in a sociology textbook? Well, Vygotsky understood that all learning, and therefore all development, took place in the context of a particular culture at a particular time in history. In fact, his work is often referred to as the cultural-historical theory. This approach was probably greatly influenced by his own experiences. He lived through the Russian Revolution of 1917. He kept a keen eye on how we learn in the context of our particular cultures and particular historical periods.

I learned my ABCs and numbers from my parents and teachers, but my godson learned his ABCs, numbers, and some simple arithmetic using educational software on his dad's computer before he started school. I'm sure that for many of you, phones, tablets, and other devices have been instrumental in your development. Therefore, as new technology is introduced into society, it alters the ways we interact with each other and the way we learn. Not only do cultural artifacts influence learning, but culturally specific practices such as classroom instruction methods, recess, physical fitness, and home life influence how children learn and construct their worlds.

Here in the U.S., as children and adolescents, we are focused on social and academic learning so we become literate, employable members of society. However, if you were a boy living among the Biaka people of the Congo River basin in central Africa, for example, your childhood learning would be concerned with gathering food, finding honey, and making music with elements found in nature. Your development and learning would focus on acquiring the skills needed to survive in your environment, which is what children around the world are doing. But culture and history influence the things they learn with and how they learn.

For example, in China, children are encouraged to appreciate the collective and learn in a collective environment in which they may share information about lessons. In contrast, in the U.S., children are taught the importance of individualism and how to be independent learners. I have a friend who taught English in China, and when he gave his class its first exam, he noticed that students immediately started sharing information and moving around the class, forming groups to complete the exam. Astonished, he asked them why they were cheating. Their response was that they were not cheating; they were just making sure everyone in the collective was successful.

Vygotsky's legacy can be found in pedagogical practices. His notion of the ZPD helps educators recognize how much assistance to afford learners by providing scaffolding. *Scaffolding* is assistance or guidance from MKOs meant to support learning until the learner has mastered the task—a sort of temporary support until a child can work independently on that task (like your parents holding you upright and running alongside you as you learned to ride your bike). His emphasis on learning and social context has highlighted the need for educators to be aware of their students' home environment and how that may detract or enhance development. For example, students who go hungry several days a week are far more likely to be less attentive in class, retain less, and have lower IQs (Jyoti et al., 2005)

Social Learning Theory

Albert Bandura (1977), the major proponent of social learning theory, argued that we learned from the environment through the process of observational learning. In part, his theory was in reaction to the behaviorist model of learning popularized by the psychologist B.F. Skinner (1953). While behaviorists argue that learning occurs when associations are formed by conditioning, positive reinforcement, and punishment, social learning theory states that learning can occur by merely observing the behavior of others. Social learning theorists refer to this as *observational learning* or modeling. Social learning theory is composed of three core concepts:

1. **People learn through observing others**: In his now-famous Bobo doll studies, Bandura showed that children learned and imitated the actions of adults (Bobo dolls are inflatable toys that have a weighted base so when you kick or punch them, they just wobble about but don't fall down). In his studies, Bandura had adults act aggressively toward Bobo dolls while young children watched; later, when the children were put in a room with toys, including Bobo dolls, they acted aggressively toward the dolls, imitating the adults' behavior (Bandura and Ross, 1961).

   Bandura noted that there were three *models* of observational learning. *Live model* learning involves an actual person demonstrating or acting out behaviors. *Verbal instructional model* learning involves someone verbally instructing or describing behavior. Finally, *symbolic model* learning can include real or fictional characters demonstrating or describing behaviors in books, movies, television, radio, the Internet, or any type of media.
2. **Mental states are important to learning**: It is not just about observing others. Your internal dialogue and how you feel about your behaviors influence learning. Bandura called this *intrinsic reinforcement*—internally rewarding yourself with a feeling of satisfaction or sense of accomplishment is a key element to learning. For example, if a child holds a door open for an elderly person and the child's parent says "what a kind person you are," the child will feel happy and take pride in themselves, leading to persistence in the behavior. This is important because this concept links the cognitive element to the behavioral/social.
3. **Learning does not necessarily lead to a change in behavior**: In contrast to the behavioral approach, which views learning as leading to permanent change in behavior, social learning theory holds that people can learn new information but not change their behavior. In a different study, Bandura (1965) found that children did not always imitate learned behavior. When children witnessed adults being aggressive toward the Bobo dolls and then were punished for their violent behavior, the children did not

model adult aggressive behavior. The children had learned the aggressive behavior but did not act on it. For example, you may notice that everyone in your office who brings your boss brownies is invited to his lake home. While you have learned this little tidbit about your boss, it doesn't mean you are going to start baking brownies.

Bandura's work fueled the debate over the potential effects on children (and adults) of viewing violence on TV. In fact, a 1982 study indicated violent programs on TV led to aggressive behavior in children who watched those programs (National Institute of Mental Health, 1982). Since then, the American Psychological Association has shown that the harmful effects of TV violence do exist (Huston et al., 1992). Subsequently, producers of children's television began to tone down overtly violent behavior among their most popular characters.

Moral Development: Kohlberg and Gilligan

Morality—making the distinction between right and wrong and good and bad behavior—is significant in the development of our personal identities. Society in general has an interest in the moral development of its members to ensure conformity and social order. Through the process of socialization, individuals are encouraged to adhere to morally appropriate social values, beliefs, and behaviors. Throughout our lives, we are faced with a number of moral dilemmas that must be resolved, and how we resolve them reflects our personal moral reasoning and level of moral development.

Lawrence Kohlberg was a professor at Harvard for most of his academic career and established the area of study called *moral development* within his discipline of psychology. He studied a number of school-age boys over several years until they were young adults. Kohlberg used his *Moral Judgment Interview*—a series of short stories that present the reader with moral dilemmas—designed to evaluate the respondent's level of moral development (Kohlberg, 1958, 1976). Kohlberg wasn't interested so much in whether the boys found the behavior in the stories to be right or wrong; he wanted to know the reasoning they used to arrive at their decisions. He believed that their reasoning indicated their level of moral development. From this research, he proposed a theory of moral development composed of three levels:

1. **Pre-Conventional level (infancy–9 years):** Children at this level have not yet internalized society's standard of right and wrong. Essentially, children try to get their way by avoiding punishment or seeking reward. This level is characterized by selfishness—children determine what is right based on what will satisfy their needs. If a child gets his way, that's good; if he doesn't, that's bad—*it's all about me*. For example, the child who sneaks cookies from the cookie jar and doesn't get caught views his behavior as right because he got his snack without suffering negative consequences.
2. **Conventional level (9 years–adulthood):** At this level of moral development, people have internalized society's standards of right and wrong. Obeying laws and other social

rules is expected not because of the fear of consequences as much as it is the right thing to do for others and society at large. People at the conventional level see their moral decisions in a larger social context that is bounded by some sense of identity, such as Americans or middle class—it's no longer just about me, *it's about people like me.* A middle-class American who is making a decision about whom to vote for president, for example, may base his decision on which candidate's platform would be best for the middle class.

3. Post-Conventional level (adulthood): In contrast to the conventional level, those at the post-conventional level of moral development don't see adherence to laws or social rules as important as maintaining higher moral ideals such as basic human rights, justice, and freedom. These post-conventional individuals understand that social rules are necessary for social control and social order, but they are not always just or evenly applied. Ultimately, these individuals act only on what is just for *all*, not only themselves or others like them, even if it means breaking conventions or laws. I think that Mahatma Gandhi, Martin Luther King, Jr., and Nelson Mandela are fine examples of those who operated on the post-conventional level of moral development. This post-conventional perspective is illustrated in this quote from Mahatma Gandhi: "An unjust law is itself a species of violence. Arrest for its breach is more so."

Along Comes Gilligan

Kohlberg's theory of moral development has persisted even in light of criticisms, mainly that he included *only* males in his original study. Interestingly, one of Kohlberg's most strident critics was also one of his former graduate students and collaborators, Carol Gilligan. While working with Kohlberg, she observed that his theory failed to incorporate the moral reasoning of women.

Fig. 4.6 Carol Gilligan demonstrated that males and females use different moral reasoning processes to navigate the social world.

In her book, *In a Different Voice* (1982), Gilligan argues that Kohlberg's androcentric (male-oriented) work failed to be generalizable to females and described the moral development of females as inferior to males. Her work showed that men and women reason differently when it comes to solving moral dilemmas. Rather than the reasoning of one gender being superior or inferior to the other gender, Gilligan argued that men and women used *different* moral "voices" to articulate their moral reasoning. Male "voices" reasoned that social rules are in place for a purpose, and that violation of them must be met with punishment to ensure social justice. Female "voices," argues Gilligan, call for understanding human relationships and connectedness in judging moral decisions. When considering the differences in moral reasoning between males and females, we could view their reasoning as coming from two different perspectives:

Justice Perspective (males): This view maintains that moral transgressions or violations of laws have to be punished so that justice is served and that the law is applied equally. Think about it this way: this perspective assumes that we live in a society in which we know the rules/boundaries, and if we break those rules, we know there will be consequences. Justice, then, is concerned with individual rights, fairness, and duty: laws protect our rights, and if they are violated, there will be consequences. Fairness implies knowing that whenever a rule is broken, the offender will suffer the consequences regardless of who they are. We all have a duty to uphold the laws. This "voice" is, in a sense, the voice of the conventional standards of society of which we are all aware. From the justice perspective, for example, a desperate man who steals expensive new cancer drugs from a pharmaceutical company to save his dying wife should be arrested and jailed; he knows stealing is wrong, he has violated the rights of others, and he may have put other cancer patients at risk by stealing their drugs.

READ MORE

- *In a Different Voice* by Carol Gilligan (1982). In this book Gilligan reveals fundamental differences in the way men and women approach and solve moral dilemmas. Women in general use moral reasoning that includes the notion that we all have responsibilities toward others. So, for women considering how relationships can be affected by moral decisions is of primary importance. Men, on the other hand, tend to view morality as imposing restrictions on behaviors through the use of rules and laws. Violation of the rules must be meet with prescribed consequences, even if this damages relationships. Ultimately, the author makes a powerful portrayal of gender differences in moral reasoning.
- *Soul Repair: Recovering from Moral Injury after War* by Rita Nakashima Brock and Gabriella Lettini (2014). This book examines the moral injury that soldiers experience in time of war. The book explores the effect of *moral injury*—the pain that results from the damage to a person's moral standards—on themselves, their families, and their communities. The book relays stories of how many young soldiers return from war not scarred by fear, but by the injury of violating their sense of right and wrong when they are forced by either command or circumstances to take the low moral ground. Living with these decisions pains their souls, leading them to violent behavior, addiction, and failed relationships. Ultimately, they are seeking some way to reconcile their battlefield behaviors with how they see themselves as moral individuals (Wood, 2014).

Care and Responsibility Perspective (females): This perspective takes into consideration interpersonal relationships when attempting to understand moral/legal transgressions. The focus of this perspective's "voice" is on the connectedness of individuals, interpersonal relationships, and concern for others. These factors should be considered when contemplating moral dilemmas and be viewed as mitigating circumstances when dispensing justice. If we use the same example from above and apply the care and responsibility perspective, we might reason that the man was trying to save his wife's life and keep his family together; his intent was not profit but to save a loved one's life. These factors should be given more weight than the fact that he broke the law when deciding his fate.

It should be noted that not all males see the world through the lens of the justice perspective and not all females are guided by the care perspective. But as we discussed earlier in this chapter, we raise our girls differently than we raise our boys in our culture, which results in differences in styles of communication, expression of emotions, and the way we view our bodies. So, with socialization practices that result in a range of differences between the genders, there should be no surprise that men and women use different styles of moral reasoning.

Re-socialization and Total Institutions

When we talk about **re-socialization**, we are referring to a radical change in one's identity to accommodate a new or altered social environment. I would not consider becoming a college freshman to be a form of re-socialization. While some sociologists think transitions such as becoming a parent is re-socialization, I consider a life transition like that as part of the process of adult socialization, which we discussed earlier in the chapter. My discussion on re-socialization focuses on more dramatic life changes in general and in the context of total institutions such as joining the military or a religious cult or being sentenced to prison.

Fig. 4.7 Soldiers marching in formation and wearing identical uniforms, which are all elements of resocialization in the context of a total institution.

Re-socialization occurs in the context of a **total institution**—an isolated social system where nearly all aspects of an individual's life are controlled and all freedoms regulated by some authority. These can include orphanages, mental hospitals, prisons, the military, monasteries, and religious cults. When individuals join the military, their free-acting, free-thinking, butterfly-chasing, sleeping-until-noon personalities do not fit that institution. New recruits in the military are, in a sense, broken down, then reshaped into a new identity that is appropriate for that institution. Erving Goffman (1961) argued that in total institutions, individuals are first broken down or *de-socialized*—stripped of the symbols of their self like clothing, hair, name, and ways of behaving and thinking—then rebuilt or *re-socialized* into an appropriate identity that fits that total institution.

Total institutions achieve this transformation among their members by creating a highly controlled and restrictive environment that strongly discourages non-conformity. These total institutions possess several characteristics:

- Members are not free to leave
- Daily life is highly structured and monitored by authority figures
- Individuality is discouraged
- Personal freedoms are severely restricted
- Contact with outsiders is highly restricted or forbidden

For example, prison inmates are certainly not free to leave, visitation is controlled, daily life is run on the prison's schedule and monitored by correctional officers, and inmates are

Fig. 4.8 Prisoners in the yard don't come and go as they please, their schedules are controlled by others.

denied personal freedoms—these encourage sameness and discourage individuality. A total institution such as a prison uses these characteristics to break inmates so they "get with the program" (conform to the institutional structure) or suffer various forms of punishments until they do. The ultimate purpose is to control the inmates. It is not that different than the military, which must know that soldiers can be controlled, or patients in a mental hospital or members of a cult. This control can only be achieved and maintained by authority and by members conforming to expected behaviors. If you think about it, this is no different from our own general socialization—in order for society to thrive, it must maintain a level of control over its members.

TRY THIS

Interview someone who was in the military. If they served in the U.S. military they experienced Basic Military Training (BMT), either boot camp or basic training. This is most recruits' first contact with the military and it acts as a transition from civilian life to a military identity. Ask them about their experience in basic training, have them describe the setting and their treatment. Ask them how their old civilian identities were broken down, and what tactics the military used do to shape them into either a soldier, sailor or marine. Also, ask them when they first saw themselves as a soldier, sailor or marine. That is, at what point did they internalize the military culture and see themselves as part of it? You can ask them more than just these questions. See if you can understand how institutions make its members "get with the program" so they fit in and allow the machinery of the institution to run smoothly.

Theoretical Perspectives on Socialization

Remember that functionalism is a theoretical perspective that views society as a complex system whose parts work together in cooperative ways to promote solidarity and stability. Therefore, functionalists view socialization as a way to reinforce social structure, maintain society (status quo), and transmit culture from one generation to the next. Additionally, the process of socialization is responsible for providing individuals with the ability to perform role expectations, which, in turn, contribute to social stability and maintaining the status quo. Functionalists believe that through socialization, members of society internalize the attitudes, values, beliefs, and behaviors that will allow them to assume and successfully fulfill the roles of obedient and productive citizens.

Conflict theorists argue that within society, there are groups that have varying degrees of power based on their access to and possession of valuable social resources, and the more powerful groups use that power to maintain their dominance and legitimize existing social inequalities. Socialization, then, is a process by which the powerful classes can replicate their privilege and reinforce inequality. According to conflict theory, for example, privileged children are socialized for positions of authority and roles of leadership, while lower-class children are socialized for positions that serve those in higher social stations and trained to respect and to defer to those above them in social class, therefore maintaining social class inequality.

Our **symbolic interactionist** friends see social reality as constructed by social interaction through the use of symbols, both verbal and non-verbal. Thus, the whole of society, institutions, and social structure only exist as a result of this human interaction. So, if social interaction is key to this perspective, the *other* becomes the primary focus of our socialization. Through socialization, we become who we are, in most part, by how we see ourselves reflected in others and how we identify with others. Interactionists emphasize that social roles and individual identities are understood through play and imitation. While playing house (identifying with parents), children may learn socially designated roles for males and females.

While interactionists would agree with both functionalism and conflict theory that individuals are socialized (shaped) by institutions, social structure, and culture, they would also point out that individuals in social interaction shape the social world, a kind of bi-directional influence on the individual and society. We are both shaped by social interactions, and we create new social relationships through interaction.

TABLE 4.1 Theoretical Perspectives on Socialization

Sociological Perspective	Key Concepts	Example
Structural Functionalism	The process of socialization serves to reinforce the values and social behaviors that help maintain social order. Individuals internalize values, beliefs, and behaviors.	In schools, children learn to obey the rules, be punctual, and play nice with others, as well as learn to read and write. Of course, all these lessons allow children to grow up to be well-adjusted citizens who obey authority, conform to social norms, and contribute to the stability of society.

Sociological Perspective	Key Concepts	Example
Conflict	Socialization is viewed as a mechanism of social control that reinforces the values and behaviors of the dominant class, perpetuating inequality in class, race, and gender, for example.	Parents reinforce gender inequality by punishing girls for acting "unladylike" and boys for acting like a "sissy." Schools perpetuate gender differences by encouraging male students to be independent in problem-solving and girls to be dependent on others to problem-solve.
Symbolic Interactionism	Through social interaction and the use of symbols, we come to understand that we are distinct from *others.* We *try out* social roles in order to understand socially appropriate behavior that is expected in a broader social context.	Through play, children come to understand social role expectations. Spiderman represents "good" behavior, while the Green Goblin represents "bad behavior." Through this interaction, they internalize social ideals of "good guys" and "bad guys." Children discover through game play that the only way for a game to progress is if all the players obey the rules, and they come to understand that rules must be obeyed to navigate the larger social landscape.

The Bottom Line

As we discussed in this chapter, the process of socialization is important for the replication of cultural values, beliefs, and behaviors, as well as producing competent members of society. From our first breath to our last, we learn from others. Family, friends, school, peers, media, and social institutions all have an investment in and a responsibility to ensure that people develop appropriate social identities and adjust to social life. For society to persist, there have to be mechanisms that constrain individuals to ensure social tasks are accomplished and social order is regulated. We have discussed how norms, cultural expectations, and a number of other social mechanisms exercise social control on members of society to ensure regularity to social life.

All societies are machines that hope to crank out good little citizens, and socialization is the process each society employs to produce those citizens. However, for this to happen, society must constrain individuals. In this chapter, I discussed how we all have desires that must be controlled in order to fit into our respective society or group—our personal desires are constrained. While we may want a large automobile, a big house, and to be rock stars, we can't rob banks or defraud people to accomplish these things. Most people realize that we must work hard, obey social rules, and defer our gratification to get what we want, and those who don't suffer the social consequences.

Also in this chapter, we explored the need for both significant human contact and interaction for us to develop into fully functioning social beings. Examples of children experiencing profound social deprivation vividly illustrate the simple fact that it takes others to make each of us an integrated, fully functioning member of society. These examples combined with research that indicates the need for involved others in our social environment only reinforce the popular idea that it takes a village to raise a child.

While the development of the self or personality is highly complex and composed of many elements, this chapter focused on three: cognitive development, gender socialization, and moral development. Cognitive stage theories focus on the successful completion of certain tasks in order to progress to the next stage, and each stage brings the individual closer to social competence in order to better cope with his/her social world. Others like Freud's insistence that humans are in a struggle between their impulsive desires and finding socially acceptable pathways to fulfilling them, implying we are driven by more base impulses.

We have seen that gender permeates our social world, and many agents of socialization behave in ways that perpetuate established gender roles and gender inequality. Much research indicates that while our concept of gender is not biologically determined, there are biological differences between the sexes. However, it is the complex interplay between these biological differences and varying social landscapes that shape our gender identities. But gender socialization is changing; research indicates that parents may be less rigid in enforcement of stereotyped gender roles than previous generations.

As we have seen, moral development can also be linked to one's gender. Kohlberg's work implied the moral superiority of males and was challenged by Carol Gilligan's approach that emphasized difference over superiority. Gilligan's work merely reinforces the larger understanding in sociology that we raise our boys very differently than we raise our girls, resulting in two different perspectives on the social world of which morality is just another component.

Figure Credits

Fig 4.0: Adapted from: Copyright © 2015 Depositphotos/ClaudiaBalasoiu.

Fig. 4.4: "Sigmund Freud," https://commons.wikimedia.org/wiki/File:Freud_ca_1900.jpg. Copyright in the Public Domain.

Fig. 4.5: Copyright © The Vygotsky Project (CC BY-SA 3.0) at https://upload.wikimedia.org/wikipedia/commons/8/8f/Lev_Vygotsky_1896-1934.jpg.

Fig. 4.6: Copyright © Ravit (CC BY-SA 3.0) at https://commons.wikimedia.org/wiki/File:Carol_and_James_Gilligan_P1010970_-_cropped.jpg.

Fig. 4.7: Copyright © Daniel Case (CC BY-SA 3.0) at https://commons.wikimedia.org/wiki/File:PLA_soldiers_marching_in_fatigues_behind_Great_Hall_of_the_People.jpg.

Fig. 4.8: Copyright © Bart Everson (CC by 2.0) at https://commons.wikimedia.org/wiki/File:Inmates_Orleans_Parish_Prison.jpg.

CHAPTER 5

SEEKING ACCEPTANCE AND FINDING OUR WAY: GROUPS, ORGANIZATIONS AND INSTITUTIONS

Skull and Bones

Imagine you're minding your own business, walking on your college campus. Suddenly, you are kidnapped by a group of large, hooded men who lead you into a darkened room in a windowless building known as the Tomb. There, your captors shout out infantile phrases like "Ooga booga," "Lick my bumhole," and "Take that plunger out of my butt!" Then they torment you with the threat of putting a plunger up your butt! You ask in a frightened tone "Are you really gonna do that?" The reply is "Shut up, neophyte!" Over several hours, you are verbally berated and physically abused to the point of exhaustion. You are told to stand in front of the great altar while holding a skull and instructed to repeat the sacred and secret oath. Over the next few weeks, you are required to perform a number of tasks to prove your loyalty to the group. Finally, you are taken back to the Tomb, where you take the pledge of secrecy and are welcomed to the Skull and Bones.

You have just been initiated into one of the most secret and powerful groups in the world. It is also elite; only about fifteen initiates are inducted each year, meaning that there are no more than eight hundred alive in the world at any given time (Rosenbaum, 2001). The other members will become like brothers; you will spend each Thursday and Sunday evening in secret meetings with them, and most of your time at Yale will be spent in their company. You will form powerful emotional bonds with them that will last your entire life. These bonds will also serve you well throughout both your personal and professional life.

Most of our lives are lived in groups. This is true because groups are so important to our development and adjustment to social life. Groups are important in everyone's life. Think about all the groups you have been a member of and all those that you are in now, such as your family, all the classes you took during your school years, friends, sports teams, math club, Girl/Boy Scouts, and your workplace. These are all social groups. However, not all these groups are the same. We behave very differently at work than we do at home; we treat family members differently than we do coworkers. Throughout this chapter, we will discuss how we define groups and differentiate between several different types of groups, the importance of groups, how groups affect us, and how we can influence groups.

I want you to take a minute and think about how many groups you belong to right now at this point in your life; as a matter of fact, write them all down or type them out. There are probably a fair number of them. But are they all groups? In sociology, we define a social group as two or more people who interact regularly and share a sense of common identity/unity—basically, a bunch of people who hang out frequently, feel like they belong, and do stuff together.

Do all the *groups* you wrote down have all three characteristics of a social group? In sociology, we make a distinction between social groups and aggregates—collections of people who simply share a physical location, such as a number of people waiting on the train platform for the T in Boston. Crowds are temporary collections of people who interact with each other but lack a sense of unity, like when several people witness an auto accident and then discuss what happened but don't feel membership in the auto accident witness group..."can't wait until the next accident, see you then!" Finally, we have categories—collections of people who do not interact with each other but share a common characteristic or trait, such as redheaded people, left-handed people, or college students.

A Note on Social Structure, Statuses, and Roles

Social structure generally refers to the underlying patterns of social relationships in groups and society (Merton, 1949). Those social relationships include small intimate groups, larger impersonal organizations, and social institutions. We will see that while social structures are not all apparent, they have a significant influence on all dimensions of the human experience.

Fig. 5.1 These people gathered on the beach represent an aggregate.

Think about it this way: Like a brick house is composed of many bricks, society is composed of many *statuses* (remember our discussion of statuses and roles in Chapter 4)—socially recognized positions that individuals occupy. Statuses are the building blocks of social groups and, ultimately, society. For each status we occupy, there are a number of accompanying *roles*—expected behaviors associated with a particular status. So, as you read through this chapter, keep in mind that each of the groups, organizations, and institutions we discuss are ultimately composed of individuals occupying statuses and fulfilling the duties of those statuses by carrying out many roles.

Primary and Secondary Groups

When I was in high school, I was really close with my two friends Dave and Andy. We did everything together: we all played on the tennis team, we carpooled to school every day, we smoked weed and watched *Saturday Night Live* every week of our senior year. Think about your closest friendship group, you and maybe two or three friends whom you are really close with. Now think about how and why you formed your friendship group. While stories about how friends meet may vary, they all have a central theme: people meet and like one another and then form strong emotional bonds with each other. These emotional or expressive bonds are the foundation of primary groups. **Primary groups** (also known as expressive groups) are usually small with strong emotional bonds, informal, enduring, and provide a range of support for their members—in other words, close-knit, face-to-face groups in which the members have a strong personal identity. Many sociologists have characterized primary groups as possessing intimate, face-to-face interactions and are integral to our development and adjustment to social life. Good examples of primary groups include families, friendship groups, and romantic couples.

To be sure, groups are important in shaping social life, but some are more important than others. If we look at less complex societies or look back at our own social history, we see that primary groups like families and kinship networks have played a pivotal role in raising young members of society and their ongoing social adjustment. In fact, Charles Cooley (1902), who coined the term *primary group*, indicated that primary groups like the family are nearly universal in all societies. That is, wherever you go in the world, whatever society you visit, you will find some basic social unit bonded by love, respect, and obligation based on familial ties.

TRY THIS

How well do you know your friends? With a group of five or six friends, gather around a table and have everyone write down three intimate things about him-self/herself. Fold all the papers alike and place them in a hat, bucket, or basket. Starting with you, reach in the basket, pull out one sheet, read the three things out loud, and see if the group can identify the correct person. Pass the hat to the next person until everyone has read an entry. In intimate primary groups, there should be many correct guesses!

Secondary Groups

In contrast to primary groups, **secondary groups** (also called instrumental groups) are larger, interactions are more formal, and there are weak emotional bonds between members; they are instruments to achieving a goal or accomplishing a task, much like this sociology class you are taking right now is an instrument to achieve the goal of satisfying an academic requirement. Your sociology class is most likely considerably larger than the household you grew up in, your bonds with your classmates are probably not emotional, but more functional, and your interactions with others in the class are more formal than those with family members. Just think about how you feel about and interact with family members and close friends versus

Fig. 5.2 School classes are secondary groups.

other members of this class. You probably don't have deep, abiding feelings for your classmates and don't feel as obligated to them as you do to your family and friends. When your boyfriend/girlfriend breaks your heart, you are feeling homesick, and your checking account is empty, are you going to ask the person next to you for help, or are you going to make that call home? Table 5.1 highlights the differences in properties between primary and secondary groups.

Fig. 5.3 In cultures like the !Kung, culture is comprised of small bands. Intimate bonds are strong between all the members.

Secondary groups become more important as societies become more complex and the needs of their members cannot be met by smaller intimate groups like the family. For example, the !Kung people of southern Africa have traditionally lived in very small, nomadic forager bands of less than thirty people, and their lives are directed by the basic social group, or what we call family. All of their needs are met in the context of the family, and their socialization and adjustment to life is regulated by the band, a sort of extended family. They don't need a formal education institution or formal religion, and while they live within the borders of various countries, they have lived as an autonomous people, taking what they need from the land.

TABLE 5.1. Properties of Primary and Secondary Groups

Group Type	Characteristics	Examples
Primary Groups	Small, intense emotional bonds, enduring, and marked by informal, personal, and face-to-face interactions.	Families, friendship groups, engaged couples, romantic partners.
Secondary Groups	Large, indirect, contractual, impersonal, temporary, and polite interactions.	Sociology classes, work groups, athletic teams, neighborhood watch groups, and your local chapter of the Young Republicans.

Group Size

Typically, when sociologists discuss group size, we describe two group sizes: the dyad and the triad. The smallest possible social group is a dyad, or a group consisting of exactly two people. This group is characterized by an intense bond (typically emotional, but not always), and it is the least stable group—if one member leaves, there's no more group!

Triads are groups that consist of just three people. Now, some interesting things happen when groups grow to three or more. The most obvious is that groups of three or more are more stable than the dyad; if one member leaves a triad, the group persists. Additionally, and perhaps more importantly, something happens in a triad and larger groups that doesn't in a dyad: alliances can be formed. Specifically, sociologists refer to coalitions—when two or more group members join forces in order to achieve a goal. That is, two members of a triad can form an alliance against the other member, or in larger groups, several members can form an alliance against other group members. Remember when you or one of your friends may have done something "uncool" that violated the norms of your tight friendship group? What happened? Most likely, you or whoever violated the rule got froze out. That is, someone got the cold shoulder from others for a period of time until everyone made up.

Fig. 5.4 Dyads are the smallest social groups and the least stable, but many times the bonds are the most intense.

The images in figures 5.4 and 5.5 illustrate a typical dyad and triad. The number of connections grows when you add just one more person to a triad. Those attachments increase the number of obligations and commitments group members have to each other. Are you a member of a group that has increased in size, such as adding a new friend? How did that affect the dynamics of the group and how you felt?

Fig. 5.5 Triads and groups larger than three possess the ability to form coalitions, something that dyads can't do.

In-Groups and Out-Groups

Many people are so invested in their groups that they feel animosity toward those groups they feel are opposed to theirs. In-groups are groups that people have membership in, identify with, and feel loyalty toward, such as your baseball team or your college. In contrast, out-groups are groups that people do not belong to and may feel opposition to; for example, your school's rival or the political party your party opposes. The best way to think about in-groups and out-groups is in terms of *us* and *them.* Think of any of your in-groups as *us* and all those groups you oppose, out-groups, as *them*. In-group out-group distinctions are particularly sharp during wartime. It is not uncommon for the opposing forces to use terms that dehumanize their opponents and spread propaganda that plays on stereotypes and misinformation to distinguish *us* from *them*.

This process of clearly distinguishing *us* from *them* is called boundary heightening— when the differences between two opposing groups are polarized or exaggerated. Our own history is littered with examples of this. In various wars, the Germans were called the Hun and Krauts and the Japanese were labeled Japs and Nips. More recent wars have brought even more hateful and divisive terms like gook, zipper head, towel head or Haji. This process extends beyond name-calling, including highlighting values, religious beliefs, and behaviors that are different from ours. Those people are not like us; they sit on the ground, eat with their hands, and devour their young. Statements like these tend to *heighten the boundary* between groups in order to distinguish one group from another, create solidarity among group members, and, many times, create a moral boundary between the groups. However, the label of us and them is relative; remember, one group's terrorist is another group's freedom fighter. During World War II, German soldiers wore belt buckles, uniform buttons, and patches inscribed with *Gott mit Uns*, which translates to "God is with us." It's all perspective.

Reference Groups

"Keeping up with the Joneses" is a common saying that implies comparison. I don't know who the Joneses are, but they're a family whom many Americans compare themselves to in terms of social success. Like the Joneses, reference groups are groups that we use to compare and evaluate our own lifestyles and behaviors. We use reference groups to evaluate the relative worth or desirability of our appearance, thoughts, feelings, and behavior and to judge the appropriateness of our appearance and behavior (Crossman, 2014). You might find other biology majors are your current reference group (if you are majoring in biology), evaluating your knowledge base, how many classes you have taken, your GPA, or if others have prepared research papers or have research experience. You are making comparisons and evaluations to gauge your standing as a biology major compared to others.

For me, I always think of reference groups when I attend a sociology conference and I see other sociologists of my age and make a kind of mental comparison between my career and theirs, gauging my relative success as a sociologist ... it's depressing, so I stop. The two examples above highlight an important point: our reference groups change over time as we take on new statuses over our life course. Right now, your reference group might be other college students, then it may shift to other graduate students in your program, then it may shift to others within your field, and eventually the Joneses down the street. Typically, we have several reference groups in our lives at any given time; our families, peers, coworkers, and community provide us with various levels of evaluation.

Reference groups not only serve as a gauge of relative success they also act as agents of socialization. Many times, we look to those in our reference groups for social cues. As a college student, you may look to other students to know what to wear, where to eat, or what professors to take. Once you graduate and take that first job, you may look to other professionals in your field for professional attire, salary expectations, work hours, and navigating office politics.

Group Dynamics: The Power of Groups

BEHOLD THE POWER OF THE GROUP

On January 13, 2015, revelers on The Ohio State University campus in Columbus set more than eighty fires, tore down a goal post, and shot guns into the air. Many of the students had been watching the NCAA national championship football game at local bars, and soon after the win, they spilled out into the streets. Caught up in the moment of jubilation and the power of the group, they started setting fire to trash cans, couches, and dumpsters. The crowd then tore down a goal post at one end of campus, resulting in the destruction of property, some injuries, and several arrests. Would any of these students set fires on their own? Would individuals destroy property just because their team wins a national title without the influence of others? (FoxSports.com, 2015)

You will never see a lone individual stroll down the streets of your college town and light police cars on fire and turn them over. However, if your college basketball team wins the NCAA national championship, celebrations may flow over into the streets, and groups of overenthusiastic fans may set cop cars on fire and roll them over, tear down street signs, get in fights, and trash the town. Of course, these are individual behaviors, but they were performed in the context of groups. We have ALL at some time given into the power of the group; whether it was jumping into freezing water, stealing a street sign, or smoking that joint, we have put aside our best judgment and taken on the judgment of the group.

Imagine you volunteer to participate in a vision test. You arrive at the psychology building on your college campus and are led to a sterile, small-groups lab. You are placed in a group of seven other students, and you are all seated next to each other at a long table. The researcher enters the room and instructs all of you on the task he wants you to perform, and it seems pretty straightforward. You are all asked to compare the reference line on the left (see figure 5.6) to the three lines on the right and indicate which line—A, B, or C—is the same in length. As you can see from below, the choices are obvious, as they were in the original experiment. Let's say you are positioned so that you will be the last person to respond. That is, the other seven students will give their responses before you. As you can see from the figure below, the answer is obviously line C. What if the first student said B was the correct line and the second, third, and fourth all responded with line B? Would you begin to doubt yourself? Would you think they need glasses or didn't understand the task? Then what if all seven responded with line B? How would you respond? Would you hesitate, stammer, or feel uneasy? Or would you just blurt out "Line C"? When I ask this of my students, nearly all of them say they would stick to their guns and answer line C.

Well, when Solomon Asch (1952) conducted his classic experiment, he found that nearly a third of people in your position gave in and answered line B. And by your position, I mean you were deceived. That is, you were the only *naïve participant*; the other seven students were his "confederates"—they were in on it. They had a script to follow and knew how to answer at each trial, or sets of lines presented. You were the only one being observed. Overall, 75% of those who were observed gave into the pressure of the group in at least one trial. Many of the subjects hesitated, stammered, or looked around for some sign of confirmation. Most who gave in reported that they did not believe their answer to be correct but just didn't want to appear to be odd or "peculiar." Interestingly, some participants reported that they believed the group was correct and answered accordingly, which is a real testament to the power of the group. Asch's work showed that we have a strong impulse to

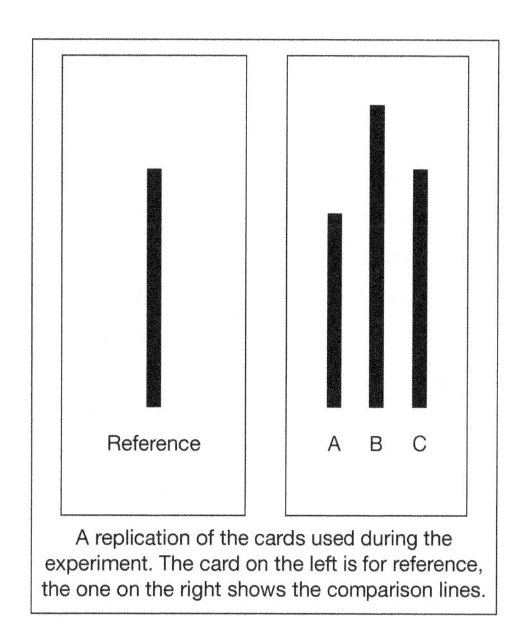

Fig. 5.6 Comparison lines like these were used in the Asch studies.

Asch was fascinated by the effects that a group could have on individuals and how people allow themselves to be pressured by group influence. His studies conducted among college students showed that many are willing to put aside their judgment for the judgment of the group. This is well-illustrated in the insert above about the Ohio State students ... I mean, does burning a couch ever seem like a good idea?

Obedience to Authority

Another classic study on conformity was inspired by tragedy. Intrigued by how the Nazi regime was able to transform seemingly mild-mannered shopkeepers, bank clerks, and machinists into brutal killers, Stanley Milgram (1963) conducted an ingenious experiment to investigate how this transformation was possible. Milgram's study focused on how people are willing to obey an apparent authority figure. The study was conducted by randomly assigning subjects into one of two groups: "teachers" and "learners." Actually, participants were only selected to be teachers; the learners were Milgram's confederates. Teachers were instructed to read pairs of words, and the learners were asked to repeat them back. The teachers and learners were in separate rooms and could not see each other, so they communicated using microphones and speakers.

Teachers were placed in a room with an *experimenter* (the authority figure wearing a lab coat) and seated in front of an imposing, industrial-looking box with a number of switches with labels that ranged from "slight shock" to "danger: extreme shock" to the last switch, which was simply labeled "XXX 450 volts" (figure 5.7 illustrates the basic layout of Milgram's study). Teachers were instructed to administer an electric shock to the learner if he gave an incorrect response and to increase the intensity of the shock with each subsequent incorrect response. If teachers hesitated to increase the shock intensity, they were reminded by the experimenter with instructions such as "The experiment requires that you continue" or "You have no other choice, you must go on." To his surprise, Milgram found that nearly 65% of the teachers in his first version of the experiment were willing to administer the most extreme electric shock, a whopping 450 volts.

Not only were the learners Milgram's confederates, there were no electric shocks administered to anyone. However, the real subjects, the teachers, did not know this; they thought they were applying electric shocks to the learners, and 65% of them pushed it to the maximum voltage! In subsequent versions of this study, Milgram (1974) had the learners cry out in pain and complain of a heart condition and even stop responding (apparently having died) when high-voltage shocks were applied. Still, 65% of the participants maxed out the shock level! Milgram mixed things up by moving the experiment from a sterile laboratory to a dingy basement, included women as subjects, and used subjects from a range of ethnic groups and social classes; he still got consistent rates of obedience. Even though no electric shocks were dispensed, some subjects were willing to shock others to the point of causing injury or death.

Of course, after the studies were completed, the subjects were debriefed, and it was revealed that they had shocked no one and injured no one. While certainly relieved that they had harmed no one, the subjects were left with the knowledge that they were the type of person who *would* have harmed another person at the behest of an authority figure. What would you have done? Would you have obeyed authority? If you are like my students, you probably believe that you would take the high road and discontinue giving shocks at a low voltage or not even agree to take part in such a study.

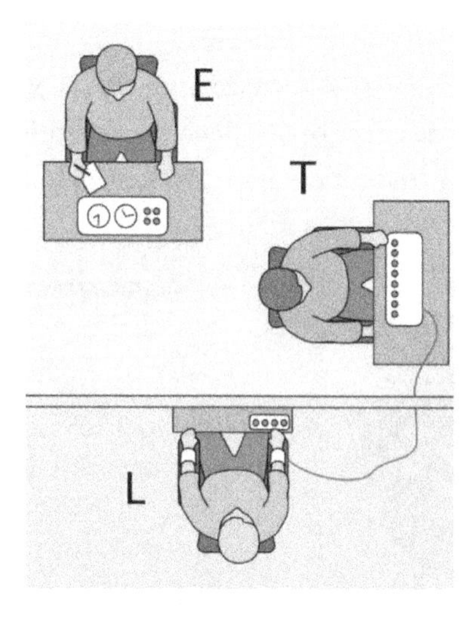

Fig. 5.7 Diagram of Milgram Study The Experimenter sat in the same room as the Teacher while the Learner was in a separate room.

What does this have to do with groups, you ask? Remember that Stanley Milgram conducted this research because of his interest in the Nazis, and through this research, he concluded (rightfully so) that individuals are willing to engage in behaviors that they most likely wouldn't engage in when they feel like they are obeying an authority figure or structure, such as what was found among the Nazi SS, Gestapo, and death camp personnel. Even Adolf Eichmann, the Gestapo's head of the Jewish section who ordered the deportation and savage treatment of countless Jews, revealed that he was obeying authority when he said while on trial in Israel, "I never had the power and the responsibility of a giver of orders," which means he was just following orders (Remember.org).

Fig. 5.8 Photo from Abu Ghraib Prison. Soldiers humiliated detainees in order to elicit conformity and information.

This effect has manifested itself more recently in the events at Abu Ghraib prison in Iraq. In 2003, a number of soldiers guarding prisoners at the Abu Ghraib committed a series of atrocities and human rights violations against their Iraqi inmates (*Washington Post*, 2005). These offenses ranged from humiliating poses to psychological torture to unsanitary conditions. The focus of the treatment was the humiliation of prisoners in front of their comrades, playing on their cultural taboos and prohibitions. Ultimately, eleven soldiers were convicted in courts-martial; some were dishonorably discharged and two were given prison sentences.

Evidence that emerged during the trials clearly indicated that the orders for this treatment came from high places, leaving those convicted to claim that they "were just following orders." Clearly, the effect of obedience to authority is not limited to Nazis or experiments; it is the dire consequence of groups and organizations that emphasize the supremacy of obeying orders.

READ MORE

- Philip Zimbardo's (2007) *Lucifer Effect* explores the social-psychological elements that influence individuals to cross the boundary of good and evil and engage in an evil act. He examines the social circumstances that are needed to push someone over that line to do evil. He also explores the organizational and interpersonal pressures that pushed good soldiers over the line to torment and humiliate their captives at Abu Ghraib and other similar events.

We all follow orders, in a sense, each day when we obey traffic laws, school policy, and rules of social engagement. This compliance with rules and laws is integral to the maintenance of social order, that regularity of daily life we have all come to expect when we wake up each morning. Above, we looked at two types of compliance: conformity and obedience. Conformity involves a change in behavior or belief in order to fit in with a group as a result of social influence, while obedience is compliance with rules, laws, or authority. Below are some other ways we comply in order to fit in and be accepted.

Normative Compliance

This is when we comply in order to align with the norms of the group. This is a result of our desire to fit into groups—we want to be liked and accepted by others, and many times, we will conform to group behaviors in order to fit in. Have you ever done something so that others would like you? Have you ever done anything so you would be accepted by a group of new friends? Of course, we all have at some point. When I was in college, I got a job at the *L.A. Times* newspaper and started working with a bunch of guys my age. Soon, we began a friendship outside of work, and one weekend, they invited me to go bodysurfing with them at the Wedge in Newport Beach, California. Those were the biggest waves I have ever seen, and they broke near a jetty—I was scared! But I wanted to be accepted, and

I wanted to be part of their friendship circle. They made it clear that only those willing to surf these monster swells were the type of people they would hang out with. I got nailed on my first few waves, but then I enjoyed some of the best bodysurfing of my life and made some lifelong friends. Would I do it today? Hell no. Would you have ridden waves like those to be accepted?

Informational Compliance

Imagine you find yourself at a state dinner at the White House. "How did I get here?" you wonder. Then, as they begin to serve the first course, you look down at the array of plates and silverware laid out before you; there is a fork above your plate and three to the left. "Uh, oh," you say to yourself, "which fork do I use first? I don't want to look like a rube and I want to fit in." So, you do what most of us would do: you look around at the other guests and carefully observe that everyone is reaching for that tiny fork to the far left, so you pick up that fork and you enjoy your salad made from vegetables grown in the White House's Kitchen Garden, and no one is the wiser. You looked around, gained information on how to behave, and conformed to the behaviors of those who knew how to behave. It is easy to understand why we call this informational compliance. You gained information about table etiquette that you did not previously have, then used that information to conform to the groups' behavior.

As we have seen above, why we conform may include seeking information, avoiding punishment, seeking reward, risking disapproval of other group members, and a lack of perceived alternatives to conformity. While there are a range of reasons we conform to group pressure, table 5.2 shows that there are three generally recognized types of conformity, with each type possessing varying degrees of intensity.

TABLE 5.2. Types of Conformity

Type of Conformity	Description	Example
Compliance (least enduring form of conformity)	Giving into pressure just to avoid punishment or gain some reward	Your mother constantly nags you to clean your room, so you finally clean your room just to avoid her vitriol. You don't necessarily believe that clean rooms are important; you just want her to stop.

(Continued)

Type of Conformity	Description	Example
Identification (lasts as long as you want to maintain the relationship with the group or person)	Giving into group pressure to maintain group membership or a relationship with an individual in the group	Jarl is a graduate student who hangs with several other grad students in his program. The group has become quite close, but most of their extracurricular activities involve heavy drinking. Jarl doesn't like to get drunk that much, but he values his relationships with the group and doesn't want to lose their friendship and support, so he drinks more than he likes.
Internalization (the most enduring form of conformity)	Integrating the beliefs and behaviors of the group into one's self-identity	Suicide bombers have internalized the values and beliefs of their radical political group so much that they view blowing themselves up as the right thing to do.

THE BYSTANDER EFFECT

In April 2010, a homeless man, Hugo Alfredo Tale-Yax, was stabbed to death while more than twenty-five passersby did nothing Hugo had come to the aid of a woman who was being robbed by a knife-wielding thug and was stabbed in his chest. He chased off his attacker then collapsed to the ground, bleeding profusely. As he lay on the ground bleeding to death, more than twenty-five people passed by, some not looking at him and some looking directly at him, and someone even took a picture of him with their cell phone. One man grabbed Tale-Yax and shook him vigorously until he saw the pool of blood underneath him, then walked away. Firefighters finally arrived nearly an hour and a half after the attack (Hutchison, 2010).

Why did so many people pass by without rendering assistance? The bystander effect—is when people fail to help an apparent victim when others are present. Have you ever seen someone lying on the sidewalk and just walked around them? Have you ever seen another motorist on the road that needed help and just kept driving? Chances are you have been in a situation in which others are present and you all see someone who needs help and you and the others do nothing. Why didn't you stop and help?

The bystander effect has three components: (1) *Ambiguity*—confusion about the situation. Witnesses are unsure if the situation calls for intervention. Many times, we are unsure about the situation and whether or not it is worth our involvement. (2) *Cohesiveness*—the extent to which witnesses feel connected to other bystanders and their sense of obligation to them and the victim. Most people in an aggregate don't perceive a sort of connectedness with others. (3) *Diffusion of responsibility*—the phenomenon in which individuals are less likely to take action or feel a sense of responsibility in the presence of others. Many times, people think that others will call 911 or render help or think help has already been called, so they don't need to intervene.

Fig. 5.9 The Bystander Effect

Recent research has indicated that the bystander effect may be much more complicated than we once thought. There are more factors involved, such as being in a confused state of mind about what to do, if anything, after witnessing a traumatic event. While it is in part influenced by group mentality—you may not want to look stupid by stepping in if help has already been called—there are personal concerns, such as the concern about also becoming a victim: if there is blood present, there is concern over blood-borne diseases like HIV (Fischer et al., 2011; Polanin, Espelage and Pigott, 2012). Whatever the reasons are, the bystander effect is a common and sometimes deadly phenomenon that has one consistent feature—the number of bystanders is related to whether assistance is rendered. Two people are more likely to help a victim than if there were a dozen people witnessing an event. Therefore, victims who think they will be helped because there are so many people around will most likely get no help. The greater number of bystanders increases the diffusion of responsibility. Moreover, we are more likely to render aid if the person is *like* us.

THE HEROIC IMAGINATION PROJECT

If you want to learn about techniques to diminish the bystander effect and stay safe, check out Philip Zimbardo's Heroic Imagination Project. The project's slogan is "Stand up. Speak out. Change the world." The project takes research findings from social psychology, sociology, and related fields and distills a number of meaningful insights, strategies, and tools that individuals can use to transform negative situations and create positive change in their everyday lives (Heroic Imagination Project, 2015).

There is still another manifestation of conformity that is nearly pathological and many times has tragic consequences. For example, in 1978, more than nine hundred people committed suicide by drinking cyanide-laced Kool-Aid (it was actually a less expensive, generic version of the Kool-Aid brand) (Hall, 1987). Why, you ask? Groupthink—decision-making by a group that is characterized by consensus at any cost, which suppresses disagreement, prevents consideration of alternatives and expects an uncritical acceptance of a group's values, beliefs, and behaviors - contributed to this tragedy and many others (Janis, 1972). Groups that fall victim to groupthink tend to ignore alternative decisions and engage in irrational actions.

The People's Temple was a cult movement that sought to create an idealized socialist community called Jonestown in the jungles of Guyana. Led by a megalomaniacal leader, Reverend James Jones, The People's Temple had ostensibly been run out of Northern California and sought utopia in South America. Like nearly all cults, once individuals were initiated into The People's Temple, they were forced to give all their money, including welfare and social security checks, to the cult and cut off ties with those outside the group, which meant family and friends. Disturbed by this behavior and suspicious, the friends and family of several cult members petitioned their congressman to investigate the cult. Congressman Leo Ryan, along with reporters and photographers, traveled to Guyana to investigate Jonestown. All seemed idyllic, but when the congressman was leaving, several cult members handed him and his associates handwritten notes asking to be taken with the congressman back to the U.S. James Jones gladly agreed, but when the congressman, defecting cult members, and others were about to board their plane, gunfire erupted and Congressman Ryan and four others were killed. Believing that the world would persecute the cult, Reverend Jones ordered that everyone prepare the poisoned concoction and drink it. Parents fed it to their children; the few who refused were executed and some fled into the jungle. But in the final analysis, more than nine hundred were dead as a result of groupthink. The vast majority of members were so devoted and socially invested in the cult and Reverend Jones that they did not question the decision, but rather accepted it uncritically.

Social Networks

There has been a proliferation of interest in social networks in recent years as a result of increased access and use of social media on the Internet. As a result of this interest in forming and maintaining virtual social networks, a wide range of definitions have emerged. However, sociologists commonly regard social networks as a set of individuals, groups, or organizations linked, bonded, or connected together either directly or indirectly.

The famous sociologist Georg Simmel (1955) wrote, "Society arises from the individual and the individual arises from interaction." In a sense, networks can be thought of as essential to the formation of society, connections between individuals forming into sets of groups that are linked.

Think about the family you grew up in; it was linked to other families, such as your aunts and uncles and cousins, your neighbors, other families and individuals at church, and the people your parents knew from work and the families of your friends. You can see that from an early age, you were the member of a network just by being a member of your family. Society, then, emerges from the interaction between these groups (which are composed of individuals), and you became who you are through interactions with family members, friends, teachers, and others (think back to Chapter 4). You can think of society as a dense web of networks that help shape our social development and adjustment. It is easy to see, then, that all individuals within society can be linked by a limited number of connections.

Maybe you have heard of the six degrees of separation effect or what the original researchers referred to as the small-world problem. That is, everyone in the country is separated by a mere six people. This idea actually comes from some research that was conducted in the 1960s and asked a number of people in Nebraska and Kansas to contact a stockbroker in Boston, Massachusetts. If they knew this stockbroker, the participants could contact him directly, or they could hand the information off to someone they thought might know him or someone that knew someone who knew him. The research found that it took an average of 6.2 people to connect strangers, the study's participants, with the stockbroker. What? While this research has its critics and limitations, it highlights the fact that society is constructed of myriad networks that may connect seemingly extremely disparate types of people (Travers and Milgram, 1969). For example, I grew up poor in New England with uneducated parents and never in my life met anyone from the Bush family, but in 2000, when George W. Bush, who came from a powerful, well-educated, and wealthy Texas family, was elected president, I could connect myself to him through just two other people. My best friend (1st connection) has a brother-in-law (2nd connection) who went to Yale with the future president. That's crazy.

Our social networks are formed in various ways and serve a number of important functions in our lives. Some networks emerge because we find other people friendly, fun to be around, affectionate, or we love them. Other networks are cultivated in order to find a job, a babysitter, or fellow scuba divers. Social networks help us all negotiate social life by providing a range of needs. Think about your network of friends and family and how they provide you with advice, support, and love. Interactions with friends and family create a familiar network of people who provide us feelings of belonging. Other networks can be more instrumental or utilitarian. Take, for example, Angie's List, an online network of consumers who rate a variety of tradespeople. Angie's List provides a network of consumers' opinions of plumbers, carpenters, and home inspectors ready to be tapped into by anyone willing to pay the fee and click on a name. The rise of the Internet has provided the population of the world with access to networks that have the potential to be worldwide—through the use of Internet social media, you may be connected to the Queen of England through just a couple of people.

Organizations

Secondary groups come in a variety of shapes and sizes; some, such as the sociology class you are in, are small, and temporary others, such as the American Sociological Association, are large and enduring. Organizations are large secondary groups designed to achieve their goals in an efficient and effective manner. Organizations contain both individuals and groups in which both statuses and roles are clearly defined. Organizations are abundant in society, and throughout our lives, we maintain membership in a number of organizations like our college, political parties, and perhaps a union or the Red Cross.

Types of Organizations

People join organizations for a host of reasons. Some people are seeking employment, some are seeking fellowship with likeminded individuals, and some are forced to join organizations. Additionally, organizations are created for a number of reasons; some are pure money-making ventures, some emerge to serve the community, and others are maintained to isolate their members. Generally, three types of formal organizations have been identified based mainly on these functions and membership affiliations (Etzioni, 1975).

Utilitarian organizations are generally regarded as organizations that people join for employment and monetary reward. A range of for-profit and non-profit organizations fit this description, such as Starbucks, McDonald's, hospitals, colleges, and churches. While organizations like Starbucks exist to make money and provide employment, others like the Methodist church pay their employees but are a non-profit and serve a different purpose or utility in the community. Most of us will join utilitarian organizations because we need to eat and pay our bills. Additionally, membership in utilitarian organizations is typically voluntary.

The Red Cross, United Way, Juvenile Diabetes Research Foundation, and Habit for Humanity are all examples of normative organizations—organizations that people join not for income and employment, but rather because they believe it to be personally or morally worthwhile. Individuals voluntarily join normative organizations because they see it as a way to give back to the community, feel it is the right thing to do, or want to advance a cause they believe in. These organizations exist in the community locally and in society at large mainly because the government and the private sector fail to provide those services or populations. Many of us will join a number of normative organizations over the course of our lives mainly because we feel connected to some cause or movement on a personal or moral level.

In contrast to the other two types of organizations discussed above, coercive organizations are characterized by involuntary membership. Prisons, some mental health hospitals and rehab facilities represent good examples of coercive organizations. Inmates *join* prison as a result of punishment by the courts. Similarly, people are regularly committed to mental health and substance abuse rehab facilities by the courts or their families involuntarily. These organizations exist because they are a necessary component in dealing with certain populations within society: those who have been deemed unable to play by the social rules and must be isolated from society. Hopefully, you will not be forced to *join* any of these types of organizations.

Bureaucracy

> *"If you are going to sin, sin against God, not the bureaucracy. God will forgive you but the bureaucracy won't."*
>
> — *Hyman G. Rickover*

Ancient Sumer, Egypt, China, and Rome all used what we would today call bureaucracy to rule their vast empires. However, the term bureaucracy wasn't coined until the mid-eighteenth century. It meant the *rule by officials* and was immediately used as a pejorative. Throughout the following centuries, bureaucracies were described variously as inefficient, impersonal, too complex, and rigid. Unfortunately, these perceptions are still with us today.

When most people hear the term bureaucracy, it strikes terror in their hearts; they envision long wait times in impersonal, sterile waiting rooms, rude, cubicle-dwelling bureaucrats, and filling out countless forms. And when your turn does come, you have invariably filled out the wrong form or you are at the wrong window—"You need form 2343ZX and you need to go to window 7, registration renewal," says the inattentive woman without even looking up! When I think of bureaucracy, I immediately think back to wasting hours and hours of my time in the waiting room of the DMV in Los Angeles.

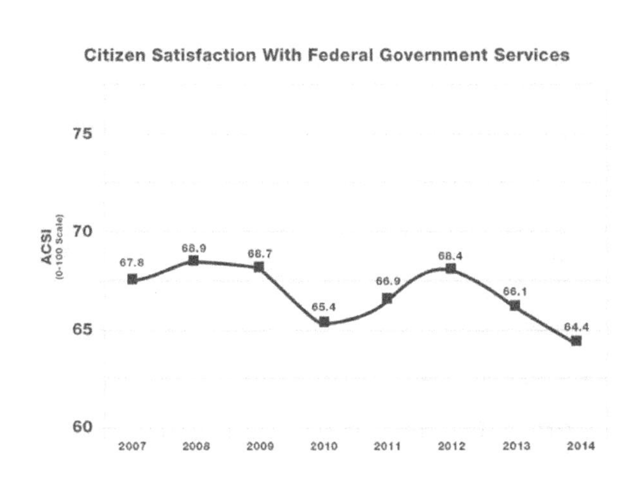

Fig. 5.10 SCI Line Chart. You can see this chart shows that satisfaction with Federal bureaucracies has decreased over time.

Bureaucracy is a system of organization characterized by a hierarchy of authority, a clear division of labor, explicit rules, and impersonality (Weber, 1922). Think DMV, hospitals, colleges, and the IRS or any number of government agencies. Over the course of your life, you most likely have encountered a number of bureaucracies, including the college you are attending. Whether you were enrolling in classes, filling out financial aid forms, or trying to transfer credits, you probably had to deal with specialized employees who had to check with their bosses because they weren't sure about some rule or regulation, all the while treating you as though you were just another number. This *red tape*—the excessive formality and routine required before any action can be taken—typifies modern bureaucracies, which most Americans view as untrustworthy, cumbersome, and inefficient (Henry J. Kaiser Family Foundation, 2000; Alvarez and Brehm, 1996). Indeed, this general dissatisfaction with bureaucracies is illustrated in figure 5.10. The chart shows the decline in Americans' overall satisfaction with federal governmental services. Citizens' satisfaction with the federal government hit a seven-year low in 2014 with a rating of 64.4 (out of 100 total satisfaction points; American Customer Satisfaction Index, 2015).

Max Weber and Bureaucracy

Max Weber (1925) argued that as societies modernized, they transitioned from traditional organizational forms to more rational, bureaucratic organizational forms. This rationalization of society involved the process of replacing traditional and emotional thought with reason and efficiency. Therefore, he saw the expansion of bureaucracy—the best administrative form for the rational or efficient pursuit of organizational goals—as necessary in modern societies, a rational solution to the complexities of large-scale social systems. Moreover, he saw the modern world as a place where rationalization was increasingly becoming a characteristic of all spheres of social life. While he acknowledged that bureaucracies had their weaknesses, he understood that they were the most rational and efficient way human activity could be organized in the modern world. Basically, he realized that while they had their problems, bureaucratic organizations were here to stay as a feature of modern society. Therefore, he figured he might as well develop a sort of template for the perfect or most efficient bureaucracy (Ritzer, 1993; Weber, 1947).

So, Weber developed what he called the **ideal type bureaucracy**, which refers to traits that a perfect bureaucracy should possess but may not be found in any real-life bureaucratic organization. Think about an ideal type this way: Imagine your ideal mate. Think of all the traits she/he would possess in order for her/him to be perfect. While this person would be ideal because she/he possesses all the traits you find to be perfect in a mate, you will never find that person, but you will find someone that has a few, some, or many of those traits. The ideal type bureaucracy, according to Weber, possessed six characteristics:

1. **High degree of division of labor and specialization**. Workers in a bureaucracy are responsible for very specific tasks. Workers will become proficient at their jobs and maximize efficiency because they are only responsible for a limited number of tasks.
2. **Hierarchy of authority**. Hierarchy is a system of ranking various positions in descending order from top to bottom of the organization. Each position has a supervisor above it and a subordinate below it with the exception of those in the highest and lowest positions. Thus, a chain of command that stretches from the top to the bottom is established in which each worker knows whom he reports to and who reports to him.
3. **Rules and regulations**. A comprehensive set of explicit written rules and regulations guarantee uniformity of interactions. These rules and regulations construct a sort of organizational structure for expected behaviors, so as workers come and go, the rules remain the same, producing organizational continuity. Strict adherence to these rules and regulations is the root of "red tape."
4. **Impersonality**. Relationships between organization members should be formal, polite, and impersonal. Rules and regulations that promote impersonality foster an atmosphere of equal treatment of personnel and maximize efficiency. The idea is that each person should come to work and do the work at hand and check any strong feelings for the organization or other workers at the door.
5. **Hiring personnel based on ability**. Only those best suited in terms of qualifications and skills are hired for any particular position. Remember, Weber is rejecting the traditional model of hiring based on nepotism, favoritism, and cronyism in favor of hiring based on a standardized set of qualifications such as skills, number of years of experience, and education. This ensures the best qualified person is hired for each position.
6. **Separation of personal and company property**. Personnel should separate their personal belongings from those that belong to the organization. Workers' desks computers and other office furniture and machinery are the property of the organization, just the right amount to get the job done efficiently. Personal property at work may be distracting, interfere with interoffice relations or promote inequality between workers, and bog down efficiency. In Weber's ideal bureaucracy, employees would not have family pictures in their work area.

Just like none of us will ever find our ideal mate, there is no ideal bureaucracy. So what is the reality of today's bureaucracies? While organizations may have widely different purposes, they are similar in the way they are structured. Typically, bureaucracies are structured with those with the most general or wide-ranging responsibilities at the top and those with narrow, sometimes singular responsibilities at the bottom. Sundar Pichai (born Pichai Sundararajan), the CEO of Google, is responsible for managing Google's image and the direction that the organization will take. Below him are various vice presidents of divisions, and below them are managers of departments filled with people like my friend Ethan, who's only responsible for writing code in his tiny cubicle.

Bureaucracies, then, are designed with a few powerful people at the top concerned mainly with the well-being of the organization and lots of people at the bottom who have a few restricted duties. Take the Roman Catholic Church, for example. The Pope is at the top and below him are cardinals, archbishops, bishops, and then parish priests. The Pope travels the world promoting the church, cardinals run the church as a sort of elected "government," bishops oversee a district of churches, and priests operate a single church. We can see, then, that the duties of cardinals and bishops are quite wide-ranging and those of a parish priest are narrow and confined. So it doesn't matter if an organization is helping us search online for a long-lost uncle or concerned with saving our eternal soul; they all use bureaucratic hierarchy to operate their organizations and achieve their goals.

We have to remember that Weber's ideal bureaucracy was designed to capitalize on the characteristics we discussed above in order to create an efficient and predictable workplace, one free of personal, irrational, and emotional elements. Even though he saw bureaucracy as the most efficient organizational strategy, he worried that it could become what he called an "iron cage," trapping individuals in an ever-growing desire for efficient, impersonal, and task-oriented solutions to modern social life (DiMaggio and Powell, 1983).

Why We Dislike Bureaucracy

Frustration with bureaucratic inefficiency, lethargy and red tape seems to be universal. While we might find them frustrating and tedious, bureaucracies are here to stay because they represent the most efficient way to organize life in our complex modern world. However, several problems have emerged from the structure of bureaucracies that impact those who work within them and those of us who frequently bump up against them.

Inflexibility. Many times, rigid adherence to rules and regulations does not allow for flexibility in seeking solutions when unexpected situations arise. The blind obedience to these rules may become an obstacle to achieving tasks or goals efficiently. This inflexibility rears its ugly head when we as patrons of bureaucracies, who do not always know the rules, encounter frustrated workers whose power is confined to their limited number of specific tasks and may take that frustration out on us.

Low Morale. Specialized jobs tend to be repetitive, and that can lead to boredom and job dissatisfaction. If employees feel that they are being evaluated on how efficiently they perform their specific tasks, this may lead to a focus on task completion and generate disincentives for creativity. The centralized structure of bureaucracies increases employee disempowerment, and can make many workers feel helpless and indifferent toward their job and the organization.

Alienation. The impersonality and the highly specialized nature of bureaucracies fosters feelings of estrangement among workers. Employees have very specific tasks to perform and are not fully connected to an end product or organizational goals and are left with feelings of alienation or being isolated from other workers and the overall process.

Parkinson's Law. This is the idea that work expands to fill the time available for its completion (Parkinson, 1957). Ever had a semester project due and had the entire term to complete it, but you waited until the last week of school? Have you ever waited until the night before an exam to study, yet known about the exam for weeks? These are examples of Parkinson's Law. (Remember, as a college student, you are a member of a bureaucracy.)

The Peter Principle. Sociologist Laurence Peter (1969) is generally credited with articulating the practice of promoting workers within a bureaucracy to the point of their incompetence. That is, employees who show ability and/or promise are promoted, and if they continue to perform well, they keep getting promoted to the point where they are promoted to a position in which they cannot handle the responsibilities—their level of incompetence. While there is a kernel of truth in the Peter Principle, if it were practiced generally, bureaucracies wouldn't last long.

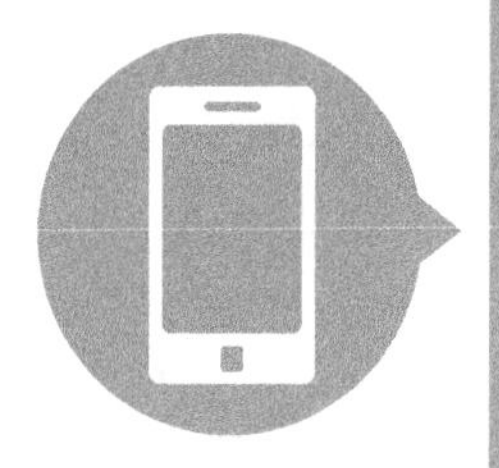

THERE'S AN APP FOR THAT

Airpaper is an app that promises to make bureaucracy "surprisingly pleasant (MightyMeeting Inc, 2016)." Specifically designed to cut through the red tape of cancelling your Comcast subscription, the app will do all the work for you, just enter your contact information and your Comcast account number—all for 5 bucks. The founder says the app will grow to handle other bureaucracy specific issues in the future. Even the police have to contend with red tape. The Palm Springs, California Police Department has started using *SceneDoc*, an app that allows them to securely digitize paperwork and slashes reporting time for incidents by an average of 45 minutes (SceneDoc Inc., 2016). This allows more officers to have boots on the ground longer because they're not at their desks bogged down with paperwork.

READ MORE

The McDonaldization of Society, 8th Edition. George Ritzer (2015).

George Ritzer (1993) suggests that the whole world is operating as though it were a McDonald's restaurant. While our man Weber suggested that bureaucracy was the most rational and efficient way to deal with complex, modern social structures, Ritzer extends and updates this idea of rationalization by using the model of the fast-food restaurant to illustrate the movement toward a sort of *sameness* to social life. Ritzer isn't referring to the restaurant itself, but the *system* it developed that has come to dominate nearly all aspects of social life.

Fig. 5.11 The McDonaldization of Society

Ritzer outlines four main principles of McDonaldization:

- Efficiency—the food is presented to you fast while minimizing cost and effort. You can get in and out of McDonald's fast because the menu is limited, many tasks are automated, and employees are working efficiently based on a kind of script. Not to mention they have you doing some of the work yourself by bussing your own table or taking the trash with you as you roll through the drive-up window.
- Calculability—you can get lots of food for little money. This concept refers to the idea that at McDonald's, you can get a lot of food for little money and not spend a lot of time doing it. Back at the dawn of time when I was a child, McDonald's advertised that you could get a hamburger, fries, and a drink *and* change back from a dollar.
- Predictability—no matter which McDonald's you walk into, you can find the same burger with the same flavor. Many Americans traveling abroad know that if they step into a McDonald's in Berlin, Istanbul, or Paris, they can count on enjoying the McDonald's experience. A reviewer on Yelp posted this about her experience in Paris, France: "My mom and I were exhausted our first day of traveling here and we wanted something quick, cheap and familiar so that we didn't have to spend too much time making a decision. Voila! McDonald's" (Natasha S., 2014).
- Control—the physical environment and procedures are designed to control the dining experience. Using a limited menu, your food choices are narrowed and controlled. Customers line up in front of a number of registers, which controls the flow of customer traffic, and seating areas are intentionally uncomfortable to encourage patrons to eat and leave the restaurant quickly.

Remember, McDonaldization refers to "the process by which the principles of the fast-food restaurant are coming to dominate more and more sectors of American society as well as the rest of the world" (Ritzer, 1993). So, according to Ritzer, the principles outlined above are being applied to many aspects of our daily lives—businesses, government organizations, and even the healthcare sector—in an attempt to make them more rational, efficient, and profitable.

You can see this process occurring in your daily life. Rather than write letters or make phone calls, we send emails or texts, get cash from ATMs, use self-checkout at the grocery store, and shop and order our clothes online. If you have done any of these things, you have fallen victim to McDonaldization, or what I call the hyper-rationalization of social life. In an attempt to get people in and out of the grocery stores fast and efficiently and reduce labor costs, many stores offer self-checkout, banks provide ATMs that outnumber real bank tellers, and healthcare focuses on getting patients in and out with a minimum of care to reduce both labor and product costs (Taylor, 2015). When I was born in 1961, my mother spent an entire week in the hospital before she was discharged, and mine was a normal birth with no complications. Today, hospitals will discharge new mothers the next day. Pretty soon, you can just go online and a connected doctor will coach you through your birth in the privacy of your own home. You can pay her through PayPal, send out birth announcements on Evite, and then have all those disposable diapers that you ordered online delivered daily.

This combination of automation, predictability, digitization, and immediacy allows us to engage in less physical contact, have nearly everything at our fingertips via the Internet, and spend less time and effort on activities of our daily lives. I'm sure that there is some guy living in his mom's basement with his computer working as an IT consultant, having his paycheck direct deposited, ordering food from Grub Hub and his clothes from L.L. Bean, and trolling for dates on Tinder or Grindr. Work, pay, food, clothes, and dates, and he never has to leave the basement!

Social Institutions

Many people use the word institution to refer to places like hospitals, prisons, churches, and even colleges, such as the fine institution in which you are enrolled. While those may be physical locations, they are not what sociologists mean by institutions. Institutions are not physical things, but rather constructs we have developed that allow us to understand how society works. Think about this: your body is made up of many structures (nervous system, cardiovascular system, muscular-skeletal system, etc.) that must function together for you to walk, talk, drink beer, and make love—in other words, live. The social analog of those bodily structures are represented in society by institutions. **Social Institutions**, then, are systems of established patterns of expected behaviors that are organized to fulfill society's fundamental needs and perpetuate social order (Durkheim, 1895 (original date)). All societies have fundamental needs that have to be fulfilled.

Therefore, social institutions are found within all societies, and while they may look different, they emerge and persist because they meet basic social needs. These fundamental needs are fulfilled through five generally recognized institutions: the family, education, religion, political institutions, and the economy—what I call the *Big 5*.

The Big 5

In most societies, the family is responsible for sexual reproduction and regulation, socializing children, and providing a range of support for members. All people of the world are involved in finding a mate, raising their children, and maintaining their households. Typically, Americans meet a mate, fall in love, get married, and then have children. While today this is not always the case, more Americans follow this path than not (Cannon, 2012). We practice monogamy, meaning we can legally only be married to one person at a time. After we marry, we *neolocate* (get our own place), where we expect parents to care for and raise their children, instilling in them values, beliefs, and expectations so that they can function appropriately in society.

Alternatively, the Yanomami people of the Amazon engage in monogamy and polygamy (we'll discuss this more in Chapter 9), allowing men to take several wives and women to take several husbands (Early and Peters, 2000). Combinations of marital arrangements occupy a common *shabono,* a kind of long house, where anywhere from twenty to a few hundred interrelated individuals live. The children are almost exclusively raised communally by their mothers, sisters, aunts, female cousins, and grandmothers. While the family form is very different for the Yanomami, the same tasks are accomplished: they raise children who embody the values, beliefs, and behaviors that allow them to navigate their culture.

Fig. 5.12 Yanomami Children

Education is the process of transmitting a range of knowledge, beliefs, values, and expectations to each generation so it may fully participate in society. In American society, we rely heavily on formal education provided by schools and colleges for members of society to gain the knowledge they need to participate in society in general and the economy specifically.

In contrast, the Yanomami do not have a formal education institution. Rather, their children stay close to their mothers during childhood, where boys are encouraged to play with toy bows and arrows so they learn how to hunt, which will be their primary adult duty, while girls watch and practice gathering, planting, and harvesting with their mothers so they are prepared to carry out women's duties later in life.

The **economy** represents the methods of producing and distributing desired goods and services to members of society. While we rely on a money market economy in which goods and services are produced and then distributed through buying and selling here in the U.S., other societies depend on other ways to produce and distribute goods. For example, the Yanomami people make and use what they need, such as bows and arrows, necklaces, or headdresses, within their small bands. They may at times trade or gift goods to other autonomous Yanomami bands. They don't need money because they simply grow or make what they need from their forest habitat.

Political institutions are represented by the rules and organizations that arise to exercise power and authority in society (Baker, 2014). These may include structures that make and enforce laws, distribute power, provide for domestic and foreign policies, and ensure the welfare of the citizenry. Our political structures and governments are comprised of some fairly large and complex organizations. There are political parties and federal, state, and local governments, not to mention the military and the courts. Our lives are influenced on a daily basis by the processes of making, enforcing, and interpreting laws.

The Yanomami have a fairly straightforward political system: all decisions are made communally. That is, whether the decision concerns punishment for some transgression or whether the band is deciding to move to a new location, everyone in the community has a right to speak his/her mind, and the final decision is made through consensus. However, the headman, the male who leads all soldiers and is typically the bravest and most successful warrior and shaman—who are exclusively men—carry more weight in their debates.

In most societies, **religion** is composed of a wide range of beliefs and practices that distinguish the difference between the sacred and the profane and help individuals deal with the issues of the meaning and purpose of life. The vast majority of Americans report that they believe in God—somewhere between 76% and 92%. However, only about 70% report attending services weekly, monthly, or yearly (Newport, 2011; Shannon-Missal, 2013; Barna Group, 2015). Religion in the United States serves mainly to help people grapple with understanding their meaning and purpose in life and to provide a reassurance of an afterlife, moral direction, and the disposition of our eternal soul. Additionally, many religions in the U.S. help individuals who may have fallen through the gaps of other institutions or charities.

Our Yanomami brethren to the south have no formal religion as we would conceive of it. Rather, they have a complex belief system that includes four planes of existence and the possession of multiple souls, and ultimately, they see magic as both the cause and cure to illness and misfortune. While in our culture we seek to understand a range of phenomenon in terms of *God's will*, the Yanomami see magic as an explanation for illness, social discord, and natural phenomenon.

As we can see, institutions help meet a variety of basic social needs, perpetuate a number of values and beliefs, and guide expected behaviors that ultimately establish a sort of regularity to daily life. However, they don't perform in a haphazard manner; institutions perform these tasks in a coordinated way. Institutions are interconnected. That is, the functions that each institution serves are linked together. For instance, families socialize children to value education and to be hard workers. In turn, through taxes collected by the government, you may be receiving federal financial aid to attend college and be trained as an accountant so that you can get a good-paying job, buy a house, and be a productive participant in the economy. Additionally, many times, religion reinforces the values of hard work and family that motivate people to work hard at their jobs, raise families, and replicate various social behaviors. Given the number of college students in the U.S., about 20.5 million, and the popular belief that education is the best way to realize social mobility, no doubt reinforced through socialization by the family and schools, it is clear that institutions reflect broadly held, shared beliefs about how to be successful in life.

Theoretical Perspectives and Groups

All theoretical perspectives are concerned with the structure and functions of social institutions. Functionalism describes institutions as interconnected and functioning in cooperative ways for the benefit of society. Functionalists assume that things in society that persist must serve some function for society. Ultimately, then, functionalism seeks to show what functions social institutions perform for the maintenance of social order. This focus on maintaining social order and avoiding change has brought the strongest criticism of functionalism—functionalism promotes the *status quo*. That is, functionalism maintains that institutions reinforce social values and beliefs and replicates behaviors that contribute to social stability and resist change.

In contrast, conflict theory seeks to understand how social institutions benefit certain segments of society and deprive others. Conflict theory sees various groups in society as acting in their own interests rather than in the interest of maintaining social order. Conflict theory assumes that not all interests are shared across all groups and that many interests are in conflict. This perspective posits that those in the ruling, powerful class in society control how institutions replicate their dominant values, beliefs, and behaviors, which benefit the ruling class, deprive other classes, and maintain the rule of the dominant class over others. While conflict theory is broad enough to include analysis of all institutions, its primary focus is on economic access, which generates its primary criticism—it focuses too narrowly on economic forces.

Holding a distinctively different perspective from both functionalist and conflict theories, symbolic interactionism argues that the individual and society are the product of social interactions. Rather than viewing macrostructures like abstract social institutions as creating society, interactionism suggests that *society* exists in our daily social interactions. Are you wondering what that means? Think about it this way: we interact with other people each day using a host of symbols, mainly language, and negotiate a social reality that has behavioral boundaries, which helps us understand our expected behaviors and how we expect others to behave, and these normative acts sustain social order. Thus, society is constructed through human interactions, not dictated as fixed social roles (functionalism) or as economic interest (conflict). The criticisms of symbolic interaction are that the perspective ignores large, abstract social institutions and overstates the subjective nature of society.

Below, table 5.3 summarizes our discussion above by distilling the central ideas of the three major theoretical perspectives and an example that helps illustrate each one.

TABLE 5.3. Theoretical Perspectives on Groups

Theoretical Perspective	Views on Groups	Example
Structural-Functionalism	This perspective sees social institutions as interconnected and they function together in a cooperative way to maintain social order or the *status quo.*	The federal *government* provides financial aid, which reduces the burden on *family* finances so children can attend *college* and become qualified to take part in the *economy* by engaging in consumerism and accruing debt like car loans and mortgages. Each of these institutions reinforces social values, beliefs, and expected behaviors that promote the status quo.
Conflict	Social institutions are instruments of the ruling class This perspective emphasizes that powerful groups define appropriate social values, beliefs, and behaviors, which less powerful groups conform to. Therefore, powerful groups maintain their dominance and perpetuate inequality through control of social institutions	The ruling class has access to lawmakers and can influence the approval of laws that favor the powerful. Powerful Americans lobby Congress using their considerable wealth and influence to effect tax laws that favor them, placing the greatest tax burden on those in the working and middle classes.

(*Continued*)

Theoretical Perspective	Views on Groups	Example
Symbolic Interactionism	Interaction between individuals constructs social reality therefore, "society" is created through human interactions These daily interactions lead to negotiated social realities, which are boundaries for expected behaviors.	An engaged couple, for example, will negotiate the parameters of their relationship using a number of symbols, mostly language, and come to an understanding of how they expect each other to behave. When they get married, they have already established their marital roles that will provide them with regularity to their married lives.

The Bottom Line

We, as humans, need other humans; we are gregarious and social creatures. According to the three major Abrahamic faiths, our very creation is based on the belief that God created humans for fellowship. God essentially created man to have someone to hang out with. There is also strong anthropological evidence to support the argument that our very survival was dependent on cooperative collectives—safety in numbers. So, however you view our origins, there is no escaping the fact that we as a species have always organized ourselves into groups.

From the day we are born and most likely until the day we die, we will be members in hundreds of groups of varying size and importance. Throughout our lives, groups, organizations, and social institutions are powerful influences on our development and adjustment to our social world. Groups like the family in part shape who we are, provide us with a "haven in a heartless world," and instill in us appropriate social values, beliefs, and behaviors (Lasch, 1977). As we have seen, groups can put considerable pressure on individuals and cause them to do things they might not ordinarily do. And in the case of The People's Temple, the group created lethal levels of conformity. Bureaucratic organizations and institutions have the capacity to constrain our behaviors and even seemingly grind our lives into a sameness in a constant search for rationality, efficiency, and profit.

Throughout this chapter, we saw that groups, bureaucracies, and institutions have a profound effect on the way we behave, see the world, and treat others. Highlighting these influences helps to debunk the myth or common-knowledge idea that motives are the single factor in determining the way we act. While it is true that we all possess the capacity of independent action or volition, the reality is that so much of our lives are spent within the context of groups, which for a variety of reasons shape the ways in which we exercise our free will. We all want to fit in, and that desire compels us all to act in ways that we think will help us gain acceptance and feel like we belong.

Figure Credits

Fig. 5.1: Copyright © Danish C (CC by 2.0) at https://commons.wikimedia.org/wiki/File:Sri_Lanka_-_Crowd_of_people_bathing_clothed_in_sea.jpg.

Fig. 5.2: Copyright © Lbaze202 (CC BY-SA 3.0) at https://commons.wikimedia.org/wiki/File:301_wiki_picture.jpg.

Fig. 5.3: Aino Tuominen, "San People," https://commons.wikimedia.org/wiki/File:Bushman-family.jpg. Copyright in the Public Domain.

Fig. 5.5: Copyright © Jorge Royan (CC BY-SA 3.0) at https://commons.wikimedia.org/wiki/File:India_-_Actors_-_0258.jpg.

Fig. 5.6: Source: https://commons.wikimedia.org/wiki/File:Ash_Lines.jpg.

Fig. 5.7: Copyright © Expiring frog (CC BY-SA 3.0) at https://commons.wikimedia.org/wiki/File:Milgram_Experiment_v2.png.

Fig. 5.8: "Prisoners being Humiliated at Abu Ghraib," https://commons.wikimedia.org/wiki/Abu_Ghraib_prisoner_abuse#/media/File:Abu_Ghraib_48.jpg. Copyright in the Public Domain.

Fig. 5.9: Copyright © رمزي زودة (CC BY-SA 3.0) at https://commons.wikimedia.org/wiki/File:Bystander_effect.jpg.

Fig. 5.10: American Customer Satisfaction Index, http://www.theacsi.org/news-and-resources/customer-satisfaction-reports/reports-2014/acsi-federal-government-report-2014.

Fig. 5.11: Copyright © Sardaka (CC by 3.0) at https://commons.wikimedia.org/wiki/File:(1)McDonalds_Cremorne-1.jpg.

Fig. 5.12: Copyright © Ambar~commonswiki (CC BY-SA 3.0) at https://commons.wikimedia.org/wiki/File:Alto_orinoco5.jpg.

CHAPTER 6

STAYING WITHIN THE LINES: SOCIAL CONTROL, DEVIANCE, AND CRIME

Eternal Love

In his book *Undying Love*, Ben Harrison (1997) documents the strange case of Carl Tanzler, a Key West radiology technician who became so obsessed with one of his tuberculosis patients, Maria Elena Milagro de Hoyos, that after her death, he stole her remains and brought them to his home, where he dressed, serenaded, and made love to her. It was reported that Tanzler's love for Maria was unrequited. This fact did not deter Tanzler from visiting her grave nightly before finally stealing her remains two years after she died in October 1931. Tanzler said that the dead Maria would speak to him and beg him to take her remains. For seven years, Tanzler kept her corpse in his bed, where he applied makeup to her, dressed her, and even had sex with her. Ultimately, Maria's sister, Florinda, caught wind of the creepy behavior and had Tanzler arrested. He was charged with "wantonly and maliciously destroying a grave and removing a body without authorization." Note that he was not charged with necrophilia—having sex with a dead body. Do you consider this deviant behavior?

Fig. 6.1 Carl Tanzler. States have not always had laws prohibiting sex with corpses (much like Florida didn't in 1933). Currently, all fifty states have statutes that prohibit sex acts with human corpses, which illustrates the dynamic nature of deviance—as norms change, so does our interpretation of deviance. However, to this day, there is no federal law that prohibits sex with a corpse.

Have you ever told a lie? Of course you have. I asked that question in my class one time, and I actually had a student raise her hand and insist that she had never told a lie—she was in her mid-thirties. Do you think she could have made it to that point in her life without telling a lie? Could you go twenty-four hours without telling a lie? Try it! From time to time in our lives, we all commit minor transgressions—lying, jaywalking, being late for class, cheating on an exam. From the sociological perspective, we have all violated standards of conduct or social norms, making us all deviants at various points in our lives. Therefore, before you judge someone's actions as deviant, you might want to step back and use your sociological imagination and consider the social forces and circumstances that may have influenced his behavior. It is not about judging deviance; it is about exploring and understanding its complex nature.

While we *all* violate society's rules occasionally, the vast majority of us would not rise to the extreme that Mr. Tanzler did. Necrophilia, or having sex with a dead person, is considered a violation of the norms of our culture—most Americans would find it rather disgusting. In fact, it would be considered criminally deviant. For sociologists, deviance refers to the violation of social norms. Therefore, strictly speaking, *all crime is deviance*, but *not all deviance is crime*. That is, crime—the violation of formal norms or *laws*—by its definition is deviance. However, there are a number of behaviors, traits, and beliefs that do not violate laws but are still viewed as deviant.

Take for example NAMBLA; the North American Man/Boy Love Association is a group that promotes love and consensual sex between men and boys, which the organization refers to as "intergenerational relationships." NAMBLA is a self-described political, civil rights, and educational organization that supports the rights of youth and adults to "... choose the partners they wish to share and enjoy their bodies with." Its focus is reforming age of consent laws, which it interprets as a form of ageism. It opposes these laws and "... all other restrictions which deny men and boys the full enjoyment of their bodies and control over their own lives." Furthermore, it feels that these laws unfairly criminalize men and boys who engage in consensual sexual relationships. It promotes and condones only consensual relationships, and it also clearly states that the organization does not engage in any behavior that violates the law and does not advocate that anyone else should (NAMBLA, 2011). Wow. This organization and its views would be seen by most as deviant in that its beliefs are far outside our cultural perspectives on children and sexuality. While not criminal, this organization and its beliefs are clearly deviant.

I should point out that it is not the function of sociology to make moral judgments about the beliefs or behaviors of individuals or groups, but rather social judgments. When we use the term *deviant,* we are simply recognizing that the belief or behavior violates a social norm of a particular group at a particular time. I am not using the term to indicate some flaw in one's moral character; when I refer to deviance, I am pointing out that some behavior or belief has violated a standard of conduct or a social convention. In American society, the mentally ill, those living as vampires, and people who identify as furries would all be considered deviants.

TRY THIS

Deviant for a day. Try being a deviant for a day at college or around your community. Wear all your clothes on inside out or get a stuffed animal, put it in a stroller, and treat it like a real human baby. High-five everyone you walk past, talk aloud to yourself while gesturing to the sky, or wear big yellow rubber dishwashing gloves all day long. These are just some suggestions; be as creative as you want. Watch the reactions of others. Do people avoid you? Laugh at you? Do they yell at you or tell you to be normal? Make mental notes of how others react. Afterward, ask some of the people you interacted with what bothered them about your behavior(s). **Be sure not to do anything criminal or anything that could potentially harm you or others.**

Some Characteristics of Deviance

Deviance depends on the social context. While actions in one social situation may be normal, they may be seen as deviant in another. If you come home after a long day of work and school and grab some food and a beer from the fridge, sit down, prop your feet up on the table, start eating with your hands, and let out a nice, long burp, that would be completely acceptable. These same behaviors would be seen as rude and unacceptable at an upscale restaurant.

Deviance can be a trait, belief, or behavior. Your behaviors are not the only things that may be viewed as deviant. Holding socially unacceptable views like being an atheist or a Satan worshipper can bring unfavorable reactions from others. A physical deformity, skin color, or a physical disability can also marginalize people by labeling them as deviant.

Perceptions of deviance can change over time: The fluidity of deviance. It is important to remember that as sociologists, we view deviance as dynamic. That is, we understand that deviance is learned in the context of a culture; therefore, deviance is interpreted differently between cultures. We also understand that deviance changes over time within cultures.

So, why was necrophilia at one point in our history not illegal? Why is it prohibited in nearly all states now? Why is it deviant in our culture but allowed in other cultures? If deviance is defined by social norms, and norms change over time, then what we consider deviant changes over time. In addition, needless to say, deviance is viewed differently from place to place. Therefore, the violation of or deviation from social norms is bounded by culture. As social norms change over time within a culture, the definition of their violation—deviance—also changes.

For example, at one time in the U.S., you could have been diagnosed as mentally ill for being gay. The American Psychiatric Association (APA) removed homosexuality from the Diagnostic and Statistical Manual (DSM: the standard classifications for mental disorders used by mental health professionals) in 1973, but it took until 1986 to get the remaining references out of the DSM (American Psychiatric Association, 1975, 1987). No thinking person today believes that gay men or women are suffering from some sort of mental illness. Being gay has moved from marginalizing people for having a psychiatric condition to all states recognizing same-sex marriages. Being gay in America has moved from being viewed as deviant to being a widely accepted sexual orientation.

When my father went into the military, he was encouraged to smoke cigarettes; today, there are entire campuses, businesses, and cities that are smoke-free. Smokers in many parts of the country have to huddle in the cold and wet weather as they smoke their cigarettes fifty feet away from the building in which they work. Smoking has gone from being ubiquitous in our culture fifty years ago to being viewed as one of our greatest health risks. On average, 40% of adults reported being smokers during the 1970s; now, about 18% of U.S. adults claim to be smokers (Saad, 2008; Centers for Disease Control, "Current Cigarette Smoking," 2015). Fifty years ago, it was completely acceptable to smoke on planes, at work, in the classroom, on TV, and in hospitals! Smoking has moved from a mainstream behavior to one that can be viewed as deviant. Our constantly changing set of social norms creates a fluidity of deviance.

Deviance varies across cultures. Our standard of normal may be very different from the standards of other cultures. What kind of society would allow women to leave their infant children with complete strangers in a non-home environment for more than eight hours a day? Well, Americans do it about 6.7 million times a day. About 33% of households with children under the age of five use non-relative childcare facilities (Laughlin, 2013). Most cultures of the world would view this practice as deviant (bordering on reprehensible); they would assume that childcare would be the duty of blood relatives, kin, fictive kin, or a known, trusted member of the community. However, in the U.S., this is completely acceptable and a practice that serves our social needs.

Food serves as another good example. Food choices in many ways help define a culture. Food is one of the most powerful ways that cultures define themselves. Some cultures do not eat meat, some see eating dogs as acceptable, and many cultures practice entomophagy (eating insects). Food can be one of the most distinguishing characteristics of a culture and what separates it from other social groups.

Fig. 6.2 Bull penis with rice. Probably not something you find on restaurant menus in your neighborhood, but commonly consumed in some cultures due to its properties of male strength and virility.

What if someone opened a restaurant in your town that served only animal penises? While we have quite an eclectic palate in the states, a penis restaurant would be viewed as odd and maybe a bit off-putting by many. However, if you would like some boiled, sautéed, fried, and even baked penis, all you have to do is travel to Beijing, China (Deemer, 2012). There, the Guolizhuang restaurant will serve you the penises of a variety of animals as well as stewed deer face, sheep fetus in a brown garlic sauce, and peacock claws! Eating body tokens (foods that resemble male genitalia) such as snakes and rhinoceros horns was a common practice for millennia by the people of many cultures (Orth, 2008; Zhao, 2015). Therefore, eating the actual penis or testicles of large or ferocious animals is viewed as a more potent way to imbue an individual with powers of potency and fertility as well as strength. While this is completely understandable in the context of the Chinese culture, it is deviant by our standards (Kahn, 1993; Simoons, 1990). Men in our culture simply take a little blue pill.

A RESTAURANT THAT ONLY SERVES PENISES

Guolizhuang is a Beijing restaurant that exclusively serves the penises of a number of animal species. You can get snake penis, yak penis, deer penis, and even seal penis. These delicacies are served in a variety of ways: in broth, stir-fried, baked, and raw. (Orth, 2008.) Food is one of the most obvious ways that cultures define themselves, and constructing food norms is part of that definition. In China, where there is a long tradition of imbuing foods with specific spiritual and physical benefits, the penises of various animals are said to be potent agents for healing an array of conditions or illnesses. (Zhao, 2015.) Would a restaurant like this fly in your neck of the woods? Why or why not? What would be the reason for resistance?

Deviance is constructed by dominant groups. In society today, there are groups that have the power to label others as deviant, such as those in the judicial system, the penal system, the media, wealthy people and politicians. Sound familiar? Those who are most invested and have the most power in society have the power to decide which individuals and groups are labeled as deviant. Let's take a quick look at how black men are over-criminalized in our judicial system here in America, for example. There are more African American adults under correctional control today—in prison or jail, on probation or parole—than were enslaved in 1850, a decade before the Civil War began (Alexander, 2012). The over-criminalization of black men in the U.S. by a powerful, mainly white, justice system has acted to marginalize this population and drive into the American psyche the image of the young black male thug.

Deviance is not absolute: There Are No Absolutes (Except that there are no absolutes!?)

> *"No act is inherently deviant in and of itself. Deviance is defined socially and will vary from one group to another."*
>
> — *Emile Durkheim*

This is one of my favorite quotes because I believe it is true. If deviance were an absolute, we would see the same traits, behaviors, and beliefs labeled as deviant in every culture of the world. However, we do not. Pedophilia, bestiality, incest, and necrophilia are not inherently deviant. These acts have been and are currently practiced by a number of cultures around the world. Therefore, this variation in cultural practices shows us that deviance is relative to time and place. In a cultural vacuum, these acts are just acts like walking, running, or sleeping. However, none of us lives in a cultural vacuum; we live in cultures that have developed a set of rules whose transgressions carry consequences, such as being viewed as deviant. Deviance, then, is relative to *where* and *when* you are.

Can Deviance Be Good for Us?

When you hear the word deviance, what thought or image jumps to mind? Is it something negative? Deviance does have a negative connotation for most people, typically conjuring up images of traits or behaviors that are viewed to be annoying, disgusting, dangerous, or even immoral (Kooistra and Harrison, 2007). However, deviance can be viewed differently. Emile Durkheim (1893) saw deviance as a natural and necessary part of society. Our man Durkheim lays out four ways in which deviance and crime can act as mechanisms to reinforce social order and bring about social change:

Deviance can affirm cultural values and norms. Understanding that deviance can result in punishment reinforces what a society views as acceptable or unacceptable. When criminals are sent to prison, our culturally held values that crime is unhealthy for society are affirmed. While we recognize that deviance will be part of our social world, we also believe that it will be dealt with appropriately so that it does not threaten or diminish our way of life.

Deviance defines moral boundaries. I think most people would respect the funeral of a fallen soldier. Regardless of your political views, funerals are typically a solemn and private event. However, the Westboro Baptist Church (WBC) regularly protests the funerals of soldiers and Marines while brandishing banners that read "Thank God for Dead Soldiers," "Soldiers Die 4 Fag Marriage," "Thank God for Sept. 11," and "God Hates America." This church is filled with hate, but Durkheim sees a purpose in its madness. Most people would find all of these slogans morally reprehensible, seeing them as crossing some unspoken moral boundary.

Therefore, the deviant vitriol of this organization creates a sort of moral boundary that most Americans are not willing to cross, clearly creating two groups of people: *us*—who would not engage in hate speech and defile funerals, and *them*—deviants who are willing to defile funerals, inflict emotional injury on grieving loved ones, and spew venomous hate speech. These WBC people are whack jobs. They believe that the fallen soldiers are "... troops whom God has killed in Iraq/Afghanistan in righteous judgment against an evil nation," meaning that because we as a nation do not condemn or put gay people to death and we support gay marriage and gay rights, God will punish us by killing our troops—you read it right (Westboro Baptist Church, 2016). Moreover, they believe God is getting back at gay-loving America by killing soldiers, who deserve to die because we as a nation have chosen human rights over some vengeful God. What rock did they climb out from under?

Deviance can promote social unity or solidarity. That is, deviance and/or criminal acts can foster the feeling of us vs. them. In our history, there have been two glaring instances of deviance that created a sense of solidarity among Americans. The attack on Pearl Harbor and September 11, 2001, were both monstrous criminal acts perpetrated against America. In the aftermath of both of these events, Americans came together in variety of ways to show their unity. In the wake of Pearl Harbor, Americans expressed their solidarity in a variety of ways, such as record numbers of men and women volunteering for military service, conserving food and needed materials, and watching what they said and whom they said it to. During World War II, many Americans would not buy any German products, and some went as far as not eating frankfurters (the German term for the hot dog).

After the 9/11 attacks, I remember seeing more American flags than I had ever seen before: people were flying them in front of their homes, some firefighters raised a flag at ground zero that very day, and it seems like everyone had American flag stickers on their cars. Some stores had a hard time keeping American flags in stock for some time after 9/11.

Deviance can lead to social change. On December 1, 1955, Rosa Parks boarded a Montgomery, Alabama, bus and headed home after another long day of work. The white section of the bus was full, and the bus driver ordered Parks to give up her seat in the colored section to a white male, but she refused. She was subsequently arrested for the violation of a local segregation code but was tried on charges of disorderly conduct as well as violating the local code. Her arrest and trial led to the Montgomery bus boycott. In fact, just over a year after her arrest, on December 21, 1956, Montgomery buses were legally integrated. Her act of defiance, her recognition that some laws are unjust, and her being just flat-out tired of being mistreated as a human, set in motion a movement that was eventually successful in striking down Jim Crow laws, and culminated in the passing of the Civil Rights Act of 1964.

AN UNKIND ACT

The bus driver that got Rosa Parks arrested that day was a pretty unsavory fellow. Twelve years earlier he made Rosa Parks exit the bus, after she paid her fare, so she could re-enter at the rear of the bus through the entrance for colored people (Hanson, 2011). She exited the bus, but before she could make it to the rear entrance, the bus driver drove off, leaving her to walk home in the rain. What an asshole.

How Do We Explain Deviance?

For a long time, many people have attempted to explain deviance. What have emerged are a number of discredited theories and a number that have persisted. These attempts to explain deviance can be placed into four basic categories: the supernatural, biological, psychological, and sociological.

Supernatural Explanations of Deviance

For millennia, deviant behaviors were explained by spiritual temptation or possession. The belief that spirits, angels, and especially the devil actively influenced the lives of men, women, and children and were the explanations for a host of phenomena, including crop failure, illness, and witchcraft, helped define deviance until the modern era. The Bible is filled with examples of individuals who are described as suffering a range of afflictions, and their deviance is attributed to God's wrath, blasphemy, or demonic possession—all supernatural explanations.

This supernatural or spiritual world was real and a part of everyday life for the inhabitants of 1692 Salem, Massachusetts, where twenty people were executed for being witches. Unbelievably, twenty innocent people were either hanged or pressed (stones placed on top of the person until he was crushed to death) because of fear and supernatural explanations of deviant behavior, specifically witchcraft (Wilson, 1997). People, mostly women, were routinely accused of witchcraft, and once labeled as witches, the women either confessed or denied the accusations. Oddly enough, those who confessed to being witches were not tried and lived out their lives marginalized from the community or simply moved away. Those who proclaimed their innocence (because they were) rarely escaped the hangman. (Contrary to popular belief, no witches were ever burned to death in the colonies).

Wow, glad we're done with that nonsense, right? Think again: witch-hunts are still around. In Ghana, West Africa, there a number of *witch camps* that house hundreds of women that have been accused of being witches or blamed for the death of family members or other villagers (Whitaker, 2012). They are believed to have supernatural powers that have resulted in injury, death, or the outbreak of disease. Their punishment for their perceived deviant behavior is banishment to the camps. Apparently, we still fear what we do not understand, and moreover, some still seek an irrational supernatural explanation.

Fig. 6.3 Women are banished to "Witch Camps" because they are wrongly believed to be responsible for a range of illnesses or tragedies that have befallen their communities.

Biological Explanations of Deviance

Phrenology, or the study of the shape and size of one's skull to determine character and personality, was an attempt by Victorian-age pseudoscientists to map the mind. A phrenologist would run his hands over the skull, feeling the indentations and enlargements, and from this assessment determine the relative size of the various regions of the mind and determine the temperament and character of the individual. Then, a map of one's skull would be drawn, illustrating the location and relationship between all the regions. It was further believed by phrenologists that through this process, they could determine criminal or deviant tendencies in people. Ultimately, this practice was shown to be meritless and has been completely discredited. It should be noted that while they could not predict criminal intentions, phrenologists advocated rehabilitating criminals rather than warehousing them, which was a progressive idea at that time.

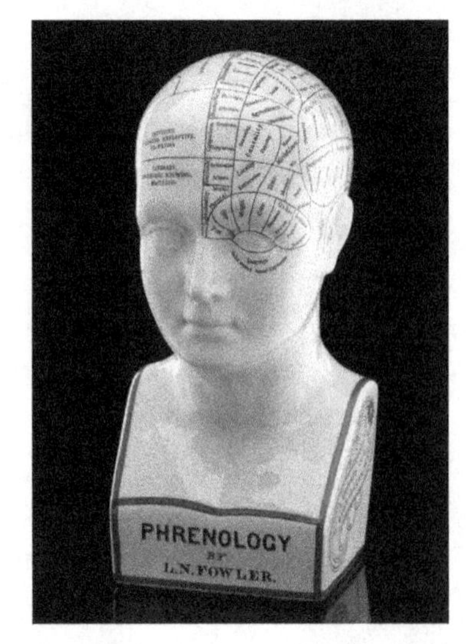

Fig. 6.4 Fowler's Phrenological Head

Body Types

In the 1940s, a psychologist named William Herbert Sheldon (1954) attempted to predict criminal or deviant behavior based on an individual's body type. That's right, he believed that for each of his designated body types, there was a set of corresponding personality characteristics—intelligence, temperament, and moral worth—that were set in genetic stone, as it were, unwavering over the life span. Basically, this guy thought he could tell who you were as a person from looking at the shape of your body. Body type as destiny? Sheldon proposed three body types (somatotypes):

- *Ectomorph*: Tall and thin with a flat chest, lightly muscled with a delicate build.
- *Mesomorph*: Muscular, rectangular shape with thick skin and an upright posture.
- *Endomorph*: Short and corpulent with underdeveloped muscles and a round shape.

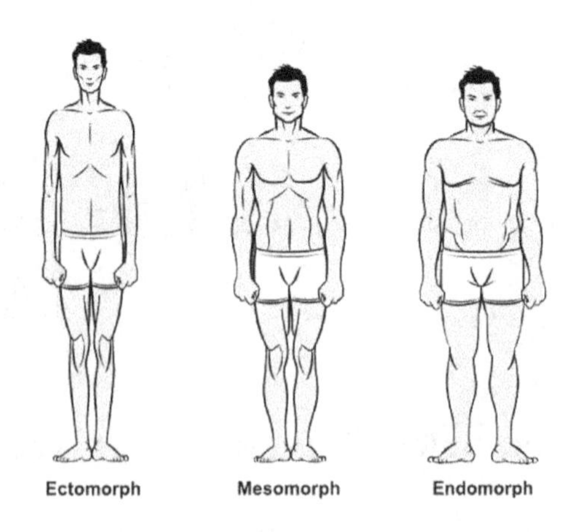

Fig. 6.5 Sheldon's Three Body Types. Believed to be associated with temperament, personality characteristics and propensity toward crime. Does your body type influence your personality or world view?

Sheldon proposed that mesomorphs were far more likely to engage in delinquency and have criminal tendencies. However, there really is no sound scientific evidence to show a significant connection between one's body shape and a propensity to engage in deviant or criminal behaviors. Sheldon's longtime research assistant even went as far as to claim that Sheldon fudged his data, falsifying data to fit his theory. Sheldon held both a Ph.D. and an M.D., which seemed to legitimize his work until a female freshman complained to her parents about his data collection methods, which began his rapid descent into scientific disgrace. Fortunately, his work has been discredited and viewed by many as quackery. While his science was crap, there could be a grain of truth in it (Butler et al., 1992; Vertinsky, 2007). Do you think that body shape and attractiveness can influence how others perceive us and how we view ourselves?

TABLE 6.1. Sheldon's Body Types and Personality Characteristics

Body Type	Temperament
Endomorph	Sociable, fun-loving, love of food, tolerant, even-tempered, good-humored, relaxed, a love of comfort, and the need for affection. Endomorphs are gregarious and just like to chill.
Ectomorph	Self-conscious, private, introverted, inhibited, socially anxious, artistic, intense, emotionally restrained, and thoughtful. Ectomorphs are uptight, private people.
Mesomorph	Adventurous, courageous, indifferent to what others think, assertive, bold, physically active, competitive, desire to dominate and engage in risky activities. Mesomorphs are outgoing, action-oriented people whom Sheldon thought of as criminal types.

Take a look at the characteristics Sheldon associated with each body type. Do we hold stereotypes about certain body types? Are large people viewed as lazy and unhappy? Are mesomorphs viewed as more competent and likable? Do you think your friends or family members are stereotyped by their body shape? Do people come to be who they are in part because of how people perceive what they are like because of their body shape?

TRY THIS

For each of your friends or other people you know well, consider what body type they would be, and then see if their personalities or temperaments match up to characteristics listed for their body type in table 6.1 above. You really shouldn't see a strong association between the characteristics listed and your friends' personalities. You can see that many of the traits listed are vague or traits that we all possess—like the need for affection—regardless of our body type.

NUDE POSTURE PHOTO PROJECT

How did Sheldon collect data on body types? For decades, he and a colleague, Earnest Albert Hooton, took nude photos of incoming freshmen at a number of Ivy League schools and affiliated colleges, amassing thousands of nude pics. The nude "posture photo" program began, independently of Sheldon's research, around the turn of the twentieth century. It was ostensibly designed to determine the goodness of students' posture, thought at the time to be a key indicator of health. Sheldon and Hooton hijacked that program to collect data for their body type theory. Yep, college freshmen were required to strip naked and be photographed from the front, in profile, and behind as part of freshman orientation. What would you say if you were told to strip naked for freshman orientation? Hell no! If that wasn't creepy enough, at least two past presidents, a number of celebrities, and other notable Americans whose names you would easily recognize were photographed nude during that period. The program was finally discontinued in the 1970s. For decades, rumors abounded that the photos and/or their negatives had been stolen and were being circulated. Not to worry: the nude pics were located and destroyed by either the respective colleges or the Smithsonian Institution, which mysteriously acquired some of them (Rosenbaum, 1995).

The Extra Y Chromosome Theory

Along similar lines, researchers looking for a connection between our biology and criminal behavior proposed the extra Y chromosome theory. This theory attempted to show a connection between men who possessed an extra Y chromosome (XYY versus XY) and a propensity for criminal behavior. The condition known as 47, XYY or so-called "supermale syndrome" was believed to be linked to violent criminal behavior due to hyper-aggressiveness. Therefore, many researchers thought these men would be found in greater numbers among violent offender populations. Well, it is not that simple. The best evidence indicates that while these 47, XYY males may be taller on average than XY males and slightly more aggressive, they do not have a higher incidence of violent behavior toward others (Beckwith and King, 1974; Beckwith, 2002; Jacobs, 2006).

While there is slightly increased criminality among 47, XYY males, it tends to manifest in crimes against property and rarely against people. The real explanation is most likely not in the simple connection between aggression in 47, XYY males and criminality (even regular XY males in prison exhibit higher levels of aggression than the general population), but rather in a more complex connection between lower IQs, behavioral issues, and criminal behavior among the 47, XYY population. Being overtly taller than their classmates and suffering from severe acne (common among 47, XYY males) may compound any behavioral or cognitive issues these adolescent males already exhibit, leading to impulse control, poor judgment, and, ultimately, to deviant or criminal behavior. However, this is very likely the same set of circumstances and characteristics that predict criminality for all populations (Gardner, Griffiths, and Hamelin, 2012; Ratcliffe, 1994; Walzer, Bashir, and Silbert, 1990). The overwhelming majority of 47, XYY males live out normal lives, oblivious to their condition. Therefore, the extra Y chromosome theory provides no real explanation for criminal behavior.

Psychological Explanations of Deviance

Unlike supernatural explanations for deviant behaviors, psychological explanations seek to understand deviance as pathology of the individual and not some spiritual or demonic force controlling the individual. There are a range of psychological theories attempting to explain deviance. Some invoke psychic struggles, others show us that missteps in developmental stages lead to pathologies, and still others reduce it to reward and punishment.

Basically, Freud argued that all humans are in a psychological struggle between two opposing forces: our *id*, or our base impulses for food, sex, and pleasure, and our *superego*, the internalized understanding of our society's rules and conduct for satisfying those impulses. (Remember our discussion in Chapter 4?) Freud believed that we are all involved in this grand psychic struggle between satisfying our immediate impulses to have sex and poop and realizing that we have to wait until we get home to our partner to have sex and use a toilet. Typically, those individuals who cannot control their impulses end up engaging in any number of deviant acts such as rape, murder, or pooping on your front lawn. Many experience severe consequences of their actions, such as ending up in prison or dead.

Sociological Perspectives

Bumps on your head, your body type, and the possession of an extra Y chromosome do not provide valid or adequate explanations of deviance. In addition, while psychological approaches to deviance can be useful and provocative, observing the inner workings of the human mind is difficult, making the connection to deviance sometimes hard to establish. So, where can we look for some strong explanations of deviance? Sociology, of course! The following are some theories commonly used to explain deviance from the sociological perspective.

Cultural Transmission

A culture of deviance can be transmitted and is learned through interactions with others. Individuals who grow up and live in deviant subcultures/communities come to adopt the behaviors, beliefs, and values of those groups. If engaging in criminal behaviors are common and necessary ways for people in a particular subculture/community to survive, make a living, and provide for their families, then it will be viewed as normative for that group. Younger members are then socialized into this community of criminals and hustlers—to a certain degree, they are products of their environments; the culture of deviance has been learned through a range of experiences and interactions.

Shaw and McKay (1942) were two pretty smart cats who noticed that the high-crime areas of Chicago remained the same year after year. They found that as one ethnic group moved out of a high-crime area, another one took its place, then juvenile delinquency rates for the new group climbed, and the relocated group saw a drop in delinquency. Many young Latinos in Los Angeles grow up in neighborhoods where gang activity is bound up in the daily lives of its members. Criminal activity is a way of life, viewed as necessary for survival, and is transmitted from one generation of gang bangers to another (Parra, 2001).

READ MORE

- *The Cultural Matrix* by Orlando Patterson (2015). This work explores the complex world of urban black youths and how both structure and their crime-filled neighborhood cultures interplay with their own decisions to engage in crime. The book explores cultural transmission theory with an ear to hearing the voice of these urban youths. It's not just the environment; they make conscious choices and know that their values, attitudes, and actions are not the same as the dominant culture.

Differential Association

The primary conduit for the transmission of these criminal values, beliefs, and behaviors is in peer groups. This process is illustrated by Edwin Sutherland's (1947) theory of **differential association**—association with intimate groups that are engaged in criminal behavior will result in members' conformity to the values, beliefs, and behaviors of that group. Deviant values, beliefs, and behaviors are learned in context of intimate groups. Like me, Sutherland understood that people have a basic desire to fit in. That desire to be accepted by a group leads to conformity. No one hangs out with a group of people hoping she/he will be rejected—"Oh, I can't wait until these people I like don't accept me" is not something you hear people say!

So, if you are hanging out with a bunch of people involved in computer hacking, at some point you will conform to the behavior and ultimately be accepted by that group. The *differential* in this theory alludes to the notion that if you associate with *different* crowds, you will get different results. Think about the distinctive groups that could be identified in your high school: the stoners, the jocks, band geeks, student government types. Kids who hang out with the stoners are at one point going to have to smoke pot to be accepted by them and become a stoner. However, the kid who associates with the student government kids will most likely raise her grades, run for office, and conform to the more mainstream dominant norms of the school.

Labeling Theory: Primary Deviance, Secondary Deviance, and Stigma

She's a "ho" and he's a "playa." People are often labeled by others, which can many times result in negative social consequences. Rooted in symbolic interactionism, labeling theory argues that deviance exists once the label of deviance has been applied: "... deviance is *not* a quality of the act the person commits, but rather a consequence of the application by others of rules and sanctions to an 'offender.' The deviant is one to whom the label has successfully been applied; deviant behavior is behavior that people so label" (Becker, 1963).

That is a great quote, but what is Becker saying here? Basically, that no behavior and no one is deviant until a label of deviance has been applied to the behavior or person. **Labeling theory** has three main parts: (1) people are deviant once they have been labeled as deviant, (2) deviant labels can affect the way labeled individuals view themselves and how others view them, and (3) deviant labels are applied by those with social power. Think about it in terms of our discussion earlier in the chapter about the relative nature of deviance (nothing is inherently deviant). Deviance for labeling theorists is like beauty: it is in the eye of the beholder (Simmons, 1969).

Labeling theorists believe that until the group labels a person as deviant, neither the act nor the person are deviant, but once labeled, others' negative reaction to the label, and therefore their reaction to the person, can cause the individual to alter his self-perception and continue the deviant behavior. **Primary deviance**—deviant acts that elicit little reaction from others and have little to no effect on one's self-image—are minor norm violations that we all engage in frequently (Lemert, 1972). For instance, many of us are guilty of a number of minor infractions such as speeding, littering, or jaywalking. If you are speeding and littering and not being ticketed (which happens to many of us), this is not altering your self-image, and others aren't shouting out "there goes that litterer" when you walk by. Typically, we rationalize our behavior, telling ourselves we were speeding to get to class on time and that jaywalking when no cars are approaching saves us time.

However, habitually engaging in behaviors like drug abuse, heavy drinking, or sexual promiscuity so that "others take notice" will get us labeled as a tweaker, alcoholic, or ho. Once the label of deviance has been applied, people react negatively toward the individual, which may lead the individual to adopt a deviant identity. Thus, secondary deviance occurs when labeled individuals accept the label as part of their own identity, which leads them to act in ways that are consistent with others' expectations (Lemert, 1951).

A stigma is a powerful, negative social label that leads individuals to be devalued, discredited, and socially rejected. Stigmatized individuals experience negative social treatment that greatly impacts their self-concept. While stigmas can be the result of criminal activity, such as "sex offender," "felon," "rapist," or "pedophile," many other social groups are stigmatized for just being themselves. Erving Goffman (1963) identified three types of stigma: Physical, group identity, and character trait. *Physical stigma* refers to a physical deformity or defect, such as people with Down syndrome, amputees, and the blind. Many disabled people report a feeling of social isolation because of their physical disability. They feel as though they are irrationally stigmatized by nondisabled people, making it doubly hard to interact with others and feel socially included (Weiss, Ramakrishna, and Somma, 2006; Kittle, 2011). Stigmas, then, are labels that are so powerful they can prevent people from fully participating in society. Many times, stigmatized individuals are pushed to the margins of society, isolated, and discriminated against.

Group identity stigmas come from being a member of a particular religion, race, ethnic group, etc. Unfortunately, some people are stigmatized not for deviant or criminal behaviors, but simply being born a particular race or affiliating with a certain religion.

Character trait stigmas include things such as mental illness, drug addiction, alcoholism, and criminal background. Character trait stigmas might include labels such as "sex offender," "drunk" or "junkie." Stigmatized individuals come to accept their deviant identity and many times resign themselves to that identity. They experience a "self-fulfilling prophecy," assuming behaviors that are consistent with their stigma. Let's take my boy Jonathan for example.

Jonathan, who comes from a working-class family, was caught smoking pot when he was seventeen by his parents, and while they were a bit upset, they realized that he was just experimenting, and it was, after all, the 1970s. No police were involved, and it was dismissed as an innocent juvenile behavior typical of the times. At age twenty-three, Jonathan was arrested for brewing up some methamphetamines; he was tried, convicted, and sent inside for seven years. When he got out and returned to his hometown, he found it difficult to get work because he was labeled as a felon and drug dealer. As a result of not being able to find straight work, he started dealing drugs again. He figured if everyone was going to treat him like a drug dealer, he was going to be a drug dealer; besides, no one would hire him, and he had to make a living. This criminal label affected the way people reacted to and interacted with him, and it profoundly changed the way he viewed himself.

Central to the labeling perspective is the idea of power. That is, those with social power can determine what actions are labeled as deviant and who is more likely to be labeled. As painful as it may be, let's go back to high school again. Remember earlier in the chapter, we identified a number of social groups or cliques in our high schools like the jocks and geeks, etc. High schools, like human societies, have dominant cultures. In high school, those with power in the dominant culture are the most popular, high-achieving, good-looking kids. Let's call them the *pleasers*. The pleasers decide what "cool" is and what "uncool" (deviance) is. This group is the arbiter of cool and has the power to label others as uncool or deviant. For example, one of the pleasers comes to school wearing his clothes inside out, and they all think it is hilarious and creative—a statement to the absurdity of the fashion industry and how we are all just slaves to fashion.

Soon after that, a few of the stoners come to school wearing their clothes inside out, and a number of the pleasers notice and ridicule them for how stupid they look, telling them that they are so stoned they can't dress properly. Other groups will most likely join in deriding the stoners because the pleasers set the standards of deviance by having the power to label others, and members of other groups do not want to take the chance of being painted with the same brush of ridicule and embarrassment.

However, within each of the social groups we identified at our high schools, there is typically a hierarchy of power. So, even within these groups, there are members who have the power to label other members as deviant—especially if they stray from what the group considers cool. A stoner who refuses to skip school to get high one day in order to take an exam may be labeled as teacher's pet by others in the group and possibly be ostracized or given the silent treatment for a few days because he violated the expected behaviors of the group.

Social Control

Above, I discussed a variety of theories that attempt to explain how people come to be viewed as deviant and/or engage in deviant behaviors—essentially, explanations of how people come to be deviant. While that's necessary to explore, to me, it is not nearly as interesting as how most of us will not engage in any seriously deviant or criminal behavior over our lifetimes. Sure, like we discussed above, from time to time we all engage in "primary deviance," minor infractions that do not draw attention from others and do not affect our self-image: a little underage drinking here, a little littering there, and maybe a bit of drunk texting.

What is more interesting is how most people will do what I refer to as "color within the lines." Remember that as a kid, your parents and teachers would praise or reward you for coloring within the lines of the images in your coloring books. You were encouraged to color within the lines because everyone told you that was the right way to color. Moreover, most of us learned to color within the lines because we sought praise and came to believe it was the right thing to do.

Social control involves the social processes and practices that promote conformity and obedience among members of society. Social control, then, encourages all of us to stay within the lines of normative boundaries. There are a number of mechanisms at work in society that lead us to believe that we are doing the right thing and to act according to those beliefs. Social control comes both from within all of us and from influences outside of all of us. As we have seen in chapters 3 and 4, people learn how to navigate their social worlds through learning and accepting appropriate beliefs and behaviors—the process of socialization. The internalization of social values and beliefs is necessary for individuals to conduct themselves in socially appropriate ways and ultimately to be integrated, productive citizens who conform to societal norms—they *fit in*.

Like the renowned criminologist Travis Hirschi (1969), I prefer *not* to ask the criminal why she/he does crime, but why the great majority of us *do not* do crime. The answer for Hirschi can be found in the pro-social bonds we form with others and our communities. In his *social bond/social control theory*, he argued that bonds are responsible for controlling us when we are tempted to engage in criminal or deviant behavior. He said that these bonds come in four interconnected forms:

Attachment: The strong social attachments we create with others, communities, and institutions encourage conformity to social norms. Throughout our lives, we establish a number of emotional attachments to others—our parents, friends, our neighborhood, and romantic partners. These attachments, in turn, constrain our behavior because we do not want to disappoint our loved ones or lose the relationships we have with them by committing crimes. Have you ever thought to yourself, "My mom/dad would be so mad with me if I (insert deviant act/crime)"? These thoughts inform our decisions not to take part in deviant or criminal behavior. The stronger our attachments to parents, friends, and others, the greater the level of social control we experience. Alternately, weak emotional attachments leave individuals at great risk for performing deviant or criminal acts.

Commitment: The more committed individuals are to legitimate opportunities, the more likely they are to conform to social norms. Commitment can include marriage and family, jobs, mortgages, and membership in a range of organizations. People who are married with kids and have a mortgage to pay, neighbors to help, and Girl Scout cookies to sell are far less likely to engage in deviant and criminal behavior. Most of us do not want to jeopardize our marriage, employment, or standing in the community by committing deviant or criminal acts. Those with few commitments are more likely to be attracted toward deviance and crime. Again, these bonds of commitment, like attachment, serve as sources of social control.

Involvement: Attachments and commitments take up a great deal of our time. We spend most of our time living our lives, doing legitimate activities such as taking the kids to basketball practice, mowing the lawn, preparing dinner, and going to work. If we are engaged in all these legitimate, time-consuming endeavors, then we don't have the time for crime.

Belief: The stronger the belief in conventional social values and behaviors, the greater the likelihood of social conformity. Most people do not engage in deviant/criminal behaviors *not* because they are afraid of breaking the rules and being punished, but rather because they are too busy following the rules because they *believe* their behavior is appropriate. Think about it: do you struggle each day deciding whether you should rob a bank for money, or are you too busy working and going to school—behaviors that most individuals *believe* to be the socially correct thing to do?

This internalization of social values, beliefs and behaviors that lead people to engage in appropriate social interactions when no one else is around is what sociologists refer to as **internal social control.** Most societies rely heavily on internalization through the process of socialization to establish social order. If people failed to internalize this kind of self-control, then there would have to be law enforcement, paramilitary, and military personnel on every street corner to ensure that people conformed and complied with all the rules.

External social control is when others respond to one's behavior with approval or disapproval. That is, others will either approve or not approve of our behavior. This approval and/or disapproval can be thought of as rewards and punishments that strive to guide behavior toward desired social conduct. **Sanctions** are the rewards or punishments given in response to individuals' behaviors, which seek to either encourage or discourage those behaviors. **Positive sanctions** are actions that reward behaviors that are considered desirable, such as getting a raise at work for being innovative or enjoying a high credit score for being responsible with your credit, paying bills on time, and buying stuff with credit cards.

There are many programs around the country that reward designated drivers by providing them with free non-alcoholic drinks, free cover charges at clubs, and free appetizers. Obviously, these programs are designed to promote designated driving and decrease driving under the influence. These are commonly used positive sanctions. Take a look at a creative use of positive sanctions in the insert Police Hand out Rewards.

POLICE HAND OUT REWARDS

In early 2015, the Farmington, New Hampshire, police department struck upon an interesting idea. In an attempt to both boost the police department's image and reward good civic behavior, the police began handing out coupons for free pizza slices to law-abiding citizens (Keady, 2015). So, if you find yourself in rural New Hampshire and you use the crosswalk, keep your pooch on its leash, or pick up litter off the streets, you may have a run-in with the police—and get some free pizza.

Negative sanctions are actions that punish behaviors that are perceived as socially undesirable. For example, being put on academic probation because you partied too much last semester or being arrested for hacking the school's computer system and giving yourself all A's for the last three years. Alternatively, for example, your wife withholding sex from you because you got drunk at her company's holiday party and embarrassed her by dancing around with a lampshade on your head.

Both positive and negative sanctions are used to control behavior, and these sanctions can be applied by agents of social control—individuals, groups, and institutions that have the official or unofficial ability to sanction deviance. Those who have power or authority, such as police, parents, umpires, deans and college professors exercise formal social control. It's easy to see how formal social control is exercised in the world. For example, police make arrests, judges sentence criminals to prison, deans can expel students, and parents ground their children. On the flip side, parents can reward their child with a new car for good grades, and a fraternity president could honor the pledge who drank the most Pabst Blue Ribbon. Those with the power and authority society or organizations have vested in them perform formal social control.

These *agents of social control* can take many forms; they can have positions of power and/or authority, or they can be ordinary citizens. Informal social control is used by ordinary people in everyday interactions to approve or disapprove of behaviors. These could include the disapproving look you get from your partner for your insensitive comments or being flipped off by the angry driver you just cut off in traffic. Getting a standing ovation for your riveting oral report on informal social control or the cheers from the crowd that has gathered to watch you rescue a cat from a tree represent positive informal social control.

Think about it this way: social control is necessary for all societies to maintain social order. Some societies, such as North Korea, are not subtle about their control mechanisms. They sustain propaganda campaigns against free Western nations, stage large, festival-like events that exalt the leadership, and starve and imprison their citizenry to maintain tight social control. Other nations use less obvious and more insidious methods like maintaining religious ideologies that constrain and control the behaviors of both men and women. Ultimately, social control is maintained through a combination of agents of social control, internalization of values and beliefs, and sanctions.

Crime and Punishment

Hacking the cloud in order to release nude photos of celebrities, shooting up an elementary school and killing more than twenty people, bilking thousands of investors out of billions of dollars, trafficking young girls around the world and forcing them into prostitution, or poaching rhinoceroses (cutting off their horns, and leaving them to die in the hot African sun). All of these are examples of crime, but all are very different types. Crime, as noted earlier in the chapter, is the violation of formal social norms or laws. However, when we think of crime, we are more likely to think of the response to it than the violation. That is, crime brings with it severe consequences for the violation of laws. Those responses vary by the type of crime, the severity of the crime, the age, sex, and race of the offender, and the prevailing social climate.

Measuring Crime

When you hear newscasts about the crime rate going up, going down, or staying the same, you probably imagine that someone, somewhere, is calculating all the crime that was committed in the last year. Is this true? Yes and no. Yes, the FBI produces the annual Uniform Crime Report (UCR), the official measure of crime in the United States. No, the UCR is not a measure of *all* crime reported. The FBI calculates the UCR by tabulating the number of crimes reported by more than 18,000 law enforcement agencies from around the country. For inclusion in the UCR, however, the FBI only counts eight types of crime that fall into two categories (see table 6.2 below): *violent crimes* and *property crimes*.

TABLE 6.2 The Uniform Crime Report's Crime Index

Violent Crime	Property Crime
Murder	Burglary
Aggravated Assault	Larceny-Theft
Rape	Motor Vehicle Theft
Robbery	Arson

The violent crimes category includes murder, forcible rape, aggravated assault, and robbery. The property crimes category is made up of motor vehicle theft, burglary, larceny-theft, and arson. It's obvious that the reports you hear about are not a complete accounting of all crime committed; moreover, they are only a record of those crimes *reported* to law enforcement. However, the UCR is a useful tool in tracking both trends and patterns in crime. The UCR allows criminologists to view trends in crime over time and can locate patterns in criminal activity, such as comparing urban vs. rural crime rates.

So, how can we get a fuller picture of the number and types of crimes committed? In 1973, the Department of Justice started the National Crime Victimization Survey (NCVS) in an attempt to capture those crimes that were not reported to law enforcement. The NCVS compiles data from law enforcement agencies as well as surveying more than 90,000 households, representing about 160,000 individual responses about crimes that were not reported to law enforcement, producing national

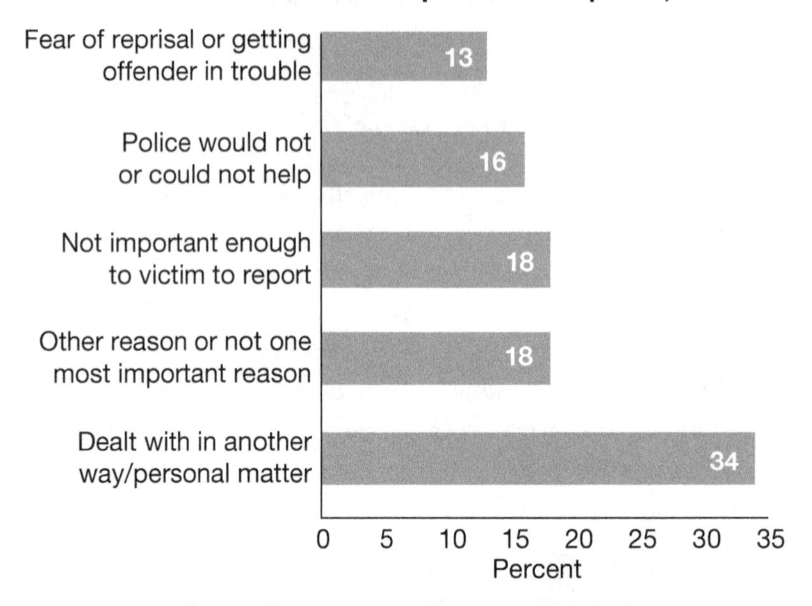

Fig. 6.6 U.S. Department of Justice Special Report: National Crime Victimization Survey

estimates of criminal victimization (Bureau of Justice Statistics, "National Crime Victimization Survey," 2015). Even with this effort, a significant amount of crime continues to go unreported. Therefore, the combination of reported crime contained in the UCR and unreported crime captured by the NCVS gives us a more accurate idea of the number and types of crimes committed nationally.

Why do you think people are reluctant to report crimes? Can you come up with at least three reasons why people are reluctant to report them? Now, take a look at figure 6.6 and see if your choices match up with what victims had to say.

In the period from 2006 to 2010, nearly 3.4 million violent crimes went unreported; that is more than half of all violent victimizations. As you can see from figure 6.6, most people (34%) dealt with the crime in another way, whether handling it personally or reporting it to non-law enforcement personnel such as a superior or school counselor. I think it is interesting that 16%, or more than a half-million victims, did not think the police could or would do anything about it. While Americans report a number of reasons for not reporting crime there are some categories of crime that are more underreported than others. Even though there is an underreporting of all crimes, rape and sexual assaults are grossly underreported, along with other violent crimes like assault and robbery (Truman, Planty and Langton, 2013; Wolitzky-Taylor et al., 2010). Why do you think these types of crime are so underreported?

Trends in Crime

A comprehensive description and exploration of trends in crime is beyond the scope of this chapter, but we can get a good look at the general trends in crime and then examine some crimes that seem to be on the rise. From about 1960 through the early 1990s, violent crime rose fairly steadily, but then unexpectedly, violent crime rates fell dramatically through 2001 and then began a general decline that continues to today (Fox and Zawitz, 2007). In figure 6.7, the chart illustrates these general trends. Sometimes referred to as the "1990s crime decline," this dramatic fall in crime rates has been attributed to several factors that include demographics, economics, policing strategies, gun laws, and prison expansion.

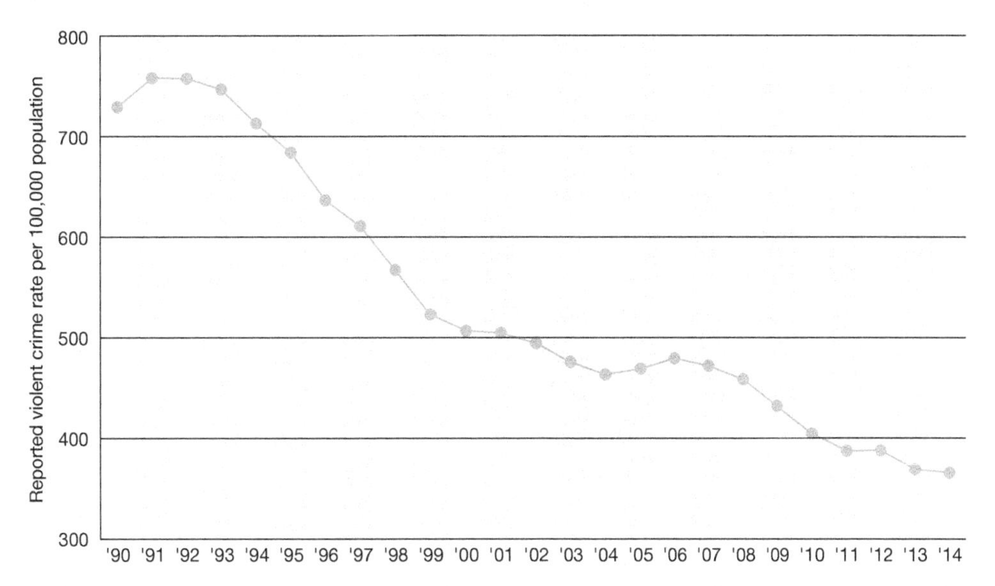

Fig. 6.7 The Crime Decline, 1990 through 2014. This graph illustrates the fall of violent crime in the U.S. over a twenty-four-year period.

Unfortunately, these explanations are woefully inadequate in fully accounting for the dramatic fall in violent crime that we have witnessed since 1991. Because of a demographic bulge of juveniles, John DiIulio, Jr. (1995) infamously predicted that millions of young men that he referred to as "juvenile super-predators" would wreak havoc on our society by creating a surge in violent crimes. This prediction was based on the belief that an increase in young males in a population is accompanied by a rise in the rates of violent crime. DiIulio, Jr. (2005) stated, "... nothing affects crime rates more than the number of young males in the population," predicting that as a result of these millions of young men being added to the population, we, as a society, will suffer waves of violent, predatory crimes over the next two decades. So much for predicting the future. The demographic bulge showed up, but there was no wave of juvenile super-predators roaming the streets, driving the rest of us indoors for fear of falling victim to testosterone-driven, violent criminals. In fact, the violent crime rate has kept on dropping during the last decade since DiIulio made his prediction, even in the face of this demographic event. Yep, more young men in the population but less violent crime (less crime overall), which does not bode well for a fully demographic explanation of violent crime rates.

So much for a strong demographic explanation. As we have seen in other chapters, economic factors seem to be instrumental in explaining various social phenomena. Let's take a look at the economic impact on crime rates. If a strong economy is associated with a decline in crime, and economic downturns are associated with increases in crime rates, then we would expect that the booming economy of the 1990s would be linked to dropping crime rates, and that is indeed what we saw. Then the argument would be that between 2008 and 2012, we would see an upswing in crime due to the severe economic downturn resulting from the mortgage debacle. However, this was not the case.

Let's take murder, the most accurately recorded and most serious crime, for example. If we look at figure 6.8, we see that murder rates from 1990 to 2013 have dropped almost in half, and universally, murder rates have plummeted in every major American city and in every region of the country (FBI, "Crime in the United States, 2013," 2014). If we look specifically at homicide rates for the years 2008–13, we see a steady decline in murder rates even in the face of serious economic troubles. It seems that economic explanations come up short in explaining the continuing decline in crime. In fact, econometrics give researchers a number of sophisticated tools to work on the problem of crime decline, but unfortunately, econometrics consistently fail to account for most of the variation in crime rates (Manzi, 2012).

Along comes economist Steven Levitt (2004), who shows that factors commonly associated with crime decline, such as innovative policing strategies, gun control laws, increased reliance on prisons, strong economy, and demographic changes, do *not* account for the decline. Rather, he identifies four factors that account for "... virtually the entire observed decline in crime," and these include the waning crack epidemic, increased number of police, the rising prison population, and the legalization of abortion. Unlike other attempts at explaining crime decline, Levitt suggests that a specific combination of factors is responsible for the decline. These include putting more police on the streets, incarcerating more people, having fewer people involved in crime to support a crack habit, and fewer "unwanted" babies born to mothers who, he believes, will abuse and/or abandon them to the streets, where they will ultimately become the juvenile super-predators that DiIulio warned us about.

While these explanations account for some of the decline in violent crime, no single sociological theory or combination of theories adequately explains the huge drop in violent crime. I would like to show that sociological explanations account for nearly all the decline in crime so I

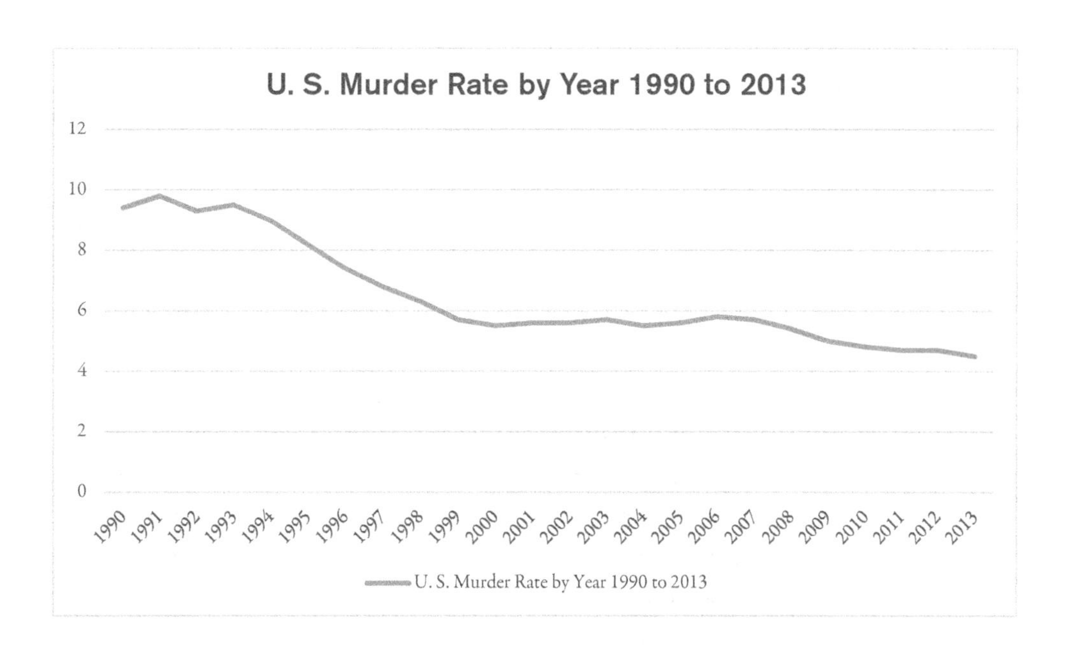

Fig. 6.8 U.S. Murder Rate by Year 1990–2013

could proudly and conspicuously strut around my college's campus, feeling secure and a bit smug in the knowledge that sociology can accurately and fully explain social phenomena, but I can't.

What does provide us with a fuller answer to this crime decline, you ask? Wait for it ... lead. More precisely, tetraethyl lead, the stuff they started adding to gasoline in the 1920s. That's right, leaded gasoline. Compelling research and arguments have demonstrated a powerful connection between the drop in lead levels and the decline in violent crimes (Needleman, 2004; Nevin, 2000; Reyes, 2007; Wright et al., 2008). Here is how the proponents of this perspective lay out their argument.

Kids growing up in the era between the 1940s and the 1970s were exposed to high levels of atmospheric lead as a result of the post-war economic boom that allowed all their parents to buy cars. All these new cars spewed record amounts of lead-laden exhaust into the atmosphere, where the kids' developing brains were affected from ingesting all the airborne lead. Recent research shows that even moderate levels of lead in the body results in a host of neuroanatomical abnormalities, including permanent loss of grey matter in the prefrontal cortex, the part of the brain associated with aggressiveness, impulsivity, emotional regulation, attention, verbal reasoning, and mental flexibility. To top off all those issues, for decades, we have known that increased lead levels in children result in lowered IQs. Breathing in all that lead affected the brains of all those generations of kids and resulted in an array of behavioral difficulties and cognitive deficits, almost all of which are associated with criminal profiles.

Fast-forward twenty years, and we see the rise in violent crime rates of the 1960s, '70s and '80s. What we have is a couple generations of lead-soaked kids with all kinds of emotional, behavioral, and cognitive issues, doing lots of crime and driving up the crime rates. Beginning in the 1970s right through 1996, when it was banned in the U.S., leaded gas production and consumption falls, dramatically reducing the amounts of lead in the atmosphere. Therefore, the crime decline we started to witness in the 1990s should just be the front edge of an overall continuing decrease in crime (Cecil et al., 2008; Drum, 2013). Perhaps most interesting is that this lead level-crime connection has been detected at the international, national, state, local, and individual levels.

Unraveling the complex nature of the crime decline is not an easy task and demands that we take into account all the variables that can help us explain this phenomenon. I am not abandoning the more traditional sociological, econometric, or demographic approaches to explaining the crime decline, but evidence from them is not adequate for any one of them to be the main cause. Including the lead level-crime connection is just good science sleuthing that will lead to a more comprehensive understanding of the crime decline. Because the crime decline was so unexpected and dramatic, sociology has been unable to produce adequate explanations for it. Ultimately, the crime decline we have been witnessing for the past two decades will no doubt only be fully understood by including all of the factors we have discussed.

The Demographics of Crime

Who is committing crime in the United States? While knowing how much crime there is and where it is most likely to happen is important, understanding what types of people are more likely to commit and be the victims of crime is essential to understanding the cause of crime. There are several variables that are involved in understanding who is engaging in crime: *age, race, gender, and social class.*

Age: Young people overwhelmingly commit more crime than any other group. This has been the case in the United States since the mid-1930s. The peak ages for criminal activity are between fifteen and twenty-four. In 2013, those aged fifteen to twenty-four made up nearly 35% of all arrests in the U.S., while those aged fifty and older comprised just 10.7% of arrests and those sixty-five and older accounted for a mere .9% (FBI, "Crime in the United States, 2013," 2014). These age differences in criminal activity are explained in part by what criminologists refer to as *aging out of crime.* As people *age out of crime*, they take on more responsibilities and new statuses and roles such as wage earner, parent, spouse, etc. The possibility of jail time becomes a relatively more serious matter because of the impact it will have on the perpetrators' lives and responsibilities.

Other reasons we see these age differences may be that younger criminals are engaged in more visible crimes like gang activity, assault, and robbery, while older people are more likely to engage in crimes that are more difficult to detect like insider trading or embezzlement. Additionally, the belief that young people are more likely to be criminally active may motivate the police to harass (stop and frisk), accuse, and arrest young people more than seniors.

Gender: Males are far more likely to engage in crime than females, and this is a global phenomenon. In 2013, of all people arrested in the U.S., 74% were male and 26% were female. If we focus on violent crimes, males account for 88% of homicide arrests and a predictable 98% of arrests for rape. Overall, men account for 80% of all violent crimes arrests compared to 20% for women. When attempting to explain gender patterns in crime, researchers typically focus on three general areas: socialization, socioeconomic status, and differential treatment of the genders by the criminal justice system (Farrington and Painter, 2004).

In general, boys are encouraged to be more aggressive, competitive, impulsive, and rebellious, and girls are expected to be more dependent, passive, and expressive. These gendered traits become reinforced in society as children grow older, preparing girls for home life and boys for roles outside the home, affording them more opportunity for criminal activity (Lindsey, 2015). Basically, boys will be boys and be aggressive and get in trouble and that is expected, but a good girl has no business getting into trouble. However, these gender roles are changing; women have many more opportunities outside the home, and this is reflected in their economic power and crime rates.

Low crime rates among women were traditionally tied to their low socioeconomic status (SES). Traditionally, women were more financially dependent on men and they had children who depended on them. Both these factors contributed to women refraining from criminal activity. However, in recent years, there has been a surge in female arrests, convictions, and incarceration. As social change allows women more latitude in activities outside the home, finances become a driver for crime, especially when we see these increases primarily in property crimes and drug offenses.

The number of females incarcerated increased 33% between 2000 and 2008, and arrest rates for women increased 11.6% compared to a decrease of 3.1% for men in the same period. With more recent data, an alarming trend emerges: Overall arrests were down for both sexes in the period covering 2004–13, a significant decrease of 18.3% for men but only a drop of 5.2% for women. However, if we look across all UCR crimes, we find a decline in arrests for *all* crimes for men but an overall increase of 15.5% in property crime arrests for women (FBI, "Crime in the United States, 2012", 2013).

According to the *chivalry hypothesis*, police, prosecutors, and judges are reluctant to arrest, prosecute, and incarcerate women precisely because they are women: maternal, loving, caregiving, and "weak" (Embry and Lyons, Jr., 2012). There was strong support for this hypothesis in the past, but recent data shows support weakening, mainly because of the increased number of women being arrested and having more frequent encounters with the courts. Additionally, more women, like male offenders, are subject to mandatory minimum sentencing and "three strikes you're out" laws.

Race: Differences in race can be seen across the board regarding the criminal justice system. Differential treatment of people of color is reflected in arrest, conviction, and incarceration rates. While more whites are arrested each year, they represent a much smaller proportion of the total white population. Of those arrested in 2013, 69% where white and 28.3% were black. Blacks make up less than 13% of the U.S. population but represent 28% of all arrests and 39% of arrests for violent crimes.

For example, America's war on drugs is expensive, inefficient, and racially biased. Let's take smoking pot, for example. While marijuana use rates are roughly the same between whites and blacks in the U.S., if you are black and like to puff, you are nearly four times more likely to be arrested than your white pot-smoking friends are. In 2010, the black arrest rate for marijuana possession was 716 per 100,000 but only 192 per 100,000 for whites (American Civil Liberties Union, 2013).

Seeing such stark differences in arrests between races, we have to ask why this is happening. In general, cops tend to focus their attention on neighborhoods with high rates of crime. Those neighborhoods tend to be populated by members of low-income minority groups. Cops patrolling those neighborhoods are often empowered to stop and frisk residents on the slimmest of pretexts, and because of that, they are likelier to find people who are carrying marijuana (ACLU, 2013).

Here is a disturbing fun fact that influences police departments' motivation for busting people for minor drug infractions. A federal program called the Byrne Justice Assistance Grant gives money to local police departments based on the number of drug arrests they make (U.S. Department of Justice, "Byrne Justice Assistance Grant", 2016). With many local police departments struggling with thin budgets, they may see federal programs like this as necessary for their survival, providing incentive for them to keep on busting tokers.

Social Class: The same argument we used above applies to the issue of social class. Police concentrate more resources in low-income neighborhoods, and subsequently, those in poorer areas are more likely to be targeted, arrested, convicted, and incarcerated than those in middle-class, suburban enclaves. This targeting and arresting of those in lower socioeconomic areas helps foster the impression that poor neighborhoods have high rates of crime.

Surveys of prison inmates show that about 68% have less than a high school education and only 11% report having any college education (Harlow, 2003). Those with a lack of education, which translates into fewer resources like money, property, or connections, are more likely to have an overworked and underpaid public defender. On the other hand, someone with more resources could afford their own attorney, who would most likely be more invested in a client who could pay and may even be a friend. More than 90% of those on death row were represented at trial by public defenders ... and look where it got them (ACLU, 2012).

The impact of social class on public and police perceptions is well-demonstrated in William Chambliss' (1973) study *The Saints and Roughnecks*. The Saints was a pseudonym for a group of upper-middle-class boys who came from well-respected families in well-to-do neighborhoods, and society expected them to do well in life. While the Saints were perceived as "good" kids, Chambliss reported that they engaged in an array of delinquent behavior such as drinking and stealing automobiles. But they were outwardly obedient toward authority figures and therefore labeled as "good boys." The Roughnecks, however, came from less well to do families and in general members of the community didn't expect them to be successful. While both groups engaged in deviant behaviors the two groups experienced very different reactions from adults. Most adults in the community dismissed the Saints' behavior because they perceived them as decent kids just being teenagers. However, those same members of the community defined the Roughnecks as troublemakers and were more likely to label them as deviant and punish their behaviors. Both groups of boys engaged in deviant behaviors but had different labels attached based primarily on their social class, and others treated them differently based on those different labels.

This is played out day after day in less well-to-do neighborhoods all over the country. When police roll into poorer neighborhoods, they have already decided that the youth there are up to no good and are more likely to stop and frisk them than their counterparts in wealthier neighborhoods. For example, the police in Miami Gardens, Florida, a working-class, predominately African American neighborhood with a population of about 111,000, made more than 99,980 "field contacts" (stop and frisk and/or question) on citizens between 2008 and 2013 (Chappell, 2013; Brennan and Lieberman, 2014). The number of these *same types of stops* for the entire Miami metropolitan area, with a population of about 5 million, in *the same period* was 3,753. The Miami Gardens police even stopped a five-year-old black youth who was described by police as a "suspicious person."

It is important to remember that the variables we have just discussed above—age, gender, race, and class—are interrelated. Black youth in poorer neighborhoods will be treated differently by the police and courts than wealthy, white, highly educated, older men—it's never just one thing. *Intersectionality* is the perspective that seeks to understand the complex interplay of race, gender, age, class, religion, sexual orientation, education, and even our geographic and historical location (Crenshaw, 1989). This perspective is sensitive to the connections between many of the variables we examine in sociology. For example, the police do not just harass young men—they stop and frisk lower-class, young, black males with few resources in high-crime neighborhoods.

Types of Crime

We have already seen two types of crime in our discussion of the FBI's Uniform Crime Report. Crimes against the person (violent crimes) involve bodily harm, the threat of bodily harm, or other actions committed against the will of an individual, including, but not limited to: murder, forcible rape, stalking, kidnapping, and hate crimes.

Crimes against property are any criminal acts that destroy another's property or deprive an owner of property against the owner's will. These may include such acts as motor vehicle theft, burglary, shoplifting, arson, and vandalism. Both crimes against the person and property are included in computations for national crime rates, but there are a number of other categories of crime that are not included in national calculations yet still impact our social world.

While I believe it to be a misnomer, **victimless crimes** are those offenses that are clearly violations of the law but have no identifiable victim. Some view these offenses as victimless because those involved are adults who are willingly exchanging goods or services. Common examples of victimless crimes are prostitution, gambling and recreational drug use. The reality is there are always victims of crimes. The person's house that is burgled so an addict can cop his heroin is the victim of his drug use. Crack babies and abused and discarded children are many times the victims of drug use and prostitution. Ultimately, the offenders are the victims. In a study that looked at street prostitutes, nearly all of those who responded reported being ripped off, assaulted, or physically abused by their johns (Venkatesh, 2010). Also, think about the harm that long-term drug use has on the addict and how many times that cost is passed on to the larger community through treatment and medical expenses.

In 2008, Bernard Madoff was arrested for bilking thousands of investors out of more than $50 billion in what today is still the largest Ponzi scheme ever uncovered. He stole all this money without ever threatening a single person, without taking a single purse or wallet, and without using any violence. People, businesses, and other investors gave their money to him, some even forcing him to take their investments. His reputation of being able to produce huge returns on investments had grown over the previous two decades. However, it was all a scam designed to enrich himself at the expense of all those who had entrusted him with everything from retirement funds to life savings. Ultimately, this all came crashing down, and his scheme was exposed for what it was: a pyramid scam that left investors from old ladies to charities penniless. Madoff is the poster child for **white-collar crimes**—crimes committed by affluent individuals who hold high status occupations (Sutherland, 1949). Typically, these offenders commit crimes in the context of a business that they are familiar with—bank executives that commit bank fraud, the insurance executive who defrauds his company, or the stockbroker practicing insider trading.

Unlike crimes against persons and property, which have immediate visible effects, white collar crimes can be less obvious, but still have disastrous effects on individuals and businesses. It is estimated that white-collar crime costs Americans between $300 and $600 billion each year, and that amount is projected to increase (Kane and Wall, 2006). The costs are not just monetary; workers in companies that collapse due to criminal mismanagement can lose their jobs, like in the case of Enron Corporation in 1996, where four thousand employees were dismissed. Other non-financial fallout from white-collar crime may include such things as retirees forced back to work due to drained retirement accounts, individuals having to depend on relatives for living situations, and other unexpected, life-disrupting events. While all violent crime and property crimes are down, white-collar crimes are among a small number of crime categories that are on the rise. (The FBI's UCR data for 2013 shows all property and violent crimes are down 5% from the same period in 2012.)

A related category of crimes includes corporate crime—offenses committed by corporate officials and offences of the corporation itself (Clinard and Yeager, 1980). These crimes may range from polluting the environment to knowingly manufacturing and selling defective or dangerous products. A prime example of corporate crime would be the 2010 BP Deepwater Horizon oil spill, considered the largest accidental oil spill, which dumped an estimated 210 million U.S. gallons into the Gulf of Mexico, killing eleven people, and leaving in its wake dead and injured marine life and thousands of miles of oil-soaked coastline (Pollardy, 2015). Total cost for this accident now approaches $50 billion; one estimate puts losses just for Gulf Coast anglers at $585 million (Xu, 2014). However, losses are more than economic; downstream effects include continued loss of marine life and loss of livelihood among the inhabitants of coastal communities in a number of states. The fallout from this disaster has been so profound that many residents have relocated in order to find work; those who stay face economic loss and disruption of their lives.

Many times, corporate crime is committed by individuals who believe that their criminal activity is merely a means to promote their organization. Sometimes referred to more specifically as *organizational crime*, these offenses are committed by individuals who believe that their crimes with serve to further the goals of an organization or movement. Something like flying jet airliners into the World Trade Center or setting off sarin gas bombs on a crowded Tokyo subway are examples of organizational crime. Those who flew the planes into the World Trade Center did so in part to promote their cause/organization, Al-Qaeda, and to prove their allegiance to the cause to show that they were "true believers."

Extortion, controlling gambling outlets, prostitution, drug and human trafficking, and more sophisticated electronic crimes like credit card fraud and identity theft are typical criminal enterprises that describe organized crime. Organized crime refers to any group which possesses a formalized structure and whose primary objective is to profit from crime (FBI, "Organized Crime," 2016). The United States has experienced waves of ethnically linked criminal organizations through the centuries. As various ethnic groups settled in America, criminal organizations emerged in their communities, many times in response to the discrimination they encountered here.

Most of these organizations began in their respective ethnic enclaves, and while many remain local, such as the Cuban, African American, and Vietnamese organizations, others spread out into the larger society. The Italian mafia is a high-profile example of a criminal enterprise that eventually left the Italian neighborhoods of New York City and over the decades has gone global. In a constant search for new criminal endeavors, the mafia now has its hands in credit card fraud, identity theft, hacking financial institutions, and Internet porn (FBI, "Italian Organized Crime," 2015). Probably the most damaging to society is its involvement in government corruption. From the cop on the beat, to the local building inspector, to the judge on the bench, to the senator on the Hill, the mob has wide influence that can affect laws and social policies. This corrupting influence it has on the local government and the criminal justice system leads many to believe that it can control local officials and influence the outcome of trials. Ultimately, the criminal acts of organized crime degrade the public trust in the integrity of local government, the police, and the judicial system.

Hate crimes are defined by the FBI as any "criminal offense against a person or property motivated in whole or in part by an offender's bias against a race, religion, disability, sexual orientation, ethnicity, gender, or gender identity" (FBI, "Hate Crimes," 2016). The vast majority of hate crimes are violent crimes that have the added element of being motivated by hatred for the victim's religion, race, sex, sexual orientation, or disability. While the term hate crime is relatively new in the popular culture, hate crime laws (not titled as such) date to the end of the Civil War, and the hate crime laws in the modern era can be dated back to 1968 with an amendment to the Civil Rights Act.

California passed the first state hate crime law in 1978; now, forty-five states and the District of Columbia all have hate crime laws. Federal statutes start to catch up beginning in 1990, leading to a more comprehensive Hate Crimes Prevention Act in 2009. Unfortunately, the United States has a long and illustrious history of hate crimes represented by organizations like the Ku Klux Klan, Skinheads, the Black Panthers, and the U.S. government—yes, our own government. Take, for example, the treatment of the Native American population, Chinese immigrants, and Japanese Americans during WWII. In an attempt to reconcile past cases with current hate crime statutes, the FBI actively investigates hate crimes retroactively. That is, it investigates unsolved cold-case crimes that at the time were not categorized as hate crimes but now can be prosecuted as such. Most of this effort has been concentrated on crimes committed in the South during the height of the civil rights movement.

Crimes involving computers are extensive in their scope, but not all crimes using a computer are considered cyber-crimes. Cyber-crimes are defined as "offenses that are committed against individuals or groups of individuals with a criminal motive to intentionally harm the reputation of the victim or cause physical or mental harm to the victim directly or indirectly, using modern telecommunication networks such as Internet (Chat rooms, emails, notice boards and groups) and mobile phones (SMS/MMS)" (Halder and Jaishankar, 2011). The intent of cyber-crimes is as wide-ranging as the type of cyber-crimes. Cyber-crimes range from conning people into sending money to your long-lost uncle in Nigeria to secretly installing malware on the computers of unsuspecting users. Frequently, these criminals are pursuing financial gain by stealing credit card information, robbing bank accounts, creating bogus online charity sites, or stealing identities. However, a growing number of cyber-crimes are aimed at either infecting computer networks with malware and/or viruses in order to disable or crash a system or spreading malicious bots and viruses simply to be, well, malicious. It seems that financial gain is a much stronger motive than others are. Both the FBI and Bureau of Justice Statistics indicate that the fastest-growing crime in the United States is identity theft, mainly through cyber tactics (FBI, "Identity Theft", 2015; Javelin Strategy & Research, 2013; Harrell, 2015).

Recently, nude photos of several celebrities were distributed on the Internet without the knowledge or consent of those celebrities. Where did these pics come from? They were hacked from the iCloud, where those celebrities had stored them in what they believed to be a secure digital environment. In December 2013, Brian Curtis Hile was sentenced to five years in federal prison for interstate stalking (FBI, "Interstate Stalking," 2013). In an ironic twist, Hile was the victim of a "catfishing" cyber-romance scam in which a South African man posed as an attractive woman and maintained an online-only, two-year romance with Hile, exchanging intimate photos and letters.

When Mr. Hile discovered the true identity of his online lover, he became enraged and sought revenge, but South Africa was too far away, so he focused on the identity of the woman whose image the scammer had used as his female alter-identity. Hile discovered who the woman in all those intimate pics was and tracked her down in San Diego, where he was arrested. Apparently, Hile had determined that the woman was somehow complicit with the South African scammer and she had to pay (the woman had no idea that her photos from a hacked email account were being used to lure young men into fake relationships). The FBI determined that Hile had intended some violent end for the woman and her family when they found a knife, zip ties, and chloroform on him when he was arrested.

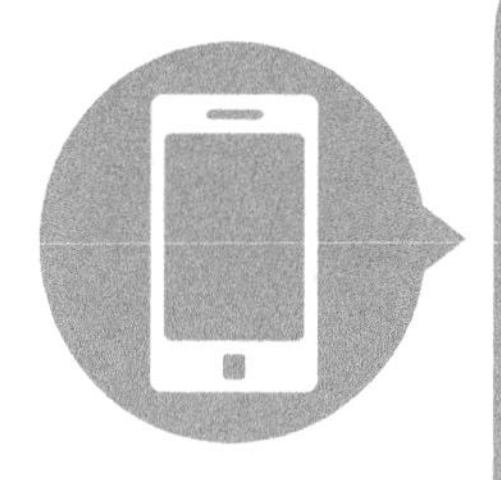

THERE'S AN APP FOR THAT

Below I have listed some crime-fighting apps:

- *iSpotACrime* allows users to report crimes directly to their local police. The app allows you to use GPS to pinpoint the location of the crime, upload pics, text and make voice recordings. So, you can witness crimes and send photo, video and audio evidence right to the police (Vorpal Fox.com, 2016).
- *Tip Submit* allows users to snitch anonymously to a range of agencies including Crime Stoppers, police, and local school administrators (Public Engines Inc., 2014).
- *iWitness* this smartphone app lets you capture and broadcast video and audio while maintaining real time tracking of your location via GPS. The data then is retrievable only by you and with your permission law enforcement. One feature allows you to alert trusted contacts with your location if you feel endangered (iWitness, 2015)

BLACK HATS, WHITE HATS, AND GRAY HATS

Not all hackers are the same. Black hat hackers, or black hats, as they are known, are people who hack computer systems for personal gain or other malicious reasons. They will hack a bank's computer system just to rob it or steal confidential information from a large retail organization in order to commit identity fraud. Sometimes, they merely want to inflict damage to a system or shut it down. For example, the large retailer Target was hacked in late 2013, and it was reported that the personal and credit card information from nearly 70 million customers was compromised ("Target: 40 Million Credit Cards," 2013).

White hats are typically computer security specialists who breach computer systems and networks to assess their security. Typically, they are hired by organizations to expose any vulnerabilities present in their systems in an attempt to head off malicious black hat attacks. While they may employ similar or identical techniques, white hats have permission to hack their clients' systems and many times are doing so to improve customer security. Today, many financial institutions, businesses, and even the federal government hire white hat cyber-security firms to probe the vulnerability of their systems and report ways that their security can be enhanced.

Gray hats are hackers who fall somewhere in between black hats and white hats. While gray hats may breach a computer system or network, they will not crash it or seek to profit from the breach. Gray hats may compromise a bank's computer network and then publicly expose the flaw rather than privately notifying the organization. While they have compromised a computer system, which is illegal, they typically do not seek personal gain from the intrusion. However, there is a time lag between publicly announcing the flaw and the organization's response, which leaves plenty of opportunity for black hats to strike.

The Criminal Justice System

The criminal justice system in the United States is represented by a number of linked organizations involved in policing, adjudicating, sentencing, and jailing those involved in crime. It includes, but is not limited to, law enforcement, courts of law, and prison. Unfortunately, by any metric, the criminal justice system is seriously flawed. The chances of an individual being arrested, convicted, and sentenced in the U.S. are greatly increased if he/she is a person of color and/or poor (The Sentencing Project, 2013).

Law Enforcement

Police are the first point of contact with the criminal justice system and, therefore, are in a position to either enhance or detract from their public image. Through this daily contact with members of the community, they have the potential to escalate or deescalate volatile situations and ultimately have the ability to make decisions about who will and will not be detained or arrested. They are armed with their most powerful weapon: discretion.

Currently, police play many roles: law enforcement, peacekeeping, and public relations. However, police are only effective if they secure public trust. Police, after all, are public servants, but when they are viewed as adversaries rather than allies in achieving social goals, distrust in them grows. This may arise from changes in police practices, as was evinced in New York City in the early 1990s when the city adopted a zero-tolerance police policy (arresting people for small infractions as well as more severe ones) that has led to fear and mistrust of police (Staples, 2012). This mistrust of law enforcement has only been exacerbated by a series of high-profile, police-involved homicides during 2014 and 2015, most notably the choking death of Eric Garner, an unarmed black man, by NYPD officers and the shooting death of Michael Brown, an unarmed black man, in Ferguson, Missouri, in August 2014 (Goldstein and Schweber, 2014; Chuck, 2014). These deaths sparked both violent riots and peaceful protests that lasted for months.

In large part, this mistrust is fueled by the staggering difference in arrest rates between whites and people of color in the United States. Black men are far more likely to be arrested than white men are. Brame et al. (2014) found that by age eighteen, 30% of black males, 26% of Hispanic males, and 22% of white males had been arrested, and by age twenty-three, 49% of black males, 44% of Hispanic males, and 38% of white males had been arrested.

These are big differences. However, the question remains—why do we see such differences? Are law enforcement officers just discriminating? For example, research indicates that police training, professional socialization, stereotypes and experience, can lead police to suspect, "stop and frisk", and arrest members of certain minority groups and the poor (Alpert et al., 2005; Alpert, Dunham and Smith, 2007; Gelman, Fagan and Kiss, 2007).

In general, in the U.S., you are far more likely to be stopped and arrested if you are poor than if you appear well to do, and if you are black in America, you are far more likely to be in poverty than if you are white (Brown and Males, 2011). Unlike the wealthy, who typically commit crimes that evade police detection, the poor are more likely to commit street crimes that are more visible to the police. Moreover, political and peer pressure may make police less likely to confront and arrest more affluent citizens.

The Courts

After being arrested by law enforcement, the accused have to deal with the criminal courts system, which serves to adjudicate offenses, determine guilt or innocence, and pronounce sentences. Again, the differences in treatment between the poor and affluent and blacks and whites are present in the courtrooms of America.

From their initial contact with the courts, differences emerge. Poor people are far less likely to be able to afford bail; therefore, they have to spend their pre-trial time in jail (Justice Policy Institute, 2012). This may affect their ability to aid in their own defense, they may lose their job, and they are separated from their family and friends. Imagine how being led into the courtroom by bailiffs and perhaps wearing a bright orange jail uniform could influence the judge or jury, whereas someone with more resources is able to post bail and can show up in court with his lawyer wearing a suit. Research indicates that defendants who can pay their bail and afford their own attorney are more likely to be acquitted than someone who cannot afford these things (Frederique et al., 2015).

Poor people are far less likely to be able to afford an attorney. While they may get a court-appointed attorney, most are working for lower wages or pro-bono, which can motivate them to rush the case along or, more often than not, plea-bargain the case. On the other hand, affluent defendants who can afford their own attorneys will most likely get off as a result of a number of legal maneuvers executed by their well-paid attorneys. Additionally, the reality for the poor in the United States is that on average they are more likely to receive harsher penalties and do more time than their wealthier counterparts.

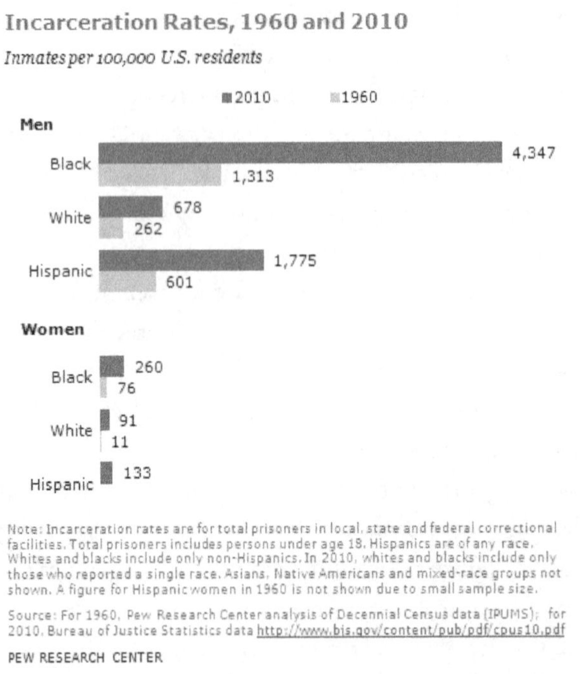

Incarceration Rates, 1960 and 2010

Inmates per 100,000 U.S. residents

	2010	1960
Men		
Black	4,347	1,313
White	678	262
Hispanic	1,775	601
Women		
Black	260	76
White	91	11
Hispanic	133	

Note: Incarceration rates are for total prisoners in local, state and federal correctional facilities. Total prisoners includes persons under age 18. Hispanics are of any race. Whites and blacks include only non-Hispanics. In 2010, whites and blacks include only those who reported a single race. Asians, Native Americans and mixed-race groups not shown. A figure for Hispanic women in 1960 is not shown due to small sample size.

Source: For 1960, Pew Research Center analysis of Decennial Census data (IPUMS); for 2010, Bureau of Justice Statistics data http://www.bjs.gov/content/pub/pdf/cpus10.pdf

PEW RESEARCH CENTER

Fig. 6.9 Bar chart showing incarceration rates for whites, blacks, and Latinos, 1960 and 2010

Blacks are arrested far more often than whites, are more likely to do time than whites, and are more likely to be handed stiffer prison terms. Therefore, there is no question that the courts are treating black and white defendants differently. For instance, when it comes to sentencing for homicide those who kill whites are more likely to get the death penalty than those who murder minorities. The reality is that if a white man and a black man were to be arrested on identical charges, have the same criminal history, be the same age, and have similar family and employment backgrounds, the black man is more likely to be convicted and do time than the white man (Kochel et al., 2011; Walker et al., 2004).

TRY THIS

Visit your local courthouse for a day. Most court cases, criminal and traffic, are open to the public. Sit and watch the process. Notice how judges, prosecutors, and defense attorneys interact. Who has a public defender? Who has their own counsel? What types of charges are being adjudicated? Are those defendants with street clothes treated differently than those in jail uniforms? Do you think age, sex, race, or physical appearance factor in how they are treated? Are there many plea bargains being made? A day in a courtroom will serve as a window into our criminal justice system. Do you like what you see?

Punishment

Ultimately, court convictions lead to some form of punishment or penalty. These punishments can take several forms: fines, restitution, probation, community service, or incarceration. Overwhelmingly, in the United States, the trend has been toward incarceration. In 1971, there were fewer than 200,000 inmates in our federal and state prisons; by 1996, we approached 1.2 million—the prison population sextupled in that twenty-five-year span. As of 2013, there were nearly 2.2 million inmates in state and federal prisons. We really like to lock people up. Is it because there is so much more crime? Well, earlier in the chapter, I showed you that all violent crime is down and only cyber-crimes and hate crimes are on the rise, but not enough to account for incarceration rates. In their book, *Why Are So Many Americans in Prison?* Raphael and Stoll (2013) show what drove up imprisonment rates was not crime—it was policy.

That's right, the public concern over the growing crime rate of the '70s and '80s led politicians, afraid of appearing to be soft on crime, into enacting minimum sentencing laws. The thinking went something like this: in order to remove criminals from society, police need to arrest all offenders, minor and major alike, and deter future crime through harsh sentencing. From 1975 through 2002, all fifty states adopted mandatory sentencing laws, specifying minimum sentences. Many also adopted "three strikes" laws to punish recidivists. Judges lost the discretion they previously had in determining sentences, their hands were tied, they had to pronounce minimum sentences. This combined with tougher policing strategies like the zero-tolerance policy adopted by the NYPD help put more and more offenders inside. For the most part, minimum sentencing guidelines have led to the swollen prison population. Unbelievably, today the United States has a greater proportion of our population in jail and prison than China, India, and Russia. Yes, while the U.S. has the world's third-largest population, the percentage of our population that is behind bars is the highest in the world! Think about it this way: The United States represents just 5% of the world's population, yet those we have incarcerated represent 25% of the world's prison population. Table 6.3 below shows the top ten countries with the largest prison populations. The United States tops the list. Take a look at the other countries that top this list; they are also countries that have long records of human rights abuses. The United States should not want to top a list like this.

TABLE 6.3 Top Ten Countries Ranked by Number of Incarcerated

Rank	Country	Incarcerated Population
1	United States	2,217,000
2	China	1,657,812
3	Russian Federation	649,500
4	Brazil	607,731
5	India	411,992
6	Thailand	308,111
7	Mexico	255,138
8	Iran	225,624
9	Turkey	165,033
10	Indonesia	161,692

Source: Institute for Criminal Policy Research 2015

Who Is More Likely to Be in Prison?

While there may be more white males in prison than black males, the proportion of black males imprisoned is far greater than for whites (Glaze and Herberman, 2013). Blacks in America make up less than 13% of the country's population, but they represent nearly 40% of the nation's prison inmates. As a matter of fact, all black men are six times more likely to be in prison than all white men. Estimates put the black prison population at 1 million out of 2.3 million inmates in American prisons. Take a look at table 6.4 below for a clear picture of who is in prison in America.

TABLE 6.4 Inmate Race

Race	Number of Inmates	Percentage of Inmates
Asian	2,927	1.5%
Black	73,557	37.6%
Native American	3,963	2.0%
White	115,046	58.8%

Data from the Federal Bureau of Prisons, April 2016

These rates of incarceration are compounded by level of education. Figure 6.10 shows that the greatest rates of imprisonment are associated with lack of education. Low levels of education are associated with greater levels of poverty, which, in turn, are linked to criminal activity. This creates a cycle of high arrest rates for poor black men, who cannot afford attorneys, who then are more likely to be convicted and are more likely to be sentenced to prison. It seems that as a society, it would benefit us greatly to focus our resources more

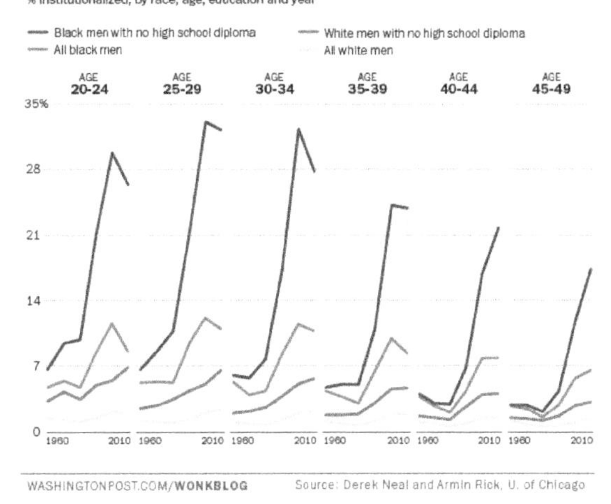

Fig. 6.10 Incarceration Rates by Education Level, Blacks and Whites, 1960 and 2010.

heavily on education to reduce poverty and crime rather than to focus on prison as a solution to crime.

READ MORE

- *Race, Incarceration and American Values* by Glenn C. Loury (2008); *Let's Get Free: A Hip-Hop Theory of Justice* by Paul Butler (2009). Both of these books explore our broken criminal justice system, putting it in a social context of racism, prejudice, and discrimination. They expose how unfairly people of color are treated by the system and how the system reproduces its practices. These books will open your eyes to the truth of how our criminal justice system treats people of color.

Why Do We Put People in Prison?

There are four main motivations for imprisoning someone: retribution, deterrence, rehabilitation, and removal from society. Remember, these motivations represent expressions of formal social control. Each is seen as a way to reinforce social norms and promote conformity.

- *Retribution* means exacting punishment on the offender—an eye for an eye and a tooth for a tooth. This rationale goes something like this: if you commit a crime, you should be held accountable and have to "repay" society by being punished. Retribution is about society exacting its pound of flesh from the criminal offender, and this may include time in jail or prison.
- *Deterrence* refers to structuring punishments in a way that the cost of crime will appear so great that would-be criminals will refrain from crime in order to avoid harsh punishments. The death penalty is, in theory, a deterrent to crime. The belief is that the threat of death is so severe that it will deter criminals from engaging in capital crimes. However, there seems to be no credible evidence to support this position.
- Those who argue for a process of *rehabilitation* seek to design prisons as institutions that have the capacity to educate and/or train inmates so they will have legitimate job skills when they re-enter society, becoming productive members of society and ultimately reducing recidivism rates. Rehabilitation programs like prison-based education and training programs should be seen as a way for former inmates to gain employment and feel more integrated into their communities, therefore feeling less inclined to engage in criminal acts.

- At the end of the day, prison represents the criminal justice system's ability to take away offenders' freedom by *removing them from society*. Removing offenders from the rest of society is one of the most fundamental acts of social control a society can perform. Denying individuals their freedom to move about in society and separating them from friends and family is nearly a universal form of punishment—a sort of *time out* for adults.

Theoretical Perspectives on Social Control, Deviance, and Crime

In sociology, there are three broad approaches to understanding deviance and crime. They should sound familiar: we have been discussing them in every chapter. Remember, these theoretical approaches are attempts to explain existence and causes of deviance in society. In general, functionalism views deviance as present in all societies and the response it provokes functions to maintain social order. Functionalism recognizes that individuals within a society need to feel integrated or connected to others and society for them to contribute to the various social institutions that maintain social order. Dysfunctions occur when people do not feel connected and engage in deviant and criminal behavior, which is disruptive to social order. Some functionalists argue that there is positive value in deviance that contributes to maintaining social order, while others see it as a result of modern society's constant pressure for material success, which leads to norm violations to achieve success.

Conflict theory focuses on social inequality and how that can result in the differential definitions and treatment of deviants. Adherents to this approach see the powerful in society as having the ability to influence the passing of laws that can serve them and maintain dominance over the less fortunate. Those disadvantaged like the poor and minorities are more likely to be viewed as deviant than the affluent and, consequently, are treated differently by law enforcement and the criminal justice system, as we saw in our discussions above.

In contrast to both functionalism and conflict theories, symbolic interactionism has a microsociological focus on deviance and crime. That means that deviance and crime are constructed out of the interactions between people. Nothing is inherently deviant but may become defined as such through the responses of others, the reactions of others are highly variable, and labeling someone as deviant may lead to the development of secondary deviance and deviant careers.

Table 6.5 summarizes each of the three main theoretical perspectives. For each perspective in the table, I have included a brief distillation of its main points and an example that helps illustrate the major proposals.

TABLE 6.5. Theoretical Perspectives on Deviance and Crime

Theoretical Perspective	View of Deviance and Crime	Example
Structural-Functionalism	Deviance and crime are a result of weak social integration—the less attached, committed, and obligated individuals are to others and society, and the less they believe in conventional social values and behaviors, the more likely they are to commit deviant or criminal acts.	Depression is most commonly associated with suicide. However, there is a large body of research that shows that most suicides are the result of a host of social factors that can lead to depressive feelings. Shortly after the collapse of the housing market in 2008, Kathy lost her job in Boston. She had recently moved there and had no real friends. She was an only child whose parents had died. She could not seem to find a job, started feeling isolated, did not have anyone to turn to, and was evicted from her apartment. Soon after, she fell down the stairs at the motel she was staying in and had to be treated as an indigent. The motel manager found her dead in her room a week later. She had taken all the pain pills she had recently been prescribed. Her note stated that it seemed the best solution given she had no friends and family and felt disconnected from the world. Such an individual act is usually seen as a result of some pathology, but deviant acts like suicide are commonly impacted by social forces and circumstances that conspire to make individuals feel disconnected from the social world.
	Deviance and crime can serve positive social functions for society, such as establish moral boundaries, create solidarity, affirm social norms and values, and promote social change.	In August 2014, an unarmed young black man was killed by a police officer in Ferguson, Missouri. The ensuing protests, riots, and looting eventually led to more protests and a dialogue between the police and community leaders, who demanded a thorough investigation. Ultimately, the protests lead to a Department of Justice investigation of that police force, which resulted in a 102-page report filled with recommendations for changes in police practices and procedures. The report highlighted rampant racism and the overcriminalization of the black community. This led to the resignation of the police chief, among other officials, and these changes will hopefully result in less criminalization and police violence against the black community. (Berman and Lowery, 2015; U.S. Department of Justice, "Investigation of the Ferguson Police Department", 2015).
	Deviance and crime can be a reaction to social strain—when individuals feel like they cannot achieve social goals through legitimate means, they may turn to crime.	In the movie *Fun with Dick and Jane* (1977), Dick losses his job and can't seem to find work, and the couple have a hard time maintaining their middle-class lifestyle—keeping up with the Joneses. Exhausted from job hunting, stressed over mounting bills, and afraid they may lose their house, Dick and Jane start robbing banks and other businesses to pay the bills and keep the house!

Theoretical Perspective	View of Deviance and Crime	Example
Conflict	Conflict theory is all about inequality in society. It maintains that laws and social norms reflect the interests of the powerful in society. They can pass laws to their benefit and influence the justice system in other ways that allow them to define deviance and crime.	Take for example the CEO of an auto parts manufacturing plant who was busted for drug possession at the same time one of his machine operators was also arrested for the same offense. The CEO was able to pay a high-priced lawyer to keep moving his court date until the lawyer could work out a deal with the prosecutor (whom he went to law school with) to dismiss the charges and keep it all out of the press. Unfortunately, the machine worker could not afford an attorney, got a court-appointed lawyer, and took a plea bargain that sent him to jail (under minimum sentencing laws passed by the powerful) for five years. He lost his job, home, and family.
	The poor and minorities are more likely to engage in more visible street crimes, making them vulnerable to arrest, conviction, and imprisonment, unlike the more affluent or powerful members of society.	White-collar criminals, such as our friend Raj in the story below, are much more likely to go undetected because of the complex nature of their crimes and because many times, there is no identifiable victim. Often, the companies do not want the bad press and will try to bury the crime by not prosecuting the offender. White-collar criminals are sometimes able to use their power and influence to avoid prosecution. Because of their social and economic influence, white-collar criminals are less likely to face criminal prosecution than less affluent criminals. When prosecuted, they are much less likely than members of lower social classes to receive a prison sentence. They are more likely to pay a fine as punishment for their crime.
Symbolic Interactionism	Deviant and criminal behaviors are a result of our need for acceptance by others—our association with criminal groups will lead to conformity with the criminal group's values, attitudes, techniques, and motives so we are accepted.	Raj was recently promoted to a special investment section at Global Bank. He worked on multimillion-dollar accounts with just five other brokers. After a few months, Raj and the others were working hard together and socializing outside of work. Raj felt privileged because he felt he was fortunate to work with who he felt were his best friends. After work one night, the others confided in Raj that they had worked out a scheme that allowed them to skim thousands of dollars each day undetected by anyone—after all, they all worked hard and never got any bonuses. Raj did not want to lose his friendships or job, and there was a lot of money to be made from a multinational company that does not recognize its employees. Within a few weeks, Raj had mastered the scheme and started filling his own offshore account with embezzled funds. He and his friends became even closer.
	Deviance can be the result of negative social labels—individuals are labeled as deviant, leading others to react to that label, which, in turn, can marginalize the individuals and impact their own self-perception.	People who have been labeled as sex offenders report having difficulty fully engaging with others and society. Many times, their label prohibits them from finding employment, housing, and even companionship. Others may avoid them or even recoil in disgust when they learn of their label. This ultimately affects how they interpret their value as a human.

The Bottom Line

No thought or action is inherently deviant. Therefore, what is deviant in one culture may not be in another, and what is considered deviant may change over time in any society. While deviance is typically interpreted negatively, there seem to be some clear positive functions it can serve society. For example, Martin Luther King, Jr., was arrested many times during his marches and protests in the 1950s and 1960s. He broke laws, making him a criminal and therefore deviant ("Martin Luther King Jr.—Biography," 2015). History has shown that while his past actions might have been criminal, now those actions are accepted and legal. Moreover, his deviant actions and those of other Freedom Marchers laid a foundation for social change.

Throughout history, there have been many attempts to understand what causes deviance in humans, including the supernatural, the bumps on our heads, our body types, and the human genome. While many have been discredited and some need more investigation, sociological approaches offer promise in understanding the presence and causes of deviance. The sociological explanations for deviance center on one's social environment, the pressure to conform, desire for valuable social resources, social power, and labels that affect the way others treat us and how we view ourselves.

As we have seen, some crimes in America are at all-time lows and others are declining. Explaining this decline has tasked criminologists, economists, historians, and sociologists alike. Currently, there is still a vigorous debate about why we witnessed such a dramatic decline in violent crime from 1993 until 2010. The connection between lead and crime rate decline is highly controversial; at first glance, it seems outside the purview of sociology, but upon closer inspection, it considers variables such as social class, race, and the urban-rural divide.

Figure Credits

Fig. 6.1: Copyright © Florida Keys-Public Libraries (CC by 2.0) at https://commons.wikimedia.org/wiki/File:Carl_Tanzler_(1940).jpg.

Fig. 6.2: Copyright © joo0ey (CC by 2.0) at https://commons.wikimedia.org/wiki/File:Bull_penis_in_restaurant.jpg.

Fig. 6.3: Jane Hahn/ ActionAid, "Ghanan Witch Camp," actionaid.org. Copyright © by ActionAid International. Reprinted with permission.

Fig. 6.4: Copyright © Fæ (CC BY-SA 4.0) at https://commons.wikimedia.org/wiki/File:Fowler%27s_phrenological_head,_Staffordshire,_England,_1879-18_Wellcome_L0057592.jpg.

Fig. 6.5: Copyright © Granito diaz (CC BY-SA 4.0) at https://en.wikipedia.org/wiki/Somatotype_and_constitutional_psychology#/media/File:Bodytypes.jpg.

Fig. 6.6: U.S. Department of Justice, Bureau of Justice Statistics, "Most Important Reason Violent Victimizations were Not reported to the police 2006-2010," http://www.bjs.gov/content/pub/pdf/vnrp0610.pdf. Copyright in the Public Domain.

Fig. 6.7: Source: http://www.statista.com/statistics/191219/reported-violent-crime-rate-in-the-usa-since-1990/

Fig. 6.8: Source: http://www.pewresearch.org/fact-tank/2013/09/06/incarceration-gap-between-whites-and-blacks-widens/

Table 6.4: Source: Federal Bureau of Prisons, https://www.bop.gov/about/statistics/statistics_inmate_race.jsp.

Fig. 6.10: Source: http://www.pewresearch.org/fact-tank/2014/07/18/chart-of-the-week-the-black-white-gap-in-incarceration-rates/

THE HAVES AND HAVE NOTS: Exploring Social Inequality

3

CHAPTER 7

RANKING SOCIETY: SOCIAL STRATIFICATION, SOCIAL CLASS, AND POVERTY

The Bohemian Grove

Every July in Northern California, the most powerful men in the world gather at the Bohemian Grove, a 2,700-acre private reserve protected by waterways and a private security crew (Flock, 2011). This exclusively male enclave is composed of politicians, CEOs of multinational corporations, heads of pharmaceutical corporations, and other giants of industry. While there, in the forests of Northern California, these powerful men agree to refrain from doing business, but that really does not stop them from brokering some of the most important deals of the past centuries.

These men spend two weeks every July relaxing, reading, socializing, and doing some business, but their stay is kicked off by a ceremony so secret that the one person (a non-member) who managed to sneak onto the property and smuggle out grainy video has had his life threatened. The Cremation of Care ceremony, which represents a banishing of worldly cares, is performed on a stage in front of a small lake over which a 40-foot-tall concrete owl looms. All of the participants wear long, hooded robes and speak in ominous tones while burning the figure of care in effigy; they then end the ceremony with fireworks. Some, however, believe that the Cremation of Care really represents a ritualized burning of conscience and empathy to assuage their guilt for having so much power and wealth.

Fig. 7.1 The Owl Shrine at the Bohemian Grove

The Bohemian Grove represents the exclusivity and excess available to the socially elite in America. You and I will never have access to such privilege and power. The members of Bohemian Grove are the power elite in America, the 1% whose wealth and power maintain inequality in America and globally.

In general, stratification refers to layering. Think geology, specifically the Grand Canyon, all those colorful layers (strata) of sedimentary soil and rock, or the layers you see in a wedding cake or in a seven-layer bean dip. Stratification applied to society simply refers to how categories of people are conceptually layered one on top of the other based on some definition of social rank. **Social stratification**, then, is the hierarchical ranking of the members of society based on their possession of and access to valuable social resources. All societies have a system by which they rank their members: the poor, the rich, and those in the middle. As Pitirim Sorokin (1957) makes clear, a society with real equity among its members is a myth and has never been achieved in the history of humankind. We would like to believe that at some point in our past or somewhere in some forgotten place, there is a truly egalitarian society where there are no class distinctions, but this is fantasy.

Characteristics of Social Stratification

That's right, all societies are unequal, and because social inequality has persisted over time and we find it in every society, common elements of stratification have emerged. Sociologists refer to these as the four principles of social stratification:

1. **It is a trait of society, not a reflection of individual differences.** The poor in society have just as much of a desire for a high standard of living or decent living conditions as the wealthy do. So, while those born to wealthy families are more likely than those born into poverty to enjoy high incomes, academic achievement, good health, and live well into old age, neither class is responsible for creating social stratification, yet it shapes the lives of them all.
2. **It persists from generation to generation.** The vast majority of you reading this book will live out your lives in the same social class as your parents. Overall, there is little social

mobility in the U.S. (Breen, 2010). The most powerful predictor of one's social class is parental education. That is, generally, middle-class parents with college educations will have children who attain college educations, and those in the lower class who have little more than high school diplomas will have children who may or may not graduate high school. All stratification systems persist because they are supported by both beliefs and behaviors. The structure of stratification systems remains while people just pass through it.

3. **Stratification is universal but variable.** While there are myriad differences in the social mechanisms and resources that create differences between ranked social groups, there is little variation in structure. For the Nuer people of the Sudan, the most valuable resource in their culture is cattle; the number of cattle and their condition are indicators of one's social standing. Meanwhile, back in the United States, one's social class is defined in part by the possession of valuable resources that include income (money), wealth, and education. We can see that cattle are different than high incomes, but the results are the same: those with all the cattle/money get more social prestige, privilege, and enhanced life chances (we'll discuss this later). Nuer men with more cattle have more social prestige, can support more wives, and, therefore, have more children to tend the cattle and to assure the later years of their lives are comfortable (Evans-Pritchard, 1940). Someone in the U.S. with a low-paying job enjoys no privilege, little power, and is at greater risk for certain injuries and/or disease. Therefore, even though those things that determine rank (cattle or money) are different across cultures, the structural outcome is the same: some get a lot of the stuff, many are somewhere in the middle, and others are left with little to none of the valued resources.
4. **It involves inequality and beliefs.** While Americans recognize that their social class system is unequal, when surveyed, most believe that it promotes competition and motivates people to work hard and achieve (Kraus and Tan, 2015). Unfortunately, the very inequality that we acknowledge is the greatest barrier to social mobility. Pickett and Wilkinson (2009) have shown that countries like the United States that have a high rate of inequality also have the lowest levels of mobility, while countries like Norway with little inequality have high rates of social mobility. Yet belief in the folklore of social achievement (the stories of Abraham Lincoln and Barack Obama), meritocracy, or religious beliefs, such as those that help maintain India's caste system, are the factors that allow these systems to persist. Systems of beliefs, or ideologies like meritocracy, are needed to maintain the structure of social stratification.

Open Systems and Closed Systems

Stratification systems can be broadly separated into two major types: open and closed systems. **Open stratification systems** allow for movement between the strata, and there are mechanisms within these systems that allow for this movement, albeit limited and unequally available. The

American class system is a fine example. Closed stratification systems do not allow for movement between the ranks. Typically, the strata or layers of a closed system are designated by some ascribed status, such as occupation, skin tone, or religion. The *Jati*, or caste system of India, and the slave caste system of Mauritania provide excellent examples.

Closed Systems

A caste system is a *closed system* of social stratification that prohibits any upward mobility. In a caste system, one's social rank is determined by birth and maintained by a rigid set of social rules that determine social interactions, occupation, and marriage. In caste systems, you are born into a given caste, you marry within that caste, you live out your life among those of that caste, and you die within that caste. Caste systems can be so rigid as to regulate individuals' social interactions. In India's past, those of the *Dalit* or untouchable caste lived their entire lives in an extremely limited social environment; they would socialize only with other untouchables, marry only other untouchables, and take up the occupations of the untouchables—handling corpses or cleaning the streets of human and animal waste. This rigidity was universal; even those of the highest caste, the *Brahmin*, were bound by the requirements of the caste system. While the Brahmin certainly enjoyed more privileged social lives and greater latitude in social interactions than the untouchables, they, too, were destined to marry within the caste and take up Brahmin occupations—priesthood, landowners, and government service. The now-outlawed caste system of India is typically referenced when describing castes; however, caste systems are not limited to India—they are found in Sri Lanka, Mauritania, and Nepal.

Mauritania's Slave Caste

Mauritania became the last country in the world to abolish slavery in 1981 (not criminalizing it until 2007), but its particularly rigid caste system reinforces and maintains a *slave caste* to this day. At the top of Mauritania's caste system is a Berber minority comprised of light-skinned "White Moors" who control the majority of the country's wealth, while depriving black Africans and darker-skinned Moors of real economic opportunity or freedom. It has been estimated that of the 3.5 million citizens of Mauritania, nearly 800,000 of them remain enslaved (Mark, 2012; Bales, 2012; Conway-Smith, 2015).

How does a society maintain a system that does not allow movement between castes, where your birth determines your social standing, and where individuals have no hope of improving their living conditions or standards of living? Power, corruption, and tradition are identifiable forces that maintain Mauritania's rigid caste system. White moors maintain their chokehold on society by power that emanates from their relatively enormous wealth and their ties to a corrupt government whose members come from their own ruling caste. Barely literate and afraid of the fallout from protesting their plight, black moors, the slave caste, do no more than follow social and economic tradition. Additionally, there are deep psychological and economic bonds between slaves and masters. Slaves themselves deny they are enslaved, some even believe that they are slaves by the will of God, and they are dependent on their masters for food, clothing and essentials. As you can see, the structures of stratification systems are shaped and maintained by recognizable social and economic forces (Boustany, 2008; Townsend, 2015).

Slavery Around the World

Possibly one of the most despicable practices to ever manifest itself in our world is slavery. Slavery is an extreme form of inequality in which one group of people (slaves) is owed by others (slave owners). Consequently, slaves are treated as property or commodities to be traded, bought and sold or even destroyed (Global Slavery Index, 2014). Slavery has a long and sorrowful history throughout the world, and as deplorable as slavery is, it still exists in various forms around the world. Traditional slavery, chattel slavery, commonly associated with the slave practices of the Americas in the eighteenth and nineteenth centuries, has nearly been eradicated globally; unfortunately, there is evidence that it is still practiced in some isolated regions of the world like Niger, Sudan, and Mauritania. Regrettably, other forms of slavery, such as debt bondage, forced labor, forced marriage, and sex slavery, have been on the rise. It is estimated that there are approximately 35.8 million people enslaved in some form worldwide, with India topping the charts with nearly 14 million. Debt bondage, or pledging oneself against a loan, is the most frequently occurring form of slavery in the world and is most prevalent in South Asia (Falola, 1994; Miller, Vandome and McBrewster, 2009). Essentially, an individual works off a loan, but the amount of time and labor required to pay off the loan is undefined, and additional debt is frequently tacked onto the original debt, increasing the time enslaved. It is not uncommon for the children of debtor parents to have to repay the parents' debts, therefore condemning the children to slavery.

SLAVERY NUMBERS AROUND THE WORLD

- An estimated 27 million people, spread across countries such as Nigeria, Indonesia, and Brazil, live in conditions of forced bondage.
- Approximately 700,000 people each year are trafficked across borders and into slavery.
- Nearly 300,000 children are forced to fight as child soldiers in thirty armed conflicts worldwide. Many female child soldiers are also forced into sexual slavery.
- An estimated 2,600 women are working in the sex industry in England and Wales, having been trafficked from abroad.

Sources: U.S. Department of State, 2014; UNICEF, 2011; Bales, 2012; BBC News, 2010

While slavery is outlawed in every country of the world, unfortunately, the practice has been reinvigorated through the criminal enterprise of human trafficking and sex slavery. Perhaps the most disturbing global development is the growing magnitude of trafficking in humans. However, finding reliable and accurate numbers on human trafficking is difficult. Even the U.S. State Department acknowledged this in its 2015 Trafficking in Persons (TIP) report. Trafficking is a criminal endeavor and therefore those engaged in these crimes operate in the shadows and in secret. Those who have fallen victim to trafficking seldom come forward, many feel shame or fear retribution from the traffickers.

Some estimates indicate that across the world, there are nearly 21 million men, women, and children who are victimized by forced labor and sex trafficking, including in the United States (International Labour Organization, 2016). Slavery is ultimately an economic system because the slave owners generate their earnings and maintain their lifestyles off the sweat of the backs of slaves.

READ MORE

Here is a website you can visit to better understand the plight of those worldwide who are trapped in the horror of slavery. You can also find out what you can do to prevent and/or reduce local and global slavery. Or you can read any of the books I've listed below for an eye-opening look at the reality of global slavery.

- The International Labour Organization. ilo.org
- *Blood and Earth: Modern Slavery, Ecocide, and the Secret to Saving the World* by Kevin Bales (2016).
- *Disposable People: New Slavery in the Global Economy* by Kevin Bales (2012).
- *Sex Trafficking: Inside the Business of Modern Slavery* by Siddharth Kara (2009).
- *The Slave Next Door: Human Trafficking and Slavery in America* by Kevin Bales and Ron Soodalter (2009).

Social Class

Earlier, I noted that unlike closed caste systems, class systems of stratification are open, allowing movement between the classes. A class system is one in which the population is divided into classes whose members are defined by their possession of and access to valuable social resources. In addition, a class is a category of similarly ranked people distinguished from other categories by such traits as income, occupation, education, and wealth (Gilbert, 2014). Class systems like the one in the United States encourage—and, to a certain extent, allow—individuals to improve their social position.

A Note on Meritocracy

Meritocracy refers to an ideology in which the belief that an individuals' efforts, talents, and abilities will be rewarded with social advancement. In other words, one's hard work is rewarded. "Work hard, get ahead" is a familiar phrase that sums up the idea of meritocracy. The ideology embodied in meritocracy is fundamental to the persistence of our social class system. Everyone knows that the United States is the land of opportunity. I travel all over the U.S., and when I travel to large/medium cities, I make a point to take a few taxi rides. Invariably, I encounter a number of cab drivers who are originally from other countries, and I ask them where they are from and why they are here. Without exception, they tell me that they are here because only in the United States can they enjoy such a wonderful life and know that their children will enjoy an even better life than they will. Millions, perhaps billions, of people worldwide view our class system as a vehicle of opportunity that will deliver a better life for them and their children. Even we Americans believe in the system of "work hard, get ahead." To be sure, meritocracy is an ideological system that maintains our structure of social inequality. That is, our unequal social class system is perpetuated in part by the belief that one's talents, skills, education, and hard work will result in the reward of upward social movement.

Mobility

Essential to the maintenance and success of an open system is the concept of social mobility—the ability of individuals or groups to move between social classes. As we saw in our discussion above, not all stratification systems allow for social mobility. Additionally, social mobility varies widely across societies. Let's take a look at several patterns of social mobility that are found in open systems.

Intragenerational mobility is the movement up or down the social ranks *within* one's own lifetime, and it is a common feature in the mobility stories in our culture. Abraham Lincoln did it, as did Henry Ford; they rose from humble beginnings to the top of society. American society is built on the belief that anyone can rise from the depths of poverty to become doctors, lawyers, captains of industry, and even the president of the United States. However, this may be more myth than reality in society today. Americans experience less mobility than their Western European and Canadian counterparts do. Moreover, recent research clearly shows that there has been very little upward mobility in America for more than forty years ("Mobility Measured," 2014).

On average, Americans experience less social mobility compared to similar Western industrialized nations. Moreover, of those American men born in the bottom one-fifth of earners, only 8% can expect to reach the top one-fifth of earners in the U.S. The chances of an American born into poverty becoming the CEO of a Fortune 500 company is about 1 in 14 million, and his/her chance of becoming president is 1 in 10 million; he/she is more likely to win the lottery or be struck by a meteor (Carter, 2012).

While on average in the United States, there is little social mobility, there are those who still experience movement between classes within their own lives. For example, growing up in my family, there was an emphasis on getting an education in order to live a better life (having a high income, owning your own home, etc.). My father dropped out of tenth grade, and my mother left school in the eighth grade. Both of them were laborers who saw education as the path to a better life. My brother and I have earned Ph.D.'s and live typical middle-class lifestyles that are very different from our parents' lives and our lives growing up. We both experienced upward social mobility in our own lifetime, or *vertical intragenerational mobility*. Typically, intragenerational mobility is measured in two directions:

Horizontal mobility involves movement within the same social class. Think about it as not up-or-down movement, but rather side-to-side movement. Examples could include an auto technician who quits his job at a Chevrolet dealership to take a raise and a new position at a Ford dealership or a nurse who leaves one hospital to work for another hospital closer to his home; neither has moved up or down in social class but moved within his social rank.

Vertical mobility, in contrast, is movement up or down the social classes. While we typically think of vertical mobility in terms of moving up in social class, both upward and downward mobility can occur in an open system. *Upward mobility* refers to movement from one social class to a higher social class, while *downward mobility* refers to movement from one social class to a lower social class. Most discussions of mobility focus on upward mobility, but after the economic downturn of 2008, many people lost well-paying jobs and found themselves living lives that were not middle-class. For example, Michael, a mortgage broker from Washington, D.C., lost his job in 2008 and could not find work for nearly five years. He finally found work in retail sales, making less than half of his old salary and radically changing his lifestyle and reducing his standard of living.

When people experience mobility between generations or from one generation to the next, sociologists refer to this as **intergenerational mobility**. A good way to think of this is to compare one's own achievement with that of his/her parents' generation, to see if there is a change *between* the generations. A vivid example of this is the success of many Vietnamese in Southern California. When I started college in Southern California, I met many Vietnamese students, many of whom had just arrived from Vietnam in the last couple of years. Several of them became my friends, and I learned about how they and their families were living. It was not uncommon for several generations of their families to share small apartments in which everyone contributed to the economic efforts of the family. That is, everyone had a job and everyone kicked in to make ends meet. Most of their meals were rice and some protein, but mostly rice. Many of my friends' families had few possessions, many times using lawn furniture and boxes to furnish their modest, cramped apartments. They made little money and had few belongings while pursuing their educations. Almost all of them eventually graduated, got good jobs, bought homes, and moved their extended families in. Fast-forward thirty years, and many in that community either have moved or are moving into some of the most affluent neighborhoods in Los Angeles. Many of them are business owners, engineers, physicians, and lawyers and have amassed considerably more income, wealth, and social prestige than their parents have. Their thoroughly middle-class lifestyles are nothing like the lives their parents experienced in Southeast Asia. Another illustration of intergenerational mobility is how Americans born into poverty are almost guaranteed to live out their lives in poverty. That is, if you are born poor in America, you can just about count on being poor throughout your life. Research on poverty clearly shows this to be true; there is little intergenerational mobility in the U.S. Poor children will live out poor lives, and rich children will live out lives of privilege (Mazumder, 2005).

These examples highlight what we refer to as **individual mobility**—movement that is a result of individual effort or educational attainment that results in a change in social class. However, not all social mobility is a result of the will and effort of an individual; many times, shifts in social or economic structures can affect the fortunes of entire groups of people.

Mobility that affects large sectors of society is **structural mobility**—movement up or down classes that results from social, industrial, or economic changes that affects large numbers of individuals across social classes. Structural mobility is particularly apparent when there are large-scale economic changes such as the Great Depression, the dot-com boom and, more recently, the mortgage/housing crash of 2008. "A rising tide lifts all ships" is a common saying that means that as the tide rises, all ships, no matter where they are or how large or small they are, will be lifted by that rising tide. As America industrialized, we saw the standard of living of all people rise; even the poor enjoyed an increase in their condition. The rise of the Internet and dot-com industries is another example of structural mobility; many people saw an increase in their standards of living as a result of the boom in Internet companies. The demand for a host of workers, from programmers to salespeople, and the construction of new office buildings rippled through the economy for nearly four years, raising the boats in most social classes.

However, structural mobility has a dark side, as we saw in the Great Depression and the housing crash. When the stock market crashed in October 1929, it plunged the United States and much of the world into the worst economic crisis in history. By 1933, nearly one-third of the workforce was unemployed and the gross national product (now the gross domestic product, GDP) fell from $103.8 billion to $55.7 billion. The entire economy shifted downward, bringing whole classes of people down with it (Marcuss and Kane, 2007). Huge numbers of those in the upper-middle, middle and working classes found themselves in poverty, and for many, there was no going back. Similarly, in 2008, when the housing mortgage market crashed, it sent the economies of many nations into a tailspin that took more than five years to correct. Hundreds of thousands of Americans lost their jobs and their houses, forcing many into long-term unemployment or into jobs that they were overqualified for and that paid very little, resulting in widespread downward mobility across classes.

Raghuram Rajan, an economist at the University of Chicago who correctly predicted the 2008 crash at a Federal Reserve meeting in 2005, suggests that the housing market crash was less about greedy Wall Street bankers and more about income inequality. The widening gulf between the rich and poor was in part the impetus for the extension of housing credit to those in the lower-income levels. Making home ownership accessible to more and more people in order for them to feel invested in society may have brought the economy to its knees. Think about it this way: "... in Greece the government buys off its people with early pensions and great social services and the U.S. buys off its people with easy credit" (Rajan, 2010). As the rich get richer and the poor get poorer, one way to make the poor feel less marginalized and more included socially and economically is to make buying a house a reality. It's like a sleight-of-hand trick — "Pay no attention to the rich getting richer at your expense ... look over here; you, too, can have a shiny, new house."

Inequality: The Rich Get Richer and the Poor Get Poorer

If you think that income and wealth differences between those at the very top and the rest of us are the result of a system that rewards those who work the hardest and therefore creates a just social world, you have not been paying attention. Those at the top make the rules and guard the gates to privilege. Through a complex interplay of foundations, elite universities, policymaking groups, and think tanks, the powerful in the U.S. maintain a system of inequality that favors the maintenance of their wealth and privilege and grows the gap between themselves and the rest of us. During the recent economic downturn in the U.S., sometimes referred to as the *Great Recession,* which toppled the housing market in 2008 and created worldwide economic distress, those in the top 1% saw their incomes grow by 31.4%, or 95% of the total gain in incomes from 2009–12. During the same period, the bottom 99% (the rest of us) saw a growth in incomes of a measly 0.4% (Saez, 2013). While most were having a tough time making ends meet, or even finding work, the top 1%, the social elites in the U.S., earned nearly all gains in income—they got richer.

A considerable body of research has shown that mobility in any society is in part a function of the inequality in that society. Generally, the *more inequality* in a society, the *less social mobility* that is experienced (Pickett and Wilkinson, 2009; Corak, 2006). Looking at figure 7.2, you can see the clear linear relationship between social inequality and social mobility. In countries like the United States and the UK, where there is considerable inequality, there is also very little social mobility. In fact, of all the countries that were examined in this study, the U.S. had both the highest rate of social inequality and the lowest level of social mobility. By contrast, countries that have little social inequality like Denmark, Finland, and Norway experience higher levels of intergenerational mobility.

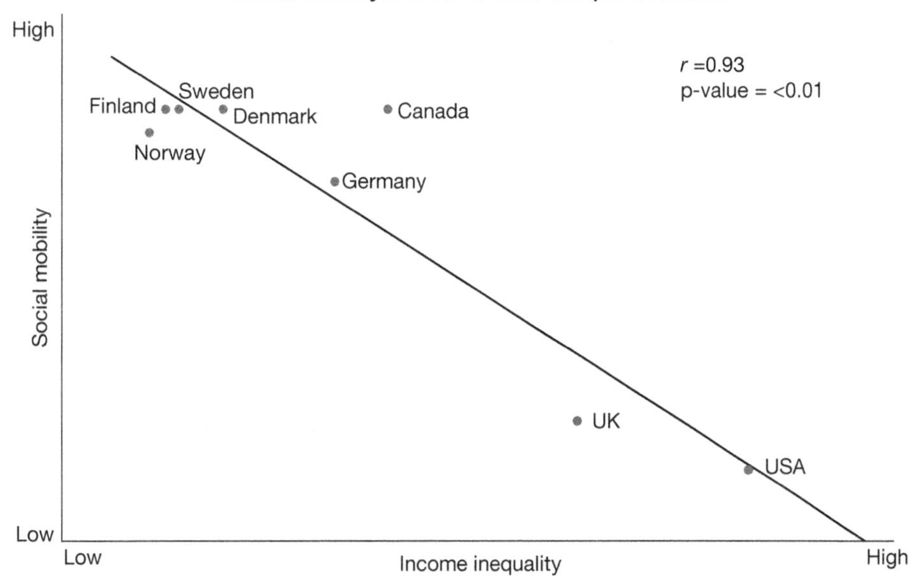

Source: Wilkinson and Pickett, 2009

Fig. 7.2 Income Inequality Compared to Social Mobility

Inequality: Wealth and Income

A great deal of the discussion in this chapter concerns inequality. While several dimensions of inequality such as social, educational, and capital inequality are examined in this chapter and throughout the book, they are all linked to both income and wealth. Obviously one's income and wealth are directly related to relative levels of deprivation or privilege. That is, those with low incomes and little wealth will have less access to and possess fewer valuable social resources than those with greater incomes and wealth. Income typically refers to how much material reward (money, mainly) one gets from work, investments or the government. So, when we discuss *income inequality* we are looking at the uneven distribution of individual or household incomes across a given society. While there has always been income inequality in the U.S., in the past thirty years the top earners have taken a bigger and bigger share of the overall income, making the gap between them and the rest of America one of the widest in history. The income inequality we are currently experiencing in the U.S. hasn't been seen since before the great depression (Atkinson, Piketty and Saez, 2011; Saez and Zucman, 2016; Piketty and Saez, 2012). In fact, one renowned economist, Thomas Piketty, said that "The United States is getting accustomed to a completely crazy level of inequality" (Lowery, 2012).

Social scientists vary widely in their interpretation and definition of wealth. Additionally, sociologist don't all agree on how to measure wealth, but that larger discourse is beyond our discussion here. However, there are some common elements of wealth that most sociologists agree on, and it is these elements I include in my definition. So, I think it is best to think about wealth this way: wealth is the accumulation and ownership of money, property, or other material goods. We all have the potential to have wealth—the stuff we own outright, such as bikes, cars, homes, or retirement accounts. However, when we think of the *wealthy* many times we conjure up images of people who don't necessarily have work-a-day jobs but have plenty of money, property, and influence, and live a more leisurely lifestyle than most. Someone can have a high income but have little wealth and vice versa. A surgeon, for example, may have a very high annual income from her work, but have a high mortgage, car payments, and lots of student loan debt. She may make good money but has to keep working to maintain her lifestyle or else she would sink financially; she has high income, very little wealth. On the other hand, someone who inherits a great amount of property and makes little income off that property may never have to work for an income, but can maintain a very high standard of living and a more leisurely lifestyle; they have great wealth, but low or no income from work.

When we discuss wealth inequality we are examining the uneven distribution of wealth across the population of a given society. As we mentioned above, the income gap in America is large and widening. In fact, the top 10% of households in the U.S. earn 28% of the overall income. That's bad enough in terms of income inequality, but it gets even worse when we look at wealth. The wealthiest 10% of American households control an eye-popping 76% of all wealth in America (OECD, 2015). It seems that no matter how it is measured, the income and wealth gap between the rich and everyone else is widening at a record pace. Why do you think the income and wealth gap in the U.S. is so great?

WEALTH MEASURED AS NET WORTH: WARNING, THIS COULD BE DEPRESSING

Some sociologist and other social scientists use net worth as the measure of wealth. For them wealth is an individual's or family's net worth. Wealth then, is the total value of everything a person or family owns minus any debt (Domhoff, 2013). So, how do you calculate your wealth or net worth? Simply add up all the stuff you own (a dollar figure for your bikes, phones, computers, etc.) then subtract all the debt you have—all you owe. You may find that your total is a negative number, which means you have no wealth. Don't feel bad; many, many Americans have no wealth. If you got a positive number, then that is your wealth. Obviously wealthier people will have much larger positive numbers than most of us who have either small positive numbers or negative numbers, making this an easily interpreted measure of wealth. You can see that this is a much easier and more efficient way to determine wealth, but does it get at what it means to be wealthy?

Are You Middle Class?

Well, are you? If you are like most of my students, you probably said, "Sure, I'm middle class." OK, you're middle class; now tell me what middle class is. Take a breath and think about it ... what do you mean by middle class? Is it how much money you make? Is it the amount of education you have, how much you have traveled, how much you know, what you do for a living, or is it how you live your life? Yes, social class is all of these things and more. In this section, we will explore the parameters/descriptions of each of the social classes so we have a better idea of what we mean by lower, working, middle, upper-middle, and upper class.

The Social Classes

Let's discuss social class. When we talk about social class, what do we mean? Social class is not an easy concept to wrap our minds around; your idea of social class may vary from my idea of social class, but in general, Americans have a vague idea of what we mean by social class. It includes mode of dress, standard of living, the means of recreation, and the material goods one is able to enjoy. Unfortunately, when we ask Americans about social class, nearly 51% of us claim to be middle class (Newport, 2015). Obviously, more than half of Americans cannot be middle class, so why do so many of us think we are middle class? Seeing ourselves as middle class is easy enough to do because the language does not present much to go on in terms of what the label describes. In a sense, we look around and see that we are not globetrotting millionaires with homes all over the world and we are not sleeping on a park bench, so we must be in the middle. While those who view themselves as middle class do so through an arbitrary measure of relative social standing, those in the upper classes are aware of who they are and are raised to be conscious of their status and their obligations. And certainly, those living at or near the bottom of society are painfully aware of their social position.

The Upper Class

In the United States, we have no monarchy, but some have dubbed the upper class the American royalty. The upper class is made up of about 1–3% of the U.S. population, making them as few as 3.1 million to as many as 9.3 million. The upper class is a homogenous, white, insular population whose wealth is inherited and wields considerable political, economic, and social power. Members of the upper class enjoy high incomes from occupations in the business, banking, and investment worlds. They are graduates of and send their children to Ivy League and highly selective universities, where they strengthen the bonds of their privileged class and cultivate the connections that will afford them access to political, industrial, and military spheres. They own multiple homes, enjoy international travel, and live luxurious lifestyles that tend to buffer them from the social and economic reality of other classes. As a group they wield considerable political power, mainly through the amount of access they have to various political offices, including the presidency.

The Upper-Middle Class

Members of the upper-middle class have substantially less wealth and prestige than the upper class but enjoy a higher standard of living than the working or lower class. America's upper-middle class consists of highly educated professionals and senior executives, for example, who earn high wages for occupations that require advanced degrees and that typically afford them considerable autonomy. In addition, this group also tends to have some local political power and prestige (Harrison and Dye, 2008). They are almost all homeowners, have a buffer against economic downturns, and their children will attend prestigious and selective colleges.

The Middle Class

The idea of middle class is the subject of considerable debate and discussion and is interpreted broadly by scholars, politicians, pundits, and laypeople alike. For example, a 2008 Pew study of Americans found that 40% of those with incomes of $20,000 or less reported being middle class and about one-third of those with incomes over $150,000 considered themselves middle class (Taylor et al., 2008). Politicians of all stripes use the term middle class frequently and regularly as if they have a firm handle on the concept. In a 2012 speech, Senator Marco Rubio used the term middle class thirty-five times (Weigel, 2012). President Obama mentioned the middle class more than a half-dozen times in his 2013 State of the Union address and seven times in his 2015 address to the union ("State of the Union Text," 2013; McAuliff and Siddiqui, 2015). Perhaps because so many Americans consider themselves middle class, using this rather hazy concept, politicians can appeal to a large segment of America, and make them feel included in the larger political discussion. While many like to freely bandy the term around, a firm definition of middle class remains elusive. Below, rather than provide a definition, I give a broad-brushed description of middle class-ness. Also, take a look at figure 7.3 below and notice the range of occupations and incomes the middle class covers compared to the other class categories.

Those in the middle class have less education, make less money, and have jobs with less social prestige than those in the upper-middle class. Typical middle-class occupations include schoolteachers, registered nurses, small business owners, bank managers, semi-professionals, and lower-level white-collar employees. Members of this class consist of college graduates and those with specialized education who have higher-than-average incomes; most are homeowners with little to no savings. Their children will most likely attend state colleges and universities.

A Note on the Middle Class

The middle class has been shrinking for decades, but it did not draw that much attention in the past because most of those leaving the middle class were upward-bound. In contrast, since 2000, those leaving the middle class are more likely doing so because they experienced a downturn in their economic situations. Moreover, the composition of today's middle class has changed. The fastest-growing segment of the middle class are those sixty-five and over, while the number of middle-class households composed of married couples with children has shrunk. The last three decades have witnessed a distinct change in social class membership, typifying widening social inequality. While the majority of those who exit the middle class leave and move downward, the greatest gains in economic growth have been experienced by those at the very top of the social hierarchy (Gilbert, 2014; Duncan and Murnane, 2011).

The Working Class

Those in the working class tend to have less education, lower wages, and jobs that require little education and are more physically demanding than those in the middle class. Those identifying as working or lower class has increased in the past few years. A series of Gallup surveys revealed that Americans who call themselves working or lower class rose from 33% in 2000 to 48% in 2015 (Newport, 2015). Members of the working class usually have a high school diploma or some college education and work in low-skilled to semi-skilled occupations. Occupations in the working class range from manual laborers to retail sales to plumbers and carpenters. These are typically not salaried, but rather hourly positions. Just over half of those in the working class are homeowners, and they tend to have no savings or protection against economic downturns. Children of the working class have considerably less chance of attending or completing college compared to children from the middle, upper-middle, and the upper classes.

The Lower Classes

A 2012 study found that one-third of Americans consider themselves to be lower class, which is up from a 2008 report. Members of the lower classes report that they feel more "powerlessness" than those in the middle classes. That is, they don't feel that they can change their environments, social conditions or society, the world is the way it is and they must endure it. They also say that they are less content and healthy than those in higher social classes. Overall, those in the lower classes view the future as bleak for themselves and their children (Morin and Motel, 2012; Narayan, 2000). The lower class represents those on the lowest end of the income, education, and occupation spectrum. Members of the lower class are engaged in low-paying service industry jobs, manual unskilled labor, and menial occupations. This class also includes the seasonally employed, partially employed, unemployed, and those on public assistance.

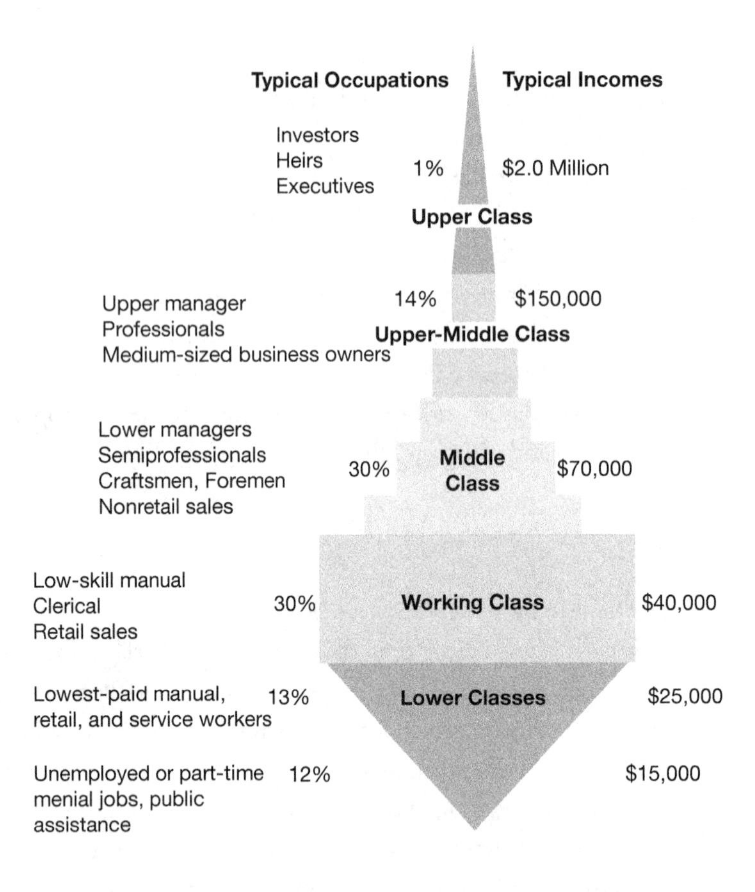

Source: Gilbert and Kahl, 1992

Fig. 7.3. How social class is distributed by income and occupation.

Measuring the Complexity of Social Class: S.E.S. (Socioeconomic Status)

Social class is one of the most complex and important concepts that sociologists discuss, yet its definition remains elusive. Social class is so much more than what I have shown above. There are a number of variables to consider when describing social class in the United States: What type of job do you have? Do you have a job? Do you have job benefits? Do you have paid vacation? Do you have vacation? How much does your job pay per year? What magazines/books/blogs do you read? Do you watch tennis or NASCAR? What is your favorite food? What neighborhood do you live in? Do you own or rent your home? Have you ever traveled abroad? Do you know how the stock market works (really works)? *Honey Boo Boo* or CNN? What does Hermes make? What is foie gras made from? Single malt scotch, wine, or beer? What is the difference between sushi and sashimi? You getting the picture? All of these questions are indirect ways of measuring social class; some are economic measures (How much does your job pay per year?), some are social measures (What neighborhood do you live in?), and some are cultural questions (What is foie gras made from?). However, when measuring social class, most people would not want to answer so many questions just to get at a single concept. You would have to burden people with a thirty-page questionnaire to get a reliable image of their social class. So, how do we measure social class? Many disciplines, including sociology, use a *proxy* for social class called **socioeconomic status** (SES), which is a measure of social class based on *income, education,* and *occupation.* This single variable has been shown to be a powerful predictor of the complex construct of social class (Hotchkiss and Borow, 1996). You have probably heard of SES and may even have bandied the term about or used it in a term paper. We social scientists use it because it connotes a person's position in the social hierarchy, how the hierarchy is constructed, and is a powerful indicator of one's consumption choices and life chances. Like social class, SES indicates one's access to and possession of valuable social resources, whether that's education, money, power, social networks, healthcare, or leisure activities. SES, then, becomes an important measure of social class because it allows us to understand social stratification, levels of inequality, amounts of mobility, and it is strongly related to life chances. Therefore, SES can and is used synonymously with social class (Oakes, 2012).

Life Chances and Social Class

> *"Everything from the chance to stay alive during the first year after birth to the chance to view fine art; the chance to remain healthy and if sick to get well again quickly; the chance to avoid becoming a juvenile delinquent; and very crucially, the chance to complete an intermediary or higher educational grade–these are among the chances that are crucially influenced by one's position in the class structure of a modern society"*
>
> — *Weber, 1925*

When the *Titanic* sank in April 1912, more than 1,500 people perished. Of those who died in the North Atlantic that night, the vast majority were of the lower classes. Fully 60 % of those in first class survived, 36% of those in second class survived, and less than a quarter (24%) of those in the lowest passenger class, third class, survived the disaster. The White Star Line (the company that owned the *Titanic*) only had an evacuation plan for first- and second-class passengers. Those in third class were only notified to abandon ship *after* the first two passenger classes (Hall, 1986; "*Titanic* Survivors," 2011; "*Titanic* Disaster Hearings," 2011). Clearly, the chances of survival on the *Titanic* were linked to what class one was traveling in and the treatment of the social classes at that point in history. By the way, there were enough lifeboats to save every single soul on board.

These differences illustrate how the various classes of travelers were treated, and it is emblematic of how your social rank can affect your life chances. How long will you live? What types of diseases and injuries will you encounter in your life? Will you go to jail or prison? How much education will you achieve? The answers to these questions are directly tied to your social class. Life chances—the opportunities experience a quality of life and the extent to which individuals can access social resources such as education, employment, healthcare, and even travel—are profoundly impacted by your social position (Weber, 1947). Social class matters!

Life Expectancy, Disease, Injury, and Social Class

> *"If you are poor, you are not likely to live long."*
>
> — *Nelson Mandela*

The average life expectancy of those earning below $25,000 a year in the United States is sixty-eight, while those who earn more than $100,000 a year can expect to live, on average, to the ripe old age of seventy-eight. In fact, a 2012 study revealed that for those with less than a high school education, life expectancy actually went from seventy-eight in 1990 to seventy-four in 2008 for women and from seventy-four to seventy-one for men in the same time period (Duleep, 1989; Singh and Siahpush, 2014; Singh-Manoux et al., 2004; Smith et al., 1997; Waldron, 2007). Why should those who make more money expect to live longer? Are they buying more years from the gods? No. They are living longer on average because life expectancy is highly correlated with education, occupation, and income. Those in the middle, upper-middle, and upper classes hold positions that require a college degree or more, pay well, and afford them significant health benefits, vacations, and retirement options. This combination of income and benefits allows members of these classes to practice health maintenance through regular visits to their doctors, exercise, and eating healthy by creating diets that are informed through education, and they have very little exposure to injury in the course of their occupations. While stockbrokers may work in a pressure-cooker environment, they are at little risk for disease or injury as a direct result of their occupations. As a professor, my greatest concern would be that a book might fall off a shelf and hit me on the head, and I am sure there has never been a professor who contracted black lung from teaching sociology in college classrooms. By contrast, those in the working and lower classes are less likely to have extensive health benefits, nutritional education, and safe work environments, putting them at greater risk for workplace injury and a variety of diseases. In fact, a 2014 report by the National Institute for Occupational Safety and Health found that rates of black lung disease among Appalachian coal miners are at their highest in forty years (Lee et al., 2014).

What other health risks are those in the lower classes prone to? Duncan and Magnuson (2011) found that those who were below the poverty line, receiving food stamps, and who had lower incomes in general were more likely to be obese. Research also indicates that lower socioeconomic status, defined as less than a high school diploma and making below $12,000 a year, was an independent risk factor for developing cardiovascular disease (Franks et al., 2011). Even sleep deprivation is linked to social class and health issues (Buxton, 2010; Benedict et al., 2012; Cockerham, 2007).

Fig. 7.4 Coal miners are at considerably greater risk for injury and disease than people with typical middle class occupations like bankers, business executives or college professors. Their life chances are impacted by their lower level of education, lower wages and their dangerous occupation.

People in the middle and upper classes can afford to take time off from work to see a doctor, and as informed consumers, they maintain their health by visiting healthcare professionals on a regular basis. These factors, along with eating healthier diets, have a positive impact on life chances like life expectancy, injury, and disease. On the other hand, those in the lower classes are more likely to wait for a medical crisis and then visit an emergency room, the most expensive healthcare venue, and have diets higher in carbohydrates and fat, putting them at greater risk for cardiovascular disease, diabetes, and obesity.

Judicial Treatment

"Law grinds the poor, and rich men rule the law."

— Oliver Goldsmith

In June 2013, a sixteen-year-old Texas boy struck and killed four pedestrians with his pickup truck while driving drunk. After a trial lasting a few months, the judge in the case sentenced the youth to ten years' probation and ordered him to attend a rehabilitation program in Newport Beach, California. An expert testifying on behalf of the white teen, who came from an extremely affluent and prominent family, said that the youth suffered from "Affluenza," a condition caused by family wealth, indulgence, and a household of parental discord, in which the child was largely ignored or placated with material possessions. His attorney argued, successfully, that their client had never experienced and serious consequences for his behaviors, therefore he really didn't know right from wrong (Voorhees, 2013). What if this had been a poor sixteen-year-old or a black or Latino youth? Do you think the punishment would have been the same? Probably not, according to national statistics that indicate the law is unequally applied across social classes.

More than half of all prisoners in the U.S. were at or below the poverty line when they began their sentences. Studies have shown that while the poor go to jail at higher rates, their time in prison compounds an already dire economic landscape by reducing their future earnings potential and increasing their unemployment rates. Moreover, this is not a temporary effect. In fact, a 2010 Pew study demonstrated that 67% of released inmates who were among the bottom fifth of all U.S. earners stayed at or below that level over a period of twenty years (Western and Pettit, 2010).

Consumption Patterns

> *"Expensive clothing is a poor man's attempt to appear prosperous."*
>
> *— Mokokoma Mokhonoana*

People who occupy different social classes buy and use different things like cars, houses, food and TV. These **consumption patterns** refer to the different ways that people consume goods and services based on their class positions. These patterns are connected to social class. It makes sense, right? The more education you have, the more money you're likely to make and the more prestigious your occupation is likely to be, and these all influence what you consume. I mean, Jay Z probably drinks a lot more Ace of Spades champagne than you (not Cristal), he drives a nicer car, eats at fancier restaurants, pays more for his designer clothes, jets around the world, and lives in a better neighborhood. Face it, he has 99 problems but money ain't one.

Have you ever heard of a magazine called *The Atlantic*? In my classes, I ask students to raise their hands if they have ever heard of *The Atlantic* magazine ... and I rarely see any hands in the air. Then I ask them if they have ever heard of *People* magazine and everyone's hands go up. If you are like most of my students, you probably wouldn't raise your hand for *The Atlantic*. What does this mean? It probably says more about the social class you grew up in than what you like to read. Those who subscribe to *The Atlantic* have incomes well above the national average, are well-educated, and have highly desirable occupations. Oh, *The Atlantic* is a literary magazine and *People* magazine ... well, you know. What we eat, drink, read, wear, watch, and listen to is influenced to a certain degree by our social class. Have you had chateaubriand or caviar and champagne in the last thirty days? Have you had fast food in the past thirty days? If you are like most of my students, and me, you have had fast food recently and don't even know what chateaubriand is. Social ranking greatly influences how we think, act, and decide, and this is reflected in our consumption choices.

Food is perhaps like no other consumption choice we make. Food is bound up with how we were raised, food exposure, availability, education, health consciousness, and class lifestyle.

Members of the middle classes tend to eat healthier diets compared to those in the lower classes. Much of this is explained through the food choices that better-educated middle-class parents make, usually with an eye to nutritional value and a balanced diet and less concern for cost. My mother, who only has an eighth-grade education, struggled with putting balanced meals on the table due to the lack of nutritional education and cost. When I was nine, my mother took me to the doctor because I had very little energy. Much to his shock, the doctor diagnosed me as malnourished and anemic. He prescribed giant iron pills for me and helped my mother understand the value of preparing meals that were nutritionally balanced.

Not all foods are available to all people. That is, the social class circumstances we grow up in many times set boundaries on the types of food we come to see as desirable. Middle-class families typically enjoy a wider range of foods than their lower-class counterparts due to cost, accessibility, and familiarity. So, what we find in our social class environments influences what we consume. Our food choices, then, are influenced by our living arrangements. That is, many working/lower-class urban dwellers may find themselves in food deserts with little access to general grocery stores or those that sell whole or organic foods (Morton et al., 2005; Proscio, 2006; Baker et al., 2006; Treuhaft and Karpyn, 2012). Retailers that specialize in whole/organic foods tend to locate themselves in more upscale neighborhoods, where a more educated, wealthier consumer base is likely to live. It is no coincidence that grocery stores with wider selections end up in the suburbs or toney urban enclaves and less robust urban areas are left with overpriced convenience stores offering little in the way of nutritional food. I grew up in a small New England town, and this class difference in food availability was apparent even there. The poor working area that I grew up in had no grocery stores, but there was a convenience store about four blocks from my house that had necessities like toilet paper, milk, soup, cleaning products, cigarettes, and soda but no whole, unprocessed foods. Yet in a much more affluent neighborhood in my hometown— "up on the hill"—not more than a mile from my house, there was a market that offered a variety of fresh fruits, vegetables, and meats that it would happily deliver to its upper-middle class customers. Even though it was so close to the neighborhood I grew up in, I did not know it existed until I was in the eighth grade.

Think About This

Social class is not real. That is, it is a *construct.* A social construct is any idea or behavior that is seen as natural and real to people, and whose meaning emerges through social interaction. Social class only has meaning because society gives it meaning. We have seen how much social class can influence your life—how much education you will attain, who you will marry, what you will read, what you eat, how you dress, and how long you will live. Social class has all these effects on your life ... and it does not even exist! If something that doesn't even exist has this much influence on your life, imagine how powerful those things that do exist are.

TRY THIS

Conduct some social research in your neighborhood. Take a look around your community and see what types of food are available. Are there fast food franchises? Are there grocery stores? Convenience stores? Now travel to different parts of your city or town and see what food choices are available in those areas. Everyone knows his/her town—go to less desirable neighborhoods, then travel to the more affluent and desirable parts of town. Are the choices different? What did you notice about the differences in food availability, quality, and number of food outlets?

Types of Capital

The concept of capital has a long social history, but it was fundamentally transformed by our man Adam Smith, when he decided that we should treat physical assets and people just like we do money—as *capital*. This meaning has lingered in a number of disciplines, including sociology (Doob, 2013). The amounts and types of capital that you accrue over your lifetime is linked to your social class position. Typically, increased amounts and types of capital are highly correlated with an increase in social class. The higher one's social class the greater amounts and types of capital one acquires.

Capital refers to an array of resources that people either possess or have access to and find useful in a range of social situations (Doob, 2013; Spillane, Hallet, and Diamond, 2003). Let's simplify this and think about capital this way: it allows you to get stuff done. You can't buy that latte without money (financial capital), you can't carry on a party conversation about Hemingway if you haven't read him (cultural capital), you can't get those concert tickets you really want without knowing someone who knows a guy who can get them (social capital), and you can't get your dream job as an accountant without the investment in an accounting degree (human capital). See, these various forms of capital allow us to get stuff done!

People accrue various types of capital over their lifetime just as we accrue things across our lives; we collect friends, knowledge, education, and a certain amount of sophistication. It is easy, then, to see the connection to the types and amounts of capital that members of the various social classes may accrue through their class experiences and across the life course. As noted above, there are four types of capital that I will discuss here briefly.

Financial Capital: This is pretty straightforward: monetary things like income from a job, investments, or things that you can buy to gain other resources. Financial capital represents, in part, access to and possession of other forms of capital. That is, with money comes some privilege. For example, families with high incomes (highly correlated with education and occupation) are more likely than families with low incomes to have children who will attend prestigious colleges and graduate from those schools (acquisition of cultural capital). Furthermore, those children are more likely to create social networks (social capital) with future leaders of government and industry, which could be advantageous to their careers and family. With money, you can get a lot of stuff done

Cultural Capital: Cultural capital is broadly understood as the acquisition of non-economic social assets that can aid in social mobility. Say you are up for a job, and during the interview, you notice a picture of the person interviewing you on a sailboat. You might mention how you recently sailed from Cape Cod to Virginia Beach and that you have been a competitive sailor for more than ten years. This could quite possibly give you a leg up on the competition.

Cultural capital includes, but is not limited to, things like worldviews, knowledge, skills (sailing), and behaviors. We accrue cultural capital over our lifetime through education, travel, and social interaction. For example, you can learn how the stock market really works by taking an economics class, find out that Hemingway was the greatest novelist of the twentieth century in college, or travel to Japan and learn the difference between sushi and sashimi; you might fly to France and taste foie gras or know which fork to use for your salad by attending fancy dinner parties. Cultural capital lets us get lots of stuff done, such as impress people with our knowledge of exoteric trivia, fit into various social groups/situations, and even land a job.

Social Capital: Think of social capital as your social networks and your ability to create social connections. It seems obvious that we all seek out connections with others as a function of being a member of our families, communities, and society. However, those who research social capital stress that our social relations have productive benefits. That is, in part, we develop networks to help us acquire resources, meet others, and benefit materially—get stuff done. Let's say you and your partner want to go out and celebrate your birthday, but you do not have a babysitter. You may call your sister, whose best friend has a wonderful babysitter, and ask her if you could call him to get the babysitter's contact information. Perhaps you have asked someone in your social circle to introduce you to a potential mate or used contacts to get a job interview. Social capital, then, is the acquisition of and maintenance of interpersonal connections that we employ to perform a range of beneficial tasks, from getting a date for your cousin's wedding to meeting the right people to help move your career along. Moreover, the digital age has increased the potential for greatly expanding our social networks. For example, LinkedIn.com is a social networking service focused on the business community where users can post their resumes, look for jobs, obtain introductions to potential employers through people they know, and follow companies they like to see if they are hiring.

Human Capital: This refers to all the knowledge and skills that people acquire throughout their lives that enable them to succeed in their occupational and social endeavors. We can think of human capital as an investment in ourselves. Your college education is an investment in your future; learning a foreign language, learning to juggle, and taking self-defense classes are all investments in you and your future. It is important to mention that not all human capital is equal. In the past decade, for-profit universities have flourished, but many times, these degrees do not translate to a higher standard of living because they are not as valued as a degree from an established college or university. Not all skills are similarly valued. I have mad fly-fishing skills, but they will not help me land a job as a college professor. While not all skills, education, and training are valued equally, some skills are seen as universally valuable, such as effective communication and interpersonal skills. So, what kind of stuff does human capital let us accomplish? It prepares us and makes us qualified for a range of jobs and vocations.

I know what you are thinking—it seems that all four types of capital are interconnected. That is, it seems that each of the four types is inexorably linked to the others. Well, you are right. Think about it this way: Your parents have money (financial capital) and can afford to send you to Yale for a really good liberal arts education and an investment in your future (human capital). There, you learn all kinds of wonderful stuff from some of the best minds in the world. You also travel abroad to amplify your educational experience (cultural capital). While at college, you meet and hang out with a range of other privileged people who will become lifelong friends and help you navigate a bright social future (social capital). All this still applies even if you don't go to Yale. Take a moment and think about how you experience all these types of capital.

Poverty

"Poverty is the worst form of violence."

— Mahatma Gandhi

The poor are a common feature in every society, and it is how any given society deals with their poor that highlights that society's values and beliefs about social ranking. About half the world's population lives on $2.50 or less per day. Think about that: could you survive on $2.50 per day? If you only had $2.50 a day to live on, what would your life be like? Most likely, you would be unable to satisfy your hunger, provide shelter for yourself, or maintain relationships with others. You would have to rely on either government or private-sector help to feed, clothe, and shelter yourself (Chandy and Geertz, 2011; Shah, 2013). These would be your day-to-day miseries; your lifestyle would not include a vehicle, travel, entertainment, shopping, that daily latte, or any number of comforts many of us have grown accustomed to.

LIVING ON ONE DOLLAR

In this documentary, a group of college students travel to Guatemala for their summer break to find out if they can live on $1.00 a day. They discover that hunger is pervasive, and daily life becomes measurably difficult as they struggle with making a living, dealing with illness, and negotiating social life. Do you think that you could live a life on $1.00 a day? Probably not in our economy. The documentary highlights many issues of inequality.

http://livingonone.org/livingonone/film/

What is Poverty?

In sociology, when we discuss poverty, we make a distinction between absolute poverty and relative poverty. **Absolute poverty** is the minimum level of income needed to meet basic needs such as food, clothing, and shelter. This concept, however, is not concerned with broader issues that affect the poor such as quality of life and social and cultural needs. This measure, then, becomes a line in the sand that separates those who are above the line from those below the line. In the United States, absolute poverty is measured by the federal government, which sets annual *Federal Poverty Guidelines* (see Table 7.1 below) that result in what is known as the *poverty line* (sometimes referred to as the Federal Poverty Level). This measure of poverty is used to determine individuals' and families' eligibility for various types of aid and services; it also indicates how many Americans are struggling financially each year and over time.

Federal Poverty Guidelines have been roundly criticized for many reasons but mainly because they are calculated by identifying how much it would cost to feed a family of three or more for one year, then multiplying that number by three. However, this formula was developed in 1963 based on the Agriculture Department's economy food plan for a family of three or more and multiplied by three. Why multiply by three? Because a 1955 Agriculture Department Household Food Consumption Survey found that for families of three or more, the average dollar value for all food for one week accounted for about one-third of their total income after taxes (Glennerster, 2002). Moreover, poverty guidelines for all years since 1963 were updated using only the Consumer Price Index (inflation). Those numbers are over fifty years old! Not only is the age of the base calculation a critical issue, but living costs and standards have changed in many ways since 1963. In fact, research on U.S. household budgets indicates that food now comprises only about one-seventh of an average family's expenditures (Orr, 2009). Because of the use of an antiquated computation that simply adjusts for inflation annually, they fail to recognize the diminished ratio of food costs to overall living costs, which means these poverty guidelines no longer represent anything in relation to family incomes or costs. The U.S. Congress actually funded a study by the National Academy of Sciences to improve the way the poverty guidelines are calculated, and two legislatures proposed an act to "modernize" the way poverty in the U.S. is measured, all to no avail (Citro and Michael, 1995). Current poverty guidelines simply fail to accurately measure and portray real poverty in the U.S. Can you think of reasons why congress would ignore or not deal with such an important issue like poverty in the U.S.?

Other international organizations such as the World Bank and the United Nations Development Programme define absolute poverty (sometimes called extreme poverty) as any individual who lives on $1.00 or less per day (Ravallion et al., 2008). Currently, there are an estimated 1.1 billion people worldwide in extreme poverty.

TABLE 7.1 2015 U.S. Federal Poverty Guidelines

Persons in Family/Household	Poverty Guideline
1	$11,700
2	$15,930
3	$20,090
4	$24,250
5	$28,410
6	$32,570
7	$36,730
8	$40,890

For families/households with more than 8 persons, add $4,160 for each additional person.

Imagine you have a family of four and have to live on the income presented in these guidelines in your city. Try creating a budget for your family using costs in your area. Could your family survive on this amount of money? If you could, what would your standard of living be like? What would your quality of life be like?

In contrast, relative poverty measures how poor a person or group is compared to other people or groups within the community or society. Whereas absolute poverty is an objective measure of poverty (a dollar amount that draws a line between individuals or groups), relative poverty is a subjective assessment of poverty that people use to gauge the difference between their own resources, the average cost of living and the perceived resources of others in their area. That is, you feel more or less poor relative to those around you. When I was in fifth grade, I overheard someone say that I wore "poor kids' clothes," whatever those are. It made me realize that relative to the other kids in my school, I wore less expensive clothes and sneakers, I rode a much less expensive bike, and my family did not eat meals out or drive a *nice* car. So, while my family ate regularly and we always had clothes to wear, we wore much less expensive fashions, and relative to most of the families in our city, we were poor. Relative poverty changes in relation to the standard of living in an area. A person who lives in relative poverty in the United States is likely to be wealthy compared to a person with an average lifestyle in a third-world country.

If your family income is $10,000 a year or greater, you make more than 84% of the world, and if your annual income is $50,000 or more a year, you are richer than 99% of the world (Hovde, 2012). Many poor Americans are quite well off compared to those in developing and undeveloped nations (Worstall, 2013). Those Americans who account for the bottom 5% of incomes are richer than nearly 70% of the remaining citizens of the world. Indeed, the poorest Americans in the lowest 5% income range still enjoy a greater amount of wealth than the top 5% of earners in India (Milanovic, 2013). It would seem that our poorest are among the world's wealthiest.

A Note on Relative Poverty

Some are quick to point out that the poor in America have it pretty good relative to the poor in many other parts of the world. This, of course, is a false argument. While a single woman in the U.S. who makes about $9,000 a year has a much larger income than the average worker in Bangladesh, she doesn't live in Bangladesh; she lives in America, where, according to the Federal Poverty Guidelines, she is poor. By all other measures, she will have a tough time putting food on her table and sheltering and clothing herself. That $9,000-a-year income makes it quite difficult to fully participate in our society; no matter where you are poor, you experience deprivation, marginalization, and, to a certain extent, a sense of powerlessness. So, while the poor in the U.S. may be more likely to have a car or a phone than the poor in the rest of the world, they are not living large; they are struggling to feed themselves and their families and feel disenfranchised, just like the poor in the rest of the world!

Who Are the Poor?

According to the U.S. Census Bureau, there were approximately 46.7 million poor Americans, or about 14.8% of the total population, in 2014, which approached the largest number of poor ever recorded in the nearly fifty-two years of keeping statistics on poverty, which makes sense because the U. S. population has swelled in the past half-century. However, as you can see in figure 7.5, the percentage of Americans in poverty has been steadily increasing since 2000.

Since Lyndon B. Johnson declared war on poverty in 1964, poverty in the United States has not changed that much overall, but the demographics of the poor have changed significantly in the past fifty years. When I was in high school in the 1970s, I remember watching the nightly news and seeing stories about old people in America being so poor and their pensions and Social Security being so inadequate that thousands of them had been reduced to eating dog food. Now the elderly represent some of the richest people who have ever lived on Earth. In 1966, nearly 29% of those sixty-five and over were in poverty; as of 2014, only 10% of the elderly are poor. Today, most poor Americans are in their prime working years. As of 2014, 57% of poor Americans were aged eighteen to sixty-four, versus 41.7% in 1959. Sadly, 33% of all children under age 18 are in poverty in the U.S.

Race is also linked to poverty in the U.S. More than 26% of the black population and 23% of Hispanics are poor. Asian Americans fare much better with about 12% of that population in poverty. In contrast 12.7% of those who identify as white and 10% of white non-Hispanic Americans are among the poor (DeNavas-Walt and Proctor, 2015). So, who are the poor in the U.S.? Well, those most likely to be poor in the U.S. are minority women and children. What factors do you think contribute to the different poverty rates across races and ages? Also, why are there so many poor people in a country that is so wealthy? Below we will discuss some of the factors contributing to poverty and those most likely to be in poverty.

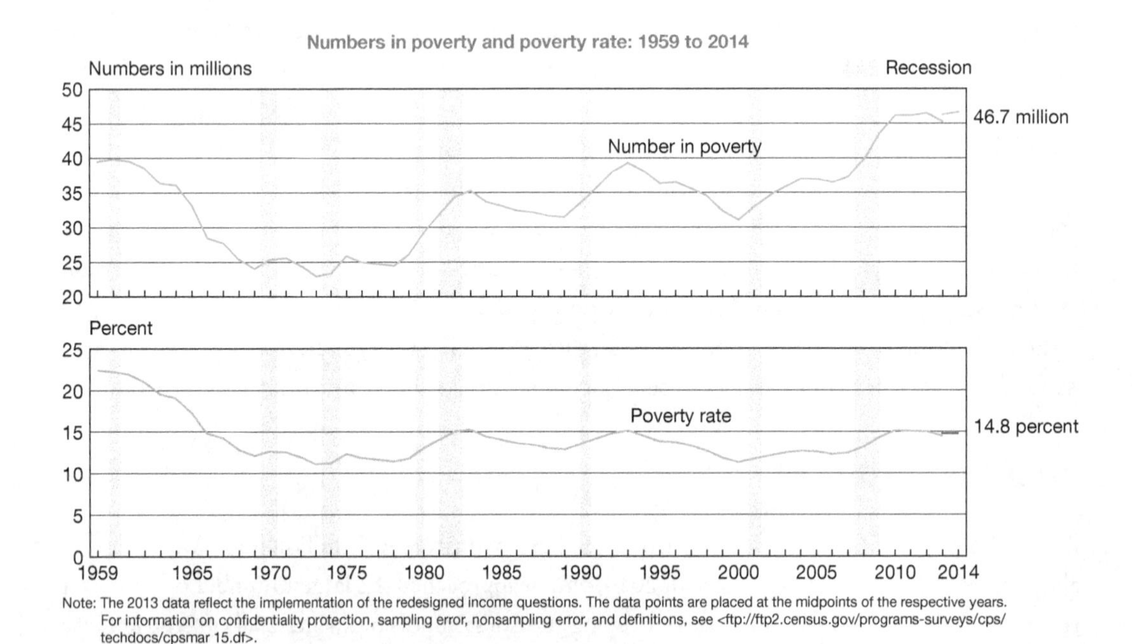

Fig. 7.5 Poverty in the U.S. has been on the rise since the beginning of this century, increasing from just over 11% in 2000 to nearly 15% in 2014.

Women and Poverty

The most significant change in the poor has been the feminization of poverty— a trend in which women increasingly represent a disproportionate amount of the world's poor. Even though this term was coined 1978, women have constituted an increasing proportion of the poor since the end of World War II (Pearce, 1978). Each year, more women slip below the poverty line than any other group. As of 2014, more women than men in the U.S. were living below the poverty line (Entmacher et al., 2014). The poverty rate for women between eighteen and sixty-four was 15.4%, compared to 11.9% for their male counterparts. By 2014, 25.9 million women lived in poverty, which means about one in six American women live in poverty. Lower wages compared to men, discrimination, lack of sufficient support systems, social attitudes, and even religions all have a part to play in the feminization of poverty around the world. Here in the U.S., the most powerful influences on women and poverty are high divorce rates, maternal custody, and unmarried childbearing. Most women tend to bring children with them when they fall below the poverty line.

Single parent households in the U.S. are far more likely to be made up of a mother and her children than to be headed by a man. Households headed by a single woman are at a greater risk of poverty, nearly 31% of female headed households live below the poverty line, which is nearly five times the rate for married couple households (see figure 7.6). For households made up of a father and his children, the poverty rate is 16.4%, which represents just over half the poverty rate of female headed households. The poverty differential between men and women even persists into old age. The poverty rate for men aged sixty-five and older is 6.6%, but for women aged sixty-five and older the rate is almost double that at 11%. Moreover, new research indicates that this gender gap persists into retirement. On average, women in the United States live on about $16,000 a year, while men enjoy an average annual retirement of over $27,000. Women in retirement are also more likely than men to rely almost entirely on Social Security benefits (Hicken, 2014; Hess et al., 2015).

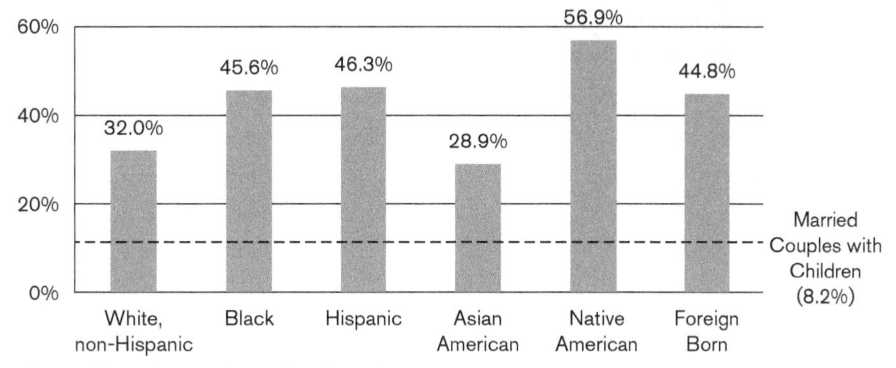

Figure 7.6 Poverty Rates for Single Mothers with Children by Race

Poor Children in the U.S.

A 2013 UNICEF study concluded that of thirty-five developed nations that were studied, the U.S. ranked thirty-fourth in child poverty (Fisher, 2013). As of 2014, more than 21% of children in the U.S. live in poverty, which represents about one-third of all those in poverty. Research has demonstrated that the effects of poverty are amplified for children, and that living in poverty has an array of negative effects on their well-being (Gunnar et al., 2009; Miller et al., 2006). According to researchers at the American Psychological Association:

- "Poverty is linked with negative conditions such as substandard housing, homelessness, inadequate nutrition and food insecurity, inadequate childcare, lack of access to healthcare, unsafe neighborhoods, and under-resourced schools ..."
- "Poorer children and teens are also at greater risk for several negative outcomes such as poor academic achievement, school dropout, abuse and neglect, behavioral and socioemotional problems, physical health problems, and developmental delays."

Source: American Psychological Association, 2016

Child poverty in the U. S. also takes an economic toll, with some estimates putting the total cost at $500 billion a year. This is a result of lost productivity and economic output, cost to the criminal justice system and increases in healthcare expenditures (Holzer et al., 2008).

Poverty also has a negative effect on the academic performance of children. Children living in poverty experience higher levels of stress than their wealthier classmates, living in poverty is stressful. These elevated stress levels are associated with disrupted concentration and memory, which in turn can impact their ability to learn. In fact, students who come from low income families are about 4.5 times more likely to dropout than students who are better off financially (Snyder, Dillow, and Hoffman, 2009; Chapman et al., 2010). Things get even worse for poor minorities. The gap in academic achievement widens for both low income black and Hispanic students compared to whites from higher income families. Children living in these poorer communities attend underfunded schools that lack the resources to help their students fully develop academically. The product of these under-resourced schools is an inadequate education, which makes it more difficult for these students to attend college, get good jobs and rise out of poverty.

THERE'S AN APP FOR THAT

Text4baby is a free nationwide app that sends texts messages to soon to be and new moms. The texts help them navigate pre- and post-natal care. The service is completely free and available in both English and Spanish. The developers have put special effort into promoting this in low income areas especially in poor black and Hispanic communities (Voxiva, 2016).

Race, Ethnicity, and Poverty

In absolute numbers, there are far more poor whites in the U.S. than any other group: about 22 million. However, this represents about 10% of the white population, while 26% of the black population, 23% of Latinos, and about 12% of Asians find themselves in poverty. Clearly, people of color are far more likely to be poor in America. For example, black families in America earn about 65 cents for every dollar a white family earns, which explains in part why blacks are about three times more likely to be poor than whites. Surprisingly, this gap has not changed in more than four decades. (DeNava-Walt and Proctor, 2015; Macartney et al., 2013). Figure 7.7 shows that while poverty rates have improved for all groups over time, racial minorities are still more likely to be poor than whites in the U.S.

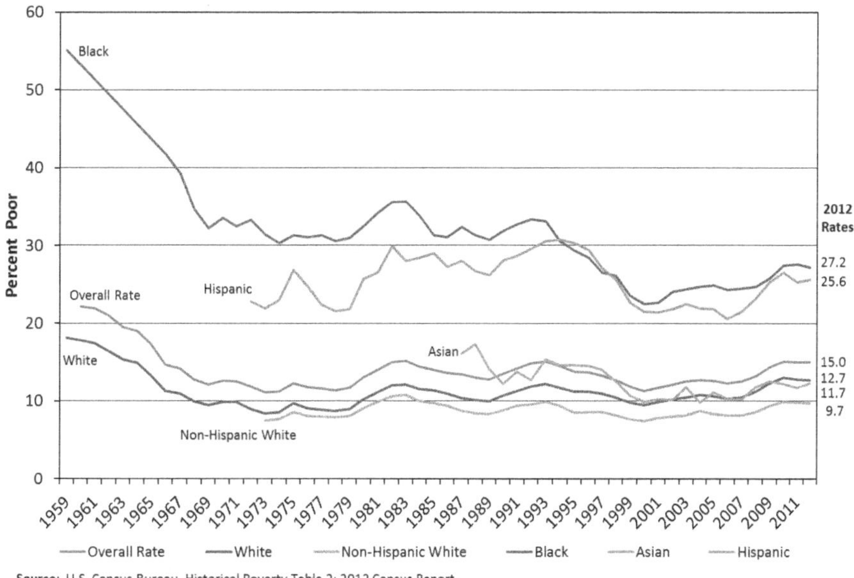

Source: U.S. Census Bureau, Historical Poverty Table 2; 2012 Census Report.
Note: Black poverty rate data from 1960 to 1965 is not available. The line shown connects the 1959 rate of 55.1 percent to the 1966 rate of 41.8 percent and is included to represent the trend but not to imply specific numerical data.

Fig 7.7 U.S. Poverty Rates by Race/Ethnicity, 1959–2012

While we will explore this topic in more detail in Chapter 8, I will outline two general categories of factors that seem to greatly influence the persistence of minority poverty: Cultural/Behavioral and Structural/Economic. Cultural/behavioral factors that are linked to the reproduction of poverty among racial minorities include such things as teenage and out of wedlock pregnancies, crime and drug use/abuse (Patterson, 2000). Essentially those who advocate a cultural/behavioral perspective on minority poverty argue that it is these behaviors that perpetuate their low socioeconomic standing. Moreover, those behaviors reflect dysfunctional values and beliefs, relative to mainstream society, about work, family and education. It's their own fault they're poor. Those who support a structural/economic position argue that economic factors and other structures/institutions including education and the government create and maintain institutional and structural discrimination, which act as barriers to movement out of poverty. Job markets and wage structures, for example, create barriers for many minorities who are forced to accept jobs that don't pay enough to keep families out of poverty. The lack of social safety nets, institutional discrimination in higher education are other structural barriers that contribute to the reproduction of poverty among racial minorities (Wilson, 1987; Eggers and Massey, 1991; Rank, Yoon and Herschl, 2003). Social structures combine to create obstacles that keep people poor. A small, but growing group of researchers see the value in both approaches and believe that all factors are involved in creating and maintaining minority poverty (Jordan, 2004, Patterson and Fosse, 2015).

THERE'S AN APP FOR THAT

Neat Streak is a two-way communication device for those in the cleaning service industry. The developers noticed that one of the biggest barriers for cleaners was the language barrier. This app lets clients choose tasks from a menu, select and send. The app generates an agreement and sends it to the cleaner and client. Now both know what is to be done, when it is to be done, and the price to be paid (Significance Labs, 2014).

Region and Poverty in the U.S.

One facet of poverty has remained stable over the past fifty years: those in the South are far more likely to be poor than those living in any other part of the United States. We should not forget nor ignore the obvious and significant structural influence of regionality. That is, poverty is distributed unevenly across the country. As figure 7.8 indicates, those in the South are most likely to be poor, and residents of the West have seen nearly a 10 percent growth in poverty since 1969. Loss of manufacturing sector jobs, outsourced labor, immigration, and educational failure rates are only partial explanations. Some of the differences in poverty rates found across regions can be attributed to something as simple as the availability of full-time and good paying jobs. That is, many times families have the capacity and willingness to rise out of poverty, but jobs in their region may be hard to find, leaving employable household members without work (Rupasingha and Goetz, 2003; 2007; U.S. Department of Agriculture, 2015).

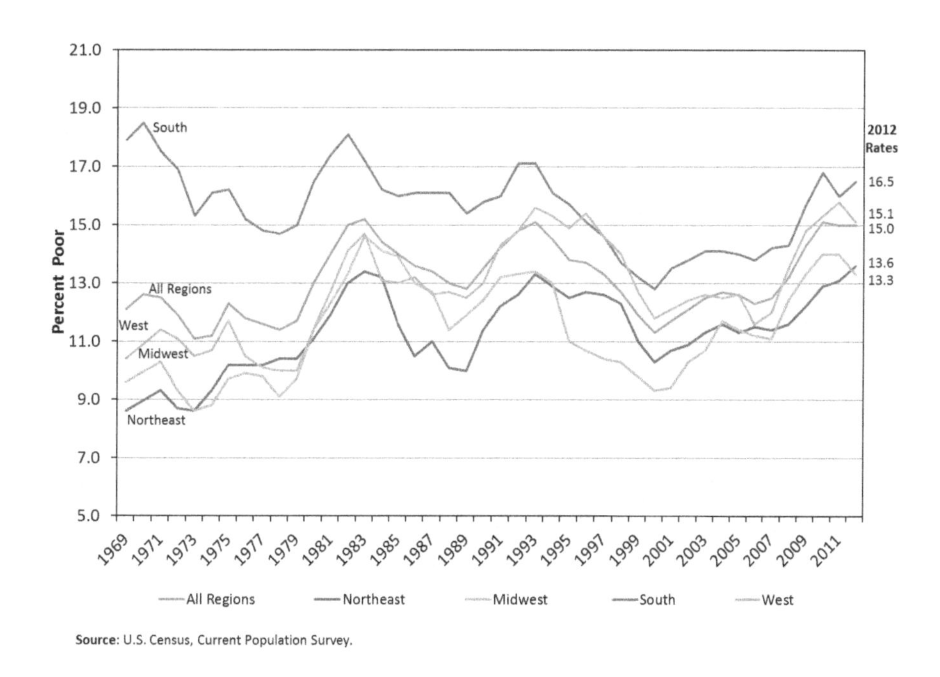

Fig. 7.8 Poverty Across Regions, 1969-2012

Inadequate and incomplete educations are significant contributing factors to poverty across the country but these factors are particularly pronounced in the South. Southern states consistently rank in the bottom 20 % for school funding and student per capita spending. Fewer resources are devoted to education in the South than any other region. As a result, this region produces a less well educated work force and greater number of high school drop outs, which reproduces the conditions of poverty (Triest, 1997; Hoyt, Jepson and Troske, 2008; Educational Finance Branch, 2015)

Global Poverty

Poverty is a global concern. Every year, more and more people worldwide slip into poverty, and each year, more women and dependent children make up the bulk of those who fall into poverty.

That's right; children and women are more likely to be among the poor than any other group. Somewhere between 72 and 80% of the world's population lives on the equivalent of $10 or less per day. By any standard, most of the world is poor and growing poorer.

In addition, as I have shown above, there are a number of problems for children in poverty, and, more importantly, there is an array of downstream negative effects for both poor women and children. Those effects become the burden of each society, therefore straining the resources of all nations. Which begs the question: why don't most societies focus on reducing poverty? Well, worldwide, there are identifiable forces or regimes that pressure governments (or pay through bribes) to maintain relationships with industry so that the resources they desire are made available. That is, a number of industries rely on the corruption of a host of national governments to turn a blind eye to those industries' activities and their exploitation of workers. To be sure, corrupt governments and greedy multinational industries are not the only influence on global poverty. Like the social stratification system in Mauritania, which we discussed earlier in the chapter, many societies are structured in such a way that poverty is maintained through wage structures, cultural traditions, corruption, and the legacy of colonial rule (Blakely et al., 2005).

Causes of Poverty

While there is wide agreement that poverty is a growing social issue, there is considerably less agreement on the causes of poverty and considerable disagreement on what to do about poverty in America. The public discourse on poverty seems to have two distinct voices. One voice echoes a long-held belief that the poor are to blame for their own circumstances through a variety of individual behaviors and moral deficits like laziness, criminality, and educational failure. This voice is perhaps the loudest from the public and many of our elected representatives in Washington, D.C. However, there is another voice—unfortunately, a quieter voice—that recognizes clearly identifiable causes of poverty embedded in social structure. This voice is attempting to tell the story of how a host of social structures/forces such as low wages, economic restructuring, educational inequities, and changing social policies have impacted poverty.

In a sense, then, these voices are battling for your ears. Which will you listen to? Are the poor to blame for their life circumstances, or are there a number of social forces that influence the lives of the poor? On the other hand, as the sociologist Sudhir Venkatesh states, "As always, the answer is probably somewhere in between" (National Public Radio, 2009). Thus, it is important to remember that it is never *one thing*; there are a number of factors that contribute to the causes of and the maintenance of poverty. Indeed, there is a growing voice that recognizes that the reality of poverty lies somewhere between cultural values and behaviors of the poor and identifiable structural barriers. In their new book, *The Cultural Matrix: Understanding Black Youth*, Orlando Patterson and Ethan Fosse (2015) explore the interaction between the cultural and structural factors that conspire to perpetuate poverty, especially in the urban black communities of America.

The Culture of Poverty

This perspective attempts to explain poverty by blaming the poor for creating a lifestyle of poverty that is transmitted from one generation of poor to the next. Originally conceived by anthropologist Oscar Lewis (1959, 1998) while studying the urban poor of Mexico City in the 1950s, he described the culture of poverty as a "design for living," which is passed down generation to generation. He showed that the urban poor felt marginalized, helpless, even inferior, and they exhibited feelings of powerlessness and personal unworthiness. Many of the families he studied were composed of mothers and children who had been abandoned by their fathers, creating a community of female-headed families. Lewis argued that the culture of poverty reproduces poverty. He wrote, it "tends to perpetuate itself from generation to generation because of its effect on children. By the time slum children are aged six or seven, they have usually absorbed the basic values and attitudes of their sub-culture and are not psychologically geared to take full advantage of changing conditions or increased opportunities which may occur in their lifetime."

However, Lewis clearly indicates that this culture of poverty is a part of third-world and emerging nations, and he did not consider it an element of modern industrialized societies. However, in a uniquely American way, Lewis' idea is coopted and transformed into seeing the poor as lazy, personally irresponsible, and passing these values on to their children. The culture of poverty is highlighted in the work of a number of American scholars but most famously popularized in 1965 by Assistant Secretary of Labor Daniel Patrick Moynihan (later to be Senator Moynihan) in what has come to be known as the Moynihan report (Frazier, 1939; Harrington, 1962; Moynihan, 1965).

The Moynihan report focuses on the structure of the black family and attempts to show that it is the breakdown of the nuclear family and the increase in single mother families in black communities that perpetuates poverty through the transmission of a set of values that devalues family. Moynihan argued that without adequate access to employment, black males would be alienated from their positions as head of household and increase the number of out-of-wedlock births and abandoned families, creating a "tangle of pathology" that would be passed on to the following generations. While the report focuses on the black family, it is like many versions of the culture of poverty that generally seek to blame the poor for their conditions by highlighting irresponsibility, poor moral judgment, laziness, and educational failure.

This perspective straddles a very fine line. On one side it has the potential to at least start the discussion on poverty, and on the other it could act as a mechanism to perpetuate racial stereotypes and marginalize the poor. So, how does a perspective like this gain traction? In part from the myth that in America, all you have to do is work hard and you will rise in social ranking. That is, regardless of who you are, as long as you are motivated and work hard, you can be a success.

This perspective puts the blame for poverty squarely on the shoulders of the poor while ignoring the myriad barriers to social mobility.

Those who advocate the culture of poverty stereotypically focus on the concentrated urban poor. For example, in early 2014, while discussing the poor in America, Representative Paul Ryan said, "We have got this tailspin of culture, in our inner cities in particular, of men not working and just generations of men not even thinking about working or learning the value and the culture of work, and so there is a real culture problem here that has to be dealt with" (Delaney, 2014).

Three things are going on in this quote. First, he is promulgating the idea that there is a culture of poverty based on the laziness of "inner-city males," ignoring in great part how the social conditions in urban areas such as low wages, few jobs, high crime, and poor schools contribute to poverty. He confuses a culture of laziness causing unemployment with social structure creating a subculture of poverty and crime. Second, whom is he referring to as the inner-city men? He was roundly criticized as racist for this statement. Some black organizations came forward to denounce the statement as "highly offensive"; others referred to Ryan's references to "inner-city men" and "culture" as code words for black inner-city men. Finally, this statement alludes to the belief that poverty is concentrated in urban areas and persists for generations. Research by Mark Rank (2013) has shown that poverty in the United States is not concentrated in urban areas or among urban populations. He found that at least 40% of Americans between the ages of twenty-five and sixty will experience at least one year below the poverty line during those years and 54% will spend one year in or near poverty. He adds that when accounting for a number of related conditions such as unemployment, near poverty, and use of social aid programs (SNAP, WIC, TANF), four out of five Americans will experience one or more of these events.

Other related research has shown the poor among the middle class. That is, there are poor within middle-class families in America, and this phenomenon is on the rise. "Put simply, poverty is a mainstream event experienced by a majority of Americans. For most of us, the question is not whether we will experience poverty, but when" (Coleman-Jensen, Gregory, and Singh, 2014; Rank, 2013). While a broad range of people will experience poverty, for the majority, it will be a temporary event.

Social Structure and Poverty

In contrast to the culture of poverty position discussed above, which essentially acknowledges poverty as a social problem but finds the causes of poverty in the attitudes and lifestyles of the poor themselves, the structural approach views the causes of poverty as located in the behaviors of the government and/or wealthy along with social and economic changes. A range of structural theories of poverty can be identified.

One key structural change in the last fifty years has been in the labor market. There has been a fundamental transformation in the United States (and many other countries) from a manufacturing economy to a post-manufacturing service economy. This significant decline in the manufacturing sector of the labor market has essentially eliminated an entire sector of semi-skilled and skilled jobs that paid relatively well and provided job security (e.g., auto parts, apparel, and the electronics industries). This decline is chiefly a result of the rise in manufacturing capacities by other countries and relocating labor outside of the United States, where production costs are considerably less (offshore labor). A related structural development that should be noted is **globalization**, or the worldwide integration of culture, ideas, media, and technology through cross-cultural exchange due to advances in communication systems and economic interests ("Globalization," 2015). The globalization of the telecommunications and computer technologies, for example, have allowed companies to employ cheaper laborers in countries like India and Bangladesh to service customers in the U.S.

Alongside this long-time decline has been a general increase in those employed in the service industries (e.g., banking, fast-food, and retail sales). It is relatively easy to see the fallout from this change. It is manifested in unemployment rates as many workers are displaced from manufacturing jobs. As manufacturing jobs are moved overseas to exploit cheap labor, the rise of less stable, lower-paying service jobs are many times the only options for these displaced workers. Additionally, most service-industry jobs require less education and can be occupied by high school students, those who have never completed high school, and immigrant workers, creating a secondary displacement of those semi-skilled and skilled employees.

What does this mean? Well, the *labor-force participation rate*—the percentage of the population who are 16 years and over who are employed or unemployed and looking for work - has been falling in recent decades and reached 62.6% in December of 2015, a thirty-eight-year low—nearly 95 million Americans are not participating in the workforce (Bureau of Labor Statistics, "The Employment Situation", 2016). Many people cannot find the type or amount of work they need or want, and some become discouraged from long-term unemployment. Consequently, they stay out of the workforce and this pushes some over the brink and into poverty.

So, the fallout from this general shift away from skilled, relatively stable and well-paying manufacturing jobs is unemployment and lowered wages from less stable service sector jobs, pushing many over the financial brink and into poverty. It should be noted that there is one important demographic reason the labor force participation rate dropped that is not directly linked to the economy. Those of the baby boomer generation, about 76 million strong, are retiring in large numbers. Historically boomers have been a powerful influence in shaping the social, political and economic landscapes, and it appears that now their exit from the workforce will be no different (US Senate Committee on Finance, 2015).

Theoretical Perspectives and Stratification

Theoretical perspectives are useful for explaining how stratification systems operate, but they are not as useful for describing and understanding the structure and functions of a phenomenon such as social stratification. Therefore, as I have done in earlier chapters, I have constructed table 7.2 below, which includes a brief description of three popular sociological theories and an example that illustrates each perspective.

TABLE 7.2 Theoretical Perspectives on Social Stratification and Social Class

Theoretical Perspective	View on Social Stratification	Example
Structural Functionalism	Functionalists view stratification as inevitable and necessary for society. Not everyone in society has the same talents, skills, and drive, resulting in a distribution of occupations that is necessary for society to function properly. All social positions serve a function, and some are viewed as more important than others are. Functionalism assumes that there is consensus concerning what jobs are more and less socially important. The more education, training, and perceived social importance, the greater the rewards. The basic idea here is that incentives like high income and social prestige act to attract the best people for important occupations. This unequal distribution of rewards creates social strata or class differences. The stratification system essentially acts as a motivator for occupational aspirations (Davis and Moore, 1945).	Remember structural functionalists believe that people occupy positions that they are best suited for. Let's take the CEO of a multinational energy corporation who has an MBA from the Wharton School of Business, many years of management experience, and top-notch social and industry connections. His company employs tens of thousands of workers, damages the environment, exploits international workers, and makes billions of dollars in profit each year. Functionalists argue that in order for someone to take on such tremendous responsibility, incentives such as a large salary, multimillion dollar bonuses, company cars, houses, and paid vacations are needed to attract the most qualified person. Functionalists, then, see the stratification system as functional for society by providing CEOs to run corporations needed by society.

Theoretical Perspective	View on Social Stratification	Example
Conflict	In contrast to functionalism, conflict theory views social stratification or class differences as harmful for society. These differences are harmful because stratification systems favor the rich at the expense of the poor, creating classes of privileged individuals who have the social resources to reproduce their dominance. Any system of social stratification is created and perpetuated by the rich and powerful. Essentially, those who have greater access to and possession of valuable social resources want to keep them, and those who do not have them want to get them. Therein lies the rub—or conflict.	Conflict theorists view the stratification systems as a struggle between the haves and the have-nots. The rich and powerful in society maintain their wealth and power by controlling social institutions and therefore control popular values, beliefs, and behaviors. Recently, many employers have opted to reduce their employees' hours to avoid providing them with healthcare benefits. Putting profits ahead of the welfare of workers is symptomatic of an unequal class system, argue conflict theorists, and this is clearly harmful for workers (Guidetti and Rehbein, 2014). In 2013, billionaire Warren Buffett commented that even though his tax rate had increased from 15 to 20%, he was paying less taxes than his secretary (Isidore, 2013). Comments like this highlight the fact that the richest Americans pay the least in taxes proportionally because they can influence lawmakers to protect their tax status. Again, this is harmful to all of us who bear the bulk of the tax burden because we do not have the money and power to change things.

(*Continued*)

Theoretical Perspective	View on Social Stratification	Example
Symbolic Interactionism	This perspective departs dramatically from both functionalism and conflict theories because it focuses on how inequality (class difference) is reproduced through the interactions between individuals, as well as how language and other symbols can be used to perpetuate social inequality. So, rather than concentrating mainly on economic forces, interactionists focus on how those at various positions in the stratification system strive for those things that are symbolically important. Those in higher positions can define symbolically those things that are socially desirable. "Power ... is achieved by controlling, influencing, and sustaining your definition of the situation." In this sense, inequality is constructed through differential abilities, which are derived from variations in social standing (social class) of individuals to define the situation (Schwalbe et al., 2000). Therefore, class differences can be reinforced by the symbols used by high-status individuals.	Keep in mind that symbolic interactionists seek meaning in symbols we use to negotiate social reality, therefore establishing behavioral boundaries, which leads to the reproduction of social classes. Imagine you have a doctor's appointment. You show up, pay your *co-pay*, then wait in the outer *waiting room* (making you wait in a segregated area). Then you are called in by your *first name*, and then you *wait* for your doctor in an exam room. Your doctor finally shows up wearing a *white lab coat* and her *name embroidered on it*, perhaps with a *stethoscope* around her neck and a *chart* in her hands. She will use your first name while you address her as doctor, and *she stands* while *you sit* on the exam table. Typically, she will use *specialized language* and tell you what is best and you will *defer to her knowledge and experience.* Notice that I have italicized the symbols used in this interaction. Individuals in higher positions in our stratification system use symbols to create and reinforce their elevated social positions, which confirms each person's position in the social hierarchy.

The Bottom Line

All societies create systems that rank their members, and these stratification systems have the potential to shape the lives of whole groups of people who share similar social circumstances.

Some systems of social stratification are open and some are closed. Open systems contain mechanisms that allow for social mobility. The class system of the United States, for example, allows people through individual hard work and education to experience social mobility, which is socially desirable. Closed systems, on the other hand, base social position on some ascribed status such as skin color, religion, or gender. Closed systems, such as the caste system of Mauritania, are designed to prevent movement between castes. As we have seen, Mauritania represents an extreme version of a caste system that contains a slave caste. Moreover, various forms of slavery are alive and well, and the number of enslaved is growing globally. While closed systems are rigid and there is no real expectation of mobility, open systems contain barriers to mobility.

As we have discussed, there are several types of mobility. Vertical mobility refers to mobility up and down the social class hierarchy, while horizontal mobility is movement within the same class (a sort of side-to-side mobility). While intragenerational mobility happens within one's own lifetime, intergenerational mobility is movement with the stratification hierarchy across generations. Intergenerational mobility was common in the U.S. as we emerged from WWII and each successive generation enjoyed a higher standard of living. However, in recent decades, we have seen little movement across generations.

Social inequality is a universal feature of all societies. However, the amount of inequality varies across societies. We have seen that those countries with high-income inequality tend to experience lower levels of social mobility than countries that have little income inequality. The United States has high- income inequality relative to other developed nations. But, more importantly, mobility in the United States has been stagnant for several decades, and the gap between middle- and upper-income earners is grower wider, deepening inequality.

In the brief description of the United States' class system, we saw that the upper class is unique in its composition and the amount of wealth its members control. The portraits of the other classes illustrate that they differ mainly on levels of income, education, wealth, and occupational categories. The measure of socioeconomic status (SES) reflects these class differences by measuring income, occupation, and education, providing sociologists and others with an accurate measure of social class.

In the United States, social class has a powerful impact on our lives, from how long we will live to the types of people we will meet to what hobbies/activities we will enjoy. Ultimately, social class affects our life chances. Our social class also influences how much access to and possession of valuable social resources we have. These resources, however, are not available equally to all members of society. Inequality, then, becomes the one social reality that all people will experience.

Capital, as we discussed in the chapter, comes in several forms that are related. One's financial capital can be directly related to investment in human capital, which, in turn, can produce greater levels of cultural and social capital. Applicants to highly selective colleges, for example, are more likely to gain admission if they have greater financial capital, more connections (social capital), and can demonstrate their preparation for college (human and cultural capital) more than those who have lower levels or lack capital.

Poverty is a global epidemic that affects billions of people worldwide. Most of the world survives on $10 or less per day, and many live on $2.50 or less per day. The number of people in poverty has been increasing for the last few decades. Additionally, there is a global feminization of poverty; each year, more women and young children slip into poverty than men. This trend is also true in the United States; nearly 60% of the poor are women and young children. In 2013, 14.5% of the U.S. population was officially poor. However, as we discussed, the way we define poverty is flawed and most likely does not represent the true number of poor in the U.S.

Functionalism argues that inequality exists and persists because it serves necessary social functions. This perspective maintains that inequality acts to motivate those who are best qualified to achieve socially desirable occupational positions. In contrast, the conflict approach suggests that the differential access to and possession of valuable social resources promotes social conflict between the powerful and others. The dominant positions of the powerful are reinforced by their control of social institutions, which allow them to maintain levels of inequality. Symbolic interactionism focuses on the symbolic nature of how the powerful manipulate symbols to create, maintain, and perpetuate class differences.

Figure Credits

Fig. 7.1: Copyright © Aarkwilde (CC BY-SA 3.0) at https://commons.wikimedia.org/wiki/File:Owl_Shrine.jpg.

Fig. 7.2: Source: https://www.equalitytrust.org.uk/social-mobility

Fig. 7.3 : Adapted from: The Gilbert-Kahl Model of The Class Structure in the U.S.," http://www.sagepub.com/sites/default/files/upm-binaries/17446_Gilbert_Chapter_1.pdf.

Fig. 7.4: Jack Corn/U.S. National Archive, "Miners at the Virginia-Pocahontas Coal Company Mine," https://commons.wikimedia.org/wiki/File:Miners_at_the_Virginia-Pocahontas_Coal_Company_Mine.jpg. Copyright in the Public Domain.

Table 7.1: "2015 Poverty Guidelines for the 48 Contiguous States," http://aspe.hhs.gov/2015-poverty-guidelines. Copyright in the Public Domain.

Fig. 7.5: "Poverty in the U.S. 1959-2014," http://www.census.gov/hhes/www/poverty/data/incpovhlth/2014/figure4.pdf. Copyright in the Public Domain.

Fig. 7.6: Source: http://www.nwlc.org/sites/default/files/pdfs/povertysnapshot2014.pdf

Fig. 7.7: Source: http://www.irp.wisc.edu/faqs/faq3.htm

Fig. 7.8: Source: http://www.irp.wisc.edu/faqs/faq3.htm

CHAPTER 8

RACE AND ETHNICITY

What's in a Name?

What's in a name? Researchers Marianne Bertrand and Sendhil Mullianathan (2004) found that employers seem to like the sound of some names better than others. These researchers sent out five thousand resumes to various employers in the Boston and Chicago areas between 2001 and 2002. These were not their own resumes; they were phony resumes with fictitious names. They sent out resumes with either stereotypically African American- or white-sounding names, and then measured the number of callbacks each resume received for interviews.

They found that job applicants with African American-sounding names, such as Lakisha Washington or Jamal Jones, needed to send out *fifteen resumes* to get *one* callback for an interview. Those with white-sounding names, such as Emily Walsh or Greg Baker, needed to send only *ten resumes* to get one callback. The authors calculated the difference in callback rates represented the equivalent of an additional eight years of job experience. What does this suggest to you? Can you think of ways to explain this difference?

Whether the potential job was cashier, clerical worker or management, black sounding names consistently received fewer calls. In addition, the results were the same for federal contractors, large employers, or those who explicitly stated they were equal opportunity employers. Perhaps what is most disturbing about these research findings is that employers were willing to dismiss qualified potential employees based solely on the ethnic *sound* of a name. Would you like to be judged on how *ethnic* or *non-ethnic* your name sounds?

Do you find this surprising? I think most of us would like to believe that in an age with laws and social policies that prohibit racial discrimination in hiring, we would not find such overt discrimination. Unfortunately, it is alive and well and evident from this example. Today in the U.S., African Americans are twice as likely as whites to be unemployed and they earn about 25% less than similarly employed whites do (United States Bureau of Labor Statistics, "Employment Status," 2015). Even in an occupational field like mine, which is perceived to be liberal and progressive, black faculty earn less on average than their white academic colleagues (Bhopal, 2016).

Sociology, Race, and Ethnicity

Race and ethnicity are frequently studied by sociologists because they influence our lives, social interactions, and how we perceive others. Our racial and ethnic identities shape the way others view us and how we view others. These concepts are key to our development as individuals and our social adjustment. Our racial and ethnic identity also affects our life chances, which include things like life expectancy, the types of diseases we may contract, and whether we will live in poverty. What race do you identify with? What is *your* ethnic identity?

Same or Different: Race, Ethnicity, and Minority Groups

In daily conversations, people tend to use the terms race and ethnicity interchangeably, implying that they mean the same thing. What is race? What is ethnicity? Are they the same? Are there real differences between race and ethnicity? In sociology, we make a distinction between the terms race and ethnicity but recognize that both concepts are social constructions.

In sociology, each of these terms has a different meaning and a specific use. Much like the distinction we make between sex and gender, our understanding of race and ethnicity are associated with biological and social factors. **Race** refers to a set of physical characteristics such as hair color, eye color, and skin color shared by a group of people. You see, while there are physical differences between groups of people, there is no significant genetic difference between groups of humans. Sure, physical differences in hair color and texture are evident between whites and blacks, but they are just superficial. If there were *real* individual and distinct biological races, there would be groups of humans who shared different DNA profiles, but there aren't. There is no evidence to suggest that there are groups of biologically distinct human beings that correspond to what people commonly refer to as races. Humans of the world hold more than 99.99% of their genetic material in common (National Human Genome Research Institute, 2016). There is only one race, the human race.

"Race is not an element of human biology (like breathing oxygen or reproducing sexually); nor is it even an idea (like the speed of light or the value of pi) that can be plausibly imagined to live an eternal life of its own. Race is not an idea but an ideology. It came into existence at a discernible historical moment for rationally understandable historical reasons and is subject to change for similar reasons" (Fields and Fields, 2012).

Because we are human, we have a need to categorize elements of the social world. Sociologists recognize that race is a social concept, not a purely biological one. Race, then, is viewed in sociology as a *social construct*, an artificial distinction, which is culturally created and allows us to place people into categories based on physical attributes. However, by placing people into groups based on these differences, it stigmatizes some as different and reinforces the privilege of others (we will discuss this more later). Because race is a social construct, it is bound to culture; its definition and interpretation changes over time and from place to place. How one identifies his/her race is a result of social context. For example, someone who identifies as black in the United States may be considered white in Brazil and colored in South Africa (Harris, 1964; Inciardi, 2000).

In contrast, **ethnicity** refers to cultural factors such as language, cultural traditions, nationality, and ancestry shared by a group of people. While I do not have a strong identification with French culture (except for the wine and cheese), my ethnic heritage is French. Earlier in America's history, many immigrant groups sought to become American as soon as possible, discarding their ethnic identity. This desire to fit in and be indistinguishable from others created what came to be referred to as the melting pot of America. This metaphor implies that many ethnic identities "melt together" and become indistinguishable forming a new single American identity. Today, people are eager to embrace their ethnic background. America can be better described as a big garden salad; together, all the ingredients make the salad (America), but each individual part is distinguishable—African Americans, Mexican Americans, and even French Americans.

People are interested in their ethnic heritage; just do a quick search of the Internet for genealogy websites and you will find plenty of them. Ancestry.com, myheritage.com, legacytree.com, and genealogy.com are just a few examples. There is even a popular television show called *Who Do You Think You Are?* that investigates the family background of celebrities. We are curious about our ethnic backgrounds for many reasons. Some people want to validate family lore, some want to know if they are related to famous or wealthy people, and some want to know if they are somehow connected to important historical events. Many want to know how they got to America, a land of immigrants. Both our racial and ethnic identities help place us in a larger social context historically and contemporarily.

Dominant and Minority Groups

The interesting thing about dominant and minority groups is that they aren't about numbers. A dominant group—the group in society who has the most power, privilege, and social standing—does not have to be numerically superior. Take for example the National Party of South Africa, which ruled that nation until 1994 ("National Party", 2015). It was a numerical minority, about 10 percent of the population, yet managed to maintain dominance through apartheid—an oppressive system of separation based on race - over the country's majority-black population. Under apartheid, blacks could not vote, had limited access to education, had their land seized, and were placed on reservations. Dominant groups create and maintain ideologies that perpetuate their dominant social positions. The dominant ideology— a set of beliefs and behaviors that shape the perception of social reality so dominant groups can maintain social control—uses language, laws, symbols, and other devices to maintain its dominance over minority groups. Therefore, minority groups are subjugated by the dominant group through the application of a dominant ideology. The former government of South Africa, for example, used laws, political power, and restricted access to education as mechanisms to apply its dominant ideology of apartheid to control non-whites.

A minority group is any group of people who have considerably less power, privilege, and social standing than the majority group. Minority group status can be determined by physical or cultural characteristics such as religion, sexual orientation, gender, skin color, or ethnic identity. African Americans, Latinos, Vietnamese, Muslims, and the Amish are all minority groups in the United States. Even though women are the majority gender in the U.S., they are a sociological minority. (Jiobu, 1990.) Women are denied the same control over their bodies and lives as men and have less political power and privilege than men.

The Continuum of Dominant and Minority Group Interactions

Minority groups have been treated in a variety of ways by dominant groups throughout history. Many Western nations pay a great deal of lip service to the protection and equality of minority groups in other countries but have tenuous race relations within their own borders. Both the United States and the United Kingdom, for example, have historically had difficult relations with minority groups. At different times through history, the United States has attempted to eliminate Native Americans, enslaved blacks, and excluded Chinese from coming to America. The British have had similar difficulties with racial groups from Pakistan and India and blacks from the West Indies. The interaction between dominant and minority groups in society is complex. Below are ways that dominant groups have historically dealt and currently deal with minority groups that they live among. Think of these methods of dominant-minority interaction as running along a continuum from intolerance to tolerance. At the most intolerant end of the continuum is the despicable act of genocide, with segregation and assimilation being more tolerant, and finally, the holy grail of social acceptance and equality, pluralism.

Fig. 8.1 Bodies pile up in Rwanda, a result of an attempted tribal genocide.

Genocide

Genocide is the intentional destruction of a particular group of people. This can include national, ethnic, racial, or religious groups. In 1948, the United Nations declared genocide an international crime, and in 1998, the International Criminal Court was established to prosecute crimes such as genocide. History is replete with examples of genocide, in which attempts were made to wipe out entire groups of people. For example, in an attempt to wipe out the native Indian population in colonial America, Jeffrey Amherst, a British army officer, gave smallpox-infected blankets to local Indians. During his despotic rule of the Soviet Union, Joseph Stalin was responsible for the death of upward of 50 million people between 1930 and 1953. This was in an attempt to eliminate entire national groups such as the Kurds, Tartars, and Ukrainians (Pohl, 1999). More recently, in 1994, the dominant Hutu tribe of Rwanda massacred 800,000 minority Tutsis in a mere one hundred days (Dallaire, 2004). Rather than tolerate, assimilate, or absorb these minority groups, dominant groups saw their elimination as their best option in order to maintain social, political, or economic control.

Segregation

Genocide is an extreme treatment of minority groups by any measure. Less drastic, but still as damaging and humiliating, is the practice of segregation, which is the physical and social separation of minority groups from the dominant group. We have a long and sad history of racial segregation in the United States. The era of Jim Crow laws created *de jure*, or legally, mandated segregation between blacks and whites in the American South. These laws created "separate but equal" public facilities for blacks, keeping black Americans separate from whites on trains, buses, in bathrooms, and even in theater seating. However, in 1954, the *Brown vs. Board of Education of Topeka* Supreme Court decision declared racial segregation laws unconstitutional. A number of federal laws that made racial segregation in education, voting, and employment illegal followed this decision. Despite numerous changes outlawing racial segregation, we still experience *de facto*, or non-official, segregation in the United States. Racial steering, for example, is the practice of real estate agents steering minority homebuyers away from desirable, predominately white neighborhoods. Unfortunately, the widespread use of this method systematically denies minorities access to good neighborhoods with better schools, services, and a range of social and economic opportunities (Pager and Sheppard, 2008; Briggs de Souza, 2005).

RACIAL STEERING IS ALIVE AND WELL, AND STILL A BAD IDEA

In 2011, the Fair Housing Council of Suburban Philadelphia conducted a real estate "sting" in Allentown, Pennsylvania, and found minorities were far more likely to be steered toward homes in urban areas, while white potential homebuyers were guided to the suburbs. These potential homebuyers were identical by income, credit worthiness, employment history, and family composition. The only difference was their race. In 73% of the cases, white buyers were steered to affluent suburbs, and the minority buyers were encouraged to buy in less desirable urban areas (Lash, 2012).

TRY THIS

See if you can identity distinct neighborhoods by race or ethnicity. Are the "bad sections" and "good sections" of your town or city well-known? Do you avoid certain neighborhoods? Look for billboards in different parts of your town/city. You won't find any in the affluent areas, but you will find them in lower socioeconomic neighborhoods. What do you think billboards advertise in low-income areas? Can you locate some examples?

Assimilation

Minority and dominant group interactions are not always as draconian as genocide or as damaging as segregation. Assimilation refers to the process of socially absorbing minorities into the dominant culture as they conform to social and cultural practices. Again, we have a long history of cultural assimilation in the United States. As wave after wave of immigrants hit the shores of the U.S., many of them wanted nothing more than to be American; they quickly learned English and adopted "American" ways of living. Why? Learning the language and adopting the dominant culture gives groups greater access to social and economic opportunities. More importantly, the more minorities emulate the values, beliefs, and actions of the dominant culture, the less they appear to be different. This process is easier for some groups than others. White ethnic minority groups such as the Irish and Italians have been more successful in blending into the dominant social landscape than, say, Vietnamese, Mexican, and Arab Americans. Their "visibility" as racial and ethnic minorities can be triggers for prejudice and discrimination, barring them from full social participation.

NATIVE AMERICAN INDIAN BOARDING SCHOOLS

There are examples of less benign assimilation woven into the history of the United States. The forced assimilation of many of the Native American Nations, for example, shows that assimilation can be a burden to bear as opposed to an emblem of inclusion. From the mid-1800s through the 1920s, the federal government established a number of boarding schools designed to "civilize" Indians. Based in the belief that separating children from their native culture would help them assimilate into the larger society faster and easier, the U. S. government separated American Indian children from their families and put them up in these boarding schools. If you are interested in reading more about this subject, check out *Education for Extinction: American Indians and the Boarding School Experience 1875-1928* by David Wallace Adams.

Pluralism

It has been argued that the process of assimilation, in some ways, places a burden on minority groups; they are the ones that must do the changing. The process may make some ethnic groups feel pressured to abandon many of their cultural values, traditions and behaviors. In addition, one could argue that assimilation is just a form of "cultural genocide." By contrast, pluralism is a social condition in which the distinct cultural differences of minority groups are preserved while enjoying equal participation in the larger society. The United States is frequently referred to as a pluralistic society because, in theory, all people have equal social standing, and minority groups are free to express their culture. This freedom to express cultural identities is most evident in "ethnic enclaves" frequently found in large cities. I lived in Los Angeles for many years, and communities like "Little Tokyo," "Koreatown," "Tehrangeles," "Little Armenia," and many others proudly displayed and practiced cultural traditions in unrestricted ways. While they may live in ethnic neighborhoods, these residents are not socially isolated; they participate in the larger society by commuting to other parts of Los Angeles for work, school, and recreation.

The United States is more of a *multicultural* society than a pluralistic one. We like the idea of having many cultures in America, but these multiple cultures are not viewed nor treated as equals. In other words, multiple cultures may live side by side and feel free to maintain their cultures, but many minority groups do not share equal social standing. As we will see in later in this chapter, there are racial and ethnic groups that experience prejudice and discrimination, which hinders their full acceptance and participation in society.

THERE'S AN APP FOR THAT

There *was* an app called *Ghetto Tracker* that allows users to identify the "good" and "bad" parts of cities they are unfamiliar with. The app also allows locals to rate the safety of different parts of their home city. You can see why this didn't last long. The makers of the app quickly changed the name to *Good Part of Town,* but that didn't stop the app from promoting racism and classism (O'Connor, 2013). Thankfully, it died a quick death.

Prejudice, Stereotypes, and Discrimination

Any negative or positive attitude, thought, or feeling toward an entire category of people is defined as prejudice. Prejudices are attitudes we hold about people *just* because they are members of a particular racial or ethnic group. Prejudice is a prejudgment not based on any evidence or experience, but assumed about the person because of his/her group membership. Feelings of prejudice are not just held by the dominant group about minority groups; anyone can harbor prejudice against any group.

We may dislike others just because they are a different race or ethnicity than us, and these feelings may lead us to make assumptions about each and every member of that group. Therefore, many of our prejudices toward members of minority groups are based on stereotypes. **Stereotypes** are exaggerated characteristics of every member of a particular group. Assumptions like "All Asians are good at math," "White people have no rhythm," or "All black people are athletic" are expressions of stereotypes. You can see how exaggerated these claims are, and any opinion about an entire racial group cannot be correct.

These preconceived notions about other groups, while often negative, can be positive, but still stereotypical. I teach on an urban campus, and the majority of my students are African American. In the beginning of each semester, I ask my students what they can tell about me from my membership in a particular group, professors who are middle-aged white men. Their answers usually include a number of stereotypes about middle-aged white male professors and some about white people in general. Most think I am wealthy, I grew up in a nice home with parents who went to college, and I lived a "comfortable" middle-class life growing up. While these stereotypes about me are essentially positive, none of them are true.

Stereotypes on their own are only verbally offensive. It's when stereotypes generate feelings about a certain group (prejudice) and *if* people act on those feelings that holds the potential for harm. **Discrimination** is the unfair *treatment* of individuals based *solely* on their membership in a particular group. Therefore, if prejudice is how someone *feels* or *thinks* about a minority group, discrimination is how they *act* toward members of that group. When individuals are denied employment because of the color of their skin, their gender, or their age, they have been discriminated against. Remember the opening story of this chapter in which job applicants were not called back because their names sounded ethnic? They were discriminated against just because their names sounded black.

Fig. 8.2 The Manzanar Japanese internment camp, located in California's Eastern Sierra Nevada Mountains, was one of the largest of its type. The camps were constructed after the U.S. entered WWII in an attempt to manage the U.S. Japanese population who were believed by many, including government officials, to be a threat to national security. What if we did this today with Muslims? Would Americans allow this to happen again?

Sometimes, prejudice, stereotypes, and discriminatory practices can lead to unfairly blaming groups for events that, in reality, they are not responsible for. **Scapegoating** is the practice of unfairly blaming minority groups for social problems. Frequently, the cause of the social event or condition of interest is unknown or lies elsewhere. The term originated in ancient Hebrew culture (see Leviticus 16:8). On the holy day of atonement (Yom Kippur) in Hebrew villages, the sins of the locals are symbolically placed on the head of a goat, and then it is sent into the wilderness, carrying the *burden* of the sins of the community with it. A sad example of scapegoating from America's history is the internment of Japanese Americans during WWII. In an attempt to assuage feelings of hatred for the Japanese Empire's sneak attack on Pearl Harbor, Japanese Americans were uprooted from their homes and communities and relocated to internment camps. The American government essentially took out its anger and blamed patriotic and loyal Japanese Americans, most of whom were born in the United States, for the cowardly actions of the Japanese Empire. The conditions in the camps were deplorable. Many young Japanese American men joined the armed forces to both escape conditions in the camps and prove their loyalty to America.

It's probably important to know that just because someone is prejudiced against a particular group does not mean he/she will discriminate based on those feelings or thoughts. Also, those who hold no ill will toward a minority group may discriminate against a member of that group unwittingly. Take a look at table 8.1 to see how the various relationships between prejudice and discrimination can exhibit themselves in everyday life.

TABLE 8.1 Relationships Between Prejudice and Discrimination

	Discriminator	**Non-Discriminator**
Prejudice	This is someone who's a hater and acts on his/her prejudices; for example, your garden-variety bigot who believes Mexican Americans are lazy and will not hire them because of that belief.	This person is a hater but will not act on his/her prejudices out of fear or cowardice. This person, for example, hates African Americans but treats them fairly for fear of being revealed as a racist.
Not Prejudice	This person has no real opinions or feelings toward any minority group but discriminates. For example, a white realtor who believes that the steering of minorities to less desirable neighborhoods by other realtors is wrong, but he steers minorities to less desirable areas because he's afraid of losing the sale.	This is what most of us strive for. People like this, for example, hold no ill feeling toward any group and try to treat everyone they encounter equally. An example is a business owner who believes that we are all socially equal and hires the best person for the job, regardless of his/her race, age, religion, or gender.

Source: Adapted from Merton, 1968

Discrimination can come in a variety of forms. Individual discrimination is when an individual acts unfairly toward a minority group member based on his/her own prejudice. Institutional discrimination is when institutional policies intentionally or unintentionally differentiate between individuals based on their membership in a minority group. For example, after the shooting death of Michael Brown, an unarmed black teenager, by a white police officer in Ferguson, Missouri, that police department was investigated (Perez, 2015). The Civil Rights Division of the United States Department of Justice found that its unlawful police procedures, policies, and practices consistently discriminated against people of color, specifically African Americans. Moreover, it was determined that the local municipality, including local government, police, the courts, and jails, systematically discriminated against poor people, but most directly against the poor black citizens of the city. This structural discrimination—when the policies of most dominant institutions, which are intended to be neutral, unfairly target members of minority groups—was widespread across all governmental institutions in Ferguson (Pincus, 1996). It was determined that the city's focus on generating revenue rather than the safety of the public at large shaped the racially discriminatory practices of the police, city officials, and judges (Department of Justice Civil Rights Division, 2015).

Fig. 8.3 Riot Police in Ferguson, MO. The U.S. Department of Justice found that the policies and practices of the criminal justice system of Ferguson was designed to discriminate against African Americans in that community.

Individual discrimination can easily be avoided by simply avoiding that individual. Institutional discrimination can be avoided, albeit not as easily, by going to a different school or getting a different job. However, it is difficult to avoid structural discrimination because it is so pervasive. The policies and practices of our social institutions such as schools, government, and businesses do not always intend to discriminate against minority groups but do so unintentionally, creating an entire society that treats certain groups unjustly. The only way to escape this discriminatory environment would be to move to another country ... and you don't know what life is really like there.

FRIED CHICKEN AND WATERMELON

Take the stereotype about all African Americans loving fried chicken and watermelon. This is based mainly on media images of African Americans from the mid-1800s right up through the 1980s. Imagery of black people eating fried chicken with their hands in advertisements, postcards, cartoons, and in the movie *Birth of a Nation* (1915) were used to portray them as savages. Watermelon was used to portray black Americans as lazy and simple. Again, images in books, cartoons, and advertisements were used as tools to reinforce stereotypical beliefs about blacks. These images implied that blacks were quite happy as long as they had fried chicken and watermelon. Therefore, when someone invokes this stereotype, it carries with it all the oppressive power and imagery of lazy, savage blacks. The history of this stereotype is a good example of racial formation theory (see page 289 for more on racial formation theory).

Racism

The belief that one race is superior to or inferior to another race is **racism**. Hating or treating someone unfairly or unjustly based just on his or her skin color is racism. Above, we examined different types of *discrimination* in broad terms, but those types of discrimination can be applied to racism. A landlord, for example, who dislikes Vietnamese Americans and refuses to rent to them is perpetrating *individual racism*. There is *institutional racism*, in which the policies of institutions seem innocuous but ultimately discriminate against minority racial groups. A vivid example of institutional racism can be seen in the segregated public school systems in the U.S. prior to 1954 (even though the Supreme Court decision made public school segregation unconstitutional, it took more than three decades for all school districts to desegregate).

Fig. 8.4 Segregated drinking fountains were familiar features throughout America's South through the 1960's.

Before the desegregation (integration) of public schools, black students received an education that was designed to be inferior. That system was commonly described as a "dual track system," one well-supported system for whites and one all-but-ignored system for blacks. Black schools and majority-black schools were poorly funded, under-resourced and dilapidated. Their athletic teams and extracurricular organizations were routinely denied participation in majority-white divisions/conferences. Moreover, teacher pay was substandard, and those low wages drove the well-qualified away and attracted only the truly committed educator, but more frequently, the truly incompetent. Even in northern, mid-western, and western states, there was a *de facto* practice of "separate and unequal" treatment of blacks in schools (Green, 2013). The substandard education they suffered damaged the lives of generations of African Americans. This purposeful institutional racism put millions of blacks at a distinct economic, social, and political disadvantage.

Institutional racism today is more subtle; it seems innocent and it ultimately seems normal, and people do not question normal or business as usual. This form of racism is so ingrained in our education system that it often goes unnoticed, ignored, or denied. Make no mistake, institutional racism is still here. So, what does institutional racism look like? It looks like normal, the taken for granted, and the way things work. What kinds of messages are being sent to young African American children when their teachers may be people of color but their deans and principle are white? And what does a Thai student aspire to when she sees no familiar faces in her teachers, coaches, or school leaders? These are the ways institutional racism is manifested.

THERE'S AN APP FOR THAT

Everyday Racism is an app aimed at challenging your ideas about racism. This game/education app challenges you to live as someone from another race for 7 days. The app allows you to immerse yourself in a new environment and face daily real life scenarios as someone of another race. This seven-day journey is designed to improve your understanding of racism (All Together Now, 2014).

The examples above are indirect effects of institutional racism, but it can have a more direct effect, especially on the lives of students of color. Black students in the United States are more likely to be placed in special needs classes than white students. White students are more likely to be tracked into high-achieving, gifted, or advanced-placement classes than their minority counterparts. In fact, black and Hispanic males make up nearly 80 percent of all special needs students ("The Urgency of Now", 2012). In the U.S., only those who identify as Asian/Pacific Islanders are more likely than whites to be in gifted education programs, while blacks and Hispanics are about half as likely to be in gifted programs as whites (Snyder, Dillow, and Hoffman, 2008; Committee on Scientific Principles for Education Research, Shavelson, & Towne, 2002). Additionally, black and Latino minority students, who are more likely to come from lower socioeconomic families, tend to start off on an uneven footing. That is, school inequality for blacks, Hispanics, and other racial minorities starts with the lack of access to and participation in developmental preschool programs. This puts them on a road to educational inequality, and this lack of adequate early schooling has lasting effects, especially for Hispanic students. One lasting effect is the underrepresentation of students of color in "exam schools"—high-achieving public high schools that admit students based on their performance on the school's entrance "exam." This low representation of students of color, primarily Hispanics, in prestigious public high schools has created what Jonathan Kozol has termed "a post-modern version of a dual track system," reminiscent of the dual system of inadequate and unequal education for blacks before school desegregation (Balonon-Rosen, 2015). Think back to your public school experience if you attended public schools. What groups were the majority of the students in your gifted or talented programs? Who were the kids in the special needs programs?

Forget about schools for a while; think about hotels. My wife and I travel frequently, and we stay in a lot of hotels. The one thing that we notice wherever we travel is that nearly all the front desk personnel and hotel management are white, but those who clean our rooms and serve us food and drinks are far more likely to be people of color. Think about your experience at hotels. Are most of those doing the serving and cleaning racial or ethnic minorities? Unfortunately, you can name just about any type of institution in the United States and it probably has some elements of institutional racism (or sexism or ageism).

TRY THIS

Go to a few of the "upscale" hotels in your area. Sit in the lobby, relax, and have a cocktail; you're going to be there a while. Now, do some people watching. Watch the employees and the guests. Start with the guests; notice the racial/ethnic mix of the guests. Is there a racial mix? Now turn your attention to the employees. Take notice of who gives orders and who takes them; who is involved with service and housekeeping? Who is at the front desk, and who are in management positions (sometimes pictures of managers are hung on the walls at the front desk, and sometimes managers walk around the place glad-handing people, people like you). Make mental notes (or pen and paper ones) about how the races of the employees are distributed across job categories like service, cleaning, front desk help, lower management, and top brass.

Multicultural America: Racial and Ethnic Minorities in the United States

> *"The interaction of disparate cultures, the vehemence of the ideals that led the immigrants here, the opportunity offered by a new life, all gave America a flavor and a character that make it as unmistakable and as remarkable to people today as it was to Alexis de Tocqueville in the early part of the nineteenth century."*
>
> *— John F. Kennedy, A Nation of Immigrants*

The United States is a nation built by immigrants. From before the formation of the United States, people from many parts of the world came to the "new world" to seek new opportunities, reinvent themselves, and to seek their fortunes. However, they did not show up to an empty land; before Columbus sailed the ocean blue, there were hundreds of nations of Native Americans already there. It has been estimated that the total population of those nations ranged anywhere from 10 to 50 million indigenous peoples. Then white people started to show up in greater numbers, and relations with the indigenous people deteriorated. The immigrants who landed on the shores of the United States came at different times and for different reasons. Whatever their reasons for coming to America, there are distinct features of their migration: they displaced native people, they came in waves, and some arrived under the yoke of slavery.

American Indians

> *"When the blood in your veins returns to the sea, and the earth in your bones returns to the ground, perhaps then you will remember that this land does not belong to you, it is you who belongs to this land."*
>
> *— Unknown*

Pre-Columbian America was a land filled with the robust cultures of native peoples. These were not "simple" people or "savages." The cultures of native Americans thrived in all corners of what is now the U.S., from the forests of what is now Maine (the Wabanaki) to the shores of Southern California (the Tongva). These people flourished, developing complex ways of living and interpreting the natural world. Among their beliefs was the notion that the earth is a living being and the native people were the stewards of her natural resources. In contrast, the Spanish, French, English, and Dutch came to America for the conquest of land and its people. These cultural differences between the indigenous population and Europeans resulted in social disruption and ethnic violence. While violence toward Indians was common, it was an unseen enemy that took the most Indian lives in the early colonization of America. Having no natural biological immunity to foreign pathogens, more Native Americans died from the diseases the whites brought with them than in combat (Johansen, 2006). From the early days of the colonization of America, Europeans subjugated local Indians by forcing them to swear loyalty to their kings and convert to Christianity. Converting them to Christianity was believed to prevent them from pursuing their "savage" ways and find a place in heaven.

While Indians were subjected to disease and violence by early settlers before the establishment of the government of the United States, the newly formed nation took a legal, organized approach toward Indians. Early in the nineteenth century, the U.S. government got really serious, passing a series of laws meant to subjugate Indians and keep them from gaining any military, economic, or political power. The Indian Relocation Act of 1830 began the exodus of Indians from their native lands east of the Mississippi River to designated "Indian territories" west of the Mississippi. This series of forced relocations of Indians is commonly referred to as the "Trail of Tears." The establishment of reservations was a ploy to move Indians off land that white settlers and the U.S. government wanted. With the administration of the Dawes Act of 1887, Indians were taken off reservations and placed on individual properties among white settlers. Ostensibly, this was done to prevent Indians from consolidating power as a group. Right around this time, the U.S. government began a concerted effort to "civilize" Native Americans by creating a system of "boarding schools." "Civilizing" Indians was a strategy of assimilation, forcing Indians to give up their language, dress, beliefs, and customs and take up "white ways" of thinking and acting. Many times, this process was begun in children, who were forcibly removed from their homes and placed in "boarding schools," where they were taught to dress, talk, and think like white people (see the box on page 271 about boarding schools). While some schools were on reservations, most were situated off reservations so children would be separated from their families, language, and cultural practices. This process of "civilizing" and "Christianizing" was an effort to help Indians blend into society and be productive, law-abiding citizens. Unfortunately, these schools were places of terrible physical, emotional, and sexual abuse.

Changes to the legal status of Native Americans began in the 1960s. In 1968, the Indian Civil Rights Act guaranteed Native Americans many, but not all, of the rights guaranteed to all other Americans under the U.S. Bill of Rights. At one time in history, there were an estimated 20 million or more Native Americans within the boundaries of what is now the U.S.; today, there are about 5.2 million American Indians and Alaska natives combined (this includes people who identify as American Indian or Alaska native *and* another race), which made up about 2% of the population in 2013. When compared to all Americans, American Indians are less educated and have lower incomes. They are also far more likely to live in poverty than any other group in the U.S. (DeVoe, Darling-Churchill, and Snyder, 2008).

READ MORE

- *Bury My Heart at Wounded Knee: An Indian History of the American West* by Dee Brown (1970). This book looks at the history of western expansion of the United States from the perspective of the Native Americans who were betrayed, relocated, and eliminated. A very interesting view on the winning of the west from the vantage point of the vanquished. You will gain much respect for the native people of America and gain a more balanced view of the settling of the west than you ever did in your history classes.
- *A People's History of the United States* by Howard Zinn (1980). As a historian, Zinn recognizes that history is written by the victors. This book presents a history of the U.S. from the perspective of all people, not just the elites. In the book, Zinn argues that the history of the U.S. is a history of the oppression of minority groups by the elites and how that subjugation reverberates in today's society. You will find yourself arguing with the book as you read, because this is NOT the history we all learned. This book will blow your mind in a good way.
- *A Nation of Immigrants* by John F. Kennedy (1964). This book reveals President Kennedy's view on immigration reform. He believed that the future of America was dependent on immigrants, just as America's history was beholden to immigrants. The book briefly outlines the history of immigration in the U.S. and emphasizes the important role that immigrants played in creating a multicultural nation. Given the current political debate over immigration law and the role of immigrants in the U.S., this is an important read. It will give you a perspective you cannot get from Fox News.

African Americans

> *"Stolen from Africa, brought to America*
> *Fight on arrival, fighting for survival"*
>
> — *Bob Marley ("Buffalo Soldier")*

While Native Americans represent the only non-immigrant minority group in the United States, African Americans have the unfortunate distinction of being the only group forcibly brought to America. Bob Marley's lyrics above echo that unique status of African Americans—they were stolen from their homelands, brutally transported to a strange country where their families were torn apart and then sold off as property. They had to fight for their survival daily under the yoke of slavery. The first documented slave in the New World dates to 1502, when a Spanish merchant sent a single African slave. The first record of Africans arriving in the colonies was from a Dutch sea captain trading nineteen black Africans for food in Jamestown, Virginia, in 1619 (Kolchin, 2003). It is unclear from records whether they were sold into slavery or made indentured servants, but most scholars think they were most likely indentured. However, that fate was not for all Africans who ended up on the shores of America.

The transatlantic slave trade was an unfortunate fallout from the trade in gold, spices and other goods along the West African coast by powerful European nations. At some point in the sixteenth century these European voyagers discovered that trading in human beings was much more lucrative than precious metals and spices. As the demand for this new human commodity grew, the slavers' destination changed from Europe to the Americas where the plantation industry proved to have an insatiable appetite for their human cargo. It is estimated that between 11 and 12 million Africans were forcibly taken from their homelands to the Americas during this slave trade period. From this number about one-half million were transported to what is now the United States (Curtin, 1969; Klein, 1999; Gilder Lehrman Institute of American History, 2016).

African Americans, who number about 45.7 million or 14.3% of the total population, represent the second largest minority group in the U.S. (U.S. Census Bureau, Population Division, 2014). This includes those who identify as black only and black in combination of another race. However, they accounted for 27.2% of all those in poverty, and 42.5% of single parent-headed black households were poor. While the annual household incomes of African Americans have outpaced whites since 1960, they still lag behind. The median household income for whites is $59,754, compared to the black median household income of $35,416 (Sentier Research, 2014). Blacks are also less likely to own homes: about 43% own homes compared to almost 75% of whites. Unemployment rates among blacks are double that of whites, 13.1% compared to 6.5% (Bureau of Labor Statistics, "Employment Status of the civilian population", 2015). This may be linked to educational attainment. African Americans are less likely than white Americans to graduate from high school, complete college, or pursue post-baccalaureate degrees.

However, since 1980, African Americans have made remarkable educational and economic progress. The rate of black high school dropouts has declined; the black middle class is the fastest-growing of all minority groups and whites. African Americans have also made political progress; many U.S. cities and states are headed by African American politicians. In 2008, Americans elected its first biracial president, lifting the hopes of not just blacks but many in the United States. America has struggled with racial inequality throughout its history, and even as laws, policies, and practices are enacted in an attempt to reduce racial inequality, there remains, as W.E.B. DuBois wrote, a "color line" in America (Du Bois, 1903).

Hispanics (Latinos)

Fig. 8.5 Hispanic households will represent the largest number of ethnic households by the middle of the 21st century.

"Latino" or "Hispanic": Which term is the correct one? Well, I don't know which one is "correct," but here I will use Hispanic, which is the term the U.S. Census uses to describe the category of people who trace their ethnic heritages to the many cultures of Mexico, Central America, South America, and the Caribbean. While their ethnic origins lie in a number of countries, nearly all groups that constitute the category "Hispanic" share the Spanish language as part of their heritage. In 2015, there were 55.4 million Hispanics in the United States, which represents 17.4% of the total population, making them the largest ethnic minority group.

Some Mexican Americans trace their origins to the part of the American southwest that the U.S. forced Mexico to sell after its defeat in the U.S.-Mexican War (1846–1848). Large-scale immigration of Mexicans to the U.S. ramped up in the early part of the twentieth century due in large part to labor demands in the United States and political unrest in Mexico. Since 1980, the U.S. receives more immigrants from Mexico than any other country in the world (De Leon and Griswold del Castillo, 2012).

At around 35 million, Mexican Americans constitute the largest single group of Hispanics in the U.S. Concentrated mainly in America's Southwest and West, they are the majority ethnic population in both New Mexico (47%) and California (39%) (Krogstad and Lopez, 2014). In other words, the Mexican American population has surpassed the white population to be the largest racial/ethnic group in both states. In fact, in Los Angeles, nearly one in every two people is Hispanic (United States Census Bureau, "Los Angeles", 2015). Despite their large numbers, Mexican immigrants have lower educational attainment than others in the U.S. Additionally, many still work at occupations in low-paying business sectors like agriculture and the service industry. The median income in the U.S. in 2014 for all Americans was roughly $53,657; however, Mexican American households' annual income was just $42,491. Mexican Americans are also more likely to live in poverty: 23.6% of Mexican American households were poor in 2014 compared to 14.8% of the U.S. population overall (DeNavas-Walt and Proctor, 2014).

The unauthorized immigration of Mexicans into the U. S. has become a political hot-button topic and much of the political discourse has focused on inflaming animosities toward this group by using certain verbal imagery and inaccurate data. Therefore, it should be noted that the common belief that unauthorized Mexican immigration is on the rise is false. Since 2007, it has been on a sharp decline, dropping from 6.9 million to 5.6 million immigrants in 2014 (Gonzalez-Barrera and Krogstad, 2015).

In contrast, Cuban Americans have had a very different immigration and social experience than Mexicans Americans. Once Fidel Castro came to power in 1959, his Communist party began to restructure Cuban society. This included appropriating privately owned land, buildings, and businesses in the name of the new Communist state. Many of his political opponents and middle-class Cubans who had suffered economic ruin and feared reprisals from the new regime, fled to the United States. Unlike most other Hispanic immigrant groups, many Cuban immigrants who came to America were educated and had marketable skills and some money. These characteristics made their transition into American life a bit smoother than other Hispanic groups.

It is important to remember that many of these Cuban immigrants came not because they sought their fortunes in America, but rather that conditions in their homeland became unbearable. As a result, Cuban Americans tend to maintain a strong ethnic identity more than other Hispanic groups. Little Havana, for example, is the Cuban community in Miami, Florida, where you can read signs in Spanish, hear people speaking Spanish, and enjoy the aroma of Cuban street food. In fact, eight out of ten Cuban American families speak Spanish at home, more than other Hispanic group. While they cling to tradition, Cuban Americans have prospered in the U.S. Compared to other Hispanic groups, Cuban Americans earn the most with a median individual annual income of $24,400. They also have the lowest poverty level compared to other Hispanic groups. Additionally, Cuban Americans tend to be better educated than other Hispanics (Motel and Patten, 2012; Brown and Patten, 2013).

We can see that the experience of Cuban Americans has been qualitatively different from that of Mexican Americans. Mexican immigrants come to the U.S. seeking economic opportunity, with little education and money. They are willing to take low-paying, sometimes migrant work, and they attempt to assimilate quickly into American culture. Those Cuban immigrants who fled the chaos of post- revolutionary Cuba came with money, education, and skills. They do well in the larger society while still maintaining strong ethnic identities and networks.

In 1980, a new wave of Cuban immigrants reached the shores of the United States. The Mariel Harbor boatlift brought as many as 125,000 Cuban immigrants to America in a six-month time span. Triggered by a downturn in the Cuban economy, Fidel Castro, Cuba's despotic ruler, announced that anyone who wanted to leave Cuba was free to do so. Among these immigrants were the mentally ill, violent criminals, homosexuals, and religious sectarians (such as Seventh Day Adventists and Jehovah's Witnesses), what Castro referred to as "*escorias*," or the scum of society. Unfortunately, all boatlift immigrants were painted with the same brush of undesirability. Although the vast majority of the "Marielitos" were law-abiding citizens looking to make their way legitimately in America, anti-Latino prejudice led to negative opinions about them. Many Americans believed the new Cuban immigrants were causing crime, unemployment, and economic declines in the U.S. (Aguirre, Sáenz, and James, 1997; Ojito, 2005; Doss, 2003). While there were some difficulties with this wave of Cuban immigrants, most criminals were imprisoned or deported, those who needed psychiatric help got it, and the vast majority of these immigrants

THE NEW CUBAN IMMIGRANTS

Encouraged by President Obama's announcement of normalizing relations with Cuba in 2014, the number of Cubans entering the U.S. spiked in 2015 to 43,000. This represents a 78% increase over the previous year. But these new immigrants are not coming to America by sea, but rather by land. While the U.S. Coast Guard reports that Cubans still try to reach the U.S. by raft, the vast majority are arriving by land. In the past few years most Cubans seeking to enter the U.S. have been flying into Ecuador, which did not require visas for Cubans until late 2015, then trekking their way through South and Central America to reach their final destination, the U.S. However, in late 2015 Nicaragua closed its borders stranding a group of about 8,000 Cubans. As a result, in part, of the president's announcement about the new state of U.S. Cuba relations, some Central American countries organized flights for the 8,000 Cubans so they could ultimately reach Mexico where they crossed over into the U.S. (Krogstad, 2015).

Why are they coming in such large numbers if things between the countries are normalizing? Well, there are several reasons. In 2009, the U.S. eased restrictions on Americans traveling there and sending money to relatives there. Then in 2013, Cuba eased exit controls on those seeking to leave the island nation. The topper, however, was President Obama's announcement about normalizing relations with Cuba. According to the 1966 Cuban Adjustment Act, Cubans receive preferential treatment with immigration, Cubans are assumed to be "political refugees" and are almost always granted asylum in the U.S. And after being in country for one year, they can apply for legal permanent residence. So, Cubans fearing that their immigration privileges would evaporate once relations between the two countries were re-established, and armed with money from American relatives and an easy exit from Cuba, thousands fled.

This new wave of Cuban immigrants is different from those who fled Castro's oppression and those who left later during boat lifts. And these new immigrants are becoming the majority, fully 56% of Cubans in the U.S. came here after 1990. The newest wave of Cubans is also better assimilated than those who came to the U.S. earlier, they are more likely to speak English at home and are less likely to "self-marginalize"—socially isolate themselves in ethnic enclaves. This new group feels that Cubans in America share "a lot" of values in common with Cubans still in Cuba. However, those who came to the U.S. before 1990 think that they have "very little" in common. Political party affiliation has done a flip-flop with these new immigrants. Of those who arrived in the U.S. after 1990, 57% lean towards the Democratic Party and only 19% report being Republican. In sharp contrast, those Cubans who entered the U.S. before 1990, 48% report being Republican, and only 35% say they are Democrats. Perhaps more importantly 80% of these new Cubans believe that the U.S. embargo on Cuba should be lifted and relations between the two countries should be normalized. However, only 47% of their older, more established counter parts think this should happen. (Lopez and Krosgstad, 2014).

were integrated into the Miami Cuban American community. While the majority of the 2 million Cubans in the U.S. call Miami home, they are more dispersed than ever before.

Asian Americans

By nearly all measures, Asian Americans fare the best of all ethnic groups in the United States. Asian Americans have been referred to as the "model minority" because of their perceived success in the U.S. They are viewed as academic overachievers, professionals, and small business owners who have assimilated and been upwardly mobile and socially accepted. However, this stereotype belies the incredible diversity of this minority group. The term Asian American encompasses people from a vast geographical area. According to the U.S. Census, Asians include those "having origins in any of the original peoples of the Far East, Southeast Asia or the Indian Sub-Continent" (Humes, Jones, and Ramirez, 2011). Table 8.2 shows the incredible geographic range—and therefore the linguistic, and cultural diversity - of the more than twenty different countries that constitute Asian Americans.

TABLE 8.2 The Geography of Asian Americans

	Countries That Constitute Asian American
Asian American can mean you come from, identify with, or descend from people from these twenty-six countries	**Native Hawaiian/Pacific Islander**: Hawaiian Islands, Samoa, Guam, Northern Mariana Islands, Micronesia, Polynesia, and Melanesia **East Asian**: China, Japan, Korea, Taiwan, Mongolia, and Tibet **South Asian**: India, Pakistan, Bangladesh, Nepal, Sri Lanka, and Bhutan **Southeast Asian**: Cambodia, Vietnam, Laos, Thailand, Myanmar, Indonesia, Malaysia, Singapore, and the Philippines (The Hmong and Mien peoples are distinct groups of Asian Americans whose origins are located within the countries listed)

According to the U.S. Census, as of 2011, there are 18.2 million Asian Americans in the U.S., representing about 6% of the total U.S. population. Of that number, Chinese Americans make up the largest group (4 million), followed by Filipino Americans (3.4 million), Asian Indians (3.2 million), Vietnamese Americans (1.9 million), Korean Americans (1.7 million), and Japanese Americans (1.3 million). While Asian Americans live in all parts of the U.S., 57% of Hawaii's population reports being of Asian descent. The U.S. Census predicts by the year 2060, the Asian American population will be nearly 40 million, representing almost 9% of the total U.S. population (Colby and Ortman, 2015).

The path taken by many of the early Asian immigrants is a similar one. They arrived in the U.S., took low-paying, undesirable jobs, lived collectively many times in ethnic enclaves (such as Chinatown), and over a few generations prospered as assimilated Americans. In fact, Asian Americans have the highest average annual income of any racial/ethnic group in the United States at $74,297 (DeNavas-Dewalt and Proctor, 2015). This high level of income is driven by a few factors. Asian Americans are the best-educated racial/ethnic group in the United States. Only 28% of the general public holds a college degree, compared to nearly 51% of Asian Americans. Nearly half (49%) work in professional, management, or related occupational fields, and more than 20% of Asian Americans hold advanced degrees (such as a master's, M.D. or PhD), compared to 10% of the general population of the U.S. (Le, 2015).

Remember, Asian Americans are an intensely diverse group, representing multiple cultures and languages; they are not a monolithic group. When combined, they may have high levels of education and income, but there are some subgroups like the Hmong, Laotians, and Cambodians who have encountered more difficulty assimilating into the U.S. These subgroups have considerably lower levels of education and income than other Asian Americans (Pew Research Center, 2013).

Middle Eastern Americans

Like Asian Americans, Middle Eastern Americans are comprised of people from a number of countries who represent dozens of languages, religions, and cultural traditions. The U.S. Census considers immigrants from Western Asia and North Africa (commonly referred to as the Middle East) to be Middle Eastern Americans. This diverse group of people can trace their heritage to such places as Morocco, Afghanistan, Lebanon, Israel, Turkey, and Azerbaijan. Regardless of which country in the Middle East they come from, as of the 2010 census, they are categorized as "white." However, organizations that represent Middle Eastern Americans have lobbied the U.S. Census Bureau and requested that it includes a new ethnic category on census forms. Activists encouraged those of Middle East descent to indicate some other race on 2010 census forms; their slogan was "Check it right, you ain't white" (Krogstad, 2014).

As a result of the census bureau's practice of counting Middle Easterners as "white," it is difficult to get an accurate count and portrait of Middle Eastern Americans. The census bureau has been categorizing and counting Arab Americans since 1980, and that population is estimated to be 1.8 million, a 76% increase since 1990. However, Arab Americans are just one piece of a larger Middle Eastern mosaic of people possessing a wide range of languages, religions, and cultures. Today, most Middle Eastern Americans identify with Arab ancestry. However, according to the Arab American Institute Foundation, the Arab American population is more than double the census count at 3.7 million ("Adding a MENA Category", 2015).

Lebanese, Syrian and Egyptian Americans combined make up 53% of all Arab Americans. In general, Arab Americans are well-educated; 40% hold college degrees compared to 28% for the average U.S. resident (Brittingham, & Patricia de la Cruz, 2005). Partly a result of their higher education levels, Arab Americans enjoy high incomes; in 2010, the median household income for all households in the U.S. was $51,914, while the median income for Arab American households was $56,433. Lebanese households enjoyed the highest median household income of all Arab American subgroups at $67,264 (Asi and Beaulieu, 2013). However, not all Arab Americans are prosperous; Yemeni and Iraqi Americans earn about half of what Lebanese, Egyptian and Syrian Americans do. Those with Yemeni and Moroccan ancestry are less likely to be homeowners, and those with Yemeni or Iraqi ancestry are more likely to be poor than other Middle Eastern groups.

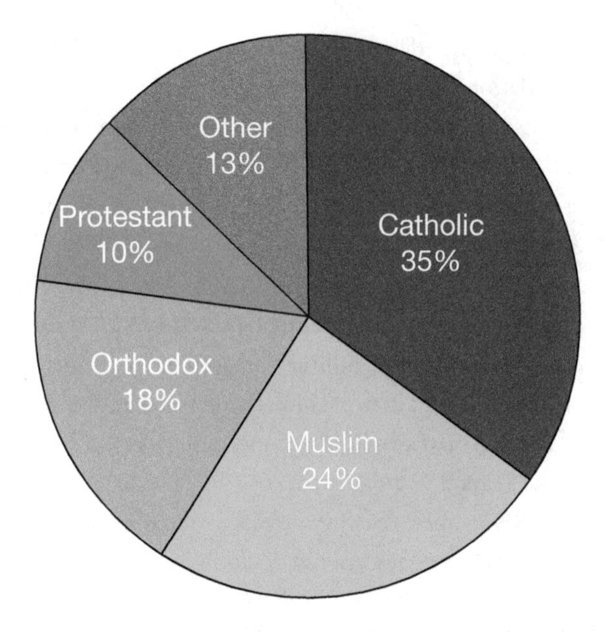

Fig. 8.6 While Arab Americans are perceived as a monolithic Islamic religious group, that's not the reality.

While there is variation in levels of education, income, and homeownership between the subgroups of Arab Americans, overall, they are a well-integrated minority. Despite enduring the stereotype that "Arab" means the same as "Muslim," (in fact, the majority of Arab Americans are Christian; take a look at the pie chart in figure 8.6) and the prejudice and discrimination after September 11, 2001, this ethnic group has done well. In general, Arab Americans are well-educated and have higher incomes. In addition, the majority are homeowners, they experience very low unemployment rates, and about three-quarters of all Arab Americans speak only English at home. These are all indicators that Arab Americans are well-assimilated into American culture and contribute to the common good.

America is a multiracial, multiethnic, multilinguistic, multireligious, and multicultural tapestry of people, some of whom were born elsewhere and came to the United States to escape religious, economic, or political oppression or strife. Others are native-born but retain their racial or ethnic identity, which is what makes the United States a "salad bowl" of racial and ethnic diversity. However, the racial and ethnic profile of America is changing rapidly as more immigrants make their way here and as resident racial and ethnic minority populations grow. As of 2015, racial and ethnic minorities are growing more rapidly than whites, and it is estimated that by 2043,

America's white majority will be gone (U.S. Census Bureau, "U.S. Census Bureau Projections," 2012). So, in the not-so-distant future, the United States will be a nation numerically dominated by the descendants of racial and ethnic minorities.

Theoretical Perspectives on Race

Racial formation is "...the socio-historical process by which racial categories are created, inhabited, transformed, and destroyed" (Omi and Winant, 2015). Racial formation theory states that race is a socially constructed identity that is *formed* by social, economic, and political forces. This perspective emphasizes that the conception and perception of race is always historically situated, therefore it is dynamic and fluid, changing over time. So, throughout history, using different imagery, media, and social attitudes of the time, racial formations come into existence, change, become contested, and are re-created anew. For example, blacks were portrayed in early movies as listless, slow-talking, simple service workers, following their bosses around uttering "yesum" in deferential agreement. Today's movies are more likely to portray a young black man as a criminalized street thug straight out of Compton or an action hero. Media images help create racial identities as well as reinforce them in the public's mind and reflect popular images of race. More importantly, this theory shows the connection between social structure and our perceptions of racial groups, which influences our attitudes and behaviors toward them. For example, differences in education and income based on race helps shape what we believe to be true about various racial groups. They further argue that racial meanings operate at all levels of society from our own individual perceptions to the social policies of the federal government.

Critical race theory seeks to *critically* analyze social structure, culture beliefs, meanings, and ideas that may be racially oppressive and expose them. Critical theory, like racial formation theory, understands that race is a social construction. Racial categories such as African American, Hispanic and Asian American, critical theory contends, are socially constructed through social interactions, meanings, and social institutions like law, politics, and education. Critical race theorists contend that the construct of race and the practice of racism emerge from social thought and the power arrangements between the races. They argue that racial inequality is reproduced by the policies and practices of institutions such as schools and the courts, and appear as normal and business as usual (Delgado and Stefancic, 2012). There are five central principles to critical race theory:

- Racism. Racism is embedded in the very fabric of social life. It is viewed as so prevalent and so nuanced into media, law, economics, and politics that most of us cannot distinguish it from what are normal social interactions.

- **White supremacy**. Because whites overwhelmingly control the political, economic, and social spheres that act to subordinate racial minorities, they are privileged by default. Whites essentially enjoy the privilege of *not* being a person of color and therefore not subject to the racist social, political, and economic forces that subjugate racial minorities.
- **Convergence of interests**. Racism works to maintain and reproduce white privilege, so whites have little interest in ending racism. However, there are times when greater equality for racial minorities may serve the interest of whites, and it is when the interests of both groups "converge" that change for greater equality can take place.
- **Intersectionality**. While the theory focusses on racial inequality, it does not disregard or ignore other forms of oppression. It recognizes that intersecting categories such as race, gender, age, and class create and reproduce oppressive regimes.
- **Voices of people of color**. Only those who are marginalized by racist ideologies can best illustrate its damaging effects. Giving voice by telling their stories of racial oppression, racial minorities have the potential to transform racist social attitudes and policies.

Some people have a hard time buying into this perspective because it shines a very bright light onto a number of socially sensitive topics, many of which polarize racial groups in the U.S. This approach essentially challenges practices that are largely ignored, taken for granted or believed not to be true. It also implies that as a people we are in denial about the way people of color are portrayed and treated in the U.S. However, this is why it is called *critical* race theory.

Structural functionalism, if you recall, emphasizes conformity, social stability, and social order. Therefore, race and ethnicity can be viewed in a way that ultimately promotes social stability. Conforming to social values, beliefs, and behaviors in order to encourage social stability is important to this approach. Therefore, functionalism views the assimilation of racial and ethnic groups as necessary to ensure conformity to the dominant culture, which helps preserve social order. For racial and ethnic groups not to be socially disruptive, they should take up the beliefs and practices of the dominant culture. This conforming to and cooperating with social rules makes things run smoothly, safeguarding social order.

In all societies, according to the **conflict approach**, there is always inequality between certain groups. There is clearly inequality between the white dominant group and racial and ethnic minorities in the United States. Inequality of income and educational opportunities combined with discriminatory treatment of racial and ethnic minorities has led to their overrepresentation among the poor, the incarcerated, and the disenfranchised. Clearly, racial and ethnic minorities have not benefited from this system of socioeconomic inequality. Frustration with social arrangements, prejudice, and discrimination has boiled over several times in our history, resulting frequently in positive social change. The Civil Rights Act of 1964, for example, was the result of both peaceful and violent demonstrations stemming from the unfair treatment of blacks.

Remember that symbolic interactionism, in contrast to both functionalism and conflict theory, focuses on social context rather than social structure. This perspective also emphasizes identity formation, and race and ethnicity are important elements of identity. We assign meaning to symbols like our race and ethnicity, and we rely on those meanings when we interact with others. Central to this approach is the idea that we interact with others based on what we believe, not on what is objectively true. So, when we interact with individuals of a different race, we respond to them based on what we believe about their race by creating a symbolic exchange of language and behaviors that demonstrates our racial identity. An African American, for example, may use African American Vernacular English, frequently referred to as "Ebonics," when interacting with friends and family. This person interprets their racial identities as similar to hers and uses language, body language, and behaviors that are appropriate for those interactions. However, if this person is in her college classroom among a variety of racial identities and a white professor, she may use "standard English" as part of her symbolic exchange for that social context.

TABLE 8.3 Theoretical Perspectives on Race/Ethnicity

Theoretical Perspective	Their Take on Race/Ethnicity
Structural Functionalism	Functionalists are all about social stability and social order. In order for racial and ethnic groups to contribute to social stability and social order, they must assimilate into society. They need to jettison their ways and absorb, in a sense, the values, beliefs, and behaviors of the dominant culture. Therefore, they contribute the most to social order by being like everyone else. For example, people who immigrate to the U.S. from, say, Uganda should learn English, get jobs, pay taxes, and take part in "American" customs and traditions. This "joining in" prevents social disruption and benefits social order while allowing the minority groups to acquire the skills needed for social mobility and to be similar to the dominant culture.

(Continued)

Theoretical Perspective	Their Take on Race/Ethnicity
Conflict Approach	This approach emphasizes use of power and coercion to maintain and reproduce the oppression of racial and ethnic minorities. The dominant white regime uses an ideology of prejudice, stereotyping, and discrimination to reproduce the racist social order. As we discussed earlier in the chapter, the murder of Mike Brown in Ferguson, Missouri, resulted in mass protests and riots. This physical *conflict* with the police symbolized the unequal treatment that the black community experienced at the hands of its police, courts, and local government. However, if you recall, the Department of Justice investigated the police, courts, and local government and found that there was systematic unfair treatment, which maintained the oppression of blacks in that city.
Symbolic Interactionism	The approach recognizes that race is a socially constructed concept. This perspective argues that our day-to-day interactions with others are guided by the meaning/labels we assign them. So, the social meaning we have come to understand about white skin, black skin, or brown skin will shape our interactions with those of another race. We encounter someone with a certain skin color, and based on that cue, we interact with that person based on our social assumptions about him or her. Two women, one white and one black, are shopping at an upscale boutique on Rodeo Drive; the white sales associate will most likely treat the two women differently. Why? According to symbolic interactionism, the sales associate holds different meanings for the symbols white skin and dark skin and will interact with each woman based on those social ideas of what white people are like and what black people are like.

The Bottom Line

Race and ethnicity, as we have seen, are complex social constructs. While race has some basis in biology, such as physical characteristics we can use to group people like hair texture, skin color, and eye color, there is no separate genomic sequence that sets blacks apart from whites or Asians. All humans share more than 99.99% of our genetic material. (National Human Genome Research Institute, 2016.) On the other hand, ethnicity is widely recognized as a set of characteristics shared by a group such as language, beliefs, customs, and practices that help them maintain an identity separate from other groups. While both racial and ethnic groups are frequently identified as minority groups, minority group status is more about access to valuable social resources and equal treatment and less about identity. Minorities do not have to be numerically inferior to maintain dominance (apartheid), and they can be numerically superior and be a social minority (women).

Dominant groups throughout history and from place to place have treated minority and immigrant groups in a variety of ways. These dominant-minority group interactions have ranged from the intensely intolerant act of genocide to the inclusive and fully tolerant practice of pluralism, with the moderately tolerant practices of segregation and assimilation falling in between the two extremes. Attitudes and behaviors toward minority groups vary by the level of tolerance present in societies. People in highly intolerant societies tend to have high levels of prejudice toward minorities, which, in turn, is acted upon through discrimination. In intolerant societies, stereotypes of minorities are part of the dominant ideology, used as tools of hate. In some instances, this can lead to the scapegoating of a particular minority group. This practice of promoting racial stereotypes and blaming a certain racial group for social, economic, and political problems in the larger society was evident in the Nazi's treatment of the Jews.

When feelings about or actions toward a given racial group are powered solely by skin color, racism emerges. Racism has a long history in the United States and in many other societies. From slavery to the Jim Crow era, America was an intolerant and hostile land for blacks. Fortunately, changes in laws and social attitudes have vastly improved social circumstances for African Americans and other people of color. However, vestiges of institutional racism remain in the United States. Differential educational resources, for example, for those in economically deprived areas, which are heavily populated by racial minorities, still plague the U.S. These deficits in education harm young people of color by putting them at a disadvantage for college admissions and the workplace. Unfortunately, a number of high-profile killings of unarmed black men by white police officers between 2014 and 2016 has raised the specter of institutional racism in law enforcement.

This movement away from intolerance toward tolerance is a pattern experienced by many minority groups in the United States. As the United States formed and expanded westward, American Indians paid a heavy price for "manifest destiny." They were driven from their homelands, put on reservations, and had their children taken from them and put in boarding schools in order to "civilize" them.

African Americans hold a unique position in America's racial history. They are the one racial group that was forcibly brought to the United States—forced onto ships on the west coast of Africa, enduring the middle passage, and then disembarking in the new world as slaves. African Americans represent the oldest "immigrant" minority group in the United States. Enduring centuries of oppression, prejudice, and discrimination, African Americans, despite the Civil Rights Act of 1964 and countless changes to discriminatory laws, policies, and practices, remain a disenfranchised group.

As America expanded and immigrant groups started to arrive in large numbers, many of them experienced periods of marginalization, widespread prejudice, discrimination, and finally, for most groups, assimilation and acceptance. For some Western European groups like the Germans, Dutch, and Scottish, it was easier to "blend" in because of their appearance and cultural similarities. Others, however, had more difficulty with fitting in. The Chinese, Japanese, and Hispanics, for example, with their perceived exotic cultural traditions and their physical differences from the dominant white groups, had a more difficult time being accepted. However, these groups have managed to find their place in the United States despite continued discrimination. Hispanics have had a more difficult time finding prosperity in America, with the exception of Cuban Americans. Other racial/ethnic groups that have arrived to the United States relatively recently like the Vietnamese, South Asians, and Middle Eastern immigrants have enjoyed economic success but endure racial stereotyping, prejudice, and discrimination. Middle Eastern and some South Asian immigrants such as Pakistanis and Arabs are more likely to be targeted for discrimination based on religious affiliation more than ethnic identity.

We discussed some more progressive theoretical perspectives on race such as racial formation theory and critical race theory. Racial formation theory argues that our attitudes and actions toward racial groups are constructed using media, symbols, and language in a historical context. Therefore, images of racial groups are created in the context of history, are fluid, and change over time. A more critical analysis of race is presented by critical race theory. This perspective argues that the continued marginalization of people of color is a result of structural discrimination, the discrimination against people of color embedded in social structure and institutions. The approach also focuses on the intersectionality of oppressions and recognizes that race alone cannot account for disempowerment.

Finally, we looked at the three major theoretical perspectives in sociology as they are applied to race. Structural functionalism assumes that racial/ethnic minority groups will conform to the dominant culture and assimilate. This, according to functionalism, is the best way for these groups to gain access to social acceptance and mobility while contributing to social stability. On the other hand, we have the conflict approach, which emphasizes that social change results from social conflict, thus reducing inequality between the dominant and minority groups. The conflict approach argues that minorities must use social conflict like demonstrations, civil disobedience, and protests to affect change in society and gain equality. Symbolic interaction is more concerned with how we interpret the symbolic meaning of skin color than with structural influences like laws and the economy. This approach focuses on how our meaning of race shapes everyday interactions and, ultimately, how we perform differently with different racial/ethnic groups based on our perceptions of what their race/ethnicity means.

Figure Credits

Fig. 8.1: MSGT Rose Reynolds, "Bodies from the Rwandan Massacre," https://commons.wikimedia.org/wiki/File:Bodies_of_Rwandan_refugees_DF-ST-02-03035.jpg. Copyright in the Public Domain.

Fig. 8.2: Ansel Adams, "Japanese Americans at Manzanar Relocation Camp in California," http://www.loc.gov/pictures/item/2002695984/resource/. Copyright in the Public Domain.

Fig. 8.3: Kane Farabuagh, "Riot Police line up in Ferguson, Missouri," https://commons.wikimedia.org/wiki/File:VOA_Ferguson_protests.jpg. Copyright in the Public Domain.

Fig. 8.4: Russell Lee, "Separate but Equal?," https://commons.wikimedia.org/wiki/File:%22Colored%22_drinking_fountain_from_mid-20th_century_with_african-american_drinking.jpg. Copyright in the Public Domain.

Fig. 8.5: National Cancer Institute, "Hispanic Family enjoying a meal," https://commons.wikimedia.org/wiki/File:Family_eating_meal.jpg. Copyright in the Public Domain.

Fig. 8.6: DinajGao, "Arab American religions," https://commons.wikimedia.org/wiki/File:Arab_American_religions.png. Copyright in the Public Domain.

CHAPTER 9

SEX AND GENDER

His and Hers or Zirs and Hirs?

The students who started college in the fall of 2015 at the University of Tennessee at Knoxville were encouraged to use language that is more inclusive and sensitive to gender. In an attempt to make the campus more gender-inclusive, the Office of Diversity and Inclusion asked students and faculty to use gender-neutral language (Braquet, 2015). It has even suggested the use of "ze" rather than he or she as a gender-neutral alternative. Other suggested gender-neutral language includes "hirs" rather than hers and "zirs" rather than his. What is the reason behind the use of these alternative pronouns? Believing that students do not always identify with their assigned birth gender, officials want to give transgender students and those who do not identify with the gender binary (male/female) a way to express their identity using gender-neutral language. Table 9.1 shows some gender-neutral alternatives to the standard English subjects, objects, and pronouns.

TABLE 9.1 Gender-Neutral Alternatives to Gender Binary Speech

	Subject	Object	Pronoun	Pronunciation
Gender Binary	She	Hers	Hers	As it looks
	He	Him	His	As it looks
Gender Neutral	They*	Them*	Their*	As it looks
	Ze	Hir	Hirs	Zhee, Here, Heres
	Ze	Zir	Zirs	Zhee, Zhere, Zheres
	Xe	Xem	Xyr	Zhee, Zhem, Zhere

**Used as singular. Source: University of Tennessee at Knoxville, Office of Diversity and Inclusion*

The university is not requiring students to use gender-neutral language. It is not official policy, just a suggestion so all students feel welcomed, included, and accepted. What do you think? Is it a good idea? Will using uncommon language make people feel accepted or uncomfortable?

TRY THIS

For a whole day, at school, work, and home, either use the gender-neutral alternatives from the table above (you might want to carry a "cheat sheet" with you) or for everyone you meet, ask which pronoun he/she prefers to be referred to by. You might start a trend in gender-neutral language use.

Sex and Gender

Issues surrounding gender are becoming more mainstreamed in American culture. In 2015, Olympic gold medal winner Bruce Jenner came out as a transgender person, appearing on the cover of *Vanity Fair* dressed in a bustier as Caitlyn Jenner. Take, for example, Amazon network's biggest hit show *Transparent*, whose main character is a family man and father who is transitioning to a woman, or The Learning Channel's *I am Jazz*, a reality TV show that follows a teenage transgender who insisted at age three she was a girl, *not* a boy, and has been living as Jazz ever since. Additionally, the legalization nationwide of same-sex marriage has made the LGBTQ community highly visible.

With all this visibility, people still struggle with the associated terminology, even the basic terms of sex and gender. Some people conflate them, some use them interchangeably, and some get them wrong altogether. Do you know the difference between the terms sex and gender? Stop here. Before you read on, see if you can define, in twenty-five words or less, the terms sex and gender. Go ahead.

In sociology, we have fairly standardized definitions for both terms. Sex refers to anatomical and biological differences between males and females. These differences include primary sex characteristics—genitalia, hormones, and chromosomes—and secondary sex characteristics— a variety of characteristics specific to males or females that develop at puberty. These include lowering of the voice and increased body hair in boys and the development of breasts and menstruation in girls (Warnke, 2007; Dozier, 2005).

Intersex

Although we tend to think of sex in binary terms, boy and girl, male and female, sex isn't always that clear-cut. Some people are born as intersex— "is a general term used for a variety of conditions in which a person born with a reproductive or sexual anatomy that doesn't seem to fit the typical definitions of female or male" (formally referred to as *hermaphrodites*). For example, someone may be born with the genitals of a male and have the internal reproduction organs of a female (Intersex Society of North America, 2015). Other times, a person is born with incomplete genitals of both sexes, which appear to be in-between the usual male and female types. The intersex condition is not always evident at birth. It may be determined at puberty or when someone is discovered to be infertile, or it may never be discovered).

Parents of intersex newborns are usually confused and distressed by the child's condition. In the past, most parents and surgeons have followed a Concealment-Centered Model of treatment for intersex children. This model essentially encouraged parents to pick a sex for their child and raise them as that sex, even if it meant lying to them. In an attempt to improve how intersex parents and children are cared for, the Intersex Society of North America (ISNA) has created a Patient-Centered Model of care. This model is designed not to conceal, but to make the process transparent. Children and parents should be fully informed, have access to support, and avoid unnecessary surgery. This approach is aimed at reducing the potential harm to both intersex children and their parents.

READ MORE

- *As Nature Made Him* by John Colapinto (2000) is the story of David Reimer, who was born a biological male. During a botched circumcision, nearly his entire penis was burned off. His parents had him "sex-reassigned" through surgery, hormonal treatment, and therapy and elected to raise him as a girl. When David finally learned of this, he rebelled and reassumed the social identity of a boy. It's a compelling read.

Gender—the widely accepted ideas about masculinity and femininity that are typically attributed to individuals based on their biological sex. Gender represents cultural ideas, or constructions, of what it means to be masculine and feminine. In our culture children are frequently taught that masculine men don't cry, and feminine women are emotional. Therefore, we are born either male or female, but our gender is learned. Characteristics of gender vary greatly across cultures. Our ideas of traditional male and female roles are reversed among the Aka people of Central Africa, for example. The men stay with and care for the young—infants actually suckle their father's nipples—while the women hunt, fish, and decide where to set up their next camp. By their cultural standards, Aka dads are quite manly (Hewlett, 1991).

The Social Construction of Gender

All cultures create ideas that over time, through use and practice, seem to become real and inevitable. While gender, how maleness and femaleness are defined seem natural, it is actually created or "constructed" by humans. And that construct of gender varies widely because cultures vary widely. Therefore, the social construct of gender is bound to culture. Gender is something that is socially constructed and defined; its meaning and significance varies within a culture over time, as well as between cultures. Each culture has different ideas about what it means to be masculine and feminine. These constructs are reinforced using language, imagery, and symbols, making them seem real in our everyday lives. In other words, we all act in ways that reinforce their existence, which makes them appear real. (Elder-Vass, 2013; Kimmel, 2010).

Our understanding of gender is created and maintained largely through gender-binary ideology, which separates gender into two distinct and opposite forms: man/woman or masculine/feminine. This is achieved largely through the use of cultural values, beliefs, and attitudes that are widely shared by members of society and shape our gender identities. Our language, for example, reinforces the gender-binary when we use such words as he/she or his/hers. Gendered language is so pervasive, and we are so habituated to its use, that we don't even notice it. From our use of pronouns to titles such as policeman, chairman, and mankind, linguistic gender labeling abounds in our culture. Language and other symbolic mechanisms are embedded in gender ideology as a way to regulate, police, and reproduce the definitions of masculine and feminine. There are glimmers of change. Target department stores, for example, recently created new store policy that eliminates gendered signage for bedding and toys. So no more "girl toys" and "boy toys"; now it's just "toys." Can you think of other ways we reinforce our cultural versions of masculine and feminine?

TRY THIS

Go to your local department store like Target or Wal-Mart and pick out ten health and beauty care items for women and ten made for men. Try to match them identically (like choosing unscented deodorant for women and unscented deodorant for men), and compare the ingredients to see if they are identical; using store brands is a good way to ensure this. Now add up the total cost of the ten female products and the ten male products. Which gender pays more for the same stuff? Try doing this at a few stores and see if one gender is being ripped off.

Gender ideology shapes our images of masculine and feminine not only through language, but also through our expectations of how boys/men and girls/women should behave. People may disapprove of the man who is seen as too effeminate or the woman who is overtly masculine. Some grow uncomfortable when their cultural image of masculine/feminine doesn't match up with the physical body. This is referred to as *gender non-conformity*—behaving and appearing in ways that are contrary to one's physical appearance. We expect *gender conformity*—one's behaviors and appearance should conform to the social expectation of one's physical appearance. For women, they should appear and act feminine. Therefore, the way we view gender is guided by our *gender ideology*—one that is narrow and, while changing, traditionally allows for only two genders, male and female (Roberts, et al., 2012; Roberts et al., 2013).

By no means is the binary view of gender a cultural universal; there are many cultures that allow for multiple genders. Among the ancient Kanaka Maoli people of Hawaii, the *mahu* were both biological males and females who could occupy a gender somewhere between or completely encompassing both the feminine and masculine. They were held in high esteem, were educators, and conducted sacred rituals (Robertson, 1989). The *hijra* of India, Pakistan, and Bangladesh are homosexual, intersex, transgender, or castrated males who live as a third gender. They are both revered and reviled. Their blessings, especially for weddings, are highly valued. However, many people are wary of them, and consequently, they have been pushed to the margins of society. Typically, they live communally to pool their meager financial resources and for protection (Roughgarden, 2004). Recently, legal rulings in India, Bangladesh, Pakistan, and Nepal have granted them legal status as a third gender. Legal rulings in other countries highlight the global awareness of variations in gender identities. Australia now uses "M" for male, "F" for female, and "X" for transgender on its passports. Germany now allows for a third gender designation on birth certificates for intersex infants. Table 9.2 below describes a range of cultural interpretations of gender.

TABLE 9.2 Variations on Gender around the World

Title	Description	Region of Origin
Xanith	Xanith (HA-neeth) are biological males who are either gay or transgender. They occupy a cultural place that is neither male nor female. They dress unlike men and more like women, and they are allowed to occupy both male and female social space.	Oman
Two-spirit (formerly *berdache*, an adulterated Persian/French term denoting a male prostitute) Nadle (Navajo)	The *two-spirit* people are viewed as possessing both the masculine and the feminine spirit. They are typically intersex, masculine females, or feminine males. Revered for possessing two spirits, they are allowed to live as whichever gender they choose, and they are allowed to marry. Among the Navajo, *nadle* means "changing one" or "one who is transformed." These are either intersex or transgender individuals. They are allowed to pursue the lifestyles of the gender they feel most comfortable in. Nadle who are shaman are highly valued, and nadle, like the two-spirit, are imbued with supernatural abilities.	North American Indians (two-spirit people are recognized by over 130 Native American Indian nations) Navajo (nadle)
Ashtime	These are either eunuchs or non-gender-conforming men. Unfortunately, today it is a pejorative term referring to any non-gender-conforming man. They are an oppressed and marginalized minority.	Ethiopia
Bugis	On the island of Sulewesi in Indonesia, the ethnic Bugis recognize three sexes (male, female, and intersex), and five genders (male, female, calalai, calabai, and bissu). • Calalai—biological females who identify as the male gender • Calabai—biological males who identify as the female gender • Bissu—considered a "transcendent gender," possessing either all genders or none. They function as holy people in their culture.	Indonesia
Bakla (Bayot)	Biological men who dress and live as women, are exclusively attracted to men, and are considered a third gender. Many *bakla* receive hormone treatment and have breast implants, but sex reassignment surgery is rare. Once viewed as scholars, healers, and shaman, now they are widely viewed and accepted as gay, cross-dressing men.	Philippines

Title	Description	Region of Origin
Acault	These men take on the appearance and social roles of women. They are viewed as neither men nor women and are believed to possess spiritual abilities. Men are allowed to have sex with *acault* without violating the prohibition against homosexuality.	Myanmar (formerly Burma)
Kathoeys	Also known as "lady-boys," these are biological males who identify and live as females. They view themselves as a third gender. Thai culture holds that the kathoeys are neither male nor female, but inhabit the space between genders. They are said to have the heart of a woman.	Thailand
Meti	These are biological men who dress and live as women and do not consider themselves gay by Western standards. Rather, they see themselves as a true male-female hybrid.	Nepal
Sworn Virgins	Women who take up the appearance, behaviors, and occupations of men. This is usually a result of financial hardship. Only men have access to good-paying jobs, and women may have to become sworn virgins to support their family. The sworn virgin may enjoy the status and all the rights of a man, but in return, she must remain a virgin her entire life.	Albania
Binabinaaine and Binabinamane	The *binabinaaine* are biological men who live as women, and *binabinamane* are biological women who live as men. Both are viewed as a third gender and are allowed to marry and adopt children.	Kiribati/Micronesia (Pacific Islands)
Saami	Transgendered men, viewed as a third gender in the *saami* culture, were thought to possess shamanistic powers and once held positions of authority.	Lapland (the northern reaches of Sweden, Norway, Finland, and Russia)

Sources: Robinson, 2000; Garcia, 2008; Hutton, 2001; Aggleton, 1999; Nanda, 1990, 2000; Wilson et al., 2011; Roscoe, 1991; Donham, 1990; Peletz, 2009; Coleman, Colgan, and Gooren, 1992; Young, 2001; Winter, 2003; Farran, 2010

Gender Identity, Gender Roles, and Socialization

Our gender identity—the perception of ourselves as masculine or feminine—is an important part of our self-identity. So, how do we develop our gender identity? Gender identity is one dimension of our overall personality, which develops through socialization (remember Chapter 4?). As soon as we are freed from our nine months of womb captivity, the process of socialization begins: pink blankies for the girls and blue blankies for the boys. In fact, by age two, girls chose pink objects more often than their male counterparts, and by two-and-a-half, they preferred pink to all other color choices. By the same age, boys learned to avoid pink (LoBue and DaLoache, 2011).

A great deal of the work of socialization is devoted to shaping our gender and gender identities. A great deal of this is done through learning our *gendered social scripts*—common ways of feeling and acting male and female, which are largely shared and accepted in society - starts early, and most of us adopt and manifest appropriate gender scripts. These are much like scripts actors use when performing a given part, they learn what to say, how to say it and how to move and stand. We learn how to behave and appear as boys and girls and men and women (Messner, 2000; Martin and Ruble, 2004; Lucal, 1999). Girls learn how to sit with their legs crossed, wear dresses and carry purses, while boys learn to "shake it off," open doors for females, and wear "boy clothes." While most of us learn and express these gender scripts in socially expected ways, some find these scripts so inadequate or confounding that they just feel wrong (we will discuss this later in the chapter).

Fig. 9.1 Louis XIV in high heels. Think about fashions now, what elements have "crossed" genders?

These scripts are embedded in gender ideology. As we grow, we learn the scripts consistent with how girls should think, feel, and behave and how boys should think, feel, and act. Specifically, gender roles— widely shared expectations on how to behave male and female—are social guidelines (boundaries, if you will) for each gender's behaviors. Gender identity is self-identified, and is a combination of genetic and environmental factors. Gender roles, on the other hand, are manifested within society by observable factors like behavior and appearance. If someone considers herself a female and is at ease with referring to her personal gender in feminine terms, then she self-identifies as female. However, she is conforming to female gender roles only if she demonstrates typically female behaviors, appearance, and comportment.

These elements of behavior, appearance, and mannerisms are culturally scripted and are subject to change. Believe it or not, high heels were once the height of male fashion. In the mid-1600s, men all over Europe started wearing high heels to emulate the look of soldiers of the Persian army. The Persian Cavalry had recently been very successful at defeating its enemies while wearing high heels, which kept men from falling out of their stirrups when they stood to fire their weapons. Believing that high heels would associate the wearer with this macho image, they became all the rage. In fact, King Louis XIV of France was a high heel-wearing monarch (Semmelhack, 2008). High heels are mainly a fashion staple for women in our society, but times do change.

All these traits of gender-appropriate behavior, appearance, and mannerisms are learned through the socialization process, which teaches people to behave according to social norms. Children learn at a very young age the differences between boys and girls and the expectations for the two genders. Research indicates that by age two, children are aware of differential gender roles, and by four or five, most children have firmly established their culturally appropriate gender roles (Bornstein et al., 2000; Dionne et al., 2003; Murray, Johnson, and Peters, 1990; Roulstone, Loader, and Northstone, 2002). So, what are these differences due to? Even though there are some people out there who just cannot handle it, there are innate biological differences between males and females. The way our brains process language, for example, is different between the genders. Females tend to use both hemispheres of their brains to process language, but males tend to be hemispherically specialized, processing language primarily in the left hemisphere of their brains. This may be part of the reason girls, on average, learn to speak and read earlier than boys (Burman, Bitan, and Booth, 2008).

Biology cannot account for all gender differences. If so, we would not see the tremendous cultural variation in gender roles. We know that our environment shapes who we are, and that is also true of our gender identities. Our family is a powerful force in shaping our gender identity and guiding us toward performing certain gender roles. Parents, without intending to do so, may socialize their offspring in gendered ways. The toys parents select for their children, for example, may guide their child's behavior in subtly gendered ways. Giving little girls dolls to play with is a way to shape their desire to nurture and care for the young, therefore preparing little girls for motherhood. Boys, on the other hand, are very often given toys central to occupational roles: the doctor's bag and stethoscope, toy tool kits, and chemistry sets. These are clearly aimed at developing skills and fostering independence and achievement. Sometimes though, simply labeling toys as "boy toys" or "girl toys" can be a turnoff for children if the label doesn't match their gender (Weisgram, Fulcher, and Dinella, 2014). However, this process of gendered socialization is not only found in families. The promotion of gender differences, subtle and overt, is evident in our educational systems, most forms of media, the government, and the economy.

Doing Gender

As we discussed above, social categories such as race, class, and gender are not universally defined or naturally occurring, but emerge through a process of social construction, which helps us understand them within the context of a cultural framework. **Doing gender** is a term used to describe how one's gender is expressed through everyday interactions. Gender is not just who you are, it is also what you do in interaction with others. We "do gender" all the time when we interact with others; we behave in gendered ways to maintain the image of our gender. It's not just the social expectation of gender roles, it is how we perform or "do" our gender (West and Zimmerman, 1987). We do gender when we *display* our gender in social interactions. In most Western countries, including the U.S., it is uncommon for men to hold hands and kiss in public. This would be breaking the gender rules, putting offenders at risk of social mockery or punishment. Yet, in the cultural context of Egypt and Saudi Arabia, men walking arm in arm or holding hands would be "doing gender" as men.

Doing our gender also means we tend to follow what Wade and Ferree (2015) have termed **gender rules,** which are essentially social instructions on how to look and act like men and women. We behave in ways that match up with the way our culture expects a man or woman to look and act. Think about how wallets and purses help us do gender. Men typically carry wallets, and when they use their wallets, they are doing gender by displaying a symbol of masculinity. Others recognize this as consistent with being a man. Wallets contain the essentials, no frills or objects that others may need or want. Men are not asked for aspirin or a Band-Aid. Where would they keep them? The purse is highly gendered. Not only is it a cultural object that conveys femininity, it is a caregiver's bag of tricks. Women's purses contain things like gum, tissues, breath mints, aspirin, and hand sanitizer. The female gender is imbued with notions of nurturing, helpfulness, and compassion. The purse symbolizes these attributes by giving women a place to carry around all their nurturing, helpful goodies. Children often turn to their moms and ask if they have gum, lotion, tissues, or a Band-Aid, fully expecting them to have those things in their purses. Wallets and purses therefore, are gendered objects that help us do gender (Bridges, 2013).

SEXUALIZED LANGUAGE

There are far more derogatory terms for women in the English language than for men. Many of these derogatory terms are highly sexualized. Bitch, cunt, slut, ho, cum-dumpster, cock tease, Mother I would Like to Fuck (MILF), yummy mommy, and sex kitten, for example, are all sexualized pejoratives for women, and the list goes on and on. Notice these terms all refer to sex acts, genitalia, or sexual promiscuity, strongly suggesting women are merely sex objects to be used or abused. Linguistic practices like these are highly insulting to women and reinforce sexual objectification of women.

Men frequently use these terms to insult other men. Moreover, the list of derogatory terms for men is tiny in comparison, and many of the terms like asshole, shithead, dick, or scumbag are used across genders. For a man, the insult is to be slapped with a female label, like pussy or cunt, cutting deep into his masculinity and implying he doesn't have a penis—he is not a man.

Gender Inequality: Perpetuating a Gendered Society

Differential treatment of boys and girls in the classroom is fairly well-documented. In the past, studies that examined the gendered treatment of school-age children pointed to the overwhelmingly gender bias toward girls. Boys were called on more, encouraged to work independently, and challenged more by teachers to solve problems on their own. Boys were traditionally seen as more analytic and presumed to be better at math; therefore, boys were encouraged to work harder at math and pursue additional math classes (Thies and Travers, 2006). High school guidance counselors were more likely to encourage them to pursue science degrees and careers and discourage girls from those majors and careers.

Things seem to be changing; more than a decade of research suggests that girls are outpacing boys in terms of education. Boys falling behind their female counterparts starts in kindergarten and progresses through college. This deficit, or "boy-gap," in the early years seems to be linked to two factors: a lag in reading proficiency and teachers' negative perceptions of boys' "comportments." A study recently found that teachers rewarded girls' classroom behaviors and punished boys' behaviors. Additionally, teachers were willing to base students' grades on this perceived classroom comportment (Grossman, 2004). Who do you think got better grades based on classroom behavior?

Girls are more likely than males to finish high school, they are more likely to apply and be accepted to college, and they are more likely to graduate from college. This is true across all racial and ethnic groups but strongest among Hispanics and blacks. In 1994, 63% of female high school graduates headed off to college, and 61% of males did the same. By 2012, the percentage of women enrolling in college rose to 71, while it remained unchanged for men at 61% (Lopez and Gonzalez-Barrera, 2014). What do you think will be some of the economic and social consequences if this trend continues?

Even with this "gap" between women and men in education, fewer women pursue an education or careers in the science, technology, engineering, and math (STEM) fields. Career fields are still very much segregated by gender. Our social ideas about who should be doing what jobs are still linked to gendered ideas of who does what kind of work. Why are women less likely to pursue careers in STEM professions? There is certainly evidence that women experience discrimination and intimidation in what invariably ends up being very male-occupied workplaces. Many women may not want to endure male-dominated workplaces where many times they are viewed as interlopers, intruding on male career turf. In addition, it may be social expectations of female work vs. male work; many jobs in the STEM fields are viewed as men's work. After all, women aren't as good at math as men (this is sarcasm). Maybe there are other reasons. Other research suggests that women do not gravitate to STEM jobs because they have too many career choices, not because they lack the abilities. Research indicates that women with both high math and verbal skills viewed the employment landscape as richer in terms of their career choices. They eventually chose jobs that they felt afforded them a better use of a range of skills, not just a concentration on math (Wang and Degol, 2013).

Some Pitfalls of Gendering

As a result of socialization, widely held beliefs about gender can become a lens for viewing our entire social landscapes, and while the world is complex, and to deal with its complexities, many times we revert to simplicity. Life seems simpler if we divide the world into gendered categories. Therefore, many elements of our lives like objects, animals, occupations, behaviors, and ideas slip into these gendered categories. Cats are perceived as feminine and dogs as masculine, pick-up trucks are masculine and cute little cars are feminine, surgeons are men and dental hygienists are women. We become so socially immersed in this practice we fail to see that not everything or everyone fits the category, but we stuff them in there anyway because it makes the world tidier. Stuffing things and people into our neat little categories creates **gender stereotypes**, which attribute characteristics to individuals based solely on their gender. Women are emotional, men don't talk much, and women are not good at math are gender stereotypes, for example.

Try to list ten or more gender stereotypes. Look at your list. Most stereotypes reinforce male dominance, right? Women are emotional, men are logical, men are better at science, women are better with kids, men are stronger. Male stereotypes contain traits that are viewed as more socially desirable: logic, good at science, and strength. Female stereotypes either emphasize less valuable traits like emotions or work that is less valued like childcare. Gender socialization teaches us the differences between the genders and stereotypes compound them. These stereotypical beliefs lead to differential treatment of the two genders. Differential treatment of individuals based solely on their sex or gender, is sexism. Sexism in society is most frequently used to establish and maintain male dominance over women. Sexism ranges from seemingly harmless statements by men about their female coworkers' appearance to the gender wage gap, which denies women the same pay for the same work as men. The extreme form of sexist belief is misogyny, which is the hatred of women. This sexist ideology promotes physical, sexual, and psychological violence against women just because they are women. While misogyny exists in societies at varying levels, highly misogynistic cultures allow and even encourage brutality against girls and women. Women in these societies are viewed either as second-class citizens, subhuman or property, which excuses the violent treatment against them. Many times in these societies, misogyny is institutionalized. That is, laws allow men to beat or kill their wives or female relatives for certain social infractions; many of these infractions are described as insults to men's honor (International Center for Research on Women, 2015; World Health Organization, 2016).

Gender and the Workplace

My wife is an operating room nurse and works with several male nurses. When I was introduced to two of them at a social function, one said he worked in the "health field," and one said he "worked in the O.R." Later, I asked them why they didn't reveal that they were nurses. Both replied that they loved being nurses and valued their profession, but others don't see it that way. They both said that when they tell other men they are nurses, it's not uncommon for them to assume they are gay or they couldn't hack medical school (neither one of them ever thought about medical school). This illustrates the assumptions many people make about those who pursue careers in fields that are traditionally filled by the opposite gender.

Interestingly, each of those male nurses was hired at a higher pay rate than my wife, even though she has more experience than them. While women today are experiencing the most educational success and the greatest access to the workplace ever in our history, there remains a substantial difference in pay between the genders. Moreover, the workplace is still an environment that affirms differences and entrenches inequality.

The Pay Gap

Women comprise almost half the entire workforce in the United States. Despite this and federal laws that prohibit unequal pay based on gender, differences between male and female earnings persist. This gender pay gap is the difference between the average incomes of men and women who work full time. Women who work full time and year-round earn just 79 cents for every dollar their male counterparts make (DeNavas-Walt and Proctor, 2015). This represents an average across all occupations, although some jobs pay more and others pay considerably less.

While this unequal earnings pattern holds across all racial/ethnic groups, across all education levels, and across all ages, black and Hispanic women, as well as less educated and older women, tend to take a greater hit ("The Simple Truth", 2013). Here are some statistical snapshots of the differences by race/ethnicity, educational level, and age.

Women's earnings differ by race and ethnicity. Asian/Pacific Islander women are the highest female earners in the U.S. with median annual earnings of $46,000, followed by white women at $40,000. Both Hispanic women at $28,000 and Native American women at $31,000 have median annual earnings less than black women do at $34,000. Take a look at table 9.3, which shows the percentage of pay each racial group makes compared to white men's pay. While pay relative to white men's earnings has improved over time, they still remain significantly less for all racial groups.

While higher levels of education increase women's earnings, they do not eliminate the gender wage gap. Education level is directly linked to earnings. Women with a bachelor's degree earn twice as much, on average, as women with less than a high school diploma. Again, if we compare full-time, year-round annual earnings of women to men with the same educational level, women still earn less. The greatest differences in earnings are between women and men with graduate

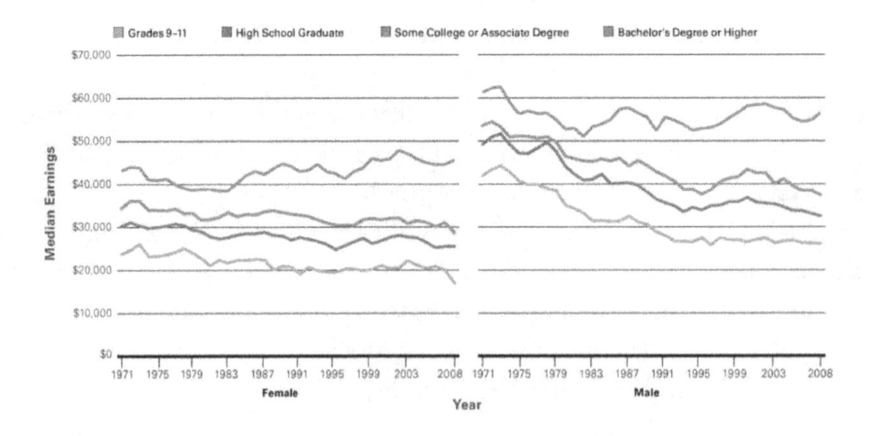

Fig. 9.2 Median Earnings of Men and Women by Education Level (includes full-time year-round workers ages 25-34, shown in constant 2008 dollars).

degrees. At that educational level, women only make 69 cents to a man's dollar earned ("The Status of Women", 2015). The chart in figure 9.2 clearly shows that a pay difference between men and women exists at all educational levels. What do you think accounts for these differences?

There are profound implications for the gender pay gap. There is a cumulative effect of lower earnings over the course of a woman's lifetime. For instance, it has been estimated that the average woman in the United States will earn somewhere between $430,000 and $530,000 less than the average man over her lifetime (Arons, 2008). That amount grows to nearly $800,000 for highly educated women. This has a direct effect on how much women can contribute to their retirement and how much social security they receive. This also has an impact on women's quality of life in old age. Women seventy-five and older are more than twice as likely to live in poverty as men of the same ages (Bureau of Labor Statistics, 2013).

Because of this intersectionality—the concept that suggests we cannot separate race, class, and gender, but rather, they are intersecting systems of oppression—we can see the connection between the lower earnings of both Hispanic and black women, who are members of minority groups that are typically underrepresented in higher educational attainment (Veenstra, 2013) are members of minority groups underrepresented in higher educational attainment (Veenstra, 2013). While the pay gap has closed somewhat over time there remains significant differences in pay between all minority groups (including white women) and white men. Figure 9.3 shows the median earnings of black men and women, Hispanic men and women, and white women as a percentage of white men's median annual earnings.

TABLE 9.3 The Wage Gap, by Gender and Race

Year	White men	Black men	Hispanic men	White women	Black women	Hispanic women
1970	100%	69.0%	n.a.	58.7%	48.2%	n.a.
1975	100	74.3	72.1%	57.5	55.4	49.3%
1980	100	70.7	70.8	58.9	55.7	50.5
1985	100	69.7	68.0	63.0	57.1	52.1
1990	100	73.1	66.3	69.4	62.5	54.3
1992	100	72.6	63.3	70.0	64.0	55.4
1994	100	75.1	64.3	71.6	63.0	55.6
1995	100	75.9	63.3	71.2	64.2	53.4

(Continued)

Year	White men	Black men	Hispanic men	White women	Black women	Hispanic women
1996	100	80.0	63.9	73.3	65.1	56.6
1997	100	75.1	61.4	71.9	62.6	53.9
1998	100	74.9	61.6	72.6	62.6	53.1
1999	100	80.6	61.6	71.6	65.0	52.1
2000	100	78.2	63.4	72.2	64.6	52.8
2003	100	78.2	63.3	75.6	65.4	54.3
2004	100	74.5	63.2	76.7	68.4	56.9
2006	100	72.1	57.5	73.5	63.6	51.7
2010	100	74.5	65.9	80.5	69.6	59.8
2013	100	75.1	67.2	78	64	54

Source: U.S. Current Population Survey and the National Committee on Pay Equity; also Bureau of Labor Statistics: Weekly and Hourly Earnings Data from the Current Population Survey.

Gendered Job Segregation

Have you ever heard the terms "white-collar jobs" or "blue-collar jobs"? You probably have. How about "pink-collar jobs"—have you ever heard that term? Most likely you haven't, but given our topic of discussion, you can probably hazard a guess at what it means. Pink-collar jobs are occupations that were traditionally filled mainly by women and many that still are. Secretaries, childcare workers, nurses, and elementary school teachers are all examples of pink-collar occupations. It's kind of an outdated term in sociology, but I use it to make a point: there is still job segregation. Job segregation refers to the practice of filling certain occupational categories mostly with women and others mostly with men. In the United States, 89% of registered nurses are women; more than 94% are secretaries and nearly 81% of elementary and middle school teachers are female (Bureau of Labor Statistics, "The Employment Situation," 2016).

By contrast, about 5% of truck drivers, 9% of airline pilots, and about 18% of movers and laborers are women. Even though we recognize this practice as exclusive and discriminatory, many people see jobs as gendered; they see some jobs as "female jobs" (secretaries and nurses) and some jobs as "male jobs" (truck drivers and construction workers). Male jobs and female jobs are not naturally occurring; we socially construct jobs to be masculine or feminine.

Using stereotypes, myths, and physical differences between the sexes, cultures socially construct gendered occupations. Think about it this way: if a job is a "male job," it must have always been a "male job," right? Wrong; think beer. Up until the Industrial Revolution, when brewing beer became a massive industrial undertaking and men were given those factory jobs, women brewed the beer. Dating back over 4,300 years to ancient Egypt, we know that brewing beer was seen by many societies as a female domestic task. Women historically were the beer brewers in many cultures, even in Europe. Today, women make up less than 1% of those employed in beer manufacturing (Biba, 2014; Hornsey, 2003). The industrialization of societies created huge numbers of brewery jobs that were given to men, who were viewed as stronger and as family providers, which displaced women from brewing.

Beer brewing, in a sense, underwent a "gender flip," when an industry flips from being dominated by one gender to the other. This is not uncommon; societies construct and deconstruct gendered occupations frequently. Occupations like cheerleaders and airline stewards, for example, were male-dominated professions that also went through a "gender flip." When occupations undergo a "gender flip" from male- to female-dominated, there is a clear pattern of pay and prestige decline. Occupations that flip from male to female experience a pay decrease and are viewed as less desirable. Jobs that flip from female to male do the opposite: pay goes up and those positions are seen as more prestigious.

If jobs were "naturally" male or female, we would see no variation in who does what job across cultures. Therefore, men would do all construction work, and all nurses would be women in any given society. In India, the construction industry is comprised mainly of women; this is "natural" in Indian culture because women are viewed as responsible for the home, including construction and repairs (Women in Informal Employment, 2016). In Malaysia, computer science occupations are seen as "women-friendly" professions; men don't really compete for them. Indeed, 50 to 60% of the computer industry's workforce is female, and women hold many of the mid- and upper-level management positions. In Malaysia, indoor work is not perceived as masculine; therefore, office-based computing jobs are best suited for women. Women are discouraged from working outdoor, "male" jobs. Women who hold outdoor, physical jobs are stigmatized as lower class (Joseph, 2014).

Not only is there gendered segregation between jobs, as we discussed above, there is segregation within occupations. My wife has worked in the operating room for over twenty years, and in all that time, she has only worked with five female surgeons. In the United States, only 15% of all surgeons are women, while over half of all pediatricians are women. Gender in many occupations is associated with specialty or prestige. Men, for example, make up 94% of all airline pilots in the U.S., while 81% of flight attendants are women ("Women in Aviation", 2013). This gap becomes an abyss for African American women. Of all 71,000 pilots in the U.S., only twenty are black women.

As we have discussed, racial and ethnic minorities tend to be overrepresented in occupations requiring less education, which, in turn, pay less. Take a look around your college campus: who are the people cleaning the buildings, emptying the trash, and maintaining the grounds? Depending on what part of the country you're in, they are mainly black or Hispanic, and many are women. Why do you think so many minority women take low-paying jobs?

What creates a job market that is gendered? Do men and women naturally gravitate to work they are better suited for? Does it reflect the way we are raised? Is it just plain old discrimination? Well, as we have discussed many times in many chapters, it is never just one thing. Let's take a brief look at the combination of factors that lead to gender job segregation.

Several of the factors that influence gender segregation in the workplace include socialization, hiring practices, and what some have called the "discomfort factor." In a sense, we are steered into certain occupations by the way we are raised. Gender role socialization is so powerful that it shapes our ideas about what types of occupations we should pursue. Typically, it begins at home, where mom and dad work in gendered jobs and mom does most of the unpaid household work (women's work). When we role-play gender-appropriate jobs, boys are cops and girls care for dolls, and many times these roles are encouraged by parents and others. However, when we act out cross-gendered job roles, we are discouraged, especially boys (Cross and Bagilhole, 2002; Miller, 2013). The media, peers, and the educational system compound this gendered approach to job segregation, guiding people into occupations that are viewed as gender appropriate.

There are many women who do work in occupations dominated by men and thrive—to a point. Many women who work in male-dominated occupations find that they encounter a point that they can't progress beyond. They no longer receive promotions or raises; it seems as though they have hit some invisible barrier to their upward professional mobility. These women report bumping into the glass ceiling—unseen barriers that prevent women from reaching top positions in male-dominated industries. Glass ceilings are constructed based on gender stereotypes the top-tier male management hold about the competence of women and what type of jobs they should hold (Carter and Silva, 2010; Wellington et al., 2003).

In contrast, men in female-dominated occupations experience the opposite effect. The glass escalator is an accelerated rise to top positions for men in female-dominated fields. In nursing, for example, male nurses, on average, make more than female nurses even though they only account for approximately 8% of the workforce. Male nurses are also more likely to be promoted faster than their female counterparts (Landivar, 2013).

Stereotypical beliefs about the difference between men's and women's aptitudes and abilities influence hiring practices. Employers tend to hire men for what they perceive to be masculine jobs and women for what they believe to be feminine jobs. For instance, women are far more likely to be hired for childcare jobs than men because women are perceived as more nurturing, patient, and compassionate. We are all products of our gendered culture, even those who do the hiring.

Many workers who take jobs in fields that are dominated by the opposite sex leave at higher rates than gender-typed employees. Employees in opposite sex-dominated occupations experience a "discomfort factor" and leave those jobs in which their gender is non-dominant. Research by David Maume Jr. (1999) showed that over a ten-year period in male-dominated occupations,

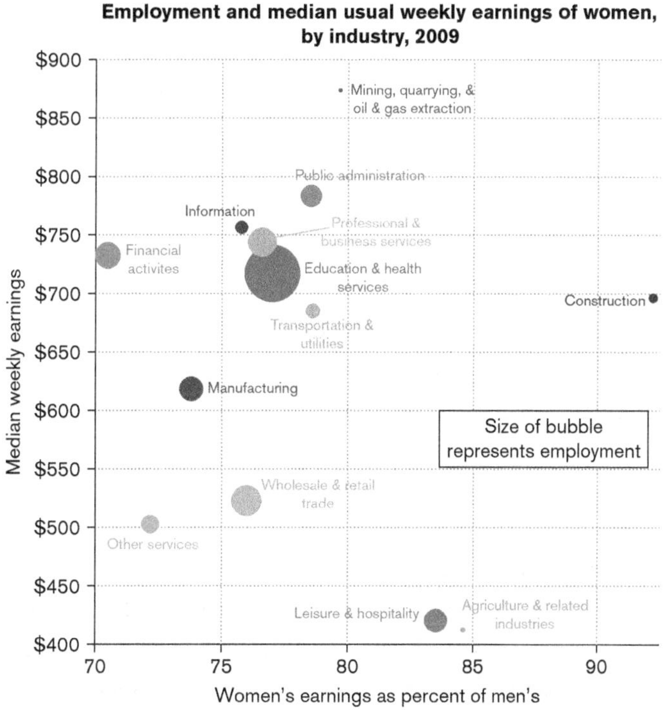

Fig. 9.3 The size of each bubble represents womens' employment percentage in each category. For example, women are more likely to be employed in the education and health services sector as opposed to the construction sector. However, on average women make less than men across all occupational categories. It is interesting to note that women are more likely to have pay parity if they work in construction than if they work in financial services. Why do you think this is so?

women left such jobs at more than twice the rate that men did. Interestingly, more than half of those women moved into female-dominated occupations. Would working in an environment in which nearly everyone else was the opposite gender make you feel uncomfortable?

The chart in figure 9.3 below shows two interesting things. Women make less than men in every occupational category but one. The one category where women and men earn the same is an occupation typically viewed as fiercely masculine—construction. What factors do you think affect this phenomenon? Why is this the case?

Gender and the Family

One commonly discussed topic in popular culture is the changing patterns of family arrangements. Women make up nearly half the workforce in the United States, and most moms work outside the home. In fact, of all moms with children age six or younger, 64% worked outside the home, and of moms with children between the ages of six and seventeen, 75% were in the labor force (Employment Characteristics, 2015). With either mom or mom and dad working outside the house, many families face the task of finding time and energy to do all the things that have to be done around the house. When parents come home after a full day of work outside the home, they are confronted with their second shift, all those duties that must be done to maintain the household (Hoschschild and Machung, 1989). After the workday ends, there is a list of tasks to perform that keep the household chugging along: meals have to be prepared, laundry needs to be done, homework has to be supervised, bathrooms have to be cleaned, and bills have to be paid.

The second shift is highly gendered. That is, women in all types of families report doing most of second-shift work. Single parents have no one but the kids to help them out around the house. However, most report that they still do nearly all the housework. Married women who work outside the home also report doing the majority of second-shift work. In a 2011 study, working women reported doing ten hours more per week of housework and childcare than married men (Offer and Schneider, 2011). This unequal distribution of household work by gender often leads to marital disputes. Housework and childcare becomes gendered work that is most frequently left to women because of perceptions of what female housework is and what male housework is.

Housework is gendered. Research on all male living arrangements illustrates how housework is perceived as female work. Kristin Natalier (2004) interviewed several all-male households, living arrangements in which several men shared an apartment. They reported that housework was not very important to them, and anyone too interested in cleanliness was perceived as "girly." So, anyone too keen to engage in housework or who complained about others' participation in cleaning up faced gender policing—the act of enforcing gender rules in order to promote conformity (Kimmel, 2012). These gendered expectations of the division of labor around housework seem to be changing in married households. Compared to their counterparts in 1965, men today do twice as much housework and three times as much childcare (Bianchi, Robinson, and Milkie, 2006). This does not mean that women don't do the bulk of second-shift work—they still do. Once they return home from work, women report doing almost twice as much housework and childcare as men (Parker and Wang, 2013).

Why do women still do more of the unpaid work? Some people still believe that there is a "natural" order to housework and childcare; women are seen as the natural caregivers and, by extension, are responsible for peripheral work like cooking, laundry, and grocery shopping. Nevertheless, this is changing, especially among younger people. In research that asked eighteen- to thirty-four-year-olds how they would ideally split careers and household work, the overwhelming majority of both men and women wanted relationships with "flexible gender boundaries." They wanted both partners to do an equal share of breadwinning, childcare, and household chores (Gerson, 2010). Therefore, in terms of sharing household and caregiving tasks, it seems that younger generations want marriages that are more egalitarian and flexible.

Sexuality

Sexual Identity and Sexual Orientation

Some people say your sexual identity is who you are, and your sexual orientation is whom you want to have sex with. However, sexual identity—the way we view ourselves as male and female and how we express ourselves sexually—is complex. As we grow and develop, we form our sexual identity, which is a complex mix of who we are attracted to, our sexual behaviors, and how we come to understand our sexual beliefs and actions. Our sexual identity is an important part of who we are (Reiter, 1989). Included in our sexual identity is our sexual orientation, which is our preference in sexual partners. Do you think your preference for sexual partners is an innate or learned characteristic? Once thought to be biologically "set in stone," new research and a greater understanding of sexual orientation reveal a range of individual preferences:

- Heterosexual: This describes people who are sexually attracted to people of the opposite gender.
- Gay: Men who have a sexual preference for other men.
- Lesbian: Women who have a preference for and sexual attraction to other women.
- Bisexual: Are people who are sexually attracted to both genders.
- Pansexual (Omnisexual): People who are attracted to people of any sexual orientation or gender identity.
- Asexual: The category of people who experience either no or low sexual attraction to any gender.

Sexual identity, orientation, and behaviors are all influenced by the culture in which we are raised. Some societies are much more progressive and accepting of a wide range of sexual orientations, while in others you could be put to death for being a gay man.

QUEER THEORY

Emerging in the 1990s and rooted in gay and lesbian studies, queer theory examines how sexual identity and sexual orientation are socially constructed. The "queer" in queer theory is an attempt to reclaim the term that had become derisive. Queer theory challenges the notion of normative sexualities by examining the social construction of all categories of normative and deviant sexual behavior. Queer theory challenges normative understandings of sexuality, sexual identity, and sexual practices. It rails against the "binary sexual regime" (Chauncey, 1994). It emphasizes that sexuality, in all its forms, is shifting and fluid, bound to cultural time and space. So, if our ideas about sexual identity and sexual orientation are culturally constructed, there are no absolutes with reference to sexual orientation, behavior, values, beliefs, and actions (Green, 2007).

Transgender and Transsexual

What about those whose gender identity does not conform to their biological sex? Individuals whose gender identity is opposite of their biological sex are transgender. For example, the reality TV show *I am Jazz* centers on a teenage girl named Jazz. She was born a biological male but always felt that she was a girl. Her gender identity as a female was so strong she started living as a girl at age four. The fact that this show and others like it are on the air and well-received is an indication of greater social acceptance of a wider range of gender identities.

Transgender individuals know in their minds and hearts they were born in the wrong body, and this severe identity issue, in the context of a culture that holds relatively rigid ideas about gender roles, results in a lot of suffering throughout their lives. Although the exact cause of transgender identity is not fully known, it is most likely a result of a combination of biological and socio-psychological factors. Additionally, it is hard to gauge the prevalence of transgenderism in the population. The most recent estimate suggests that 0.3% of the U.S. population identify as transgender (Harris, 2015).

Transsexuals are individuals who wish to alter their bodies so their physical bodies are better aligned with their gender identities. Not all transgender people alter their bodies with medical interventions. Some do not surgically alter their bodies and live as the opposite gender. Some choose, for personal or financial reasons, to have only some hormonal therapy or minor to moderate cosmetic or reconstructive surgery. Still other transgender individuals want their physical bodies to match their gender identities so strongly that they seek out sex reassignment surgery (SRS). SRS is a set of surgical procedures available to transgender people that allows them to alter their physical appearance and change their external genital organs to align with their identified sex (Bevan, 2014).

Larger, more powerful, and more visible communities like lesbians, gays, and bisexuals have joined with the transgender community in a sign of solidarity and to facilitate social awareness and change. Education about transgender people and media exposure has resulted in changing social attitudes about the transgender community. Although social attitudes are improving, those in the transgender community still face discrimination and abuse. Transgender individuals are twice as likely to face discrimination or assault as non-transgender individuals (Ahmed and Jindasurat, 2014).

THERE'S AN APP FOR THAT

Thurst is a dating app specifically designed for trans, queer and gender non-conforming people. The app was created in part as a response to the frustration many non-gender conforming users had with standard dating apps like Okcupid and Tinder. In fact, Tinder has banned many trans users simply because of their trans gender identities. So in an effort to create a space where people of all gender identities could feel safe, comfortable and interact with like-minded users, Thurst was born. Thurst has become a place, as their motto states, "Where queer people of all genders date" (Dickey, 2015).

Women, Poverty, and Violence

We have discussed several dimensions of gender inequality so far. Now I want to broaden the scope of inequality. I do not think that most people realize that gender inequality is a worldwide pandemic. Women everywhere in the world, on average, are more likely to earn less than men, live in poverty, and be the victims of violent crime.

Feminization of Poverty

Poverty has a woman's face. Women in America are more likely to be poor than men. Of the more than 45 million poor Americans, over half are women. Nearly 60% of children in poverty live in a single mom-headed household. In 2013, 16% of adult women lived in poverty, compared to 11% of adult men. Women are more likely to be poor than men at any age, but it gets even worse for the elderly. For those older than sixty-five and poor, fully 11% are women and only 6.5% are men.

While women are more likely to be poor than men across all racial and ethnic groups, women of color fare worse than white women. One-quarter of African American women live in poverty, it is nearly the same for Hispanic women at 24.8% and more than one-third of American Indian women live in poverty (Hess et al., 2015).

This is not just a domestic issue; the *feminization of poverty*, which is the trend in which women increasingly represent a disproportionate amount of the world's poor, is a global crisis. In every country of the world, women are far more likely to experience poverty than their male compatriots. As inequality—the gap between the wealthy and the poor—deepens worldwide, more women and children fall into poverty each year (Chant, 2006; Pearce, 1978). Women account for 70% of the world's poor, and one out of two children worldwide are poor. Moreover, women are more likely than men to live on $2.50 or less per day and have less access to bank accounts and other financial services (United Nations, "Human Development Report", 2013; World Bank, 2013).

The causes of the feminization of poverty are multidimensional and complex. Women are devalued in most societies of the world, and in some, they are treated as male possessions, with few or no rights but tremendous responsibilities. Often, women are not allowed to own land or businesses and are denied education. This puts them at greater risk for unemployment than men because they lack job skills, which places them at greater risk of poverty. While in undeveloped nations, women are poor along with men, they are less likely to be employed and earn less when they are. Even in economically emerging nations whose infrastructures and economies are improving, deeply held beliefs concerning gender roles reinforce discrimination against women, barring them from employment. Even in wealthier nations like the U.S., issues of discrimination, the gender pay gap, and gender job segregation leave more women in low-paying jobs. It is not hard to stumble into poverty if you are living on the edge to begin with. Many women and single mothers report that all it takes is a serious illness or an unexpected car repair, which they can't afford, and they have lost their job. Poverty among women leads to social exclusion in terms of access to public transportation, healthcare services, and decent housing. Globally, women earn less, own less, and are at far greater risk of falling victim to injury, disease, violence, and sexual exploitation. Poverty for women, then, becomes a sort of *deprivation multiplier*, increasing women's risk for social isolation, disease, violence, and sexual exploitation (Mykyta and Renwick, 2013).

READ MORE

- *Rachel and her Children: Homeless Families in America* by Jonathan Kozol (1988). A powerfully moving ethnographic sketch of what life is like on the streets when you're a family. Kozol interviews a number of women and children to understand how they became homeless and what forces keep them there. A gritty look at homelessness and families.

Gender Violence

While poor women are at much greater risk for physical violence and sexual exploitation, all women face the potential of domestic and stranger violence all over the world. Rape, female genital mutilation, and gender violence are just some of the things that women face in some countries. Violence against women is rooted in gender role norms and cultural and religious beliefs, and it is institutionalized through laws and the courts. Some places are more notorious for gender violence than others. Table 9.4 below displays the top ten most dangerous countries to be a woman. Notice there are a range of factors that make them dangerous places. Is there a common thread?

TABLE 9.4 Top Offenders of Violence Against Women

Country	Frequent Types of Violence Against Women
Afghanistan	Eighty-six percent of females are illiterate. Most are married before they are twenty years old. Maternal mortality rate is one of the highest in the world. Domestic violence is common, but courts make it difficult to prosecute because by law, family members cannot testify.
Democratic Republic of Congo	One of the worst offenders of gender-based violence, it is estimated that there are 1,150 women raped every day—adding up to about 420,000 per year.
Pakistan	Cultural practices such as forced marriages, acid attacks, and stoning make Pakistan a very dangerous place for women. Approximately 1,000 women per year are the victims of "honor killings."
India	An estimated 50 million cases of female infanticide over the last three decades along with child marriage, bride burning, and sex trafficking make India a deadly place for women.
Somalia	In a country that lacks law and order, 95% of the women there can expect to experience female genital mutilation sometime between ages four and eleven.
Colombia	There were 45,000 instances of violence against women in 2010. Few to no systems to provide post-violence care leave most women with no medical treatment.

(Continued)

Country	Frequent Types of Violence Against Women
Egypt	Violence against women escalated in the wake of Egypt's revolution in the spring of 2011. However, women have little recourse because domestic violence is not criminalized and women's legal rights are ignored.
Kenya	Even though women do most of the agricultural work, their wages are a fraction of what they should be. Girls are given a substandard education or none at all, while boys are given far better educations. Women have little control over their sex lives. As a consequence, HIV rates are highest among women. Forty-four percent of all households are headed by women; nearly all are in poverty or extreme poverty.
Mexico	Between 2011 and 2012, over 4,000 women went missing in Mexico, their remains often found in garbage heaps. Mexico's judicial system does not protect against domestic or sexual violence. Women rarely come forward with accounts of sexual violence because the courts typically treat them with disregard.
Brazil	Data show that a woman is assaulted about every fifteen seconds and killed every two hours in Brazil. Reproductive rights are extremely limited, and a woman who gets an abortion and does not meet the narrow set of criteria can be jailed for up to three years. Some estimates suggest 100,000 women have been killed inside their own homes over the past thirty years because of domestic violence.

Sources: "Issues Facing Women", 2015; Peterman, Palermo, and Bredenkamp, 2011; "World Report", 2015; Zelinger, 2012; "Violence Against Women", 2015; Rama and Diaz, 2014.

The common thread that connects these ten nations is sustained high levels of violence against women. This table just represents some of the worst countries. Violence against women can be found in every single society. The World Health Organization (WHO) found that among women aged fifteen to forty-nine in Ethiopia, 71% reported sexual violence by an intimate partner. It also found that 24% of women in Peru and 30% of women in Bangladesh reported their first sexual encounter was forced. WHO researchers also found that in over eighty countries, more than 35% of women reported being the victim of some type of violence (World Health Organization, 2016).

That's just a tiny glimpse of the pandemic of violence against women. Women around the world are subjugated by men, routinely denied education, used as forced labor and sex workers, and killed routinely for violating masculine codes of "honor." Why do you think there is so much violence against women? One obvious reason is that men are, on average, larger and stronger than women, which can make them easy targets for violence. What allows this level and frequency of abuse to persist are **patriarchal regimes**, which are male-dominated systems of control that oppress women and privilege men. These regimes produce and maintain dominance through civil society, the economy, and the government. Using civil entities like religion, the dominance of men is reinforced through language (God the Father), beliefs (the man is the head of the family), and practice (women must cover themselves and avert theirs from men). Many countries deny girls and women any access to education, and some have a two-tier educational system, with the least funded designated for girls (Miller, 2001). As we discussed above, women face lower wages and less access to upper-management positions, and in some countries like Saudi Arabia, women are denied entry to the workforce. Aung San Suu Kyi was under house arrest in Myanmar (Burma) for fifteen years by a military patriarchal regime ("Aung San Suu Kyi", 2015). She represents a democratic movement that advocates education and employment for girls and women; her imprisonment is symbolic of that regime's oppression of women in the larger society. Women around the world live in the shadow of male-dominated institutions and suffer the abusive consequences.

THERE'S AN APP FOR THAT

Krousar Koumrou, Safe Agent 008 and 7 Plus are apps that hope to educate women and men and protect women against both domestic and stranger violence. All were developed and released in Cambodia in 2015. Krousar Koumrou, which means "model family" in Khmer, is designed as an educational app meant to change negative attitudes toward women. In Cambodia, where women are devalued and their oppression is reinforced through common verbal imagery like "Men are gold, women are cloth," this app hopes to change those attitudes through a variety of educational tools accessible by its users.

Safe Agent 008 is an app that allows women to send their GPS coordinates to family and friends if they feel in danger and it lets them report violence anonymously. The app *7Plus* was originally designed by a beer promotor who wanted bar and restaurant employees to feel safe from sexual harassment and violence in their workplace (The Asia Foundation, "Krousar Koumrou", 2015; "Safe Agent 008", 2015; Everett, 2015).

The Three Waves of the Women's Movement (Three Waves of Feminism)

Feminism—the belief that men and women should have equal rights and opportunities—has been advanced significantly in three major waves of social change. When most people talk about the women's movement, they typically refer to the "women's liberation" (women's lib) movement of the 1960s and '70s. Most people are unaware that this movement only represents the second wave of three waves of feminism in the United States.

The birth of the women's movement is commonly attributed to the Seneca Falls Convention held in upstate New York in 1848. The convention issued a *Declaration of Sentiments*, which aimed at ending discriminatory practices against women and called for equality between the sexes. This gathering set off the first wave of the women's movement in the United States. Members of the Seneca Falls Convention made several demands; among them was that women be given the right to vote. Noting that women had to submit to laws that they did not help create, the right to vote became a fundamental step in establishing women's rights. Consequently, *suffrage*, the struggle to win the vote for women, is forever linked with the first wave of the women's movement. Interestingly, the resolution to seek the vote for women passed by a slim margin: many women at that time believed they could attain equality without the vote. Although it took another seventy-two years, the right to vote was finally extended to women in 1920 (Marlow, 2001; Talbot, Charlesworth and Talbot, 2014).

Fig. 9.4 Suffragettes. Securing the vote for women was the central focus of the first wave of feminism.

The second wave (1960–1980s) of the women's movement came of age as the United States entered into some of its most socially turbulent times. Children of the baby boom were coming of age, the sexual revolution was getting a kick-start from the introduction of the birth control pill, and many young people were rejecting their parents' generation's notions of masculinity, femininity, and family (not to mention experimentation with drugs and the anti-war movement). Millions of young people were questioning traditional ideas about society in general and women's roles in society specifically. While the right to vote became the issue about which the first wave of the women's movement revolved, the second wave centered on empowering women through education and employment.

There were two key catalysts for this wave of the women's movement. The first was the 1963 publication of Betty Friedan's *The Feminine Mystique*, which articulated women's dissatisfaction with the social expectation that women should be completely fulfilled in the role of mother-wife. Women's feelings of social, political, and economic limitation, Freidan wrote, was "the problem with no name" (Friedan, 1963). This book had the powerful effect of raising the awareness of the limited opportunities and oppression women faced in society.

The second was the founding of the National Organization of Women (NOW). NOW sought to raise public consciousness about the condition of women in society. The organization demonstrated, rallied, and pushed for changes in laws, policies, and practices that hindered women's equality with men ("National Organization for Women", 2015). NOW was most likely successful because of its moderate approach—in contrast to many radical and militant groups of the time—and because it was originally led by white, middle-class women. Ultimately, the legacy of the second wave of the women's movement is visible in our everyday lives today. Equal opportunity laws, legislation prohibiting sexual harassment, women's increased access to education, and an overall change in the perception of women in society are all the direct or indirect result of the second wave.

Recognizing that not all women were being helped by the second wave of the women's movement, the third wave of the women's movement focuses on the inclusion of women from marginalized groups and the plight of women globally. Emerging in the 1980s and '90s, the third wave of the women's movement seeks inclusion of all races/ethnicities, sexual orientations, and a global perspective. Third-wave feminists reject the view of *women* as one category, essentially white and middle class, therefore they strive to reach out globally to marginalized groups such as lesbians, women of color, and women in poverty. While the first two waves of the women's movement were focused on conditions faced by women in America, this movement attempts to draw attention to the conditions women suffer at the hands of oppressive religious, cultural, and political regimes around the world (Gillis, Howie and Munford, 2007; Freedman, 2007).

Feminist Theories

Because of perceived weaknesses with the second wave of the women's movement over inclusion, the scope of oppression, and methods used to affect change, several feminist theories have emerged that are more in line with the goals of the third wave. This range of theories attempts to address women's conditions in a comprehensive way. These theories seek a broader understanding of the global oppression of women through "intersectionality." Acknowledging *intersecting systems of oppression* is necessary to develop a complete framework for understanding women's subjugation and the patriarchal regimes that maintain it. While these theories identify a range of problems and suggest various strategies to solve them, they all share some common fundamental principles (Sandoval, 2000; Davis, 2011; Serano, 2013). All feminisms promote equality between men and women, promote the idea that women should have control over their bodies and lives, and believe that changes in social institutions and regimes will realize gender equality. Table 9.5 on the next page gives a brief description of the varieties of feminism.

TABLE 9.5 Variations on a Theme: Types of Feminism

Type of Feminism	Perspective
Liberal Feminism (mainstream feminism)	This is your mother's feminism. The basic premise of liberal feminism is equality of opportunity regardless of gender. Both men and women suffer under sexism, so eliminating it requires the efforts of men as well as women and with free both genders. Society does not have to be completely reordered to achieve gender equality. Through gender-neutral socialization of children, social awareness, and mobilization, gender equality can be achieved. The focus is on legal, political, and economic change. This perspective is represented by the National Organization for Women (NOW).
Radical Feminism	This approach argues that all institutions are male-dominated and designed to oppress women and perpetuate sexist ideology. Radical feminism advocates the creation of women-centered institutions that value female attributes such as nurturing, conflict resolution, and cooperative work. Radical feminists seek to create businesses and institutions that are owned only by women and serve only women. This is an inclusive (if you are female) and separatist feminism.
Socialist Feminism (Marxist feminism)	This approach views the family as a reflection of capitalist oppression in which the husband-father represents the oppressor class and the wife-mother and children are the oppressed. Like Marxism, and Liberal feminism, socialist feminism argues that men and women have to work together to create a more equitable society.
Cultural Feminism	This perspective views women's roles in society as undervalued. A cultural shift in valuing female roles such as cooperation, caring, and nurturing is necessary for equality between the sexes. Unlike Liberal feminism, this approach promotes substantial cultural shifts in education, socialization, media and the economy to achieve gender equality.
Multicultural/Global Feminism	Focused primarily on the intersection of gender, race, and social class among oppressed women in the developing world, global feminism seeks to eliminate oppressive regimes globally. By empowering women in societies where they are underpaid, enslaved, sexually abused, and denied education, this version of feminism seeks to eliminate conditions that oppress women worldwide.

Type of Feminism	Perspective
Ecofeminism	This type of feminism links the global exploitation of the environment with the oppression of women. As patriarchal multinational industries encroach on fragile environments in developing countries, women are exploited as sex workers and underpaid or slave laborers. Healing the planet, according to ecofeminism, does not just mean fixing the physical world, but the social world as well. This represents an intersection between eco-awareness meets feminism.

Sources: Wade and Ferree, 2015; Deckard, 1983; Gordon, 2013; Shelton and Agger, 1993; Bunch, 1993; Ruether, 2005; Salleh, 2009; Blair et al., 2009.

Theoretical Perspectives on Sex and Gender

The functionalist theoretical perspective on gender roles reflects its emphasis on social equilibrium. Therefore, within the general framework of the functionalist theory, a gendered division of labor contributes to social stability. Functionalism argues that in order for the family to function efficiently, adults must adopt complementary, specialized roles based on their gender. Functionalism proposes that men take on instrumental roles—task-oriented behaviors like providing food and shelter and connecting the family to the larger world and other social institutions. Mothers assume expressive roles—providing emotional support and engaging in nurturing activities with the aim of maintaining harmony in the household. Mom stays home and takes care of the kids, cleans up, and cooks the meals so dad can go out into the work world and bring home the bacon (Parsons and Bales, 1955). As each spouse performs his or her set of specialized tasks, the division of labor becomes functional for the family unit, which in turn promotes social stability.

While traditional conflict theory focused on class struggle between two economic classes, contemporary theories realize that struggles happen on a wider level across various social groups. Conflict theorists, then, recognize that gender differences are a reflection of the subjugation of women by men. Men originally rose to dominance over women because of their physical strength, and women were historically tied to the home by childbearing and children. These factors are not as important in contemporary societies; however, beliefs about the differences between men and women persist and have established men as the more powerful gender. These perceived differences between the genders are perpetuated by cultural beliefs that men's lives and work are more valuable than women's lives and work. For conflict theorists, this subordination of women by men contributes directly to lower wages for women, the devaluation of housework and childcare, and violence against women.

Recall that in symbolic interactionism (the interactionist perspective), social processes such as gender identity formation emerge from our interaction with each other. Central to symbolic interactionism is the use of symbols in our everyday interactions. Symbols can be things like our clothing, objects, the social positions we hold, and our behaviors. We interact with others using a number of symbols; we interpret the meaning of the symbols and the social situation to construct a negotiated reality. People do not respond to the world around them but to the meaning they collectively apply to it. And meaning emerges from people interacting.

Gender socialization and gender-role internalization are central concerns to symbolic interactionism. Typically, children are taught to act in ways that are consistent with their physical sex, which is a symbol that elicits expected behaviors—females learn to act like "girls" and males learn to act like "boys." Girls are taught to play with "female symbols" like dolls, which encourage girls to take on female gender roles of caregiver and nurturer. Parents and others encourage girls take on female symbols like wearing dresses, keeping their hair long, and being "lady-like." This gender socialization encourages us to internalize widely agreed-upon ideas of how girls and boys should appear and behave—gender roles. Therefore, when we encounter someone who appears and acts feminine, according to our social standards, we know how to interact with her and how to interpret her words and actions.

TABLE 9.6 Theoretical Perspectives on Gender Roles

Theoretical Perspective	View on Gender Roles
Structural-Functionalism	Functionalism views gender roles as necessary mechanisms that establish a division of labor that promotes social stability, especially in the context of the family. Women carry out expressive roles—caregiving and nurturing. Men perform instrumental roles—providing materially for the family by breadwinning, establishing social position.
Conflict	According to this approach, in order for men to maintain domination over women, a belief system must emerge that supports this gender inequality. This belief system, or gender ideology, is maintained through beliefs such as women are more valuable in the home and less valuable in the workplace.
Symbolic Interactionism	For symbolic interactionism, gender identity and gender roles are learned through socialization. The process of socialization involves the use and interpretations of gendered symbols. The meaning of these symbols help to shape our gender identities, equipping us with the ability to perform or "do gender" in our day-to-day interactions.

The Bottom Line

Sex and gender are terms people use in a variety of ways. However, as we have discussed, sex refers to the biological characteristics that distinguish males from females, and gender refers to socially constructed behaviors, attributes, and activities that society considers appropriate for men and women. Therefore, our sex indicates whether we are male or female, and gender makes us masculine or feminine.

Gender, then, is a product of social interaction. We make efforts to distinguish things that are male and things that are female. We start with pink and blue blankets and move on to football for boys and cheerleading for girls. We construct gender. We know this because it changes over time and from culture to culture. How women appear and behave has changed considerably in the United States. Women were forbidden, by law, to wear pants until early in the twentieth century. Pants were not considered feminine attire. Skinny jeans are a long way from that idea. In fact, women could not wear pants on the Senate floor (even female senators) until 1993 (Henderson, 2015).

The gender-binary concept is prevalent in Western industrialized nations; however, we have looked at a number of societies that see gender as more expansive. Some societies allow for three or more genders, affording homosexuals and transgender people cultural space by recognizing their "in-between" status. In fact, several countries have granted those who identify as other than the gender-binary legal standing. Transgender people in the United States have no legal standing unless they have sex reassignment surgery; then they can have full legal recognition, but not as transgender, only as their newly assigned sex. In the United States, we do not have cultural space for transgender people, and consequently, they are victimized and socially marginalized. However, the acceptance of high-profile transgender celebrities like Caitlyn Jenner and the legalization of same-sex marriage indicates that society is becoming more tolerant and accepting of all a wider range of gender identities and sexual orientations.

The gender-binary is reproduced in our society by a collection of values, beliefs, attitudes, and expected behaviors. This ideology perpetuates gender differences and inequalities by legitimizing prejudicial and discriminatory behaviors. This gender inequality has many faces. We see gender in the workplace in the form of the gender pay gap; on average, women in the U.S. earn less than men for the same work with the same qualifications.

Sociologists focus on the powerful influence the family has on gender socialization. We discussed how family members tend to reinforce gender conformity with the use of gender-appropriate clothing, toys, and behaviors. Girls have a much greater range in clothing and toy choices than boys. Parents are much more likely to encourage their little girls to play with cross-gender toys while discouraging little boys from playing with "girl toys." Even gender-appropriate appearance and mannerisms are monitored by family and peers. Same-sex playgroups "police" gender roles by calling out offenders, thus promoting gender conformity.

Women all over the world are far more likely to live in poverty and become victims of violence. We have seen that there has been a feminization of poverty in the United States for several decades. The majority of the poor in the U.S. are women and children, and this is a much older issue in all other countries. Worldwide, women are denied access to education, employment, healthcare, and birth control. Without basic education, women are forced to take the least desirable, lowest paying, and often the most demanding work. This economic oppression combined with their low social position make women and their children dependent on men. This dependency puts them at greater risk for domestic violence, having to tolerate abuse in order to survive economically and socially.

While most people commonly think that the women's liberation movement of the 1960s and 1970s was *the* women's movement, we have discussed a much fuller view. In fact, three distinct waves of the women's movement or feminism were explored. We traced the origins of the women's movement in the U.S. to the Seneca Falls Convention of 1848, and then showed its connection to the suffrage movement (first wave) that won the vote for women. Then we examined the women's liberation movement (second wave) set against the backdrop of tumultuous social change of the 1960s and 1970s. This movement sought to empower women through education and employment. Emerging in the early 1990s, the current wave (third wave) of feminism recognizes that many groups of women were not fully included in earlier feminist movements. This wave attempts to include more diverse groups of women in the struggle for equality, many of whom were excluded by earlier feminist movements.

We also examined feminist theoretical perspectives on gender. These theories share the common thread of equality for the sexes but describe different paths to get there. In a way, liberal feminism is the old guard, represented by the accomplishments of the women's liberation era and the National Organization for Women. Other, more radical feminists seek freedom from male oppression by maintaining separate, female-only organizations and businesses. Still others see capitalism as the engine that drives male dominance and female subjugation by replicating gender roles and devaluing women's unpaid domestic work. Another feminist theory argues that the physical environment is linked to oppressive human social regimes, and global environmental healing is directly connected to reforming human societies.

Finally, we looked at sociological theoretical perspectives on gender. Structural functionalism, as we discussed, is primarily concerned with gender role socialization and performance. Functionalism argues that gender role socialization is one of the primary duties of the family. Reproduction of normative gender roles promotes social stability. In contrast, the conflict approach recognizes that like the oppression of the less powerful lower social classes by the elite class, men dominate women. This pattern of domination is maintained and reproduced through the application of dominant gender ideology. All things male are typically viewed as more desirable and valuable, while female roles, beliefs, and behaviors are devalued. This gender dichotomy becomes institutionalized and ultimately is reproduced socially and viewed as normal.

The symbolic interactionism approach focuses on socialization and performance of gender roles. Through interaction with their children, caregivers use gendered symbols such as "girls' toys" and "boys' toys" to shape gender identities. Additionally, through play, children learn socially appropriate gender role appearance and behaviors. Internalized gender role expectations supply us with the tools to appear and act gender-appropriate; therefore, we can "do gender" as we interact with others.

Figure Credits

Fig. 9.1: Hyacinthe Rigaud, "Luis XIV, rey de Francia (Rigaud)," https://commons.wikimedia.org/wiki/File:Luis_XIV,_rey_de_Francia_(Rigaud).jpg. Copyright in the Public Domain.

Table 9.3: Source: http://www.infoplease.com/ipa/A0882775.html.

Fig. 9.2: Source: http://trends.collegeboard.org/education-pays/figures-tables/median-earnings-gender-and-education-level-1971-2008.

Fig. 9.3: Source: http://www.bls.gov/opub/ted/2011/ted_20110216.htm.

Fig. 9.4: Library of Congress, "Picture of Suffragettes," https://commons.wikimedia.org/wiki/File:The_Library_of_Congress_-_(Suffragettes_with_flag)_(LOC).jpg. Copyright in the Public Domain.

4

SOCIAL INSTITUTIONS: The Structure of the Daily Grind

CHAPTER 10

MARRIAGES AND FAMILIES

The Ghost Marriage Ritual and Grave-Robbing in China

In 2013, in China, four men were arrested, convicted, and imprisoned for exhuming the bodies of recently deceased women in order to sell them on the "ghost marriage" black market. They were apparently going around the countryside digging up female corpses for the purpose of trafficking in corpse brides. Each man was sentenced to at least two years in prison for digging up more than ten corpses over a two-year time period. After digging up the bodies, they cleaned them and altered their medical records in order to fetch higher prices. Their entrepreneurial endeavors were fueled by the millennia-old Chinese belief that an unmarried man who dies and is buried alone will be lonely in the afterlife, his spirit being so restless that he may even haunt his own family. In hopes of soothing the dead man's spirit, and to avoid any unwanted visits from the angry, unmarried dead, families are willing to pay large sums to find a corpse bride to bury next to their bachelor relatives.

The fate of these men is just a recent example of corpse bride trafficking. More recently, the body of a woman who died in February 2012 was sold by her family to the family of a young man who had recently died. Not long afterward, police discovered a corpse purveyor selling her now twice-exhumed body to another family. The belief that these men need a bride to lie next to them for eternity in order to rest peacefully is so powerful that it compels families who can afford it to purchase corpses, which promotes grave-robbing.

However, the buying and selling of corpse brides is not driven only by deep-rooted, long-held cultural beliefs; economic and class issues are also at play. China's superheated economy has created a surge in coal-mining activity and accidents, sending unmarried men to their graves with some frequency. An influx of coal money to some rural regions in China, populated by less sophisticated and more superstitious locals, has led to a significant increase in the area's underground corpse trade. Armed with coal cash, these Chinese hill folk can now afford to pay premium prices, some even buying freshly dead corpse brides from local hospitals; these just-dead brides are highly desirable and much more expensive (Xiao, 2013).

The practice of ritual ghost marriage is believed to date back to the seventeenth century BCE and was outlawed decades ago, but it has been on the rise due to China's booming economy. This perfect storm of deeply held beliefs coupled with newly found economic resources has led to a surge in the demand for corpse brides, which has re-invigorated the grave-robbing business. This belief and ritual underscore the importance of marriage and family in Chinese culture. One's eternal soul is linked to marriage and family; it is more important to find an unmarried dead son a bride than to find his killer if he was murdered. Ghost marriage is not only found in China; it is a fairly widely practiced ritual, which underscores the importance of marriage and family across many cultures and beyond the grave.

What is Marriage?

Marriages

Will you get married someday? Are you already married? Well, whether you are married or you want to be, you are in good company. The vast majority of Americans who are not married say that they would like to marry at some point in their lives. And for what reason will you marry? For companionship? A lifelong commitment? To have children? For financial stability? If you are like most people, you will choose love over any other factor (Cohn, 2013).

Marriage is an essential institution in most, but not all, societies. In many cultures, marriage marks the transition from childhood to adulthood. Frequently, marriage is the first step in building a family, and it is instrumental in forming familial and kin networks. The current heated debate in the United States and worldwide about same-sex marriage highlights the importance of marriage. Marriage is seen as such a central part of a person's life that many societies currently restrict or previously restricted people from marrying outside their group or marrying a partner who was not approved of by the family. Children have been disowned by their families for marrying the "wrong" person (Beattie, 2014; Fox, 1967; Faruqui, 2010). I think the number of ways people around the world come together to form families would surprise most of you; however, you would probably be less surprised to know that some form of the family is found in all societies.

As we saw in the story above, marriage is so important in some cultures that people will go to extremes to find a mate for a loved one, even if he is dead. In Nepal, among the *Nyinba* people, women are allowed to be married to several men at the same time; in fact, the men are brothers. It is customary for Nyinba brothers to take a single wife, and if the brother's parents have another son, the wife is expected to help raise her future husband. The *Mosuo* minority group of China practice *axia* (visiting marriage), a system in which there is no formal marriage. Mosuo couples simply engage in romantic relations until the woman decides to end things by boarding up her *azhu* house, indicating to her lover the affair is over. If children are produced in a relationship, they live with the mother, and the father is not expected to maintain any ties with the child ("Mosuo: A Mysterious Matriarchal Group", 2003).

In the United States, we practice **monogamy**, a marriage between two individuals. Worldwide, this is the most common type of marriage. At one time, this type of marriage was designated as a union between one woman and one man. However, as of 2015, more than fifteen counties recognize same-sex marriages, and as of June 2015, same-sex marriage is legal in all fifty states and the District of Columbia. Due to the high rates of divorce and remarriage in many post-industrial nations, such as the United States, some sociologists have labeled the pattern of engaging in a number of monogamous marriages over one's lifetime **serial monogamy** (I'm using marriage in the definition, but the term also applies to a series of monogamous romantic relationships over one's lifetime). Some notable serial monogamists include Martin Scorcese, who married five times; Larry King, who married eight times, twice to the same woman; Billy Bob Thorton, married five times and, Elizabeth Taylor who walked down the aisle eight times, twice with Richard Burton. While monogamy is the most commonly practiced form of marriage globally, there are many types of marriages found in a variety of cultures. Table 10.1 below shows a number of marriage forms.

TABLE 10.1 Marriage Forms Found Around the World

Type of Marriage	Description	Function (Rationale)	Region(s) Where Practiced
Child Marriage	A marriage form in which one or both partners are under the age of eighteen.	Deeply rooted in tradition, the practice is most prevalent among the poor. These are usually arranged or forced marriages. One purpose is to ensure the bride is a virgin. Other reasons include creating bonds between two families or villages, economic survival, and debt repayment.	The Middle East, Africa, Asia, Bangladesh, India, Papua New Guinea, and Guatemala

(Continued)

Type of Marriage	Description	Function (Rationale)	Region(s) Where Practiced
Group Marriage (Also referred to as Polygynandry and Polyamory)	Marriage arrangement where several men are married to several women at the same time—mostly expressed as more of a household arrangement consisting of several married couples and their children.	Mostly seen as a way to communally raise children, pool resources or maintain peace by uniting rival groups.	Caingang people of Brazil, ancient Hawaiians, Melanesia, Europe, North America, and Australia The Oneida community in upstate New York 1848–1878 The Kerista Commune in San Francisco, California, between 1971 and 1991
Same-Sex Marriage	A marriage type in which both partners are of the same sex.	Affords same-sex couples the same marriage rights as heterosexuals in many Western industrialized nations including the U.S. Among the Lovedu of South Africa, the "Rain Queen" (the highest recognized social position) is presented with many "wives." The custom of "bride-giving"—offering young women as *symbolic* brides—ensures loyalty from local chiefs. Male "two-spirit" people from many Native North American nations can take a same-sex spouse. Among the Nuer people of South Sudan, a barren woman can be married off as a "husband" to another woman, who is then impregnated by a secret boyfriend. The infertile women are socially recognized as the father.	Legal or recognized in approximately twenty-two countries, including the United States Third-gender marriages among Native North Americans. South Africa (symbolic)

Type of Marriage	Description	Function (Rationale)	Region(s) Where Practiced
Levirate Marriage	The practice of a widow marrying her dead husband's brother.	The brother is considered a proxy for his dead brother—therefore, any offspring from the new union are considered that of the first husband (dead brother). This allows for the continuation of the bloodline and keeps wealth within the family. It also maintains the existing ties between the two families.	Americas, Africa, India, and Australia
Sororate Marriage	A type of marriage in which a woman marries her dead sister's husband.	Like levirate marriage, this type of marriage is used to maintain existing bonds between the two families. In some sororate societies, that husband may have sex with his wife's sister if the wife is infertile.	Native North Americans, India, Africa
Ghost Marriage	A marriage in which one or both partners are dead	In Chinese culture, it is necessary for dead unmarried men to have a wife buried next to them to ensure a peaceful afterlife. Also in Chinese culture, families may tempt a living woman to marry their dead unmarried son so that the mother will have a daughter-in-law as her servant. Among the Nuer people, a woman may marry the "ghost" of a deceased man to keep her wealth and power. She is seen as married, but there is no one she has to share her wealth and power with.	Asia, Africa, Europe

(Continued)

Type of Marriage	Description	Function (Rationale)	Region(s) Where Practiced
Line Marriage (Fictional)	A form of group marriage in which spouses are constantly being added so the marriage never ends.	So that the marriage and all its attendant benefits never end.	In the fictional writings of Robert A. Heinlein (on a lunar penal colony)

Source: "Oneida Community", 2014; Lewis, 2002; Jones, 2001; Evans-Pritchard, 1990; Graburn, 1971; Heinlein, 1966

Polygamy is the general term for having multiple spouses at the same time. This type of marriage is illegal in all fifty states and the District of Columbia despite that there are television shows that depict it like *Big Love* and *Sister Wives*. How do you think the marriages in these shows get around the law? Even though polygamy is illegal in the U.S., there are an estimated 30,000 people involved in polygamous marriages, mostly associated with breakaway sects from the Mormon Church, specifically The Fundamentalist Church of Jesus Christ of Latter-Day Saints (Giddens, 2006). Additionally, an estimated 50,000 to 100,000 Muslim Americans are secretly involved in polygamous marriages in the U.S. (Hagerty, 2008).

Polygamy may be gaining some popularity here in the United States. The Polygamists Rights Organization argued that when the Supreme Court struck down the Defense of Marriage Act in 2013, it was a step in the right direction for recognizing alternate marriage forms like polygamy (Vorwerck, 2013). In her 2014 Daily Beast article "Is Polygamy the Next Gay Marriage?" Sally Kohn (2014) wonders if, in light of widespread acceptance of gay marriage, our society will be open to other marriage patterns like polygamy. Regardless of its recent popular exposure, polygamy is probably not coming to a church near you soon, as it remains outlawed in about 75% of the world's nations.

More specifically, **polygyny** refers to one man having more than one woman at the same time. In many cultures of the world, polygyny is practiced as a secular custom, and it is encouraged in nearly all Muslim nations as a religious expectation. Even though it is the most common form of polygamy, it is legal or tolerated in only about one-quarter of the world's countries. A variant of polygyny is **sororal polygyny**, in which one man takes two or more wives who are sisters. It is believed in some cultures that sisters are more agreeable and cooperative, which makes for a more harmonious home. Polygyny has a distinct advantage for producing many children, which are often needed in agrarian cultures where it is practiced. Additionally, having many children provides a sort of "social security" for the husbands and wives, as they have someone to care for them in their advanced years. Regardless of which version is allowed, nearly all cultures that practice polygyny insist that the man treat each wife *equally* and that he must able to financially *afford* multiple wives.

Today, nearly all organizations that oppose polygyny do so on the basis of human rights; they view the practice as a violation of women's rights. Citing that it violates the dignity of women, the United Nations has called on all nations to outlaw the practice. However, there is tremendous variation in the way polygyny is practiced, and this view may not fit the reality in all societies.

Fig. 10.1 While monogamy is the most commonly recognized and practiced marriage pattern globally, there are many cultures and religions that practice polygyny.

The flip side of polygyny is polyandry—one woman married to two or more men at the same time. Once believed to be extremely rare, practiced mainly by groups living in India, Nepal, China, and the Marquesas, research by Starkweather and Hames (2012) has identified an additional fifty-three societies that permit polyandry. The Nyinba people of Nepal and the Toda of Southern India both practice fraternal polyandry—when two or more brothers marry one woman. This is an infrequently practiced marriage form; most times, it is used to preserve family-owned land so that it can sustain a family. Imagine a married couple has three sons; the couple is getting too old to farm the family land, so it splits the family farm into three equal portions, one for each son. While the size of the original family farm was large enough to sustain a family, each of the three parcels is not. If each son were to take a wife and have a family, his one-third share of the family farm is not large enough to support his new family. However, if all three sons inherit the entire farm jointly, and they all take one wife, now there is enough land to support a growing family. In addition, this family will grow slower than three families with three wives. Other advantages of polyandry include allowing one husband to be away from the family without necessarily disrupting the family and providing economic security for the wife if one husband were to die.

Same-sex marriages—in which two people of the same sex marry—are now legal in all fifty states and the District of Columbia, and as of the writing of this book, twenty-one countries recognize same-sex marriages. The fact that so many societies of the world resist recognizing same-sex marriages indicates how strong the link is between marriage, family, and reproduction. However, same-sex marriages are viewed by advocates as a human rights issue; people should not be denied the right to marry just because of their sexual orientation. This position has been successful in changing marital laws in more than twenty countries. Some societies allow symbolic same-sex marriages to maintain family lineage, wealth, power, or to preserve bonds between families. Some societies like the Omaha Nation, for example, allow "two-spirit" or third-gender individuals (remember from Chapter 9?) to take same-sex marriage partners.

DO YOU HAVE TO MARRY A PERSON?

When people tell you they were just married, you may not know what gender, how old, what religion, or how rich or poor their spouse is, but you do assume they married another human. Below is a short list of people who found their soulmates in objects or animals.

- An American woman, Erika Eiffel, married the Eiffel Tower in a 2007 ceremony.
- Eija-Riitta Berliner-Mauer has been married to the Berlin Wall since 1979.
- A Japanese man who goes by the name Sal-9000 married a video game character named Nene Anegasaki from the Nintendo game "Love Plus" in 2009.
- A Korean man, Lee Jin-Gyu, married his "dakimakura," a kind of large huggable pillow, usually bearing the image of an anime character.
- A woman in India's state of Orissa married a cobra in 2006.
- In 2007, Liu Ye of China married himself. In a simple ceremony, he married a foam board cutout of himself in a stunning red dress.
- In the Sudan, if you are caught sleeping with an unmarried woman, you must marry her immediately. In 2006, Sudan applied this law to goats. Subsequently, Charles Tombe was caught *in flagrante* with a goat and had to marry it.
- In some parts of India, if your partner leaves you at the altar on your wedding day, you may marry a clay pot in his or her absence. In 2005, a young Indian woman named Salvita couldn't wait for her fiancé, who was late to the wedding, so she placed a picture of him on a clay pot and continued the ceremony.

Source: Snow and Brady, 2009; Alleyne, 2008; Lah, 2009; Phillips, 2010; Thompson, 2014; Landin, 2015

All societies enforce a number of rules about marriage, both prescriptive and proscriptive, in order to control who marries whom. Here in the United States, we have few rules that would restrict anyone from marrying whomever he or she wants. However, many cultures of the world strictly enforce rules of endogamy and exogamy. **Endogamy** refers to social rules that require individuals to marry someone from within their group. Religion, race, ethnicity, class, caste, tribe, or language can define that group. Marrying within one's family was widely practiced by royalty throughout history. Royals believed they could keep their bloodlines pure by keeping it all in the family. In fact, Cleopatra's parents were brother and sister. Traditionally, in the caste system of India, you must marry within your own caste; Orthodox Jews still require members to marry only other Orthodox Jews. Can you think of any rules of endogamy in the United States? Are Americans, in general, required to marry within a certain group? Other than those who practice religious endogamy, the only endogamous requirement in the U.S. is to marry within our own species.

For example, we can show that people in the United States are far more likely to marry someone of the same race. Of all those who married in 2013, the most recent data available, only 12% married someone of a different race. Moreover, if we look at all marriages in the United States, about 6.3% are between spouses of different races (Wang, 2015). While interracial marriages represent a small number of all U.S. marriages, the practice is on the rise. In 1970, only 1% of all marriages in the U.S. were interracial. I use this as an example to show that people overwhelmingly marry those of the same race, but the same can be said of religion and social class. Research from 2014 indicates that nearly seven in ten (69%) people reported being married to someone who shares their religion (Murphy, 2015). Similarly, people from the same socioeconomic background marry more frequently than those from different social classes.

Exogamy, on the other hand, is the requirement of individuals to marry outside of some designated group. At one time in the U.S., you were required to marry outside your sex; that is, a woman had to marry a man and a man had to marry a woman. Until 1967, when the United States Supreme Court ruled them unconstitutional, anti-miscegenation laws prohibited individuals from marrying outside of their race. These laws criminalized interracial marriage and, in some cases, sexual activity between people of different races.

Common exogamy practices include the prohibition of marrying family members; in nearly all cultures, people are required to marry outside their family. This reinforces the **incest taboo**—a cultural rule that prohibits sexual activity between closely related persons. However, in the U.S., twenty-six states allow first cousins to marry, and despite the stereotypes, West Virginia is *not* one. Does your home state allow first cousin marriages?

Even the looming specter of divorce is not a deterrent to marriage in the U.S.; most Americans either are married or plan to marry at some point. When I ask students in my classes if they are married or plan on marrying, almost every hand goes up. Even though people are staying single longer and delaying first marriage (the average age for men is twenty-nine and twenty-seven for women), most will marry. Marriage in the U.S. is a $70 billion industry, which is more than we spend on coffee, childcare, toothpaste, and toilet paper combined (The Week Staff, 2013; IBISWorld, 2015; Franchise Direct, 2014). In addition, you really need those things. Do you really need to be married? And what about starting that family? Pushing off marriage has led to delaying birth of the first child, and that late start has resulted in families having far fewer children.

TRY THIS

Ask all the married people you know where/how they met. Also, ask all your friends who are in serious committed relationships where/how they met. Then think about the relationships you have had or have now. How/where did you meet your partners? Then ask all those married, seriously involved people and yourself to describe how similar they are to their partners. Not in terms of personality traits but in socio-cultural traits things like religion, race, social class, interests, political leanings even geographical region. You'll probably be surprised that the majority of your respondents are married to or involved with people pretty similar to themselves. It's a phenomenon sociologists refer to as *homogamy* - the tendency to select mates who are socio-cultural similar to ourselves. We will discuss the concept more below.

Courtship and Mate Selection

When most of us think about courtship and mate selection, we imagine meeting that someone special, falling in love, and marring him or her. That's usually the way it goes in the United States and many Westernized cultures. However, in many societies, you may have little to no input into whom you will marry. Your marriage partner may be selected for you or you may have to steal your mate. There are three types of mate selection processes that are generally recognized: free choice, arranged, and marriage by capture.

In the United States, our marriage partners are typically not selected for us—we choose our own. This is commonly referred to as a "participant-run" mate selection process; the participants run the show. This process is also called free-choice mate selection. Some have called the mate selection process in the U.S. a "marriage market" due to the practice of comparing the positives and negatives of potential partners, then choosing the best mate. Regardless of which label you apply the process serves several important functions. It gives participants socially acceptable ways to experience a number of partners for fun, explore sexual expression/intimacy, find companionship, and ultimately decide with whom they are most compatible. We have the ability to test drive as many makes and models as we want before we buy.

Even with all this freedom of choice, most people end up marrying someone similar to themselves. **Homogamy** is the tendency for individuals with similar backgrounds to marry. Similar backgrounds may include religion, race, ethnicity, social class, or geographical region. Homogamy is not a social rule, ritual, or custom; it is merely a descriptive concept. Why do "likes" marry "likes"? Researchers have proposed a number of factors that explain who marries whom, and I cannot cover all of them. So, I will briefly discuss the factor I think is the most intuitive and convincing in explaining the tendency toward marital homogamy - propinquity.

Propinquity is geographical closeness, being close to someone or something. The people we have frequent contact with are people who tend to share our beliefs and activities: those we run into at the gym, school, work, coffee shops, and church share similar backgrounds and attitudes. Take the TV sitcom *How I Met Your Mother*, for example. The characters are all white, college-educated, middle-class professionals of which two have married. The others end up dating each other or people similar to themselves (usually meeting at their local bar). We tend to date and marry people we bump into in our social circles.

TINDER

There are many different ways to meet a potential mate: through family and friends, at work, school, church, or running on the beach. However, if your life is too busy for any of that nonsense, try Tinder. If you are not familiar with Tinder, it is a hook-up app that uses location-based profile matching with text chatting. You are presented with a series of photos of possible matches. Think about the set of pictures like a stack of cards: for each pic, you either swipe left (discard, not interested) or swipe right (interested) as you work your way through your "stack" of photos. If you both swipe right, it's a "match." The match leads to conversation, which leads to meeting in person, which may lead to a hook-up. Whether this techno-sexual app is or isn't the wave of the future, using technology to meet others is a growing practice and industry. Tinder, for example, has tens of millions of users that say they find the app fun and no different from real life. You usually approach someone you initially find attractive; if he or she chats you up, fine, and if he or she blows you off, oh, well. This is not really any different from swiping right or left. Even though this app can broaden your potential mate horizons, geography rears its ugly head. *Propinquity* (remember that from above?) still reigns supreme. Users on Tinder were 54% more likely to hook up if they were within one mile of each other; that percentage drops in half for every two miles they move out from where they are (Gazibara, 2015). The digital world is wonderful, but people still have to meet, and apparently, the closer you are, the better.

According to sociologists Michael Rosenfeld and Reuben Thomas (2012), 30% of heterosexual married couples met through friends, and another 10% met their spouse at work. A very interesting 2013 study by Facebook Data Sciences found that 28% of their members married college sweethearts. Interestingly, the top three schools for men to meet their spouses, according to the study, were all religiously affiliated colleges. The study also showed that the top three colleges for women to meet their future husbands were all technical schools. You really can't avoid running into someone who is similar to you in social class, religious background, or interests at those schools.

I know what you are thinking: the Internet blows the idea of propinquity out of the water. Remember our man Rosenfeld from the paragraph above? Well, he found that the Internet has only partly displaced traditional meeting places like school, work, neighborhood, and family. His research indicates that about 20–24% of people make initial contact with their spouses online. Even if you live in the U.S. and meet your soulmate online, and he or she happens to live in Bhutan, one of you has to move so you can get married. You really cannot start a family over the Internet. At least I don't think you can.

In contrast to the free-choice model of mate selection is the arranged marriage. The partners in **arranged marriages** are chosen by parents, community leaders, matchmakers, or clergy. The bride and groom typically have little or no say in the matter. Arranged marriages are still commonly practiced today in Iran, Iraq, Afghanistan, and India. Arranged marriage was once an extremely common practice, but it has since fallen out of favor in many societies like China and India. This is due to the diffusion of Western cultural practices and the liberalization of social customs.

Often in cultures, whom one marries is far too important a decision to be left to someone so young and inexperienced. Marriage, in these societies, is the union of two families, not two individuals. Marriages should be the result of careful negotiations, not from young people following impulses of the heart. These decisions are a common way of securing alliances so that families can enjoy increased status, political power, economic gain, or to clear a debt. It is commonly believed that while they do not know each other, their love will grow for each other as time passes. This process of choosing a mate is difficult for many of us to understand because it is at odds with our values, beliefs, and customs. Would you want your marriage arranged? Who would you trust to arrange it?

Arranged marriages are many times secured with either a bride price or dowry. *Bride price* is the price paid by the groom's family to the bride's family for the loss of her services. This can be paid in the form of livestock, shells, money, services, years of labor, or other valuables. A *dowry*, on the other hand, is an incentive for a man to marry a woman and relieve her family of the burden of having a daughter. This is paid by the bride's family in the same forms as bride price. In fact, a Kenyan lawyer offered President Obama fifty cows, thirty goats, and seventy sheep as a bride price for the his daughter Malia (Leopold, 2015).

THERE'S AN APP FOR THAT

While I mentioned Tinder above there are a number of alternatives to this popular app. Below I have listed and briefly described some alternative mate-finder apps.

- *Hot or Not.* I don't think I have to say more (Or Not Limited, 2016).
- *Clover.* Like Tinder this is a location based profile match app that lets you sift through potential mates/hook-ups by the type of relationship they are looking for. You can also sort by things like ethnicity and height (Clover Inc., 2016).
- *Wingme.* Find a mate with the help of your friends, they have input on each of your selections. You can be the dater or act as a wingman for your friends (Wingme, 2014).
- *Stitch Companionship.* Tinder for older adults (Stitch Holdings Pty Ltd, 2016).
- *Grindr.* The all gay version of Tinder, for finding a lasting relationship or a casual hook-up (Grindr LLC, 2016).
- *3nder.* Meet like-minded people who want three-ways. This is an open minded app where trios are made easy and discretely, your friends and family will never know (3nder Ltd, 2015).

Arranged Child Marriages

Although now illegal, arranged child marriages are common in the Rajasthan region of northern India. Children as young as five years old are forced to accept their parents' choice of whom they will marry. In 2011, three young girls, aged fifteen, thirteen, and five, were all secretly married on a hilltop in northern India. National Geographic reporter Cynthia Gorney (2011) describes the scene and circumstances as three young Indian girls are married to boys they have never even seen.

> "Because the wedding was illegal and a secret, except to the invited guests, and because marriage rites in Rajasthan are often conducted late at night, it was well into the afternoon before the three girl brides in this dry farm settlement in the north of India began to prepare themselves for their sacred vows. They squatted side by side on the dirt, a crowd of village women holding sari cloth around them as a makeshift curtain, and poured soapy water from

> a metal pan over their heads. Two of the brides, the sisters Radha and Gora, were 15 and 13, old enough to understand what was happening. The third, their niece Rajani, was five. She wore a pink T-shirt with a butterfly design on the shoulder. A grown-up helped her pull it off to bathe. The grooms were en route from their own village, many miles away. No one could afford an elephant or the lavishly saddled horses that would have been ceremonially correct for the grooms' entrance to the wedding, so they were coming by car and were expected to arrive high-spirited and drunk."

This scene is not that uncommon. The practice of child marriage crosses many continents, languages, religions, and cultures. It is a common practice in parts of India, Yemen, Afghanistan, Nepal, Bangladesh, Nicaragua, and more than fifteen African nations. In fact, in Niger, 75% of women were married before they turned eighteen (United Nations, "Motherhood in Childhood", 2013; International Center for Research on Women, 2015). Whether the child bride is married off by her family to unite communities, resolve a feud, or to repay a debt, the results are the same: she is exploited by the husband's family, and her health and safety are put at risk. Essentially, her future is stolen.

A 2013 report from the United Nations Population Fund (UNFPA) indicates that between 2011 and 2020, more than 140 million young girls will be exploited through arranged child marriage. Of these 140 million child brides (girls under eighteen years), fully 50 million of them will marry under the age of fifteen. While both young boys and girls may be involved in child marriage, the practice is far more common among young girls. These young brides are frequently married off to men who are five, ten, or even thirty years older than they are. Most importantly, child brides are a far greater risk for a range of health and social issues. Their education is effectively ended, opportunity to gain vocational skills is blocked, and they are at increased risk for intimate partner sexual violence. Moreover, they are exposed to the "risks of too-early pregnancy, childbearing and motherhood before they are physically and psychologically ready". In addition, this population is at an increased risk of HIV infection. Child marriage is recognized by most international health and economic assistance organizations as a violation of the rights of girls.

READ MORE

- *I am Nujood, Age 10 and Divorced* by Nujood Ali and Delpine Minoui (2010). This book recounts the story of Nujood, a ten-year-old Yemeni girl who found the strength and courage to travel alone to a courthouse seeking a divorce. She wanted a divorce from her husband, a man in his thirties her father had forced her to marry. I also highly recommend Stephanie Sinclair's photographs and accompanying stories of the sorrow, abuse, and bravery of child brides.

Marriage by capture is the practice of taking a wife by force or deceit. This is almost always performed without the consent of the woman or her family. Unfortunately, it is practiced in many places, such as Asia, Africa, the Middle East, the Caucasus and even the Americas. While there is some variation in methods, the practice goes something like this: A frustrated man waits until the woman he wants is alone, grabs her, and takes her back to his place, where he quickly marries her, therefore claiming her as his property. Sometimes, the bride's family is able to dissuade the kidnapper to let her go but more often they must fight, or pay for her safe return. Many times, men who marry by capture are the least desirable members of their society: poor, of low status, and without resources. Therefore, for these men, the capture is viewed as their only access to a mate (Barnes, 1999).

Another common technique is to rape the woman, attempting to impregnate the "bride," which allows the "groom" to lay claim to her. Historically, and on a larger scale, this practice is common during times of war. Think the rape of the Sabine women, the French during the Napoleonic Wars, the Russians in WWII—basically, any and every war. You can even find marriage by capture in the Bible (Deuteronomy 21:10–14). More recently, for example, Boko Haram, a Jihadist terrorist group operating mainly in Nigeria, kidnapped more than two hundred schoolgirls in April 2014. Some of the girls managed to escape, but most were beaten, executed, or forced into marriage by their captors ("Nigeria frees dozens", 2015; Oduah, 2015).

Fortunately, marriage by capture in most countries is considered a crime. The practice of marriage by capture, in many cultures, has evolved into the custom of bride price. Apparently, it seems more civilized to pay for your wife rather than kidnap her. Either way, these practices perpetuate the treatment of women as objects to be bought and sold or taken by force.

Residence Patterns

After all the excitement of the wedding and the honeymoon is over, where do you live? Where newlyweds live is based as much on cultural custom as it is practicality. The most common residence pattern for newlyweds worldwide is patrilocality—newly married couples live with the groom's family. Anthropologists estimate that about 70% of world societies are patrilocal. Patrilocal households are used to pool resources and foster economic development. When sons bring their new wives to their parents' home, the young brides become household laborers. Typically, these new additions fall to the bottom of the household pecking order and must do everyone's bidding. The residence pattern of patrilocality is very often exploitative of women. Additionally, in many societies, patrilocality leads to adultery, wife stealing, and fights, creating considerable disharmony within those communities (Divale, 1975).

A less common residence pattern is matrilocality—an arrangement where the newly married couple live with the bride's family—found in only about 10% of the world's societies.

Although not practiced by many societies, matrilocal cultures can be found on every continent except Antarctica. In contrast to patrilocal societies, matrilocal societies tend to experience less fighting and disharmony within households and communities. Matrilocality is typically practiced in *matrilineal* societies, those in which wealth and status is passed from mother to daughter. The practice of this residence pattern ultimately concentrates offspring and resources in the matrilineal household (Jones, 2011).

The typical residence pattern practiced in the United States and in nearly all industrialized nations is neolocality—the newly married couple establishes their own residence separate from their parents. This is the least common residence pattern in the world. It is usually practiced in societies in which kinship is minimized and there is a great deal of mobility, such as the United States. However, as a result of the Great Recession (2007–09), many newlyweds found neolocation economically untenable. Therefore, many couples had no choice but to move in with their parents.

What Is Family?

Family has variously been labeled the basic unit of society, the backbone of society, and the universal social group. These terms imply that family is instrumental in organizing societies, important to holding societies together, and found in all societies. While some form of the family is found in all cultures, its form varies widely across societies and over time. We often talk about "the family" as if there was just one type, yet we know there are many types of families around the world and in our own society. Those types may include some with children, some without, some with two parents, and some with just one. Other families may include grandparents, uncles, cousins, nieces and nephews, or same-sex parents.

There are many definitions of family, and I really haven't found one that I like. However, I know there are students who need definitions. The U.S. Census Bureau defines a family as a group of two or more people related by birth, marriage, or adoption and residing together. As of 2013, only 66% of Americans fit this definition, down from 81% in 1970 (Vespa, Lewis, and Kreider, 2013). What do you think about this definition? Is it inclusive enough? It does cover many living arrangements, but it may exclude some that many people consider to be their "family." Think about the family you were raised in. Would this definition include the household in which you grew up?

When we discuss change and family in sociology, we consider both its structure (shape) and its function (purpose). That is, we examine what families look like—nuclear, blended, single parent—and what society expects the family to do—provide support, raise children, etc. Moreover, in sociology, we study the family as both a social institution and as a system of intergenerational relationships. We analyze the family from both a macrosociological and a microsociological perspective.

Change in the Family: Structure and Function

- Structure: The shape of marriage and family
  - What do marriages and families look like?
  - How and why have they changed?
- Function: The social and cultural purpose of marriage and family
  - What purpose do marriage and family serve in society?
  - How and why have they changed?

Family Forms

Family is embedded in culture; therefore, so are our perceptions of family. What family is changes across time and space; what did you think family was when you were ten years old, what do you think family is now, and what will you think family is when you are much older? Our perceptions of family have changed and will continue to change as our society embraces the growing number of alternate family forms. The events in your life such as marrying, having children, divorcing, remarrying, and becoming a stepparent will no doubt influence your thoughts on what family is. Most people will move through several family types over the course of their lives. Let's take a look at what families look like in today's society and how they have changed.

Perhaps the most salient feature of change in society in the past one hundred years has been the family. Some lament that the "family" is disappearing. Politicians and pundits alike bemoan the decline of the American family. Statements like "The American family is at its worst state in the history of the country," "... the nationwide decline of the family unit," and "The American family is no more" all seem to indicate there is no more "family" in the U.S. (Ginsborg, 2005; Dodrill, 2013; Bidwell, 2013). What family are they referring to? Nearly all are referring to a family that was present in the U.S. as a majority family type for less than twenty years: The *Leave It to Beaver*, nuclear, "traditional" family of the 1950s and '60s.

However, this is just a longing for a "family" that never was. In her book *The Way We Never Were: American Families and the Nostalgia Trap* (1992), Stephanie Coontz presents a compelling argument that shatters our image of the family from "the good old days." Neither the 1950s nor any other time in our past lines up with the mythical image of the "traditional family." The historical evidence shows that families were always complex, dynamic, and sorting through crises like many families today, just trying to make things work. This nostalgia for a mythical past is a dangerous obsession that hinders our ability to embrace the ever-changing landscape of modern family arrangements.

The **nuclear family**—married parents and their biological or adopted children sharing a common residence—is a waning family type. In 1960, the nuclear family—the *Leave it to Beaver* version of mom, dad, and two kids—accounted for about 44% of households; now that number is around 19% (Laughlin, 2013). Many times, politicians and others point to the nuclear family as the "normal" family, which we should all strive to achieve. In fact, the nuclear family was a relatively new type of family springing up mostly after WWII. For decades, it was common for Americans to live in families comprised of several generations. For the great number of rural farming families, these large, multigenerational families made sense. Before 1935, there was no Social Security, and the elderly counted on their children and grandchildren for housing and support, a sort of all-in-the-family social security. Additionally, The Great Depression forced many family members to come together for economic reasons. In 1940, just before the outbreak of WWII, extended families accounted for one-quarter of all U.S. households (Taylor et al., 2010).

The extended family, as the name suggests, extends the nuclear family by including additional family members. This is a common family type found in many societies. *Vertical extended* families include grandparents, their children, and their grandchildren. Imagine you, your parents, and your grandparents all sharing a residence. *Horizontal extended* families usually include two or more siblings living together with their families, so you get a mix of uncles, aunts, nieces, nephews, and cousins. Try this out: you, your brothers and sisters, mom and dad, mom's no-good brother, his wife, their five kids, and a goat all in the same house, with one bathroom. Many times, extended families are cultural expressions of reverence for older generations, consolidation of labor, or economic necessities. When they first come to the U.S., many immigrant groups live in extended family arrangements to pool their resources, and some are continuing cultural patterns.

While a common family pattern at one time in America's past, its popularity bottomed out in 1980 with only 12% of households reporting extended family living arrangements. However, the extended

Fig. 10.2 Extended families are found more frequently among certain ethnic groups in the U.S. However, in recent years the overall number of extended family households has been on the rise.

family has made a resurgence in the past decade. Between 2000 and 2010, those living in extended family households increased from 15% to 16.7%, spiking after the Great Recession of 2008. While the increase has been across all age segments, millennials (those born between 1982 and 2000) are the major contributors to the rise in extended family households. They are part of what sociologists call the boomerang generation—because they leave home and come right back, like a boomerang. Some of the factors contributing to the boomerang generation include the Great Recession, increased cost of college, and an inclination to postpone marriage (Pew Research Center, "A Portrait of Stepfamilies," 2011).

The **blended family** (stepfamily) is a family in which at least one spouse has children from a previous marriage or relationship. Blended families are quickly becoming one of the most common family patterns in the U.S. Currently, blended families comprise about one-third of all U.S. families. Why do you think there are so many blended families? Why are their numbers increasing? The majority of blended families are formed when parents decide to remarry. Divorce is the driving force behind the large and growing numbers of blended families. However, some blended families can be formed by previously unwed parents who have decided to marry.

The number of single parent families has nearly doubled since 1960, according to the U.S. Census. **Single parent families** are living arrangements that involve one parent and his or her dependent children. These families make up just over 30% of all U.S. families. Fully one-quarter of all U.S. households are single female-headed, and 6% of single households are male-headed. This represents a tripling of single parent households since 1960. I think by now you are getting the sense that single parent families are growing, and growing fast. In fact, the fastest-growing family form in the U.S. is the single parent-headed household. Let's break it down. Single parent-headed families are formed in a variety of ways like divorce, desertion, death of a spouse, or by choice. Below, I present a brief overview of the structure of single parent-headed households.

- Of all single parent-headed families, 84% are headed by a woman, and only 16% are dad-only households.
- Births to teenage unwed mothers have dropped in half since 1991. Today, unmarried single moms are more likely to be in their twenties or thirties.
- Education level is a factor: about 90% of women with a college degree marry before giving birth to their first child. However, of women with some college education, 40% are unmarried when they have their first child. In addition, for women with a high school diploma or less, 57% are unmarried at the birth of their first child.
- About 46% of female-headed households are at or below the poverty line, which is over four times that of married families.
- Non-marital births vary by race. It is highest for black women at 72%, followed by Hispanic with 53%, whites with 29%, and Asians with just 17%.
  (Sources: U.S. Census, 2012; Department of Health and Human Services, "Information on Poverty", 2014; Livingston and Cohn, 2010)

Cohabitation

In the past, it has been referred to as "shacking up" or "living in sin," but cohabitation—unmarried couples living together in a committed, non-marital relationship—is on the rise. Between 1990 and 2007, the number of unmarried cohabitating partners increased 88% (Kreider and Elliot, 2009). While cohabitation is more popular than ever, who is doing it is changing. More and more, the age of those who cohabitate is on the rise. Fully half of those aged thirty to forty-nine have cohabitated at some point in their lives; those twenty-four and younger make up only 20% of people living together (Fry and Cohn, 2011).

Some people are not ready for marriage, some do not want to marry, and some just want to take a committed, long-term relationship for a spin. Others just want to share the cost of running a household. Whatever the reason, Americans like to cohabitate. Many view cohabitation as a viable alternative to marriage. Of all married women in the United States, 60% cohabitated with someone at some point in their lives before they married (Manning, 2013). Cohabitation, apparently, is a gateway drug to marriage.

Does cohabitation bode well for marriage? Two years ago, I would have written an emphatic no. Recent research by Arielle Kuperberg (2014) has cast some doubt on decades of research that showed cohabitation leads to divorce. Her research showed no correlation between cohabitation before marriage and divorce. Why? Well, we know that those who marry young are at considerably greater risk for divorce than those who marry at older ages. Therefore, she adjusted for age of cohabitation. That is, young people who live together and then marry are at greater risk for divorce. It's not that cohabitation leads to divorce; it's that young people establish their marital roles during their cohabitation and carry those roles over into their marriage, essentially dooming them. So, the younger that a couple who eventually marry begin cohabitation, the greater their risk for divorce. If you are going to shack up with someone while you are young, do not marry him or her. You could always wait until your mid-twenties to live with someone before marriage, which dramatically reduces your risk of divorce.

Those with lower education levels and lower incomes are more likely to cohabitate. Moreover, working-class and poor cohabitating couples are more likely to have children. More educated, wealthier live-in partners are more likely to marry their partner than their less educated, poorer counterparts. Educated live-ins with higher incomes are more likely to use cohabitation as a *launching pad* for marriage, while those with less education and income are more likely to use cohabitation as an *alternative* to marriage.

A Note on Change

The family is not on the decline, it is simply changing. The growing variations in family arrangements are just responses to a rapidly changing social landscape. Many of the changes in family structure in the past fifty years have been a result of the impact of the women's movement of the 1960s and '70s. In fact, I think that of all possible influences, the women's movement has had the most profound effect on the changing American family—in a good way. The women's movement affected changes in federal and state laws, hiring practices, college admissions, economic policy, and social attitudes. While these changes were focused primarily on women, their downstream effect has affected men, the family, and society in general.

Although profound, the effects of the women's movement do not stand alone in their influence on the changing American family. The shift from a manufacturing to a post-industrial economy, powerful political and educational changes, demographic changes, as well as a general movement away from formal religion in the U.S. have all influenced the changing face of the family. Knowing that there is an interplay between the various parts of society, in which changes in one sphere of social life can affect other spheres, we should not be surprised by changing family patterns. We cannot realistically expect the family to stand still while society is changing all around it; I don't know if we would want it to. So, rather than pine for some bygone, idealized version of family that never was, let's embrace the resilience and adaptability reflected in our incredible diversity of families.

Family Functions

We have seen that families come in a variety of shapes and sizes. While families may vary in their appearance, they are all working toward some common goals. Families everywhere function in ways that benefit their members and society. Families seek to reproduce, prosper, raise healthy, well-adjusted children, and provide a range of support for their members. Sociologists may disagree on the number and types of functions modern families are responsible for, but there is considerable consensus on the ones I have outlined below.

Socialization: By my estimation, the most important function families perform. Society looks to the family as the primary agent of socialization; we expect families to teach children at least the basics about how to function in society. Children around the world are being raised to learn, internalize, and abide by their cultural standards so that they fit in, prosper, and have families of their own.

Sexual Regulation: Every society has rules that regulate sexual behavior within the family and in the larger society. Most cultures enforce an *incest taboo*, the prohibition of sexual activity with closely related people. Regulation of sexual activity includes the idea that sex should only be between the spouses and not with others outside of the marriage. Additionally, children learn about a range of socially acceptable sexual behaviors. These may include whom they can have sex with, at what ages, for what purposes, and the consequences of sex.

Reproduction: In order for human societies to continue, we need to reproduce; most societies look to the family to perform this function. As families replace dying members of society, they ensure the continuation of society. Reproduction in the context of a family ensures that we know whom the offspring belong to, who is responsible for the offspring, and that there is system of support for them.

Provide a range of support: Families are expected to provide support, ranging from financial to emotional. We expect families to feed, clothe, and shelter their members, as well as provide moral support by showing up at baseball games, ballet recitals, and school plays. The family is expected to provide warm and intimate relationships so that its members can feel secure. Ideally, the family provides an environment in which we are understood, cared for, and comforted, a sort of safe port or a "haven in a heartless world" (Lasch, 1977).

Social status: Without any consultation or input, we are born into a family. It may be a rich family or a poor family. It may be an Asian family or a Hispanic family. Our social position is based on that of our parents. In addition, family resources can influence children's development as well as their social opportunities. Our social position is fixed initially, but we have the ability to attempt social mobility later in life.

Think about it this way: families are essentially all doing the same things, just in different ways. For example, every family feeds its children but goes about it in a variety of ways. I think about when I would stay overnight at my friend's house when I was younger. I would dread breakfast at my friend's house because, invariably, his mother would ask us what cereal we wanted, put it in a bowl, and then pour the milk. That was the painful part: watching her pour out a tiny amount of milk, leaving me to choke down some pasty version of my favorite breakfast cereal. At my house, we poured our own milk, and I let it flow, making sure the cereal was covered by milk. Can you think of experiences you have had that highlight how families are doing the same things, just differently?

READ MORE

- *Haven in a Heartless World* by Christopher Lasch (1977). A critical look at society and how the changes in other spheres of our social life have eroded the sanctity of the family. Once the family was a "haven in a heartless world," it is now besieged on all sides from changing social forces and attitudes.
- *The Black Family in the Age of Mass Incarceration* by Ta-Nehisi Coates in *The Atlantic*, October 2015 issue. The author vividly connects structural social factors such as poverty, crime and incarceration rates with the plight of the black family in today's society. This is a compelling story of how black families are uniquely affected by the criminalization and over incarceration of black men.

Work and Family

We have discussed a number of changes in marriage and families, but our discussion would not be complete without a look at how work, especially women's employment, has influenced those changes. Below, I have indicated the factors that have been most influential on families over the past few decades.

- Women make up nearly half of the workforce. Fully 47% of all workers are women, up from 38% in 1970. Additionally, women are increasingly becoming the household breadwinners. Nearly all the growth in family incomes in the past several decades can be attributed to women's increased earnings. For all households, more than 40% of moms are now the sole or primary source of income. In 1970, only 7% of working women earned more than their husbands; today, 24% do. In fact, since the 1970s, nearly all the rise in family income has come from women's earnings (Bureau of Labor Statistics, 2014).
- Education is linked both to earnings potential and to likelihood of employment. Over the past few decades, women's college attendance and graduation rates have approached and then surpassed that of men. Today, substantially more women graduate from college than men. Therefore, they will soon be the majority of college-educated workers, positioning them to be the bulk of the highest wage earners in the workplace.
- This increase in women's earnings and presence in the workplace has affected the caregiver roles in families. Fathers are playing larger roles in caregiving. In households where mom is employed, one in five dads are primary caregivers. Stay-at-home dads with working moms have doubled since 1990. This trend in dad as the primary caregiver is reflected in the number of father-only families, which have tripled in the past forty years (The Council of Economic Advisers, "Nine Facts", 2014).
- With the decades-long increase in both dual-earner homes and working single parents, 60% of children live in homes where all parents work. In addition, it's not just childcare that can strain families: with more people living longer, more families are facing issues surrounding elder care. This has created what some have called "the sandwich generation," those sandwiched between care for their own children and care for their aging parents (Bureau of Labor Statistics, 2011; Bureau of Labor Statistics, 2012).
- Searching for flexibility in the workplace: Workers who are struggling to balance work and family are looking for employers that understand the changing needs of families in relationship to workplace flexibility and are willing to respond to those needs. Almost half of parents with kids under eighteen at home have passed up a job because it conflicted with their family obligations. Women, research indicates, are seeking career paths that offer more autonomy and flexibility (The Council of Economic Advisers, "Work-Life",

2014; Goldin, 2006). Not coincidentally, careers that can accommodate childcares needs and offer both high levels of autonomy and flexibility require more education, which more women are pursuing.
- Balancing work and family: Both men and women report they are increasingly pressed for time. Frequently, this creates conflicts between managing work and home responsibilities. Men and women are increasingly likely to report that work interferes with family, not the other way around. A 2011 study revealed that 60% of men in dual-earner families reported some form of work/family conflict, which was an increase from just 35% in 1977. In 2010, 46% of working men and women reported that work interfered with some family obligation, which was an increase over reports from 2002 (Galinsky, Aumann, and Bond, 2011; King, 2005).

Divorce and Remarriage

No chapter on marriage and family would be complete without a discussion on divorce. Divorce is nearly as popular as marriage is in the U.S. **Divorce**—the legal dissolution of marriage—is not recognized in some cultures and perhaps a little too recognized in others. The Philippines and the Vatican do not allow divorce, and in just the last twenty years, Ireland, Chile, and Malta have allowed divorce.

You have probably heard that 50% of all marriages in the U.S. end in divorce. It's not true. The cumulative percentage of those divorced from a first marriage in the U.S. is just about 41% (Goodlight, 2012). However, the percentage of those who seek a divorce from a second marriage is over 60%. Moreover, divorce is not on the rise; in fact, it has been on the decline since around 1981.

Let's take a quick peek at divorce rates and their slow decline over the past thirty years. A **divorce rate** is measured as the number of divorces per one thousand people. That number was 5.3 divorces per thousand people when divorces peaked in 1981. By 1990, that rate had dropped to 4.7 divorces per thousand people. In addition, by 2012, the divorce rate hovered right at 3.4 divorces per thousand people (Centers for Disease Control, "National Marriage", 2015). Clearly, the divorce rate in the U.S. is falling.

More people who married in the 1990s were still married at the fifteen-year mark than couples married in the 1980s. In addition, so far, those who married in the 2000s are divorcing at even lower rates. According to economist Justin Wolfers, if current divorce rate trends continue, nearly two-thirds of those who marry will never experience divorce (Miller, 2014).

In figure 10.3 below, you can see the historical pattern of divorce in the United States. In 1950 just after the end of WWII, divorce rates were relatively low, declining steadily until 1960. Divorce rates then climbed steadily until they peaked in 1980. Since then, divorce rates have been falling slowly but remain high.

Fig. 10.3 Divorce rates climbed steadily after 1960, but peaked in 1980. Since then divorce rates have slowly dropped.

Given these patterns, we have to ask two things. Why the dramatic rise in divorce from 1960 to 1981? In addition, why have divorce rates been slowly declining in the past thirty years? Led mostly by the baby boomers, the 1960s and 1970s were times of tremendous social upheaval in the U.S. and many Western nations. Not only were the previous generations' marital and sexual norms being challenged, but so was nearly all institutional authority. Positions on the war in Vietnam, civil rights, censorship, and educational policies were being revised as many institutions experienced a general liberalization. During these decades the United States emerged from a sort of social and cultural dark ages. Drugs, music, and the sexual revolution played a key role in transforming society, altering many long-held views on social arrangements like marriage and family. Think about it this way: there were 76 million baby boomers coming of age in a very short time period. It was as though the United States was a house filled with millions of teenagers and twenty-somethings. Moreover, like many adolescents, in order to establish their own identities, they felt they must reject the conventional moral beliefs of their parents.

As the baby boomers vocalized their opposition to and rejection of their parents' institutional view of marriage, they adopted a more "self-fulfillment" model of marriage (Coontz, 1992). Rather than view marriage as a duty to spouse, offspring, community, and, ultimately, country, this generation looked to find love, self- fulfillment, and gratification in marriage. Also, the women's movement had increased educational and economic freedoms that allowed women to exit unfulfilling marriages. The rise of "no-fault" divorce laws made divorce less expensive, easier to obtain, and unilaterally exercised (one spouse could divorce another even if he or she did not want a divorce). Additionally, the more it was practiced, the less stigma was connected to divorce, making it more socially acceptable. These and several other social factors led many to believe in the disposability of marriage.

Understanding what elements have converged to produce both a decline in marriages and divorces is a complex task and well beyond our discussion here. Therefore, let's take a look at just a few factors that have contributed to the thirty-year slide in divorce rates. Much interest has focused on the delay of first marriage, increased average age at first marriage, cohabitation, and the increasing view by younger cohorts that marriage is not that important. Obviously, as more people choose not to marry, the potential for divorce is reduced. However, even taking into account the decrease in the number of marriages, divorce is still declining. Additionally, as people, specifically women, pursue more education, they tend to delay marriage. The median age at first marriage for men is nearly twenty-nine and almost twenty-seven for women (U.S. Census, "Decennial Censuses, 1890 to 1940", 2014). This increase in age at first marriage bodes well for success in marriage.

Today, couples are increasingly more likely to cohabitate before marriage. More than 65% of married people report cohabitating with someone of the opposite sex before marrying (Donevan, 2014). Cohabitation is quickly becoming the "gateway relationship" to marriage. Previous research suggested that cohabitation was a likely predictor of divorce. Recent analyses have speculated that divorce-prone people cohabitate rather than cohabitation causing divorce. Flipping the once commonly held idea that cohabitation increases likelihood of divorce on its head, Stevenson and Wolfers (2007) suggest that without cohabitation, divorce may be more likely. Experimenting with various elements of a relationship through cohabitation may better prepare couples before they marry.

Divorce rates, however, vary across groups in the United States. African Americans have the highest divorce rates. Whites run a close second, followed by Hispanics, and Asian Americans have the lowest divorce rates. The differences in rates are tied to a number of social variables, including income, education levels, religion, and cultural influences.

While it is clear that divorce is on the decline in the United States, it is still a part of the marital landscape. Research has identified a number of factors that put some at greater risk for divorce than others. Here are some factors that seem to increase the risk of divorce:

- Marrying young. Those who marry for the first time young (as teenagers) tend to have high divorce rates. Those rates decrease as age increases for first marriages. Marriage can be challenging without the necessary life skills, education, and employability. The high divorce rate among young couples tends to be associated with education, which is linked to income levels and economic stability (Lehrer, 2008).

- Education levels. Those with college degrees are less likely to divorce than those with a high school diploma or less. Those who attend college tend to be older at the time of first marriage and have a greater range of dating, courtship, and sexual experiences. Their college degree is also associated with higher incomes and better benefits, which may translate to more stable households (Martin, 2006).
- Income. Those married couples with higher incomes tend to experience lower divorce rates. Income is highly correlated with education. Research indicates that those households with annual incomes of $50,000 or more run a lower risk of divorce than those with incomes of $25,000 or less (Lewis and Kreider, 2015).
- Parents' divorce. You cannot control all risk factors for divorce. However, if your parents divorced, that doubles your risk of divorce, and if your partner's parents were divorced, that can just about triple the risk (Dennison, 2014).
- Childless marriages. Married couples without children are more likely to divorce than those with kids. With fewer reasons to remain in an unhappy marriage, those without children can find divorce easier. The divorce laws in many states make dissolution of the marriage easier if there are no children involved (Bronson, 2006).
- Religious affiliation. Those who report belonging to a religion are slightly less likely to divorce than those who claim no religious affiliation. Moreover, if you and your spouse share a common religious affiliation, risk of divorce is further reduced (White, 1990).

The Graying of Divorce

Divorce rates in the United States are on an overall downturn except for one group: those over age fifty, our beloved baby boomers. In 1990, a mere 10% of all divorces were among those fifty and older. Today, those calling it quits with their marriages over age fifty make up 25% of all divorces. In addition, those who do divorce after age fifty are far more likely to hold at least a bachelor's degree (Brown and Lin, 2012). We don't know exactly why we are seeing this rise in divorce among older people, but researchers have speculated that this rise in "gray divorce" is due in part to an increase in life expectancy—believing you have enough years left to do marriage one more time. Perhaps it is due to increased financial stability for both spouses, which translates to a greater financial ability to divorce. Other reasons may include a shift in marital expectations. Marriage was once expected to simply provide stability and security; now, the added expectations of self-fulfillment and personal satisfaction may be deal-breakers. Now that the nest is empty and couples being to "recouple" they may find that through the years they have drifted too far away from their partners or they simply realize they no longer like them. After decades of distractions from intimacy as a couple like juggling careers, childrearing, and keeping the household together, couples may realize they don't like the person on the other side of the breakfast table. Whatever the reasons, make no mistake: just as boomers have driven other economic and social changes, they could be reshaping divorce.

Remarriage

Along with both first marriages and divorce, remarriage—any marriage in which at least one spouse was previously married—is also on the decline. The remarriage rate in the U.S. has declined by 40% since 1990. Men are twice as likely to remarry as women; either they are more eager to remarry or have greater resources to help them find a new spouse (Payne, 2015). Interestingly, about 6% of those who remarry do it with their ex-spouse (Kalish, 2005). People are also taking longer to remarry than in past decades; today, most remarry within four years, although on average, women take longer to remarry than men. Why do you think women take longer than men to remarry?

Often, remarriage means the formation of complex families. Nearly half of all remarried couples already have children in the home. Overall, men are more likely than women to be the stepparents in newly formed blended families, which makes sense given the greater likelihood of women retaining custody of children. Therefore, women are more likely to bring children to the marriage than men. While blended families have become far more common, evidence suggests that the children in those families do not fare as well as those raised by two biological parents or a single parent (Stewart, 2007). Why do you think children in blended families don't do as well as those raised by either one or both of their biological parents?

Even though remarriage is on the decline, people are still taking a second, third, or fourth ride on the marriage-go-round. Americans love the idea of marriage. However, these remarriages are forming complex blended families with a mixture of step, half, and biological siblings, many of whom are in variety of custody situations. This can create a sense of impermanence or transience, which can undermine the stability of the new family. In addition, unfortunately, this is evident in the divorce rates among second and third marriages. There is a 67% divorce rate among second marriages, and 73% of third marriages end in divorce.

Theoretical Perspectives on Marriage and Family

The structural functionalist view emphasizes the importance of social institutions and the particular functions they perform in maintaining social stability and keeping society chugging along. Therefore, a functionalist understanding of the family stresses how the family, as a social institution, performs several important functions that contribute to social order. Functionalists see the family as the primary agent of socialization, responsible for the development and social adjustment of its members. Families help their younger members understand and internalize acceptable social values, beliefs, and behaviors, which are central to maintaining social solidarity and stability. Functionalists also view the family as a source of a range of support, from physical to financial to emotional. Not only do we expect families to provide food, shelter, and clothing for their members, but we also expect families to provide love and comfort—to care for us and be there when we need them.

Families also provide their members with a social identity. When children are born, they assume their families' social status, race/ethnicity, religion, etc. While for some this can bring advantage, for others it can mean lifelong deprivation. Whatever a family's status, functionalists expect it to transmit to each new generation the central social values, beliefs, and behaviors that will help duplicate social statuses, roles, and, ultimately, social structure, all with the aim of promoting social order. Consequently, functionalists see family types that vary from the conventional as a threat to the well-being of children, the family, and, by extension, society itself.

Like functionalists, conflict theorists recognize that the family as a social institution serves many functions. However, while functionalism focuses on reproduction of social statuses and roles for the maintenance of social stability, the conflict approach sees families as a locus of the reproduction of inequality and patriarchy. Primarily, the conflict perspective focuses on how the capitalist system maintains inequality between the powerful and less powerful classes, which, in turn, shapes other institutions such as the family.

For instance, families with the resources to do so pass their wealth from one generation to the next. This concentration of wealth in a small number of families reinforces existing social and wealth inequality. Family, for conflict theorists, is essentially an institution that reproduces social class. Patterns of inequality affect families across the social class spectrum. Poor families experience a deprivation of social resources, while advantaged families enjoy social privilege. The lack of social resources becomes a source of stress and contention within poor families, which can impair family functioning and relationships. On the other hand, wealthier families have access to better schools, extracurricular activities, and travel, therefore enhancing their children's social and human capital.

The family is also seen as replicating patterns of patriarchy. The family is a microcosm of the capitalist system in which power is directly related to earnings. Historically, men have been the top wage earners in most households; therefore, they exercise the most power over other family members. This has led to the control of women and children by men. Some feminists suggest this power imbalance and control leads to domestic violence when family members resist. The conflict approach maintains that the capitalist system creates family relations that mirror inequality in the large society.

The interactionism perspective examines the family at a more microsociological level than either functionalism or the conflict approach. Rather than seeing family roles as automatically adopted by family members as part of preexisting social structure, this approach contends that families and households operate on a system of expected behaviors that have been constructed from their day to day interactions (McLennan et al., 2000). Much work by symbolic interactionists focuses on socialization and gender roles. For example, symbolic interactionists might examine how gender role conceptions influence the boundaries of spousal responsibilities or how male and female children may be treated differently. Also, socialization is viewed as a reciprocal process in which parents guide children's social development and adjustment while they are socialized into the role of parent. These daily interactions between family members are how each individual family is formed and maintains its internal order.

TABLE 10.2. Theoretical Perspectives on Marriage and Family

Theoretical Perspectives

	Structural Functionalism	Conflict Approach	Interactionist Approach
Marriage	The social value of marriage encourages couples to marry. Marriage is the foundation of the family unit, which is needed to fulfill its social functions. Therefore, marriage should be encouraged. Other institutions reinforce the value of marriage by offering cooperative rules and practices. There are more than 2,000 legal benefits marriage in the U.S. including tax advantages.	The institution of marriage is designed to replicate the larger social economic conditions. A man essentially takes a wife as chattel—his possession. He puts a ring on her finger to show is possession and she will take his name at marriage further solidifying his control.	Marriage is a social reality negotiated between two people using symbols. Engagement parties and engagement rings act as highly visible symbols that establish the social acknowledged relationship between the engaged couple.
Family	The family is an important social institution for socializing younger members of society and reproduction. The family is necessary for the transmission of social values, beliefs, and norms, which are key factors in stabilizing society and maintaining social order.	Families are arrangements that reproduce the economic relations in the larger society. This is played out within the family as patriarchal control. The father-husband has his wife and children adhere to family "rules" and "ideology" that reinforces his dominance.	Through daily interactions, family members create a negotiated reality—a shared understanding of what your "family" is—which sets boundaries for each family member's roles, fostering social regularity in the context of the family.

The Bottom Line

It is clear that the family is an essential thread in our larger complex social fabric. For many societies, the family is formed through marriage. We have seen that there are a variety of marriage patterns available in many cultures, but monogamy is the preferred marriage form worldwide. There is tremendous variation in how the cultures of the world define marriage and structure their families. In the United States, there have been profound changes in the arrangement of families and even considerable debate about marriage and how that is defined.

Shifts in demographics, economic conditions, and social attitudes have given rise to a number of different, flexible, and practical family patterns. While some lament the bygone days of "the family" and fear that its changing complexion is a harbinger of the end of civilization, others see these changes as necessary adaptations to a changing society. Families are not in danger: they are thriving, and they are as meaningful as ever. American households have never been more diverse, more baffling, or more accepted. Because there are so many different living arrangements, most people will pass through several different types in the course of their lives.

The last sixty years have brought about significant change in family patterns. Specifically, the second wave of the women's movement has had a profound influence on the complexion of the family. Women seeking more education and career stability have been delaying age at first marriage, age at birth of first child, and are having fewer children. The increased economic power of women along with changes in no-fault divorce laws make exiting a bad marriage easier. While divorce rates peaked in 1981, they have been falling steadily ever since, but not terribly fast.

There was also a shift in our attitudes toward marriage. Those of the boomer generation transformed the meaning of marriage away from duty and obligation to an institution in which one finds self-fulfillment and gratification, from the marriage of *we* to the marriage for *me*. Some social critics have pointed out that among past generations, spouses felt an obligation to the marriage and the larger community. Now, they say if one spouse or both don't find personal happiness in the marriage, they just divorce. These changing attitudes toward marriage and divorce have led some to speculate that many see marriage as disposable.

The changing face of the American family is evident from just these few statistical profiles I have presented below. Today, we are:

- Marrying later, staying single longer
- Choosing not to marry at all, even when there are minor children involved
- Cohabitating in record numbers
- Forming a greater variety of family arrangements
- Having smaller families (the average number of people per household dropped from 3.1 in 1970 to 2.5 in 2013)

- Having fewer children (average number of children per family in 1970 was 1.3; that dropped to 0.9 children per family in 2013)

While divorce is slowly declining, it is still a common event, leaving many to remarry. While the number of first marriages is at a low point, remarriage is still as popular as ever. Fully 84% of those who divorce will remarry. Most of them remarry in five years or less; men are faster to return to the altar than are women. Even though divorce rates are down overall, they are on the rise for those fifty and older. Older, better-educated, wealthier Americans are experiencing a gray divorce boom.

In the historical long view, the functions of the family have changed. We no longer expect the family to be a unit of economic production *and* consumption. The family is no longer responsible for educating the young, and even religious instruction is conducted largely in the community. However, if we look at the great many changes in the demographics of the family in the past sixty years, we still expect the family to perform some basic functions. We certainly expect the family to socialize the young, provide physical, emotional, and financial support for its members, and provide us with a place in the world. While there may still be the expectation of having children within the context of a marriage, this requirement of the family is becoming increasingly less important.

Figure Credits

Fig. 10.1: "Man with Multiple Wives," https://commons.wikimedia.org/wiki/Category:Polygamy#/media/File:Rua_Kenana_and_four_of_his_wives.jpg. Copyright in the Public Domain.

Fig. 10.2: Henry M. Trotter, "Extended Family," https://commons.wikimedia.org/wiki/File:Coloured-family.jpg. Copyright in the Public Domain.

Fig. 10.3: Copyright © Rcragun (CC BY-SA 4.0) at https://commons.wikimedia.org/wiki/File:Marriage_and_Divorce_Rates_1960-2011.png.

CHAPTER 11

EDUCATION AND RELIGION

Too Good to Be True?

When asked to name the surest way to get ahead in America, the vast majority of people respond with education. I know in my family, education was seen as the path out of the working class. My father was a tenth-grade dropout who would use any occasion to stress the need for an education. Honestly, part of me was afraid not to get an education for fear my father would hunt me down and berate me or worse. But this nearly sacred belief that education is a pathway to social mobility was betrayed by Corinthian College Inc. (CCI), a for-profit collection of colleges that is now defunct. Thousands of students filled with the hope of a better life enrolled at Everest University, Wyo Tech, and Heald College, schools operated by CCI, only to have those dreams dashed and find themselves in tremendous debt. Preying on potential students' deeply held belief in education as a sort of up elevator to financial, occupational, and social success, CCI has been accused of grade manipulation, bogus job placement statistics, using false and predatory advertisements, and mismanaging billions of dollars of federal financial aid. Using the slogan "Get in. Get out. Get Ahead." CCI appealed to the working poor and single-parent households that wanted to get an education to improve their lives without having to attend a traditional college.

CCI focused on the money. CCI typically lured students by claiming a 100 percent job placement rate for its graduates; once students were enrolled, CCI employees would focus on maxing out students' financial aid. They used tactics that forced many students into loan debt without exploring

Fig. 11.1 College attendance is becoming more common among Americans. Most people in the U.S. see higher education as the path to the middle class and a higher standard of living.

other financing or class options that could have avoided the debt. Additionally, CCI's recruiters and counselors guaranteed employment even if it was unrealistic. One student in Georgia, for example, spent two years and thousands of dollars studying medical billing only to find out before graduation that her criminal record prohibited her from ever working in the medical or billing industry. Her advisors failed to mention this to her (Kieler, 2014). There are hundreds of horror stories about CCI students who were misled, lied to, and defrauded. Many have been left with thousands of dollars in school debt, course credits that are nontransferable, and degrees that are worthless.

How did so many students fall victim to this educational scam? The reason that CCI was so successful is because it tapped into several elements of our culture: the belief that education is the pathway to success, a growing social sentiment that a college education should be career directed as opposed to education directed. That is, a college education should prepare you for a job, not waste your time with frivolous classes like sociology. CCI's recruiters and counselors promised better jobs, more income, and improved standards of living. The allure of a college degree and all the social benefits that go along with it is too hard to resist, especially for those who can see the American dream but can't touch it. These opportunities sounded too good to be true for many students, because they were (Lagemann and Lewis, 2012).

The Symbolic Nature of Education

Education is viewed by many Americans as the single best way to obtain the American dream. People simply believe that getting an education will improve their lives by giving them access to better jobs, higher incomes, and a bit of social respect. I teach at a community college, which has an open enrollment policy. That means if you have a few minutes to fill out the admission application and can afford the reasonable registration fees, you can be a college student. Open enrollment colleges have reduced barriers to higher education for many underrepresented groups for decades. Community colleges then, serve as a symbol of access to higher education for many who might have otherwise believed college to be out of reach. The overwhelming majority of my students are seeking a better life through education. Education has become a symbol of social success, and we have made access to it wide ranging, from public schools to community colleges, junior colleges, technical colleges, private and public colleges and universities, and even for-profit schools like CCI. The brief success of CCI was due to what it symbolized—access to the American dream. While access to education in the United States is abundant and all good evidence indicates that more education is correlated with more income and social prestige, the story of CCI acts as a cautionary tale of the cost of social success through education. *Caveat emptor*—buyer beware.

An Extremely Brief History of Public Education in the United States

For millennia people relied on the experiences of daily life as their source of education. Watching parents and other members of the community labor, hunt, cook, and care for the young, their instruction came from those in their social environments. There was no need for a specialized institution of education. Until recently in our history nearly all, except those of the upper classes, followed this same tradition. However, as many Western nations like the United States transitioned from the traditional agrarian to more complex industrialized and urbanized societies, the social institution of education emerged.

Early education in America tended to serve to maintain certain religious beliefs. In Puritan New England, education arose as a way to teach everyone to read the Bible in order to save their eternal souls. Later in post-Revolutionary America, education became the pathway to a literate electorate; it would take an educated citizenry to govern themselves. While usually at odds politically, John Adams and Thomas Jefferson, the second and third presidents of the United States respectively, both agreed that their new nation needed a tax-funded system of public education (Butts, 1978; Goldin and Katz, 1999; Goldin, 1998).

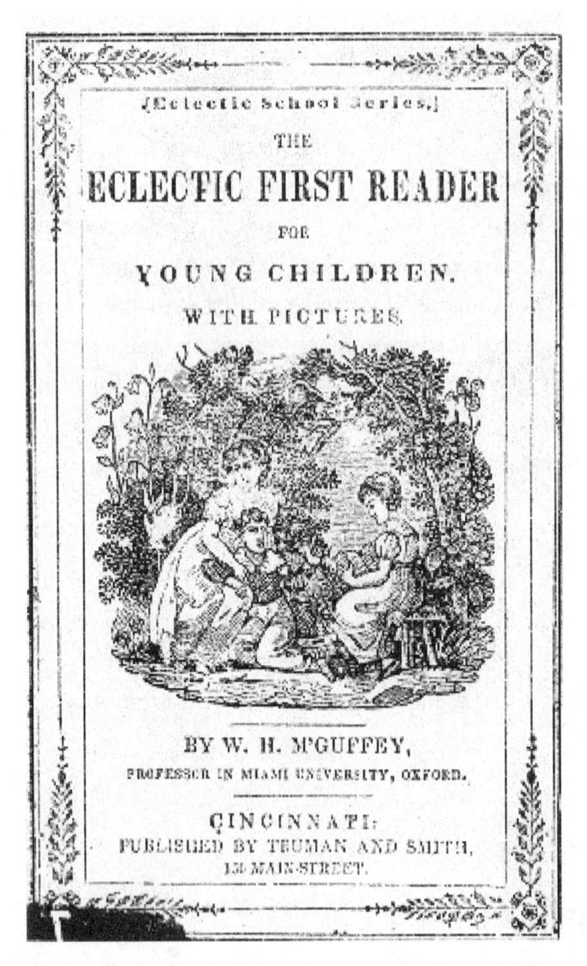

[Eclectic School Series.]

THE

ECLECTIC FIRST READER

FOR

YOUNG CHILDREN.

WITH PICTURES.

BY W. H. M'GUFFEY,

PROFESSOR IN MIAMI UNIVERSITY, OXFORD.

CINCINNATI:

PUBLISHED BY TRUMAN AND SMITH,

[illegible] MAIN-STREET.

Fig. 11.2 The McGuffey readers attempted to reinforce the values, beliefs, and norms of their time. Do today's textbooks do the same thing?

The textbooks used in early American education emphasized nationalism, patriotism, and American heroes, an attempt at nation building (Nash, 2009). As more and more immigrants began arriving in America, education became a tool for cultural indoctrination. Education was an important way for newcomers to "melt" into the American "pot." One highly visible element of education in the mid-nineteenth century was the McGuffey Reader. This primitive textbook stressed morality, sobriety, and diligence as the essential traits of American citizens. These readers also pointed out the value of education as a pathway to social mobility. Overall, these books showed their readers the importance of embracing American values, beliefs, and behaviors in order to ensure social acceptance and success (Westerhoff, 1978; Mosier, 1947; Cubberley, 2013).

Despite the fact that mass education was taking root and spreading by the early 1900s, most poor Americans and much of the immigrant populations did not attend or graduate high school. These children had to leave school to help support their families financially. However, as child labor laws improved and child labor decreased, school attendance increased (Tyack and Cuban, 1995). Public mass education was successful and becoming increasingly functional for a society that was rapidly modernizing. Over the past several decades, literacy rates, school attendance, and high school graduation rates in the United States have steadily increased. In fact, the high school graduation rate for the 2012–2013 school year was 82 percent, an all-time high (see figure 11.4) (US Department of Education, "The Condition of Education: Public High School Graduation Rates," 2016). Along with more students finishing high school, fewer than ever are dropping out (see figure 11.5). In 2013 just 7 percent of high school students dropped out, a record low (Fry, 2014).

EDUCATION FOR THE UPPER CLASSES

Access to an exclusive, rigorous education based on social class membership has a long history in the United States. Before the American Revolution ended, many of today's most prestigious preparatory schools had been established for the sons of wealthy colonists. Schools such as Phillips Exeter Academy and Phillips Academy Andover were established in 1787 and 1781 respectively. They served to prepare early American elites for the rigors of Ivy League universities like Yale and Harvard, and they continue that tradition even today. Exeter was for most of its existence a "feeder" school for Harvard, while Andover grads went to Yale. To this day the graduates of these elite schools are far more likely to attend an Ivy League or highly selective private college than any other type of college or university (Staff Writers, 2012). These "prep" schools were insular, the bastion of upper-class, white maleness, not admitting female students and becoming coeducational until the early 1970s. These schools are also exceedingly monochromatic, with an average of 80 percent of their student bodies being white (Reardon and Yun, 2002).

Fig. 11.3 Picture of the grounds of an elite prep school

Social and political power becomes concentrated in those that attend these elite schools; their social advantages are legion. Students at these schools rub shoulders with future leaders of financial markets, industry, and politics. It shouldn't surprise you that alumni of these two schools include past presidents of the United States, secretaries of state, members of Congress, attorneys general, and several notable writers and thinkers. For example, Mark Zuckerberg, Facebook's cofounder, attended Exeter. Their educational experiences allow them to amass copious amounts of cultural, social, and financial capital and to enhance their life chances. In a sense there are two tiers of education in America. At the top is an elite tier of private, well-endowed, architecturally stunning schools situated on park-like settings in which the power and dominance of wealthy whites is maintained and reproduced. Below this is a second, less well-founded tier, built for the utility of mass education and subject to the decay of much of America's infrastructure—public schools. Besides what I have discussed above, can you think of other advantages of attending elite prep schools?

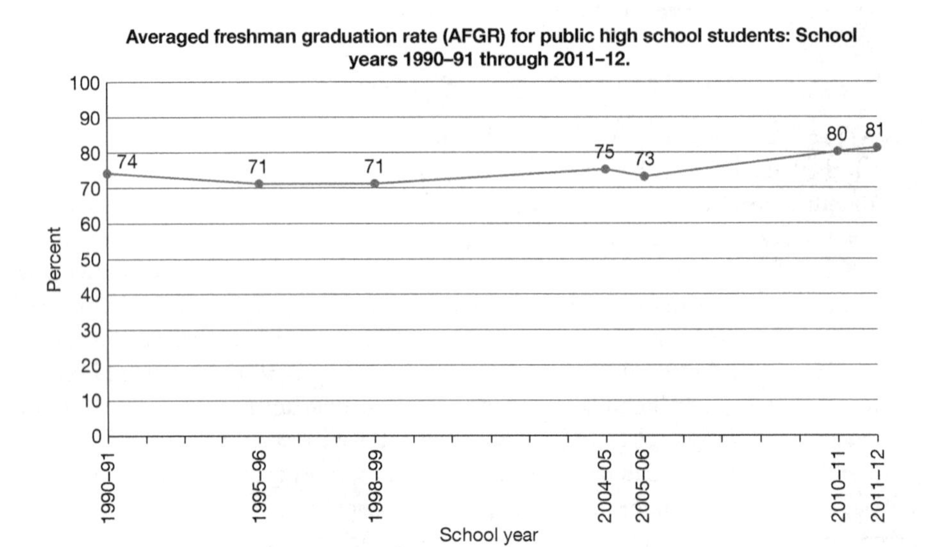

Fig. 11.4 High school graduation rates, 1990–2013

Mass education in the United States has been successful for a number of reasons. It took children out of the workplace and gave them hope and opportunity. Mass education created generations of literate citizens who were better prepared to take part in the modernizing workplace. It helped elevate generations of Americans out of poverty and inform generations of voters. To a large extent public education in the United States has accomplished many of the functions our forefathers envisioned it would.

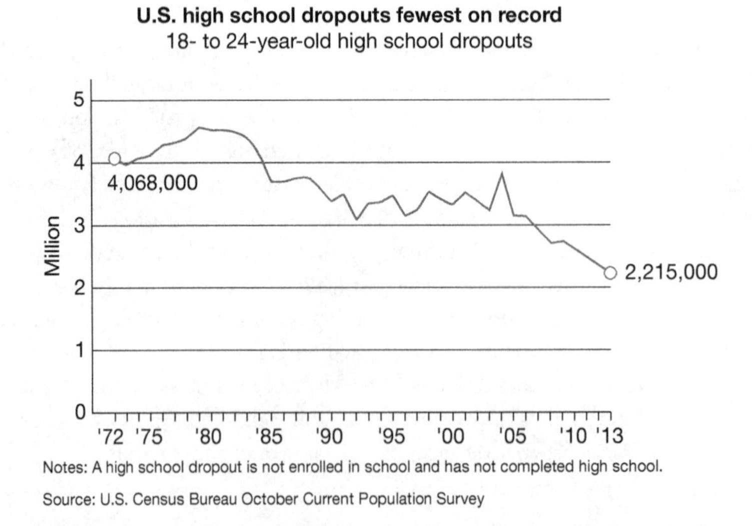

Fig. 11.5 Dropout rates, 1993–2013

Today's educational system faces new criticisms and challenges. In a highly technical postindustrial economy, there is a demand for greater amounts of education beyond high school with more technical skills. Public education is under greater scrutiny with regard to inadequacies such as preparing students for college, equality of opportunity, and the achievement gap (we'll discuss this in detail later in the chapter).

Education Is a Social Institution

Education is an important element of all societies. Every individual's education begins at birth. Parents, family, and friends are sources of informal education for children the world over. We learn a great deal about our social world, interpersonal interactions, and self-identity from those around us in our early years. At some point, however, we enter the education system, the formal source of education.

When describing any social institution in sociology, we typically focus on its structure and function and the change in both. Like many other topics in this book, the area of education is wide ranging and impossible to cover comprehensively in a single chapter. So our discussion of the social institution of education will include an examination of its structure (what it looks like); its function (what purpose it serves in society); the change in both of these; how it creates, maintains, and reproduces social inequality; and how it is perceived and acts as a mechanism of social mobility.

Structure of Education: How Are Schools Configured in the United States?

While there is some variation, generally in the United States, public education is structured fairly uniformly. Most students attend an elementary school, which typically includes kindergarten through sixth grade. This can be followed by middle school, junior high school, or a combined junior/senior high school (see figure 11.6). Junior high schools (grouping seventh, eighth, and ninth grades) are less popular now; many states switched to the middle school configuration (grouping either fifth through eighth grades or sixth through eighth grades). In fact, between 1970 and 2000, the number of middle schools in the United States ballooned from 1,500 to 11,500 (Rockoff and Lockwood, 2010). Research begun in the early 1960s indicated that the earlier maturation of students (onset of puberty) was a major factor in the change in grade grouping configurations (Myers, 1970; Hillyer, 1972). Other studies found that grouping grades six through eight was beneficial for students because it put students who are similar in terms of physical, social, psychological, and intellectual abilities together. Smith and Brantly's research showed

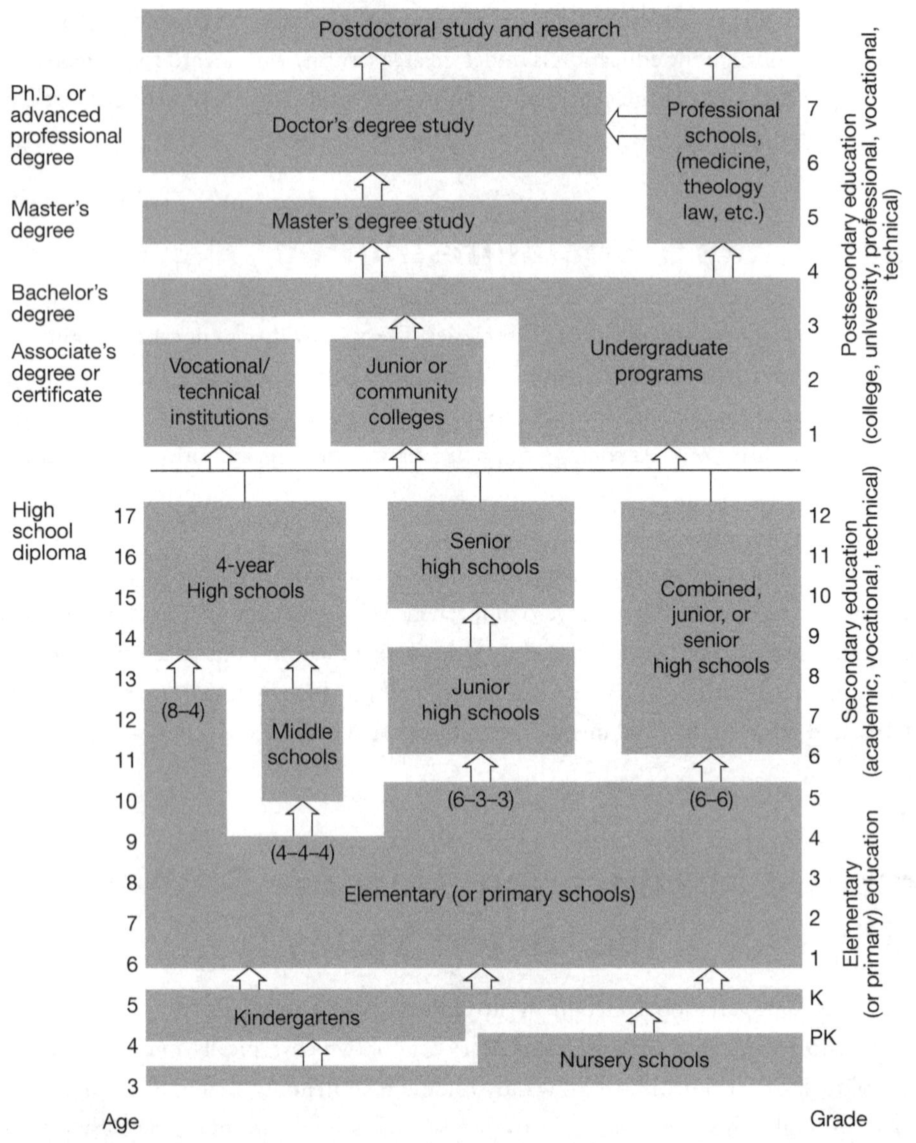

Fig. 11.6 The figure above shows the typical patterns of progression through the education structure of the United States.

that students had better reading, math, and science scores in middle schools (sixth through eighth grades) (Combs, 2008). Growing up in New Hampshire in the mid-1970s, I attended a junior high school that included seventh, eighth, and ninth grades only.

The times, they are a changing. In the past few years the school districts in about a dozen states have challenged the middle school model. Rockoff and Lockwood (2010) have shown that students who transition to a middle school in sixth grade experience significant declines in math and English scores compared to their fellow classmates who stay in a K–8 elementary school arrangement. Moreover, it is not just a matter of adjusting to the transition to middle school. We tend not to see a "rebound" in the academic performance of those who transition to middle school; their lower academic achievement persists throughout middle school. It's not just academic performance that suffers when kids transition to middle schools; their attendance decreases compared to those who stayed in a K–8 school.

Why do we see these differences? Some explanations put forth by these researchers include level of parental resources or the socioeconomic status of students' families and the size of the class making the transition. Students who come from backgrounds with few educational resources may fare worse when transitioning to middle school than more affluent students. And the size of your incoming class or cohort seems to have a significant effect on middle school academic performance. That is, if you started middle school with two hundred other sixth graders, your academic performance suffered more than if you started your middle school experience with seventy-five other sixth graders (Yecke, 2005). Can you remember your middle school experience? Did you experience similar effects? What explanations for these differences would you suggest?

Most high schools in the United States include ninth through twelfth grades, although some have just grades ten, eleven, and twelve (like my hometown high school did). Still, some school districts combine all grades (K–12) in a single school. While there is very little debate over high school configuration, relative to the firestorm surrounding middle schools, of the top ten–rated high schools in the United States in 2015, nine of them consisted of grades nine to twelve. That doesn't necessarily mean the nine-to-twelve configuration created great schools, it's just that there are far more configured that way, and the odds were that the best schools would be in that configuration. High schools in large part prepare students for college, but this can vary by region, social class, gender, and race/ethnicity. In October 2014 slightly more than 68 percent of all 2014 high school graduates in the United States were enrolled in colleges or universities (Bureau of Labor Statistics, "College Enrollment," 2015).

However, if you are a student of color, male, and live in the rural South or the inner city, you are more likely to go into the workforce after high school than to attend college. For some, high school was a cherished time; for others, an experience to forget. Either way, don't worry; I focus on higher education in this chapter for several reasons. First, I'm a college professor. Second, you are a college student. Higher education is important, immediate, and relevant for both you and me.

Homeschooling

When I was growing up, I didn't know of any kids who were homeschooled, but the number of homeschooled children in the United States has grown in the past few decades. During the 2011–2012 academic year, there were about 1.77 million homeschooled children, which represents about 3.4 percent of all school-aged children (Broughman and Swaim, 2013). There are stark differences between races among homeschoolers in the United States. About 83 percent of all homeschooled children are white, 7 percent Hispanic, 5 percent black, and nearly 2 percent identify as Asian or Pacific Islander (US Department of Education, "Fast Facts," 2015). While the common perception is that Christians or religious families are more likely to homeschool, recent research indicates that Christian homeschoolers are now in the minority among all homeschooling families (Medlin, 2013; Ray, 2010; 2013).

The reasons why parents choose to homeschool their kids and who is homeschooling have changed in the past two decades. While once perceived as something that religious fundamentalists did, only about 36 percent of homeschool parents said that providing "religious or moral instruction" was the most important reason they keep their kids out of school. Concerns over their children's safety was central for a majority of homeschooling parents, with 91 percent of them claiming issues over the school's environment was an important reason for homeschooling. Parents who homeschool are an increasingly diverse group, including a growing number who are well-educated and well-off. Homeschooling families in the U.S. are not a monolithic group, rather they are more ethnically and economically diverse than ever (Bielick and Chandler, 2001; Ray, 2009).

Unfortunately, homeschooling regulation is wide ranging; in the United States, these regulations vary from state to state. In some states, in order to homeschool, you must hold at least a high school diploma, your curriculum must be approved, and you must test your kids regularly. In other states you don't have to notify anyone that you are keeping your children at home for schooling.

So much of a child's social adjustment is influenced by the school environment. Because public school is such a common experience for the majority of Americans, the greatest criticism aimed at homeschooling has been the perceived deficit in socialization. That is, many people think that isolated homeschooled children will lack the social skills needed to adequately adjust to the larger social world. In order to address this criticism, many homeschool families join homeschool "districts" that allow them to engage in athletic competition and hold proms. Many homeschoolers who transition to college may have played on a homeschool football team, competed in debates with other homeschoolers, and taken their sweetheart to the homeschool prom. The homeschooling environment is changing, and the number of homeschooled kids is growing, making homeschooling a permanent element of our educational landscape.

Higher Education

If you are reading this textbook, you are most likely taking a college-level introductory sociology class. You could be at a community college, a state college or university, or a private college or university. Your class may be face-to-face or online. Regardless of where you are taking your class or what type of class you're enrolled, in there is tremendous access to higher education in the United States. In 2014 there were 20.6 million college students in the United States, which is a record number (US Department of Education, "The Condition of Education," 2015). Getting a college degree is increasingly seen as a necessity for anyone who wants to maintain or rise to middle-class status and enjoy the American dream. However, this was not always the case. In 1947 there were just over 2 million people enrolled in colleges and universities in the United States, compared to nearly 21 million today; that's just about ten times as many (US Department of Education, "The Condition of Education," 2014). I know what you are thinking—the population in 2014 was more than double the population in 1947. True. However, the proportion of the population that were college students in 1947 was a mere 1.5% compared to 6.5% in 2014. Either way you look at it more people are in college now than ever before and they look very different from the college students of a generation ago.

THERE'S AN APP FOR THAT

Having a hard time balancing your budget at college? Mint is an app that can help you with that. All your accounts are in one location, and it tracks all your transactions, keeping a real-time eye on your budget (Intuit Inc., 2016).

- iHomework is a virtual organizer that lets you keep life on track by organizing your schedule, homework, papers, teachers, and classes. It will even notify you when assignments are due and what your professor's favorite food is (I made that part up, but it's a good idea) (Pilone, 2015).
- WiFi Finder: Do I really have to describe this (JiWire Inc., 2013)?

The Demographics of Higher Education

Who goes to college? The image of the "traditional" college student as an affluent, white, middle-class male aged eighteen to twenty-four is a thing of the past. The student body of colleges and universities around the country are changing (see figure 11.7). In fact, the University of California

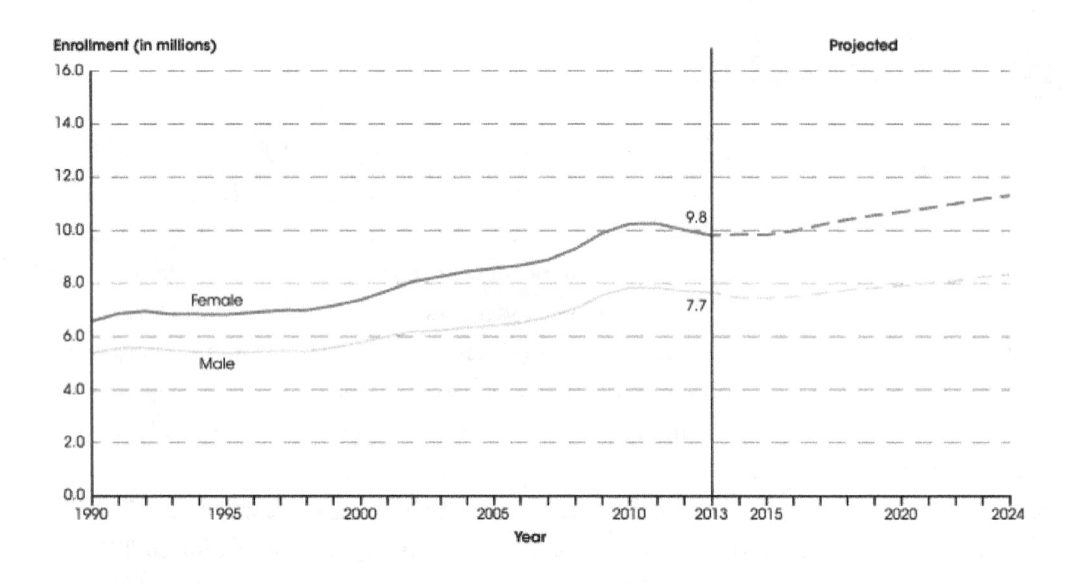

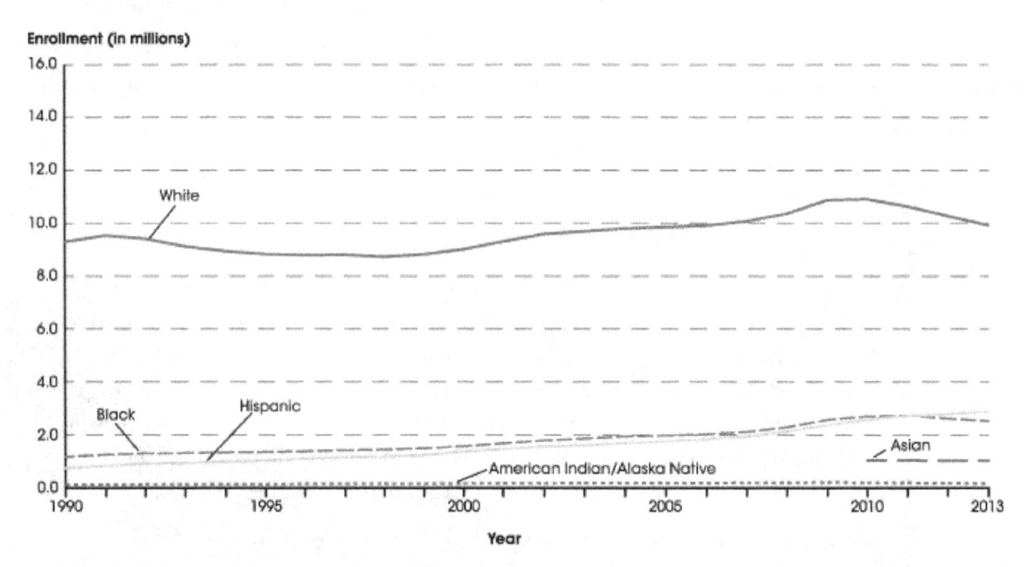

Fig. 11.7 Graphs (a) above and (b) below both show the change in college enrollment by gender and race in the 100 plus years.

(UC) system announced that for the 2014 academic year, it admitted more Latino students (29 percent) than white students (27 percent) (UC Office of the President, 2014). College students today are overwhelmingly female, and minority college students along with older students and first-generation (first-gen) college goers are all on the rise, changing the complexion of college campuses all over the country.

Gender

The gender of college students has definitely changed. In 1947 women made up just 29 percent of all college students, but today they represent 57 percent of all college goers. Additionally, women are about three times more likely to graduate from college than their male counterparts. Women are more likely than men to graduate with a bachelor's degree, and in a shorter amount of time than men (Lewin, 2006). Women, however, are less likely to pursue degrees in science, technology, engineering, and math than are men. While women represent the majority of undergraduate students in the United States, their numbers decline significantly if we look at enrollments in medical schools, law schools, and dental schools (Contorno, 2014).

Race and Ethnicity

Despite the lingering urban myth—and contrary to what then senator Barack Obama said in a speech to the NAACP in 2007—there are not more black men in prison than there are in college. In 2013 there were 1.4 million black men enrolled in college and about 516,900 black men incarcerated (Carson, 2015). While college enrollment for blacks in the United States has skyrocketed in the past few decades, their presence at top tier colleges and universities is actually down since 1994 (Krogstad and Fry, 2014; Rothwell, 2015). Why do we see a surge in college enrollment among blacks overall but an underrepresentation among top tier schools? Tougher admission requirements at top schools, which emphasize superior performance on standardized tests, put many potential black students at a disadvantage, and high school counselors are far more likely to steer black students to community or state colleges than toward highly selective schools. Perhaps the most influential barrier to black admission to top tier schools is institutional discrimination. Some research has shown that the schools themselves are complicit in maintaining barriers to admission for minorities (Carnevale and Strohl, 2013).

From 1976 to 2012 Hispanics, Asian Americans, and blacks all experienced a dramatic rise in college attendance. Alternately, the white college student population during the same period decreased from 84 percent to 60 percent. The greatest gains have been among Hispanics, who now represent 19 percent of U.S. college students, while blacks make up about 14 percent. While more and more minority students are going to college, they are less likely than their white counterparts to complete their degrees. Asian American college students are a notable exception; they are more likely than any other minority group to complete a college degree (Ogunwole, Drewery, and Rios-Vargas, 2012). Sometimes referred to as the "model minority" (because of their perceived educational, social, and economic success), Asian Americans, it should be noted, are not a monolithic minority group. Within the Asian American population there are wide variations in college attendance and completion. South Asians (students of Indian, Pakistani, and Bangladeshi descent) as a group are highly successful in college, while other groups like the

Hmong, Laotians and Cambodians in the United States rarely attend college (Krupnick, 2015). Whites, on the other hand, represent three out of every four students completing a bachelor's degree. What would be some sociological explanations for these differences?

Social Class

Most college graduates in the United States come from upper- or middle-class family backgrounds. But this too is changing. First-gen college students—students whose parents did not pursue any postsecondary education—are on the rise, but they face a number of obstacles. Most first-gen college goers are disproportionately overrepresented among the most disadvantaged economic groups—the poor, low-income families, and racial minorities—who have no experience with the admissions process or financial aid. First-gens typically do not enroll in college directly out of high school, need academic help, and are less likely to finish their degrees than their more affluent non-first-gen classmates (Balemian and Feng, 2013). First-gens are more likely than their non-first-gen counterparts to have financial hardships apart from the cost of college, be a minority, be older, be married, need remediation, work while attending college, and be less prepared for college (Engle, 2007; Saenz et al., 2007; Chen, 2005; Choy, 2001). Many delay college because they need to work to help their family financially, making many of them older than "traditional" students when they start college. Most come from impoverished or underserved communities and high schools and are not prepared for the rigors of college. While more affluent students see college as an extension of their life experience and a path to independence, first-gens are more likely to view a college degree as an instrument to improve their family's circumstances. Even with all these challenges and obstacles, those who come from families who have no experience with higher education see a college degree as a way to improve their standard of living.

These students can't ask their parents for advice about what college they should attend, what to major in, or what classes to take. Up until very recently, they have essentially been on their own, in a strange environment surrounded by people they have no social connection to. I know; I am a first-gen who came from a poor background, and when I got to college I was lost and lonely. Not because I was away from home, but because I was among others whose life experiences were so very different from mine. First-gens on many college campuses have formed first-gen organizations, not so much for others to gain awareness of them but for them to own their identity and support one another. For example, Ana Barros, a first-gen at Harvard, heads the Harvard First Generation Student Union, which is only two years old. She expressed her feelings about being a first-gen this way: "This is a movement, we are not ashamed of taking on this identity" (Pappano, 2015). If you're a first-gen college student, check out I'm First at www.imfirst.org. It's an online community that supports and celebrates first-gens.

Age

People of all ages attend college. I have had students in my classes who ranged from sixteen to seventy-five years old. While the majority of currently enrolled college students are of "traditional" college age (eighteen to twenty-four years old), nearly 40 percent are classified as "adult learners"—a college student who is twenty-five or older (National Student Clearinghouse, 2012). Many of those adult learners are accessing community colleges, for-profit colleges and universities, and public four-year colleges, and they are increasingly first-gen college students (Giancola, Munz, and Trares, 2008). While the majority of college student bodies are composed of students of "traditional" age, there are more and more older students finding their way to college—some for the first time, some returning to continue an interrupted degree, and some who see a college degree as a path to a promotion or a better life. I have noticed that when I walk on campus at the large urban university where I teach, students defer to me, and other (I assume) faculty members greet me as a peer. However, when I walk around the campus of the community college I teach at, people are unsure of my status because the student body is much more age diverse. Next time you see some old guy walking across campus, don't assume he's a professor; he may, like you, be headed to his next class.

TRY THIS

Look around at your classmates in all your classes and notice the racial, age, and gender compositions. What is the composition of your sociology class versus a science or engineering class (if you are taking one)? Do they look like you? That is, are they similar to you in age, race/ethnicity, and gender, or are they very different?

Is a College Degree Worth It?

It's not just the face of college student bodies that is changing; colleges themselves are changing, and so is the national dialogue about a college education. Today's college students have a wide variety of educational opportunities. Potential students can choose from junior colleges, community colleges, and public and private colleges and universities. There is also a growing number of for-profit schools that offer two-year degrees and bachelor's degrees that can be completed in less than four years (like ITT Tech). Many schools advertise programs that allow learners to go at their own pace and do course work on their own schedules—no need to show up for pesky face-to-face classes, get your degree online. Schools like the University of Phoenix offer associate, bachelor's, and master's degrees completely online. However, these for-profits are not alone; major universities now offer online degrees. Penn State, Arizona State University, the University of North Dakota, and Drexel University all offer online degrees (*U.S. News & World Report*, 2015). You can earn a degree from any of these universities without having to set foot on their campuses. You don't even have to be in the same state or for that matter the same country to earn a degree. Even these big-name schools recognize the demand for online educational access.

The rise of for-profit schools, accelerated degree programs (both traditional and online), and wholly online degree programs reflects changing student demographics, economic conditions and reevaluation of the necessity of a traditional liberal arts education. During the economic downturn of 2007–2012, community colleges like the one where I teach saw a dramatic rise in enrollment, as did other technical and vocational schools, as displaced workers attempted to "retool" themselves. They were looking for fast ways to get degrees or certificates so they would be more "employable." During this same period, a number of colleges offered three-year bachelor's degrees to reduce the cost of a college education (Hopkins, 2012). Interestingly, those with college degrees fared better during the economic downturn than those with a high school diploma or less (US Department of Education, "Employment Rates," 2015).

Recently, there has been a rising national dialogue that pits a liberal arts education against majors that prepare students for careers and hopefully ensure employment. For instance, Bill Gates implied in a speech he gave to the National Governors Association that states were wasting taxpayer money by supporting academic majors at public universities that don't contribute to jobs of the future. Never fear, you majors of sociology, psychology, and the liberal arts; research indicates that in terms of your future income, you will catch up with those who majored in jobs of the future about ten years after graduation (Kolowich, 2011; Ross et al., 2012). So, whatever you choose to major in, getting a degree is worth it in the long run. In fact, economist Susan Dynarski (2012) testified to the U.S. Senate Finance Committee in 2011 and had this to say about a college education:

> *A college education is one of the best investments a young person can make. Even with record high tuition prices, a bachelor's degree pays for itself several times over, in the form of higher income, lower unemployment, better health and enhanced civic engagement. Within ten years of college graduation, the typical BA will already have recouped the cost of her investment.*

Moreover, a study from the Pew Research Center found that an overwhelming majority of college graduates said that given what they and their families have invested in their education, it was worth it (DeSilver, "5 Facts", 2014). Clearly, a college education is valuable, and it is certainly perceived as being necessary in today's world (see figure 11.8). As discussed above, college student demographics are changing, and as a society, we are becoming more educated. In fact, as of 2014, about 34 percent of all U.S. adults aged twenty-five to twenty-nine had earned a bachelor's degree or higher. However, not all groups in the United States have enjoyed this level of academic success. Some racial minorities and the poor have not seen the same academic achievement of whites and the more affluent, and the differences between these groups begin early and have a cumulative and lasting effect on college enrollment and completion.

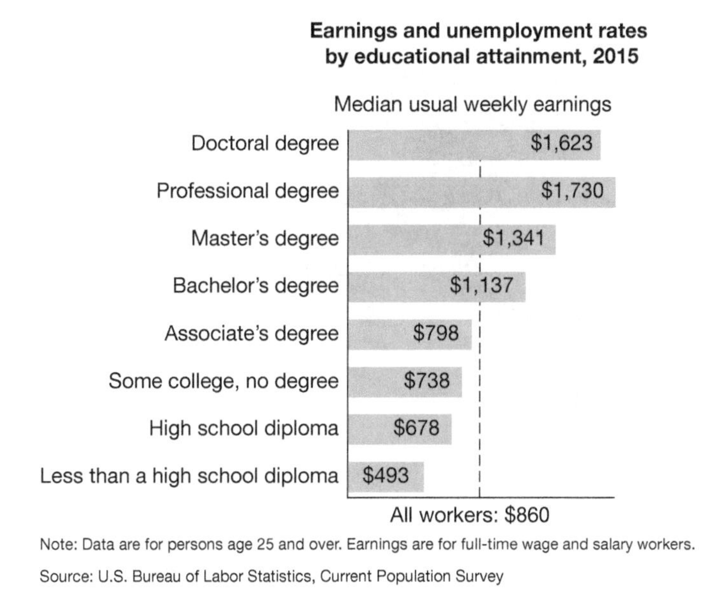

Fig. 11.8 Chart showing the relationship between income and level of education

The Achievement Gap in Education

The achievement gap refers to the differences in observed academic performance between groups of students, most often defined by socioeconomic status and race/ethnicity. This gap is commonly measured using standardized tests, grade point averages, dropout rates, college enrollment, and completion rates.

As a college education has grown more valuable, it has also grown more unequally distributed. Children born in the poorest quarter of the income distribution are unlikely to earn a bachelor's degree; just 9 percent manage to do so. In the richest quarter of the income distribution, 54 percent

Disparity among Millennials Ages 25–32 By Education Level in Terms of Annual Earnings ...

(*median among full-time workers, in* 2012 *dollars*)

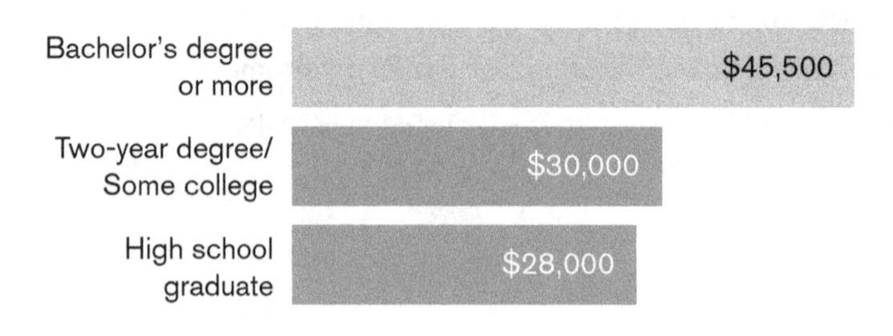

Unemployment Rate ...

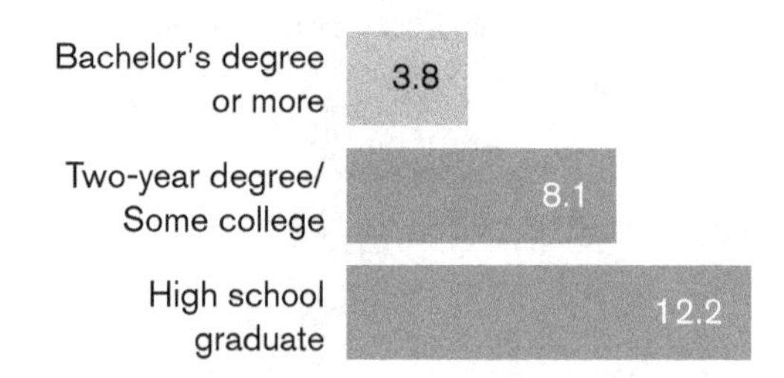

And Share Living in Poverty ...

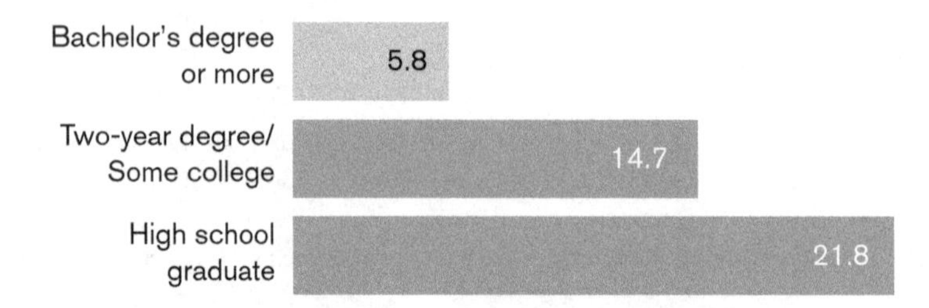

Notes: Median annual earnings are based on earnings and work status during the calendar year prior to interview and limited to 25- to 32-year-olds who worked full time during the previous calendar year and reported positive earnings. "Full time" refers to those who usually worked at least 35 hours a week last year. The unemployment rate refers to the share of the labor force (those working or actively seeking work) who are not employed. Poverty is based on the respondent's family, income in the calendar year preceding the survey.

Source: Pew Research centertabulations of the 2013 March Current Population Survey (CPS) Integrated Public Use Micro Sample

Fig. 11.9 Earnings, unemployment, and living in poverty—the cost of not going to college of children go on to earn a bachelor's degree. Troublingly, this gap has increased substantially over the past twenty years (Bailey and Dynarski, 2011). This gap in educational attainment is enormous and translates into a significant gap in economic opportunity. Disparities of this magnitude in the educational outcomes of rich and poor children bode ill for our democratic society. Education has long been a vehicle for opportunity in our country, a path to prosperity for every class. This growing gap between rich and poor in educational attainment could act as a disincentive for less privileged groups, further restricting economic mobility (see figure 11.9).

READ MORE

- *What Is College For?* by Ellen Condliffe Lagemann and Harry Lewis (2012). A thoughtful, academic examination of higher education and its civil purpose. This book is a series of essays about the state of higher education in the United States, what its fundamental purpose is, and how it has strayed from that.
- *What's College For?* by Zachary Karabell (1998). This book, based on interviews of college students, staff, and faculty, examines the changing and conflicting expectations of these groups. Like the title asks, this book attempts to understand what college is for in our postindustrial modern society.

Manifest and Latent Functions of Education

All social institutions serve a number of functions in all societies; that's why they exist. Institutions arise in society to fulfill the needs of its people. All institutions serve both *manifest functions*—an institution's expected, intended, and recognized purpose—and *latent functions*—unintended and many times unexpected consequences of an institution's operation. Of course, over time these institutions and their functions transform as social needs, social attitudes, and technologies change.

The institution of education is no exception; it serves both manifest and latent functions. Below I briefly describe the commonly recognized functions of education.

- Perpetuate societies by *transmitting knowledge* from generation to generation. While we all learned basic academic subjects in school, we also learned about our culture. Through the process of education, we gain a wide range of knowledge about our society.

- Schools act as agents of *socialization*, teaching students not only academic subjects (manifest functions) but also necessary social skills needed for participation in the social world (latent functions), such as punctuality, courtesy, and cooperation (Durkheim, 1956; Parsons, 1959).
- Education helps with the *social integration* of individuals. That is, children need to internalize a common set of values and beliefs in order for them to integrate into social life. Learning to respect authority, believing in the value of hard work, being patriotic, and even speaking English are key to fitting in to our social world (Schildkraut, 2005).
- *Social control*. Schools teach adherence to rules and obedience to authority figures. Respect for other students, teachers, and the community (Pledge of Allegiance) are emphasized so that good students will become hardworking, tax-paying, law-abiding citizens.
- Institutions of higher education produce *social and cultural innovation*. Each year in the United States, billions of dollars are spent on research largely conducted at universities and colleges that results in new discoveries, inventions, and innovations. These forward leaps benefit both the scientific community and society at large (e.g., pharmaceuticals, genetics, and video games).
- One result of education is *social placement*. This refers to the process of matching students' academic performance with an appropriate curriculum. Grouping students based on academic abilities creates a hierarchy of academic achievement (e.g., tracking or ability grouping). Those at the top do well academically, and that translates to greater occupational, economic, and social success than those at the bottom of the academic hierarchy.

The concept of the **hidden curriculum**—beliefs, attitudes, and behaviors that are learned in school but are not part of the intended curriculum—is similar to Merton's (1949) idea of *latent* functions. However, the hidden curriculum typically refers to the process by which the dominant ideology and inequality are reproduced through education (Jackson, 1968). While latent functions of a public school education include things such as providing day care for working parents, understanding the structure and pace of a workday, learning how to socialize with peers, and later on finding potential mates; implied by its name, the hidden curriculum is more sinister. The differential treatment of males and females in schools reinforces gender inequality when teachers or coaches discourage girls from engaging in "boy" activities, and vice versa. And later in high school, girls may be steered away from "male" subjects like physics and higher math. School guidance counselors recommend "female" college majors such as social work or sociology for girls while guiding boys to majors like computer science and engineering. The institutional structure itself can reinforce ideas about traditional gender roles and gendered employment. The overwhelming majority of elementary school teachers are women, which may foster children's impressions that women are particularly suited for the care and instruction of young children (Reay, 2000, 2001).

It's not just gender inequality that is propagated by the hidden curriculum; messages about race and social class inequality are passed along during interactions among students and between faculty and students in schools every day. The standards of behavior at many public schools may impact minority students more than middle-class white students. Langhout and Mitchell (2008) found that Latinos, blacks, and males were more likely to be reprimanded than other students. This sends signals about who the troublemakers are and who "belongs in school," reinforcing racial stereotypes. This pattern of continuous reprimand also leads to academic disengagement and increased dropout rates among minorities, leading to difficulty with employment and lower earnings. That schools in high-income communities are better off than schools in low-income neighborhoods is no surprise. I taught high school before I went to graduate school, and I had an opportunity to teach in two economically distinctly different neighborhoods. I taught in a school in an area of Los Angeles that was exclusively African American and Latino. The students at that school had to share textbooks, which were outdated and missing pages and sometimes their covers. There was hardly any lab equipment, so we couldn't conduct any chemistry experiments; rather, I had to describe what we would do if we had equipment. Then I moved to a middle-class area of Pasadena, California, and taught at a high school there. Students there all had their own books, we had plenty of lab equipment, and there was new playground equipment as well. Even these material differences send messages about what groups are valued. More importantly it stressed that material deficits can profoundly impact students' educational experience and performance. Which group of students do you think will be best prepared for college?

Schools in economically distinct communities prepare students for different educational and occupational paths. Schools like the one in Pasadena encourage students to excel academically and prepare them for middle-class occupations, while schools like those in the Los Angeles neighborhood are simply trying to graduate as many students as they can. Many times students in these communities are encouraged to enter the workforce or the military right out of high school, rather than pursue a college education. The hidden curriculum, in effect, reinforces and reproduces systems of gender, racial, and class inequalities (Bowles and Gintis, 1976; Kozol, 2005).

Theoretical Perspectives on Education

Functionalism: Education Is Good for Society

You should be familiar with functionalism's take on things by now. Functionalism views education like it does other social institutions; a system that encourages conformity and promotes the adherence to conventional social values, beliefs, and practices, thereby creating social cohesion and stability. Mainly, education is seen as binding members of society together by teaching a common knowledge base and core cultural values and beliefs. Ultimately, functionalism sees education as a way to reproduce the status quo and maintain social stability by instilling in each student the need to conform to social norms, obey authority, and be a productive citizen.

Conflict Perspective: Education Is Good for the Powerful

In contrast to functionalism, which stresses consensus and cooperation between groups in order to maintain social order, conflict theory argues that dominant social classes use institutions like education to reproduce their ideology and class differences; for example, the use of a selective curriculum in public schools that emphasizes conformity and obedience to social rules. Students in public schools have limited resources relative to those who have access to elite prep schools. These two tiers of education reproduce class differences. Those with wealth and power have access to elite schools, which allow entrance to government, business, and military occupations, therefore solidifying their class positions. Meanwhile, the children of the less wealthy are prepared for less-prestigious and less-powerful occupations via public education.

Feminist Theory: Education Is Good, But Provides Unequal Treatment Of Males and Females

Similar to the conflict perspective, the feminist view of education stresses the reproduction of inequality. However, instead of social class, feminist theory focusses on the reproduction of gender inequality. Feminist theory argues that boys and girls are treated differently in schools. Young boys and girls taught not only that they are physically different, but that they are intellectually different and should pursue different educational and occupational paths and that they should expect different things out of life. Feminists contend that this is achieved in part through the use of a *gendered hidden curriculum.* Researchers have suggested that this gendered hidden curriculum is advanced in key ways (Heaton and Lawson, 1996; Hernández, Gonzáles, and Sánchez, 2013; Davis, Fuentes, and Sparkes, 2005):

- *Readings.* Textbooks portray women in stereotypically female roles such as caregiver and homemaker and depict them as dependent on men. Women figures in science, engineering, and the computer industry are absent. And men are prominently shown as leaders, scientists, and those with greater social status (Kelly, 1987).
- *Lack of positive/high-status role models.* While there may be many female teachers at the elementary level, their superiors, deans, assistant principals, and principals are far more likely to be men than women. Additionally, the male-to-female teacher ratio tilts toward males as students advance through middle and high school (Bitterman et al., 2013).

- *Teachers*. Subtly, teachers allocate classroom duties by gender; boys move desks around while girls wash up or tidy up common space. It has also been demonstrated that teachers are more likely to encourage independent problem solving among boys and dependence among girls (Jussim and Harber, 2005; Connell, 1996; McKnown and Weinstein, 2008).

These elements of the hidden curriculum, feminists argue, are instrumental in shaping students' perception of gender and gender roles in society at large, which in turn influence girls' and boys' decisions about how they should appear and act as well as what careers they should pursue. Thus, according to feminist theory, gendered academic pursuits, occupations, and ultimately social roles are reproduced, maintaining male dominance (Thorne, 1993; Connell, 1989).

Race Theory: Education Is Good for Everyone, but Better for Whites

One focus of race theory in relation to education is the practice of *tracking* (sometimes referred to as *ability grouping*)—assigning students to different educational pathways based on academic performance. Race theory argues that students of color, especially blacks and Hispanics, are more likely to be "tracked down"—placed in a slower-paced and lower-performing curriculum (Ansalone, 2006: Oakes, 2005). Therefore, students who are tracked down are treated as though they are less academically capable, learn less, think less of themselves, and ultimately do poorly in school (Cole, 2009; Grodsky, Warren, and Felts, 2008; Hanushek and Woessmann, 2009).

Race theory points to tracking as one of many policies and practices that helps construct institutional and structural racism. Ostensibly designed for the benefit of students, tracking has become an institutional mechanism that keeps students of color from performing well academically and discourages them from pursuing education past high school. Tracking combined with other institutional policies, procedures, and practices conspire to negatively affect high school performance and dropout rates among blacks and Hispanics. Moreover, this leads to minority students being less prepared for college than their white counterparts. While blacks and Hispanics make up a mere 14 percent and 19 percent of all college students respectively, they are less likely to finish college compared to their white counterparts. Blacks and Hispanics make up only 10 percent and 9 percent respectively of those with bachelor's degrees, compared with 77 percent for whites (US Department of Education, 2012). Thus, practices such as tracking perpetuate racial inequality in public schools, whose downstream effect is low college attendance and success among students of color, which culminates in occupational, economic, and social inequality for racial minorities.

MISMATCH THEORY

Mismatch theory argues that driven by compensatory programs like affirmative action, colleges are anxious to accept minority students who may not be well "matched" for a given institution. That is, because minority students are typically underprepared for the academic rigors of a top tier college, programs like affirmative action may get these students in the door, but they are "mismatched" for that school and are destined to failure. They would be better suited, argue those who hold with the mismatch thesis, to attend a lower tier school, where they would be surrounded by a student body more like themselves and ultimately be more successful. Sounds like an argument to legitimize discrimination. Do you think this sounds racist, patronizing, and like another way to reproduce white privilege? Or is it a legitimate argument?

READ MORE

- *Mismatch: How Affirmative Action Hurts Students It's Intended to Help, and Why Universities Won't Admit It* by Richard H. Sander and Stuart Taylor Jr. (2012). In this book the authors use new research to show that compensatory programs such as affirmative action place minority students in academic settings where they are sure to fail. The authors argue that many minority students are underprepared and therefore falter in rigorous academic programs. The authors claim that many colleges and universities refuse to acknowledge the reality of affirmative action's failure, fearing the response from students, alumni donors, and the public at large. No matter how you feel about affirmative action, this book gives those with certain agendas some misguided ammunition.

Symbolic Interactionism: Education Is Good Depending on How You Are Labeled

Symbolic interactionism argues that social interaction in classrooms and other school venues is instrumental in shaping students' understanding of gender roles. Moreover, teachers' perceptions of pupils' intellectual abilities influence what and how much students learn and whether they are academically successful. According to this perspective, teachers interact with students based on a set of symbols that can include labels generated by the tracking process, students' behaviors, or students' appearances (Adler, Kless, and Adler, 1992; Skelton, 2006; Skelton, Francis, and Valkanova, 2007).

Like race theory, symbolic interactionism views tracking as an important component in understanding educational performance. However, symbolic interactionism focuses on the effects that are produced by the labels placed on students as a result of their track status. Students who are put into advanced classes are labeled as "bright," while others who track low may be labeled "dim." Teachers ultimately interact with students differently based on various symbols that students possess, such as labels of "bright" or "dim," skin color, gender, type of clothing, or hygiene. Teachers give more time and attention to "bright" students; they are more attentive to students who appear well kempt and better dressed than to students who appear dirty and poor. Symbolic interactionism uses patterns of play at school to understand how gender roles are socially maintained and reproduced. Schools, according to this perspective, are places where traditional gender roles are learned in part through play. Symbolic interactionism contends that girls are more likely to engage in interactive role-play while boys are more likely to take part in more competitive play. Interactions in same-sex play tend to reinforce the differences between boys and girls by demanding conformity to gendered play. Boys may tease other boys if they engage in "girl" games, and girls may do the same if a girl wants to take part in "boy" activities. This gender role policing keeps boys and girls in their gendered place.

TABLE 11.1 Theoretical Perspectives on Education

Theoretical Perspective	View of Education	Example
Functionalism	Good for society in general because it helps create educated, socially well-adjusted citizens who work and pay taxes, which ultimately contributes to social cohesion and stability.	Schools act as training grounds for the workplace and stress social obedience.
Conflict	Education serves to produce and reproduce the ideology of the powerful classes and contributes to the maintenance of their dominance.	Elite prep schools serve to concentrate and perpetuate the economic and social power of the dominant class.

(Continued)

Theoretical Perspective	View of Education	Example
Feminist	Differential treatment of boys and girls reinforces and reproduces gender differences that benefit males.	Boys are more likely to be taught to be independent problem solvers, while girls are encouraged to be dependent when solving problems.
Race Theory	Institutional and structural racism and de facto segregation perpetuate racial differences in academic performance and achievement, creating and reproducing an achievement gap. This ranking of students based on various performance criteria has a cumulative effect that deepens over time. This benefits those at the top, while those at the lower levels suffer academic deficits.	Students of color who are concentrated in impoverished and underserved communities experience de facto segregation in substandard schools, creating institutional barriers to academic achievement.
Symbolic Interactionism	Students' performance labels can influence the way their teachers and others interact with them and the way they view themselves, ultimately affecting their academic achievement.	Students labeled as "bright" get more time with and more praise from teachers. Those who are labeled as "less bright" are somewhat ignored and considered less capable by teachers.

The Boy Who Went to Heaven ... or Did He?

A tragic car accident in 2004 left six-year-old Alex Malarkey paralyzed from the neck down and in a coma for more than two months. When he awoke from his coma, he had an incredible tale to tell. Young Alex began to relay stories of the crash, his treatment in the hospital emergency room while he was unconscious, passing through the very gates of heaven and hearing "unearthly" music, and meeting Jesus. Alex apparently died, went to heaven, and then returned to earth as he awakened from his coma. Along with his father, Kevin, Alex wrote a book about his supernatural near-death experience.

In *The Boy Who Came Back from Heaven: A Remarkable Account of Miracles, Angels, and Life beyond This World (2010),* Alex and his dad chronicle his near-death experience and his encounters with angels, the devil, and Jesus all in colorful detail. The book, which seems to reinforce a Christian interpretation of the afterlife, became an immediate best seller. The faithful flocked to buy a book that seemed to prove their belief in miracles, heaven, and Jesus. In the four years it was out, it sold more than 1 million copies. Alex and his story reinforced the beliefs of the faithful and made nonbelievers sit up and take notice. In the wake of the book, churches around the country saw double-digit growth, lapsed Christians returning to the flock, nonbelievers coming to Jesus, and the faithful reinvigorated all because a young boy said he saw heaven.

Was this confirmation that God and Jesus are real? Should nonbelievers and people of other faiths repent, live their lives right, and find salvation and eternal life in Jesus? Alex's tale would have massive implications for all people and religions of the world ... if it were true. In late 2014 Alex came clean about his near-death experience. It never happened. As he stated in a press release, "I did not die. ... I never went to heaven." He did it for attention. But even at his young age, Alex was aware that power of a story that involved validating that there was life after this one surely held a special appeal (Charles, 2015). People in general want to know what lies beyond this world, what our lives mean, and how it all fits together. For the most part that is what religion is designed to do, and that is why so many people of the world claim to believe in some form of religion. Do you identify with a particular religion? Do you believe there is life after this one?

Religion

"The purpose of religion is to control yourself, not to criticize others."
— *The Dalai Lama*

"I challenge you to find one good or noble thing that cannot be accomplished without religion. It is impossible. You cannot do it."
— *Christopher Hitchens*

Religion has long been with us as a species, and we find it in some form in nearly all cultures of the world. While many people find that religion brings them great comfort and reassurance, others view it as unnecessary in our scientifically enlightened times, while still others see it as downright dangerous. So much ink and blood has been spilled over religion, so many of the world's people believe in and take part in religion, there are so many forms of religion throughout the world and history that in this book I can only sketch out a very basic sociological understanding of religion for you.

Religion is at once seen by some as important and necessary for humankind, and by others as an enemy of culture and, by extension, the enemy of humankind (Hitchens, 2007). Nonetheless, most of the world's population believes in a god or some higher being, and more than 80 percent of people globally identify with some religious group. Since the events of September 11, 2001, religion has taken a prominent position on the world stage, in the public discourse, and in political rhetoric. Unfortunately, those events lead many to view Islam as a militant religion. The backlash against Muslims in the United States and around the world took on many forms. Some claimed a "holy crusade" pitting the Christian world against Islam, while other actions included a number of hate crimes committed against innocent Muslims and a threat to publicly burn the Quran. All of this has put a sort of media spotlight on a religion that was not well understood by most and now must plead with those outside the religion to believe its members are not all suicide bombers. However, organizations such as Al Qaeda, Daesh (also known as ISIS), and Boko Haram have done a disservice to the advancement of a better understanding of the basic tenets of Islam and its peaceful nature.

Religious belief is rooting in faith—a firm belief in something for which there is no proof—making it very difficult for people to accept criticisms of their religion. The truth is that most people know very little about other faiths and not a lot about their own, which makes fostering tolerance of other religions an immensely daunting task.

Traditionally in sociology, religion is viewed as another of the social institutions that meets the needs of the members of society. Remember in the first part of this chapter, I wrote that all institutions have both a structure (shape or form) and function (its purpose). So in this portion of the chapter, we will examine the structure and function of religion and look at how those have changed over time in our society.

READ MORE

- *World Religions: The Great Faiths Explored & Explained* by John Bowker (2006). A comprehensive view of religion and religions. A surprisingly in-depth exploration of the religions of the world. The real value in this book is that the author goes beyond a simple description of each religion and explains the symbolism, meaning, tenets, and iconography of each religion. Super fascinating.

What Is Religion, and Where Did It Come From?

Before we head off to our discussion of religion as a social institution, let's think about what religion is. Religion, I have often thought, is one of those concepts that you know until someone asks you what it is, like the middle class or what time is or what love is. Definitions of religion abound. Try searching the Internet for a definition of religion; you will get hundreds of millions

Fig. 11.10 People of different faiths worship in different ways, but they all worship to a higher power or being that they believe has supernatural abilities, which can intervene in the lives of humans.

of results. I didn't like any definition I came across, so I came up with the following quasi definition of *religion*. It could be said that religion is a number of beliefs and ritualized practices that individuals use to seek comfort and cope with the unknown. It does not necessarily have to be theist in nature, meaning a religion does not have to recognize a god or gods.

I think it is best to list what I call the elements of religion, common attributes of all religions. While all these elements are not found in all religions, all religions contain at least some of them. So the following elements cover all religions (Beversluis, 2011; Levinson, 1996).

- *A belief system or worldview*: A set of beliefs that fit together to help explain our place in the world and universe. This may or may not include a deity or deities. For example, the Christian worldview sees the universe and humans as created by a supernatural God who sent his only son, Jesus, to earth to die for the sins of the world, and belief in Jesus is the only path to eternal salvation. Moreover, accepting Jesus as your personal savior is the "one way" to heaven and life everlasting; if not, you're going to hell. Whereas the Buddhists believe in the four noble truths: (1) All life is suffering; (2) Suffering is caused by craving and aversion; (3) Suffering can be overcome and happiness attained;

(4) Following the noble eightfold path will end suffering (right thought, right action, right speech, right understanding, right livelihood, right effort, right mindfulness and right concentration). Essentially, Buddhists strive to live a moral life that is right in all they think, say, and do, while injuring no living thing as they seek enlightenment. Unlike Christians, Buddhists' salvation is not predicated on divine assistance. Ultimately, the worldview of a given religion guides the thoughts and actions of its followers.

- *Delineation of the sacred and the profane*: All religions assign all objects and phenomena into one of two categories, the sacred and the profane—that which is revered (good) and that which is reviled (evil). The sacred for any given religion may be people, places, objects, actions, or events. The Pope is considered a sacred person by Catholics, as the Dalai Lama is for Buddhists. Mecca, Medina, and Jerusalem are sacred locations for Muslims, Jews, and Christians. Profane objects, people, or places are those feared or hated by members of a given religion, which typically represent an opposition to their beliefs or practices. Satanic worship is profane to most mainstream religions, the devil is profane, and so are blasphemers.
- *Ritual(s)*: Ceremonies that are practiced uniformly and in a prescribed manner. Rituals are thought to explain, teach, and make real the religion's beliefs.
- *Ethics*: These can be thought of as rules of behavior for members of a given group. Some religions believe these guidelines are divinely inspired or come directly from a supernatural deity or force, while others believe their rules evolved over time through the actions of the group.
- *Material expression*: Religions use material things to perform rituals or to express or represent beliefs. The Catholic Church is rich with iconography. The crucifix, the altar, the priests' robes, communion wafers and wine, and even the dried blood of a saint. The Bunlap people of Pentecost Island in the South Pacific make and use masks that represent various spirits they believe inhabit the world.
- *Community*: There are others that share the same worldview and engage in practices that reinforce your united sense of your place in the world. Coming together for Sunday worship services for Christians or payer at a local mosque for Muslims are expressions of community.
- *Central myths or stories*: All religions contain myths and stories that attempt to teach or reinforce critical element of the religion. The creation of the universe and then Adam and Eve by the all-powerful God is a common creation myth among the Jewish, Muslim, and Christian faiths. P'an Ku, who lived in a cosmic egg for eighteen hundred years before creating the earth and humans, is central to Chinese folk religions. The parting of the Red Sea by Moses, as well as Jesus and the loaves and fishes, serve as vehicles to illustrate the miraculous nature of God and how we must put our faith in him, not in ourselves (Leeming, 2010).

- *Characteristic emotional expression:* Most religions have commonly shared emotions that may be central to their practice. Loving Jesus, for example, is central to Christianity. Inner peace, while central to Buddhist teachings, is not a prominent emotional feature of Judaism or Christianity.

No doubt in an attempt to understand and explain the workings of the physical world in which they found themselves, early humans attributed *agency*—the ability to act on its own accord—to objects that had no agency, such as storm clouds or moving grass. This tendency to attribute agency to inanimate object by humans is sometimes referred to as the hyperactive agency detection device (Barrett and Johnson, 2003).

Perhaps religion emerged from our own fear. The day-to-day existence of early humans was filled with difficulties such as finding enough food to eat, fending off predators, avoiding injury, and dealing with what must have been terrifying natural phenomena like thunder, lightning, and volcanoes (Clark, 2014; Palermo, 2015). The idea of gods was created to help explain those things that were beyond the control of early humans, like natural phenomena or why some fell victim to disease and death. Aware that they were not responsible for these events, our ancestors attributed them to some unseen, unknown force, power, or spirit, which no doubt eased their fears and gave them some comfort because now they had a way to explain the things they witnessed. These characteristics of easing fear, granting comfort, and even instilling courage in individuals are still attributed to religion and gods. Also, it is not uncommon for people in times of crisis to find religion, relying on faith to see them through tough times. Have you ever heard the phrase "There are no atheists in foxholes?"

Regardless of how or why they emerged, all religions are constructed by humans and therefore fallible and malleable. Religions change over time; for example, one original doctrine of the Mormon Church was plural marriage, meaning a man could take several wives, ostensibly ended in 1890 (although it continued and was finally ended in 1904) when the president of the Mormon Church issued an official manifest declaring the end of polygamy in the church. Currently the only official form of marriage recognized by the Mormon Church is monogamy ("The Manifesto and the End of Plural Marriage," 2015; Cannon, 1983). The Roman Catholic Church no longer tortures Jews in order to persuade them to convert to Christianity. And animal sacrifices are no longer conducted during Jewish holidays. Religions also may look different as you move from one society to another, reflecting local cultural influences. This syncretism—the practice of blending or joining two or more different belief systems—is common throughout history and around the world. It is common for indigenous populations to adopt Christianity or Islam and combine that faith with their local religious rituals and practices.

For instance, both the United States and the Philippines are majority Christian countries, but the way Americans and Filipinos celebrate Easter is both similar and divergent. Among Christian denominations in the United States, Easter is a high holiday. It represents one of the two days of the year in which church attendance soars. Members of congregations all over the country sport their finest Sunday church clothes, and women wear their Easter hats to service. The Easter meal typically includes ham and/or lamb, and there is an Easter egg hunt. While Easter is also a high holiday in the Philippines, in this mainly Catholic country many will fast on the Friday and Saturday before Easter Sunday, and shops and businesses will alter their hours or close altogether for weeks running up to Easter. Many of the faithful will walk for miles while beating themselves with mini multi-stranded whips, tearing the flesh open and causing serious bleeding. At the end of their masochistic walk, they are crucified. They are placed on a cross, nails are driven through both their hands and feet, and the crossed is raised up. They will remain on the cross for as long as they find necessary. (Cabrera, 2013.) Here is a holiday that is common for both Christian cultures, but the common faith is expressed differently.

While the religions of the world may look different, have different central figures, possess different iconography, and practice different rituals, they all serve some basic human needs. Regardless of how you feel about religion, it serves an important and perhaps essential role in society, like family, education, and the law. It is part of the complex system of human social arrangements that allow us to live orderly lives. So, for the purposes of our discussion here, we will not focus on the origins of religion but on its structure and functions.

The Face of Religion

To many people of the world, their church, temple, or mosque represents religion. Worldwide, nearly 8 in 10 people adhere to some form of religion. The three major Abrahamic religions of the world—Christianity, Judaism, and Islam—account for nearly 4 billion of the world's 7.2 billion people. Add Hinduism (1 billion) and Buddhists (500 million), and these five religions account for about 5.4 billion people. The balance of the world's population, about 1.8 billion, is composed of those practicing folk religions (e.g., Chinese folk religion, African tradition religions, Native American

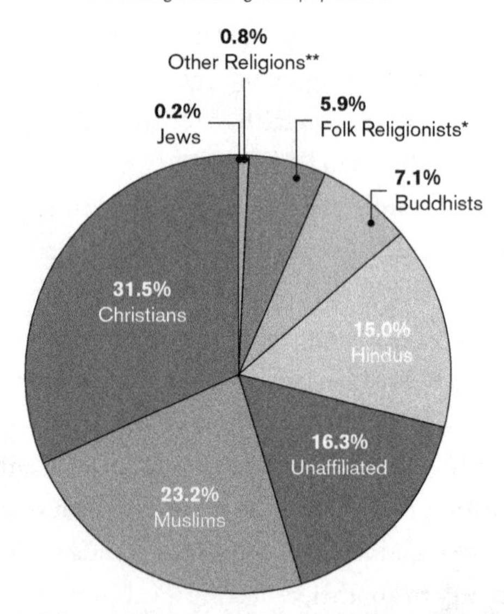

Fig. 11.11 Major religious groups around the world

and Australian Aboriginal religions) or other religions (e.g., Baha'i, Jainism, Wicca, and others), and about 1.1 billion people worldwide (that's about one in six) claim no religion (Pew Research Center, 2012). Interestingly, if having no religion was a religion, it would be the third-largest one in the world. Take a look at the chart in figure 11.11 to see the size of major religious groups as percentages of the world population.

In the United States, things break down differently. As you can see in figure 11.12, we are an overwhelmingly Christian society, with about 244 million followers, or a little more than three out of every four Americans claiming Christian religious affiliation. Those Americans claiming no religious affiliation make up the second-largest group. The Jewish population, at nearly 5.7 million, is the largest single religious group outside of Christianity in the United States. Surprisingly, there are more than 3.5 million Buddhists in the United States, larger than the U.S. Muslim population, which is about 2.8 million. (I should note that there is a tremendous amount of debate about the actual U.S. Muslim population. The numbers I have used here are estimated and come from a Pew Research Center study published in 2012.)

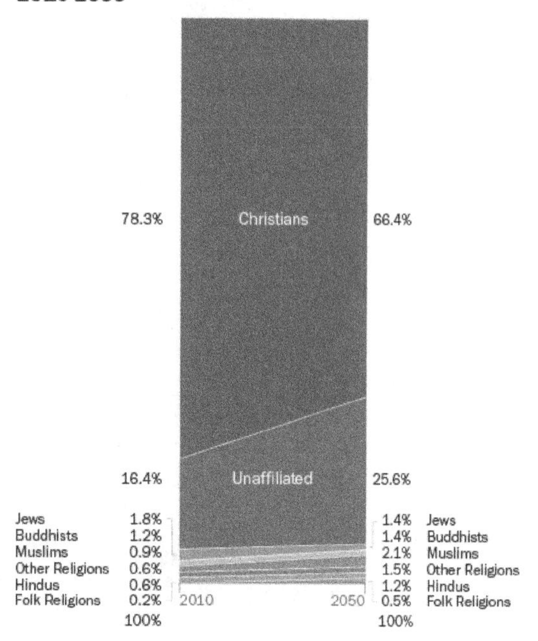

Fig. 11.12 The graph above shows the distribution of religious affiliation in the United States.

These numbers are changing. Lipka and Hackett (2015) predict that by 2050 the global Muslim population will have grown 73 percent to 2.8 billion followers, while Christianity will grow by 35 percent to 2.9 billion believers. In the next four decades, Hinduism will be the only other major world religion that will see growth, collecting about 350 million new followers. Buddhism, Judaism, and those affiliated with other religions will see little to no change in their worldwide populations (see figure 11.13). Nonbelievers and those claiming no religious affiliation will decline globally, while their ranks will increase in the United States by 2050. It's predicted that by 2050 in the United States, Muslims will make up the second-largest religious group, surpassing those who identify as Jewish (Lipka, 2015).

Fig. 11.13 Map of the world showing the distribution of major religions (2015). The religious complexion of the world may change as predicted growth in some religions may alter the distribution of major religions from what it is now.

Why such major growth for Islam? There seem to be two major factors influencing the predicted significant increase in the global Muslim population. First, on average Muslims are younger than adherents to other religions, positioning them in the childbearing years in the upcoming decades. Second, Muslims have more children on average then members of other religions. Muslim women have an average of 3.1 children, compared to 2.3 for all non-Muslims. During the same period (2010–2050), the number of Christians will also grow worldwide to about 2.9 billion. In 2050 Christians will make up a bit more than 31 percent of the world's people, about what it was in 2010 (Pew Research Center, 2015).

THERE'S AN APP FOR THAT

- The Bible app makes the word of God available at your fingertips. You can access favorite scripture, your bookmarks, notes, and reading plans from any mobile device (Life.Church, 2016).
- NaanMap for the iPhone lets you map out places to find halal foods (food that is permissible by Islamic law). One tap and it locates all possible halal food locations near you, in the United States (Qurtaba, 2012).

The Functions of Religion: What Role Does It Play in Society?

Government provides order through laws and courts; the economy provides goods, services, and livelihoods for members of society; family provides social instruction, reproduction, and support for its members; and education educates and socializes. But what does religion do? Does religion free us or help control us? Does it bring us together or maintain differences between social groups? It really depends on your perspective. In the following section, I will explore the various functions of religion through the lenses of the three major sociological perspectives.

Theoretical Perspectives on Religion

Functionalism: Religion Is Good for Social Cohesion

While Auguste Comte, the father of sociology, hoped that the new science of sociology would eliminate the "irrational" and "backward" influences of religion on human society, modern functionalism recognizes the social utility of religion (Comte, 1842). The thrust of functionalism's perspective on religion is that it is a form of social control. Religion, for functionalists, is an institution, like education, that serves society by providing a mechanism for social control. Religions demand that their followers adhere to a set of tenets such as the belief in a resurrected Jesus, the immutability of the Torah, or praying five times a day. Followers seeking acceptance will obey these tenets and conform to beliefs and practices that seem consistent with them. Religions for the most part stress civil as well as spiritual obedience.

Think about your own experiences at church, temple, or mosque. Have you ever heard the person in the front of the congregation, usually wearing robes and/or holding some religious object like a Bible, tell his or her followers to break the law, be lazy, quit their jobs, or abandon their families? Probably not. Rather, religious leaders tell their flocks to be productive citizens, pay their taxes, work hard, and care for their families. Messages about social behavior that is rooted in the fundamental tenets of religions promote civil obedience—social control—which results in social cohesion and stability.

Functionalism further argues that religion provides people with a set of beliefs that give them comfort and an understanding about their place in the universe and purpose in life. The major religions of the world provide their followers with an understanding of their position in the grand scheme of things and a belief that through faith and obedience they will be reward with some version of heaven or closeness to God for eternity; a kind of cosmic reward for doing what you are told. Moreover, all the major religions of the world have prohibitions that emphasize care of oneself, like don't abuse your body with chemicals or masturbation and don't kill yourself.

Do you remember Emile Durkheim? We discussed him in Chapter 1 and his work on suicide. We also discussed his near obsession with society's transition from a traditional to a modern form and the problems that could create. Specifically, Durkheim (1912) was concerned with maintaining the significance of the collective and fostering social integration. In his book *The Elementary Forms of Religious Life*, he recognized the social origin of religion. Durkheim contended that religion served to bring people together and provide them with a common identity. Rituals like Sunday mass for Catholics allow members of a parish to come together and bond over their common beliefs and practices, which are central to their Catholic identity. Therefore, through ritual and identity, religion reinforces larger, widely held social norms such as being kind to others, working hard, and raising a family. Durkheim argued that religion was a necessary element of society precisely because it provided needed social control and solidarity.

Conflict Perspective: Religion is the Opiate of the Masses

> *"Religion is the sigh of the oppressed creature, the heart of a heartless world, and the soul of soulless conditions. It is the opium of the people."*
>
> — *Karl Marx*

While there was no systematic treatment of religion in the writings of Marx, Marxism generally views religion as a mechanism of the capitalist classes, which allows them to maintain control over the working classes. Religion creates an illusory version of the world by offering divine explanations for material conditions. In other words, religion asserts that neither individuals nor classes of people have control over their social conditions; rather, they are subject to supernatural forces beyond their control. The conflict approach argues that the belief by individuals that their fates are in the hands of some god makes them vulnerable to a capitalist system that exploits them. That is, they believe they are poor because it is God's will, not because of structural inequality. This comfort that people believe they find in religion, according to the conflict approach, is the drug that keeps the subordinate classes numb to the reality of the true income disparity, for example. Since the mid-1970s real incomes have dropped sharply, while those at the top of the income distribution have grown considerably. The top 1 percent of income earners in the United States average more than 38 percent more income than the bottom 90 percent of earners (Saez, 2013). So, while those of us in the middle- and lower-income-earning classes have been binging on our drug (religion), the rich get richer.

Like functionalism, the conflict approach views religion as an agent of social control. However, unlike functionalism—which sees the element of social control acting in the common good for the stability of society—conflict theory argues that social control is maintained by the powerful classes in order to reproduce their dominance. Religion becomes, for conflict theorists, a tool of capitalism, a method to promote and reinforce social inequality by forcing the subordinate classes to conform to the ideologies of the dominate classes. As in the example above, clergy members are not in the habit of telling members of their congregations to break laws and quit their jobs; rather, they encourage them to be obedient, go to work, and provide for their family, not for social good but to keep the economy going so the powerful can maintain their stranglehold over the economy and society through their disproportionate control of wealth.

A more contemporary perspective like feminist theory, which has its roots in Marxism, would similarly argue that mainstream religions act to reproduce gender inequality. The entire hierarchy of the Catholic Church is male. While catholic girls may view nuns as role models, nuns are always under the direction of the male hierarchy and subordinate to male clergy. Moreover, the ideologies of the Catholic Church, for example, do not allow women to be ordained (this includes nuns), and they deny women control over their own bodies by not allowing the use of contraceptives and by prohibiting abortion. Women in the Muslim world must cover themselves and walk behind men, many are not allowed to work or leave their homes, and young Muslim girls are not as valued as their brothers. Oppressive religious regimes like these, feminist theory argues, maintain the low status of women worldwide and contribute to the continued violence against women. Rates of violence against women are highest in nations with majority populations that are Catholic, like Mexico, Brazil, and Colombia; and in majority Muslim countries such as Pakistan, Afghanistan, and Egypt ("Violence against Women," 2015; "World Report," 2015). While these and other religions do not cause violence against women, their worldviews and practices that devalue and subjugate women certainly contribute to it.

Symbolic Interactionist Perspective: Religion Is Up for Interpretation

While functional and conflict theories take a macrosociological perspective on religion and society, symbolic interactionism takes a microsociological perspective. According to this perspective, we understand religion through symbols, just as we construct daily life through the use of ordinary symbols. Religion comes into being through the use of symbols, and the collection of symbols of any given religion ultimately defines it. What do you think when you see a woman wearing a hijab? What do you think when you see a woman in a burka? These symbols create an image of that person and her life based on the interpretation of those symbols. A cross to more than 1 billion Christians worldwide, the Star of David for Jews, and the crescent moon and star are all symbols with deeply religious significance. Symbols can also act as sacred objects no to be defiled or destroyed, but to be revered.

These symbols not only invoke meaning for members of a given religion, they conjure up images and ideas about that religion by nonpractitioners based on how those symbols are interpreted in the current social and historical period. As social and historical contexts change, they give rise to different religious beliefs and practices. During the Black Death, many of the faithful in Germany walked from village to village while beating themselves with flagellates, believing that the mortification of the flesh was necessary to atone for whatever mankind had done to bring such horror upon them. (Ziegler, 1971.) You don't find people doing that today. Context, then, is an important feature of symbolic interactionism because it frames the meaning of religious belief. Therefore, symbolic interactionism helps us understand how the same religion can be interpreted differently by different groups or at different times throughout history.

TRY THIS

Attend the worship service of a religion that is not yours. If you are Christian, try attending a Jewish temple or an Islamic mosque; if you are Muslim or Baptist, try attending a Catholic mass. If you are an atheist, try attending an Orthodox worship service. Take a look around the worship area and pay attention to the symbolism of the iconography, and to how people orient themselves to the worship leaders and each other. Are certain groups segregated? That is, do women and men or the young and old worship separately? How do people interact before, during, and after the service? Do the symbols make sense to you? How different are they from your worship experience? Can you figure them out? Do you think that all people are searching for similar things, just using different paths to find it? It may sound intimidating, but you will find that people are incredibly kind. I have done this several times in different cities in the United States. It really is eye opening.

TABLE 11.2 Theoretical Perspectives and Religion

Theoretical Perspective	View of Religion	Example
Structural Functionalism (Functionalism)	Functionalism sees religion as a necessary social institution that provides believers with meaning, serves as a mechanism of social control, promotes physical and psychological well-being, and reinforces social unity and stability.	Clergy do not encourage members of their flocks to break the law, quit their jobs, stop paying taxes, or abandon their families. On the contrary, they encourage members of the community to conform to social convention and be obedient citizens, thus reinforcing the status quo and maintaining social stability.
Conflict Perspective	Religion is viewed as an instrument of capitalism, designed to essentially keep people in their economic place. Marx believed that religion was an opiate of the masses ... it gave people a false sense of economic reality, convincing them that there were divine reasons for economic deprivation, thus shifting perception of the real cause of economic conditions away from inequality shaped by the powerful classes.	Religion instills a fatalistic perspective on one's economic circumstances: "I'm poor because it is God's will." This denies the economic reality—income inequality is maintained by the wealthy to assure their dominance.
Feminist Theory	Religion reinforces and promotes gender inequality. Religious doctrine helps convince women to accept their lot in life. Women are enslaved, married off young, raped, and killed in many parts of the world because it is consistent with the ideologies of oppressive religious regimes. Patriarchal religions that promote the dominance of men and devalue women shape oppressive practices toward women and produce increased violence toward women.	In April 2007 a seventeen-year-old Yazidi girl, Du'a Kahlil Aswad, was stoned to death by members of her own community in Iraqi Kurdistan because they believed she was planning to run away to marry a Sunni Muslim man. Yazidis must adhere to a rigid rule of religious endogamy—Yazidis ONLY marry other Yazidis.

(*Continued*)

Theoretical Perspective	View of Religion	Example
Symbolic Interactionism	Religion comes into being through the use of symbols. Religion is therefore defined in part by symbols. However, social and historical context shapes the interpretation of religion. So, while the symbols remain the same, their meaning can change over time.	Taking multiple wives once symbolized prosperity and strong religious belief for Mormon men. Now it symbolizes defiance of official church policy. The symbolism of polygyny is interpreted differently in different historical periods, creating new understanding of how one appears prosperous and faithful.

Sources: Terman, 2010; Lattimer, 2007; Schmidt, 2009; Hardy, 1992; Van Wagoner, 1989

The Bottom Line

Education

This chapter examined two important social institutions, education and religion. While teaching younger members of society is a universal practice, the level of development of an educational social institution is related to the needs of a given society. In the United States we have a highly developed and rather sophisticated educational system, in part because we have such a large and diverse population and our economy demands a technically trained workforce. While this may be true, most Americans view education as the path to social mobility.

Originally, educational instruction was merely a vehicle to teach members of the community to read and understand the Bible. Education beyond interpretation of the Bible was for the privileged and remained that way for nearly two hundred years in the United States. Education was reserved for the social elites, who created schools that reinforced their ideologies and position, preparing their offspring to assume the mantle of leadership in government, industry, science, and the arts.

Public education grew in part as a reaction to the industrialization of America and the growing need for a literate workforce. Big cities also needed a place to warehouse the children of all those workers who were flooding into large urban areas and taking all the new factory jobs. Changes in child labor laws took children off the factory floor and put them classrooms. By the early part of the twentieth century, Americans flowed through school systems that were fairly uniform, with the familiar elementary schools followed by middle schools and capped off with high schools.

Public education isn't the only game in town. Elite private schools create a tier of schools that insulate the powerful classes and help preserve their way of life. While there is more diversity among these schools than ever before, elite private schools remain the bastion of white privilege. Some opt out of formal education altogether by homeschooling their young. Homeschooling is growing in popularity, and not just among religious fundamentalists; more well-educated, wealthy, not necessarily religious parents are choosing homeschooling. Most parents cite concerns about the safety of public schools as an important factor in deciding to homeschool their children.

As we discussed, higher education has become much more accessible in the past forty years, and college enrollments are at record levels. More women and people of color are attending and completing college than ever before, and the composition of today's college goers is not your traditional eighteen- to twenty-four-year olds. College is more popular than ever, in part because it is so accessible and is perceived as a path to success. Research clearly indicates that there is a strong positive correlation between level of education and income—the more education you have, the more money you make. Even while Americans are attending college in record numbers, some are still falling behind. The achievement gap is widening for many in the United States.

Schools still serve an important function in society, especially in today's workplace, where technical training is so necessary. While creating literate citizens through instruction of basic academic fields is one major manifest function education serves, it also serves a number of latent or unintentional functions, like learning about punctuality and how to socialize with your peers. Other lessons also learned in school have the potential to be more dangerous, like the reproduction of inequality of gender and social class. This hidden curriculum tends to reproduce the dominant ideologies of inequality.

In the final section on education, we discussed theoretical perspectives and education. We noted that functionalism viewed education as a necessary institution that teaches the young about our values, beliefs, and practices and strongly encourages conformity in order to maintain social cohesion. The conflict approach sees education as another tool of the powerful classes used to reproduce class differences and maintain their dominance by promoting adherence to their ideologies. And lastly we discussed the interactionist's view that labeling can affect students' performance and self-perception.

Religion

Religion is an ever-present cultural institution. It has emerged in every culture as a way to understand and cope with the world around us and discover our place in it. Some view religion as necessary to the human condition, while others find it a useless vestige of a bygone era in human social evolution. Whatever you think of religion, it is here to stay, and adherents to the various forms of it are growing.

What is religion? I couldn't find an adequate definition, but I presented eight elements that were comprehensive enough that we can identify at least several of them in all major religions. No one is sure where and when religion emerged, but we know it has been with us as a species for a considerable time. We do know that it is human-made like all components of culture, and therefore it is fallible and malleable. It changes over time and from place to place; the same religion can appear different, given its location in time and space.

More than eight out of every ten people of the world identify with some religion, and while Christians and Muslims make up the greatest number of believers worldwide, there is still plenty of room for other faiths. As we look to the future, most faiths will witness either an increase or a leveling off among their faithful. In the United States the face of religion is changing, with Muslims making up the second-largest religious group by 2050.

What role does religion play in today's world? According to functionalism, it is an important element in making people feel like they belong by providing a set of values and beliefs that are widely shared in society, therefore promoting conformity and social cohesion. Other perspectives, like the conflict approach, see religion as a tool of the powerful classes used merely to spread an ideology that perpetuates inequality between the classes and solidifies their dominance. On the other hand, symbolic interactionism seeks to understand the meaning that the faithful find in the symbols of religion. Held in the symbols of religion is the meaning that constructs believers' interpretation of what the religion means to them in that social and historical context. Changing social and historical contexts bring changing interpretations of the religion, giving us a constantly changing version of religion.

Figure Credits

Fig. 11.2: William Holmes McGuffey, "McGuffey Reader," https://commons.wikimedia.org/wiki/File:Cover_of_McGuffey%27s_First_Eclectic_Reader.jpeg. Copyright in the Public Domain.

Fig. 11.3: Tomwsulcer, "Entrance to the posh Phillips Academy in Andover Mass.," https://commons.wikimedia.org/wiki/File:Andover_Massachusetts_Phillips_Academy_Abbot_campus_entranceway_with_Draper_Hall_in_background.JPG. Copyright in the Public Domain.

Fig. 11.4: National Center for Education Statistics, "High School Graduation Rates 1990-2012 (Use first Line graph)," http://nces.ed.gov/programs/coe/indicator_coi.asp#info. Copyright in the Public Domain.

Fig. 11.5: Source: http://www.pewresearch.org/fact-tank/2014/10/02/u-s-high-school-dropout-rate-reaches-record-low-driven-by-improvements-among-hispanics-blacks/ft_14-10-01_h-s-dropout_2/

Fig. 11.6: National Center for Education Statistics, "[image]: The structure of education in the United States," http://nces.ed.gov/programs/digest/d01/fig1.asp, ~1. Copyright in the Public Domain.

Fig. 11.7: National Center for Education Statistics, "Demographics of College Students," http://nces.ed.gov/programs/coe/indicator_cha.asp. Copyright in the Public Domain.

Fig. 11.8: Bureau of Labor Statistics, "Relationship between education level and income," http://www.bls.gov/emp/ep_chart_001.htm. Copyright in the Public Domain.

Fig. 11.10a: Copyright © Depositphotos/Rawpixel.

Fig. 11.10b: Copyright © Depositphotos/iphemant.

Fig. 11.10c: Copyright © Depositphotos/avalanchez.

Fig. 11.10d: Copyright © Depositphotos/Buurserstraat38.

Fig. 11.11: Source: http://www.pewforum.org/2012/12/18/global-religious-landscape-exec/

Fig. 11.12: Source: http://www.pewresearch.org/fact-tank/2015/04/14/muslims-expected-to-surpass-jews-as-second-largest-u-s-religious-group/

Fig. 11.13: Usergreatpower, "Map of the distribution of the world's major religions," https://commons.wikimedia.org/wiki/File:Major_religions_distribution.png. Copyright in the Public Domain.

CHAPTER 12

ECONOMY AND GOVERNMENT

The Economy Can Be a Bully

Many of my students, perhaps like you, view a college education as a necessity in today's economic climate. Indeed, some type of postsecondary education has become all but required for a well-paying career in today's economy. Most college students believe that in order to enjoy a "comfortable" or "middle-class" lifestyle, they have to complete a college degree. In fact, the results of the *College Decision Survey* indicated that 91 percent of respondents said "To improve my employment possibilities" was the most important reason for going to college (Fishman, 2015). The results also showed that 90 percent of those surveyed said "to make more money," and 89 percent stated "to get a better job" rounded out the top three most important reasons to go to college. A Pew Research Center study revealed that 94 percent of parents in the United States expect their children to attend college (Pew Research Center, "Is College Worth It," 2011). So in today's society, not only do most people expect to attend college, they also feel that it is the most direct and efficient path to the American dream.

It seems then, that the economy is a bully, forcing people to go to college in order to be successful in today's economy. It's as though the bully is saying, "Look at this nice comfortable lifestyle, this middle-class standard of living; you can have it, but you have to go to college. And if you don't go to college, you won't be eligible for all the 'good' jobs, you will make less money than those who do, and you will enjoy a lower standard of living than college grads." What if

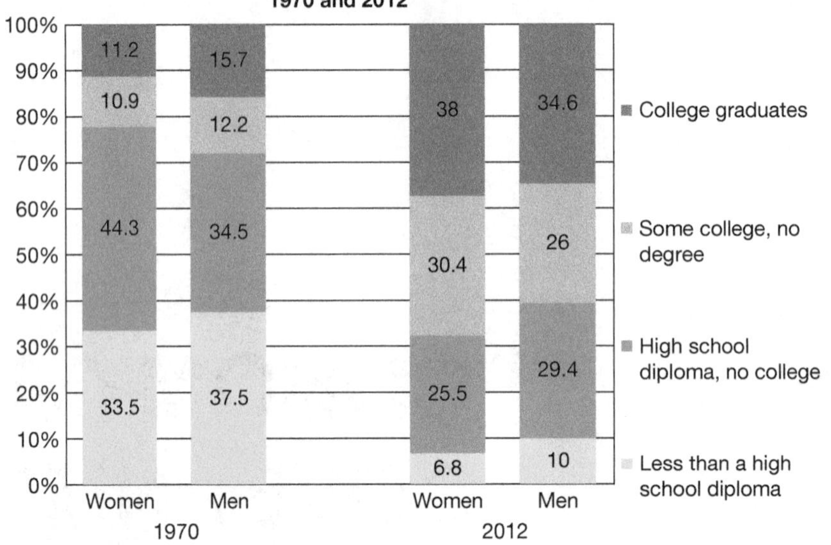

Fig. 12.1 Since the 1970s, the percentage of female college graduates has more than tripled, and, for men, the rate has more than doubled. More and more people are earning college degrees in order to be more competitive in the job market.

you don't go to college and just go from high school right into the workforce? What kinds of jobs will you be qualified for? What kind of money can you expect to make? In this sense the economy is a bully, coercing us into taking a particular path to attain desired social goals.

While the economy may be a powerful influence on students' decision to go to college, it's not the only social force compelling them to go. The economy is interconnected with other institutions like the government, whose actions have allowed many students to attend college. Laws enacted by the federal and state governments make college accessible to just about anyone who wants to go, regardless of their gender, race/ethnicity, religion, age, social class, or abilities. How do 20.2 million students afford college? In 2015 the federal government alone gave out $239 billion in financial aid to college students (College Board, 2015). On average, more than 83 percent of students pursuing any type of higher education (four-year, two-year, for-profit, and not-for-profit schools) receive federal financial aid (US Department of Education, *The Condition of Education 2015)*. Additionally, local and state governments have made higher education much more accessible by establishing community and junior colleges. In an effort to meet the economic demands for well-educated workers, the state of Tennessee now allows state residents to attend any two-year public community college for free (known as the "Tennessee Promise") ("Tennessee Promise," 2016).

You can view government and the economy as working together cooperatively, or you could see the economy as a bully that not only pushes individuals around, but also bullies the government into enacting new laws and policies, providing financial aid, and creating greater access to higher education. Either way you see it, the functions of these two institutions are intertwined in many ways.

In this chapter, we will examine the institutions of both the economy and the government. Just like I have done with other institutions in previous chapters, I will explore both the structures and functions of these institutions. We will examine how economies of the world vary and pay close attention to what they look like and what they do, and we'll do the same for government. So let's start by taking a look at a number of economic systems.

READ MORE

- *Will College Pay Off? A Guide to the Most Important Financial Decision You'll Ever Make* by Peter Cappelli (2015). In this book, the author explores the connection between education and good jobs, as well as the state of education in the United States and whether college really does pay off. The author surveys the current educational landscape and presents arguments for why certain schools and programs are better investments than others. Not all degrees from all colleges will pay off. In broad terms, he suggests some of the best bets and some of the wrong moves. This is a book both for those preparing to attend college and for parents with children either in college or about to enroll.

Economy

The economy—a system used by society to produce, distribute, and consume goods and services—is a unique social institution. The vast majority of people can easily navigate its complexities, but few know, in a detailed way, how the economy works. We get jobs, pay taxes, purchase homes, invest in communities, and buy all kinds of stuff. Most of us operate on a pretty straightforward understanding of basic economics. Having jobs allows us to buy and invest in the things we feel are best for us and our families. Additionally, as we have seen in the discussion above, the economy has an influence on decisions that we make as well as our behaviors.

THERE'S AN APP FOR THAT

Are you having a tough time balancing your household budget or just keeping track of where all your money goes? Well, there are several apps for that.

HomeBudget, GoodBudget, and Spendbook are all, well, apps that help you manage your household budget. Enter in all your financial information and whatnot, then the apps track spending, help you set financial goals, and help keep your budget on track. Each of these apps works across platforms and operating systems. HomeBudget and GoodBudget will cost you a few dollars, but Spendbook is free (Anishu, Inc., 2016; Dayspring Technologies, 2015; Lab304, 2015). Features vary somewhat between these apps, but they all provide you with instant access to a user-friendly and well-organized version of your financial life.

An Extremely Brief History of the Market Economy

Many point to the *Neolithic revolution*—when humans began domesticating plants and animals, and groups became less nomadic—as the point at which market economies emerged. This revolution gave rise to agricultural economies. This improved efficiency in food production freed many from work in the fields. As agriculture developed, new jobs emerged along with new technology. New ways of processing, transporting, and storing surplus crops had to be developed, new farm tools and irrigation technology had to be built, and herds of livestock needed to be tended to and sheltered. New economies developed because people now had goods and services to trade.

Market economies— a *free market* is a general term for any number of exchanges that take place in society, which are voluntary exchanges between two parties trading in goods and services (Ross, 2015). These markets have existed for millennia, but certainly not in the complex ways they operate now. Even before money, we engaged in trade with one another. No doubt early trade was barter based, but as civilizations and consequently economies grew larger and more complex, most societies created some medium of exchange that could be used universally for all types of trade. You can see how using some commonly recognized and valuable medium would make things easier. Say you had a cow but wanted some grain; you would have to find someone with grain who also wanted a cow, and this could take some time. However, if you had, say, a gold coin, you could exchange that coin for some grain, and the grain seller could use that gold coin to buy a chicken or a nice chair (Corn, 1999).

Most reliable historical evidence indicates that cattle was the oldest "currency," dating back to about 9000 to 6000 BCE. Then around 1000 BCE, metallic "coins" were produced in China. Since then moneyed economies spread and grew all over the world. However, the movement toward market economies, which required a simultaneous rise in a banking system, was met with great resistance in Europe, mainly from the church (today's Roman Catholic Church). Initially, the church condemned *usury*—the practice of lending money at high rates of interest. Slowly over time, as markets emerged and flourished and the church saw the potential for profit, attitudes and policies began to change about profit, business, and new markets (Weatherford, 1998; Ferguson, 2009). Incidentally, the Catholic Church became one of the most powerful financial institutions during the rise of banking. Today the Vatican Bank controls hundreds of billions of dollars, and the Catholic Church is one of the world's wealthiest institutions (Manhattan, 1983)

One prominent struggle in establishing market economies in societies that featured feudal-, caste-, or religious-based social systems was moving control of the economy out of the hands of a central authority. Obviously, the central authority and elites, who controlled and directed the economy, were resistant to free market economies that were no longer under their centralized control. Additionally, capitalism, industrialization, and mass production were challenged by those who viewed it as a threat to their traditional production model. Karl Marx helped frame a political and economic model that advocated state control of the means of production, taking it out of the hands of private citizens. This struggle between market economies and central authority–planned economies is commonly framed as *socialism* versus *capitalism*. Below we will explore both capitalist and socialist economic systems (McMillan, 2003).

Economic Systems

In the world today we find a variety of economic systems, but the most frequently occurring are capitalism and socialism. While these two systems are commonly portrayed as opposites and sometimes pitted against each other as a metaphor for how a society should be run and treat its citizens, the reality is that most economies are some mixture of both. Other systems, such as command and traditional economies, are also found in a few countries of the world.

Capitalism

Capitalism is the economic system in which the means of production (capital) is controlled by private owners for profit. It is the prevailing economic model in the United States and in many countries around the world. In its original or "raw" form, capitalism was free from nearly all regulation and restraint by the state. Workers were routinely exploited, including child labor;

Fig. 12.2 In its "raw" form capitalism provided unsafe work environments and exploited a range of workers like the children pictured here.

the workplace was unsafe; and workers had little if any rights. However, as industries came under mounting scrutiny and workers became increasingly disillusioned with working conditions, capitalism became reined in by governmental regulation such as the implementation of restrictive child labor laws, workplace safety regulations, and environmental protection laws (Appleby, 2010). The system proved to be flexible, withstanding increased regulation while still thriving. While capitalism has evolved and grown more complex than its original "raw" form found in the beginnings of the Industrial Revolution, it retains some distinctive characteristics:

- *Private ownership of the means of production.* In a capitalist economy the means of production, such as factories and businesses, are privately held. While the government may control some industries, like space exploration, most commerce is owned by private citizens. These privately owned businesses respond to market demands, not the will of the government.
- *Free competition.* Ideally, the market will demand the best product or service for the lowest price. Competition in the marketplace, free of government or other outside forces, stimulates invention and innovation, which brings the best product with the best price to market.

- *Profit.* The goods and services produced and consumed are intended to make a profit. Businesses exist to make a profit. The motive for businesses is to produce goods for far less than they sell them for, thereby generating profits. Businesses and their products and services don't exist just to meet people's needs; although some products and services meet needs, they are only available if people have the resources to pay for them (Beaud, 2001; Neal and Williamson, 2014).
- *Economic inequality.* A natural and perhaps necessary characteristic of capitalist economies is the existence of inequalities of income, wealth, and power. Through the feature of private property and the practice of inheritance, these inequalities tend to be intensified. The potential for vast amounts of wealth and power to be concentrated in the hands of a few people is a risk, and perhaps an inevitability (Roche, 2014).

The above characteristics are present in all capitalist systems in varying degrees. In Israel, for example, capitalism and entrepreneurship are highly encouraged and developed, yet the airline EL AL is state owned and operated (EL AL Israel Airline, Inc., 2016). The U.S. Postal Service is what's known as an "independent establishment of the executive branch of the United States government" (US Postal Service, 2012). This makes it a mix of a privately operated business that is subject to congressional control. Additionally, many businesses such as airlines, the petroleum industry, telecommunications, and the financial sector are highly regulated by the U.S. government. Over time the complexion of capitalism has changed. Our capitalist economic system has a long history of change that has allowed it to bend and persist rather than break and fail.

The rise of unions in the United States in the 1920s and 1930s serves as a vivid example of how capitalism proved to be malleable. Many capitalists who controlled vast production empires feared that union labor would reduce profits and workers would have too much control over the workplace. After many violent clashes between union organizers, workers, scabs, and industrial thugs, unions prevailed. The workers' case was too strong. They were simply asking for what we all enjoy today; a forty-hour workweek, safe working conditions, time off, the ability to bargain collectively, and health benefits. Capitalism not only survived unionization, it thrived for many decades after, proving that capitalism could change and still be a productive economic system. However, the unions have not fared as well in recent years. In 1983 more than 20 percent of the U.S. workforce was unionized, but by 2015 that numbered had dropped to 11 percent (Bureau of Labor Statistics, "Union Members," 2016).

Fig. 12.3 While many think that capitalism is criminal, most nations of the world have incorporated at least some of its features into their economies.

Socialism

As I mentioned earlier, many perceive socialism and capitalism to be mortal enemies, yet above I gave several examples of how capitalist systems have taken on features that are typically associated with socialist economies. While one of the hallmarks of capitalism is the fierce pursuit of valuable social resources like income, education, wealth, and power (which often results in a wildly unequal distribution of such resources), socialism seeks to reduce inequality by "spreading the wealth." That is, the aim of socialism is to distribute valuable social resources equally and provide a number of economic security programs, thus ensuring the welfare of all members of society and reducing economic inequality.

Socialism is an economic system characterized by state or collective ownership of the means of production, land, and capital, and the cooperative allocation of resources (Rosser and Rosser, 2004; Arnold, 1994; Badie, Berg-Schlosser, and Morlino, 2011). While the nations of the world provide a variety of socialist economies, as they do with capitalism, all retain some common components or features:

- *Common or state ownership* of the means of production. The means of production, such as factories, railways, and farms, are owned by public enterprises, cooperatives, and/or the state, unlike in a capitalist economic system, in which the means of production are owned privately by individuals or businesses.
- *Central planning.* Economic planning is done centrally by cooperatives and/or state agencies and is based on human consumption needs and economic demands. Economic decisions regarding the allocation of resources to various ends, the goods to be produced, and the methods of production are taken by a central authority and not left to individuals, as in the capitalist economies (Lindemann, 1984).
- *Equal opportunity for all.* Because large-scale industries are commonly owned, the gains or "profits" from these industries are returned to society to benefit all.
- *Redistribution of income.* Believing that inequality is socially damaging, socialist economies provide a host of social welfare programs such as "cradle-to-grave health care," employment assistance, and guaranteed pensions. These programs are designed to increase the well-being of and guarantee a minimum standard of living for the less privileged. This is typically achieved through placing a high tax burden on incomes. The broad objectives of a socialist economy are to increase the material and cultural standards of the people so they may attain full employment and achieve economic equality (Mises, 1951).

There are few if any national economies in the world today that possess a "pure" version of socialism. Like capitalist countries, socialist economies mix state ownership and control of industries with privately owned businesses and free markets. China is a perfect example of the combination of a once rigidly state-planned and state-controlled economy that has allowed, even encouraged, people to engage in private financial enterprises. The phrase "To get rich is glorious" has been attributed to China's former leader Deng Xiaoping and is believed to have set China on a path to unbridled capitalism (while reported widely by many media outlets, there is no proof he actually said this). From all outward appearances China has become a capitalist juggernaut; however, much of the industry and banking remain in the hands of the state. For example, even though the major banks in China were officially transformed into "joint-stock" companies, which means shares (stocks) are sold to private individuals and companies, they are still effectively controlled by the state. China now operates more of a hybrid than either a socialist or capitalist economy (Breslin, 2014; Hersh, 2014).

Command Economies

There are a few countries that have highly rigid socialist economies, which are called command economies. A command economy is a system in which all means of production are state owned and a centralized government body determines what goods should be produced, how much to produce, and the prices of goods (Dunmore, 1980). The only real choice consumers have is among those goods produced by the state. Even occupations are chosen for the members of a command economy by the state. Essentially, a centralized government body commands (designs and runs) the economy; every aspect of the economy is regulated by the government rather than market forces, as in capitalism. Zimbabwe, Cuba, North Korea, and Laos all operate command economies (Lane and Ersson, 2002).

It is interesting to note that while we believe we have a free market economy and are not under the rigid economic control of the state, the United States actually has some features of a command economy. While we don't have a central economic plan, there is an annual federal budget, wherein government spending helps set the priorities for the country. This almost always includes stimulating economic growth. Through the allocation of taxes, some activities are discouraged and others are subsidized, like agriculture. The federal government has complete *command* of important national industries such as NASA and the National Oceanic and Atmospheric Administration. Other countries also possess some characteristics of a command economy, like China, Belarus, Canada, and Iran (Amadeo, "Command Economy," 2016).

Traditional Economies

At the other end of the economic spectrum from a command economy is the traditional economy—a system in which economic activity is based on habits and customs that have been handed down through many generations. Whereas in a command economy individual economic behavior is shaped by a central government plan, all economic activity in traditional economies is decided by the individual mostly for their own survival. Traditional economies typically possess four key features:

- They are based on agriculture, hunting, fishing, and gathering but are usually organized around a combination of these activities.
- These subsistence behaviors are based on traditions such as rituals, habits, and customs that have been handed down through generations. Additionally, in traditional economies social roles—especially gender—roles are rigidly defined by custom.
- Traditional economies may use barter instead of or in combination with money. The Mbuti people of Africa's Congo region, for example, trade meat for tools and pots and pans (Mukenge, 2002).
- People in these societies usually live in families, small bands, or tribes. Again, the Mbuti live in small bands ranging in size from fifteen to sixty people (Amadeo, "Traditional Economy," 2016).

People in these cultures grow, kill, or gather what they need to survive. Farming, fishing, hunting, and gathering have been done the same way for generations in these societies. The legacy of this way of life includes the traditions that have emerged that shape the lives of people in these societies. Those traditions then become the basis of their economy. The Inuit people of northern

Fig. 12.4 The Inuit dry fish during the warm season to sustain them through their long winters. Frugal members of the community who dry and store surplus fish can use them to barter within their traditional economies.

Canada, for example, have a traditional economy. Traditions of hunting, fishing, shelter building, and making clothes have been handed down through countless generations (Stern, 2010; Corriveau, 2002). Gaining these survival skills allows individuals to provide for themselves (hunting food and making clothing and shelter) and to take part in the larger economy (bartering meat or clothing for other desired goods or services).

Through their traditional practices, people in traditional economies provide themselves with food, clothing, and shelter, whereas we, in a large market economy, typically buy our food clothing and shelter using money. Those in traditional economies rely on themselves and family members for economic survival, whereas we rely on the markets for our economic survival. Traditional economies are found around the globe in Africa, South America, North America, Asia, and Oceania. It is commonly thought that the economies of the world emerged from traditional economies and that tradition economies will eventually transition into market economies.

Mixed Economies

A pure form of any economic system is difficult to find in the world today. The vast majority of economies are mixed economies—systems that possesses elements of two or more economic models. All modern economies are mixed, being composed of some combination of private enterprise and government control of some industries or sectors. The United States, the United Kingdom, Spain, France, Germany, Italy, Greece, and the Netherlands are all examples of modern mixed economies. Because these countries have a combination of private and state-owned and state-run economic features, they are sometimes referred to as *dual economies* (Johnson, 2013; Blass and Foster, 1993). Most European nations have economies in which heavy industries are controlled by the state, such as mining and steel production, while other market sectors can be privately owned and controlled. The key feature of nearly all European mixed economies is that while they allow free markets to flourish, the state controls mechanisms such as universal health care and guaranteed state pensions, which tend to "level the playing field" by reducing inequality.

Fig. 12.5 Here a mixed economy is represented by a statue of Lenin (the former leader of the communist Soviet Union- which had a command economy) and his shopping bag symbolizing capitalism.

Typically, the term *mixed economy* refers to economies where the means of production are shared between private and public sectors, but the term doesn't necessarily have to be limited to that narrow interpretation. Mixed economies can include those that contain a combination of features of traditional, capitalist, and/or command systems. Cambodia, for example, is a nation that has seen major economic growth in the past few decades. Once a command economy, it was reformed in 1989 and has been transitioning to a capitalist open market economy since. However, Cambodia lacks well-developed infrastructure like roads and bridges, and a large portion of the rural population remains involved with traditional economies, growing and hunting their own food and producing many of their daily goods. While it has an established banking industry and a financial center located in Phnom Penh, the capital city, barter is still practiced in rural Cambodian communities. Cambodia has features of a command economy, capitalism, and a traditional economy (Naron, 2012; Chandler, 2008; Brinkley, 2012; IFAD, 2007).

Emergent and Frontier Economies

Some countries are described as having **emerging economies** (or markets)—economies that have a basic banking industry and a stock exchange but still have underdeveloped infrastructure and may be politically unstable. Emerging economies are rapidly growing but are also volatile; they have tremendous potential for growth but also pose significant political, financial, and social risk. Countries like Peru, for example, are recognized as having economic stability but lacking infrastructure like roads, dams, and bridges. While it has made giant strides in the past two decades, Peru still struggles with the inequality of opportunity and radical political insurgents. As emerging economies, countries like Peru, Mexico, and Brazil represent investment opportunities for individuals and businesses around the world. Most countries strive to grow their economies, and as they "emerge," other countries and businesses invest in them, giving them the money they need to improve infrastructure, income opportunities, health care, and standards of living; which in turn brings more investment and more improvement, until these countries' economies are no longer considered emerging, but seen as developed (Enderwick, 2012; de la Torre and Schmukler, 2007).

Frontier economies (or markets) are less developed than emerging markets; they do not possess a stock exchange, may have rudimentary banking, have low gross domestic product (GDP), and are politically and socially volatile. Myanmar (formerly Burma) is a good example of a frontier economy. While Myanmar's economy is agriculturally based, it most closely resembles a traditional economy; most people grow, consume, and sell their own crops. Due to pervasive government controls, inefficient economic policies, corruption, and high rates of poverty, social and economic conditions are difficult. Myanmar's economy is weak, and the country has experienced outbreaks of violence. This makes the country too risky for many investors, which results in little money coming into the country, limiting economic and social growth. Frontier economies essentially represent the stage before economies become emergent (Standard & Poor's Rating Services, 2016; Serkin, 2015; Mataen, 2012; Brown, 2013).

However, the democratic elections of 2015 may be a signal that the country is ready to move toward opening free markets, allowing foreign investment, and further developing its industrial sector (currently only about 10 percent of the workforce is engaged in the industrial sector). Additionally, the government has relaxed banking regulations and has allowed foreign banks to operate within the country, and both Ford and Coca-Cola have begun to penetrate the market. These are positive signs for Myanmar's economy and the social and economic conditions of its people (Asian Development Bank, 2016).

Work, the Economy, and You

Above we discussed economic systems in broad brush strokes, giving us a sort of overview of what features economies of the world have and how they operate in a general sense. However, most of us are not involved in stocks, futures, derivatives, or commodities trading. Additionally, most of us are not involved with international banking or high finance. Most of us do, however, have jobs, invest, and buy stuff. By the time we have graduated high school, we have had enough interaction with the economy that we are aware of the things we have to do to be successful in society. These most likely include going to college, getting a job, buying a house, and paying bills and taxes.

Work

> *"If one works to live, one has something worth working for. If one lives to work, hopefully one does not get fired."*
>
> — *Siam Luu*

If you are reading this textbook, you are most likely taking an introductory sociology course at some college or university. You are most likely attending your college or university because you think it is important to get a college education so you can get a good job or start a good paying career. The one thing that nearly all humans will face at some point in their life is work. **Work** is any physical and/or mental activity that is performed in exchange for income. According to the Bureau of Labor Statistics, in the United States those born between 1957 and 1964 held an average of 11.7 jobs between the ages of eighteen and forty-eight, and that number is expected to increase (Bureau of Labor Statistics, "Number of Jobs Held," 2015). Today's youngest workers—that would be you—are projected to hold 12 to 15 jobs in their lifetime (Meister, 2012).

How Has Work Changed in the United States?

The fact that there is such a demand for well-educated workers in our society is evidence that there has been a change in the economy, shaping a different type of workforce. Factors such as shifting labor markets, the loss of manufacturing industries, and continued globalization have changed the composition of the U.S. labor force. As a result of offshoring and outsourcing (we will discuss this later in the chapter), much of America's manufacturing industry has been transferred overseas to countries like China, Vietnam, and Cambodia, leaving fewer manufacturing jobs and shifting those workers to the low-paying service sector. Consequently, many of the heavily unionized industries have shrunk or disappeared, due in part to ever-increasing globalization, leaving those workers to take jobs with less job security and few or no benefits. While wages and benefits have increased overall in the past forty years, occupations like those in manufacturing have dwindled, creating a labor market with a thin middle, the low-wage service sector jobs on the bottom and white-collar jobs on top (Lerman and Schmidt, 1999). The composition of the U.S. workforce and labor force participation rates (see figure 12.6) have also been influenced by changes in the population; the workforce now includes a greater number of women, minorities, and older people (Bureau of Labor Statistics, "Labor Force Statistics," 2016).

Fig. 12.6 Labor force participation rates, 1948–2015

The Postindustrial or Service Economy

In my lifetime, the U.S. economy has gone from a mainly industrial manufacturing economy to a postindustrial or service economy. A **postindustrial** economy (or society) is one in which the primary focus has shifted from producing goods to primarily providing services. That is, the service sector of the economy accounts for more of the income, wealth, and economic growth than the manufacturing sector does (Bell, 1973). That's why this type of economy is also referred to as a *service economy*. In this type of economy, the importance of blue-collar, unionized work, including manual labor, declines, while professional and technical jobs like scientists, teachers, and IT professionals are in greater demand, growing in value and prevalence. Occupations based in behavioral and information sciences such as behavioral economics, cybernetics, and information architecture develop and will emerge as an important sector of the labor force. Additionally, knowledge becomes a highly valued form of capital. For example, knowledge derived from the Human Genome Project has led to thousands of patents, inventions, and health care innovations. Knowledge produced in this way, from research and scientific inquiry, becomes a main way to grow the economy (Tripp and Grueber, 2011).

The United States and many European nations have developed postindustrial economies, mainly because these countries industrialized sooner than many other nations of the world. In fact, the United States was the first country in the world to have more than 50 percent of its workforce occupying service sector jobs. Obviously, this transformation to a service economy, where information, services, and research are important and in high demand, will have a profound impact and change society as a whole. In the 1999 edition of his book *The Coming of Post-Industrial Society: A Venture in Social Forecasting*, Daniel Bell describes seven important ways the United States has changed as it transforms into a postindustrial society:

1. *The rise in service sector jobs.* The production of goods like toys, cars, and clothing declines as the production of services such as fast-foods restaurants, researchers, and life coaches increases. In the United States in 2014, those employed in the "goods-producing" sector represented a mere 12.7 percent of the workforce, while those employed in the "service-providing" sector made up 80.1 percent of the total workforce (Bureau of Labor Statistics, "Industry Employment," 2015).
2. *A rise in the number of technical and professional jobs and workers.* Jobs such as app developer, market research data miner, social media manager, chief listening office, and user experience designer didn't exist in 2000. However, with the incredible growth in social media and virtual technology, whole new occupational categories have emerged (Casserly, 2012).
3. *A rise in education being viewed as the best path to social mobility.* Education becomes the pathway to more prestigious and well-paying occupations, translating into a higher standard of living. Historically, inheritance of family wealth, a family business, or a family occupation was the way to social privilege. With the increasing demand for highly educated workers to take on well-paying occupations, education becomes the direct path to high-income, prestigious jobs. Between 2008 and 2018 it is projected that the economy will create 55 million new job openings, and 65 percent of these jobs will require some postsecondary education or training (Carnevale, Smith, and Strohl, 2010).

4. *The rise of the importance of other types of capital over financial capital.* For nearly the entire economic history of the United States, financial capital, the amassing of money and land, was viewed as the only form of capital. However, human and social capital is the way to gauge the strength of postindustrial societies. An investment in higher education in order to compete in a job market that is increasingly demanding postsecondary education is an investment in one's human capital—self-improvement. Additionally, social capital—the extent to which one has access to opportunities and social networks—is becoming increasingly important in finding work and getting ahead. In 2014, 43 percent of employers reported using social networking sites to research job candidates, which was up from 39 percent in 2013 (Grasz, "Number of Employers," 2014).
5. *The rise of intellectual technology.* For Bell, intellectual technology is the marriage of knowledge, information, and computers, especially using computers for data transmission, which is essentially what the Internet does. It is what is provided to retailers, charities, politicians, and the government by people using the Internet—big data—that can be described as "intellectual technology." According to Bell, computers would facilitate decision making, specifically the use of algorithms. Whether it is a politician deciding what her message should be for her voting demographic or eHarmony deciding who would make the best life mate for you, big data is being crunched and funneled through a gauntlet of algorithms to make the best decision.
6. *A change in the fundamental infrastructure of society from transportation to communication.* In industrial economies raw materials need to get to manufacturers and the goods that are produced have to get to their markets; ships bring raw materials to port, trains ship these materials to manufacturing centers, workers have to get to work, and finally, trucks deliver goods to wholesale and retail outlets. Therefore, transportation becomes the single most important element of an industrial economy's infrastructure. In contrast, in a postindustrial society the movement of information becomes the single most important piece of infrastructure. The "information superhighway" was how the Internet was once described; the ability to transmit enormous amounts of information instantly without geographical restriction has transformed the way we live, interact with others, and view the world.
7. *A knowledge theory of value versus a labor theory of value.* Industrial economies are based on the labor theory of value. That is, the value of goods is based on how much labor it took to produce the goods. Say you stop by your favorite hamburger place and order your favorite bacon and bleu cheeseburger. The cooks in the back take raw hamburger meat and raw bacon, cook them up, toast the buns, and pour on the bleu cheese. Their labor and capital (the grill and toaster oven) have added value to those ingredients, and you are willing to pay for that tasty snack because it has value to you. You would not be willing to pay for the raw ingredients if they just handed those over the counter to you.

They have no value to you in that form. However, Bell believes that knowledge, in our postindustrial economy, will add value through invention and innovation, which in turn can save labor and capital. If you have a navigation system built into your car, all you have to do is jump in, buckle up, and tell your navigation system where you want to go, and he or she will gladly direct you as you drive to your destination. Through the invention and innovation of a navigation system, your labor and time has been saved. No finding a map, writing down directions, then trying to read them as you drive. All that labor has been saved, and now you have more time to eat cheeseburgers.

All of these features of a postindustrial society are with us. However, it doesn't mean that the production of goods has stopped; it has just lessened as we place greater value and rely more heavily on other sectors of the economy. After all, even in a postindustrial society we still have to wear underwear, skinny jeans, and shoes, and most importantly, we need our mobile devices. So where did the production of all those goods go? Well, in today's world much of the manufactured goods we buy and use are made in places other than the United States.

Offshoring, Outsourcing, and Reshoring

Many American manufacturing industries began **offshoring**—the practice of relocating the production of goods to foreign countries while still selling those goods to the U.S. market—in the 1970s, and it is a pervasive practice today. Rising wages among American workers, cheap offshore labor, and a nonunionized workforce were all factors that made offshoring appealing to U.S. companies, and the economic benefits of offshoring have been considerable for many different groups. Workers in low-cost countries have enjoyed a rise in their standards of living and access to a greater array of goods. Multinational businesses have managed to cut labor costs and realize higher profits. And consumers in Western industrialized nations have enjoyed access to more goods at far lower prices. But offshoring by Western countries has contributed to job losses in wealthier countries. Globalization has become a double-edged sword for Western industrialized nations; on one edge they enjoy an abundance of cheap goods, and on the other they fear the loss of jobs and preeminence in the global workplace (Bhagwati and Blinder, 2009; Buttonwood, 2016).

The whole world has become offshore to American businesses that send the production jobs to places like Canada, Mexico, Vietnam, the Philippines, Venezuela, and even Russia. However, China and India are the two countries that have received more offshored U.S. jobs in the past two decades. In fact, between 2001 and 2013, 3.2 million U.S. jobs were lost to a single country—China. Of those, 2.4 million, or 75 percent, were manufacturing jobs (Kimball and Scott, 2014). Apple, for example, puts "Designed by Apple in California" on all its products. While that may be true, Apple products are not manufactured in California or any other state. The manufacturing of Apple products has been offshored to China, Taiwan, Mongolia, and South Korea (Odekon, 2015). When asked why Apple doesn't make its products in the United States, CEO Tim Cook (2015) said the primary reason is "it's skill." He said Americans have lost their vocational skills, and jobs like machinist are rare in the United States but plentiful in Asian countries. However, Steve Jobs, cofounder of Apple, said that while cost is a factor in offshoring manufacturing processes to China, the real reason Apple makes products there is that Chinese workers can do things fast, really fast, and on a much larger scale (Duhigg and Bradsher, 2012). While China offers lots of workers who can produce goods fast and on a large scale, India's attraction is that it has a workforce than can do low-level jobs like data entry as well as high-end work like research and engineering. The bonus is much of India's tech workforce can speak English, making them valuable across the labor spectrum (Bhate, 2009; Federation of Indian Chambers of Commerce & Industry, 2013).

Many times offshoring is mistakenly called outsourcing. **Outsourcing**—obtaining or contracting certain services or products from a third party—does not mean that the jobs needed to perform the service or make the product have been sent to another country, as in offshoring. Outsourced jobs can be found right in your hometown. There are many small, medium, and large companies that contract with accountants to keep their books; rather than doing it in house, they outsource their accounting. If I'm manufacturing baseball bats, for example, and outsource my accounting, I haven't created job loss at my production facility, where I make bats, not employ accountants. However, if I decide to now make my bats in Estonia, I have offshored my manufacturing jobs and people are out of work, because what I do is make baseball bats. Figure 12.7 shows that outsourcing continues to increase and that people see it as harmful to Americans and, no surprise, CEOs see it as good for business—which has the potential to create friction between companies that outsource heavily and consumers who use their goods or services.

An NBC News and *Wall Street Journal* survey conducted in 2010 showed that 86 percent of Americans polled said that offshoring and outsourcing of jobs by local firms to low-wage locations was a leading cause of their country's economic problems ("The Story So Far," 2013). As a result of the economic downturn of 2007–2008, unemployed workers in some Western countries began to perceive these practices as the major reason many of them couldn't find work. Even politicians have jumped on the anti-offshoring wagon, using the issue to vilify their opponents (Mansfield and Mutz, 2013). During his 2012 presidential campaign, Barack Obama accused Mitt Romney, his Republican opponent, of transferring thousands of jobs overseas. In response, Romney pointed out that Chrysler was planning on manufacturing Jeeps in China, which the company did and continues to do (Killough, 2012).

In response to American's fears of losing more jobs and opportunities to overseas workers, a reshoring movement has gained traction. The *Reshoring Initiative* is on the vanguard of

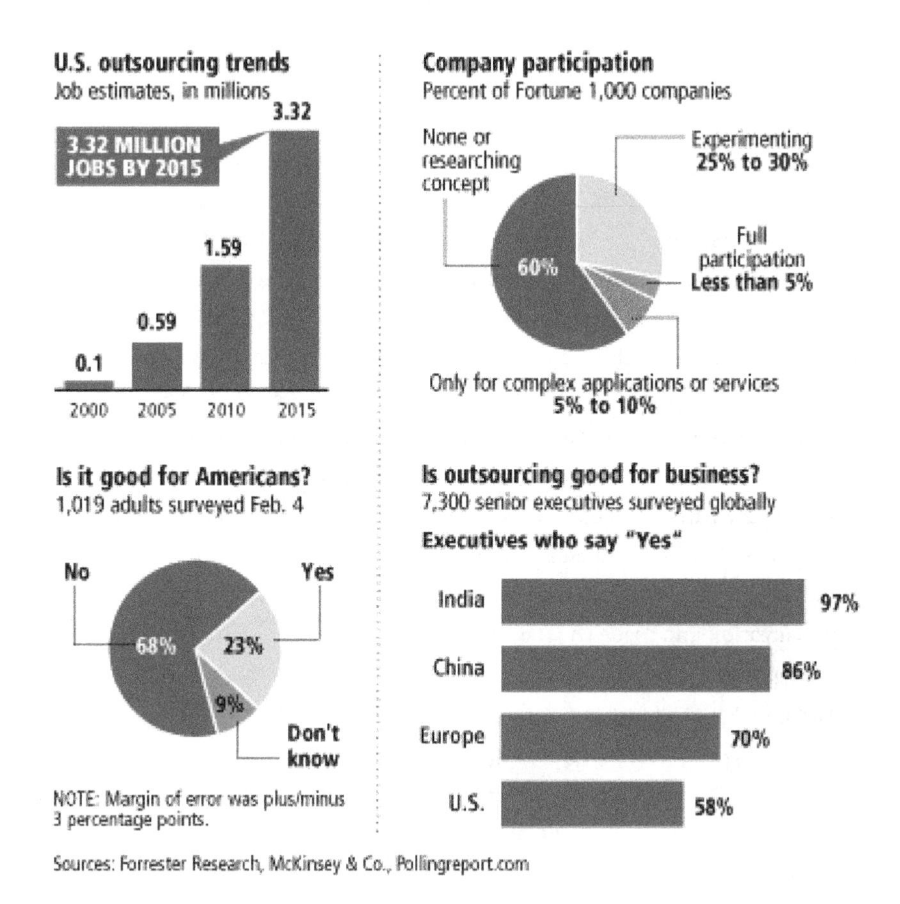

Fig. 12.7 Outsourcing: Figures and Feelings. The charts and graphs above clearly indicate that outsourcing has been on the rise for over a decade and that most companies participate in it. Why is it that while outsourcing seems to be wildly popular with U.S. companies, both American business executives and Americans in general think it is a bad idea?

this movement. Founded by a former president of a machine tool–making company who grew up working summers in the now defunct Singer Sewing Machine factory in New Jersey. the Reshoring Initiative's mission "is to bring good, well-paying manufacturing jobs back to the United States by assisting companies to more accurately assess their total cost of offshoring, and shift collective thinking from *offshoring is cheaper* to *local reduces the total cost of ownership*" ("Reshoring Initiative", 2016, italics added). Basically, they hope to persuade U.S. businesses to bring their manufacturing back, put American workers back to work, and make America less dependent on foreign labor and thus economically stronger.

Globalization

Offshoring manufacturing processes and job outsourcing became two of the key features of the movement to a postindustrial society in an increasingly globalized economy. Historically, human societies around the world have engaged in complex interactions through trading, wars, and cultural diffusion. So global integration is not new, it has just accelerated dramatically in the past few decades. Globalization—the increased interconnectedness and interdependence of the people, governments, and businesses of different countries of the world—is driven by international trade and investment and is propelled by information technology (Levitt, 1983; Al-Rodhan, 2006). Globalization is not new; for thousands of years, people have been trading goods and spreading language, customs, and ideas to each other across great distances. The Silk Road connected China and Europe during the Middle Ages, and as an infant nation the United States established trade partnerships in Europe, Africa, and Asia (Hansen, 2012; Frankopan, 2015).

Unparalleled changes in communications, transportation, and information technology have accelerated globalization and made the nations of the world more interdependent than ever. Now multinational corporations like Apple and Levi Strauss manufacture their products in many different countries and sell to consumers around the world. These multinationals have tremendous economic power and use it to influence regional trade agreements, which can coerce less-developed countries into economic cooperation. These powerful companies have so much influence and money that they can convince or pay off these countries' officials, which results in reduced tariffs and relaxed environmental and labor standards. Consequently, these changes make poor countries much more attractive to the multinationals, and their workers more susceptible to exploitation (Stiglitz, 2002, 2006; Bhagwati, 2004; Bishop, Reinke, and Adams, 2011; Visto, 2002).

Money, raw materials, and information move ever more rapidly across national borders. It's not just money and goods that are moving effortlessly across borders, ideas and elements of cultures also spread more freely. As a result, there is a great amount of cultural diffusion; ideas, beliefs, and practices previously unknown in some countries are being adopted by their people. For example, rapping is not an indigenous performance style in Estonia, but when countries that were isolated for decades started trading freely with the West, it brought more than just cell phones. People like G-Enka, an Estonian rapper, was influenced by the beats from the West, and he now ranks among a host of multinational rap performers. While these trends may be seen as inevitable in an increasingly profit-driven world, billions of people have been uprooted, their livelihoods threatened, and their cultural beliefs and practices disrupted (Machida, 2012). Who do you think most benefits from globalization? Who is most harmed by it?

Even as the world seems to prosper as a consequence of the international flow of money, goods, and information, globalization remains controversial. Proponents argue that globalization has encouraged economic development in poorer countries while allowing their citizens to enjoy

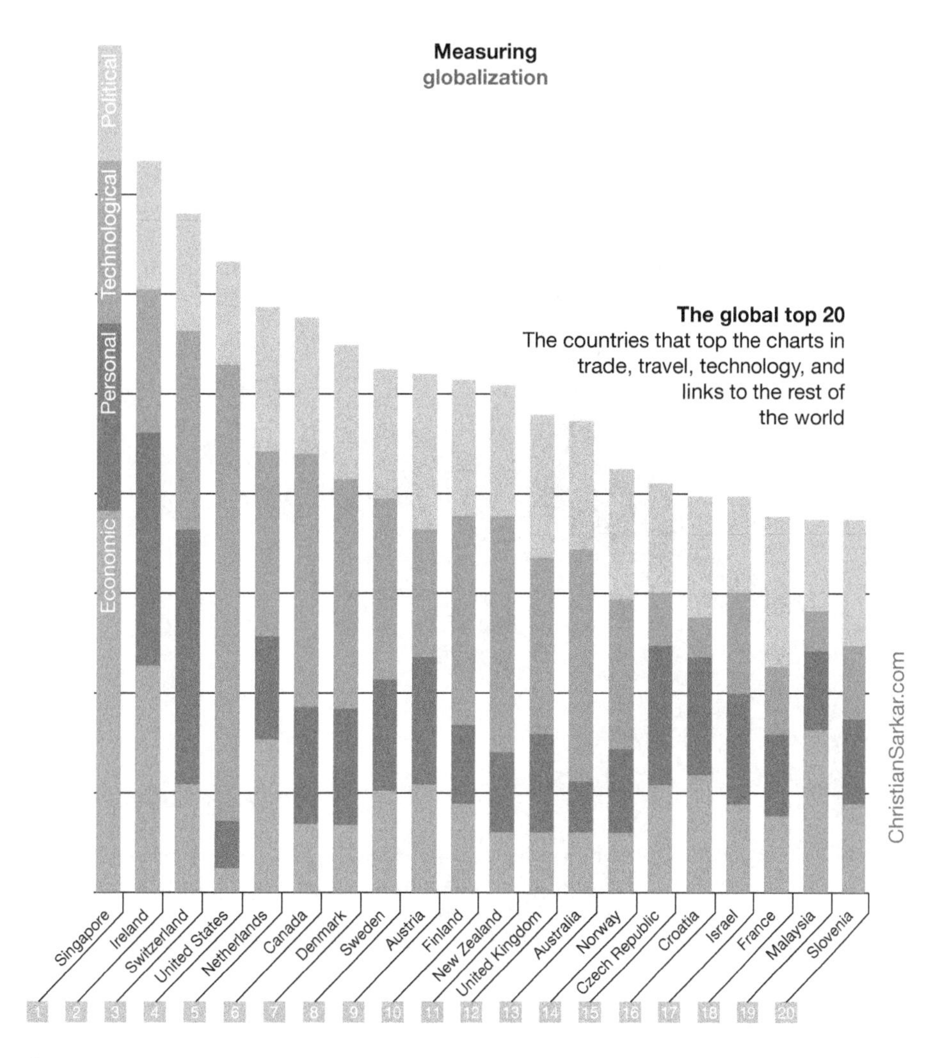

Fig. 12.8 The United States ranks fourth in the top twenty globalized nations of the world. Notice that it's our technology that is our greatest strength in linking up with other nations of the world.

and increase in their standards of living. People in many developing countries who before had very little now enjoy more economic freedom and access to affordable goods. Opponents believe that free trade, as well as access to new and emerging markets and their cheap labor and natural resources, has benefited multinational corporations while harming the environment and local cultures. Globalization, opponents say, continues to exploit poor workers in developing countries, creating grinding poverty and forcing many into slavery, while endangering and destroying local cultures and habitats (Bales, 2016). Do you benefit from globalization, directly or indirectly? Are you harmed by globalization, directly or indirectly? How have you benefited or been harmed by globalization?

Globalization:

Fig. 12.9 A cynical perspective on globalization. However, opponents of globalization argue that in their search for cheap labor and goods, developed Western nations benefit much more from globalization than do poorer nations. The people of less wealthy nations are exploited, subjugated, and even enslaved as a result of globalization.

TRY THIS

Go through your house and look at the labels on all the stuff you own. Where is your phone made? How about your clothes, where are they made? Go through the labels or owner's manuals of the things you own and see where things are made. You may find that some things are assembled in the United States but all the parts are made in other countries. You may find that some things are made in countries you may never have heard of. Some Levi's jeans are made on Saipan in Micronesia, Barbie figures are made in Hong Kong, and there are no TVs made in the United States. Where are most things you own made? Is the majority of the things you own made outside the United States? Well, that's a result of globalization.

Women and the Workforce

The growth seen in the U.S. labor force in the past few decades is clearly related to two main factors: an increase in the overall population and a growing number of women participating in the labor force. There is an array of factors affecting the rise in women's workforce participation. As we discussed earlier in the chapter, there has been a decline in the demand for jobs requiring manual labor, while many more jobs requiring more education, such as white-collar jobs, have been created in the past forty years. This change in employment demands had the effect of opening up more jobs for women. Other greater educational opportunities for women have led many to pursue careers that allow them to use their diplomas and degrees. Also, increased divorce rates have returned or brought more women into the workforce. Finally, changes in a number of laws and social policies make it more difficult and costly for employers to discriminate against women (Bureau of Labor Statistics, "Women in the Labor Force," 2014; Lavery, 2012). Figure 12.10 shows that as of 2015, 56.7 percent of women of working age participated in the labor force, and that number is predicted to *decrease* to 55.8 percent by 2024.

It's not just economic reasons that make women enter the workforce. In the past few decades, women have increasingly decided to delay marriage and childbirth or forego them altogether, instead choosing to pursue an education or develop their careers. Not having children or being married frees up time otherwise devoted to child care, leaving many women more time to pursue job opportunities. Even if women have children later, their increased life expectancy gives them

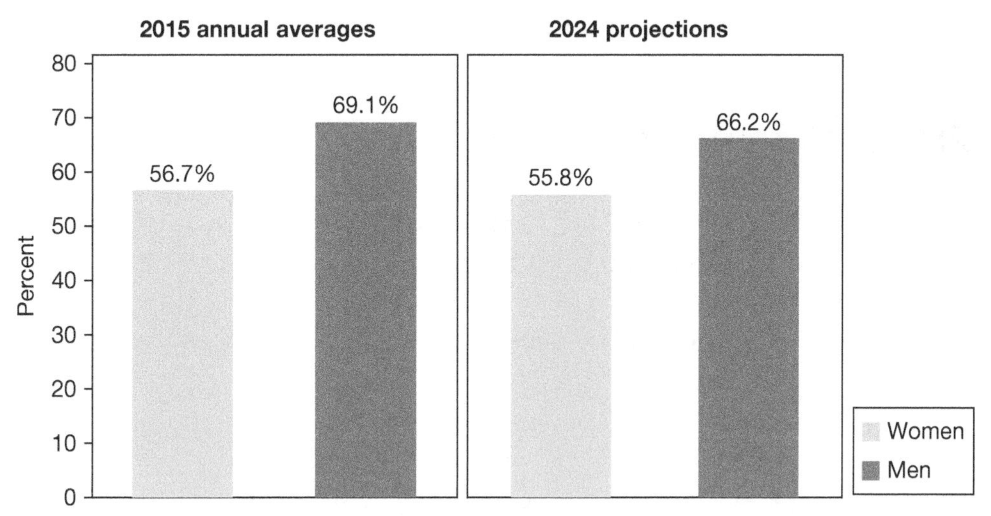

Fig. 12.10 Labor force participation by sex

Fig. 12.11 Chart showing gender wage gap over time. Median woman's salary as a percentage of median man's salary.

more years of potential work life once the nest is empty or close to empty (Glynn, 2014).

Even though women are entering the workforce in record numbers, their pay continues to lag behind that of men. Take a look at figure 12.11, which shows the gender wage gap over time. On average, women make about 79 cents for every dollar a man makes (Hegewisch and DuMonthier, 2016). This holds true even when comparing the pay of men and women in the same job sector, with comparable skills, education, and experience. Younger women fare better than those in the last years of their work life. For women aged twenty-five to twenty-nine, the annual wage gap is about $1,700. However, for women in the last five years of their careers before retirement, that gap widens to $14,352. That ever-widening gap over a woman's forty-year work life becomes a chasm, losing the average working women a staggering $431,000. With all the legal protections women (among others) are afforded in the workplace, why do you think the gender pay gap persists?

Minorities and the Workforce

In just over a decade, several minority groups have gained ground in the U.S. workforce. Since the U.S. population is more racially and ethnically diverse today than in 2001, so is the workforce. In 2014 Hispanics made up 13 percent of the U.S. workforce, up from 11 percent in 2001. Asian Americans represented 5 percent of the workforce, a modest increase from 4 percent in 2001. In 2014 African American were 12 percent of the workforce, no change from 2001. White workers lost a share of total employment, dropping from 71 percent to 69 percent from 2001 to 2014. Hispanic/Latino workers, Asian workers, and black/African American workers all experienced major growth in the diversity of their occupations (Grasz, "CareerBuilder," 2015). While racial minorities make up more of the workforce in the United States than they have in the past, with the exception of Asians, they still lag behind the wages of whites (US Equal Employment Opportunity Commision, 2015).

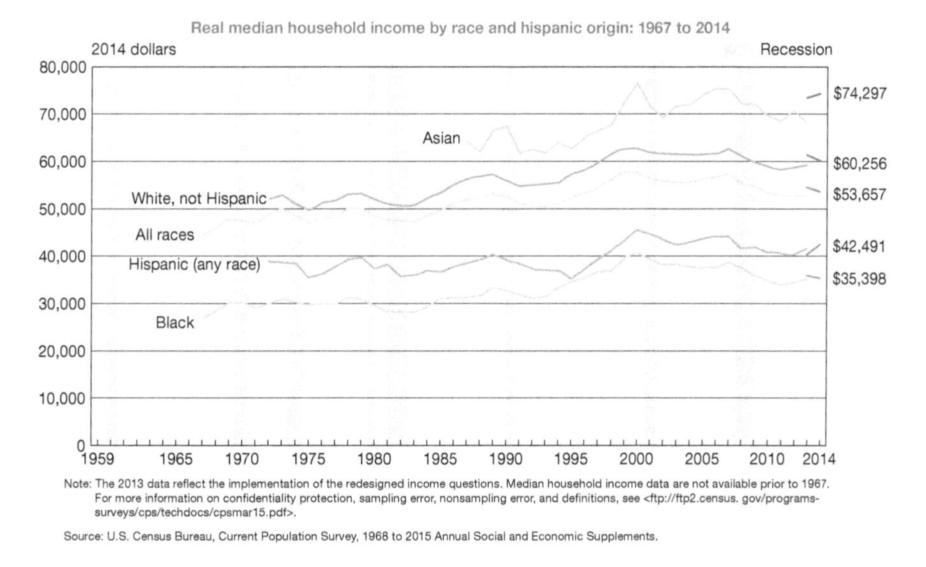

Fig. 12.12 While median household incomes have increased over time, the earnings of both blacks and Hispanics lag behind those of Asians and whites.

If you look at the earnings of blacks and Hispanics compared to whites in figure 12.12, you can see that in 2014 the median household income for whites was $60,256, compared to $42,491 for Hispanics and $35,398 for black households. Asians were the exception for minority groups, earning more than whites with a median household income of over $74,000. If you break income down by both sex and race, being a woman compounds the earnings differential. In 2014 all women earned on average less than men; however, white women had the highest median annual income followed by black women, while Hispanic women had the lowest earnings among these groups. So the combination of being black or Hispanic and female results in earnings that are the lowest among all racial groups and both sexes. Men earn more than women across all racial/ethnic groups. These earning differences between sexes and racial/ethnic groups is present across all occupational categories. That is, whether you are a truck driver or brain surgeon, if you are black or Hispanic, you will make less than your white counterparts. And if you are a woman you will make less on average than men, regardless of your race/ethnicity or occupational category (Bureau of Labor Statistics, "Usual Weekly Earnings," 2016; DeNavas- Walt and Proctor, 2015).

Underemployment, Unemployment, and the Great Recession

Even though at times we have all complained about our jobs, working conditions, coworkers, or superiors, most people want to work. We have been taught to "be a hard worker" and that "hard work

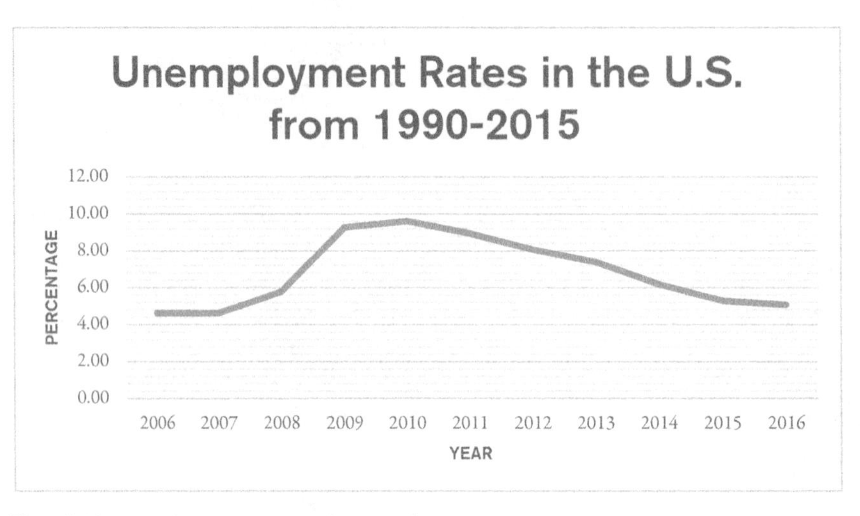

Fig. 12.13 Unemployment rates in the United States, 1990–2015

never hurt anyone." However, not everyone can find enough work or any work at all. Those who are not working are typically represented by the **unemployment rate**, which is all people who are jobless, looking for work, and available for work as a percentage of the total labor force. You can see from figure 12.13 that the unemployment rate in the United States was relatively low before the great recession but soared from 4.6 percent in 2007 to 9.6 percent in 2010, illustrating the downstream effects of the housing market crash (Bureau of Labor Statistics, "Labor Force," 2016). Many lost their jobs as companies went out of business, and some employees were the victims of **downsizing**—an intentional reduction in a workforce in order for a business to stay afloat or profitable.

Businesses in several industries offshored or outsourced much of their labor during this turbulent period in order to maintain their profitability, further damaging the labor market. Those in male-dominated job sectors like construction and manufacturing were hardest hit, leading some economists to refer to the great recession as the "mancession." Job markets like these are populated mostly by men with lower levels of education and fewer resources to cope with lost wages and jobs (Thompson, 2009; Negra and Tasker, 2014; Perry, 2008). However, in mid-2010 a Pew (2010) study showed that 55 percent of adults in the U.S. labor force experienced some type of work-related hardship between 2007 and 2010. Particularly hard hit during this period were blacks, who had an unemployment rate of 16 percent, and Latinos, with 13 percent unemployment, while the national unemployment rate peaked at 10 percent in late 2010. Additionally, young workers fared much worse than did older workers during the recession.

However, the economy and the labor market have improved. The unemployment rate slowly dropped to 7.4 percent in 2013 and has been in a freefall since, reaching 4.9 percent as of March 2016. While the unemployment rate has improved dramatically, the employment landscape has changed. Nearly 6.6 million of the jobs added to the economy since 2010 are "good jobs," those paying at least $53,000 for full-time employees (Carnevale, Jayasundera, and Gulish, 2015).

And almost all those good jobs, 97 percent, went to college grads. During the recession many college-educated people found themselves **underemployed,** a situation where employees are working fewer hours than they wish or working in jobs that don't match or that underutilize their skills/education/training. Many were forced to take **Mcjobs**—low-paying, low-skill jobs that they were overqualified for, such as mathematicians cleaning offices or engineers handing out lattes at Starbucks (Etzioni, 1986; Coupland, 1991). But the job market has changed; while Mcjobs have returned after the recession, they aren't growing like well-paying jobs are.

The future of the labor market for well-educated individuals seems bright, while for those with little or some education it looks bleak. The labor market that has emerged from the great recession is one that is somewhat polarized. That is, as of the writing of this chapter in early 2016, good jobs, those with the best pay and conditions, have rebounded and were the first to come back. While low-wage jobs, those that pay less than $32,000 per year, have fully recovered (800,000 jobs above the prerecession employment) from the recession, they are growing much slower than good jobs. And the middle seems to have dropped out. Middle-wage jobs, those that pay between $32,000 and $53,000 per year, have yet to find their way back from the recession—about 900,000 jobs short of prerecession employment (Carnevale, Jayasundera, and Gulish, 2015). This job market landscape represents the postindustrial or service economy. Jobs demanding high levels of education that pay well, like those in high-tech, research, and health, are plentiful; so too are jobs at the lowest end of the job spectrum, like fast-food worker, cleaning person, and delivery person. And the middle-wage jobs that were once represented by manufacturing industries have largely been offshored or outsourced and aren't coming back anytime soon. Have you ever been underemployed or unemployed? Can unemployment be symbolic? Do you think others see unemployed people differently? Do you think others treat unemployed people differently?

READ MORE

- *The Great Recession: Profit Cycles, Economic Crisis (A Marxist View)* by Michael Roberts (2009). Michael Roberts predicted the greatest economic downturn in U.S. history since the Great Depression of the 1930s. His book explores how this most recent market crash happened, and using a Marxist perspective he makes predictions about whether and when it could happen again. Be warned, this book is not for the faint of heart.
- *The Great Recession: History, Ideology, Hubris and Nemesis* by Michael S. Heng (2010). The author takes a much broader historical and sociological view of the great recession. Placing it in historical context, Heng examines the financial egos, multinational economic struggles, and social forces that led up to the collapse of the U.S. housing market, and the subsequent global economic downturn. This book jettisons the myopic financial view of the great recession and paints a backdrop of myriad social, political, and economic factors against which the recession seems inevitable.

DEFINITIONS OF UNEMPLOYMENT: VARIATIONS ON A THEME

But does looking at just those without jobs give us an accurate picture of the health of the labor market? We humans like to put things into discrete categories like right or wrong, pass or fail, and Democrat or Republican. We are conditioned to do this, but evolutionary psychologists have shown that we need to do it so we can manage the complexities of life and succeed as a species. We tend to do this with the labor market as well; we tend to think of people as either employed or unemployed. The U.S. labor market is complex to say the least, so it is impossible to represent it with a single measure like the total number of people employed or the unemployment rate.

This narrow measure of the condition of the labor market may be misleading because using broad characterizations like this discards important information. Therefore, it is important to consider not only the unemployment rate, but a number of other measures of labor market health. A more comprehensive measure of the condition of the labor market should include not just the unemployment rate, but other indicators like:

Involuntary part-time workers—those who want full-time work, can't find it, and settle for part-time work.

Marginally attached workers—workers who want a job, are available to work, but have become so discouraged that they stopped looking for work and as a result are not counted among the officially unemployed.

Believe it or not, the U.S. government does attempt to capture a full picture of unemployment, but those figures are not typically presented in the national media—we just get the one number, the unemployment rate. As a matter of fact, there are six different measures of unemployment used by the federal government. Below are the six different ways (U-1 through U-6) you can slice unemployment; these definitions come directly from the Bureau of Labor Statistics. You can see some measures are narrow, like U-1 and U-2, and some are broader and more comprehensive measures of unemployment, like U-4 through U-6 (Bureau of Labor Statistics, "Table A-15," 2015).

- U-1, persons unemployed fifteen weeks or longer, as a percentage of the civilian labor force.
- U-2, job losers and persons who completed temporary jobs, as a percentage of the civilian labor force.
- U-3, total unemployed, as a percentage of the civilian labor force (this is the definition used for the official unemployment rate).
- U-4, total unemployed plus discouraged workers, as a percentage of the civilian labor force plus discouraged workers.
- U-5, total unemployed, plus discouraged workers, plus all other marginally attached workers, as a percentage of the civilian labor force plus all marginally attached workers.
- U-6, total unemployed, plus all marginally attached workers, plus total employed part time for economic reasons, as a percentage of the civilian labor force plus all marginally attached workers.

Theoretical Perspectives on the Economy and Work

Functionalism: Work and the Economy Is Good for You, Me, and Society

An economy is essential to any society because it provides a system of producing and distributing goods and services as well as providing people with jobs, which ultimately allows society to exist (Smelser and Swedberg, 2005). Functionalists would argue that the economy acts as a sort of engine for society, providing subsistence, producing productive labor, and creating and reproducing statuses and roles, thereby promoting conformity, which enhances social cohesion and ultimately ensures social order.

Functionalists believe that in part, work gives people purpose and defines their place in the social word. Going to work and contributing to the economy and society in general promotes social stability and social order. Functionalists stress the positive aspects of work and the economy and not the limitations it can place on people. For example, functionalists would argue that people derive satisfaction from work. Using the 2015 Society for Human Resource Management's Employee Job Satisfaction and Engagement Survey as evidence, functionalists would point out that 86 percent of workers in the United States reported overall satisfaction with their current job.

Conflict Perspective: Work and the Economy Is Good for the Elites but Not the Workers

In contrast to functionalism, the conflict approach views the economy as controlled by an elite class whose power extends to all sectors of the economy. These wealthy classes are the true beneficiaries of labor in the economy, not the workers. In other words, according to conflict theorists, while the elite class may own the means of production, like factories and other business, it is the workers' labor that adds value to those things. So the real work in the economy is done by the workers, yet the elites reap the rewards because they control capital and exploit the workers. Compensation for CEOs, for example, has risen from 20 times greater than an average worker's pay in 1965 to 303 times greater than the average worker's pay in 2014 (Bakija, Cole, and Heim, 2012; Bivens et al., 2014). From 1978 to 2014, CEO compensation increased by 997 percent, compared to a measly 10.9 percent increase in a typical worker's annual income over the same period. American workers are more productive than ever, while at the same time they are experiencing stagnating wages, and their CEOs are experiencing unprecedented earnings growth.

They pay differentials between CEOs and average workers, conflict theorists would contend, is discouraging, not a motivator for workers to work harder. Conflict theorists argue that rather than providing motivation for workers, low wages and poor working conditions just alienate them further, negatively impacting employee morale (Leidner, 1993). The conflict approach recognizes that no matter what steps workers take, like more education or training, there are structural and individual barriers to getting better jobs. Institutional racism, sexism, ageism, and plain-old discrimination prevent workers from advancing at work no matter what steps they take to improve themselves. For example, the glass ceiling, conflict theorists (feminist theorists) would contend, is evidence that even the most-qualified women are barred from the upper reaches of corporate America, simply because they are women (Matthaei, 2015).

Symbolic Interactionism: Work Brings Meaning to Our Lives, and That's Good

When I attend social functions and mingle with others, the conversation invariably includes something like, "So, what do you do for a living?" Our jobs are central features of our lives and in some way define who we are, both by the way others react to our job titles and by the meaning and self-worth our status gives to each of us. Symbolic interactionists would argue that even our occupations act as symbols and that others react to us in ways that are consistent with the meaning our jobs hold. Say you're at a cocktail party and discover the person you are chatting with is a grocery store cashier; you may interact with him differently than if he had told you he was a neurosurgeon. I have experienced this. I have been at social gatherings, and when I tell someone that I'm a professor, they have actually changed the way they speak and begin moving the conversations to weightier topics. Remember that this perspective stresses that during our daily interactions, we react to the meanings attached to symbols, which help us define social situations, interpret actions, and behave appropriately. For example, police officers, like employees in other workplaces, use a number of symbols to manage the impression they wish to project. Police officers want to give the impression that they are in control and that they are competent, so their appearance is always clean, neat, and organized; they use specific language to convey they understand the situation and have control, pay great detail to information from dispatchers so as not to make mistakes, and perform well on the firing range. The rules of behavior and the meanings behind these behaviors are well understood in the law enforcement community, which helps officers project an image of control and competence, enhancing their work identity—they feel good about themselves (Rubenstein, 1993).

TABLE 12.1 Theoretical Perspectives on Economy

Sociological Perspective	Level of Analysis	View of Economy	Example
Functionalism	Macro	Functionalism views the economy as a social institution that is interconnected with other social institutions. The economy represents a necessary social institution. The economy makes society possible by providing its members with goods and services. Jobs provide workers with money so they can participate in the economy and society in general. This social participation includes conforming to social conventions, which promotes social cohesion and stability.	The government and the economy are interconnected through the regulations government applies to certain industries in the public interest. Higher education produces highly trained workers to fill jobs in the workforce, which promotes economic growth. Without jobs, we could not provide basics such as food, clothing, and shelter and fully participate in society.
Conflict	Macro	The conflict perspective views the economy as controlled by the elite classes, who use the economy to maintain their dominance over the subordinate classes.	Rather than realize fewer profits, corporations fire or lay off workers, sending many individuals and families into poverty and impeding their ability to experience improvements in standards of living.
Symbolic Interactionism	Micro	Individuals interact at work using symbols to negotiate a social reality, which establishes a set of expected behaviors so the workplace runs smoothly.	Bosses use symbols like private offices and private executive bathrooms to establish physical boundaries, which in turn establish behavioral boundaries and make the workplace run smoothly. In many businesses subordinates must knock on a superior's door before entering, but superiors can just show up at subordinates' cubicles.

The Interconnectedness of the Economy and Government

Our discussions of both the economy and government will reveal how intimately linked these two institutions are. The government has to regulate industries in order to fulfill one of its main functions, protection of its people, for example. In turn, industries lobby members of Congress to encourage them to support their various interests. The government understands how vital the economy is to society and that preserving it is vital to the well-being of its citizens and the preservation of society.

The Troubled Asset Relief Program (TARP) and the Dodd-Frank Wall Street Reform and Consumer Protection Act (Dodd-Frank Act) are vivid illustrations of how interdependent the economy and government are. In response to the great recession, in 2008 the U.S. government provided several sectors of the economy with a bailout that Congress originally approved at $700 billion (TARP), but which was reduced by the Dodd-Frank Act to $475 billion (US Office of Management and Budget, 2012). Below I've shown how this money was allocated. Notice who got the least amount of aid; you and I are directly affected by credit and housing markets.

- **Approximately $250 billion** was committed to programs to stabilize banking institutions ($5 billion of which was ultimately canceled).
- **Approximately $27 billion** was committed to programs to restart credit markets.
- **Approximately $82 billion** was committed to stabilize the U.S. auto industry ($2 billion of which was ultimately canceled).
- **Approximately $70 billion** was committed to stabilize American International Group (AIG) ($2 billion of which was ultimately canceled).
- **Approximately $46 billion** was committed to programs to help struggling families avoid foreclosure, with these expenditures being made over time (US Department of the Treasury, 2016; Webel, 2013).

There are many ways the economy and government are connected. For example, the federal financial aid you may have received to attend college was an investment in you so you could be better prepared for jobs in an economy that is increasingly demanding well-educated workers to fill more technically demanding positions—what a bully.

Government

"How can you be expected to govern a country that has 246 kinds of cheese?"
— Charles de Gaulle

There are more than 320 million people in the United States. Therefore, there are more than 320 million "social agendas." These agendas put individuals and groups in competition for valuable social resources such as income, education, health care, power, and so on. However, who gets what and when and how they get it is determined in part by following established methods (Lasswell, 1936). Using these recognized practices or legitimate pathways to compete for valuable resources is referred to as politics. Politics encompasses the recognized practices involved in managing a state or government. Government is the political system by which a nation, state, or community is ruled. These systems of government may vary widely from the "head man" system used by the Trobriand Islanders to the complex multiparty coalition government of India.

Politics in the United States

Our Unique Two-Party System

Generally, there are three types of party systems recognized in the world: a one-party system like that of North Korea; a multiparty system like France, which has more than twenty, and India, with more than one thousand separate political parties; and a two-party system. The United States is unique among democracies because we operate a two-party system. While politics is played out on local and national stages all over the world and regardless of the structure of the political system, political groups or parties are trying to achieve one thing—to win. And by win I mean achieve enough power so a political party's particular ideology can be advanced. Any political party's ideology is a set of ideas, beliefs, and practices that have come to represent that party's political orientation.

Fig. 12.14 Most people in the United States are unaware that there are more than 30 registered political parties in the country. Most of the lesser known parties represents special interest groups, but welcome anyone as a member. Here you can see the logo of the Veteran's Party, which advances the interests of U.S. Veterans.

In the United States there are two dominant political parties; therefore, there are two dominant political ideologies. Democrats tend to view government as playing a central role in providing social programs and advancing the rights and opportunities of women and minorities. Consequently, the Democratic Party is attractive to groups like women, minorities, and the highly educated. Republicans tend to be wary of governmental intrusion into both public and private life. Generally, Republican ideology centers on reducing the size and influence of the federal government. While you might think that that the population is split between the two parties, recent research shows that 43 percent of voters are registered as independents or nonpartisan as of 2015.

Independents register this way so they can pick the best candidate, not just *their* party's candidate (Jones, 2016).

However, neither of the two parties are monolithic. That is, there is variation in political views within each party. Some consider themselves moderate Democrats, some Democrats refer to themselves as politically conservative (blue-dog Democrats), and others view themselves as radical liberal Democrats. In the previous decade many dissatisfied members of both parties created the Tea Party. This party represents the ultraconservative sector mainly within the Republican Party, and it now has considerable sway within that party. So the two-party system isn't as simplistic as it appears. Most people don't realize this, but there are a number of other political parties in the United States beyond the two commonly recognized ones. There is the Independent Party, the Green Party, the Constitution Party, the Transhumanist Party, and the Objectivist Party. In fact, there are thirty-nine distinct, ballot-qualified political parties in the United States (Ballotpedia, 2016; Library of Congress, 2016).

We affiliate with particular political parties because we feel like their ideologies or positions align with the way we think society should be run. Those ideologies have the potential to impact the lives of all people, but they may affect some groups more adversely while affording privilege to others. Political parties may have great ideas about how to organize and operate the government and ultimately society, but in order to realize those ideas, they have to get into office. Regardless of which political party is voted in to run the government, being successful always involves power and authority.

THERE'S AN APP FOR THAT

Apps you need to get if you absolutely, positively have to keep up with U.S. politics.

- Politifact. Politicians say a lot of things, and you don't always know how much of it is real and what is enhancement, exaggeration, or just plain lies. This app gives you access to a full-time team of political fact checkers. You can check just about any political statement for truth and accuracy (Times Publishing Company, 2012).
- Proud Republican & Proud Democrat. Whichever party you are fond of, this app will fill your device with all things Republican or Democrat. Constantly updating political headlines, this app gives you all the latest information about your party (Schatzisoft, 2011, 2013).
- Politico. Perhaps your best bet for nonpartisan political news. Keeps you current on all things political and has a forum where pundits and the public can chime in with their two cents' worth (Politico, LLC, 2016).

Power

All governments or political systems must be perceived as having the power and authority to rule; otherwise they lack legitimacy. Power is the ability to direct or influence the behaviors of others or events. You can see that having more power can get you more resources than someone with less power. Power does not just apply to individuals; it can be exerted by groups and governments (Dahl, 1957; Weber, 1922). The power of the U.S. government, for example, is not limited to Americans. The U.S. government regularly exercises its power to support the interests of other governments and nations and to vanquish or rule over others. For example, the U.S. government supported both the Diem government in Vietnam and the Mujahideen in Afghanistan in an effort to help those groups defeat Communist forces. Imposing economic sanctions on countries such as Cuba, North Korea, and Iran in order for them to bow to the will of the U.S. government is another way it can exercise its power. In 2001 US-led forces invaded Afghanistan in an effort to capture Osama bin Laden and destroy Al Qaeda, and possibly dislodge the Taliban. Then in 2003, U.S. forces invaded Iraq in an effort to bring down Saddam Hussein's government. All of these actions ultimately impacted not only the lives of U.S. operatives, but also the people of those nations.

Power doesn't have to be exerted through violence or domination; it can be wielded in more peaceful ways. Malala, the young Pakistani girl who was shot in the head and left for dead by a member of the Taliban, now has a powerful message that is changing the way women are viewed and treated in some Islamic countries. She has essentially *fought back* against her attackers by telling a compelling story in her book, *I Am Malala*, which raised awareness about the treatment of girls and women at the hands of the Taliban (Yousafzai, 2013). The combination of her book and the talks she gives around the world has fueled efforts to dislodge the Taliban from some of their strongholds, proving that the pen is mightier than the sword. Other endeavors to use the power of information include the marches, sit-ins, and protest rallies used by Martin Luther King Jr. and others in the civil rights movement. Fueled by social media, demonstrators who participated in the Arab Spring, for example, were able to communicate with the outside world, coordinate demonstrations, and feel a sense of solidarity as they attempted to topple a corrupt government. This illustrated how the power of youth, technology, and information could transform entire societies.

Authority

The recognized and legitimate use of power is authority. Sociologist routinely use the term in the context of obedience or compliance. That is, in order to get people to do things (comply), the power used by some authority must be viewed as legitimate. Those individuals and groups that are viewed as having legitimate authority can command compliance from others. We pay our taxes, obey traffic laws, and keep our dogs on leashes because we recognize the authority governments have.

Types of Authority

Most people within societies see their government as legitimate and tend to adhere to its rules, and they recognize its authority to govern them. However, this legitimation of authority can have very different sources. Max Weber (1922) developed a classification of authority that is still frequently used by sociologists. Weber identified three ideal types of authority: traditional, legal-rational, and charismatic authority.

Traditional authority is legitimized through long-standing custom: "It's the way things have always been." Monarchs, for example, are recognized as legitimate rulers simply by inheriting the crown. So the right of a king or queen to rule is recognized by inheritance. For example, Charles Prince of Wales will be crowned king of England when his mother, Queen Elizabeth II of England, dies or steps down. His authority to be king will be accepted because this is the traditional way royalty comes to power.

Fig. 12.15 Both Fidel Castro and Che Guevara were charismatic leaders who were able to lead the revolution in Cuba in 1959.

Legal-rational authority is derived from the perceived legitimacy of society's laws and rules. This type of authority is at the center of modern democracies. People who come to power through legitimate pathways, such as elections, are given the authority to lead. While traditional authority is granted through inheritance or by custom, legal-rational authority comes from the office that someone fills, not from the individual. The authority of the president of the United States is in the office of the presidency, not in whoever happens to be president. When one president leaves office, authority is transferred to the next president. While the president may not be who you voted for, you still recognize the person's authority as president.

Charismatic authority is based on intense personal loyalty to a powerfully magnetic leader. Many times these leaders claim that their right to lead emanates from some extraordinary powers that supersede the authority of others. Many believe their claims, and thus the leader is granted power and authority. However, this type of authority is far less stable than traditional or legal-rational authority. Each of the other two types of authority have mechanisms for replacing aging, unfit, or dead leaders, either through custom or election; but when charismatic leaders die, their authority dies as well. It is common for charismatic leaders to name a successor, fearing their death will be the end of the movement, cause, or nation. For example, due to his failing health, Fidel Castro, the charismatic leader of the Cuban Revolution, named his brother, Raul, as president of Cuba in 2008.

Charismatic authority can reside in leaders who also hold traditional or legal-rational authority. Henry VIII, king of England, came to the throne as a matter of tradition, but he was also a larger-than-life figure who was highly charismatic. So much so that he was able to severe England's tie with the Catholic Church and create his own religious denomination, the Church of England. Several U.S. presidents have been viewed as charismatic, such as Washington, Jefferson, Lincoln, Teddy and Franklin Roosevelt, Kennedy, and Reagan. It could be argued that a presidential candidate must have some level of charisma to hope to occupy the office of the president.

TABLE 12.2 Types of Authority

Type of Authority	Description	Examples
Traditional	Traditional authority is conferred by long-standing culturally accepted practices.	Kings, queens, and tribal chiefs
Legal-Rational	Legal-rational authority is established by laws and rules.	Elected officials like members of Congress, senators, and the president
Charismatic	Charismatic authority arises from the charisma of the individual or his or her claim of possessing extraordinary powers.	Political and religious leaders such as Fidel Castro, Che Guevara, David Karesh, and Jesus

Systems of Government

Democracies

> *"No one pretends that democracy is perfect or all-wise. Indeed, it has been said that democracy is the worst form of government except all those other forms that have been tried from time to time."*
>
> — *Winston Churchill*

Did you know that the word *democracy* does not appear anywhere in the Declaration of Independence or the U.S. Constitution? Probably because our founding fathers, like many eighteenth-century thinkers, believed that rule by the people leads to disruption and ultimately social disorder. Democracy—a form of government in which the supreme power lies with the people and is either exercised directly by them or by their legally and freely elected representatives—wasn't their idea anyway. The ancient Greeks practiced a form of *direct democracy* where all citizens discussed social issues then made decisions by majority rule. However, only free males were considered citizens, so much for true democracy. The problem our founding fathers faced was, how would a democracy in which everyone participates work in a new country that stretched from Georgia to Maine. Well, it wouldn't. So they designed an *indirect* or *representative democracy*. In our system we, the people, legally and feely elect representatives to make decisions for us (Dunn, 2006; Lakoff, 1996). While this sounds good, the reality is that the elected representatives

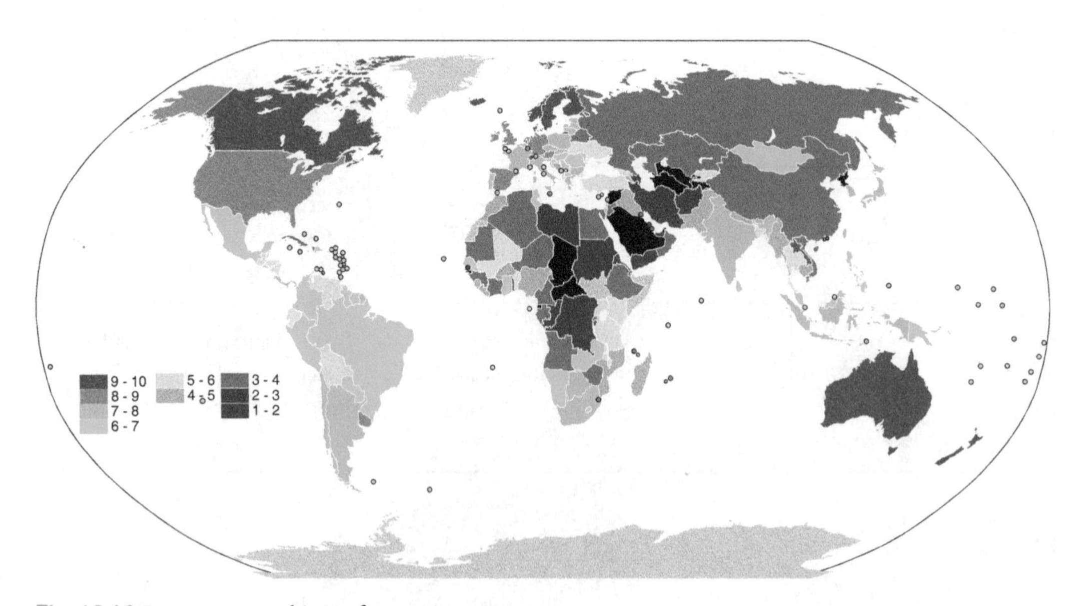

Fig. 12.16 Democracy rankings of countries, 2015.

have become social elites and serve the interests of that powerful class, so we don't live in a truly representative democracy, but a stronger one than many countries. Take a look at the map in figure 12.16. It shows each country's level of democracy by assigning it a score ranging from 0.0 (very low democracy, few freedoms for its people) to 10.0 (high democracy, people in these countries enjoy many freedoms).

While democratic governments around the world vary in their form, they all possess some basic features that are fundamental to democracy:

- Democracy is a system of government in which citizens exercise power and civic responsibility, either directly or indirectly through their elected representatives, as we do in the United States.
- Democracies hold regularly scheduled fair and free elections.
- Democracy is guided by the principles of majority rule and individual rights. However, majority rule cannot be used to abuse individual rights or the freedoms of minority groups.

The protection of its citizens' human rights is a fundamental element of democracies. In the United States we view the freedom of speech, religion, and public assembly, and the right to equal protection under the law as necessary for full participation in political and social life.

The only way democratic societies thrive is if tolerance, cooperation, and compromise are valued and practiced. Not all democratic societies, including America, are fully tolerant of all views and practices. Public debate of social issues is necessary for the exercise of democracy; indeed, it is a cornerstone of it. Without public discourse we would be unable to choose candidates for office, and only the voice of the powerful would be heard; all other interests would go unattended (Meyer-Resende, 2011; Center for Civic Education, 2007). This ideal is reflected in a quote from Mahatma Gandhi: "Intolerance is itself a form of violence and an obstacle to the growth of a true democratic spirit."

Of the 195 (this number may be disputed, I use the U.S. Department of State's count) countries of the world, 125 claim to be democracies (U.S. Department of State, "Independent States in the World," 2015). However, just because a country is democratic it doesn't mean it is a place where its citizens are totally free. Even in the United States, a paragon of democracy, freedom is not evenly distributed. In an attempt to restrict some groups' access to voting, voter identification legislation has been passed in more than thirty states. Many of these states have seen a reduction in voter turnout as a result of the new laws. In a comprehensive study that looked at fifty-one elections held between 2006 and 2012, researchers found that voter identification laws adversely affect voter turnout. Those most affected were poor voters and black, Hispanic, and young voters (Hajnal, Lajevardi, and Nielson, 2015). When groups are denied access to voting, they are denied a voice in social issues, laws, and electing representatives. These groups that are not truly free to vote will have to submit to policies and laws they did not help create.

Fig. 12.17 Freedom House freedom by region, 2015

Whatever their motivations may be, those who advocate legislation like voter identification are just putting the democratic process into action. Those voter identification laws were passed by a majority vote. This is sometimes referred to as the "tyranny of the majority" (tyranny of the masses), when the majority uses the voting process to subjugate a minority by placing their interests above those of an individual or a minority group. Laws, like voter identification, can act to oppress certain groups much like a tyrant would do. While these laws may reflect the interest of the majority, they do not serve all the people (Tocqueville, 2003; Knight, 2016).

Countries vary widely in the amount of freedom their citizens enjoy. In fact, the 2015 Freedom House Survey rated all countries on a "freedom scale," with scores ranging from 1 to 7, where 1 represents countries that are "most free'" and 7 indicates countries that are the "least free." Scores are based on the level of political rights and civil liberties the people of each country possess. Countries like the United States, Australia, and Sweden scored 1, while countries like North Korea, Saudi Arabia, and Sudan scored 7. The study noted that for the tenth consecutive year, freedom has been on the decline. That is, more countries of the world saw a decrease in their freedom scores than saw a rise in their scores (Puddington and Roylance, 2016). Take a look at figure 12.17 above and notice which regions of the world are more free and which are rated as less free. What are the common elements between countries in more free regions and those in less free regions?

From 2014 to 2015 the world witnessed many troubling events that further eroded freedoms in several democratic nations, such as "Russia's invasion of Ukraine, a rollback of democratic gains by Egyptian president Abdel Fattah el-Sisi, Turkish President Recep Tayyip Erdoğan's intensified campaign against press freedom and civil society, and further centralization of authority in China." These all stood as clear indicators of a growing contempt for democratic standards (Puddington, 2015). While many of these countries, including the United States, are variations on democratic governments, they all set some limitations on the freedoms of their people.

TRY THIS

Do you think politics seeps into other parts of society? Try watching a bunch of TV shows, such as *The Simpsons*, *The Big Bang Theory*, *Orange Is the New Black*—anything. While you watch the shows, notice if any of the characters either overtly or indirectly promotes or condemns a political ideology. Does any individual episode have a political message or meaning? Do TV shows promote certain political ideologies? Watch and listen carefully, and I think you will be surprised at how politically loaded entertainment can be.

Dictatorships, Totalitarianism, and Oligarchies

Dictatorships

For me, it is hard to believe that in this day and age there remain nations whose governments either severely or totally restrict the liberties of their people, imprison those who dissent, and even starve their own people. Unlike democracies, these types of governments centralize power and control the economy and all other aspects of social life. In a dictatorship one person, the dictator, has absolute power, many times backed by the military, over the entire nation and its people. Many times a dictator comes to power as the result of a revolution or coup, defeating a leader who is widely perceived as corrupt or ineffective, only to become the people's new oppressor, like Fidel Castro in Cuba (Sharp, 2012). Sometimes dictators come to power through democratic elections, but they soon change the system by restricting civil liberties, dispensing with all opposition, and restructuring government so they cannot be dislodged from their position of absolute power. Adolf Hitler rose to power through legitimate channels, then began to limit the rights of Germans and enact laws that ultimately denied any freedoms to Jews, homosexuals, and intellectuals (Toland, 1991; Schmitt, 2014).

Fig. 12.18 Dictators use propaganda like this painting of Kim Jong-il, the former head of North Korea, to reinforce their image of being a sort of gentle uncle who will protect and care for his people as long as they are devoted to him.

Totalitarianism

Totalitarianism, like the name implies, is a form of rule in which the government gains and maintains *total* control over all aspects of the public and private lives of its citizens. Again, like nearly all forms of government totalitarian regimes vary in their structure, but all possess some fundamental characteristics:

- *Rule by a single political party.* For example, in the former Soviet Union, the Communist Party ruled from 1917 without opposition from any officially recognized party, until it was dissolved in 1991. Similarly, the Worker's Party of Korea rules over North Korea, and Fidel Castro's Cuban Communist Party has rule over Cuba. While there are eight other parties in Cuba, they are all completely politically aligned with the Communist Party, and none of them are allowed to campaign or endorse candidates for elections (Fusco, 2015).
- *Total control over the military.* Joseph Stalin was, and Kim Jong Un is considered the supreme military leader of their respective nations. Control of the military is maintained by the single political party in a totalitarian society. Every member of Korea's Central Military Commission, the military's ruling body headed by Kim Jong Un, is a party member (Smith, 2015).

- *Police maintain control by using terror tactics.* Papa Doc Duvalier ruled Haiti with an iron fist from 1957 until 1971. The tip of his spear was his notoriously corrupt and brutal National Security Volunteers (a sort of national police force), referred to by the Haitian people as the Tonton Macoutes. This label refers to a common Haitian Creole myth about an "uncle" (Tonton), who kidnaps and punishes naughty children by snaring them in a gunnysack (Macoute) and carrying them off to be consumed at breakfast. Those Haitians brave enough to speak out against the regime where kidnapped in the middle of the night. And it was believed that those who were kidnapped by Duvalier's Tonto Macoutes never returned. Additionally, the Tonton Macoutes intimidated communities by stealing land and money and raping women (Kurczy, 2011; Ferguson, 1987; Diederich, 2005).
- *Total control over all media outlets.* North Korea, for example, keeps tight control over print and electronic media, thereby controlling what people hear about the regime and ultimately how they view the world. Newspapers, TV channels, and radio stations are all run by the central Communist Party. In fact, all TVs and radios are pretuned to government stations. Only a handful of elites have access to the Internet; other privileged cronies have access to a tightly controlled intranet called "Kwangmyong," which translates to "Bright." Other than these select few, no one in North Korea has legal access to the Internet (Kim, 2014).
- *Total control of the economy.* Totalitarian regimes all have command economies, which are centrally planned by the ruling political party. Everything from how much wheat and toilet paper should be produced is planned, prices are fixed by the government, and individuals are placed in their jobs by a centralized labor committee.

READ MORE

- *Freedom from Fear: And Other Writings* by Aung San Suu Kyi (1991). "San Suu Kyi's collected writings—edited by her late husband, whom the ruling military junta prevented from visiting Burma as he was dying of cancer—reflects her greatest hopes and fears for her fellow Burmese people, and her concern about the need for international co-operation in the continuing fight for Burma's freedom."
- *Letters from Burma by Aung San Suu Kyi* (1995). "Aung San Suu Kyi reaches out beyond Burma's borders to paint for her readers a vivid and poignant picture of her native land. Here she celebrates the courageous army officers, academics, actors and everyday people who have supported the National League for Democracy, often at great risk to their own lives. She reveals the impact of political decisions on the people of Burma, from the terrible cost to the children of imprisoned dissidents—allowed to see their parents for only fifteen minutes every fortnight—to the effect of inflation on the national diet and of state repression on traditions of hospitality."

Oligarchies

Saudi Arabia is ruled by a king and a few male princes who happen to be descended from the nation's founder, King Abd al-Aziz al-Sa'ud, who sired forty-four sons by seventeen wives. This form of an **oligarchy**—a system of government where a few powerful people rule the many—is unique because this group of ruling elites are connected through a bloodline, which is referred to as a *royal oligarchy*. There are no political parties in Saudi Arabia; therefore, total political and economic control is retained by the royal family. These princes have treated the immense petroleum and mineral wealth of their nation like their own private domain, amassing huge personal fortunes. These seven thousand to eight thousand members of the royal family secretly siphon off state revenues to fuel their extravagant lifestyles, while their citizens grow poorer. Their per capita GDP lags behind other countries in their region, and it has been estimated that one-quarter of Saudi citizens live in poverty, a sharp contrast to the opulence of the royal oligarchy (Sullivan, 2013; Aarts and Roelants, 2015).

Oligarchies can exist within other systems of government; the preceding example shows that an oligarchy can emerge within a monarchy. Oligarchies can exist even if a country's official form of government is a theocracy (rule by clergy), totalitarian, authoritarian, or a democracy. Even though Russia is officially a **federation**—a collection of states that operate under the rule of a central government while retaining control over local matters—it operates as an oligarchy. Vladimir Putin and a few other very powerful businessmen, who head up the largest industries in Russia such as oil, mining, and utilities, control nearly all matters in the Russian Federation. China, officially a Communist state, has been ruled by an oligarchy of "princelings" and "princesslings," the sons and daughters of the so-called eight elders (those who came to power with Mao in 1949) since the death of Mao Tse-tung in 1976. The offspring of these prince- and princesslings have risen to great power, heading up the country's largest state-owned industries. Collectively, the princelings, princesslings, and their families are known as the "red nobility" (Joseph, 2010; Barboza and LaFraniere, 2012). Some have argued that the United States is an oligarchy, ruled by a powerful elite class that has tremendous influence over industry, media, government, and the military (Mills, 1958; Domhoff, 2013). Do you think we live in an oligarchy? Do you think there is a small group of powerful individuals who rule over America?

READ MORE

- *Vanquish of the Dragon Shroud* by Gregory E. Seller (2015). A power struggle in China results in a battle for control of billions of dollars in hidden assets. The Shroud of the Red Dragon is a multibillion-dollar business enterprise that hides the personal wealth of families of the Red Nobility, leaders of the Chinese Communist Party. They have hidden their vast wealth from the Chinese people and from the world, but a purge of the old regime threatens to expose the secrecy of these illicit assets. While this is a novel, it weaves in true accounts of the Red Nobility and how powerful Chinese leaders hide their immense wealth from their own people.
- *Driving the Saudis: A Chauffer's Tale of the World's Richest Princesses (Plus Their Servants, Nannies and One Royal Hairdresser)* by Jane Amelia Larson (2012). A true-life account from a female chauffer who was hired to drive members of the Saudi royal family in Los Angeles. This book is amusing and gives the reader an insight into how the royal Saudis view those who are not wealthy, Americans, and the world.

Theoretical Perspectives on Politics and Government

Functionalism: Politics and Government Is a Pluralist Endeavor

The functionalist approach to political power is most commonly viewed through a pluralist perspective. The **pluralist model** argues that power is distributed among various groups that compete in the political process for resources and influence. This allows power and influence to be spread across a number of groups, argue the functionalists, and assures that it is not concentrated in the hands of a single interest group. According to this perspective, power and influence can shift between groups, as we see when the majority party shifts in Congress or when a union strikes and negotiates a new, better contract (Dahl, 1974; Dye and Zeigler, 1983).

Participation in various interest groups is how you and I can influence decisions, policies, and laws. We join and participate in groups that represent our interests. For example, members of a posh neighborhood may put out a petition, protest, and contact their local representative to oppose the building of a Walmart in their community. And Walmart may mobilize by publicizing that it will create new jobs and wealth in the community, and it may lobby local officials to permit it to build. These competing or opposing groups attempt to balance out power so it doesn't become concentrated in the hands of a few.

Many times groups can mobilize their members when they feel that their interests are threatened. Therefore, groups can attempt to exert influence so they gain some advantage, like protecting or advancing their interests. For example, in an effort to protect its interests (profits), the coal industry was mobilized when it opposed tougher coal-emission regulations proposed by the government. In fact, the coal industry took the issue to the U.S. Supreme Court and won, protecting its interests—for now (Liptak and Davenport, 2016).

DROWN THE BUNNIES: AN EXAMPLE OF COMPETITION BETWEEN INTEREST GROUPS

The president of a fairly prestigious college on the East Coast developed an unethical way to determine whether freshman students were a good fit with the college early in their first semester. This was all in an effort to force students the college perceived as "at risk" for dropping out to leave by a September deadline to boost the schools' retention rate. When confronted with the sort of underhanded way he was sniffing out "unfit" students, the president told a faculty member that you have to stop thinking of freshmen as "cuddly bunnies" and said: "You have to drown the bunnies ... put a Glock to their heads." Meaning the college would have to use tough love and force out at-risk students in order to improve the school's retention numbers. This story broke in the school's newspaper. Subsequently, the faculty advisor to the newspaper and two other faculty members, who had vocalized their opposition to the president's new retention scheme and his bunny and Glock references, were fired. They were let go via e-mail and immediately escorted off campus by security, and their e-mail accounts were blocked. One professor had to make an appointment to come back to campus to retrieve his belongings.

Needless to say, faculty at that school and around the country were furious with this college president for firing faculty who were simply articulating dissenting opinions and questioning the president's motivations and methods. The American Association of University Professors (AAUP) soon sent a harsh letter to the college, and many more followed from other individuals and interest groups. At first, the board of trustees backed the president and became engaged in a competition between several interest groups, the board of trustees and the college's administration on one side and many of the faculty and the AAUP on the other. Ultimately, the pressure from faculty, the AAUP, and even parents of students at the college forced the president to step down and the college to rehire the faculty members (Jaschik, 2016).

Conflict Approach: Politics and the Government Are Controlled by a Power Elite

In contrast to the functionalists' pluralist perspective, the conflict approach takes an opposite view of groups and power. According to this approach, power in capitalist societies is concentrated in the hands of a few wealthy individuals and organizations—or *power elites.* This power elite approach argues that economic and political power is not spread across a plurality of groups; rather, economic power is concentrated in the hands of a small number of individuals who control multiple spheres of influence, such as the media, the military, the government, and the corporate world (Mills, 1958; Domhoff, 2013).

The powerful people who make up this group move between the spheres, using a sort of revolving door to move from one powerful institution to another and further consolidate their power. Many of them have overlapping memberships on the boards of the multinational corporations, business lobby groups, universities, foundations, the military, and the media industry. They use this inordinate influence on the government to shape its decisions, policies, and laws to benefit and advance their own interests. According to the power elite approach, this powerful group controls government—or at the very least panders to its needs and interests. Tax laws, for example, benefit the wealthy, who with all their power helped craft them via their access to lawmakers.

TABLE 12.3 Theoretical Perspectives on Politics and Government

Theoretical Perspective	View of Politics and Government	Example
Functionalism	Government is viewed as a necessary social institution that is responsible for law and order, national defense, and protecting the well-being of the citizenry. Politics involves various interest groups competing for power. Power and influence is dispersed across interest groups so that it is not concentrated in a very few or a single group. Groups with opposing interests tend to balance each other, but power moves back and forth between competing groups.	The Black Lives Matter movement represents the interests of members of the black community (one group) competing with local police and municipal governments (another group) to change policies that target members of the African American community, especially young, black, urban males.

(*Continued*)

Theoretical Perspective	View of Politics and Government	Example
Conflict	Government is seen as a tool of members of the ruling class/power elite used to protect and advance their interests. The wealth and power of the elite classes help elect politicians who are sympathetic to their needs. As a result, they have access to those powerful politicians and administrators who cater to their needs and interests.	After the BP Gulf of Mexico oil spill of 2010, it was revealed that in the previous year BP had spent more than $16 million on lobbying efforts to keep the petroleum industry lightly regulated. Power elites who sit on the board of directors of BP spend this kind of money to buy the votes of members of Congress. (Stein, 2012). In turn, Congress caters to the needs and interests of the elites. (Stein, 2016.)

Source: Montopoli, 2010.

The Bottom Line

Economy

As we have seen, economies of the world may vary widely in how they are structured, but they are all trying to perform similar functions and goals. Whether economic markets are free or restricted, they attempt to provide employment so goods can be produced and services used. Additionally, economies provide methods to distribute goods and services to people within society. Economies can range from free market capitalism, in which people have open access to all goods and services, provided they can afford them, to command economies, where every aspect is controlled and planned by a ruling party, right down to the price of toilet paper and who gets what job.

Work, as we discussed, is a critical element of the economy and an important feature of our daily lives. As our economy has changed in the past forty years, so has the workplace. Both globalization and our postindustrial economy have changed the nature and type of work we do. As the dust settles from our most recent economic downturn, the labor market appears to have morphed into one in which "good jobs" and "low-wage jobs" are plentiful, but the middle seems to be missing. Unfortunately, even with these changes, women and minorities seem to suffer the vestiges of an older economy, in which they are underrepresented and underpaid.

Sociological perspectives on work and the economy vary widely. The functionalist approach stresses the cooperative nature of the economy and other social institutions, arguing that everyone benefits from a capitalist economic system, despite the huge disparities in levels of income and wealth. The conflict approach, in contrast, focuses squarely on the issue of how the wealthy control the economy at the peril of the working classes. Diverging from both functionalism's and conflict's macro view of the economy, symbolic interactionism seeks to understand how people are socialized into their occupations, how they manage impressions in the workplace, and how work brings meaning to their lives.

Government

The United States practices a unique brand of democracy with its distinctive two-party system. Regardless of how many political parties are in the game, they ultimately need power and authority to rule. Power is crucial to acquiring resources and getting things done, and those with more power typically end up having greater access to and possessing more of those desired resources, giving them more privilege. Authority, or having the right to exercise power, can be granted in different ways. Some inherit their authority, like royalty; some come by it through socially designed legitimate competition, like elected officials; and some by sheer magnetism and will.

We have seen that democracies can come in many shapes and sizes, but ultimately they afford citizens the most opportunity and liberties, relative to other forms of government. Other types of government, like dictatorships, totalitarianism, and oligarchies, leave their people with little rights or opportunity. These oppressive regimes stifle free expression, creativity, and competition, compelling people to participate in black markets for survival or risk their own lives in escaping from them.

We discussed two broad theoretical approaches that attempt to understand politics and government. The pluralist view holds that society is composed of a number of groups that compete to secure or advance their interests in fair and legal ways. In contrast, the power elite approach argues that politics and government are in the hands of small group of powerful, corporate, military, and political operatives. These power elites possess so much economic and political power, the power elite model contends, that they are able to use the political system to manipulate the economy to benefit them.

Figure Credits

Fig. 12.1: United States Department of Labor, http://www.dol.gov/wb/stats/facts_over_time.htm. Copyright in the Public Domain.

Fig. 12.2: Anonymous, "Child laborers," https://commons.wikimedia.org/wiki/File:TravailEnfantUSXIX.jpg. Copyright in the Public Domain.

Fig. 12.3: Copyright © Edal Anton Lefterov (CC BY-SA 3.0) at https://commons.wikimedia.org/wiki/File:Capitalism-stencil.jpg.

Fig. 12.4: Copyright © Depositphotos/Checco.

Fig. 12.5: Copyright © Carlos Menendez San Juan (CC BY-SA 2.0) at https://commons.wikimedia.org/wiki/File:Capitalism_(3874351882).jpg.

Fig. 12.6: Executive Office of the President of the United States, "Labor force participation rates," https://www.whitehouse.gov/sites/default/files/docs/labor_force_participation_report.pdf. Copyright in the Public Domain.

Figure 12.7: Source: http://thefutureofoutsourcing.blogspot.com/p/blog-page.html

Fig. 12.8: Source: http://greenfieldgeography.wikispaces.com/Global+Participation

Fig. 12.9: Copyright © Pascal Kirchmair (CC BY-SA 3.0) at https://commons.wikimedia.org/wiki/File:Globalisierung.jpg.

Fig. 12.11: United States Department of Labor, "Women in the labor force over time," http://www.dol.gov/wb/stats/latest_annual_data.htm. Copyright in the Public Domain.

Fig. 12.12: "Real Median Household Income by Race and Hispanic Origin: 1967 to 2014," https://www.census.gov/content/dam/Census/library/publications/2015/demo/p60-252.pdf. Copyright in the Public Domain.

Fig. 12.13: Source: http://data.bls.gov/timeseries/LNU04000000?years_option=all_years&periods_option=specific_periods&periods=Annual+Data.

Fig. 12.14: The Veteran's Party of America, "The Veteran's Party of America," https://commons.wikimedia.org/wiki/File:Veteran%27s_Party_of_America_Seal.png. Copyright © by The Veteran's Party of America. Reprinted with permission.

Fig. 12.15: "Fidel Castro and Che Guavera," https://commons.wikimedia.org/wiki/File:CheyFidel.jpg. Copyright in the Public Domain.

Fig, 12.16: Copyright © Ternoc (CC BY-SA 4.0 International) at https://commons.wikimedia.org/wiki/File:2015_Democracy_Index.svg.

Fig. 12.17: Adapted from: Copyright © Depositphotos/alekseyderin.gmail.com.

Fig. 12.18: Copyright © Kok Leng Yeo (CC by 2.0) at https://commons.wikimedia.org/wiki/File:Victorious_Fatherland_Liberation_War_Museum,_Pyongyang,_North_Korea-1.jpg.

BIBLIOGRAPHY AND FURTHER READING

"2015 State of Atheism in America." *Barna Group*. Barna Group, 24 Mar. 2015. Web. 21 May 2015.

3nder Ltd. *3nder*. Computer software. *Apple App Store*. Vers. 3.3.0 3nder Ltd, 13 Nov. 2015. Web. 26 Mar. 2016.

Aarts, Paul and Carolien Roelants. *Saudi Arabia: A Kingdom in Peril*. London: C. Hurst & Co., 2015. Print.

Abramov, Israel, James Gordon, Olga Feldman, and Alla Chavarga. "Sex & Vision I: Spatio-temporal Resolution." *Biology of Sex Differences* 3.20 (2012): 1–14. Web. 9 Mar. 2016.

"ACSI Federal Government Report 2014: Citizen Satisfaction with Federal Government Services Declines for Second Year." *American Customer Satisfaction Index*. N.p., 27 Jan. 2015. Web. 14 May 2015.

Adams, David Wallace. *Education for Extinction: American Indians and the Boarding School Experience 1876–1928*. New York: University Press of Kansas, 1995. Print.

"Adding a MENA Category to the U.S. Census." *Arab American Institute*. Arab American Institute, 16 May 2015. Web. 28 Sept. 2015.

Adler, Patricia A., Steven J. Kless, and Peter Adler. "Socialization to Gender Roles: Popularity among Elementary School Boys and Girls." *Sociology of Education* 65.3 (1992): 169–187. Web. 26 Apr. 2016.

Aggleton, Peter. *Men Who Sell Sex*. London: UCL Press, 1999. Print.

Aguirre, B.E., Rogelio Sáenz, and Brian Sinclair James. "Marielitos Ten Years Later: The Scarface Legacy." *Social Science Quarterly* 78.2 (1997): 487–507. Web. 28 Sept. 2015.

Ahmed, Osman, and Chai Jindasurat. "A Report from the National Coalition of Anti-Violence Programs: Lesbian, Gay, Bisexual, Transgender, Queer, and HIV-Affected Hate Violence in 2013." National Coalition of Anti-Violence Programs, 2014. Web. 30 Aug. 2015.

Alexander, Michelle. *The New Jim Crow: Mass Incarceration in the Age of Colorblindness*. New York: The New Press, 2012. Print.

Ali, Nujood, and Delpine Minoui. *I am Nujood, Age 10 and Divorced*. Trans. Linda Coverdale. New York: Three Rivers Press, 2010. Print.

Alleyne, Richard. "Woman 'married' to Berlin Wall for 29 years." *The Telegraph*. The Telegraph, 27 May 2008. Web. 24 Sept. 2015.

All Together Now. *Everyday Racism. All Together Now*. All Together Now. 2014. Web. 24 Mar. 2016. <http://alltogethernow.org.au/everyday-racism/>.

Alpert, Geoffrey P., Roger G. Dunham, and Michael R. Smith. "Investigating Racial Profiling by the Miami-Dade Police Dept.: A Multimethod Approach." *Criminology & Public Policy* 6.1 (2007): 25–55. Web. 18 Apr. 2016.

Alpert, G., J.H. MacDonald, and R.G. Dunham. "Police Suspicion and Discretionary Decision Making During Citizen Stops." *Criminology* 43 (2005): 407–434. Web. 29 May 2015.

Al-Rodhan, Nayef R.F. Ed. *The Geopolitical and Geosecurity Implications of Globalization*. New York: Slatkine, 2006. Print.

Alvarez, R. Michael, and John Brehm. "Are Americans Ambivalent Towards Racial Policies?" *American Journal of Political Science* 41.2 (1996): 345–374. Web. 14 May 2015.

Amadeo, Kimberly. "Command Economy: Characteristics, Pros, Cons, and Examples." *About.com*. 2016. Web. 31 Mar. 2016.

Amadeo, Kimberly. "Traditional Economy: Definition, Examples, Pros, Cons." *About.com*. 2016. Web. 31 Mar. 2016.

American Association of Medical Colleges. "What will the Psychological, Social, and Biological Foundations of Behavior Section test?" *American Association of Medical Colleges*. 2015. Web. 22 July 2015.

American Civil Liberties Union. "The Case Against the Death Penalty." American Civil Liberties Union, 2012. Web. 29 May 2015.

American Civil Liberties Union. "The War on Marijuana in Black and White." American Civil Liberties Union (2013). Web. 28 May 2015.

American Psychiatric Association. *Diagnostic and Statistical Manual of Mental Disorders*. 3rd ed. Washington, D.C.: American Psychiatric Association, 1987. Print.

American Psychiatric Association. "Minutes of the Council of Representatives." *American Psychologist* 30 (1975): 633. Web. 21 May 2015.

American Psychological Association. "Effects of Poverty, Hunger and Homelessness on Children and Youth." *American Psychological Association*. American Psychological Association, 2016. Web. 18 Apr. 2016.

Anishu, Inc. *HomeBudget with Sync*. Computer software. *Apple App Store*. Vers. 3.2.2 Anishu, Inc., 15 Mar. 2016. Web. 31 Mar. 2016.

Ansalone, G. "Tracking: A Return to Jim Crow." *Race, Gender, and Class* 13.12 (2006): 144–153. Web. 26 Mar. 2016.

Anti-Defamation League. "ADL: 2012 Hate Crime Statistics Report 'Seriously Flawed': Law Enforcement Under-Reporting Must Be Addressed." *ADL: Anti-Defamation League*. ADL, 25 Nov. 2013. Web. 29 May 2015.

Appleby, Joyce. *The Relentless Revolution: A History of Capitalism*. New York: W.W. Norton & Company, 2010. Print.

Aristotle. *Aristotle's Politics*. Trans. Benjamin Jowett and H.W. Carless Davis. Oxford: At the Clarendon Press, 1920. Print.

Arnold, N. Scott. *The Philosophy and Economics of Market Socialism*. Oxford: Oxford University Press, 1994. Print.

Arons, Jessica. "Lifetime Losses: The Career Wage Gap." *Center for American Progress*. Center for American Progress, 2008. Web. 30 Aug. 2015.

Arria, Amelia M., Laura M. Garnier-Dykstra, Kimberly M. Caldeira, Kathryn B. Vincent, Emily R. Winick, Kevin E. O'Grady. "Drug Use Patterns and Continuous Enrollment in College: Results from a Longitudinal Study." *J Stud Alcohol Drugs* 74.1 (2013): 71–83. Web. 19 June 2015.

Asch, Solomon. *Social psychology*. Englewood Cliffs: Prentice-Hall, 1952. Print.

Asian Development Bank. *Asian Development Outlook 2016: Asia's Potential Growth. Asian Development Bank*. Asian Development Bank, 2016. Web. 2 Apr. 2016.

Asi, Maryam and Daniel Beaulieu. *Arab Households in the United States: 2006–2010*. Washington: U.S. Census Bureau, American Community Survey Briefs, May 2013. Web. 28 Sept. 2015.

Association of Religion Data Archives. "Longitudinal Study of Generations, 1971." *Association of Religion Data Archives*. Association of Religion Data Archives, 2015. Web. 3 Aug. 2016.

Atkinson, Anthony B., Thomas Piketty, and Emmanuel Saez. "Top Incomes in the Long Run of History." *Journal of Economic Literature* 49.1 (2011): 3-71. Web. 12 June 2016.

Audiger, Stephan. "Thai Food Etiquette: Do's and Don'ts." *Phuket*. Hotels.com, 2016. Web. 26 July 2016.

"Aung San Suu Kyi." *Bio*. A&E Television Networks, 2015. Web. 30 Aug. 2015.

Automattic. Polldaddy. Computer software. Apple App Store. Vers. 2.0 Automattic, 30 July 2016. Web. 3 Aug. 2016.

Baczone, LLC. *iDrinkSmarter*. Computer software. *Apple App Store*. Vers. 1.5. Baczone, LLC, 25 Mar. 2014. Web. 9 Mar. 2016.

Badie, Bertrand, Dirk Berg-Schlosser, and Leonardo Morlino. *International Encyclopedia of Political Science*. Thousand Oaks: SAGE Publications, 2011. Print.

Bailey, Martha J. and Susan M. Dynarski, eds. "Gains and Gaps: Changing Inequality in U.S. College Entry and Completion." *The National Bureau of Economic Research* (2011): 1–30. Web. 26 Mar. 2016.

Baker, Andy. *Shaping the Developing World: The West, the South, and the Natural World*. Thousand Oaks: CQ Press, 2014. Web. 9 Mar. 2016.

Baker, Elizabeth A., Mario Schootman, Ellen Barnidge, and Cheryl Kelly. "The Role of Race and Poverty in Access to Foods that Enable Individuals to Adhere to Dietary Guidelines." *Prev Chronic Dis* 3.3 (2006): A76. Web. 30 May 2015.

Baker, Wayne. *United America*. Canton: Read The Spirit Books, 2014. Print.

Bakija, Jon, Adam Cole, and Bradley T. Heim. "Jobs and Income Growth of Top Earners and the Causes of Changing Income Inequality: Evidence from U.S. Tax Return Data." 2012. Web. 31 Mar. 2016.

Balemian, Kara and Jing Feng. "First Generation Students: College Aspirations, Preparedness and Challenges." *CollegeBoard*. Collegeboard, 19 July 2013. Web. 26 Mar. 2016.

Bales, Kevin. *Disposable People: New Slavery in the Global Economy*. Revised ed. Berkeley: University of California Press, 2012. Print.

Bales, Kevin. *Blood and Earth: Modern Slavery, Ecocide, and the Secret to Saving the World*. New York: Spiegel & Grau, 2016. Print.

Bales, Kevin and Ron Soodalter. *The Slave Next Door: Human Trafficking and Slavery in America Today*. Berkeley: University of California Press, 2009. Print.

Ballotpedia. "Ballet access for major and minor party candidates." *Ballotpedia*. Ballotpedia, 2016. Web. 31 Mar. 2016.

Balonon-Rosen, Peter. "4 Takeaways from Jonathan Kozol On Race, Poverty And Corporate Reform in Education." *Learning Lab*. Learning Lab, 8 May 2015. Web. 26 Sept. 2015.

Bandura, Albert and S.A. Ross. "Transmission of aggression through imitation of aggressive models." *Journal of Abnormal and Social Psychology* 63 (1961): 575–582. Web. 30 June 2015.

Bandura, Albert. "Influence of Models' Reinforcement Contingencies on the Acquisition of Imitative Responses." *Journal of Personality and Social Psychology* 1.6 (1965): 589–95. Web. 23 Aug. 2014.

Bandura, Albert. *Social Learning Theory*. Englewood Cliffs: Prentice Hall, 1977. Print.

Barboza, David and Sharon LaFraniere. "'Princelings' in China Use Family Ties to Gain Riches." *New York Times*. New York Times, 17 May 2012. Web. 2 Apr. 2016.

Barnes, R.H. "Marriage by Capture." *The Journal of the Royal Anthropological Institute* 5.1 (1999): 57–73. Web. 24 Sept. 2015.

Barrett, Justin L. and Amanda Hankes Johnson. "The Role of Control in Attributing Intentional Agency to Inanimate Objects." *Journal of Cognition and Culture* 3.3 (2003): 208–217. Web. 26 Mar. 2016.

Bartlett, Tom. "The Unraveling of Michael LaCour." *The Chronicle of Higher Education*. 22 June 2015. Web. 30 June 2015.

BBC News. "Anti-human trafficking post criticised." *BBC News*. BBC, 25 Sept. 2010. Web. 18 Apr. 2016.

Beattie, Tina. "Sex, marriage and the Catholic Church." *The Guardian*. The Guardian, 8 Oct. 2014. Web. 20 Apr. 2016.

Beaud, Michel. *A History of Capitalism, 1500-2000*. New York: Monthly Review Press, 2001. Print.

Becker, Howard S. *Outsiders: Studies in the Sociology of Deviance*. New York: Macmillan, 1963. Print.

Beckwith, Jon and Jonathan King. "The XYY Syndrome: A Dangerous Myth." *New Scientist* (1974): 474-476. Web. 9 Mar. 2016.

Beckwith, Johnathan R. *Making Genes, Making Waves: A Social Activist in Science*. Cambridge: Harvard University Press, 2002. Print.

Bell, Daniel. *The Coming of Post-Industrial Society: A Venture in Social Forecasting*. New York: Basic Books, 1973. Print.

Benedict, C., S.J. Brooks, O.G. O'Daly, M.S. Almen, A. Morell, K. Aberg, M. Gingnell, B. Schultes, M. Hallschmid, J.E. Broman, E.M. Larsson, and H.B. Schloth. "Acute Sleep Deprivation Enhances the Brain's Response to Hedonic Food Stimuli: an fMRI study." *J. Clin Endocrinal Metab* 97.3 (2012): 443–447. Web. 30 May 2015.

Benedict, Helen. *The Lonely Soldier: The Private War of Women Serving in Iraq*. Boston: Beacon Press, 2009. Print.

Bengston, Vern. "Longitudinal Study of Generations, 1971, 1985, 1988, 1991, 1994, 1997, 2000 [California] (ICPSR 22100)." *ICPSR*. University of Michigan, 2009. Web. 29 June 2015.

Berger, Peter L. *Invitation to Sociology: A Humanistic Perspective*. New York: Anchor Books, 1963. Print.

Berger, Peter L. *The Sacred Canopy: Elements of a Sociological Theory of Religion*. New York: Doubleday, 1967. Print.

Berman, Mark and Wesley Lowery. "The 12 key highlights from the DOJ's scathing Ferguson report." *The Washington Post*. The Washington Post, 4 Mar. 2015. Web. 28 July 2016.

Bertrand, Marianne, and Sendhil Mullainathan. "Are Emily and Greg More Employable than Lakisha and Jamal? A Field Experiment on Labor Market Discrimination." *The American Economic Review* 94.4 (2004): 991–1013. Web. 7 Mar. 2015.

Bevan, Thomas E. *The Psychobiology of Transsexualism and Transgenderism*. Santa Barbara: Praeger, 2014. Web. 10 Dec. 2015.

Beversluis, Joel. ed. *Sourcebook of the World's Religions: An Interfaith Guide to Religion and Spirituality*. 3rd ed. New York: New World Library, 2011. Print.

Bhagwati, Jagdish N. and Alan S. Blinder. *Offshoring of American Jobs: What Response from U.S. Economic Policy?* Ed. Benjamin M. Friedman. Boston: Massachusetts Institute of Technology, 2009. Print.

Bhagwati, Jagdish N. *In Defense of Globalization*. Oxford: Oxford University Press, 2004. Print.

Bhate, Rucha. "India: Statistical Profile." *The Sloan Center on Aging & Work*. Boston College, Sept. 2009. Web. 31 Mar. 2016.

Bhopal, Kalwant. *The Experiences of Black and Minority Ethnic Academics: A comparative study of the unequal academy*. New York: Routledge, 2016. Print.

Bianchi, Suzanne M., John P. Robinson, and Melissa A. Milkie. *Changing Rhythms of American Family Life*. New York: Russel Sage Foundation, 2006. Print.

Biba, Erin. "Women Are Taking Back Beer." *Medium*. Medium, 26 Feb. 2014. Web. 30 Aug. 2015.

Bidwell, Allie. "Study: The American Family is No More." *U.S. News*. U.S. News, 11 Sept. 2013. Web. 24 Sept. 2015.

Bielick, Stacey and Kathryn Chandler. *Homeschooling in the United States: 1999*. U.S. Dept. of Education, National Center for Education Statistics, July 2001. Web. 6 June 2016.

Bishop, Tiffany, John Reinke, and Tommy Adams. "Globalization: Trends and Perspectives." *Journal of International Business Research* 10.1 (2011). Web. 31 Mar. 2016.

Bitterman, Amy, Rebecca Goldring, Lucinda Gray, and Stephen Broughman. *Characteristics of Public and Private Elementary and Secondary School Principals in the United States: Results from the 2011–12 Schools and Staffing Survey*. U.S. Dept. of Education, National Center for Education Statistics, August 2013. Web. 26 Apr. 2016.

Bivens, Josh, Elise Gould, Lawrence Mishel, and Heidi Shierholz. "Raising America's Pay: Why It's Our Central Economic Policy Challenge." *Economic Policy Institute*, Economic Policy Institute, 4 June 2014. Web. 31 Mar. 2016.

Blair, Kristine, Radhika Gajjalaand, and Christine Tulley. eds. *Webbing Cyberfeminist Practice: Communities, Pedagogies, and Social Action*. Cresskill: Hampton Press, 2009. Web. 10 Dec. 2015.

Blakely, Tony, Simon Hales, Charlotte Kieft, Nick Wilson, and Alistair Woodward. "The Global Distribution of Risk Factors by Poverty Level." *Bulletin of the World Health Organization* 83 (2005): 118-126. Web. 9 Mar. 2016.

Blass, Wolfgang and John Foster. Eds. *Mixed Economies in Europe*. Brookfield: Edward Elgar Publishing, 1993. Print.

Bloom, Joshua, and Waldo E. Martin Jr. *Black Against Empire: The History and Politics of the Black Panther Party*. Berkeley: University of California Press, 2013. Print.

Bloy, Marjie. "The Luddites 1811–1816." *The Victorian Web*. The Victorian, 30 Dec. 2005. Web. 31 Mar. 2016.

Bogdan, R.C., and Biklen, S.K. *Qualitative Research for Education. An Introduction to Theory and Methods.* Boston: Allyn & Bacon, 1992. Print.

Bohannan, Paul. *How Culture Works*. New York: The Free Press, 1995. Print.

Bornstein, M.H., O.M. Haynes, K.M. Painter, and J.L. Genevro. "Child Language with Mother and with Stranger At Home and in the Laboratory: A Methodological Study." *J. Child Lang* 27.2 (2000): 407–420. Web. 29 Aug. 2015.

Bourdieu, Pierre. "Cultural Reproduction and Social Reproduction." *Knowledge, Education, and Cultural Change*. Ed. Richard Brown. London: Tavistock Publications, 1973. Print.

Bourgois, Philippe and Jeffrey Schonberg. *Righteous Dopefiend*. Berkeley: University of California Press, 2009. Print.

Boustany, Nora. "Ex-slave works to free others from West African tradition." *Christian Science Monitor*. Christian Science Monitor, 26 Mar. 2008. Web. 21 Apr. 2016.

Bowker, John. *World Religions: The Great Faiths Explored & Explained*. New York: DK Publishing, 2006. Print.

Bowles, Samuel and Herbert Gintis. *Schooling in Capitalist America: Educational Reform and the Contradictions of Economic Life*. New York: Basic Books, 1976. Print.

Braithwaite, J. *Crime, Shame, and Reintegration*. Cambridge: Cambridge University Press, 1989. Print.

Brame, R., S.D. Bushway, R. Paternoster, and M.G. Turner. "Demographic Patterns of Cumulative Arrest Prevalence by Ages 18 and 23." *Crime and Delinquency* 60 (2014): 471–486. Web. 29 May 2015.

Braquet, Donna. "Inclusive Practice: Pronoun Usage." *Office for Diversity and Inclusion*. University of Tennessee at Knoxville, 26 Aug. 2015. Web. 30 Aug. 2015.

Breen, Richard. "Educational Expansion and Social Mobility in the 20th Century." *Social Forces* 89.2 (2010): 365–88. Web. 22 Aug. 2014.

Brennan, Alice, and Dan Lieberman. "Florida City's 'Stop and Frisk' Nabs Thousands of Kids, Finds 5-Year-Olds 'Suspicious'" *Fusion*. Fusion Publishing Media, 9 May 2014. Web. 29 May 2015.

Breslin, Shaun. "Financial Transitions in The PRC: Banking On The State?" *Third World Quarterly* 35.6 (2014): 996–1013. Web. 31 Mar. 2016.

Bridges, Tristan. "Doing Gender with Wallets and Purses." *The Society Pages: Sociological Images*. The Society Pages, 14 Nov. 2013. Web. 29 Aug. 2015.

Briggs de Souza, X. "The Geography of Opportunity: Race and Housing Choice in Metropolitan America." *The Brookings Institution*. Washington, D.C., 2005. Web. 26 Sept. 2015.

Brinkley, Joel. *Cambodia's Curse: The Modern History of a Troubled Land*. New York: PublicAffairs, 2012. Print.

Brittingham, Angela, and G. Patricia de la Cruz. "We the People of Arab Ancestry in the United States." Washington: U.S. Census Bureau, Census 2000 Special Reports, Mar. 2005. Web. 24 Mar. 2016.

Brizendine, Louann. *The Female Brain*. New York: Random House, 2006. Print.

Bronson, Po. *"Why Do I Love These People?": Understanding, Surviving, and Creating Your Own Family*. New York: Random House, 2006. Print.

Broughman, Stephen P., and Nancy L. Swaim. "Characteristics of Private Schools in the United States: Results from the 2011–12 Private School Universe Survey." Washington: U.S. Dept. of Education, First Look, July 2013. Web. 26 Mar. 2016.

Brown, Anna and Eileen Patten. "Hispanics of Cuban Origin in the United States, 2011." Pew Research Center, 2013. Web. 10 Dec. 2015.

Brown, Dee. *Bury My Heart at Wounded Knee: An Indian History of the American West.* New York: Henry Holt and Company, 1970. Print.

Brown, Elizabeth and Mike Males. "Does Age or Poverty Level Best Predict Criminal Arrest and Homicide Rates?" *Justice Policy Journal* 8.1 (2011): 1–30. Web. 18 Apr. 2016.

Brown, Ian. *Burma's Economy in the Twentieth Century.* New York: Cambridge University Press, 2013. Print.

Brown, Susan L. and I-Fen Lin. "The Gray Divorce Revolution: Rising Divorce Among Middle-Aged and Older Adults, 1990–2010." *Journals of Gerontology Series B: Psychological Sciences and Social Sciences* 67.6 (2012): 731–741. Web. 25 Sept. 2015.

Buechler, Steven M. *Critical Sociology.* New York: Paradigm Publishers, 2008. Print.

Bump, Philip. "The New Congress is 80 Percent White, 80 Percent Male and 92 Percent Christian." *Washington Post.* Washington Post, 5 Jan. 2015. Web. 9 Aug. 2015.

Bunch, Charlotte. "Women's Subordination Through the Lens of Sex/Gender and Sexuality: Radical Feminism." *Feminist Frameworks: Alternative Accounts of the Relations between Women and Men.* Eds. A. Jaggar and P. Rothenberg. New York: McGraw-Hill, 1993. 174–178. Print.

Burman, Douglas D., Tali Bitan, and James R. Booth. "Sex Differences in Neural Processing of Language Among Children." *Neuropsychologia* 46.5 (2008): 1349–1362. Web. 29 Aug. 2015.

Butler, J. Corey, Richard M. Ryckman, Bill Thornton, and Rachel L. Bouchard. "Assessment of the Full Content of Physique Stereotypes With a Free-Response Format." *The Journal of Social Psychology* 133.2 (1992): 147–162. Web. 22 Sept. 2015.

Butler, Paul. *Let's Get Free: A Hip-Hop Theory of Justice.* New York: The New Press, 2009. Print.

Buttonwood. "Political power follows economic power." *The Economist.* The Economist Newspaper, 3 Feb. 2016. Web. 26 Apr. 2016.

Butts, R. Freeman. *American Public Education from Revolution to Reform, 1776–1976.* New York: Holt, Rinehart, & Winston, 1978. Print.

Buxton, Orfeu M., Milena Pavlova, Emily W. Reid, Wei Wang, Donald C. Simonson, and Gail K. Adler. "Sleep Restriction for 1 Week Reduces Insulin in Healthy Men." *Diabetes* 59.9 (2010): 2126–2133. Web. 30 May 2015.

Cabrera, Michaela. "Devotees nailed to cross in Philippine folk Catholicism ritual." *Reuters.* Reuters, 29 Mar. 2013. Web. 28 July 2016.

Cannon, Elaine. "Agency and Accountability." *The Church of Jesus Christ of Latter-Day Saints.* The Church of Jesus Christ of Latter-Day Saints, 1983. Web. 26 Mar. 2016.

Cannon, H. Brevy. "U.Va. Study Identifies Four Family Cultures in America." *UVA Today.* University of Virginia, 5 Nov. 2012. Web. 20 May 2015.

Cannon, Robert. "The Legislative History of Senator Exon's Communications Decency Act: Regulating Barbarians on the Information Superhighway." *Cybertelecom.* Cybertelecom, Nov. 1996. Web. 9 Aug. 2015.

Cappelli, Peter. *Will College Pay Off? A Guide to the Most Important Financial Decision You'll Ever Make.* New York: PublicAffairs, 2015. Print.

Carnevale, Anthony P. and Jeff Strohl. *Separate & Unequal: How Higher Education Reinforces the Intergenerational Reproduction of White Racial Privilege*. Georgetown Public Policy Institute Center on Education and Workforce. Georgetown University, 30 July 2013. Web. 26 Mar. 2016.

Carnevale, Anthony P., Nicole Smith, and Jeff Strohl. *Help Wanted: Projections of Jobs and Education Requirements through 2018*. Georgetown University Center on Education and Workforce, June 2010. Web. 31 Mar. 2016.

Carnevale, Anthony P., Tamara Jayasundera, and Artem Gulish. *Good Jobs are Back: College Graduates are First in Line*. Georgetown University Center on Education and Workforce, 14 Aug. 2015. Web. 31 Mar. 2016.

Carr, Deborah, James S. House, Ronald C. Kessler, Randolph Nesse, John Sonnega, and Camille B. Wortman. "Marital Quality and Psychological Adjustment to Widowhood among Older Adults: A Longitudinal Analysis." *Journal of Gerontology: Social Sciences* 55B.4 (2001): S197–S207. Web. 17 Mar. 2015.

Carson, E. Ann. *Prisoners in 2014*. Washington: U.S. Dept. of Justice, Bureau of Justice Statistics, Office of Justice Programs, Sept. 2015. Web. 26 Mar. 2016.

Carter, Andrew. "15 Things More Likely to Happen than Winning Mega Millions." *The Daily Beast*. Newsweek/Daily Beast, 30 Mar. 2012. Web. 01 June 2015.

Carter, Nancy M., and Christine Silva. "Women in Management: Delusions of Progress." *Harvard Business Review*. Harvard, Mar. 2010. Web. 10 Dec. 2015.

Cashdan, E., F.W. Marlowe, A. Crittenden, C. Porter, and B.M. Wood. "Sex Differences in Spatial Cognition Among Hadza Foragers." *Evolution and Human Behavior* 33 (2012): 274–284. Web. 9 Mar. 2016.

Casserly, Meghan. "10 Jobs That Didn't Exist 10 Years Ago." *Forbes*. Forbes Magazine, 11 May 2012. Web. 31 Mar. 2016.

Caton, Dan. "Natality and the Phase of the Moon Revisited: Do Birth Rates Depend on the Phases of the Moon?" *Birth Rates and the Phase of the Moon Revisited*. N.p., 2002. Web. 19 June 2015.

Causa, Orsetta and Åsa Johansson. "Intergenerational Social Mobility in OECD Countries." *OECD Economic Studies* 2010.1 (2011): 1–44. Web. 9 Mar. 2016.

Cecil, Kim M., Christopher J. Brubaker, Caleb M. Adler, Kim N. Dietrich, Mekibib Altaye, John C. Egelhoff, Stephanie Wessel, Ilayaraja Elangovan, Richard Hornung, Kelly Jarvis, and Bruce P. Lanphear. "Decreased Brain Volume in Adults with Childhood Lead Exposure." *PLoS Med* 5.5 (2008): 741–750. Web. 28 May 2015.

Center for Civic Education. *Elements of Democracy*. New York: Center for Civic Education, 2007. Print.

Center for Reproductive Rights. "Female Genital Mutilation (FGM): Legal Prohibitions Worldwide." *Center for Reproductive Rights*. Center for Reproductive Rights, 11 Dec. 2008. Web. 5 Aug. 2015.

Center on Budget and Policy Priorities. "Chart Book: The Legacy of the Great Recession." *Center on Budget and Policy Priorities*. Center on Budget and Policy Priorities, 13 July 2016. Web. 28 July 2016.

Chambliss, William J. "The Saints and the Roughnecks." *Society* 11.1 (1973): 24–31. Web. 28 May 2015.

Chandler, David. *A History of Cambodia*. 4th ed. Boulder: Westview Press, 2008. Print.

Chandy, Laurence, and Geoffrey Gertz. "Poverty in Numbers: The Changing State of Global Poverty." *Global News* (2011). Web. 30 May 2015.

Chant, Sylvia. "Re-thinking the "Feminization of Poverty" in Relation to Aggregate Gender Indices." *Journal of Human Development* 7.2 (2006): 201–220. Web. 10 Dec. 2015.

Chapman, Chris, Jennifer Laird, and Angelina KewalRamani. *Trends in High School Dropout and Completion Rates in the United States: 1972–2008*. U.S. Dept. of Education, National Center for Education Statistics, 2010. Web. 30 May 2015.

Chappell, Bill. "Miami-Area Police Chief Resigns Amid Charges of Racial Profiling." *The Two-Way. NPR*. Natl. Public Radio. 11 Dec. 2013. Web. 29 May 2015.

Charles, Ron. "'Boy Who Came Back From Heaven' actually didn't; books recalled." *Washington Post*. Washington Post, 16 Jan. 2015. Web. 26 Mar. 2016.

Chauncey, George. *Gay New York: Gender, Urban Culture, and the Making of the Gay Male World*. New York: Basic Books, 1994. Print.

Chen, Xianglei *First-Generation Students in Postsecondary Education: A Look at Their College Transcripts*. U.S. Dept. of Education, National Center for Education Statistics, July 2005. Web. 26 Mar. 2016.

Chetty, Raj, Nathaniel Hendren, Patrick Kline, and Emmanuel Saez. "Where is the Land of Opportunity? The Geography of Intergenerational Mobility in the United States." *The National Bureau of Economic Research* (2014): 1–104. Web. 26 July 2014.

Choy, Susan P. *Students Whose Parents Did Not Go To College*. U.S. Dept. of Education, National Center for Education Statistics, Dec. 2001. Web. 26 Mar. 2016.

Chuck, Elizabeth. "The Killing of an Unarmed Teen: What We Know About Brown's Death." *NBC News*. NBC News. 13 Aug. 2014. Web. 23 Sept. 2015.

Citro, Constance F., and Robert T. Michael, eds. *Measuring Poverty: A New Approach*. Washington, D.C.: National Academy Press, 1995. Print.

Clark, Kelly James. *Religion and the Sciences of Origins: Historical and Contemporary Discussions*. New York: Palgrave MacMillan, 2014. Print.

Clinard, Marshall B. and Peter C. Yeager. *Corporate Crime*. New York: Free Press, 1980. Print.

Clover Inc. *Clover Dating App*. Computer software. *Apple App Store*. Vers. 5.0 Clover Inc., 22 Feb. 2016. Web. 25 Mar. 2016.

Coates, Ta-Nehisi. "The Black Family in the Age of Mass Incarceration." *The Atlantic*. The Atlantic, Oct. 2015. Web. 26 Mar. 2016.

Cockerham, William C. *Social Causes of Health and Disease*. Cambridge: Polity Press, 2007. Print.

Cohn, D'vera. "Love and Marriage." Pew Research Center, 13 Feb. 2013. Web. 29 Aug. 2015. <http://www.pewsocialtrends.org/2013/02/13/love-and-marriage/>.

Colapinto, John. *As Nature Made Him: The Boy Who Was Raised as a Girl*. New York: HarperCollins Publishers, 2000. Print.

Colby, Sandra L. and Jennifer M. Ortman. *Projections of the Size and Composition of the U.S. Population: 2014 to 2060*. Washington: U.S. Census Bureau, Current Population Reports, Mar. 2015. Web. 28 Sept. 2015.

Cole, M. "The Perils of Translation: A First Step in Reconsidering Vygotsky's Theory of Development in Relation to Formal Education." *Mind, Culture, Activity: An International Journal* 16 (2009): 291–295. Web. 26 Mar. 2016.

Coleman, E., P. Colgan, and L. Gooren. "Male Cross-Gender Behavior in Myanmar (Burma): A Description of the Acault." *Archives of Sexual Behavior* 21 (1992): 313–321. Web. 29 Aug. 2015.

Coleman-Jensen, Alisha, Christian Gregory, and Anita Singh. *Household Food Security in the United States in 2013*. U.S. Dept. of Agriculture, Economic Research Service, Sept. 2014. Web. 30 May 2015.

College Board. "Trends in Student Aid: 2015." *Trends in Higher Education Series*. College Board, 2015. Web. 2 Apr. 2016.

"Columbus Police Use Tear Gas on Crowds Celebrating Ohio State Buckeyes Championship." *FOX Sports*. N.p., 13 Jan. 2015. Web. 14 May 2015.

Combs, H. Jurgen. "Middle School Configuration." *Edulink*. Edulink, 25 July 2008. Web. 26 Mar. 2016.

Committee on Scientific Principles for Education Research, Shavelson, Richard J. and Lisa Towne. *Scientific Research in Education*. Eds. National Research Council. Washington, D.C.: Center for Education, 2002. Print.

Comte, Auguste. *Cours de philosophie positive*. Paris: Rouen, 1842. Print.

Comte, Auguste. *The Course of Positive Philosophy*. Trans. Harriet Martineau. New York: Calvin Blanchard, 1855. Print.

Connell, R.W. "Cool Guys, Swots and Wimps: The Interplay of Masculinity and Education." *Oxford Review of Education* 15 (1989): 291–303. Web. 26 Mar. 2016.

Connell, R.W. "Teaching the Boys: New Research on Masculinity, and Gender Strategies for Schools." *Teachers College Record* 98.2 (1996): 206–235. Web. 26 Apr. 2016.

Contorno, Steve. "Rand Paul says more than half of students at medical, dental and law schools are female." *Politifact*. Politifact, 28 Jan. 2014. Web. 26 Mar. 2016.

Conway-Smith, Erin. "Why Mauritania has the highest percentage of slaves in the world." *The Week*. globalpost, 26 Oct. 2015. Web. 18 Apr. 2016.

Cook, Tim. Interview with Charlie Rose. "What's Next for Apple?" *60 Minutes*. 20 Dec. 2015. Web. 31 Mar. 2016.

Cooley, George Horton. *Human Nature and the Social Order*. New York: Charles Scribner's Sons, 1902. Print.

Cooley, Charles Horton. *On Self and Social Organization*. Chicago: University of Chicago Press. 1998. Print.

Coontz, Stephanie. *The Way We Never Were: American Families and the Nostalgia Trap*. New York: Basic Books, 1992. Print.

Corak, Miles "Do poor children become poor adults? Lessons from a cross country comparison of generational earnings mobility." *IZA Discussion Papers, No. 1993*. (2006): 1–64. Web. 05 Dec. 2014.

Corn, Charles. *The Scents of Eden: A History of the Spice Trade*. New York: Kodansha America Inc., 1999. Print.

Cornell University. "White-collar Crime." *White-collar Crime*. Cornell University Law School, n.d. Web. 29 May 2015.

Corriveau, Danielle. *The Inuit of Canada*. Minneapolis: Lerner Publications Company, 2002. Print.

Coupland, Douglas. *Generation X: Tales for an Accelerated Culture*. New York: St. Martin's Press, 1991. Print.

Cox, Stan. *Losing Our Cool: Uncomfortable Truths about our Air-Conditioned World (and Finding New Ways to Get Through the Summer)*. New York: The New Press, 2010. Print.

Crenshaw, Kimberle. "Demarginalizing the Intersection of Race and Sex: A Black Feminist Critique of Antidiscrimination Doctrine, Feminist Theory and Antiracist Politics." *University of Chicago Legal Forum* 140 (1989): 139–167. Web. 10 Dec. 2015.

Cross, Simon, and Barbara Bagilhole. "Girls' Jobs for the Boys? Men, Masculinity and Non-Traditional Occupations." *Gender, Work and Organization* 9.2 (2002): 204–226. Web. 30 Aug. 2015.

Crossman, Ashley. "An Overview of Qualitative Research Methods." *About.com*. 2015. Web. 29 June 2015.

Crossman, Ashley. "Reference Group Definition—Sociology." *About.com*. 2014. Web. 14 May 2015.

Cubberly, Ellwood Patterson. *Changing Conceptions of Education*. New York: Nabu Press, 2013. Print.

Curtin, Philip D. *The Atlantic Slave Trade: A Census*. Madison: University of Wisconsin Press, 1969. Print.

Dahl, Robert A. "The Concept of Power." *Behavioral Science* 2.3 (1957): 201–215. Web. 2 Apr. 2016.

Dahl, Robert A. *Who Governs?: Democracy and Power in an American City*. New Haven: Yale University Press, 1974. Print.

Dallaire, Roméo. *Shake Hands with the Devil: The Failure of Humanity in Rwanda*. New York: Carroll & Graf, 2004. Print.

Darwin, Charles Robert. *The Origin of Species by Means of Natural Selection, or, the Preservation of Favored Races in the Struggle for Life*. London: John Murray, 1859. Print.

Davis, J., J. Fuentes, and B.C. Sparkes. "What remains hidden of the hidden curriculum? Identities of gender and sexuality in physical education." *Revista Iberoamericana de Educación* 39 (2005): 73–90. Web. 26 Apr. 2016.

Davis, Kathy. "Intersectionality as Buzzword: A Sociology of Science Perspective on What Makes a Feminist Theory Successful." *Framing Intersectionality: Debates on a Multi-Faceted Concept in Gender Studies*. Eds. Helma Lutz, Maria Teresa Herrera Vivar, Linda Supik. Farnham: Ashgate Publishing Limited, 2011. 43–54. Print.

Davis, Kingsley and Wilbert Moore. "Some Principles of Stratification." *American Sociological Review* 10 (1945): 242–249. Web. 3 Aug. 2016.

Day, Jennifer Cheeseman, and Eric C. Newburger. *The Big Payoff: Educational Attainment and Synthetic Estimates of Work-Life Earnings*. Washington: U.S. Census Bureau, Current Population Reports: Special Studies, July 2002. Web. 22 July 2015.

Dayspring Technologies. *Goodbudget: Budget & Finance*. Computer software. *Google Play*. Vers. 2.4.3 Dayspring Technologies, 9 Dec. 2015 Web. 31 Mar. 2016.

Deckard, Barbara Sinclair. *The Women's Movement: Political, Socioeconomic and Psychological Issues*. New York: HarperCollins College Div, 1983. Print.

Deemer, Andy. "Beijing's Single Most Horrific Meal." *Asia Obscura*. N.p., 12 July 2012. Web. 21 May 2015.

De Guzman, Maria R.T. "Friendships, Peer Influence, and Peer Pressure During Teen Years." *NebGuide*. University of Nebraska—Lincoln, 2007. Web. 20 Sept. 2015.

Delaney, Arthur. "Paul Ryan Laments Inner-City Culture of Not Working" *The Huffington Post*. Huffington Post.com, Inc., 12 Mar. 2014. Web. 30 May 2015.

De la Torre, Augusto and Sergio L. Schmukler. *Emerging Capital Markets and Globalization*. New York: Standford University Press and The World Bank, 2007. Web. 2 Apr. 2016.

De Leon, Arnoldo, and Richard Griswold del Castillo. *North to Aztlan: A History of Mexican Americans in the United States*. 2nd ed. New York: Wiley-Blackwell. 2012. Print.

Delgado, Richard and Jean Stefancic. *Critical Race Theory: An Introduction*. 2nd ed. New York: New York University Press, 2012. Print.

DeNavas-Walt, Carmen, and Bernadette D. Proctor. "Income and Poverty in the United States: 2013." *Current Population Reports*. Washington, D.C.: U.S. Census Bureau, Sept. 2014. Web. 30 Aug. 2015.

DeNavas-Walt, Carmen, and Bernadette D. Proctor. "Income and Poverty in the United States: 2014." *Current Population Reports*. Washington, D.C.: U.S. Census Bureau, Sept. 2015. Web. 10 Dec. 2015.

Dennison, Renée Peltz. "Are Children of Divorce Doomed to Fail?" *Psychology Today*. Psychology Today, 2 Aug. 2014. Web. 26 Mar. 2016.

Dennis, Steven, and Jay Hunter. "Wealth of Congress Jumps $150 Million." *Hill Blotter*. Hill Blotter, 22 Oct. 2014. Web. 9 Aug. 2015.

DeSilver, Drew. "5 Facts about today's College Graduates." Pew Research Center, 30 May 2014. Web. 26 Mar. 2016.

DeSilver, Drew. "Who's poor in America? 50 years into the 'War on Poverty,' a data portrait." Pew Research Center, 2014. Web. 06 Nov. 2014.

DeVoe, Jill Fleury, Kristen E. Darling-Churchill, and Thomas Snyder. *Status and Trends in the Education of American Indians and Alaska Natives: 2008*. U.S. Dept. of Education, National Center for Education Statistics, Sept. 2008. Web. 28 Sept. 2015.

Dhaoudi, Mahmoud. "Ibn Khaldun: The Founding Father of Eastern Sociology." *International Sociology* 5.3 (1990): 319–335. Web. 9 Mar. 2016.

Dickey, Megan Rose. "Thurst is a Promising Dating App for Queer, Trans and Gender Non-Conforming People." *Tech Crunch*, Tech Crunch, 19 Aug. 2015 Web. 24 Mar. 2016.

Diederich, Bernard. *Papa Doc & the Tontons Macoutes*. Princeton: Markus Wiener Publishing, 2005. Print.

Dilulio Jr., John J. "My Black Crime Problem, and Ours." *Race, Crime, and Justice: A Reader*. Eds. Shaun L. Gabbidon and Helen Taylor Greene. New York: Routledge, 2005. 73–86. Print.

Dilulio Jr., John J. "The Coming of the Super—Predators." *The Weekly Standard*. Clarity Media Group, 27 Nov. 1995. Web. 28 May 2015.

DiMaggio, Paul J., and Walter W. Powell. "The Iron Cage Revisited: Institutional Isomorphism and Collective Rationality in Organizational Fields." *American Sociological Review* 48.2 (1983): 147–160. Web. 28 May 2015.

Dionne, G., P.S. Dale, M. Boivin, and R. Plomin. "Genetic Evidence for Bidirectional effects of early lexical and grammatical development." *Child Dev.* 74.2 (2003): 394–412. Web. 29 Aug. 2015.

DiSalvo, David. "Why Is Heroin Abuse Rising While Other Drug Abuse is Falling?" *Forbes*. Forbes Magazine, 14 Jan. 2014. Web. 20 Sept. 2015.

Divale, William Tulio. "An Explanation for Matrilocal Residence." *Being Female: Reproduction, Power, and Change*. Ed. Dana Raphael. The Hague: Mouton, 1975. 99–108. Web. 24 Sept. 2015.

Dixon, Mark. *Public Education Finances: 2011*. Washington: U.S. Census Bureau, Government Division Reports, May 2013. Web. 10 Mar. 2016.

Dodrill, Tara. "The Downfall of the American Family." *OffTheGridNews*. OffTheGridNews: Better Ideas for Off the Grid Living, 17 July 2013. Web. 24 Sept. 2015.

Domhoff, G. William. *Who Rules America? The Triumph of the Corporate Rich*. New York: McGraw-Hill Education, 2013. Print.

Donevan, Connor. "Millenials Navigae the Ups and Downs of Cohabitation." *All Things Considered. NPR*. Natl. Public Radio. 1 Nov. 2014. Web. 25 Sept. 2015.

Donham, Donald L. *History, Power, Ideology*. Cambridge: Cambridge University Press, 1990. Print.

Doob, Christopher. *Social Inequality and Social Stratification in U.S. Society*. Upper Saddle River: Pearson, 2013. Print.

Doss, Joe Morris. *Let the Bastards Go: From Cuba to Freedom on God's Mercy*. Baton Rouge: Louisiana State University Press, 2003. Print.

Dozier, Mary. "Challenges of Foster Care." *Attachment and Human Development* 7 (2005): 27–30. Web. 10 Dec. 2015.

Drake, Bruce. "Incarceration gap widens between whites and blacks." Pew Research Center, 6 Sept. 2013. Web. 3 Aug. 2016.

Drum, Kevin. *America's Real Criminal Element: Lead*. Mother Jones, Jan. 2013. Web. 28 May 2015.

Du Bois, W.E.B. *The Philadelphia Negro: A Social Study*. Philadelphia: University of Pennsylvania, 1899. Print.

Du Bois, W.E.B. *The Souls of Black Folk*. New York: Bantam Classic, 1903. Print.

Duhigg, Charles and Keith Bradsher. "How the U.S. Lost Out on iPhone Work." *New York Times*. New York Times, 21 Jan. 2012. Web. 31 Mar. 2016.

Duleep, Harriet Orcutt. "Measuring Socioeconomic Mortality Differentials Over Time." *Demography* 26 (1989): 345–351. Web. 29 May 2015.

Duncan, Greg J. and Katherine Magnuson. "Early Childhood Poverty." *Pathways: A Magazine on Poverty, Inequality, and Social Policy* Eds. David Grusky and Christopher Wimer. Stanford: Stanford University, 2011. 22–27. Web. 30 May 2015.

Duncan, Greg J., and Richard J. Murnane. "Introduction: The American Dream, Then and Now." *Whither Opportunity? Rising Inequality, Schools, and Children's Life Chances*. Eds. Duncan, Greg J., and Richard J. Murnane. New York: Russel Sage Foundation, 2011. 3–26. Print.

Dunmore, Timothy. *The Stalinist Command Economy: The Soviet State Apparatus and Economic Policy, 1945–53*. New York: St. Martin's Press, 1980. Print.

Dunn, John. *Democracy: A History*. New York: Atlantic Monthly Press, 2006. Print.

Durkheim, Émile. *Education and Sociology*. New York: Free Press, 1956. Print.

Durkheim, Émile. *Emile Durkheim on Institutional Analyses*. Trans. Mark Traugott. Chicago: University of Chicago Press, 1978. Print.

Durkheim, Émile. *Suicide: A Study in Sociology*. 1897. Trans. John A. Spaulding and George Simpson. New York: The Free Press of Glenco, 1951. Print.

Durkheim, Émile. *The Division of Labor in Society*. 1893. New York: Free Press, 1964. Print.

Durkheim, Émile. *The Elementary Forms of the Religious Life*. New York: Free Press, 1912. Print.

Durkheim, Émile. *The Rules of Sociological Method*. 1895. Trans. W.D. Halls. Ed. Steven Lukes. New York: The Free Press, 1982. Print.

Dye, Thomas R. and L. Harmon Ziegler. *The Irony of Democracy: An Uncommon Introduction to American Politics*. North Scituate: Duxbury Press, 1983. Print.

Early, John D., and John F. Peters. *The Xilixana Yanomami of the Amazon: History, Social Structure, and Population Dynamics*. Gainesville, FL: U of Florida, 2000. Print.

"Earth First! Journal: Media from the Frontlines of Ecological Resistance." *Earth First! Journal | Media from the Frontlines of Ecological Resistance*. Earth First!, 2015. Web. 9 Aug. 2015. <http://earthfirstjournal.org/>.

Educational Finance Branch. *Public Education Finances: 2013*. Washington: U.S. Census Bureau, Government Division Reports, June 2015. Web. 10 Mar. 2016.

Eggers, Mitchell and Douglas S. Massey. "The Structural Determinants of Urban Poverty: A Comparison of Whites, Blacks, and Hispanics." *Social Science Research* 20.3 (1991): 217–255. Web. 9 Mar. 2016.

EL AL Israel Airline Inc. "EL AL—History of Israel's National Airline." EL AL Israel Airline Inc., 2016. Web. 31 Mar. 2016

Elder-Vass, Dave. *The Reality of Social Construction*. New York: Cambridge University Press, 2013. Print.

El Gedida, El Manshia. "The Bedouin Hospitality." *Bedawi*. Bedawi, 2007. Web. 26 July 2016.

Eliot, Lise. *Pink Brain, Blue Brain*. New York: Houghton Mifflin Harcourt, 2009. Print.

Ellis, Deborah A., Robert A. Zucker, Hiram E. Fitzgerald. "The Role of Family Influences in Development and Risk." *Alcohol Health and Research World* 21.3 (1997): 218–225. Web. 19 June 2015.

Embry, Randa, and Phillip M. Lyons Jr. "Sex-Based Sentencing: Sentencing Discrepancies Between Male and Female Sex Offenders." *Feminist Criminology* 7 (2012): 146–162. Web. 28 May 2015.

Enan, Mohammad A. *Ibn Khaldun: His life and Works*. New Delhi: Kitab Bhavan, 1979. Print.

Enderwick, Peter. *Understanding Emerging Markets: China and India*. New York: Routledge, 2012. Print.

Engle, Jennifer. "Postsecondary Access and Success for First-Generation College Students." *American Academic* 3 (2007): 25–48. Web. 26 Mar. 2016.

Entmacher, Joan, Katherine Gallagher Robbins, Julie Vogtman, and Anne Morrison. "Insecure & Unequal: Poverty and Income Among Women and Families 2000–2013." *National Women's Law Center* (2014): 1–18. Web. 28 Oct. 2014.

Erikson, Erik, ed. *Youth: Change and Challenge*. New York: Basic Books, 1963. Print.

Etzioni, Amitai. *Comparative Analysis of Complex Organizations: Revised and Enlarged Edition*. New York: Macmillan Publishing Co., Inc., 1975. Print.

Etzioni, Amitai. "The Fast-Food Factories: McJobs are Bad for Kids." *Washington Post*. Washington Post, 24 Aug. 1986. Web. 2 Apr. 2016.

Evans-Pritchard, Edward. *Kinship and Marriage Among the Nuer*. Oxford: Clarendon Press, 1990. Print.

Evans-Pritchard, Edward *The Nuer: A Description of the Modes of Livelihood and Political Institutions of a Nilotic People*. Oxford: Clarendon Press, 1940. Print.

Everett, Silas. *7 Plus*. Computer software. *Apple App Store*. Vers. 1.0 Silas Everett, 24 June 2015. Web. 24 Mar. 2016.

Everything Code, Inc. *Can I Drive Yet*? Computer software. *Apple App Store*. Vers. 3.0.3. Everything Code, Inc., 24 July 2012. Web. 9 Mar. 2016.

Falola, T. "Slavery and Pawnship in the Yoruba Economy of the Nineteenth Century." *Slavery and Abolition* 15.2 (1994): 221–245. Web. 9 Mar. 2016.

Farber, Henry S. "Unemployment in the Great Recession: Did the Housing Market Crisis Prevent the Unemployed from Moving to Take Jobs?" *Papers and Proceedings* (2012): 1–6. Web. 29 May 2015.

Farran, Sue. "Pacific Perspectives: Fa'afafine and Fakaleiti in Samoa and Tonga: People Between Worlds." *Liverpool Law Rev* 31 (2010): 13–28. Web. 29 Aug. 2015.

Farrington, David P. and Kate A. Painter. "Gender Differences in Offending: Implications for Risk-Focused Prevention." *Home Office Online Report*. Home Office, Sept. 2004. Web. 11 Dec. 2015.

Faruqui, Fahad. "Saudi Arabia's cruel marriage laws." *The Guardian*. The Guardian, 3 Apr. 2010. Web. 14 Apr. 2016.

Federation of Indian Chambers of Commerce & Industry. "FICCI Quarterly Survey on Indian Manufacturing Sector." *FICCI*. FICCI, Nov. 2013. Web. 31 Mar. 2016.

Ferguson, James. *Papa Doc, Baby Doc: Haiti and the Duvaliers*. Oxford: Basil Blackwell Ltd., 1987. Print.

Ferguson, Niall. *The Ascent of Money: A Financial History of the World*. New York: The Penguin Press, 2009. Print.

Fields, Karen E. and Barbara J. Fields. *Racecraft: The Soul of Inequality in American Life*. New York: Verso, 2012. Print.

File, Thom and Camille Ryan. *Computer and Internet Use in the United States: 2013*. Washington: U.S. Census Bureau: American Community Survey Reports, Nov. 2014. Web. 21 Jul. 2015.

Fischer, Peter, Krueger, Joachim I., Tobias Greitemeyer, Claudia Vogrincic, Andreas Kastenmuller, Dieter Frey, Moritz Heene, Magdalena Wicher, and Martina Kainbacher. "The Bystander-Effect: A Meta-Analytic Review on Bystander Intervention in Dangerous and Non-Dangerous Emergencies." *Psychological Bulletin* 137.4 (2011): 517–537. Web. 9 Mar. 2016.

Fisher, Ernst. *How to Read Karl Marx*. London: Monthly Review Press, 1996. Print.

Fisher, Max. "Map: How 35 countries compare on child poverty (the U.S. is ranked 34th)." The Washington Post. The Washington Post, 15 Apr. 2013. Web. 30 May 2015.

Fishman, Rachel. "College Decisions Survey: Deciding to Go to College." *New America: EdCentral*. New America: EdCentral, 28 May 2015. Web. 31 Mar. 2016.

Fleischmann, Martin, and Stanley Pons. "Electrochemically induced nuclear fusion of deuterium." *Journal of Electroanalytical Chemistry* 261.2A (1989): 301–308. Web. 19 June 2015.

Flock, Elizabeth. "Bohemian Grove: Where the Rich and Powerful Go to Misbehave." *The Washington Post*. N.p., 15 June 2011. Web. 29 May 2015.

Fox, James Alan and Marianne W. Zawitz. *Homicide trends in the United States*. U.S. Dept. of Justice, Bureau of Justice Statistics [2007]. Web. 8 June 2016.

Fox, Robin. *Kinship & Marriage: An Anthropological Perspective*. Cambridge: Press Syndicate of the University of Cambridge, 1967. Print.

Franchise Direct. "Food Franchise Industry Report 2014: Industry Segment Overviews." *Franchise Direct*. Franchise Direct, 9 July 2014. Web. 25 Mar. 2016.

Frankopan, Peter. *The Silk Roads: A New History of the World*. New York: Bloomsbury Publishing, 2015. Print.

Franks, Peter, Paul C. Winters, Daniel J. Tancredi, and Kevin A. Fiscella. "Do Changes in Traditional Coronary Heart Disease Risk Factors Over Time Explain the Association between Socio-Economic Status and Coronary Heart Disease?" *BMC Cardiovascular Disorders* 11.28 (2011): 30 May 2015.

Frazier, E. Franklin. *The Negro Family in the United States*. Chicago: University of Chicago Press, 1939. Print.

Frederique, Nadine, Patricia Joseph, and R. Christopher C. Hild. "What is the State of Empirical Research on Indigent Defense Nationwide? A Brief Overview and Suggestions for Future Research." *Albany Law Review* 78.3 (2015): 1317–1340. Web. 10 Dec. 2015.

Freed, Andrea B. "School of Education at Johns Hopkins University-Multicultural Science Education: Myths, Legends, and Moon Phases." *Johns Hopkins School of Education*. Johns Hopkins University, 2012. Web. 5 Aug. 2015.

Freedman, Estelle, ed. *The Essential Feminist Reader*. New York: Random House, 2007. Print.

Freese, J. "Genetics and the social science explanation of individual outcomes." *American Journal of Sociology* 114. S1 (2008): S1–S35. Web. 30 June 2015.

Freud, Sigmund. *Civilization and Its Discontents*. 1930. London: Penguin, 2002. Print.

Friedan, Betty. *The Feminine Mystique*. New York: Vail-Ballou Press, 1963. Print.

Fry, Richard and D'vera Cohn. "Living Together: The Economics of Cohabitation." Pew Research Center, 27 June 2011. Web. 24 Sept. 2015.

Fry, Richard, and Rakesh Kochhar. "America's Wealth Gap Between Middle-Income and Upper-Income Families is Widest on Record." Pew Research Center, 2014. Web. 29 June 2015.

Fry, Richard. "U.S. High School Dropout Rate Reaches Record Low, Driven by Improvements Among Hispanics, Blacks." Pew Research Center, 2 Oct. 2014. Web. 26 Mar. 2016.

Fun with Dick and Jane. Dir. Ted Kotcheff. Perf. Jane Fonda, George Segal, and Ed McMahon. Columbia Pictures Corporation, 1977. DVD.

Fusco, Coco. *Dangerous Moves: Performance and Politics in Cuba*. New York: Tate, 2015. Print.

Galbraith, John Kenneth. *The Affluent Society*. Boston: Houghton Mifflin, 1958. Print.

Galinsky, Ellen, Kerstin Aumann, and James T. Bond. "Times are Changing: Gender and Generation at Work and at Home." *Families and Work Institute*. Families and Work Institute, 2011. Web. 26 Mar. 2016.

Gallo, Carmine. "Paris Considers Friendlier Service The New Battleground For Tourism Dollars." *Forbes*. Forbes Magazine, 30 Aug. 2013. Web. 19 June 2015.

Gans, Herbert J. *The Levittowners: Ways of Life and Politics in a New Suburban Community*. New York: Random House, 1967. Print.

Gao, George. "Chart of the Week: The black-white gap in incarceration rates." Pew Research Center, 18 July 2014. Web. 23 Sept. 2015.

Garcia, J. Neil. *Philippine Gay Culture: Binabae to Bakla, Silahis to MSM*. Hong Kong: Hong Kong University Press, 2009. Print.

Gardner, William I., Dorothy M. Griffiths, and Jeffrey P. Hamelin. "Biopsychosocial Features Influencing Aggression: A Multimodal Assessment and Therapy Approach." *The Handbook of High Risk Challenging Behaviors in People with Intellectual and Developmental Disabilities*. Ed. J. Luiselli. Baltimore: Paul Brooks Publishing, 2012. 83–104. Print.

Garfinkel, Harold. *Studies in Ethnomethodology*. 1967. Cambridge: Polity, 1984. Print.

Gates, Warren E. "The Spread of Ibn Khaldûn's Ideas on Climate and Culture." *Journal of History and Ideas* 28.3 (1967): 415–422. Web. 9 Mar. 2016.

Gazibara, Steve. "10 Crazy Facts from the Indiana University Tinder Study." *10Worthy*. 10Worthy, Feb. 2015. Web. 11 Dec. 2015.

Gelman, Andrew, Jeffrey Fagan, and Alex Kiss. "An Analysis of the New York City Police Department's "Stop-and-Frisk" Policy in the Context of Claims of Racial Bias." *Journal of the American Statistical Association* 102.479 (2007): 813–823. Web. 18 Apr. 2016.

Gershoff, Elizabeth T. "More Harm Than Good: A Summary of Scientific Research on the Intended and Unintended Effects of Corporal Punishment on Children." *Law and Contemporary Problems* 73.31 (2010): 31–56. Web. 5 Aug. 2015.

Gerson, K. *The Unfinished Revolution: How a New Generation is Reshaping Family, Work, and Gender in America*. New York: Oxford University Press, 2010. Print.

Giancola, Jennifer Kohler, David C. Munz, and Shawn Trares. "First-Versus Continuing-Generation Adult Students on College Perceptions: Are Differences Actually Because of Demographic Variance?" *Adult Education Quarterly* 58.3 (2008): 214–228. Web. 26 Mar. 2016.

Giddens, Anthony. *Sociology*. 5th ed. Malden: Polity Press, 2006. Web. 29 Aug. 2015.

Gilbert, Dennis and Joseph A. Kahl. *American Class Structure: A New Synthesis*. 4th ed. New York: Wadsworth Publishing, 1992. Print.

Gilbert, Dennis. *The American Class Structure in an Age of Growing Inequality*. Thousand Oaks: SAGE Publications Inc., 2014. Web. 15 July 2014.

Gilligan, Carol. *In a Different Voice: Psychological Theory and Women's Development*. New York: Carol Gilligan, 1982. Print.

Gillis, Stacy, Gillian Howie, and Rebecca Munford, eds. *Third Wave Feminism: A Critical Exploration*. 2nd ed. New York: Palgrave MacMillan, 2007. Print.

Ginsborg, Paul. *The Politics of Everyday Life: Making Choices, Changing Lives*. Bury St. Edmunds: Yale University Press, 2005. Print.

Gladieux, Lawrence E. "Federal Student Aid Policy: A History and an Assessment." *Financing Postsecondary Education: The Federal Role—October 1995*. College Board, Oct. 1995. Web. 22 July 2015.

Gläser, Jochen and Grit Laudel. "Life With and Without Coding: Two Methods for Early-Stage Data Analysis in Qualitative Research Aiming at Causal Explanations." *Forum: Qualitative Social Research* 14.2 (2013). Web. 9 Mar. 2016.

Glaze, Lauren E., and Erinn J. Herberman. *Correctional Populations in the United States, 2012*. U.S. Dept. of Justice, Bureau of Justice Statistics [2013]. Web. 10 July 2014.

Glennerster, H. "United States poverty studies and poverty measurement: The past twenty-five years." *Social Service Review* 76.1 (2002): 83–107. Web. 3 Aug. 2016.

"Global Democracy Ranking." *Democracy Ranking*. Democracy Ranking, 2016. Web. 31 Mar. 2016.

Global Slavery Index. "Findings—Walk Free Foundation—Global Slavery Index 2014." *Global Slavery Index 2014*. Walk Free Foundation, 2014. Web. 29 May 2015.

"Globalization." *Open Education Sociology Dictionary*. Ed. Kenton Bell. 2015. Web. 30 May 2015.

Glynn, Sarah Jane. "Breadwinning Mothers, Then and Now." *Center for American Progress*. Center for American Progress, June 2014. Web. 31 Aug. 2015.

"God Hates Fags." *God Hates Fags*. Westboro Baptist Church, 2015. Web. 11 Dec. 2015.

Goffman, Alice. *On the Run: Fugitive Life in an American City*. Chicago: The University of Chicago Press, 2014. Print.

Goffman, Erving. *Asylums: Essays on the Social Situation of Mental Patients and Other Inmates*. New York: Anchor Books, 1961. Print.

Goffman, Erving. *Stigma: Notes on the Management of Spoiled Identity*. New York: Simon & Schuster, 1963. Print.

Goffman, Erving. *The Presentation of Self in Everyday Life*. New York: Doubleday, 1959. Print.

Goldin, Claudia. "America's Graduation from High School: The Evolution and Spread of Secondary Schooling in the Twentieth Century." *Journal of Economic History* 58.2 (1998): 345–374. Web. 26 Mar. 2016.

Goldin, Claudia, and Lawrence F. Katz. "The Shaping of Higher Education: The Formative Years in the United States, 1890 to 1940." *Journal of Economic Perspectives* 13.1 (1999): 37–62. Web. 26 Mar. 2016.

Goldin, C. "The Quiet Revolution That Transformed Women's Employment, Education, and Family." *AEA Papers and Proceedings* (2006): 1–21. Web. 25 Sept. 2015.

Goldstein, Joseph, and Nate Schweber. "Man's Death After Chokehold Raises Old Issue for the Police" *New York Times*. New York Times, 18 July 2014. Web. 23 Sept. 2015.

Gonzalez-Barrera, Ana, and Jens Manuel Krogstad. "What we know About Illegal Immigration from Mexico." Pew Research Center, 20 Nov. 2015 Web. 24 Mar. 2016.

Goodlight, Sandra. *Why Marriages Do Not Last*. Bloomington: Author House, 2012. Print.

Gordon, Linda. "Socialist Feminism in the Second Wave." *New Labor Forum* 22.3 (2013). Web. 10 Dec. 2015.

Gorney, Cynthia. "Child Brides." *National Geographic*. National Geographic, June 2011. Web. 24 Sept. 2015.

Graburn, Nelson H.H. *Readings in Kinship and Social Structure*. New York: Harper & Row, 1971. Print.

Graff, Kristen and Rio Ramadhana. *Chinese Dining Etiquette*. Austin: Magnolia, 2011. Print.

Grasz, Jennifer. "CareerBuilder Special Report Tracks the Changing Composition of Jobs by Gender, Race and Age from 2001–2014." *CareerBuilder*. CareerBuilder, 26 Mar. 2015. Web. 31 Mar. 2016.

Grasz, Jennifer. "Number of Employers Passing on Applicants Due to Social Media Posts Continues to Rise, According to New CareerBuilder Survey." *CareerBuilder*. CareerBuilder, 26 June 2014. Web. 31 Mar. 2016.

Gray-Kanatiiosh, Barbara A. *Inuit*. New York: Abdo Publishers, 2002. Print.

Green, Adam Isaiah. "Queer Theory and Sociology: Locating the Subject and the Self in Sexuality Studies." *Sociological Theory* 25.1 (2007): 26–45. Web. 30 Aug. 2015.

Green, Andy. *The Palgrave Macmillan Education and State Formation: Europe, East Asia and the USA*. 2nd ed. New York: Palgrave MacMillan, 2013. Print.

Grenoble, Ryan. "College President Fires Professors Who Criticized His 'Drown The Bunnies' Comment [UPDATE]." *The Huffington Post*. The Huffington Post, 9 Feb. 2016. Web. 31 Mar. 2016.

Grindr LLC. *Grindr—Gay chat, meet & date*. Computer software. *Google Play*. Vers. 2.3.3 Grindr LLC, 22 Feb. 2016. Web. 25 Mar. 2016.

Grodsky, Eric, John Robert Warren, and Erika Felts. "Testing and Social Stratification in American Education." *Annual Review of Sociology* 34 (2008): 385–404. Web. 26 Mar. 2016.

Grossman, Herbert. *Classroom Behavior Management for Diverse and Inclusive Schools*. Lanham: Rowman & Littlefield, 2004. Web. Sept. 24 2015.

Guidetti, Giovanni and Boike Rehbein. "Theoretical Approaches to Inequality in Economics and Sociology. A Preliminary Assessment." *Transcience* 5.1 (2014): 1–15. Web. 24 Sept. 2015.

Guilhaumou, Jacques. "Sieyès et le non-dit de *la sociologie*: du mot à la chose." *Revue d'histoire des sciences humaines, Naissance de la science sociale (1750–1856)* 15 (2006): 117–134. Web. 22 July 2015.

Gunnar, M.R., K. Frenn, S.S. Wewerka, and M.J. Van Ryzin. "Moderate Versus Sever Early Life Stress: Associations with Stress Reactivity and Regulation in 10–12-year-old Children." *Psychoneuroendocrinology* 34.1 (2009): 62–75. Web. 9 Mar. 2016.

"Hacker Hat Colors Explained: Black Hats, White Hats, and Gray Hats." *How To Geek*. How To Geek, 2015. Web. 29 May 2015.

Hagerty, Barbara Bradley. "Some Muslims in U.S. Quietly Engage in Polygamy." *All Things Considered. NPR.* Natl. Public Radio. 27 May 2008. Web. 29 Aug. 2015.

Hajnal, Zoltan, Nazita Lajevardi, and Lindsay Nielson. "Voter Identification Laws and the Suppression of Minority Votes." 2015. Web. 31 Mar. 2016.

Halder, Debarati, and K. Jaishankar. *Cyber Crime and the Victimization of Women: Laws, Rights, and Regulations.* Hershey: IGI Global, 2011. Print.

Hall, John R. *Gone from the Promised Land: Jonestown in American Cultural History.* New Brunswick: Transaction Publishers, 1987. Print.

Hall, Wayne. "Social Class and Survival on the S.S. Titanic." *Social Science and Medicine* 22.6 (1986): 687–690. Web. 29 May 2015.

Hansen, Valerie. *The Silk Road: A New History.* New York: Oxford University Press, 2012. Print.

Hanson, Joyce A. *Rosa Parks: A Biography.* Santa Barbara: Greenwood Biographies, 2011. Print.

Hanushek, Eric A. and Ludger Woessmann. "Do Better Schools Lead to More Growth? Cognitive Skills, Economic Outcomes, and Causation." *The National Bureau of Economic Research* (2009): 1–31. Web. 26 Mar. 2016.

Hardy, B. Carmon. *Solemn Covenant: THE MORMON POLYGAMOUS PASAGE.* Chicago: University of Illinois Press, 1992. Print.

Harlow, Caroline Wolf. "Education and Correctional Populations" *Bureau of Justice Statistics Special Report* Washington: Office of Justice Programs, 2003. Web. 28 May 2015.

Harlow, Harry F. "The Nature of Love." *American Psychologist* 13 (1958): 673–685. Web. 30 June 2015.

Harlow, Harry F. "Development of Affection in Primates." *Roots of Behavior.* Ed. E.L. Bliss. New York: Harper, 1962. 157–166. Print.

Harlow, Harry F., Margaret K. Harlow, and Stephen J. Suomi. "From Thought to Therapy: Lessons from a Primate Laboratory." *American Scientist* 59.5 (1971): 538–549. Web. 30 June 2015.

Harrell, Erika. "Victims of Identity Theft, 2014." *Bureau of Justice Statistics Bulletin* Washington: Office of Justice Programs, Sept. 2015. Web. 11 Dec. 2015.

Harrington, Michael. *The Other America: Poverty in the United States.* New York: Simon & Schuster, 1962. Print.

Harris, Benjamin Cerf. "Likely Transgender Individuals in U.S. Federal Administrative Records and the 2010 Census." Washington: U.S. Census Bureau, Center for Administrative Records Research and Applications, 4 May 2015. Web. 24 Mar. 2016.

Harris, Marvin. *Patterns of Race in the Americas.* New York: Praeger, 1964. Print.

Harrison, Ben. *Undying Love: The True Story of a Passion That Defied Death.* Far Hills, NJ: New Horizon, 1997. Print.

Harrison, Brigid C. and Thomas R. Dye. *Power & Society: An Introduction to the Social Sciences.* New York: Wadsworth, 2008. Print.

Heaton, Tim and Tony Lawson. *Education and Training.* New York: Macmillan, 1996. Print.

Hegewisch, Ariane and Asha DuMonthier. "The Gender Wage Gap: 2015: Earnings Differences by Race and Ethnicity." *Institute for Women's Policy Research,* Institute for Women's Policy Research, Mar. 2016. Web. 3 June 2016.

Heinlein, Robert A. *The Moon is a Harsh Mistress.* New York: Tom Doherty Associates, 1966. Print.

Henderson, Nia-Malika. "Barbara Mikulski made it okay for women to wear pants in the Senate." *Washington Post*. Washington Post, 2 Mar. 2015. Web. 24 Sept. 2015.

Heng, Michael S.H. *The Great Recession: History, Ideology, Hubris and Nemesis*. New Jersey: World Scientific, 2010. Print.

Herdt, Gilbert. *The Sambia: Ritual and Gender in New Guinea*. New York: Holt, Rinehart and Winston, 1987. Print.

Hernández, Ma del Refugio Navrro, Prisca Icela Romo González, and Salvador Vázquez Sánchez. "Gender and Constructs from the Hidden Curriculum." *Creative Education* 4.12 (2013): 89–92. Web. 26 Apr. 2016.

"Heroic Imagination Project | Transforming Compassion into Heroic Action." *Heroic Imagination Project*. N.p., 2015. Web. 14 May 2015.

Hersh, Adam. "Assessing China's Economic Reform Agenda." *Center for American Progress*. Center for American Progress, 1 May 2014. Web. 31 Mar. 2016.

Hess, Cynthia, Jessica Milli, Jeff Hayes, Ariane Hegewisch, Yana Mayayeva, Stephanie Roman, Julie Anderson, and Justine Augeri. *The Status of Women in the States: 2015*. Washington D.C. Institute for Women's Policy Research, 2015. Web. 25 Mar. 2016.

Hewlett, Barry S. *Intimate Fathers: The Nature and Context of Aka Pygmy Paternal Infant Care*. Ann Arbor: University of Michigan Press, 1991. Print.

Hicken, Melanie. "Why Many Retired Women Live in Poverty." *CNN Money*. CNN, 13 May 2014. Web. 30 May 2015.

Hill, M.R. and S. Hoecker-Drysdale, eds. *Harriet Martineau, Theoretical and Methodological Perspectives*. New York: Routledge, 2003. Print.

Hillyer, Jack Lee. *A Comparative Study of Maturity Factors of Elementary and Middle School Pupils with Implications for School Grade Organization*. Columbia: University of Missouri, 1972. Print.

Hirschi, Travis. *Causes of Delinquency*. Berkeley: University of California, 1969. Print.

History. "The Death Spiral of Napster Begins." *This Day in History*. History, 6 Mar. 2015. Web. 9 Aug. 2015.

Hitchens, Christopher. *God is not Great: How Religion Poisons Everything*. New York: Twelve Books, 2007. Print.

Hoecker-Drysdale, Susan. *Harriet Martineau, First Woman Sociologist*. Oxford: Berg, 1992. Print.

Hokayem, Charles, and Misty L. Heggeness. Census Bureau. "Living in Near Poverty in the United States: 1966–2012." *Current Population Reports*. Washington, D.C.: U.S. Census Bureau, May 2014. Web. 30 May 2015.

Holmes, Mary. "The emotionalization of reflexivity." *Sociology* 44.1 (2010): 139–154. Web. 22 July 2015.

Holzer, Harry J., Diane Whitmore Schanzenbach, Greg J. Duncan, and Jens Ludwig. "The Economic Costs of Childhood Poverty in the United States." *Journal of Children and Poverty* 14.1 (2008): 41–61. Web. 30 May 2015.

Hopkins, Katy. "New Three-Year Degree Programs Trim College Costs." *U.S. News & World Report*. U.S. News & World Report, 29 Feb. 2012. Web. 26 Mar. 2016.

Horn, Dan. "Middle Class a Matter of Income, Attitude." *USA Today*. Gannett, 14 Apr. 2013. Web. 30 May 2015.

Hornsey, Ian S. *A History of Beer and Brewing*. Cambridge: RSC Paperbacks, 2003. Print.

Hoschild, Arlie R., and Anne Machung. *The Second Shift*. New York: Viking, 1989. Print.

Hotchkiss, L. and H. Borow. "Sociological Perspectives on Career Choice and Development." *Career Choice and Development*. Eds. D. Brown, L. Brooks, & Associates. San Francisco: Jossey-Bass, 1996. 262–307. Print.

Housseini, Khaled. *And the Mountains Echoed*. London: Bloomsbury Publishing, 2013. Print.

Hout, Michael, Claude S. Fischer, and Mark A. Chaves. "More Americans Have No Religious Preference: Key Finding from the 2012 General Social Survey." *Institute for the Study of Societal Issues* 7 Mar. 2013. Web. 22 July 2015.

Hovde, Elizabeth. "Income in Perspective: America's Poor Are among the World's Wealthy." *Oregon Live*. The Oregonian, 4 Aug. 2012. Web. 30 May 2015.

Hoyt, W.H., C. Jepsen, and K.R. Troske. *Educational Spending: Kentucky vs. Other States*. Lexington: University of Kentucky Center for Business and Economic Research, 2008. Web. 10 Mar. 2016.

Humes, Karen R., Nicholas A. Jones, and Roberto R. Ramirez. *Overview of Race and Hispanic Origin: 2010*. U.S. Census Bureau, 2010 Census Briefs, Mar. 2011. Web. 28 Sept. 2015.

Humphreys Laud. *Tearoom Trade: Impersonal Sex in Public Places*. New York: Aldine Transaction, 1970. Print.

Huston, Aletha, Edward Donnerstein, Halford Fairchild, Norma D. Feshbach, Phyllis A. Katz, John P. Murray, Eli A. Rubinstein, Brian L. Wilcox, and Diana Zuckerman. *Big World, Small Screen: The Role of Television in American Society*. Lincoln: University of Nebraska Press, 1992. Print.

Hutchison, Courtney. *Why Homeless Hero Hugo Alfredo Tale-Yax Died on NYC Street*. ABC News. 28 Apr. 2010. Web. 14 May 2015.

Hutton, Ronald. *Shamans: Siberian Spirituality and the Western Imagination*. New York: Hambledon and London, 2001. Print.

IBISWorld. "Wedding Services in the US: Market Research Report." *IBISWorld*. IBISWorld, Sept. 2015. Web. 25 Mar. 2016.

IBM. "IBM Expands PureSystems Family to Help Clients Tame Big Data." *IBM*. IBM, 9 Oct. 2012. Web. 20 Sept. 2015.

IFAD. "Enabling the rural poor to overcome poverty in Cambodia." *IFAD*. IFAD, Oct. 2007. Web. 31 Mar. 2016.

Inciardi, James A. "The Harm Reduction Roles of the American Criminal Justice System." *Harm Reduction: National and International Perspectives*. Ed. James A. Inciardi, and Lana D. Harrison. Thousand Oaks, CA: SAGE Publications, Inc., 2000. Web. 26 Sept. 2015.

Indiana University. Kinsey Reporter. Computer software. *Apple App Store*. Vers. 2.1.4 Indiana University, 15 Apr. 2015. Web. 14 Apr. 2016.

Institute for Criminal Policy Research. "World Prison Brief." *Institute for Criminal Policy Research*. Institute for Criminal Policy Research, 2015. Web. 3 Aug. 2016.

International Center for Research on Women. "Violence Against Women." International Center for Research on Women. 2015. Web. 24 Mar. 2016.

International Labour Organization. *Forced Labour, Human Trafficking and Slavery*. The International Labour Organization, 2016. Web. 9 Mar. 2016.

Intersex Society of North America. Intersex Society of North America, 2015. Web. 29 Aug. 2015. <http://isna.org/>.

Intuit Inc. *Mint: Personal Finance and Money*. Computer software. *Google Play*. Vers. 4.7.2.3 Intuit Inc., 21 Mar. 2016. Web. 26 Mar. 2016.

Isaacs, Julia B. "International Comparisons of Economic Mobility" *Getting Ahead or Losing Ground: Economic Mobility in America.* Eds. Isaacs, Julia B., Isabel V. Sawhill, and Ron Haskins. Brookings. The Brookings Institution, 2008. 37–46. Web. 7 Mar. 2015.

Isidore, Chris. "Buffet says he's still paying lower rate than his secretary." *CNN Money*. CNN, 4 Mar. 2013. Web. 24 Sept. 2015.

"Issues Facing Women and Children in Afghanistan." *UNICEF.* UNICEF, 2015. Web. 30 Aug. 2015. <http://www.unicef.org/afghanistan/about_2156.htm>.

iWitness. *iWitness personal safety*. Computer software. *Apple App Store*. Vers. 2.0.7 iWitness, 6 Oct. 2015. Web. 18 Apr. 2016.

Jacobs, Patricia A. "The Discovery and History of Trisomy X and XYY Syndrome." *National Conference on Trisomy X and XYY*, UC Davis M.I.N.D. Institute. 2006. Web. 21 May 2015.

Jackson, Philip W. *Life in Classrooms*. New York: Holt, Reinhart & Winston, 1968. Print.

Jacob, Theodore, and Sheri Johnson. "Parenting Influences on the Development of Alcohol Abuse and Dependence." *Alcohol Health and Research World* 21.3 (1997): 204–209. Web. 19 June 2015.

James, Steven R. "Hominid use of fire in the Lower and Middle Pleistocene." *Current Anthropology* 30 (1989): 1–26. Web. 5 Aug. 2015.

Janis, Irving L. *Victims of Groupthink*. New York: Houghton Mifflin, 1972. Print.

"Japanese Table Manners." *Japan-guide*. Japan-guide, 18 Feb. 2015. Web. 26 July 2016.

Jaschik, Scott. "President Quits at Mount St. Mary's." *Inside Higher Ed*. Inside Higher Ed, 1 Mar. 2016. Web. 31 Mar. 2016.

Javelin Strategy & Research. "How Consumers can Protect Against Identity Fraudsters in 2013." *Javelin Strategy & Research*. Javelin Strategy & Research, Feb. 2013. Web. 11 Dec. 2015.

Jensen, Alexander C., and Shawn D. Whiteman. "Differential Treatment and Adolescents' Delinquent Behaviors: Direct and Indirect Effects of Difference-Score and Perception-Based Measures." *Journal of Family Psychology* 28.4 (2014): 549–59. Web. 17 Mar. 2015.

Jiobu, Robert M. *Ethnicity and Inequality*. New York: State University of New York Press, 1990. Print.

JiWire, Inc. *WiFi Finder*. Computer software. *Google Play*. JiWire Inc., 16 Feb. 2013. Web. 26 Mar. 2016.

Johansen, Bruce. *The Native Peoples of North America: A History*. New York: Rutgers University Press, 2006. Print.

Johnson, Norman. *Mixed Economies of Welfare: A Comparative Perspective*. New York: Routledge, 2013. Print.

Jones, Ann. *Looking for Lovedu: A woman's Journey Through Africa*. New York: Vintage Books, 2001. Print.

Jones, Doug. "The Matrilocal Tribe: An Organization of Demic Expansion." *Human Nature* 22 (2011): 177–200. Web. 26 Mar. 2016.

Jones, Jeffrey M. "Democratic, Republican Identification Near Historical Lows." *Gallup*. Gallup, 11 Jan. 2016. Web. 31 Mar. 2016.

Jordan, G. "The Causes of Poverty-Cultural vs. Structural: Can There Be a Synthesis?" *Perspectives in Public Affairs* (2004): 18–34. Web. 9 Mar. 2016.

Joseph, Cynthia. *Growing up Female in Multi-Ethnic Malaysia*. Oxon: Routledge, 2014. Print.

Joseph, William A. Ed. *Politics in China: An Introduction*. Oxford: Oxford University Press, 2010. Print.

Jussim, L., and K.D. Harber. "Teacher Expectations and Self-Fulfulling Prophecies: Known and Unknowns, Resolved and Unresolved Controversies." *Personality and Social Psychology Review* 9.2 (2005): 131–155. Web. 26 Apr. 2016.

Justice Policy Institute. "Bail Fail: Why the U.S. Should End the Practice of Using Money for Bail." *Justice Policy Institute*. Justice Policy Institute. Sept. 2012. Web. 23 Sept. 2015.

Jyoti, Diana F., Edward A. Frongillo, and Sonya J. Jones. "Food Insecurity Affects School Children's Academic Performance, Weight Gain, and Social Skills." *Journal of Nutrition* 135.12 (2005): 2831–2839. Web. 30 June 2015.

Kahn, M. *Always Hungry, Never Greedy: Food and the Expression of Gender in a Melanesian Society*. Long Grove: Waveland Press, 1993. Print.

Kain, Edward L. "Changes in the MCAT Have Implications for Sociology Department Planning." *ASA Footnotes*. American Sociological Association, 2012. Web. 22 July 2015.

Kalish, Nancy. *Lost and Found Lovers: Facts and Fantasies of Rekindled Romances.* Lincoln: iUniverse, Inc., 2005. Print.

Kane, John and April D. Wall. "The 2005 National Public Survey on White Collar Crime." National White Collar Crime Center, 2006. Web. 10 Dec. 2015.

Karabell, Zachary. *What's College For?: The Struggle To Define American Higher Education*. New York: Basic Books, 1998. Print.

Kara, Siddharth. *Sex Trafficking: Inside the Business of Modern Slavery*. New York: Columbia University Press, 2009. Print.

Keady, Cameron. "New Hampshire Police Department Gives Out Free Pizza to Law-Abiding Citizens." *The Huffington Post*. HuffingtonPost.com, Inc., 12 Mar. 2015. Web. 8 Apr. 2015.

Kelly, Allison "The construction of masculine science." *Science for Girls?* Ed. Allison Kelly. Milton Keynes: Open University Press, 1987. Print.

Kemp, Joe. "'It was a bonehead decision': Florida dad regrets kicking 6-year-old son down skateboard ramp." *New York Daily News*. Daily News, 19 Mar. 2014. Web. 30 June 2015.

Kennedy, John F. *A Nation of Immigrants*. New York: Harper Perennial, 1964. Print.

Kieler, Ashlee. "Student: Corinthian Colleges' Demise is Like "Watching a House Fall on a Witch"." *Consumerist*. Consumerist, 17 July 2014. Web. 26 Mar. 2016.

Kille, Leighton Walter. "The low-wage recovery: Industries and jobs after the Great Recession." *Journalist's Resource*. Journalist's Resource, 1 May 2014. Web. 28 July 2016.

Killough, Ashley. "Obama campaign hits Romney as 'outsourcer in chief'." *CNN*. CNN, 22 June 2012. Web. 26 Apr. 2016.

Kimball, Will and Robert E. Scott. "China Trade, Outsourcing and Jobs: Growing U.S. trade deficit with China cost 3.2 million jobs between 2001 and 2013, with job losses in every state." *Economic Policy Institute*, Economic Policy Institute, 11 Dec. 2014. Web. 31 Mar. 2016.

Kimmel, Michael. *Misframing Men: Essays on the Politics of Contemporary Masculinities*. New Brunswick: Rutgers University Press, 2010. Print.

Kimmel, Michael. *The Gendered Society*. New York: Oxford University Press, 2012. Print.

Kim, Tong-Hyung. "Look At How Bizarre North Korea's 'Internet' Is." *Business Insider*. Business Insider, 23 Dec. 2014. Web. 31 Mar. 2016.

King, Jacque L. "Research Review: Work-Family/Family-Work Conflict." *International Journal of Leadership Studies* 1.1 (2005): 102–105. Web. 25 Sept. 2015.

King James Bible, Deuteronomy 21.10–14. Web. 24 Sept. 2015.

Kinsey, Alfred C., Wardell B. Pomeroy, and Clyde E. Martin. *Sexual Behavior in the Human Male*. Philadelphia: W.B. Saunders Company, 1948. Print.

Kinsey, Alfred C., Wardell B. Pomeroy, Clyde E. Martin, and Paul H. Gebhard. *Sexual Behavior in the Human Female*. Indiana: Indiana University Press, 1953. Print.

Kittle, Cameron. "A year after paralyzing accident, 'it could be worse' says Cooper Doucette." *The Telegraph*. The Telegraph, 31 Aug. 2011. Web. 28 Sept. 2015.

Klein, Herbert S. *The Atlantic Slave Trade*. Cambridge: Cambridge University Press, 1999. Print.

Klinkenborg, Verlyn. "Trying to Measure the Amount of Information that Humans Create." *New York Times*. New York Times, 12 Nov. 2003. Web. 20 Sept. 2015.

Knight, Wayne. The issue of Tyranny of the Majority. Personal conversation. March 2016.

Kochel, Tammy Rinehart, David B. Wilson, and Stephen D. Mastrofski. "Effect of Suspect Race on Officer's Arrest Decisions." *Criminology* 49.2 (2011): 473–512. Web. 29 May 2015.

Kohlberg, Lawrence. *The Development of Modes of Thinking and Choices in Years 10 to 16*. Diss. University of Chicago, 1958. Print.

Kohlberg, Lawrence. "Moral Stages and Moralization: The Cognitive-Developmental Approach." *Moral Development and Behavior: Theory, Research, and Social Issues*. Ed. T. Lickona. New York: Holt, Rinehart & Winston, 1976. Print.

Kohn, Sally. "Is Polygamy the Next Gay Marriage?" *The Daily Beast*. The Daily Beast, 12 Sept. 2014. Web. 24 Sept. 2015.

Kolchin, Peter. *American Slavery: 1619–1877*. New York: Hill and Wang, 2003. Print.

Kolowich, Steve. "How to Train Your Draconian." *Inside Higher Ed*. Inside Higher Ed, 1 Mar. 2011. Web. 26 Apr. 2016.

Kooistra, Paul, and Daniel M. Harrison. "Durkheim, Terrorism, and Positive Deviance." *International Journal of Crime, Criminal Justice, and Law* 2.2 (2007): 2–31. Web. 15 Sept. 2014.

Kovelant, Kevin. "The DangerMedia Innerview." *RAWilsonFansorg*. 2000. Web. 9 Aug. 2015.

Kozol, Jonathan. *Rachel and Her Children: Homeless Families in America*. New York: Three Rivers Press, 1988. Print.

Kozol, Jonathan. *The Shame of the Nation: The Restoration of Apartheid Schooling in America*. New York: Three Rivers Press, 2005. Print.

Kraus, Michael W., and Jacinth J.X. Tan. "Americans Overestimate Social Class Mobility." *Journal of Experimental Social Psychology* 58 (2015): 101–111. Web. 29 May 2015.

Kravets, David. "Napster Trial Ends Seven Years Later, Defining Online Sharing Along the Way." *Wired*. Wired, 31 Aug. 2007. Web. 9 Aug. 2015.

Kreider, Rose M. and Diana B. Elliott. *America's Families and Living Arrangements: 2007.* Washington: U.S. Census Bureau, Current Population Reports, Sept. 2009. Web. 24 Sept. 2015.

Krogstad, Jens Manuel and Mark Hugo Lopez. "Hispanic Nativity Shift." Pew Research Center, 29 Apr. 2014. Web. 28 Sept. 2015.

Krogstad, Jens Manuel and Richard Fry. "More Hispanics, blacks enrolling in college, but lag in bachelor's degrees." Pew Research Center, 24 Apr. 2014. Web. 26 Mar. 2016.

Krogstad, Jens Manuel. "Census Bureau Explores New Middle East/North Africa Ethnic Category." Pew Research Center, 24 Mar. 2014. Web. 28 Sept. 2015.

Krogstad, Jens Manuel. "Cuban Immigration to U.S. Surges as Relations Warm." Pew Research Center, 10 Dec. 2015. Web. 2 Apr. 2016.

Krueger, Alan B. "The Great Utility of the Great Gatsby Curve." *The Brookings Institute*. The Brookings Institute, 19 May 2015. Web. 9 Mar. 2016.

Krugman, Paul. "Economics in Crisis." *New York Times*. New York Times, 5 Mar. 2012. Web. 9 Mar. 2016.

Krupnik, Igor, Claudio Aporta, Shari Gearheard, Gita J. Laidler, and Lene Kielsen Holm, eds. *SIKU: Knowing Our Ice: Documenting Inuit Sea Ice Knowledge and Use*. New York: Springer, 2010. Print.

Krupnick, Matt. "These groups of Asian-Americans rarely attend college, but California is trying to change that." *PBS*. PBS Newshour, 21 May 2015. Web. 26 Mar. 2016.

Kuczynski, Leon ed. *Handbook of Dynamics in Parent-Child Relations*. Thousand Oaks: SAGE Publications, 2003. Print.

Kuperberg, Arielle. "Age at Coresidence, Premarital Cohabitation, and Marriage Dissolution: 1985–2009." *Journal of Marriage and Family* 76.2 (2014): 352–369. Web. 24 Sept. 2015.

Kurczy, Stephen. "5 reasons why Haiti's Jean-Claude Duvalier is infamous." *Christian Science Monitor*. Christian Science Monitor, 20 Jan. 2011. Web. 31 Mar. 2016.

Kyi, Aung San Suu. *Freedom from Fear: And Other Writings*. Ed. Michael Aris. New York: Penguin Group, 1991. Print.

Kyi, Aung San Suu. *Letters from Burma*. New York: Penguin Books, 1995. Print.

Lab304. *Spendbook—Personal Finance Tracker*. Computer software. *Apple App Store*. Vers. 1.1.3 Lab304, 3 Apr. 2015. Web. 31 Mar. 2016.

Lagemann, Ellen Condliffe and Harry Lewis. *What is College for? The Public Purpose of Higher Education*. New York: Teachers College Press, 2012. Print.

Lah, Kyung. "Tokyo Man Marries Video Game Character." *CNN*. CNN, 17 Dec. 2009. Web. 24 Sept. 2015.

Lakoff, Sanford A. *Democracy: History, Theory, Practice*. New York: Westview Press, 1996. Print.

Landin, Kathy. "15 of the World's Weirdest Marriages, 'I Now Pronounce You ... What?!'" *TheFW*. TheFW, 2015. Web. 24 Sept. 2015.

Landivar, Liana Christin. "Men in Nursing Occupations." *American Community Survey Highlight Report*. Washington, D.C.: U.S. Census Bureau, Feb. 2013. Web. 30 Aug. 2015.

Lane, Jan-Erik and Svante Ersson. *Government and the Economy: A Global Perspective*. New York: Continuum, 2002. Print.

Laney, Doug. "Application Delivery Strategies." *Meta Delta*. Meta Group, 6 Feb. 2001. Web. 20 Sept. 2015.

Langhout, Regina D. and Cecily A. Mitchell. "Engaging Contexts: Drawing the Link Between Student and Teacher Experiences of the Hidden Curriculum." *Journal of Community & Applied Social Psychology* 18.6 (2008): 593–614. Web. 26 Mar. 2016.

Larson, Jayne Amelia. *Driving the Saudis: A Chauffeur's Tale of Life, Liberty, and the Pursuit of Happiness on Rodeo Drive*. New York: Simon & Schuster Paperbacks, 2012. Print.

Lasch, Christopher. *Haven in a Heartless World: The Family Besieged*. New York: Basic Books, 1977. Print.

Lash, Devon. "Allentown housing sting shows whites and minorities treated differently." *The Morning Call*. The Morning Call, 26 June 2012. Web. 26 Sept. 2015.

Lasswell, Harold Dwight. *Politics: Who Gets What, When, How*. New York: McGraw-Hill, 1936. Print.

Lattimer, Mark. "Freedom Lost." *The Guardian* 13 Dec. 2007. Web. 26 Mar. 2016.

Laughlin, Lynda. "Who's Minding the Kids? Child Care Arrangements: Spring 2011." *Household Economic Studies*. Washington, D.C.: U.S. Census Bureau, Apr. 2013. Web. 21 May 2015.

Lavery, Diana. "More Mothers of Young Children in U.S. Workforce." *Population Reference Bureau*. Population Reference Bureau, 2012. Web. 26 Apr. 2016.

Le, C.N. "14 Important Statistics About Asian Americans." *Asian Nation*. Asian Nation, 2015. Web. 28 Sept. 2015.

Ledger, Kate. "Sociology and the Gene." *Contexts* 8.3 (2009): 16–20. Web. 30 June 2015.

Lee, Kyuhong, Eun Joo Lee, and Min-Sung Kang. "Resurgence of a Debilitating and Entirely Preventable Respiratory Disease Among Working Coal Miners." *American Journal of Respiratory and Critical Care Medicine* 190.6 (2014): 708–709. Web. 30 May 2015.

Leeming, David Adams. *Creation Myths of the World: An Encyclopedia, Second Edition*. 2nd ed. Santa Barbara: Greenwood Publishing Group, 2010. Web. 3 June 2016.

Lehrer, Evelyn L. "Age at Marriage and Marital Instability: Revisiting the Becker-Landes-Michael Hypothesis." *Journal of Population Economics* 21.2 (2008): 463–484. Web. 26 Mar. 2016.

Leidner, Robin. *Fast Food, Fast Talk: Service Work and the Routinization of Everyday Life*. Berkeley: University of California Press, 1993. Print.

Lemert, Edwin M. *Human Deviance, Social Problems, and Social Control*. Englewood Cliffs: Prentice-Hall, 1972. Print.

Lemert, Edwin M. *Social Pathology: A Systematic Approach to the Theory of Sociopathic Behavior*. New York: McGraw-Hill, 1951. Print.

Leopold, Todd. "Kenyan Lawyer offers Cows, Goats, Sheep to Marry Malia Obama." *CNN*. CNN, 28 May 2015. Web. 25 Mar. 2016.

Lerman, Robert I. and Stefanie R. Schmidt. *An Overview of Economic, Social, and Demographic Trends Affecting the US Labor Market*. U.S. Dept. of Labor, Office of the Assistant Secretary for Policy, 1999. Web. 26 Apr. 2016.

Levinson, David. *Religion: A Cross-Cultural Encyclopedia*. New York: ABC-CLIO, 1996. Print.

Levitt, Steven D., and Stephen J. Dubner. *Freakonomics: A Rogue Economist Explores the Hidden Side of Everything*. New York: HarperCollins, 2009. Print.

Levitt, Steven D. "Understanding Why Crime Fell in the 1990s: Four Factors That Explain the Decline and Six That Do Not." *Journal of Economic Perspectives* 18.1 (2004): 163–190. Web. 28 May 2015.

Levitt, Theodore. "The Globalization of Markets" *Harvard Business Review*. Harvard, May 1983. Web. 2 Apr. 2016.

Lewin, Kurt. *Resolving Social Conflicts; Selected Papers on Group Dynamics*. Ed. Gertrude W. Lewin. New York: Harper & Row, 1948. Print.

Lewin, Tamar. "At Colleges, Women are Leaving Men in the Dust." *New York Times*. New York Times, 9 July 2006. Web. 26 Mar. 2016.

Lewis, James R. *The Encyclopedia of Cults, Sects, and New Religions*. Amherst: Prometheus Books, 2002. Print.

Lewis, Jamie M. and Rose M. Kreider. *Remarriage in the United States*. Washington: U.S. Census Bureau, American Community Survey Reports, Mar. 2015. Web. 26 Mar. 2016.

Lewis, Oscar. *Five Families: Mexican Case Studies in the Culture of Poverty*. New York: Basic Books, 1959. Print.

Lewis, Oscar. "The Culture of Poverty." *Society* 35.2 (1998): 7–9. Web. 30 May 2015.

Library of Congress. "Party System." *United States Congress*. United States, 2016. Web. 31 Mar. 2016.

Liebow, Elliot. *Tally's Corner: A Study of Negro Streetcorner Men*. Boston: Rowman & Littlefield Publishers, 1967. Print.

Life.Church. *Bible*. Computer software. *Google Play*. Vers. 6.5.1 Life.Church, 15 Mar. 2016. Web. 26 Mar. 2016.

Lindemann, Albert S. *A History of European Socialism*. New Haven: Yale University Press, 1984. Print.

Lindsey, Linda L. *Gender Roles: A Sociological Perspective*. 6th ed. New York: Routledge, 2015. Print.

Lipka, Michael and Conrad Hackett. "Why Muslims are the world's fastest-growing religious group." Washington, DC: Pew Research Center, 23 Apr. 2015. Web. 26 Mar. 2016.

Lipka, Michael. "Muslims and Islam: Key Findings in the U.S. and Around the World." Washington, DC: Pew Research Center, 7 Dec. 2015. Web. 26 Mar. 2016.

Lippens, R. "Rethinking Organizational Crime and Organizational Criminology." *Crime, Law, and Social Change* 35.4 (2001): 319–331. Web. 29 May 2015.

Liptak, Adam and Coral Davenport. "Supreme Court Deals Blow to Obama's Efforts to Regulate Coal Emissions." *New York Times*. New York Times, 9 Feb. 2016. Web. 31 Mar. 2016.

Living on One Dollar. Dir. Zach Ingrasci, Sean Leonard, and Chris Temple. IndieFlix, 2013. DVD.

Livingston, Gretchen. "Four-in-Ten Couples are Saying "I Do," Again." Pew Research Center, 14 Nov. 2014. Web. 7 Dec. 2015.

Livingston, Gretchen and D'vera Cohn. "The New Demography of Motherhood." Pew Research Center, 6 May 2010. Web. 23 Sept. 2015.

LoBue, Vanessa, and Judy S. DeLoache. "Pretty in Pink: The Early Development of Gender-Stereotyped Colour Preferences." *British Journal of Developmental Psychology* 29.3 (2011): 656–667. Web. 29 Aug. 2015.

Lopez, Mark Hugo, and Ana Gonzalez-Barrera. "Women's College Enrollment Gains Leave Men Behind." Pew Research Center, 13 Feb. 2013. Web. 29 Aug. 2015.

Lopez, Mark Hugo, and Jens Manuel Krogstad. "As Cuban Americans Demographics Change, So Do Views of Cuba." Pew Research Center, 23 Dec. 2014. Web. 2 Apr. 2016.

Loury, Glenn C. *Race, Incarceration, and American Values*. Cambridge: MIT Press, 2008. Print.

Lowrey, Annie. "For Two Economists, the Buffet Rule Is Just a Start." *New York Times*. New York Times, 16 Apr. 2012. Web. 12 June 2016.

Lucal, Betsy. "What it Means to be Gendered Me: Life on the Boundaries of a Dichotomous Gender System." *Gender & Society* 13.6 (1999): 781–797. Web. 14 Apr. 2016.

Macartney, Suzanne, Alemayehu Bishaw, and Kayla Fontenot. *Poverty Rates for Selected Detailed Race and Hispanic Groups by State and Place: 2007–2011*. Washington: U.S. Census Bureau, American Community Survey Briefs, Feb. 2013. Web. 10 Dec. 2015.

Machida, Satoshi. "Does Globalization Render People More Ethnocentric? Globalization and People's Views on Cultures." *American Journal of Economics and Sociology* 71.2 (2012): 436–469. Web. 31 Mar. 2016.

Macskássy, Sofus Attila. "From Classmates to Soulmates." *Facebook Data Sciences*. Facebook, 7 Oct. 2013. Web. 24 Sept. 2015.

Malarkey, Kevin and Alex Malarkey. *The Boy Who Came Back From Heaven: A Remarkable Account of Miracles, Angels, and Life beyond This World*. New York: Tyndale House Publishers, 2010. Print.

Malinowski, Bronislaw. *The Sexual Lives of Savages in North-Western Melanesia*. 1929. New York: Kessinger Publishing, 2005. Print.

Manhattan, Avro. *The Vatican Billions*. New York: Chick Pub, 1983. Print.

Manning, Wendy D. "Trends in Cohabitation. Over Twenty Years of Change, 1987–2010." National Center for Family & Marriage Research, 2013. Web. 24 Sept. 2015.

Mansfield, Edward and Diana Mutz. "Us vs. Them: Mass Attitudes toward Offshore Outsourcing." *World Politics* 65.4 (2013): 571–608. Web. 2 Apr. 2016.

Manzi, Jim. *Uncontrolled: The Surprising Payoff of Trial-and-Error for Business, Politics, and Society*. New York: Basic Books, 2012. Print.

Marcuss, Rosemary D., and Richard E. Kane. "U.S. National Income and Product Statistics: Born of the Great Depression and World War II." *Survey of Current Business* (2007): 32–46. Web. 29 May 2015.

Mark, Monica. "Slavery Still Shackles Mauritania, 31 Years after Its Abolition." *The Guardian* 14 Aug. 2012. Web. 14 Oct. 2014.

Marlow, C. *Research Methods for Generalist Social Work*. 3rd ed. Belmont: Brooks/Cole, 2001. Print.

Marmor, M., R.E. Shore, S. Titus, X. Chen, and D.C. Des Jarlais. "Drug Injection Rates and Needle-Exchange Use in New York City, 1991–1996." *Journal of Urban Health: Bulletin of the New York Academy of Medicine* 77.3 (2000): 359–368. Web. 19 June 2015.

Martin, Carol Lynn and Diane Ruble. "Children's Search for Gender Cues: Cognitive Perspectives on Gender Development." *Current Directions in Psychological Science* 13.2 (2004): 67–70. Web. 15 Apr. 2016.

Martineau, Harriet. *How to Observe Morals and Manners*. London: Charles Knight and Co., 1838. Print.

Martineau, Harriet. *Society in America Vol. 1*. New York: Saunders and Otley, 1837. Print.

"Martin Luther King Jr.—Biography." *Nobel Prize.org*. Nobel Prize. 2015. Web. 23 Sept. 2015.

Martin, Steven P. "Trends in Marital Dissolution by Women's Education in the United States." *Demographic Research* 15.20 (2006): 537–560. Web. 26 Mar. 2016.

Marx, Karl. *Capital: A Critique of Political Economy, Vol. I. The Process of Capitalist Production*. 1867. Trans. Samuel Moore and Edward Aveling. Ed. Frederick Engels. London: Swan Sonnenschein, Loweey & Co., 1887. Print.

Marx, Karl. *Collected Works of Karl Marx and Frederick Engels: Volume 1*. New York: International Publishers, 1975.

Marx, Karl. *Economic & Philosophic Manuscripts of 1844*. 1844. Trans. Matin Mulligan. Moscow: Progress Publishers, 1959. Print.

Marx, Karl and Frederick Engels. *Manifesto of the Communist Party*. 1848. Print.

Marx, Karl. *The First International and After*. Ed. Fernbach, David. New York: Penguin Books with New Left Review, 1974. Web. 9 Mar. 2016.

Mataen, David. *Africa: The Ultimate Frontier Market: A Guide to the business and investment opportunities in emerging Africa*. Hampshire: Harriman House Ltd, 2012. Print.

Matthaei, Julie. "Workers, Women, and Revolution: A Marxist-Feminist Perspective on URPE (The Union for Radical Political Economics)." Boston, MA. 4 Jan. 2015. Web. 2 Apr. 2015.

Maume Jr., David J. "Occupational Segregation and the Career Mobility of White Men and Women." *Social Forces* 77.4 (1999): 1433–1459. Web. 30 Aug. 2015.

Mazumder, Bhaskar. "Fortunate Sons: New Estimates of Intergenerational Mobility in the United States using Social Security Earnings Data". *The Review of Economics and Statistics* 87.2 (2005): 235–55. Web. 16 Dec. 2014.

McAuliff, Michael, and Sabrina Siddiqui. *Obama State of the Union Address Highlights Battle for the Middle Class*. The Huffington Post, 21 Jan. 2015. Web. 29 May 2015.

McCarthy, Justin. "More Americans Say Crime Is Rising in U.S." *Gallup*. Gallup, 22 October 2015. Web. 8 June 2016.

McCarthy, Justin. "U.S. Support for Gay Marriage Stable After High Court Ruling." *Gallup*. Gallup, 17 July 2015. Web. 9 Mar. 2016.

McGovern, Michele. "The Media's Influence on Public Perception of Homosexuality." *Journal of Research Across the Disciplines Online* (2011): 1–14. Web. 24 Sept. 2015.

McGue, M., W. Slutske, J. Taylor, W.G. Iacono. "Personality and Substance Use Disorders. I. Effects of Gender and Alcoholism Subtype." *Alcohol Clin Exp Res* 21.3 (1997): 513–520. Web. 19 June 2015.

McKnown, C. and R.S. Weinstein. "Teacher expectations, classroom context, and the achievement gap." *Journal of Social Psychology* 46.3 (2008): 235–261. Web. 26 Apr. 2016.

McLennan, Gregor, Allanah Ryan, and Paul Spoonley. *Exploring society: Sociology for New Zealand students*. Auckland: Pearson Education New Zealand Unlimited, 2000. Print.

McMahan, Elysia. "The Horrific Story of 'Genie': The Feral Child Who Suffered at the Hands of Her Sadistic Father." *First to Know*. First to Know, 6 Nov. 2014. Web. 30 June 2015.

McMillan, John. *Reinventing the Bazaar: A Natural History of Markets*. New York: W.W. Norton & Company, Inc., 2003. Print.

Mead, George Herbert. *Mind, Self, and Society*. ed. Charles W. Morris. Chicago: University of Chicago Press, 1934. Print.

Mead, George Herbert. *On Social Psychology*. ed. Anselm Strauss. Chicago: University of Chicago Press, 1964. Print.

Mead, Margaret. *Sex and Temperament in Three Primitive Societies*. New York: William Morrow and Company, 1935. Print.

Meister, Jeanne. "Job Hopping is the 'New Normal' for Millennials: Three Ways to Prevent a Human Resource Nightmare." *Forbes*. Forbes Magazine, 14 Aug. 2012. Web. 31 Mar. 2016.

Medlin, Richard G. "Homeschooling and the question of socialization revisited." *Peabody Journal of Education* 88.3 (2013): 284–297. Web. 3 Aug. 2016.

Mellins, Maria. *Vampire Culture*. New York: Bloomsbury, 2013. Print.

Meredith, Martin. *Born in Africa: The Quest for the Origins of Human Life*. New York: Public Affairs, 2011. Print.

Merton, Robert K. *Social Theory and Social Structure*. 1949. New York: The Free Press, 1968. Print.

Messner, Michael A. "Barbie Girls versus Sea Monsters: Children Constructing Gender." *Gender and Society* 14.6 (2000): 765–784. Web. 13 Apr. 2016.

Meszaros, I. *Marx's Theory of Alienation*. New York: Merlin Press, 1986. Print.

Meyer-Resende, Michael. "International Consensus: Essential Elements of Democracy." *Democracy Reporting International*. Democracy Reporting International, Oct. 2011. Web. 26 Apr. 2016.

Meyer-Rochow, Victor Benno. "Food taboos: their origins and purposes." *Journal of Ethnobiology and Ethnomedicine* 5.18 (2009): 1–10. Web. 26 July 2016.

MightyMeeting Inc. AirPaper. Computer software. *Apple App Store*. Vers. 1.1 MightyMeeting Inc, 12 June 2016. Web. 3 Aug. 2016.

Milanovic, Branko. "Global Income Inequality in Numbers: in History and Now." *Global Policy* 4.2 (2013): 198–208. Web. 30 May 2015.

Milgram, Stanley. "Behavioral Study of Obedience." *Journal of Abnormal and Social Psychology* 67 (1963): 371–378. Web. 20 Sept. 2015.

Milgram, Stanley. *Obedience to Authority*. New York: Harper & Row, 1974. Print.

Milkie, Melissa A., and Catharine H. Warner. "Classroom Learning Environments and the Mental Health of First Grade Children." *Journal of Health and Social Behavior* 52.1 (2011): 4–22. Web. 19 June 2015.

Miller, A.L., R. Seifer, L. Stroud, S.J. Sheinkopf, and S. Dickstein. "Biobehavioral Indices of Emotion Regulation Relate to School Attitudes, Motivation, and Behavior Problems in a Low-Income Preschool Sample." *Ann N Y Acad Sci.* 1094 (2006): 325–9. Web. 9 Mar. 2016.

Miller, Anna. "Stigma Hinders Workplace Flexibility, Reports Special Issue." *American Psychological Association* 44.11. American Psychological Association, Dec. 2013. Web. 30 Aug. 2015.

Miller, Claire Cain. "The Divorce Surge is Over, but the Myth Lives On." *New York Times*. New York Times, 2 Dec. 2014. Web. 25 Sept. 2015.

Miller, David I., and Diane F. Halpern. "The New Science of Cognitive Sex Differences." *Trends in Cognitive Sciences* (2013): 1–9. Web. 9 Mar. 2016.

Miller, David. *Principles of Social Justice*. New York: Harvard University Press, 2001. Print.

Miller, Frederic P., Agnes F. Vandome, and John McBrewster. *Igbo People: Igbo People. Kingdom of Nri, Atlantic Slave Trade, the Igbo in the Atlantic Slave Trade, Colonial Nigeria, Nigerian Civil War, Igbo Culture, Igbo Language, Igbo Music, Igbo Art*. New York: Alphascript Publishing, 2009. Web. 9 Mar. 2016.

Mills, C. Wright. *The Power Elite*. New York: Oxford University Press, 1958. Print.

Mills, C. Wright. *The Sociological Imagination*. New York: Oxford University Press, 1959. Print.

Mises, Ludwig von. *Socialism: An Economic and Sociological Analysis*. New Haven: Yale University Press, 1951. Print.

"Mismatch." *Basic Books*. Basic Books, 2012. Web. 26 Apr. 2016.

"Mobility, Measured." *The Economist*. The Economist Newspaper, 01 Feb. 2014. Web. 29 May 2015.

Moeller, Susan, Eunryung Chong, Sergei Golitsinski, Jing Guo, Raymond McCaffrey, Andrew Nynka, and Jessica Roberts. "A Day Without Media: 24 Hours: Unplugged." *International Center for Media & the Public Agenda*. University of Maryland, 2011. Web. 3 Aug. 2016.

Montopoli, Brian. "BP Spent Millions on Lobbying, Campaign Donations." *CBS News*. CBS News, 5 May 2010. Web. 31 Mar. 2016.

Morin, Rich, and Seth Motel. "A Third of Americans Now Say They Are in the Lower Classes." Pew Research Center, 2012. Web. 29 May 2015.

Morton, Lois Wright, Ella Annette Bitto, Mary Jane Oakland, and Mary Sand. "Solving the Problems of Iowa Food Deserts: Food Insecurity and Civic Structure." *Rural Sociology* 70.1 (2005): 94–112. Web. 30 May 2015.

Mosier, R. *Making the American Mind: Social and Moral Ideas in the McGuffey Readers*. New York: King's Crown Press, 1947. Print.

"Mosuo: A Mysterious Matriarchal Group in China." *ChinaCulture.org*. ChinaCulture.org, 2003. Web. 29 Aug. 2015.

Motel, Seth and Eileen Patten. "Hispanics of Cuban Origin in the United States, 2010." Washington, D.C.: Pew Research Center, 27 June 2012. Web. 28 Sept. 2015.

Moynihan, Daniel Patrick. *The Negro Family: The Case for National Action*. U.S. Dept. of Labor, Office of Planning and Research, [1965]. Web. 30 May 2015.

Mukenge, Tshilemalema. *Culture and Customs of the Congo*. Westport: Greenwood Press, 2002. Print.

Murphy, Caryle. "Interfaith marriage is common in U.S., particularly among the recently wed." Pew Research Center, 2 June 2015. Web. 24 Sept. 2015.

Murray, Ann D., Jeanne Johnson, and Jo Peters. "Fine-tuning of Utterance Length to Preverbal Infants: Effects on Later Language Development." *Journal of Child Language* 17.3 (1990): 511–525. Web. 29 Aug. 2015.

Myers, Norman K. *Physical, Intellectual, Emotional, and Social Maturity Levels of Eighth, Ninth, and Tenth Grade Students with Implications for School Grade Organization*. Columbia: University of Missouri, 1970. Print.

Mykyta, Laryssa and Trudi J. Renwick. "Changes in Poverty Measurement: An Examination of the Research SPM and Its Effects by Gender." *SEHSD Working Paper #2013–05*. Washington, D.C.: U.S. Census Bureau, Jan. 2013. Web. 25 Mar. 2016.

NAACP. "Our Mission." *NAACP*. National Association for the Advancement of Colored People, 2015. Web. 22 July 2015.

Nakashima, Rita, and Gabriella Lettini. *Soul Repair: Recovering from Moral Injury after War*. Boston: Beacon Press, 2012. Print.

Nanda, Serena. *Gender Diversity: Crosscultural Variations*. Long Grove: Waveland Press, 2000. Print.

Nanda, Serena. *Neither Man Nor Woman: The Hijras of India*. New York: The Wadsworth Publishing Company, 1990. Print.

Narayan, Deepa. "Poverty Is Powerlessness and Voicelessness." *Finance & Development*. International Monetary Fund, 2000. Web. 18 Apr. 2016.

Naron, Hang Chuon. *Cambodian Economy: Charting the Course of a Brighter Future—A Survey of Progress, Problems and Prospects*. Cambodia: Institute of Southeast Asian Studies, 2012. Web. 31 Mar. 2016.

Nash, Margaret A. "Contested Identities: Nationalism, Regionalism, and Patriotism in Early American Textbooks." *History of Education Quarterly* 49 (2009): 417–441. Web. 26 Mar. 2016.

Natalier, Kristin. "Avoiding the Housework: Domestic Labour and Gender in Group Living Contexts." *Electronic Journal of Sociology* (2004). Web. 30 Aug. 2015.

National Conference of State Legislatures. "New Laws for a New Year: 2014." *NCSL: National Conference of State Legislatures*. National Conference of State Legislatures, 2013. Web. 5 Aug. 2015.

National Human Genome Research Institute. "Frequently Asked Questions About Genetic and Genomic Science." *National Human Genome Research Institute*. National Human Genome Research Institute, 2 Mar. 2016. Web. 28 July 2016.

National Institute of Mental Health. *Television and Behavior: Ten Years of Scientific Progress and Implications for the Eighties, Vol. 1*. Rockville: U.S. Dept. of Health and Human Services, 1982. Web. 30 June 30, 2015.

"National Organization for Women." *National Organization for Women*. 2015. Web. 31 Aug. 2015. <http://now.org/>.

"National Party (NP)." 2015. *Encyclopedia Britannica*. Web. 26 Sept. 2015. <http://www.britannica.com/topic/National-Party-political-party-South-Africa>.

National Public Radio. "The Culture of Poverty" Narr. Alison Stewart. *Talk of the Nation. NPR*. Natl. Public Radio. 23 March 2009. Web. 30 May 2015.

National Student Clearinghouse. "More than One-Third of College Students Are Over 25." *National Student Clearinghouse*. National Student Clearinghouse, 19 Apr. 2012. Web. 26 Mar. 2016.

Neal, Larry and Jeffrey G. Williamson. Eds. *The Cambridge History of Capitalism: Volume 2: The Spread of Capitalism: From 1848 to the Present*. Cambridge: Cambridge University Press, 2014. Print.

Needleman, Herbert. "Lead Poisoning." *Annual Review of Medicine* 55 (2004): 209–222. Web. 28 May 2015.

Negra, Diane and Yvonne Tasker. Eds. *Gendering the Recession*. New York: Duke University Press, 2014. Print.

Nevin, Rick. "How Lead Exposure Relates to Temporal Changes in IQ, Violent Crime, and Unwed Pregnancy." *Environmental Research Section* 83 (2000): 1–22. Web. 28 May 2015.

Newport, Frank. "More Than 9 in 10 Americans Continue to Believe in God." *Gallup Poll*. Gallup Poll, 3 June 2011. Web. 20 May 2015.

Newport, Frank. "Fewer Americans Identify as Middle Class in Recent Years." *Gallup Poll*. Gallup Poll, 28 Apr. 2015. Web. 9 Mar. 2016.

"Nigeria frees dozens from Boko Haram captivity." *Aljazeera*. Aljazeera, 31 July 2015. Web. 24 Sept. 2015.

"Who We Are." North American Man/Boy Love Association. The North American Man/Boy Love Association, 2011. Web. 28 July 2016. <http://nambla.org/welcome.html>.

Oakes, J. *Keeping Track: How Schools Structure Inequality*. New Haven: Yale University Press, 2005. Print.

Oakes, J. M. "Socioeconomic Status." *SpringerReference* (2011): *Esourceresearch.org*. Springer, 2012. Web. 29 May 2015. <http://www.esourceresearch.org/Portals/0/Uploads/Documents/Public/Oakes_FullChapter.pdf>.

O'Connor, Lydia. "'Ghetto Tracker,' App That Helps Rich Avoid Poor, is as Bad as it Sounds." *The Huffington Post*. Huffington Post.com, Inc., 4 Sept. 2013 Web. 24 Mar. 2016.

Odekon, Mehmet. ed. *The SAGE Encyclopedia of World Poverty*. Los Angeles: SAGE Publications, 2015. Print.

Oduah, Chika. "Women held by Boko Haram in Sambisa Forest describe abuse, crippling fear." *Aljazeera America*. Aljazeera America, 8 June 2015. Web. 24 Sept. 2015.

OECD. *In It Together: Why Less Inequality Benefits All*. Paris: OECD Publishing, 2015. Web. 12 June 2016.

Offer, Shira, and Barbara Schneider. "Revisiting the Gender Gap in Time-Use Patterns: Multitasking and Well-Being among Mothers and Fathers in Dual-Earner Families." *American Sociological Review* 76.6 (2011): 809–833. Web. 30 Aug. 2015.

Office for National Statistics. "Census-taking in the Ancient World." *Office for National Statistics*. 2014. Web. 17 Sept. 2014.

Ogunwole, Stella U., Malcolm P. Drewery Jr., and Merarys Rios-Vargas. *The Population With a Bachelor's Degree or Higher by Race and Hispanic Origin: 2006–2010*. Washington: U.S. Census Bureau, American Community Survey Briefs, May 2012. Web. 26 Mar. 2016.

Ojito, Mirta. *Finding Mañana: A Memoir of a Cuban Exodus*. New York: The Penguin Group, 2005. Print.

Ollman, Bertell. *Alienation: Marx's Conception of Man in Capitalist Society*. Cambridge: Cambridge University Press, 1971. Print.

Omi, Michael and Howard Winant. *Racial Formation in the United States*. 3rd ed. New York: Routledge, 2015. Print.

"Oneida Community: Utopian Religious Community." *Encyclopedia Britannica Online*. Encyclopedia Britannica, 9 Dec. 2014. Web. 29 Aug. 2015. <http://www.britannica.com/topic/Oneida-Community>.

OpenStax College, *Introduction to Sociology*. OpenStax College. 21 June 2012. Web. 10 Dec. 2015.

Or Not Limited. *Hot or Not*. Computer software. *Google Play*. Or Not Limited, 23 Mar. 2016. Web. 26 Mar. 2016.

Orr, Andrea. "Making Ends Meet on $21,834 a Year." *Economic Policy Institute*, Economic Policy Institute, 2009. Web. 30 May 2015.

Orth, Stephan. "Members Only: A Visit to Beijing's Exclusive Penis Restaurant." *Spiegel Online International.* Spiegel Online International, 25 Apr. 2008. Web. 28 July 2016.

Oxford English Dictionary "Symbol." *Oxford Dictionaries*. Oxford University Press, 2015. Web. 7 Dec. 2015.

Palermo, Elizabeth. "The Origins of Religion: How Supernatural Beliefs Evolved." *livescience*. livescience, 5 Oct. 2015. Web. 26 Apr. 2016.

Pager, Devah and Hana Shepherd. "The Sociology of Discrimination: Racial Discrimination in Employment, Housing, Credit, and Consumer Markets." *Annu Rev Sociol.* 34 (2008): 181–209. Web. 26 Sept. 2015.

Pappano, Laura. "First-Generation Students Unite." *New York Times*. New York Times, 8 Apr. 2015. Web. 26 Mar. 2016.

Parra, Fernando. "Good, the Bad, and the Ugly: Veterano (Older) Chicano Gang Members and the (Dys) Functional Aspects of the Role." *Journal of Gang Research* 8.4 (2001): 13–18. Web. 22 Sept. 2015.

Parents Television Council. *Dying to Entertain: Violence on Prime Time Broadcast Television 1998 to 2006*. Los Angeles: Parents Television Council, 2007. Web. 29 June 2015.

Parker, Kim, and Wendy Wang. "Modern Parenthood: Roles of Moms and Dads Converge as They Balance Work and Family." Pew Research Center, 14 Mar. 2013. Web. 30 Aug. 2015.

Parkinson, C. Northcote. *Parkinson's Law*. New York: Houghton Mifflin, 1957. Print.

Parsons, Paul. *How to Destroy the Universe: And 34 Other Really Interesting Uses of Physics*. New York: Random House, 2011. Print.

Parsons, Talcott. "The School Class as a Social System: Some of Its Functions in American Society." *Harvard Educational Review* 29.4 (1959): 297–318. Web. 26 Mar. 2016.

Parsons, Talcott. *The Social System*. New York: The Free Press, 1951. Print.

Parsons, Talcott, and Robert Bales. *Family, Socialization and Interaction Processes*. New York: Free Press, 1955. Print.

Patterson, James T. *America's Struggle Against Poverty in the Twentieth Century*. Cambridge: Harvard University Press, 2000. Print.

Patterson, O. "Taking Culture Seriously: A Framework and Afro-American Illustration." *Culture Matters: How Values Shape Human Progress*. Eds. Harrison, L.E. and S.P. Huntington. New York: Basic Books, 2000. Print.

Patterson, Orlando, and Ethan Fosse. *The Cultural Matrix: Understanding Black Youth*. Cambridge: Harvard University Press, 2015. Print.

Payne, Krista K. "Median Age at First Marriage, 2013." *National Center for Family & Marriage Research*. 2015. Web. 25 Sept. 2015.

Pearce, Diana. "The Feminization of Poverty: Women, Work, and Welfare." *Urban and Social Change Review* 11 (1978): 28–36. Web. 10 Dec. 2015.

Peletz, Michael. *Gender Pluralism: Southeast Asia Since Early Modern Times*. New York: Routledge, 2009. Print.

Perez, Evan. "Justice report finds systematic discrimination against African-Americans in Ferguson." *CNN Politics*. CNN, 4 Mar. 2015. Web. 19 Apr. 2016.

Perrin, Robert G. "Spencer's Four Theories of Social Evolution." *American Journal of Sociology* 81 (1976): 1339–1359. Web. 9 Mar. 2016.

Perry, Mark J. "The 2008 Male Recession? The Gender Jobs Gap." *American Enterprise Institute*. American Enterprise Institute, 5 Dec. 2008. Web. 2 Apr. 2016.

Peter, Laurence J., and Raymond Hull. *The Peter Principle: Why Things Always Go Wrong*. New York: William Morrow and Company. 1969. Print.

Peterman, Amber, Tia Palermo, and Caryn Bredenkamp. "Estimates and Determinants of Sexual Violence Against Women in the Democratic Republic of Congo." *American Journal of Public Health* 101.6 (2011): 1060–1067. Web. 30 Aug. 2015.

Pew Research Center. "A Portrait of Stepfamilies." Washington, DC: Pew Research Center, 13 Jan. 2011. Web. 26 Mar. 2016.

Pew Research Center. "How the Great Recession Has Changed Life in America." Washington, DC: Pew Research Center, 30 June 2010. Web. 31 Mar. 2016.

Pew Research Center. "Is College Worth It?" Washington, DC: Pew Research Center, 15 May 2011. Web. 31 Mar. 2016.

Pew Research Center. "The Future of World Religions: Population Growth Projections, 2010–2050." Washington, DC: Pew Research Center, 2 Apr. 2015. Web. 26 Mar. 2016.

Pew Research Center. "The Global Religious Landscape." Washington, DC: Pew Research Center, 18 Dec. 2012. Web. 26 Mar. 2016.

Pew Research Center. "The Rise of Asian Americans." Washington, DC: Pew Research Center, 4 Apr. 2013. Web. 10 Dec. 2015.

Phillips, Tom. "Man Marries Pillow." *Metro*. Metro, 9 Mar. 2010. Web. 24 Sept. 2015.

Piaget, Jean. *The Construction of Reality in the Child*. Trans. M. Cook. New York: Basic Books, 1954. Print.

Pichanick, Valerie Kossew. *Harriet Martineau, The Woman and Her Work, 1802–75*. Ann Arbor: University of Michigan Press, 1980. Print.

Pickett, Kate, and Richard Wilkinson. *The Spirit Level: Why Greater Equality Makes Societies Stronger*. New York: Bloomsbury Press, 2009. Print.

Piketty, Thomas and Emmanueal Saez. "Top Incomes and the Great Recession: Recent Evolutions and Policy Implications." *Jacques Polak Annual Research Conference*. Washington DC: International Monetary Fund, 2012. Web. 12 June 2016.

Pilone, Paul. *iHomework*. Computer software. *Apple App Store*. Vers. 2.8 Paul Pilone, 19 Dec. 2015. Web. 26 Mar. 2016.

Pincus, Fred L. "Discrimination Comes in Many Forms." *The American Behavioral Scientist* 40.2 (1996): 186–194. Web. 10 Dec. 2015.

Plato. *The Republic*. Trans. Benjamin Jowett. New York: The Modern Library, 1941. Print.

Plumer, Brad. "How the recession turned middle-class jobs into low-wage jobs." *The Washington Post*. The Washington Post, 28 Feb. 2013. Web. 28 July 2016.

Pohl, J. Otto. *Ethnic Cleansing in the USSR, 1937–1949*. Westport: Greenwood Press, 1999. Print.

Polanin, Joshua R., Dorothy L. Espelage, and Therese D. Pigott. "A Meta-Analysis of School-Based Bullying Prevention Programs' Effects on Bystander Intervention Behavior." *School Psychology Review* 41.1 (2012): 47–65. Web. 9 Mar. 2016.

Politico, LLC. *Politico*. Computer software. *Apple App Store*. Vers. 4.0.5 Politico, LLC, 22 Mar. 2016. Web. 31 Mar. 2016.

Pollardy, Richard. "Deepwater Horizon Oil Spill of 2010." *Encyclopedia Britannica*. 20 Apr. 2015. 29 May 2015.

Proscio, Tony. *Food, Markets, and Healthy Communities: How Food Stores Accelerate Local Development and Enrich Residents' Lives*. New York: Local Initiatives Support Corporation, 2006. Print.

Public Engines Inc. *TipSubmit Mobile*. Computer software. *Apple App Store*. Vers. 3.1 Public Engines Inc., 29 Oct. 2014. Web. 18 Apr. 2016.

Puddington, Arch. *Freedom in the World: 2015. Freedom House*. Freedom House, 2015. Web. 31 Mar. 2016.

Puddington, Arch and Tyler Roylance. *Freedom in the World: 2016. Freedom House*. Freedom House, 2016. Web. 31 Mar. 2016.

Pukui, Mary Kawena, and Samule H. Elbert. *Hawaiian Dictionary: Hawaiian-English, English-Hawaiian*. Hawaii: University of Hawaii Press, 1986. Print.

Pullum, Geoffrey K. *The Great Eskimo Vocabulary Hoax and Other Irreverent Essays on the Study of Language*. Chicago: University of Chicago Press, 1991. Print.

Qbiki Networks. *Beverly Hills Manners*. Computer software. *Apple App Store*. Vers. 1.1 Qbiki Networks, 20 Jan. 2011. Web. 3 Aug. 2016.

Qurtaba LLC. *NaanMap for iPhone—The Best Way to Find Halal. ...* Computer software. *Apple App Store*. Vers. 1.1.2 Qurtaba, 3 June 2012. Web. 26 Mar. 2016.

Rajan, Raghuram G. *Fault Lines: How Hidden Fractures Still Threaten the World Economy*. Princeton: Princeton University Press, 2010. Print.

Rama, Anahi, and Lizbeth Diaz. "Violence Against Women 'Pandemic' in Mexico." *Reuters*. Reuters, 7 Mar. 2014. Web. 30 Aug. 2015.

Rank, Mark. R., Hong-Sik Yoon, and Thomas A. Hirschl. "American Poverty as a Structural Failing: Evidence and Arguments." *The Journal of Sociology and Social Welfare* 30.4 (2003): 3–29. Web. 9 Mar. 2016.

Rank, Mark R. "Poverty in America Is Mainstream." *Opinionator: The Opinion Pages*. New York Times, 2 Nov. 2013. Web. 30 May 2015.

Raphael, Steven, and Michael A. Stoll. *Why Are So Many Americans in Prison?* New York: Russell Sage Foundation, 2013. Print.

Ratcliffe, S. "The Psychological and Psychiatric Consequences of Sex Chromosome Abnormalities in Children, Based on Population Studies." *Basic Approaches to Genetic and Molecularbiological Developmental Psychiatry*. Ed. Poustka, F. Berlin: Quintessenz, 1994. Print.

Ravallion, Martin, Shaohua Chen, and Prem Sangraula. "Dollar a Day Revisited." *Policy Research Working Paper 4620*. Washington: World Bank, 2008. Web. 10 Dec. 2015.

Ray, Brian D. "Academic Achievement and Demographic Traits of Homeschool Students: A Nationwide Study, 2010." *Academic Leadership: The Online Journal* 8 2010. Web. 6 June 2016.

Ray, Brian D. "Homeschooling Associated with Beneficial Learner and Societal Outcomes but Educators do not Promote It." *Peabody Journal of Education* 88(3) 2013: 324–341. Web. 6 June 2016.

Ray, Brian D. "Homeschooling: More Ethnic Minorities, Lower-Income Families, and Parents Moderately High Education." *National Home Education Research Institute*. National Home Education Research Institute, 16 June 2009. Web. 8 June 2016.

Reardon, Sean F. and John T. Yun. "Private School Racial Enrollments and Segregation." *The Civil Rights Project*. Harvard University, 26 June 2002. Web. 26 Mar. 2016.

Reason, Peter, and Hilary Bradbury, eds. *The SAGE Handbook of Action Research: Participative Inquiry and Practice*. 2nd ed. SAGE Publications, 2008. Print.

Reay, D. "Dim dross?: Marginalized voices both inside and outside the academy." *Women's Studies International Forum* 23.1 (2000): 13–21. Web. 26 Mar. 2016.

Reay, D. "Spice girls, 'nice girls', 'girlies' and tomboys: Gender discourses, girls' cultures and femininities in the primary classroom." *Gender and Education* 13.2 (2001): 153–166. Web. 26 Mar. 2016.

Reid, Robert. "Fine tune your table manners." *Lonely Planet*. Lonely Planet, May 2012. Web. 26 July 2016.

Reiter, L. "Sexual Orientation, Sexual Identity, and the Question of Choice." *Clinical Social Work Journal* 17 (1989): 138–150. Web. 10 Dec. 2015.

"Eichmann's Final Plea." Remember.org. *Remember.org*, 2015. Web. 3 Aug. 2016.

Reshoring Initiative: Bringing Manufacturing Back Home. Reshoring Initiative, 2016. Web. 31 Mar. 2016.

Reyes, Jessica Wolpaw. "Environmental Policy as Social Policy? The Impact of Childhood Lead Exposure on Crime." *The B.E. Journal of Economic Analysis and Policy* 7.1 (2007): 1–41. Web. 28 May 2015.

Ritzer, George. *The McDonaldization of Society*. Thousand Oaks: Pine Forge Press, 1993. Print.

Ritzer, George. *The McDonaldization of Society*. 8th ed. Thousand Oaks: SAGE Publications, 2015. Print.

Roberts, Andrea L., Margaret Rosario, Heather L. Corliss, Karestan C. Koenen, and S. Bryn Austin. "Childhood Gender Nonconformity: A Risk Indicator for Childhood Abuse and Posttraumatic Stress in Youth." *Pediatrics* 129.3 (2012): 410–417. Web. 10 Dec. 2015.

Roberts, Andrea L., Margaret Rosario, Natalie Slopen, Jerel P. Calzo, and S. Bryn Austin. "Childhood Gender Nonconformity, Bullying Victimization, and Depressive Symptoms Across Adolescence and Early Adulthood: An 11-Year Longitudinal Study." *J Am Acad Child Adolesc Psychiatry* 52.2 (2013): 143–152. Web. 10 Dec. 2015.

Roberts, Michael. *The Great Recession: Profit Cycles, Economic Crisis: A Marxist View*. Michael Roberts, 2009. Web. 31 Mar. 2016.

Robertson, Carol E. "Art Essay: The Māhū of Hawai'i." *Feminist Studies* 15.2 (1989): 312–326. Web. 29 Aug. 2015.

Robinson, Kathryn. "Indonesian Women: From Order Baru to Reformasi." *Women in Asia. Tradition, Modernity and Globalisation*. Eds. Louise Edwards and Mina Roces. St. Leonards: Allen & Unwin, 2000. Print.

Roche, Cullen. *Pragmatic Capitalism: What Every Investor Needs to Know About Money and Finance*. New York: St. Martin's Press, 2014. Print.

Rockoff, Jonah E., and Benjamin B. Lockwood. "Stuck in the Middle: Impacts of Grade Configuration in Public Schools." *Journal of Public Economics* 91 (2010): 1051–1061. Web. 26 Mar. 2016.

Roscoe, Will. *The Zuni Man-Woman*. Albuquerque: University of New Mexico Press, 1991. Print.

Roselle, Mike, and Josh Mahan. *Tree Spiker: From Earth First! To Lowbagging: My Struggles in Radical Environmental Action*. New York: St. Martin's Press, 2009. Print.

Rosenbaum, Ron. "At Skull and Bones, Bush's Secret Club Initiates Ream Gore." *The New York Observer (New York, NY)*. N.p., 23 Apr. 2001. Web. 20 May 2015.

Rosenbaum, Ron. "The Great Ivy League Nude Posture Photo Scandal." *New York Times*. New York Times, 15 Jan. 1995. Web. 1 Oct. 2014.

Rosenfeld, Michael and Reuben J. Thomas. "Searching for a Mate: The Rise of the Internet as a Social Intermediary." *American Sociological Review* 77.4 (2012): 523–547. Web. 24 Sept. 2015.

Ross, Sean. "What is the history of the market economy?" *Investopedia*. Investopedia, 2015. Web. 26 Apr. 2016.

Rosser Jr., J. Barkeley and Marina V. Rosser. *Comparative Economics in a Transforming World Economy*. Boston: Massachusetts Institute of Technology, 2004. Print.

Ross, Terris, Grace Kena, Amy Rathbun, Angelina KewalRamani, Jijun Zhang, Paul Kristapovich, and Eileen Manning. *Higher Education: Gaps in Access and Persistence Study*. U.S. Dept. of Education, National Center for Education Statistics, Aug. 2012. Web. 26 Mar. 2016.

Rothwell, Jonathan. "Black Students at Top Colleges: Exceptions, Not the Rule." *The Brookings Institution*. Washington, D.C., 3 Feb. 2015. Web. 26 Mar. 2016.

Roughgarden, Joan. *Evolution's Rainbow: Diversity, Gender, and Sexuality in Nature and People*. Berkeley: University of California Press, 2004. Print.

Roulstone, Sue, Sue Loader, Kate Northstone, & Mike Beveridge. "The Speech and Language of Children Aged 25 Months: Descriptive Data from the Avon Longitudinal Study of Parents and Children." *Early Child Development and Care* 172.3 (2002): 259–268. Web. 29 Aug. 2015.

Rubenstein, William R. ed. *Lesbians, Gay Men, and the Law*. New York: New Press, 1993. Print.

Ruether, Rosemary Radford. *Integrating Ecofeminism Globalization and World Religions*. New York: Rowman & Littlefield Publishers, 2005. Print.

Rupasingha, Anil, and Stephan J. Goetz. "Social and Political Forces as Determinants of Poverty: A Spatial Analysis." *The Journal of Socio-Economics* 36 (2007): 650–671. Web. 19 Apr. 2016.

Rupasingha, Anil, and Stephan J. Goetz. "The Causes of Enduring Poverty: An Extended Spatial Analysis of the Structural Determinants of Poverty in the US." *The Northeast Regional Center for Rural Development*. Pennsylvania State University, Dec. 2003. Web. 19 Apr. 2016.

S., Natasha. "McDonald's." Rev. of McDonalds. *Yelp* 13 Nov. 2014: 6. Web. 14 May 2015. <http://www.yelp.com/user_details_reviews_self?userid=7KVpIdVSWCzI5F7TGxQawA&rec_pagestart=50>.

Saad, Lydia. "U.S. Smoking Rate Still Coming Down." *Gallup*. Gallup, 24 July 2008. Web. 28 May 2015.

Saenz, Victor B., Sylvia Hurtado, Doug Berrera, De'Sha Wolf, and Fanny Yeung. "First in my Family: A Profile of First-Generation College Students at Four-Year Institutions Since 1971." *Higher Education Research Institute*. University of California, Los Angeles, 2007. Web. 26 Mar. 2016.

Saez, Emmanuel and Gabriel Zucman. "Wealth Inequality in the United States Since 1913: Evidence fro Capitalized Income Tax Data." *The Quarterly Journal of Economics* 131.2 (2016): 519–578. Web. 12 June 2016.

Saez, Emmanuel. *Striking it Richer: The Evolution of Top Incomes in the United States (Updated with 2012 preliminary estimates).* University of California Berkeley, 3 Sept. 2013. Web. 29 May 2015.

Sakala, Leah. "Breaking Down Mass Incarceration in the 2010 Census: State-by-State Incarceration Rates by Race/Ethnicity." *Prison Policy Initiative.* Prison Policy Initiative, 28 May 2014. Web. 23 Sept. 2015.

Salleh, Ariel. ed. *Eco-Sufficiency & Global Justice: Women Write Political Ecology.* London: Pluto Press and Spinifex, 2009. Print.

Salzano, Francisco M. "Studies on the Caingang Indians: I. Demography." *Human Biology* 33.2 (1961): 110–130. Web. 29 Aug. 2015.

Sander, Richard H. and Stuart Taylor Jr. *Mismatch: How Affirmative Action Hurts Students It's Intended to Help, and Why Universities Won't Admit It.* New York: Basic Books, 2012. Print.

Sandoval, Chela. *Methodology of the Oppressed.* Minneapolis: University of Minnesota Press, 2000. Print.

SceneDoc Inc. SceneDoc—*Collect. Connect. Retrieve.* Computer software. *Apple App Store.* Vers. 4.0 SceneDoc Inc, 13 June 2016. Web. 3 Aug. 2016.

Schatzisoft. *Proud Democrat.* Computer Software. *MyAppFresh.* Vers. 2.1 Schatzisoft, 4 Feb. 2011. Web. 31 Mar. 2016.

Schatzisoft. *Proud Republican.* Computer software. *Apple App Store.* Vers. 3.3 Schatzisoft, 4 Feb. 2013. Web. 31 Mar. 2016.

Schildkraut, D.J. *Press "ONE" for English: Language Policy, Public Opinion, and American Identity.* Princeton: Princeton University Press, 2005. Print.

Schmidt, Susan. *Favorite Wife: Escape from Polygamy.* New York: First Lyons Press, 2009. Print.

Schmitt, Carl. *Dictatorship.* Malden: Polity Press, 2014. Print.

Schwalbe, Michael, Sandra Godwin, Daphne Holden, Douglas Schrock, Shealy Thompson, and Michelle Wolkomir. "Generic Processes in the Reproduction of Inequality: An Interactionist Analysis." *Social Forces* 79.2 (2000): 419–452. Web. 24 Sept. 2015.

Sears, Robert R., Deborah Lapidus, and Christine Cozzens. "Content Analysis of Mark Twain's Novels and Letters as a Biographical Method." *Poetics* 7.2 (1978): 155–175. Web. 29 June 2015.

Seller, Gregory E. *Vanquish of the Dragon Shroud: Murder, Intrigue, and the Hidden Wealth of the Red Nobility.* New York: AuthorHouse, 2015. Print.

Semmelhack, Elizabeth. *Heights of Fashion: A History of the Elevated Shoe.* New York: Periscope, 2008. Print.

Sentier Research. "Household Income Down by 3.1 Percent Overall Post Recession, but Many Groups Have Started to Recover Following 2011 Low-Point." Press Release, 2014. Web. 28 Sept. 2015.

Serano, Julia. *Excluded: Making Feminist and Queer Movements More Inclusive.* Berkeley: Seal Press, 2013. Print.

Serkin, Gavin. *Frontier: Exploring the Top Ten Emerging Markets of Tomorrow.* West Sussex: John Wiley & Sons Ltd, 2015. Print.

Shah, Anup. "Poverty Facts and Stats." *Global Issues.* 7 Jan. 2013. Web. 20 Dec. 2014.

Shannon-Missal, Larry. "Americans' Belief in God, Miracles and Heaven Declines." *Harris Interactive: Harris Polls.* Harris Poll, 16 Dec. 2013. Web. 20 May 2015.

Shapiro, Charlotte. "Women Bleed. Period: An Exploration of Feminine Hygiene Companies' Print and Commercial Advertisements." *Senior Independent Study Theses.* Paper 651, 2013. Web. 9 Mar. 2016.

Sharp, Gene. *From Dictatorship to Democracy.* London: Serpent's Tail, 2012. Print.

Shaw, C.R., and H.D. McKay. *Juvenile Delinquency and Urban Areas*. Chicago: University of Chicago Press, 1942. Print.

Sheldon, William Herbert. *Atlas of Men; A Guide for Somatotyping the Adult Male at All Ages*. New York: Harper, 1954. Print.

Shelton, B.A. and B. Agger. "Shotgun Wedding, Unhappy Marriage, No-Fault Divorce? Rethinking the feminism-Marxism Relationship." *Theory on Gender: Feminism in Theory*. Ed. P. England. New York: Aldine de Gruyter, 1993. 25–42. Print.

"Shifting the Paradigm of Intersex Treatment." *Intersex Society of North America*. Intersex Society of North America, 2008. Web. 29 Aug. 2015. <http://www.isna.org/compare>.

Shover, N., and Andy Hochstetler. "Cultural Explanation and Organizational Crime." *Crime, Law, and Social Change* 37 (2002): 1–18. Web. 29 May 2015.

Significance Labs. *Neat Streak*. Computer software. Significance Labs, 26 Sept. 2014. Web. 3 Aug. 2016.

Siegler, Robert S. "The Rebirth of Children's Learning." *Child Development* 71.1 (2000): 26–35. Web. 3 Aug. 2016.

Simmel, Georg. *Conflict and the Web of Group Affiliations*. New York: Free Press, 1955. Print.

Simmons, J.L. *Deviants*. Santa Barbara: University of California Press, 1969. Print.

Simoons, Frederick J. *Food in China: A Cultural and Historical Inquiry*. Ann Arbor: 1990. Print.

Singh, Gopal K., and Mohammad Siahpush. "Widening Rural-Urban Disparities in Life Expectancy, U.S., 1969–2009." *Am J Prev Med* 46.2 (2014): 19–29. Web. 04 Nov. 2014.

Singh-Manoux, Archana, Jane E. Ferrie, Tarani Chandola, and Michael Marmot. "Socioeconomic Trajectories Across the Life Course and Health Outcomes in Midlife: Evidence for the Accumulation Hypothesis?" *International Journal of Epidemiology* 33 (2004): 1072–1079. Web. 29 May 2015.

Skelton, Christine, Becky Francis, and Yordanka Valkanova. "Breaking down the stereotypes: gender and achievement in schools." *Roehampton University*. Roehampton University, 2007. Web. 26 Apr. 2016.

Skelton, Christine. "Boys and Girls in the Elementary School." *The SAGE Handbook of Gender and Education*. Eds. Christine Skelton, Becky Francis, and Lisa Smulyan. London: SAGE Publications, 2006. Web. 26 Apr. 2016.

Skinner, B.F. *Science and Human Behavior*. New York: The Free Press, 1953. Print.

Smelser, Neil J. and Richard Swedberg. Eds. *The Handbook of Economic Sociology*. 2nd ed. Princeton: Princeton University Press, 2005. Print.

Smith, Aaron. "Smartphone Ownership 2013." Pew Research Center, 2013. Web. 30 June 2015.

Smith, G.D., C. Hart, D. Blane, and V. Hawthorne. "Lifetime Socioeconomic Position and Mortality: Prospective Observational Study." *BMJ* 314.7086 (1997): 547. Web. 29 May 2015.

Smith, Hazel. *North Korea: Markets and Military Rule*. Cambridge: Cambridge University Press, 2015. Print.

Snow, Kate and Jonann Brady. "Woman Proves Love for Eiffel Tower with Commitment Ceremony." *ABC News*. ABC News, 8 Apr. 2009. Web. 24 Sept. 2015.

Snyder, Thomas D., Sally A. Dillow, Charlene M. Hoffman. *Digest of Education Statistics 2007*. U.S. Dept. of Education, National Center for Education Statistics. Mar. 2008. Web. 26 Sept. 2015.

Snyder, Thomas D., Sally A. Dillow, Charlene M. Hoffman. *Digest of Education Statistics 2008*. U.S. Dept. of Education, National Center for Education Statistics. Mar. 2009. Web. 19 Apr. 2016.

Solaz Dazen srl. *Good Manners: Improve your etiquette*. Computer software. Apple App Store. Vers. 2.0 Solaz Dazen srl, 22 Jan. 2016. Web. 3 Aug. 2016.

Sorokin, Pitrim. *Social and Cultural Dynamics*. U.S.: Sargent (Porter), 1957. Print.

Spencer, Herbert. *Social Statics: or, The Conditions Essential to Happiness Specified, and the First of them Developed*. London: John Chapman, 1851. Print.

Spencer, Herbert. *The Principles of Sociology*. New York: D. Appleton and Company, 1898. Print.

Spencer, Herbert. *The Study of Sociology*. London: Henry S. King & Co., 1873. Print.

Spillane, James P., Tim Hallett, and John B. Diamond. "Forms of Capital and the Construction of Leadership: Instructional Leadership in Urban Elementary Schools." *Sociology of Education* (2003): 1–17. Web. 29 May 2015.

Staff Writers. "The 10 Most Legendary Prep Schools in America." *Best Colleges Online*. Best Colleges Online, 22 May 2012. Web. 26 Mar. 2016.

Standard & Poor's Rating Services. "Ratings Actions." *Standard & Poor's Rating Services*. McGraw Hill Financial, 2016. Web. 31 Mar. 2016.

Stancati, Margherita. "When Obama Quotes Gandhi." *The Wall Street Journal*. The Wall Street Journal, 2 Oct. 2012. Web. 2 Apr. 2016.

Staples, Brent. "The Human Cost of 'Zero Tolerance'" *New York Times*. New York Times, 28 Apr. 2012. Web. 23 Sept. 2015.

Starkweather, Katherine E. and Raymond Hames. "A Survey of Non-Classical Polyandry." *Human Nature* 23.2 (2012): 149–172. Web. 24 Sept. 2015.

"State Of The Union Text: Read Obama's Address [FULL TEXT]." *The Huffington Post*. The Huffington Post, 12 Feb. 2013. Web. 29 May 2015.

Stein, Sam. "BP's Influence Peddling in Congress Bears Fruit Two Years After Gulf Spill." *The Huffington Post*. The Huffington Post, 12 Mar. 2012. Web. 28 July 2016.

Stelter, Brian. "8 Hours a Day Spent on Screens, Study Finds." *New York Times*. New York Times, 26 Mar. 2009. Web. 20 Sept. 2015.

Stern, Pamela R. *Daily Life of the Inuit*. New York: Greenwood Press, 2010. Print.

Stevenson, Betsey and Justin Wolfers. "Marriage and Divorce: Changes and their Driving Forces." *National Bureau of Economic Research: Working Paper No. 12944*. 2007. Web. 25 Sept. 2015.

Stewart, Susan D. *Brave New Stepfamilies: Diverse Paths Toward Stepfamily Living*. New York: SAGE Publications, 2007. Print.

Stiglitz, Joseph. *Globalization and Its Discontents*. New York: W.W. Norton & Company Inc., 2002. Print.

Stiglitz, Joseph. *Making Globalization Work*. New York: W.W. Norton & Company Inc., 2006. Print.

Stitch Holdings Pty Ltd. *Stitch Companionship*. Computer software. *Apple App Store*. Vers. 0.1.6 Stitch Holdings Pty Ltd, 23 Mar. 2016. Web. 26 Mar. 2016.

Stoller, Paul. "Alice Goffman and the Future of Ethnography." *The Huffington Post*. 15 June 2015. Web. 30 June 2015.

Strauss, Murray A. "Criminogenic Effect of Corporal Punishment by Parents." *Transnational Criminology Manual: Vol. I*. Eds. M. Herzog-Evans, and Isabelle Dréan-Rivette. Amsterdam: Wolf Legal Publishing, 2010. 373–390. Web. Aug. 5 2015.

Stringer, Ernest T. *Action Research*. 2nd ed. New York: Sage Publications, 1999. Print.

Sullivan, Kevin. "Saudi Arabia's riches conceal a growing problem of poverty." *The Guardian*. The Guardian, 1 Jan. 2013. Web. 31 Mar. 2016.

Super Boise. *Political Fury: Primary 2012 Edition*. Computer software. *Apple App Store*. Vers. 2.1 Super Boise, 5 July 2011. Web. 31 Mar. 2016.

Supple, Andrew J. and Scott W. Plunkett. "Dimensionality and Validity of the Rosenberg Self-Esteem Scale for use with Latino adolescents." *Hispanic Journal of Behavioral Sciences* 33.1 (2010): 39–53. Web. 29 June 2015.

Sutherland, Edwin H. *Principles of Criminology*. 4th ed. Philadelphia: J.B. Lippincott, 1947. Print.

Sutherland, Edwin H. *White Collar Crime*. New York: Dryden Press, 1949. Print.

Sutherland, Edwin H. "White-Collar Criminality." *American Sociological Review* 5.1 (1940): 1–12. Web. 29 May 2015.

Tabatadze, Nino, Guangzhe Huang, Renee M. May, Anant Jain, and Catherine S. Woolley. "Sex Differences in Molecular Signaling at Inhibitory Synapses in the Hippocampus." *The Journal of Neuroscience* 35.32 (2015): 11252–11265. Web. 9 Mar. 2016.

Talbot, Mary M., Kate Charlesworth, and Bryan Talbot. *Sally Heathcote: Suffragette*. New York: Jonathan Cape, 2014. Web. 25 Mar. 2016.

Tannen, Deborah. *You Just Don't Understand: Women and Men in Conversation*. New York: HarperCollins, 1990. Print.

"Target: 40 Million Credit Cards Compromised." *CNN Money*. Cable News Network, 19 Dec. 2013. Web. 30 May 2015. <http://money.cnn.com/2013/12/18/news/companies/target-credit-card/>.

Taylor, Paul, Jeffrey Passel, Richard Fry, Richard Morin, Wendy Wang, Gabriel Velasco, and Daniel Dockterman. "The Return of the Multi-Generational Family Household." Pew Research Center, 18 Mar. 2010. Web. 24 Sept. 2015.

Taylor, Paul, Rich Morin, D'Vera Cohn, Richard Fry, Rakesh Kochar, and April Clar. "Inside the Middle Class: Bad Times Hit the Good Life." Pew Research Center, 2008. Web. 29 May 2015.

Taylor, Timothy. "ATMs and a Rising Number of Bank Tellers?" *Conversable Economist*. N.p., 3 Mar. 2015. Web. 20 May 2015.

"Tennessee Promise." *Tennessee Student Assistance Corporation*. Tennessee Government. 2016. Web. 31 Mar. 2016.

Terman, Rochelle L. "To Specify or Single Out: Should We Use the Term "Honor Killing"?" *Muslim World Journal of Human Rights* 7.1 (2010): 1–39. Web. 6 June 2016.

The Asia Foundation. *Krousar Koumrou*. Computer software. *Google Play*. Vers. 1.0 The Asia Foundation, 16 July 2015. Web. 24 Mar. 2016.

The Asia Foundation. *Safe Agent 008*. Computer software. *Google Play*. Vers. 1.0.0.2 The Asia Foundation, 3 June 2015. Web. 24 Mar. 2016.

The Birth of a Nation. Dir. D.W. Griffith. David W. Griffith Corp., 1915. DVD.

The Council of Economic Advisers. *Nine Facts About American Families and Work*. Executive Office of the President of the United States, June 2014. Web. 25 Sept. 2015.

The Council of Economic Advisers. *Work-Life Balance and the Economics of Workplace Flexibility*. Executive Office of the President of the United States, June 2014. Web. 25 Sept. 2015.

"The Culture of Poverty" Narr. Alison Stewart. *Talk of the Nation. NPR*. Natl. Public Radio. 23 Mar. 2009. Web. 30 May 2015.

The Gilder Lehrman Institute of American History. "The Origins of Slavery." The Gilder Lehrman Institute of American History, 2016. Web. 19 Apr. 2016.

"The Manifesto and the End of Plural Marriage." *The Church of Jesus Christ of Latter-Day Saints*. The Church of Jesus Christ of Latter-Day Saints, 2015. Web. 26 Mar. 2016.

The Sentencing Project. "Report of The Sentencing Project to the United Nations Human Rights Committee: Regarding Racial Disparities in the United States Criminal Justice System." *The Sentencing Project*. United Nations, Aug. 2013. Web. 3 Aug. 2016.

"The Simple Truth: About the Gender Pay Gap." *American Association of University Women*. American Association of University Women, 2014. Web. 29 Aug. 2015.

"The Status of Women in the States: 2015: Employment and Earnings." *Institute for Women's Policy Research*. Institute for Women's Policy Research, Mar. 2015. Web. 30 Aug. 2015. <http://www.iwpr.org/publications/pubs/the-status-of-women-in-the-states-2015–2014-employment-and-earnings>.

"The Story So Far: Offshoring has brought huge economic benefits, but at a heavy political price." *The Economist*. The Economist Newspaper, 19 Jan. 2013. Web. 31 Mar. 2016.

"The Truth About Abu Ghraib." *The Washington Post*. N.p., 29 July 2005. Web. 20 May 2015.

"The Urgency of Now: The Schott 50 State Report on Public Education and Black Males." *Schott Foundation for Public Education*. Schott Foundation for Public Education, 2012. Web. 10 Dec. 2015. <http://blackboysreport.org/bbreport2012.pdf>.

The Week Staff. "The Wedding Industrial Complex." *The Week*. The Week, 15 June 2013. Web. 25 Mar. 2016.

Thies, Kathleen M., and John F. Travers. *Handbook of Human Development for Health Care Professionals*. Sudbury: Jones and Bartlett Publishers, 2006. Print.

Thompson, Derek. "It's Not Just a Recession. It's a Mancession!." *The Atlantic*. The Atlantic, 9 July 2009. Web. 31 Mar. 2016.

Thompson, G. Deon. *Standing Under the Wrong Rainbow*. Bloomington: Abbot Press, 2014. Print.

Thorne, Barrie. *Gender Play: Girls and Boys in School*. New York: Rutgers University Press, 1993. Print.

Times Publishing Company. *Politifact Mobile*. Computer software. *Google Play*. Vers. 1.3.0 Times Publishing Company, 14 Sept. 2011. Web. 31 Mar. 2016.

Tinakon, Wongpakaran and Wongpakaran Nahathai. "A Comparison of Reliability and Construct Validity between the Original and Revised Versions of the Rosenberg Self-Esteem Scale." *Psychiatry Investig*. 9.1 (2012): 54–58. Web. 29 June 2015.

"Titanic Disaster Hearings: The Official Transcripts of the 1912 Senate Investigation." *U.S. Senate: Reference Home*. United States Senate, 2011. Web. 29 May 2015. <http://www.senate.gov/reference/reference_item/titanic.htm>.

"Titanic Survivors." *Encyclopedia Titanica*. N.p., 30 Sept. 2011. Web. 02 June 2015. <http://www.encyclopedia-titanica.org/titanic-survivors-video.html>.

Tocqueville, Alexis de. *Democracy in America*. Trans. Gerald E. Bevan. New York: Penguin Books, 2003. Print.

Toland, John. *Adolf Hitler: The Definitive Biography*. New York: Random House, 1991. Print.

Townsend, Jacinda. "Meet the woman freeing Mauritania's slaves." *Aljazeera*. Aljazeera, 9 Dec. 2015. Web. 18 Apr. 2016.

Travers, Jeffrey and Stanley Milgram. "An Experimental Study of the Small World Problem." *Sociometry* 32.4 (1969): 425–443. Web. 13 May 2015.

Treuhaft, Sarah, and Allison Karpyn. "The Grocery Gap: Who Has Access to Healthy Food and Why It Matters." The Food Trust. PolicyLink, 2012. Web. 30 May 2015.

Triest, R.K. "Regional Differences in Family Poverty." *New England Economic Review* (1997): 3–17. Web. 10 Mar. 2016.

Tripp, Simon and Martin Grueber. *Economic Impact of the Human Genome Project: How a $3.8 billion investment drove $796 billion in economic impact, created 310,000 jobs and launched the genomic revolution*. Batelle Memorial Institute, May 2011. Web. 2 Apr. 2016.

Truman, Jennifer, Lynn Langton, and Michael Planty. *Criminal Victimization, 2012*. U.S. Dept. of Justice, Bureau of Justice Statistics [2013]. Web. 9 Mar. 2016.

Tucker, Jim B. *Return to Life: Extraordinary Cases of Children Who Remember Past Lives*. New York: St. Martin's Press, 2013. Print.

Tyack, David, and Larry Cuban. *Tinkering Toward Utopia*. New York: Harvard University Press, 1995. Print.

UC Office of the President. "More California freshman admitted to UC for fall 2014." *University of California*. University of California, Press Room, 18 Apr. 2014. Web. 26 Mar. 2016.

UNICEF. "Factsheet: Child Soldiers." *Springer Reference* (2011): *UNICEF*. 2011. Web. 29 May 2015. <http://www.unicef.org/emerg/files/childsoldiers.pdf>.

United Nations. *Human Development Report 2013*. United Nations, 2013. Web. 10 Dec. 2015.

United Nations. Population Fund. *Motherhood in Childhood: Facing the challenge of adolescent pregnancy*. United Nations, 2013. Web. 24 Sept. 2015.

United Nations. *Report to the World Summit for Social Development*. United Nations, 19 Apr. 1995. Web. 10 Dec. 2015.

United States Census Bureau. *Decennial Censuses, 1890 to 1940, and Current Population Survey, Annual Social and Economic Supplements, 1947 to 2014*. Washington: U.S. Census Bureau, 2014. Web. 24 Sept. 2015.

United States Census Bureau. *Los Angeles County, California*. U.S. Census Bureau, State & County QuickFacts, 2015. Web. 28 Sept. 2015. <http://quickfacts.census.gov/qfd/states/06/06037.html>.

United States Census Bureau, Population Division. *Annual Estimates of the Resident Population by Sex, Race Alone or in Combination, and Hispanic Origin for the United States, States, and Counties*. Washington: U.S. Census Bureau, 2014. Web. 24 Mar. 2016.

United States Census Bureau. *USA*. U.S. Census Bureau, State & County QuickFacts, 2015. Web. 28 Sept. 2015. <http://quickfacts.census.gov/qfd/states/00000.html>.

United States Census Bureau. *U.S. Census Bureau Projections Show a Slower Growing, Older, More Diverse Nation a Half Century from Now*. U.S. Census Bureau, Newsroom Archive, 12 Dec., 2012. Web. 28 Sept. 2015.

United States. Cong. Senate. Committee on Finance. *Testimony of Dr. Susan Dynarski. July 25, 2012*. 112th Cong. Washington: GPO, 2012. Web. 26 Mar. 2016.

United States. Cong. Senate. Committee on Finance. *Statement of Justin Wolfers: Hearings on "Job Creation and a Healthy Economy", Jan. 22, 2012*. 114th Cong. Washington: GPO, 2015. Web. 19 Apr. 2016.

United States. Dept. of Agriculture, Economic Research Service. "Geography of Poverty." United States Dept. of Agriculture, Economic Research Service, 17 Dec. 2015. Web. 21 Apr. 2016.

United States. Dept. of Education, Institute of Education Sciences. *Digest of Education Statistics, 2013*. Washington: National Center for Education Statistics, 2013. Web. 22 July 2015.

United States. Dept. of Education, Institute of Education Sciences. *Fast Facts: Homeschooling*. Washington: National Center for Education Statistics, 2015. Web. 26 Mar. 2016.

United States. Dept. of Education, Institute of Education Sciences. *Employment Rates and Unemployment Rates by Educational Attainment*. Washington: National Center for Education Statistics, May 2015. Web. 26 Mar. 2016.

United States. Dept. of Education, Institute of Education Sciences, National Center for Education Statistics. *Public High School Graduation Rates*. Washington: National Center for Education Statistics, May 2016. Web. 3 Aug. 2016.

United States. Dept. of Education, Institute of Education Sciences. *The Condition of Education 2012*. Washington: National Center for Education Statistics, May 2012. Web. 26 Mar. 2016.

United States. Dept. of Education, Institute of Education Sciences. *The Condition of Education 2014*. Washington: National Center for Education Statistics, May 2014. Web. 26 Mar. 2016.

United States. Dept. of Education, Institute of Education Sciences. *The Condition of Education 2015*. Washington: National Center for Education Statistics, May 2015. Web. 26 Mar. 2016.

United States. Dept. of Education, Institute of Education Sciences. *The Condition of Education 2016*. Washington: National Center for Education Statistics, May 2016. Web. 6 June 2016.

United States. Dept. of Health and Human Services. Centers for Disease Control and Prevention. *Current Cigarette Smoking Among Adults in the United States*. Washington: Centers for Disease Control and Prevention, 23 Jan. 2015. Web. 28 May 2015.

United States. Dept. of Health and Human Services. Centers for Disease Control and Prevention. *National Intimate Partner and Sexual Violence Survey*. Washington: Centers for Disease Control and Prevention: Division of Violence Prevention, Nov. 2011. Web. 22 July 2015.

United States. Dept. of Health and Human Services. Centers for Disease Control and Prevention. *Syringe Exchange Programs—United States, 2008*. Washington: Centers for Disease Control and Prevention: MMWR: Morbidity and Mortality Weekly Report, 19 Nov. 2008. Web. 19 June 2015.

United States. Dept. of Health and Human Services. *Information on Poverty and Income Statistics: A Summary of 2014 Current Population Survey Data*. Health and Human Services, 16 Sept. 2014. Web. 24 Sept. 2015.

United States. Dept. of Health and Human Services. Centers for Disease Control and Prevention. *National Marriage and Divorce Rate Trends*. Washington: Centers for Disease Control and Prevention: National Vital Statistics System, 2015. Web. 25 Sept. 2015.

United States. Dept. of Health and Human Services. *Research Shows Needle Exchange Programs Reduce HIV Infections Without Increasing Drug Use*. Washington: HHS Archive, 20 Apr. 1998. Web. 19 June 2015.

United States Dept. of Justice. Bureau of Justice Assistance. *Byrne Justice Assistance Grant (JAG) Program FY 2014 Local Solicitation*. Washington: Office of Justice Programs, n.d. Web. 28 May 2015.

United States Dept. of Justice. Bureau of Justice Statistics. *Hate Crime*. Washington: Office of Justice Programs, 2015. Web. 29 May 2015.

United States Dept. of Justice. Bureau of Justice Statistics. *National Crime Victimization Survey*. Washington: Office of Justice Programs, 2015. Web. 21 May 2015.

United States. Dept. of Justice. Bureau of Justice Statistics. *U.S. Residents Experienced about 293,800 Hate Crime Victimizations in 2012—Unchanged from 2004.* Washington: Office of Justice Programs, 20 Feb. 2014. Web. 29 May 2015. <http://www.bjs.gov/content/pub/press/hcv0412stpr.cfm>.

United States Dept. of Justice. Civil Rights Division. *Investigation of the Ferguson Police Department.* Washington: Civil Rights Division, 2015. Web. 26 Sept. 2015.

United States. Dept. of Justice. Federal Bureau of Investigation. *Attorney General Eric Holder Announces Revisions to the Uniform Crime Report's Definition of Rape: Data Reported on Rape Will Better Reflect State Criminal Codes, Victim Experiences. The FBI: Federal Bureau of Investigation.* Washington: Office of Public Affairs, 06 Jan. 2012. Web. 22 July 2015.

United States. Dept. of Justice. Federal Bureau of Investigation. *Crime in the United States, 2012.* Washington: Federal Bureau of Investigation. Sept. 2013. Web. 1 Oct. 2014.

United States. Dept. of Justice. Federal Bureau of Investigation. *Crime in the United States, 2013.* Washington: Federal Bureau of Investigation. Sept. 2014. Web. 28 May 2015.

United States. Dept. of Justice. Federal Bureau of Investigation. *Hate Crimes.* Washington: Federal Bureau of Investigation. 2016. Web. 18 Apr. 2016.

United States. Dept. of Justice. Federal Bureau of Investigation. *Hate Crime Statistics, 2011.* Washington: Federal Bureau of Investigation. 2012. Web. 29 May 2015.

United States. Dept. of Justice. Federal Bureau of Investigation. *Identity Theft.* Washington: Federal Bureau of Investigation. 2015. Web. 11 Dec. 2015.

United States. Dept. of Justice. Federal Bureau of Investigation. *Italian Organized Crime.* Washington: Federal Bureau of Investigation, 2015. Web. 29 May 2015.

United States. Dept. of Justice. Federal Bureau of Investigation. *Organized Crime.* Washington: Federal Bureau of Investigation, 2016. Web. 3 Aug. 2016.

United States. Dept. of Justice. Federal Bureau of Investigation. San Diego Division. *Interstate Stalking Defendant Sentenced to Five Years in Prison.* Washington: Federal Bureau of Investigation, 2013. Web. 23 Sept. 2015

United States. Dept. of Labor, Bureau of Labor Statistics. *American Time Use Survey—2010 Results.* Bureau of Labor Statistics, News Release, 2011. Web. 25 Sept. 2015.

United States. Dept. of Labor, Bureau of Labor Statistics. *American Time Use Survey—2011 Results.* Bureau of Labor Statistics, News Release, 2012. Web. 25 Sept. 2015.

United States. Dept. of Labor, Bureau of Labor Statistics. *College Enrollment and Work Activity of 2014 High School Graduates.* Bureau of Labor Statistics, Economic News Release, 16 Apr. 2015. Web. 26 Mar. 2016.

United States. Dept. of Labor. Bureau of Labor Statistics. *Employment Characteristics of Families Summary.* Bureau of Labor Statistics, Economic News Release, 23 Apr. 2015. Web. 30 Aug. 2015.

United States. Dept. of Labor. Bureau of Labor Statistics. *Highlights of Women's Earnings in 2012.* Bureau of Labor Statistics, BLS Reports, Oct. 2013. Web. 30 Aug. 2015.

United States. Dept. of Labor, Bureau of Labor Statistics. *Industry employment and output projections to 2024.* Bureau of Labor Statistics, Monthly Labor Review, Dec. 2015. Web. 31 Mar. 2016.

United States. Dept. of Labor, Bureau of Labor Statistics. *Labor Force Statistics from the Current Population Survey.* Bureau of Labor Statistics, 2016. Web. 24 Mar. 2016.

United States. Dept. of Labor, Bureau of Labor Statistics. *Number of Jobs Held, Labor Market Activity, and Earnings Growth Among the Youngest Baby Boomers: Results from a Longitudinal Survey.* Bureau of Labor Statistics, News Release, 31 Mar. 2015. Web. 31 Mar. 2016.

United States. Dept. of Labor, Bureau of Labor Statistics. *Table A–2. Employment Status of the civilian population by race, sex, and age*. Bureau of Labor Statistics, Economic News Release, 2015. Web. 25 Sept. 2015.

United States. Dept. of Labor, Bureau of Labor Statistics. *Table A–15. Alternative measures of labor underutilization*. Bureau of Labor Statistic, Economic News Release, 2015. Web. 31 Mar. 2016.

United States. Dept. of Labor, Bureau of Labor Statistics. *The Employment Situation*. Bureau of Labor Statistics, News Release, Mar. 2016. Web. 19 Apr. 2016.

United States. Dept. of Labor, Bureau of Labor Statistics. *Union Members Summary*. Bureau of Labor Statistics, Economic News Release, 28 Jan. 2016. Web. 31 Mar. 2016.

United States. Dept. of Labor, Bureau of Labor Statistics. *Usual Weekly Earnings of Wage and Salary Workers Fourth Quarter 2015*. Bureau of Labor Statistics, News Release, 22 Jan. 2016. Web. 31 Mar. 2016.

United States. Dept. of Labor. Bureau of Labor Statistics. *Women in the Labor Force: A Databook*. Bureau of Labor Statistics, BLS Reports. Dec. 2014. Web. 26 Mar. 2016.

United States. Dept. of State. *Independent States in the World*. Dept. of State, Fact Sheet. 21 July 2015. Web. 31 Mar. 2016.

United States. Dept. of State. *Trafficking in Persons Report: June 2014*. Dept. of State, June 2014. Web. 18 Apr. 2016.

United States. Dept. of State. *Trafficking in Persons Report: July 2015*. Dept. of State, July 2015. Web. 18 Apr. 2016.

United States. Dept. of the Treasury. "TARP Programs." Dept. of the Treasury, 13 Jan. 2016. Web. 26 Apr. 2016.

United States. Equal Employment Opportunity Commission. *American Experiences Versus American Expectations*. July 2015. Web. 2 Apr. 2016.

United States. Office of Management and Budget. *TARP Report*. Aug. 2012. Web. 31 Mar. 2016.

United States. Federal Bureau of Prisons. "Inmate Race." Federal Bureau of Prisons, 2016. Web. 3 Aug. 2016.

United States. Postal Service. "Publication 100—The United States Postal Service—An American History 1775—2006." United States Postal Service, Nov. 2012. Web. 31 Mar. 2016.

U.S. News & World Report. "Education." U.S. News & World Report, 2015. Web. 26 Mar. 2016.

Valladares, Danilo. "Guatemalan Communities Have No Say in Exploitation of Resources." *Global Policy Forum*. Global Policy Forum, 21 May 2016. Web. 26 Apr. 2016.

Van Wagoner, Richard S. *Mormon Polygamy: A History*. 2nd ed. New York: Signature Books, 1989. Print.

Veenstra, Gerry. "The Gendered Nature of Discriminatory Experiences by Race, Class, and Sexuality: A Comparison of Intersectionality Theory and the Subordinate Male Target Hypothesis." *Sex Roles: A Journal of Research* 68.11 (2013): 646–659. Web. 10 Dec. 2015.

Venkatesh, Sudir. "Five Myths About Prostitution" *The Washington Post*. N.p., 12 Sept. 2010 Web. 29 May 2015.

Vertinsky, P. "Physique as Destiny: William H. Sheldon, Barbara Honeyman Heath and the Struggle for Hegemony in the Science of Somatotyping." *Canadian Bulletin of Medical History*, 24.2 (2007): 291–316. Web. 21 May 2015.

Vespa, Jonathan, Jamie M. Lewis, and Rose M. Kreider. *America's Families and Living Arrangements: 2012.* Washington: U.S. Census Bureau, Current Population Reports, Aug. 2013. Web. 24 Sept. 2015.

"Violence against women: Intimate partner and sexual violence against women." *World Health Organization*. World Health Organization, Nov. 2014. Web. 30 Aug. 2015. <http://www.who.int/mediacentre/factsheets/fs239/en/>.

"Violence Against Women & Millennium Development Goals." *United Nations Development Fund for Women*. UN Women, 2015. Web. 30 Aug. 2015. <http://www.unwomen.org/~/media/Headquarters/Media/Publications/UNIFEM/EVAWkit_02_VAWandMDGs_en.pdf>.

Visto, Cecille S. "Globalization's Bad Effects Discussed." *Global Policy Forum*. Global Policy Forum, 12 Sept. 2002. Web. 26 Apr. 2016.

Vlahov, D., and B. Junge. "The Role of Needle Exchange Programs in HIV Prevention." *Public Health Rep.* 113. S1 (1998): 75–80. Web. 19 June 2015.

Voorhees, Josh. "Texas Teen Avoids Prison After Defense Claims He Was Too Rich to Know Better." *Slate*. N.p., 12 Dec. 2013. Web. 30 May 2015.

Vorpal Fox. *iSpotACrime*. Computer software. *Apple App Store*. Vorpal Fox, 15 Mar. 2016. Web. 18 Apr. 2016.

Vorweck, Molly. "Polygamists find promise in Supreme Court Decisions." *USA Today*. Gannett, 2013. Web. 24 Sept. 2015.

Voxiva. Text4baby. Computer software. *Apple App Store*. Vers. 4.2.5.1 Voxiva, 20 Mar. 2016. Web. 3 Aug. 2016.

Vygotsky, Lev S. *Mind in Society: The Development of Higher Psychological Processes*. Cambridge: Harvard University Press, 1978. Print.

Wade, Lisa, and Myra Marx Ferree. *Gender: Ideas, Interactions, Institutions*. New York: W.W. Norton & Company, 2015. Web. 10 Dec. 2015.

Waldron, Hillary. U.S. Social Security Administration Office of Policy. *Trends in Mortality Differentials and Life Expectancy for Male Social Security–Covered Workers, by Average Relative Earnings*. Washington: U.S. Social Security Administration, 2007. Web. 04 Nov. 2014.

Walker, S., C. Spohn, and M. DeLone. *The Color of Justice: Race, Ethnicity, and Crime in America*. 3rd ed. Belmont: Wadsworth/Thompson Learning, 2004. Print.

Walzer, S., A.S. Bashir, and A.R. Silbert. "Cognitive and Behavioral Factors in the Learning Disabilities of 47,XXY and 47,XYY Boys." *Birth Defects Orig Artic Ser.* 26.4 (1990): 45–58. Web. 9 Mar. 2016.

Wang, Ming-Te, and Jessica Degol. "Motivational Pathways to STEM Career Choices: Using Expectancy-Value Perspective to Understand Individual and Gender Differences in STEM Fields." *Developmental Review* 33.4 (2013): 304–340. Web. 29 Aug. 2015.

Wang, Andi. "Last Call iPhone App Want You to Get Drunk Responsibly." *Gizmodo*. Gizmodo, 13 Nov. 2008. Web. 9 Mar. 2016.

Wang, Wendy. "Interracial marriage: Who is 'marrying out'?" Pew Research Center, 12 June 2015. Web. 24 Sept. 2015.

Warnke, Georgia. *After Identity: Rethinking Race, Sex, and Gender*. New York: Cambridge University Press, 2007. Print.

Weatherford, Jack. *The History of Money*. New York: Three Rivers Press, 1998. Print.

Webb, R.K. *Harriet Martineau: A Radical Victorian*. New York: Columbia University Press, 1960. Print.

Webel, Baird. *Troubled Asset Relief Program (TARP): Implementation and Status*. Congressional Research Service, 27 June 2013. Web. 31 Mar. 2016.

Weber, Max. *Economy and Society*. 1925. Eds. Guenther Roth and Claus Wittich. Berkeley: University of California Press, 1978. Print.

Weber, Max. *The Protestant Ethic and the Spirit of Capitalism*. 1905. Trans. Stephen Kalberg. New York: Routledge, 2001. Print.

Weber, Max. *The Theory of Social and Economic Organization*. Trans. A. M. Henderson and Talcott Parsons. New York: Free Press, 1947. Print.

Weber, Max. "The Three Types of Legitimate Rule." 1922. Trans. Hans Gerth. *Berkeley Publications in Society and Institutions* 4.1 (1958): 1–11. Web. 3 June 2016.

Weicha, Karin. "New Estimates on the Rate of Global Language Loss." *The Rosetta Blog*. The Rosetta Project, 28 Mar. 2013. Web. 5 Aug. 2015.

Weigel, David. "Marco Rubio Mentions the Middle Class 35 Times in One Speech." *Salon*. Salon Media Group, 5 Dec. 2012. Web. 20 May 2015.

Weiner, Steve, Qinqi Xu, Paul Goldberg, Jinyi Liu, and Ofer Bar-Yosef. "Evidence for the Use of Fire at Zhoukoudian, China." *Science* 281.5374 (1998): 251–253. Web. 5 Aug. 2015.

Weismantel, Mary. "Moche Sex Pots: Reproduction and Temporality in Ancient South America." *American Anthropologist* 106.3 (2004): 495–505. Web. Aug. 5 2015.

Weiss, Mitchell G., Jayashree Ramakrishna and Daryl Somma. "Health Related Stigma: Rethinking Concepts and Interventions." *Psychology, Health, and Medicine* 11.3 (2006): 277–287. Web. 29 May 2015.

Weisgram, Erica S., Megan Fulcher, and Lisa M. Dinella. "Pink Gives Girls Permission: Exploring the Roles of Explicit and Implicit Gender Labels on Preschool Children's Toy Preferences. *Journal of Applied Developmental Psychology* 35 (2014): 401–409. Web. 29 Aug. 2015.

Wellington, Sheila, Marcia Brumit Kropf, and Paulette R. Gerkovich. "What's Holding Women Back?" *Harvard Business Review*. Harvard, June 2003. Web. 10 Dec. 2015.

Westboro Baptist Church. "GodHatesFags." Westboro Baptist Church. *Westboro Baptist Church*, 2016. Web. 3 Aug. 2016.

West, Candace, and Don H. Zimmerman. "Doing Gender." *Gender & Society* 1.2 (1987): 125–151. Web. 29 Aug. 2015.

Westerhoff, John H. *McGuffey and his readers: Piety, morality, and education in nineteenth-century America*. New York: Abingdon, 1978. Print.

Western, Bruce, and Becky Pettit. "Collateral Costs: Incarceration's Effect on Economic Mobility." Pew Research Center, 2010. Web. 30 May 2015.

Whitaker, Kati. "Ghana Witch Camps: Widows' Lives in Exile." *BBC News*. BBC, 1 Sept. 2012. Web. 21 May 2015.

White, H.R., V. Johnson, and S. Buyske. "Parental Modeling and Parenting Behavior Effects on Offspring Alcohol and Cigarette Use: A Growth Curve Analysis." *Journal of Substance Abuse* 12 (2000): 287–310. Web. 19 June 2015.

White, L.K. "Determinants of Divorce: A Review of the Research in the Eighties." *Journal of Marriage and the Family* 52 (1990): 904–912. Web. 25 Sept. 2015.

Whitfield, Jerome T., Wandagi H. Pako, John Collinge, and Michael P. Alpers. "Mortuary Rites of the South Fore and Kuru." *Philosophical Transactions of the Royal Society* 363 (2008): 3721–3724. Web. Aug. 9 2015.

"Who We Are." *North American Man/Boy Love Association*. The North American Man/Boy Love Association, 2011. Web. 28 July 2016. < http://nambla.org/welcome.html>.

"Why Don't Americans Trust the Government? – Toplines/Survey." *The Henry J. Kaiser Family Foundation*. The Washington Post, 30 Jan. 1996. Web. 28 May 2015. <http://kff.org/other/poll-finding/why-dont-americans-trust-the-government-toplinessurvey/>.

Wiessner, Pauline Wilson. *Hxaro: A Regional System of Reciprocity for Reducing Risk Among The!Kung San*. Ann Arbor: University of Michigan, 1977. Print.

Wiessner, Polly W. "Embers of Society: Firelight talk among the Ju/'hoansi Bushmen." *Proceedings of the National Academy of Sciences* 111.39 (2014): 14013–14014. Web. 5 Aug. 2015.

Wile, Rob. "How The Great Recession Crushed The Middle Class." *Business Insider*. Business Insider, Inc, 22 May 2014. Web. 29 May 2015.

Wilkinson, Richard and Kate Pickett. The Spirit Level. London: Allen Lane, 2009. Print.

Wilsher, Kim. "France bans ketchup in cafeterias." *Los Angeles Times*. Los Angeles Times, 6 Oct. 2011. Web. 26 July 2016.

Wilson, Erin, Sunil Babu Pant, Megan Comfort, and Maria Ekstrand. "Stigma and HIV risk amon Metis in Nepal." *Cult Health Sex* 13.3 (2011): 253–266. Web. 24 Mar. 2016.

Wilson, Lori Lee. *The Salem Witch Trials*. Minneapolis: Lerner Publications, 1997. Print.

Wilson, William Julius. *The Truly Disadvantaged: The Inner City, The Underclass, and Public Policy*. Chicago: University of Chicago Press, 1987. Print.

Wimberly, Dale W. "Religion and Role-Identity: A Structural Symbolic Interactionist Conceptualization of Religiosity." *The Sociological Quarterly* 30.1 (1989): 125–142. Web. 26 Mar. 2016.

Wingme. *Wingme*. Computer software. *Apple App Store*. Vers. 1.23 Wingme, 5 Aug. 2014. Web. 25 Mar. 2016.

Winter, Sam. "Language and Identity in Transgender: Gender Wars and the Case of the Thai kathoey." *Hawaii Conference on Social Sciences, Waikiki, June 2003*. 2003. Web. 29 Aug. 2015.

Wodak, Alex, and Annie Cooney. "Effectiveness of Sterile Needle and Syringe Programming in Reducing HIV/AIDS Among Injecting Drug Users." *World Health Organization* 2004. Web. 19 June 2015.

Wolitzky-Taylor, Kate B., Heidi S. Resnick, Jenna L. McCauley, Ananda B. Amstadter, Dean G. Kilpatrick, and Kenneth J. Ruggiero. "Is Reporting of Rape on the Rise? A Comparison of Women with Reported Versus Unreported Rape Experiences in the National Women's Study-Replication." *Journal of Interpersonal Violence* 26.4 (2010): 807–832. Web. 9 Mar. 2016.

Wood, David. "Healing: Can We Treat Moral Wounds?" *The Huffington Post*. HuffingtonPost.com, Inc., 20 Mar. 2014. Web. 30 June 2015.

"Women in Aviation, International—The Facts—Current Statistics of Aviation Careers." Women in Aviation, International. 2013. Web. 24 Sept. 2015. <https://www.wai.org/resources/waistats.cfm>.

Women in Informal Employment. "Construction Workers." Women in Informal Employment: Globalizing and Organizing. 2016 Web. Mar. 24 2016.

World Bank. *Results 2013. World Bank*. 2013. Web. 10 Dec. 2015. <http://siteresources.worldbank.org/PROJECTS/Resources/40940-1367867968385/2013_WorldBankforResults.pdf>.

World Health Organization. "Eliminating Female genital mutilation: An interagency statement: OHCHR, UNAIDS, UNDP, UNECA, UNESCO, UNFPA, UNHCR, UNICEF, UNIFEM, and WHO." Geneva: World Health Organization, 2008. Web. 5 Aug. 2015.

World Health Organization. "Violence Against Women: Intimate Partner and Sexual Violence Against Women." Geneva: World Health Organization, 2016. Web. 24 Mar. 2016.

"World Report 2015: Pakistan." *Human Rights Watch*. Human Rights Watch, 2015. Web. 30 Aug. 2015. <https://www.hrw.org/world-report/2015/country-chapters/pakistan>.

Worstall, Tim. "Astonishing Numbers: America's Poor Still Live Better Than Most of the Rest of Humanity." *Forbes*. Forbes Magazine, 1 June 2013. Web. 30 May 2015.

Wright, John Paul, Kim N. Dietrich, M. Douglas Ris, Richard W. Hornung, Stephanie D. Wessel, Bruce P. Lanphear, Mona Ho, and Mary N. Rae. "Association of Prenatal and Childhood Blood Lead Concentrations with Criminal Arrests in Early Adulthood." *PLoS Med* 5.5 (2008): 732–740. Web. 28 May 2015.

Xiao, Kaijing. "'Ghost Marriages' Prompt Grave Robbing as Men Dig Up Brides." *ABC News*. ABC News, 6 Mar. 2013. Web. 29 Aug. 2015.

Xu, Daniel. "Total Cost of 2010 BP Oil Spill to Gulf Anglers Estimated at $585 Million." *OutdoorHub*. Outdoor Hub, 11 Sept. 2014. Web. 29 May 2015.

Yecke, Cheri Pierson. "Mayhem in the Middle: How Middle Schools Have Failed America—and How to Make Them Work." *Thomas B. Fordham Institute*. Thomas B. Fordham Institute, Sept. 2005. Web. 26 Mar. 2016.

Young, Antonia. *Women Who Become Men: Albanian Sworn Virgins (Dress, Body, Culture)*. New York: Bloomsbury Academic, 2001. Print.

Yousafzai, Malala. *I Am Malala: The Girl Who Stood Up for Education and Was Shot by the Taliban*. Ed. Christina Lamb. London: Orion Publishing Group Ltd., 2013. Print.

Zelinger, Julie. *A Little F'd Up: Why Feminism is Not a Dirty Word*. Berkeley: Seal Press, 2012. Print.

Zhao, Rongguang. *A History of Food Culture in China*. Trans. Gangliu Wang and Aimee Yiran Wang. New York: SCPG Publishing Corporation, 2015. Print.

Zimbardo, Philip G. *The Lucifer Effect: Understanding How Good People Turn Evil*. New York: Random House. 2007. Print.

Ziegler, Philip. *Black Death*. New York: Harper Collins, 1971. Print.

Zimbardo, Philip, and Nikita D. Coulombe. *Man Disconnected: How Technology Has Sabotaged What it Means to be a Male*. London: Rider. 2015. Print.

Zimring, Franklin E. *The Great American Crime Decline*. New York: Oxford University Press, 2006. Print.

Zinn, Howard. *A People's History of the United States*. New York: HarperCollins, 1990. Print.

CPSIA information can be obtained
at www.ICGtesting.com
Printed in the USA
LVHW06s2135250818
587791LV00030B/12/P

9 781634 874144